Credit Method Compatibility and Constraints under EU Law

Series on International Taxation

VOLUME 79

Series Editors

Introduction & Contents

The Series on International Taxation deals with a wide variety of topics in the global tax arena. The authors include many of the field's leading experts as well as talented newcomers. Their expert views and incisive commentary have proven highly useful to practitioners and academics alike.

Objective

The volumes published in this series are aimed at offering high-quality analytical information and practical solutions to international tax practitioners.

Readership

Practitioners, academics and policy makers in international tax law.

Frequency of Publication

2-3 new volumes published each year.

The titles published in this series are listed at the end of this volume.

Credit Method Compatibility and Constraints under EU Law

An Analysis of the Case Law of the CJEU

Rita Julien

Wolters Kluwer

Published by:
Kluwer Law International B.V.
PO Box 316
2400 AH Alphen aan den Rijn
The Netherlands
E-mail: international-sales@wolterskluwer.com
Website: www.wolterskluwer.com/en/solutions/kluwerlawinternational

Sold and distributed by:
Wolters Kluwer Legal & Regulatory U.S.
7201 McKinney Circle
Frederick, MD 21704
United States of America
E-mail: customer.service@wolterskluwer.com

ISBN 978-94-035-2363-7

e-Book: ISBN 978-94-035-2364-4
web-PDF: ISBN 978-94-035-2365-1

About the Author

Dr Rita Julien, LLM, obtained her doctoral degree at WU (Vienna University of Economics and Business), where she worked as a Research and Teaching Associate at the Institute for Austrian and International Tax Law. She obtained her LLM with a specialization in European and International Tax Law at the Faculty of Law, Economics and Finance of the University of Luxembourg. She is a Graduate Tax Scholar in the LLM programme at Georgetown Law, teaches in the LLM programme in International Tax Law at WU and conducts research for the focus group on unexplained wealth in the Tax Transparency and Corruption Project of the Global Tax Policy Center. She has published on various tax law topics and has taught numerous courses and seminars to students, practitioners and government officials, including on Austrian tax law, on dividends and interest under tax treaties and on the methods for the elimination of double taxation. The author's doctoral dissertation, on which this book is based, was awarded a Wolfgang Gassner Science Prize 2020 and the European Doctoral Tax Thesis Award 2020.

Table of Contents

List of Examples

List of Abbreviations

ACT	Advance Corporation Tax
AG	Advocate General
ATAD	Anti-tax Avoidance Directive
BEPS	Base Erosion and Profit Shifting
C-	Case Number for Court of Justice of the European Union
C.J.S.	Corpus Juris Secundum
CEN	Capital Export Neutrality
CFC	Controlled Foreign Company
CIN	Capital Import Neutrality
CIT	Corporate Income Tax
CJEU	Court of Justice of the European Union
CLEN	Capital and Labour *Export* Neutrality
CLIN	Capital *and Labour* Import Neutrality
DSI	Domestic-Source Income
DTC	Double Taxation Convention
E&P	Earnings and Profits
EC	European Community/Communities
EEA	European Economic Area
EEC	European Economic Community
EFTA	European Free Trade Association
ETR	Effective Tax Rate
EU	European Union
FID	Foreign Income Dividend

FIFO	First-In-First-Out
FII	Franked Investment Income
FSI	Foreign-Source Income
FTC	Foreign Tax Credit
GILTI	Global Intangible Low-Taxed Income
IBFD	International Bureau of Fiscal Documentation
ICC	International Chamber of Commerce
IFA	International Fiscal Association
IRC	Internal Revenue Code of the United States
LCF	Loss Carryforward
LIFO	Last-In-First-Out
m.no./m.nos	Margin Number/Margin Numbers
MCA	Maximum Creditable Amount
MCT	Mainstream Corporation Tax
MLI	Multilateral Convention to Implement Tax Treaty Related Measures to Prevent Base Erosion and Profit Shifting
MNEs	Multinational Enterprises
MS	Member State
n.; *supra/infra* note	Footnote external to the work; cross reference to footnote internal to the work and to its accompanying text in the work
OECD	Organisation for Economic Co-operation and Development
OEEC	Organisation for European Economic Co-operation
OJ	Official Journal of the European Union
PE	Permanent Establishment
State R	State of Residence
State S	State of Source
TEEC	Treaty Establishing the European Economic Community
TEU	Treaty on European Union
TFEU	Treaty on the Functioning of the European Union
UK	United Kingdom of Great Britain and Northern Ireland
UN	United Nations
US	United States
WHT	Withholding Tax
WWI	Worldwide Income

Preface

Under European Union (EU) law, the credit method, also commonly referred to as the foreign tax credit (FTC), has given rise to various legal challenges and questions. Its compatibility with the fundamental freedoms of the EU's internal market has been debated. Yet, a wave of recent legal and political developments, such as the Anti-Tax Avoidance Directive, has been increasing states' reliance on the credit method. Broadly speaking, EU Member States (MSs) have been asked to expand their tax bases and close loopholes, in order to prevent base erosion and profit shifting (BEPS), while simultaneously ensuring that this does not mount new obstacles to the internal market, such as, most notably, double taxation. In striking this delicate balance between the heightened concerns over BEPS and double non-taxation and the long-standing concerns over double taxation, the credit method is one of the tools at MSs' disposal; however, it must be designed, and wielded, in a way that is in line with EU law.

In light of these developments, this book offers a timely, more comprehensive study of the relationship between the credit method and EU law. To accomplish this, the first part of the study traces the historical legal developments of the credit method in order to define this relief mechanism and to distinguish its main component parts. In doing so, it forms a general framework for the features that legislators of EU MSs would have to consider or adapt when designing an FTC. Both a 'direct' credit and an 'indirect' credit are addressed. The second part of the study is dedicated to the unique EU law issues that have arisen in connection with the credit method. Given the paramount role of 'negative integration' in shaping the EU law obligations of MSs in the field of direct taxation, the research focused in particular on what guidance can be derived from the case law of the Court of Justice of the European Union (CJEU). The research identified the cases of the CJEU that may affect, directly or indirectly, the credit method and its main components. These cases were then carefully analysed in order to extract the relevant legal findings and principles that can guide MSs and help detect the contours within which they can manoeuvre in the design of an EU law compatible credit method.

Acknowledgements

I would like to express my enormous gratitude to each and every person who has made this book possible. Thank you to all of the staff, faculty, colleagues and friends at the Institute for Austrian and International Tax Law at the Vienna University for Economics and Business (WU). The doctoral research and the dissertation, on which this book is based, was made possible thanks to the countless enriching opportunities provided there to learn, to research, to teach, and to collaborate on projects and conferences with experts from around the world. Thank you to my supervisors, Prof. Dr Alexander Rust, LLM and Prof. Dr DDr h.c. Michael Lang, to Prof. Dr Claus Staringer and Prof. MMag. Dr Josef Schuch of my doctoral committee, to Prof. Dr Pasquale Pistone and all the professors, colleagues and friends who discussed my research with me for their invaluable feedback and guidance. In particular, Prof. Rust was not only my doctoral supervisor but also the professor who, thanks to his brilliant lectures in my very first tax law course and his mentorship, inspired me to pursue my studies in tax law further. All of these shared experiences and conversations, at conferences or over coffees, deepened my knowledge of international taxation and European tax law, and also formed lasting memories and friendships. Thank you to the administrative staff of the Institute whose kind, efficient help ensures the highest quality, most smoothly run and enjoyable working and learning environment. Thank you to the entire team at Kluwer Law International for their dedication, enthusiasm and expert assistance all throughout the publication process. Thank you especially to my precious family and friends for their unconditional love and always being there for me. My deepest gratitude goes to you all for the continuous encouragement throughout the process, for everything I have learned from you along the way and for making my years abroad in France, Luxembourg and Austria an invaluable experience personally and professionally.

Chapter 1
Introduction

1.1. RESEARCH SYNOPSIS

One of the by-products of the political and legal developments in the European Union (EU), from its joint international efforts to combat 'base erosion and profit shifting' (BEPS), may be a repositioning, and possible reinforcing, of the role of the credit method in the EU. Most notably, since 1 January 2019, EU Member States (MSs) have begun to apply certain measures in the Anti-Tax Avoidance Directives (ATAD I and II). In doing so, MSs must undertake a balancing act between two obligations. On the one hand, they are required to expand their taxation in certain ways to better target tax avoidance, BEPS and double non-taxation (e.g., by implementing Controlled Foreign Company (CFC) rules); on the other hand, they are asked to ensure that this expanded taxation does not lead to double taxation. Moreover, the measures in both hands, so to speak, must be administered in line with MSs' primary EU law obligations. While much attention had concentrated on the design of the former rules, attention had shifted away from the latter.

Traditionally, two main methods are used to relieve double taxation, namely the exemption method and the credit method. Generally speaking, various EU scholars, and to some extent MSs' legislators, have indicated a preference for the exemption method (*see*, e.g., references at *infra* note 18 and note 53). Yet, MSs will find themselves, perhaps reluctantly, more reliant on the credit method. Not only does the ATAD mandate the credit method in the case of CFC rules, but it also strongly encourages it in the preamble in other cases where ATAD rules lead to double taxation in general. Moreover, even beyond the ATAD, in any case where a state is seeking to recapture a part of its tax base alleged to have been diverted in some way (e.g., the 'Diverted Profits Tax' in the United Kingdom (UK)), the exemption method is less suitable than the credit method for any resulting double taxation. In this way, the credit method is being positioned as one of the necessary tools in the toolkit to strike this balance, to help MSs 'avoid creating other obstacles to the market, such as double taxation' (according to the preamble of the ATAD), by contrast with its previous more contentious reputation as being itself a potential obstacle to the market. This would not mean, however, that it is without constraints under EU law, such as the need to adhere to the fundamental freedoms.

Against this background, it would be timely to more comprehensively and closely study the relationship between the credit method and EU law, updated in light of recent developments. Moreover, if MSs are to successfully balance their current EU law obligations, as they implement and update anti-BEPS rules while seeking to avoid double taxation, it is particularly useful to study what guidance can be garnered from the case law of the Court of Justice of the European Union (CJEU) on how the credit method can be designed in line with EU law. This is relevant for both a 'direct' credit and an 'indirect' credit (which is required under the CFC rules). To accomplish this, the research identifies and compiles the cases of the CJEU that may affect, directly or indirectly, the credit method. These cases are carefully analysed so as to extract out the relevant legal findings and principles that can guide the design of the credit method under EU law.

1.2. RESEARCH CONTEXT

In the broadest sense, the field in which this research is conducted is international tax law – defined as comprising both tax treaty provisions and domestic laws that affect the taxation of cross-border (inbound and outbound) income, including those that unilaterally grant relief for double (or multiple) taxation[1] – where it intersects with EU law. More precisely, it is EU law in the field of 'direct' taxation.[2]

The state of the field could be characterized as undergoing unprecedented change. Legislative changes have been taking place around the world to counteract various practices described as base erosion and profit shifting (BEPS) practices, aggressive tax planning and unintended low- or (double) non-taxation.[3] This was particularly catalysed by the launch of the Organisation for Economic Co-operation and

1. For definitions, *see*, e.g., OECD, *Glossary of Tax Terms*, https://www.oecd.org/ctp/glossaryoftaxterms.htm (last visited 5 May 2018) (defining 'international taxation'); *International Taxation, IBFD International Tax Glossary* (Julie Rogers-Glabush ed., IBFD 7th ed. 2015). For debates on the term and meaning of 'international tax law', *see*, e.g., H. David Rosenbloom, *The David R. Tillinghast Lecture International Tax Arbitrage and the 'International Tax System'*, 53(2) Tax L. Rev. 137 (1999); Reuven S. Avi-Yonah, *International Tax as International Law*, 57(4) Tax L. Rev. 483, 483–501 (2004).
2. *See*, e.g., European Union, Summaries of EU Legislation, Glossary of Summaries, EUR-Lex: Access to European Union Law, https://eur-lex.europa.eu/summary/glossary/taxation.html (last visited 11 May 2019) (in the EU, 'direct' taxation is the term used to refer to income taxation or 'taxes on incomes or profits (direct taxes)'. It is often juxtaposed with 'taxes levied on goods and services (indirect taxes, such as value-added tax (VAT) and excise duties levied on energy products, electricity, alcohol and manufactured tobacco)').
3. *See*, e.g., OECD, *About the Inclusive Framework on BEPS*, https://www.oecd.org/tax/beps/beps-about.htm (last visited 11 May 2019) (it claims that 'over 125 countries and jurisdictions' have joined to 'collaborate on the implementation of the BEPS Package'); *see infra* note 37 (on the MLI implementing the BEPS proposals in tax treaties); *see infra* note 10 and note 25 (on certain unilateral measures that states, such as India and the UK, have taken regarding BEPS issues).

Development (OECD)/G20 BEPS Project,[4] which comprised 15 'Actions' addressing topics such as 'Countering Harmful Tax Practices More Effectively, Taking Into Account Transparency and Substance' and 'Neutralising the Effects of Hybrid Mismatch Arrangements'.[5] In the EU, legislative action was taken to implement many of the BEPS proposals via Directives, such as Council Directive 2016/881/EU (on country-by-country reporting of multinational enterprises (MNEs))[6] and the Council Directive (EU) 2016/1164 of 12 July 2016 laying down rules against tax avoidance practices that directly affect the functioning of the internal market,[7] among others. In doing so, the EU legal context, as the OECD itself acknowledged (e.g., in Action 3), entailed special consideration be given to ensure all such legislative action is in line with primary EU law.[8] Even before these were fully implemented, international talks started moving forward for yet new rules regarding the taxation of the 'digital economy'.[9] And, even outside of these more internationally coordinated measures, some states have passed their own, often innovative, measures, such as the 'Diverted Profits Tax' in the UK[10] and the 'Global Intangible Low-Taxed Income' (GILTI) tax in the United States (US).[11]

As a result of the rapid pace of developments, the open research questions have been multiplying, as legislators, taxpayers and judges seek guidance on implementing and interpreting the numerous legal changes. Indeed, for every single proposal issued by the BEPS Project and for every legislative response by the EU, a series of questions

4. OECD, *BEPS Project Explanatory Statement: 2015 Final Reports*, OECD/G20 Base Erosion and Profit Shifting Project, 4, para. 1 (OECD Publishing 2016) ('In September 2013, G20 Leaders endorsed the ambitious and comprehensive Action Plan on BEPS').
5. *Id.*, at 13–18, Annex A ('Action 1 – Address the Tax Challenges of the Digital Economy'; 'Action 2 – Neutralise the Effects of Hybrid Mismatch Arrangements'; 'Action 3 – Strengthen CFC Rules'; 'Action 4 – Limit Base Erosion via Interest Deductions and Other Financial Payments'; 'Action 5 – Counter Harmful Tax Practices More Effectively, Taking Into Account Transparency and Substance'; 'Action 6 – Prevent Treaty Abuse'; 'Action 7 – Prevent the Artificial Avoidance of PE Status'; 'Actions 8-10 – Assure That Transfer Pricing Outcomes Are in Line with Value Creation'; 'Action 11 – Measuring and Monitoring BEPS'; 'Action 12 – Require Taxpayers to Disclose Their Aggressive Tax Planning Arrangements'; 'Action 13 – Re-examine Transfer Pricing Documentation'; 'Action 14 – Make Dispute Resolution Mechanisms More Effective'; 'Action 15 – Develop a Multilateral Instrument').
6. Council Directive (EU) 2016/881 of 25 May 2016 Amending Directive 2011/16/EU as Regards Mandatory Automatic Exchange of Information in the Field of Taxation, OJ L 146, 8–21 (3 Jun. 2016).
7. Council Directive (EU) 2016/1164 of 12 July 2016 Laying Down Rules Against Tax Avoidance Practices that Directly Affect the Functioning of the Internal Market, OJ L 193, 1–14 (19 Jul. 2016) (ATAD I).
8. *See*, e.g., OECD, *Designing Effective Controlled Foreign Company Rules, Action 3 – 2015 Final Report*, OECD/G20 Base Erosion and Profit Shifting Project, 10, 17–20 (OECD Publishing 2015).
9. OECD, *Addressing the Tax Challenges of the Digitalisation of the Economy, Public Consultation Document* (13 Feb.–6 Mar. 2019), OECD/G20 Base Erosion and Profit Shifting Project (OECD 2019). *See also infra* note 52.
10. *See*, e.g., United Kingdom, HM Revenue & Customs, *Diverted Profits Tax Guidance* (31 Dec. 2018), https://assets.publishing.service.gov.uk/government/uploads/system/uploads/attachment_data/file/768204/Diverted_Profits_Tax_-_Guidance__December_2018_.pdf (last visited 19 Aug. 2018).
11. United States, An Act to Provide for Reconciliation Pursuant to Titles II and V of the Concurrent Resolution on the Budget for Fiscal Year 2018, One-Hundred-Fifteenth Congress, Session I, Public Law 115-97, 131 STAT. 2208 (US Government Printing Office 22 Dec. 2017) (Tax Cuts and Jobs Act).

arise such as, from a tax policy perspective, whether the proposals of the BEPS Actions are truly the most sound or effective or, from a legal perspective, whether the implementation or the interpretation of the proposals is in line with a given national legal system, or in line with international obligations, such as tax treaties or World Trade Organization (WTO) obligations, or for EU MSs, in line with primary EU law.

One of the overarching concerns that has arisen is that of the balance to be struck between, on the one hand, the multitude of new rules to combat certain causes of undesirable low taxation and, on the other hand, the risk for unintended double (or multiple) taxation, as new rules lead to new unexpected overlaps in tax claims.[12] For at least a century, the focus of coordination among states in the field of direct taxation, both internationally and within the EU, was primarily on the removal of barriers created by double taxation.[13] As the aforementioned recent developments show, the pendulum has swung towards the potential distortions and inequality created by double non-taxation, BEPS, etc. Some have wondered whether this could unravel the accomplishments made towards reducing double (or multiple) taxation, such as the often-touted global network of more than three thousand bilateral tax treaties.[14] Due to worries about both ongoing and potential future cases of double (or multiple) taxation and disputes, the OECD included Action 14 on 'More Effective Dispute Resolution Mechanisms'[15] and the EU enacted Council Directive (EU) 2017/1852 of 10 October 2017 on tax dispute resolution mechanisms in the EU.[16] These are much needed

12. *See*, e.g., OECD, *BEPS: Frequently Asked Questions*, https://www.oecd.org/ctp/beps-frequently-asked-questions.pdf (last visited 11 May 2019) (among its top ten most frequently asked questions was '5. Do the BEPS measures increase the risk of double taxation?' The OECD marketed the project as a means to save the system of relief for double taxation in place). But, *see*, e.g., *infra* note 14 (other practitioners and scholars remained sceptical).
13. In the international context, *see*, e.g., League of Nations, Economic and Financial Commission, *Report on Double Taxation, submitted to the Financial Committee by Professors Bruins, Einaudi, Seligman, and Sir Josiah Stamp* (1923), *in* 4 *Legislative History of United States Tax Conventions*, 4003 (United States, Joint Committee on Internal Revenue Taxation, US Government Printing Office 1962). In the EU context, *see* Chapter 3 (a longitudinal study of the Directives in the field of direct taxation evidences that early Directives focused primarily on removing barriers, as Chapter 3 of the book shows). *See*, e.g., European Commission, Proposal for a Council Directive on the Common System of Taxation Applicable to Mergers, Divisions and Contributions of Assets Involving Companies of Different Member States, COM(1969) 5 Final, OJ C 39, 1–6 (22 Mar. 1969) (which eventually led to the adoption of the Merger Directive in 1990); European Commission, Proposal for a Council Directive on the Common System of Taxation Applicable to Parent Companies and Their Subsidiaries of Different Member States, COM(1969) 6 Final, OJ C 39, 7–9 (22 Mar. 1969) (which eventually led to the adoption of the Parent-Subsidiary Directive in 1990); Commission, Proposal for a Council Directive on a Common System of Taxation Applicable to Interest and Royalty Payments Made Between Associated Companies of Different Member States, COM(98) 0067 Final, OJ C 123, 9 (22 Mar. 1998) (which eventually led to the adoption of the Interest and Royalties Directive in 2003).
14. *See*, e.g., Ryan Finley, *Practitioners See Treaty System under Siege*, 93 Tax Notes Int'l 989 (4 Mar. 2019); Daniel W. Blum, *The Proposal for a Global Minimum Tax: Comeback of Residence Taxation in the Digital Era?: Comment on Can GILTI + BEAT = GLOBE?*, 47(5) Intertax 514 (2019) (Blum considers whether certain new rules 'would arguably decrease the relevance of tax treaties').
15. OECD, *Making Dispute Resolution Mechanisms More Effective, Action 14 – 2015 Final Report*, OECD/G20 Base Erosion and Profit Shifting Project (OECD Publishing 2015).
16. Council Directive (EU) 2017/1852 of 10 October 2017 on Tax Dispute Resolution Mechanisms in the European Union, OJ L 265, 1–14 (14 Oct. 2017).

positive steps. Nevertheless, by their very subject matter, i.e., disputes, these instruments play a role at a later stage - generally, after rules regarding relief of double taxation or overlapping tax claims have failed or fallen short. If a regime of new rules ends up relying too extensively on dispute resolution mechanisms, it could be symptomatic of a malfunction at an earlier stage, in the design of the rules. Hopefully, disputes, which may be costly or clog up arbitral or court systems, could be avoided with well-functioning rules. But, of course, both (well-functioning rules and dispute resolution mechanisms) are essential.

As regards the functioning of the rules at an earlier stage, there seem to be two general approaches: (1) the avoiding of overlaps through coordination mechanisms built into the rules (such as the ordering rules proposed in Action 2 to determine which hybrid mismatch rules should apply first)[17] and (2), where such overlaps occur, relief of any resulting double (or multiple) taxation. It is in this second context that, as mentioned in the synopsis (of Section 1.1.), the credit method - a mechanism whereby taxes levied by a foreign jurisdiction can be deducted from the taxes due in the credit-granting state - seems headed for an increased role.

In the context of the EU in particular, in the past, the credit method has given rise to debates as to its compatibility with EU law[18] and, in the present, MSs may have to rely on it more. As Members of the EU, they would have the legal responsibility to do so in a way that is compatible with EU law.[19] This gives rise to the questions as to whether those doubts have been settled and, if so, even if the credit method is, broadly speaking, compatible with EU law, whether there are ways in which the credit method could be designed that nevertheless infringe EU law.

17. OECD, *Neutralising the Effects of Hybrid Mismatch Arrangements, Action 2 – 2015 Final Report*, OECD/G20 Base Erosion and Profit Shifting Project, 11–12 (OECD Publishing 2015).

18. *See*, e.g., Peter J. Wattel, *Home Neutrality in an Internal Market*, 36(5) Eur. Tax'n 159 (1996); Paul Farmer, *EC Law and National Rules on Direct Taxation: A Phoney War?*, 7(1) EC Tax Rev. 13 (1998); Moris Lehner, *Limitation of the National Power of Taxation by the Fundamental Freedoms and Non-discrimination Clauses of the EC Treaty*, 9(1) EC Tax Rev. 5 (2000); Peter J. Wattel, *Progressive Taxation of Non-residents and Intra-EC Allocation of Personal Tax Allowances: Why Schumacker, Asscher, Gilly and Gschwind Do Not Suffice*, 40(6) Eur. Tax'n 210 (2000); John F. Avery Jones, *A Comment on 'Progressive Taxation of Non-residents and Intra-EC Allocation of Personal Tax Allowances'*, 40(8) Eur. Tax'n 375 (2000); Eric C.C.M. Kemmeren, *Principle of Origin in Tax Conventions: A Rethinking of Models* (Pijnenburg vormgevers.uitgevers 2001); Klaus Vogel, *Which Method Should the European Community Adopt for the Avoidance of Double Taxation?*, 56(1) Bull. Int'l Fiscal Documentation 4 (2002); Pasquale Pistone, *The Impact of Community Law on Tax Treaties: Issues and Solutions* 177–178, 197–201 (Kluwer Law International 2002); Ben J.M. Terra & Peter J. Wattel, *European Tax Law* 210–222 (Wolters Kluwer 6th ed. 2012); Otto Marres (update of 6th ed.), *Chapter 16: Division of Tax Jurisdiction; Double Tax Relief Mechanisms; Tax Treaty Issues, in* 1 *Terra/Wattel European Tax Law* 695, 698–709 (Peter J. Wattel, Otto Marres & Hein Vermeulen eds, Wolters Kluwer 7th ed. 2019).

19. *See*, e.g., CJEU, Case C-26/62, *Van Gend en Loos*, 5 Feb. 1963, ECLI:EU:C:1963:1 (regarding the 'direct effect' of EU, at that time EEC, law); CJEU, Case C-6/64, *Costa v. E.N.E.L.*, 15 Jul. 1964, ECLI:EU:C:1964:66 (regarding the 'supremacy' or 'precedence' of EU law); CJEU, Case C-279/93, *Schumacker*, 14 Feb. 1995, ECLI:EU:C:1995:31, at para. 21; CJEU, Case C-80/94, *Wielockx*, 11 Aug. 1995, ECLI:EU:C:1995:271, at para. 16; CJEU, Case C-107/94, *Asscher*, 27 Jun. 1996, ECLI:EU:C:1996:251, at para. 36.

On the topic of the credit method, there are some detailed studies, most notably in the literature on US tax law and on tax treaty law. In the US, a seminal comprehensive and detailed study of the credit method is the work of Elisabeth A. Owens, *The Foreign Tax Credit: A Study of the Credit for Foreign Taxes under United States Income Tax Law*, published in 1961.[20] In addition, there is vast literature on the credit method (often referred to as the foreign tax credit (FTC)) and its specific design components in the US, unsurprisingly as the invention of the credit method in its standard form today is largely attributed to the US and as US legislators thus experimented numerous times with the precise design of the credit method.[21] From a more global perspective, the 2011 International Fiscal Association (IFA) Congress was dedicated to 'Key practical issues to eliminate double taxation of business income', which compiled 37 reports.[22] As for the credit method in the model conventions, drafted by the OECD, the United Nations (UN) and the US, one of the most long-standing authoritative sources of a comprehensive overview is the Klaus Vogel Commentary and, more recently, there is now the Global Tax Treaty Commentaries series.[23]

From these sources, it is clear that the term 'credit method', far from being a monolithic concept, encompasses numerous distinct technical questions, as well as different types, such as a 'direct' credit and an 'indirect' credit. The credit method is a juncture at which the most fundamental tax law questions join together, since, in order to apply credit method, one must be able to answer questions as to the notion of an income tax, the source of income and related expenses, the characterization of income, the attribution of income to a given taxpayer, the attribution of taxes paid to a given taxpayer, the tax treatment of various legal entities, the time period for which the credit

20. Elisabeth A. Owens, *The Foreign Tax Credit: A Study of the Credit for Foreign Taxes under United States Income Tax Law* (Harvard Law School 1961).
21. *See*, e.g., John P. Steines Jr., *The Foreign Tax Credit at Ninety-Five Bionic Centenarian*, 66(4) Tax L. Rev. 545, 549 n.22 (2013) ('The FTC has provoked prodigious quantities of literature addressing everything from first principles to hyper-technical issues. Some of the more important work analyzing broad principles and providing historical sweep are Elisabeth A. Owens, The Foreign Tax Credit: A Study of the Credit for Foreign Taxes Under United States Income Tax Law (1961); Michael J. Graetz & Michael M. O'Hear, The "Original Intent" of U.S. International Taxation, 46 Duke L.J. 1021 (1997); Joseph Isenbergh, The Foreign Tax Credit: Royalties, Subsidies, and Creditable Taxes, 39 Tax L. Rev. 227 (1984); Charles I. Kingson, The Foreign Tax Credit and Its Critics, 9 Am. J. Tax Pol'y 1 (1991)').
22. Gauthier Blanluet & Philippe J. Durand, *General Report: Key Practical Issues to Eliminate Double Taxation of Business Income*, 96b Cahiers de Droit Fiscal International 17 (IFA 2011) (the study looked at both domestic law and tax treaties and looked at both methods, i.e., credit and exemption. Although it also compared both methods, it shifted the focus from the well-trodden 'theoretical merits', e.g., the CEN versus CIN debate, to the under-treated 'practical problems'. The 27 reports were from Argentina, Australia, Austria, Belgium, Brazil, Canada, Chile, China, Colombia, the Czech Republic, Denmark, EU Report, Estonia, Finland, France, General Report, Germany, India, Luxembourg, Malta, Mexico, the Netherlands, New Zealand, Norway, Peru, Poland, Portugal, Romania, Russia, South Africa, Spain, Sri Lanka, Sweden, Switzerland, Ukraine, United Kingdom, United States, Venezuela. The reports are available in IBFD Online Books).
23. Alexander Rust, *Article 23 A Exemption Method and Article 23 B Credit Method, in 2 Klaus Vogel on Double Taxation Conventions* 1581 (Ekkehart Reimer & Alexander Rust eds, Kluwer Law International 4th ed. 2015); Georg Kofler, *Article 23B: Methods for Elimination of Double Taxation, in Global Tax Treaty Commentaries* (Richard Vann ed.-in-chief, Pasquale Pistone et al. eds, Global Topics IBFD updated as of February 2019).

is allowed, the computation of the credit and the limitations thereof, etc. In addition to its relationship with domestic law, the credit method of Article 23 of the OECD Model, UN Model and US Model also raises questions regarding its interaction with other treaty provisions, which may give rise to 'conflicts of qualification' and other conflicts of interpretation.[24] As a result of the OECD/G20 BEPS Project, some of these fundamental credit method questions are being re-examined, such as whether certain new taxes on the digital economy are creditable for tax treaty purposes[25] or the relationship between the new Article 1(2) treaty provision on transparent entities and the credit method under Article 23.[26] This touches upon only a few of the updates that will directly and

24. For example, where states disagree as to the allocation rule that should apply - be it due to different domestic law or due to a different interpretation of the convention or the facts - such conflicts of qualification and conflicts of interpretation can lead to cases of double taxation or double non-taxation; this may be difficult to resolve under Article 23, depending on how the states interpret Article 23 or whether Article 23 contains a specific provision to address these cases. *See*, e.g., OECD, *Model Tax Convention on Income and on Capital 2017: Condensed Version* Commentary on Articles 23 A and 23 B, paras 32.1–32.7, 56.1–56.3 (OECD Publishing 2017); Jean-Marc Déry & David A. Ward, *Canada: Interpretation of Double Taxation Conventions*, 78a Cahiers de Droit Fiscal International 259, 281–284 (IFA 1993); John F. Avery Jones et al., *Credit and Exemption under Tax Treaties in Cases of Differing Income Characterization*, 36(4) Eur. Tax'n 118, 141 et seq. (1996); Michael Lang, *2008 OECD Model: Conflicts of Qualification and Double Non-taxation*, 63(5) Bull. Int'l Tax'n 204 (2009); Alexander Rust, *The New Approach to Qualification Conflicts Has Its Limits*, 57(2) Bull. Int'l Tax'n 45 (2003); John F. Avery Jones, *Conflicts of Qualification: Comment on Prof. Vogel's and Alexander Rust's Articles*, 57(5) Bull. Int'l Tax'n 184 (2003).
25. Certain new taxes inspired by Action 1, such as an 'equalization levy' on certain e-commerce transactions in India or the digital services tax proposed in the EU, have provoked questions over the notion of income taxes, forcing legislators and taxpayers to assess whether and under what circumstances new taxes constitute creditable income taxes for tax treaty purposes. *See*, e.g., OECD, *Addressing the Tax Challenges of the Digital Economy, Action 1 – 2015 Final Report*, OECD/G20 Base Erosion and Profit Shifting Project (OECD Publishing 2015); India, Committee on Taxation of E-Commerce formed by the Central Board of Direct Taxes, Department of Revenue, Ministry of Finance, Government of India, *Proposal for Equalization Levy on Specified Transactions* (February 2016), http://www.incometaxindia.gov.in/Documents/News/Report-of-Committee-on-Taxation-of-e-Commerce-Feb-2016.pdf (last visited 23 Mar. 2016); Marjaana Helminen, *General Report: The Notion of Tax and the Elimination of International Double Taxation or Double Non-taxation*, 101b Cahiers de Droit Fiscal International 17, 43 (IFA 2016); J.P. Finet, *IRS Guidance on Treaty Benefits, PFICs Coming Next Year, Official Says*, 88 Tax Notes Int'l 666, 666–667 (13 Nov. 2017) (in the United States, IRS officials predict that this will raise the question as to when foreign taxes are considered 'compulsory' payments. 'She [Rollinson] noted that a portion of the regulations deal with the treatment of compulsory payments. "I do think that in this era of countries imposing all sorts of different taxes in relation to pressure under [the base erosion and profit-shifting project] and the OECD, the issue of what is a compulsory tax is just going to be more complicated and we will continue to need to write regs in that area," she said'); Daniela Hohenwarter, Georg Kofler, Gunter Mayr & Julia Sinnig, *Qualification of the Digital Services Tax under Tax Treaties*, 47(2) Intertax 140 (2019); Teri Sprackland, *French Legislature Amending DST to Prevent Double Taxation*, 94 Tax Notes Int'l 189 (8 Apr. 2019).
26. Questions as to the attribution of income as well as the tax treatment of legal entities will be updated in those cases where states decide to adopt the new Article 1(2) treaty provision on transparent entities proposed in Action 2. This provision will have implications for the credit method under Article 23, in some cases expanding its scope of application. The OECD itself recognizes and discusses the interaction between its hybrid mismatch proposals and Article 23 in Action 2. *See*, e.g., OECD, *Neutralising the Effects of Hybrid Mismatch Arrangements, Action 2 – 2015 Final Report*, OECD/G20 Base Erosion and Profit Shifting Project, 139, paras 434 et seq.

indirectly have an impact on the credit method, both in domestic law and in tax treaties.

Of course, the precise legal questions that arise from these contexts – e.g., within the US legal system, within tax treaties – are different from those that arise from EU law. In the field of EU law on direct taxation, the legal questions predominantly revolve around whether certain tax laws infringe the provisions of the EU Treaties on the internal market.[27] On the topic of the credit method under EU law, much has been written about the credit method as a general concept (often with a focus on its relationship with 'capital export neutrality' (CEN)) as compared to the exemption method (often with a focus on its relationship with 'capital import neutrality' (CIN)).[28] The bulk of this scholarship was published around the turn of the century. Since then, there have been developments in the CJEU case law that have touched on the credit method or certain components of it.[29] Notably, the CJEU generally found itself better positioned to address issues under the 'indirect' credit, by comparison with the 'direct' credit, as issues under the latter were often attributable to cross-border 'disparities' (as the analysis in Chapter 4 elaborates). As can be expected, each time new developments are detected in CJEU case law, scholarship is published about that specific case or line of case law.[30] This leaves open questions regarding the insights that could be gained

---

and 147, paras 445 et seq. (OECD Publishing 2015); Georg Kofler, *Some Reflections on the 'Saving Clause'*, 44(8/9) Intertax 574 (2016) (discussing the interaction between Article 1(3), Article 1(2) and Article 23).

27. *See*, e.g., *infra* note 80.
28. *See*, e.g., *supra* note 18.
29. *See*, e.g., CJEU, Case C-385/00, *de Groot*, 12 Dec. 2002, ECLI:EU:C:2002:750; CJEU, Case C-319/02, *Manninen*, 7 Sep. 2004, ECLI:EU:C:2004:484; CJEU, Case C-513/04, *Kerckhaert and Morres*, 14 Nov. 2006, ECLI:EU:C:2006:713; CJEU, Case C-446/04, *Test Claimants in the FII Group Litigation*, 12 Dec. 2006, ECLI:EU:C:2006:774; CJEU, Case C-170/05, *Denkavit Internationaal and Denkavit France*, 14 Dec. 2006, ECLI:EU:C:2006:783; CJEU, Case C-292/04, *Meilicke*, 6 Mar. 2007, ECLI:EU:C:2007:132; CJEU, Case C-379/05, *Amurta*, 8 Nov. 2007, ECLI:EU:C:2007:655; CJEU, Case C-298/05, *Columbus Container Services*, 6 Dec. 2007, ECLI:EU:C:2007:754; CJEU, Case C-194/06, *Orange European Smallcap Fund*, 24 May 2008, ECLI:EU:C:2008:289; CJEU, Case C-67/08, *Block*, 12 Feb. 2009, ECLI:EU:C:2009:92; CJEU, Case C-521/07, *Commission v. Netherlands*, 11 Jun. 2009, ECLI:EU:C:2009:360; CJEU, Case C-128/08, *Damseaux*, 16 Jul. 2009, ECLI:EU:C:2009:471; CJEU, Case C-540/07, *Commission v. Italy*, 19 Nov. 2009, ECLI:EU:C:2009:717; CJEU, Case C-262/09, *Meilicke*, 30 Jun. 2011, ECLI:EU:C:2011:438; CJEU, Joined Cases C-436/08 and C-437/08, *Haribo Lakritzen Hans Riegel BetriebsgmbH and Österreichische Salinen AG*, 10 Feb. 2011, ECLI:EU:C:2011:61; CJEU, Case C-310/09, *Accor*, 15 Sep. 2011, ECLI:EU:C:2011:581; CJEU, Case C-35/11, *Test Claimants in the FII Group Litigation*, 13 Nov. 2012, ECLI:EU:C:2012:707; CJEU, Case C-168/11, *Beker*, 28 Feb. 2013, ECLI:EU:C:2013:117; CJEU, Case C-48/13, *Nordea Bank*, 17 Jul. 2014, ECLI:EU:C:2014:2087; CJEU, Case C-47/12, *Kronos International Inc.*, 11 Sep. 2014, ECLI:EU:C:2014:2200; CJEU, Joined Cases C-10/14, C-14/14 and C-17/14, *J. B. G. T. Miljoen, X, and Société Générale SA*, 17 Sep. 2015, ECLI:EU:C:2015:608; CJEU, Case C-176/15, *Riskin and Timmermans*, 30 Jun. 2016, ECLI:EU:C:2016:488; CJEU, Case C-28/17, *NN*, 4 Jul. 2018, ECLI:EU:C:2018:526; CJEU, Case C-416/17, *Commission v. France (Précompte mobilier)*, 4 Oct. 2018, ECLI:EU:C:2018:811. In addition to CJEU case law, *see* EFTA, Case E-1/04, *Fokus Bank v. Norway*, 23 Nov. 2004; EFTA, Case E-7/07, *Seabrokers v. Norway*, 7 May 2008.
30. *See*, e.g., Werner Haslehner, *'Avoir Fiscal' and Its Legacy after Thirty Years of Direct Tax Jurisprudence of the Court of Justice*, 44(5) Intertax 374 (2016); Peter J. Wattel, *Progressive Taxation of Non-residents and Intra-EC Allocation of Personal Tax Allowances: Why Schumacker, Asscher, Gilly and Gschwind Do Not Suffice*, 40(6) Eur. Tax'n 210 (2000); Michael J. Graetz &

from the combined and cumulative effect of this case law on the credit method and, in particular, if and the extent to which EU law affects specific design components of the credit method. These are therefore the questions addressed in this study.

1.3. RESEARCH PROBLEM STATEMENT

To further elaborate on the synopsis above, according to the preamble of the ATAD, most measures of which have been in effect since 1 January 2019:

> '(5) It is necessary to lay down rules against the erosion of tax bases in the internal market and the shifting of profits out of the internal market. Rules in the following areas are necessary in order to contribute to achieving that objective: limitations to the deductibility of interest, exit taxation, a general anti-abuse rule, controlled foreign company rules and rules to tackle hybrid mismatches. Where the application of those rules gives rise to *double taxation*, taxpayers should receive *relief through a deduction for the tax paid in another Member State or third country*, as the case may be. Thus, the rules should not only aim to counter tax avoidance practices but also avoid creating other obstacles to the market, such as *double taxation*' (emphasis added).[31]

From this, the (aforementioned) balancing act of EU MSs emerges. They are obliged to implement the ATAD I[32] and ATAD II[33] and to simultaneously ensure that this expanded taxation does not give rise to double taxation. Additionally, as MSs implement a Directive, which constitutes secondary EU law, or double taxation relief measures under their domestic law, they must do so in line with primary EU law.

Typically, rules for double taxation relief apply either the 'exemption method' or the 'credit method'. Setting aside the details and debates, the methods can be explained simply.[34] Under the exemption method, double taxation is avoided by excluding the income earned from abroad (foreign-source income (FSI)) from the tax base in the state of residence of the taxpayer (residence state). Under the credit method, double taxation is relieved by reducing the total taxes owed by the taxpayer on the basis of all income earned worldwide, by an amount equal to the foreign taxes paid abroad or an amount

Alvin C. Warren Jr., *Dividend Taxation in Europe: When the ECJ Makes Tax Policy*, 44(6) Common Mkt. L. Rev. 1577 (2007); Michael Lang, *Recent Case Law of the ECJ in Direct Taxation: Trends, Tensions and Contradictions*, 18(3) EC Tax Rev. 98 (2009); Georg Kofler, *Tax Treaty 'Neutralization' of Source State Discrimination under the EU Fundamental Freedoms?*, 65(12) Bull. Int'l Tax'n 684 (2011); Georg Kofler, *Chapter 7: Double Taxation and European Law – Analysis of the Jurisprudence, in Double Taxation Within the European Union* 97 (Alexander Rust ed., Kluwer 2011); Georg Kofler, *Indirect Credit Versus Exemption: Double Taxation Relief for Intercompany Distributions*, 66(2) Bull. Int'l Tax'n 77 (2012); Eric C.C.M. Kemmeren, *Gross Withholding Taxes: Is the Court of Justice of the European Union Back on Track with Regard to Deductible Expenses?*, 26(1) EC Tax Rev. 2 (2017).

31. Council Directive (EU) 2016/1164 of 12 July 2016 Laying Down Rules Against Tax Avoidance Practices that Directly Affect the Functioning of the Internal Market, OJ L 193, 1–14, preamble recital 5 (19 Jul. 2016) (ATAD I).
32. *Id.*
33. Council Directive (EU) 2017/952 of 29 May 2017 Amending Directive (EU) 2016/1164 as Regards Hybrid Mismatches with Third Countries, OJ L 144, 1–11 (7 Jun. 2017) (ATAD II).
34. For further details, *see* Chapter 2.

that corresponds to what the residence state would collect on the FSI. Nearly all states apply a mix of these two methods, depending on the type of income and other factors.[35]

The ATAD states that, in general, regarding the application of *all* the ATAD rules, MSs should provide 'relief through a deduction for the tax paid in another Member State or third country' and, in particular, regarding the CFC rules,[36] MSs 'shall allow a deduction of the tax paid by the entity or permanent establishment from the tax liability of the taxpayer in its state of tax residence or location'. In other words, it mandates the credit method.

Moreover, in addition to the ATAD, other recent developments point towards an increasing, or renewed, recognition of the role of the credit method in the anti-BEPS, anti-double-non-taxation political climate – not necessarily as a superior means to eliminate double taxation, but as a means to do so while preventing double non-taxation or base erosion. These include: (1) the options offered under Multilateral Convention to Implement Tax Treaty Related Measures to Prevent Base Erosion and Profit Shifting (MLI) for the 'Application of Methods for Elimination of Double Taxation' (Article 5), proposing that states adopt either the credit method or a form of switch-over from the exemption method to the credit method in certain cases (*see* Option A, Option B and especially Option C);[37] (2) the European Parliament draft recommendation to the Council and the Commission following the inquiry on money laundering, tax avoidance and tax evasion (2016/3044(RSP)) proposing more withholding tax (WHT) systems with the credit method,[38] and, along similar lines,[39] the

35. For further details, *see*, e.g., Alexander Rust, *Article 23 A Exemption Method and Article 23 B Credit Method, in* 2 *Klaus Vogel on Double Taxation Conventions* 1581 (Ekkehart Reimer & Alexander Rust eds, Kluwer Law International 4th ed. 2015).
36. Council Directive (EU) 2016/1164 of 12 July 2016 Laying Down Rules Against Tax Avoidance Practices that Directly Affect the Functioning of the Internal Market, OJ L 193, 1–14, preamble recital 12 (19 Jul. 2016) (CFC rules are described in the ATAD in the following way: 'Controlled foreign company (CFC) rules have the effect of re-attributing the income of a low-taxed controlled subsidiary to its parent company. Then, the parent company becomes taxable on this attributed income in the State where it is resident for tax purposes. Depending on the policy priorities of that State, CFC rules may target an entire low-taxed subsidiary, specific categories of income or be limited to income which has artificially been diverted to the subsidiary. In particular, in order to ensure that CFC rules are a proportionate response to BEPS concerns, it is critical that Member States that limit their CFC rules to income which has been artificially diverted to the subsidiary precisely target situations where most of the decision-making functions which generated diverted income at the level of the controlled subsidiary are carried out in the Member State of the taxpayer').
37. Multilateral Convention to Implement Tax Treaty Related Measures to Prevent Base Erosion and Profit Shifting, Article 5 (text adopted 24 Nov. 2016) (MLI) (Option A is a switch-over from the exemption method to the credit method modelled after Article 23A(4) OECD Model; Option B is a switch-over from the exemption method to the credit method that is targeted at hybrid financial instruments; Option C is the credit method).
38. European Parliament, *Draft Recommendation to the Council and the Commission Following the Inquiry on Money Laundering, Tax Avoidance and Tax Evasion*, 2016/3044(RSP), B8-0660/2017, para. 24 (30 Nov. 2017) ('Calls for concerted action on the part of Member States *against low or non-taxation of outbound payments in order to combat base erosion and profit shifting (BEPS) effectively and systematically*; reiterates its position that more action is needed than is provided for in the Anti-Tax Avoidance Package (ATAP) and that such action should be binding; calls, therefore, for the introduction of a *harmonised withholding tax* by Member States on all *interest* payments and on *dividend, licence and royalty fees* to low-tax third countries,

2017 UN Model expanded WHTs under its new Article 12A on 'fees for technical services'[40] and one of the main topics debated at the 2018 IFA Congress was WHTs in the era of BEPS and the digital economy;[41] (3) the initial proposals of the Austrian Presidency of the EU included an EU Model Tax Treaty with a credit method or switch-over clause in certain cases,[42] the proposal of the ATAD originally included a rule to switch-over from the exemption to credit method in certain cases,[43] and though it was removed from the final version of the ATAD, a switch-over reappeared in the proposal for a Common (Consolidated) Corporate Tax Base (C(C)CTB) Directive;[44] (4) on the methods more broadly, the EU Commission's state aid investigation of Luxembourg's tax treatment of McDonald's militated against interpreting the exemption method of Article 23 of the US-Luxembourg tax treaty in a way that created double non-taxation,[45] before having to back down since it could not prove 'selectivity'.[46] As

---

irrespective of whether these countries are on the EU's list of non-cooperative tax jurisdictions; *underlines that such a general withholding tax system based on the credit method has the advantage of preventing double non-taxation and BEPS without creating instances of double taxation and without relying on a selective blacklisting approach which would entail significant diplomatic challenges*; calls on the Member States to agree on strong, comprehensive and enforceable CFC rules and to discard rules which are limited to vaguely defined arrangements which are not genuine, the burden of proof for which is placed on the tax authorities' (emphasis added)).

39. *See*, e.g., Chapter 4 (as can be inferred from the line of CJEU case law on 'neutralization', under EU law, a more widespread application of income withholding taxes could require a more widespread application of the credit method).
40. United Nations, Department of Economic & Social Affairs, *United Nations Model Double Taxation Convention Between Developed and Developing Countries: 2017 Update* (United Nations 2018).
41. Chang Hee Lee & Ji-Hyun Yoon, *General Report: Withholding Tax in the Era of BEPS, CIVs and Digital Economy*, 103b Cahiers de Droit Fiscal International 5 (IFA 2018).
42. Austria, Bundesministerium für Finanzen (Ministry of Finance), *Schelling-Plan: Schließung internationaler Steuerflucht-Routen* (10 Jul. 2017).
43. European Commission, Proposal for a Council Directive Laying Down Rules Against Tax Avoidance Practices that Directly Affect the Functioning of the Internal Market, COM(2016) 26 Final (28 Jan. 2016).
44. Pasquale Pistone & Dennis Weber, *Chapter 1: An Introduction to the Anti-tax Avoidance Directive and the Implementation of the BEPS Project in the European Union, in The Implementation of Anti-BEPS Rules in the EU: A Comprehensive Study* 1 (Pasquale Pistone & Dennis Weber eds, IBFD 2018); Fred van Horzen & Isabella de Groot, *Chapter 9: The Switch-Over Clause – To Exempt or Not to Exempt, That Is the Question, in The Implementation of Anti-BEPS Rules in the EU: A Comprehensive Study* 167 (Pasquale Pistone & Dennis Weber eds, IBFD 2018); European Commission, Proposal for a Council Directive on a Common Corporate Tax Base, COM(2016) 685 Final, Article 53 (25 Oct. 2016); European Commission, Proposal for a Council Directive on a Common Consolidated Corporate Tax Base (CCCTB), COM(2016) 683 Final, Article 72 (25 Oct. 2016).
45. European Commission, SA.38945 Alleged aid to Mc Donald's – Luxembourg, Decision to Initiate the Formal Investigation Procedure (3 Dec. 2015), http://ec.europa.eu/competition/elojade/isef/case_details.cfm?proc_code=3_SA_38945 (last visited 10 Mar. 2018). For an analysis of this case, *see* Rita Szudoczky, *Double Taxation Relief, Transfer Pricing Adjustments and State Aid Law: Comments, in State Aid Law and Business Taxation* 163 (Isabelle Richelle, Wolfgang Schön & Edoardo Traversa eds, Springer 2016); Werner Haslehner, *The McDonald's State Aid Case: The EU Commission Interprets a Tax Treaty*, Kluwer International Tax Blog (22 Jun. 2016), http://kluwertaxblog.com/2016/06/22/the-mcdonalds-state-aid-case-the-eu-commission-interprets-a-tax-treaty (last visited 31 Jul. 2016); Oliver R. Hoor & Keith O'Donnell, *McDonald's State Aid Investigation: What the European Commission Got Wrong*, 83 Tax Notes Int'l 975, 982–983

under the ATAD, trends emerge of expanding tax bases which then require the credit method to relieve the resulting double taxation; the exemption method by its nature (namely, exempting the tax base) is not suitable where the objective is to recapture parts of the tax base that have been eroded or shifted. For example, the UK's Diverted Profits Tax captures 'profits that have been generated by UK economic activity' which have been artificially diverted out of the UK and levies a 25% tax 'plus any "true-up interest"', but will offer an FTC in some cases.[47] As for one notable example outside of the EU, the US tax reform, passed in 2017,[48] included an unprecedented form of worldwide minimum tax on the income of CFCs that, simply put, exceeds a 10% return on tangible assets (referred to by its popular acronym, GILTI, for global intangible low-taxed income), for which an FTC will be available (capped at 80% of the foreign taxes paid).[49] In Germany, the finance minister had repeatedly encouraged EU MSs to work together on a worldwide minimum tax, a development which could entail increased reliance on the credit method or similar mechanisms.[50] The idea of some form of global minimum taxation then made its way into the OECD's proposals on

(12 Sep. 2016); Fadi Shaheen, *Tax Treaty Aspects of the McDonald's State Aid Investigation*, 86 Tax Notes Int'l 331 (24 Apr. 2017).

46. European Commission, State aid: Commission Investigation Did Not Find That Luxembourg Gave Selective Tax Treatment to McDonald's, IP/18/5831 (19 Sep. 2018), http://europa.eu/rapid/press-release_IP-18-5831_en.htm (last visited 3 Nov. 2018).
47. United Kingdom, HM Revenue & Customs, *Diverted Profits Tax Guidance* at DPT1010, DPT1030 and DPT2300 (31 Dec. 2018), https://assets.publishing.service.gov.uk/government/uploads/system/uploads/attachment_data/file/768204/Diverted_Profits_Tax_-_Guidance__December_2018_.pdf (last visited 19 Aug. 2018).
48. United States, An Act to Provide for Reconciliation Pursuant to Titles II and V of the Concurrent Resolution on the Budget for Fiscal Year 2018, One-Hundred-Fifteenth Congress, Session I, Public Law 115-97 (US Government Printing Office 22 Dec. 2017) (Tax Cuts and Jobs Act).
49. *See*, e.g., J. Clifton Fleming Jr., Robert J. Peroni & Stephen E. Shay, *Expanded Worldwide Versus Territorial Taxation after the TCJA*, 161(10) Tax Notes 1173 (3 Dec. 2018) (the authors observe that, while the tax reform includes elements of territoriality in the new exemption for dividends in certain cases, it simultaneously expanded worldwide taxation with the new GILTI rules).
50. *See*, e.g., Economic and Financial Affairs Council, *Franco-German Joint Declaration on the Taxation of Digital Companies and Minimum Taxation* (Meeting No. 3659, Brussels, 4 Dec. 2018), https://www.consilium.europa.eu/en/meetings/ecofin/2018/12/04/ (last visited 10 Dec. 2018); Johannes Becker & Joachim Englisch, *The German Proposal for an Effective Minimum Tax on MNE Profits*, Kluwer International Tax Blog (17 Jan. 2019), http://kluwertaxblog.com/2019/01/17/the-german-proposal-for-an-effective-minimum-tax-on-mne-profits/ (last visited 20 Jan. 2019). *See also*, e.g., Mindy Herzfeld, *Debate on the US Tax Reform and the EU ATAD: Can GILTI + BEAT = GLOBE?*, 47(5) Intertax 504 (2019); Francis Weyzig, *Why a Minimum Effective Tax Rate Is Urgently Needed*, Kluwer International Tax Blog (4 Apr. 2019), http://kluwertaxblog.com/2019/04/04/why-a-minimum-effective-tax-rate-is-urgently-needed/ (last visited 10 Apr. 2019); Mindy Herzfeld, *News Analysis: What the OECD Can Learn from the U.S. GILTI Regime*, 93 Tax Notes Int'l 163 (14 Jan. 2019); Stephanie Soong Johnston, *U.S. Throws Weight Behind French Push for Global Minimum Tax*, 93 Tax Notes Int'l 991 (4 Mar. 2019). On the other hand, for doubts as to the EU law compatibility of a global minimum tax, *see*, e.g., CFE Fiscal Committee, *CFE Response to the OECD Consultation Document: Addressing the Tax Challenges of the Digitalising Economy* (CFE Tax Advisors Europe, Opinion Statement FC 1/2019, 5 Mar. 2019), http://taxadviserseurope.org/wp-content/uploads/2019/03/CFE-Response-OECD-Consultation-Taxation-of-the-Digital-Economy.pdf (last visited 6 Mar. 2019); Daniel W. Blum, *Debate on the US Tax Reform and the EU ATAD: The Proposal for a Global Minimum Tax – Comeback of Residence Taxation in the Digital Era? – Comment on Can GILTI + BEAT = GLOBE?*, 47(5) Intertax 514 (2019).

Addressing the Tax Challenges of the Digitalisation of the Economy,[51] eventually leading to international agreement on an income inclusion rule, an undertaxed payment rule and a treaty-based subject-to-tax rule.[52]

In connecting the dots, so to speak, between these recent developments, an evolution regarding the credit method can be detected, which may make it a more stable fixture in the 'post-BEPS' tax law landscape in the EU. That said, one issue is that EU scholars, and arguably legislators of MSs, have been known to have a preference for the exemption method.[53] Not only did EU MSs embark on a proliferation of 'participation exemption' regimes, especially following the Parent-Subsidiary Directive, but also scholars have tended to criticize the credit method as a potential impediment to the internal market.[54]

CJEU case law has continued to further clarify the relationship between the credit method and EU law.[55] It has found that, in the current state of EU law, the credit method does not violate EU law; however, this does not mean that there are no constraints on its design. Indeed, further guidance seems merited since certain key design questions – such as whether excess credits should be carried forward into future years (credit carryforward) and whether the credit limitation (also referred to as the maximum creditable amount (MCA)) should be calculated on a per-country, per-item or overall basis – considerably alter the effect of the credit method. A mere at-a-glance comparison of different MSs' credit methods shows that the design can vary in substantial ways.[56,57] Although Directives are not intended to provide all details, as

51. OECD, *Addressing the Tax Challenges of the Digitalisation of the Economy, Public Consultation Document* (13 Feb.–6 Mar. 2019), OECD/G20 Base Erosion and Profit Shifting Project, 25–26, paras 96–100 (OECD 2019).
52. For the developments on these global minimum tax efforts since the initial writing of this book, and forthcoming developments in 2022, *see*, e.g., OECD, *Tax Challenges Arising from Digitalisation – Report on Pillar Two Blueprint: Inclusive Framework on BEPS*, OECD/G20 Base Erosion and Profit Shifting Project (OECD Publishing 2020), https://doi.org/10.1787/abb4c3d1-en (last visited November 2020); OECD, *Statement on a Two-Pillar Solution to Address the Tax Challenges Arising From the Digitalisation of the Economy*, OECD/G20 Base Erosion and Profit Shifting Project (1 Jul. 2021), https://www.oecd.org/tax/beps/statement-on-a-two-pillar-solution-to-address-the-tax-challenges-arising-from-the-digitalisation-of-the-economy-july-2021.pdf (last visited 9 Oct. 2021); OECD, *Tax Challenges Arising from the Digitalisation of the Economy – Global Anti-Base Erosion Model Rules (Pillar Two)*, (Inclusive Framework on BEPS, OECD 2021), https://www.oecd.org/tax/beps/tax-challenges-arising-from-the-digitalisation-of-the-economy-global-anti-base-erosion-model-rules-pillar-two.htm (last visited 23 Dec. 2021).
53. *See*, e.g., Georg Kofler, *Indirect Credit Versus Exemption: Double Taxation Relief for Intercompany Distributions*, 66(2) Bull. Int'l Tax'n 77, 87 n.129 (2012) ('However, the majority of scholars consider the exemption method as being more in line with the Internal Market. [...]'); European Commission, Workshop on EC Law and Tax Treaties, Annex A: The Articles of the OECD Model Convention: A Community Perspective, TAXUD E1/FR DOC (05) 2306/A, 12 n.33 (9 Jun. 2005); *see also supra* note 18.
54. *See supra* note 18.
55. *See supra* note 29.
56. To offer a few illustrative examples, Belgium offers a fixed credit (*quotité forfaitaire d'impôt étranger*) equivalent to 15/85 of net revenue in some cases. Hungary limits its credit to 90% of the foreign taxes paid. Malta operates a 'full imputation' system that grants both resident and non-resident shareholders a credit on 'dividends paid by a company resident in Malta ... equivalent to the tax paid by the company on its profits out of which the dividends are distributed'. All three apply a per-country and per-item limitation, while Finland applies a

they deliberately offer some margin of discretion for MSs to implement them in accordance with their national legal systems,[58] the ATAD offers essentially no guidance. It neglected to even specify whether an indirect credit should be offered for taxes levied on sub-subsidiaries, something which the Parent-Subsidiary Directive by comparison did address. The anti-BEPS rules are noticeably more detailed than the relief-for-double-taxation rules. This is indicative of the broader trend at the time of writing. As MSs must implement Directives, and all measures for that matter, in line with EU law, as interpreted by the CJEU, this research seeks to contribute some clarity and a more structured framework to update the discussion of the credit method under EU law.

1.4. RESEARCH QUESTION

The year 2019 marked the hundred-year anniversary of the legal birth of the credit method (in its current form).[59] Its centenary moment also coincided with the birth of the ATAD,[60] touted as a major turning point in EU tax policy.[61] Tying these two topics

per-basket limitation and Luxembourg a per-country and per-basket limitation. Belgium does not permit a carryforward of excess credits, Luxembourg permits the excess of foreign tax to be deducted from the tax base, and Finland allows a carryforward for five years. *See* respectively Stefan Geluyckens, *Belgium: Individual Taxation*, Country Analyses IBFD Section 7 (last visited 1 Jul. 2018); Gauthier Cruysmans, *Belgium: Corporate Taxation*, Country Analyses IBFD Section 7 (last visited 1 Jul. 2018); Levente Torma, *Hungary: Individual Taxation*, Country Analyses IBFD Section 7 (last visited 4 Jul. 2018); Levente Torma, *Hungary: Corporate Taxation*, Country Analyses IBFD Section 7 (last visited 4 Jul. 2018); André Zarb & Pierre Portelli, *Malta: Individual Taxation*, Country Analyses IBFD Section 7 (last visited 10 Jul. 2018); Conrad Cassar Torregiani, *Malta: Corporate Taxation*, Country Analyses IBFD Section 7 (last visited 10 Jul. 2018); Laura Ambagtsheer-Pakarinen, *Finland: Individual Taxation*, Country Analyses IBFD Section 7 (last visited 3 Jul. 2018); Kirsi Hiltunen, *Finland: Corporate Taxation*, Country Analyses IBFD Section 7 (last visited 3 Jul. 2018); Pierre-Jean Estagerie, *Luxembourg: Individual Taxation*, Country Analyses IBFD Section 7 (last visited 10 Jul. 2018); Chiara Bardini & Michel Lambion, *Luxembourg: Corporate Taxation*, Country Analyses IBFD Section 7 (last visited 10 Jul. 2018).

57. Moreover, approximately half of EU MSs had no CFC rules, prior to ATAD, and thus less experience with indirect credit under such rules (i.e., Austria, Belgium, Bulgaria, Croatia, the Czech Republic, Ireland, Latvia, Luxembourg, Malta, the Netherlands, Romania, Slovak Republic, Slovenia, and Greece only since 2014).
58. *See* Treaty on the Functioning of the European Union (TFEU), Consolidated Version, Document C:2012:326:TOC, OJ C 326, 47–390, Article 288 (26 Oct. 2012) (hereinafter 'TFEU').
59. *See* United States, Revenue Act of 1918, Sixty-Fifth Congress, Session III, Chapter 18, Public Law 65-254 (US Government Printing Office 1919) (this assumes the date of entry into force of the Revenue Act of 1918 can be considered the date of birth, which, as Chapter 2 reveals, is arguably the case, when referring to the credit method in its standard version most commonly used today. For other versions of the credit method, *see* the historical legal developments in Chapter 2).
60. Council Directive (EU) 2016/1164 of 12 July 2016 Laying Down Rules Against Tax Avoidance Practices that Directly Affect the Functioning of the Internal Market, OJ L 193, 1–14 (19 Jul. 2016) (according to Article 11 on 'Transposition', 1 Jan. 2019 is the general rule, subject to some exceptions).
61. *See*, e.g., Pasquale Pistone & Dennis Weber, *Chapter 1: An Introduction to the Anti-tax Avoidance Directive and the Implementation of the BEPS Project in the European Union*, *in The Implementation of Anti-BEPS Rules in the EU: A Comprehensive Study* 1 (Pasquale Pistone & Dennis Weber eds, IBFD 2018); Aloys Rigaut, *Anti-tax Avoidance Directive (2016/1164): New EU Policy Horizons*, 56(11) Eur. Tax'n 497 (2016); Daniel Gutmann et al., *The Impact of the ATAD on Domestic Systems: A Comparative Survey*, 57(1) Eur. Tax'n 2, 2–20 (2017). *See also*, e.g., Pasquale Pistone, *BEPS, Capital Export Neutrality and the Risk of Hidden Tax Protectionism.*

and the broader trends together, this book posits an increased role for the credit method in the EU in light of recent developments. The credit method, properly designed, is one of the tools currently needed to assist MSs in balancing obligations to counteract BEPS practices while avoiding double taxation.

Unpacking this proposition requires two things: first, this requires engaging with a broader academic debate on the compatibility of the credit method with the EU internal market; second, it calls for a practical study on the design of the credit method. For assessing 'properly designed', the framework of analysis is of course EU law; thus 'properly' refers to 'correctly' or 'duly', 'in an appropriate or suitable manner'[62] under EU law.

To conduct this assessment, this book proposed the following research question: to what extent and in what ways does EU law influence the design and application of the credit method? It is timely to take stock of the CJEU decisions thus far to see what MSs should keep in mind moving forward, identify what open issues remain and reflect upon some responses to those open issues.

Research of the credit method reveals certain key components that compose it, such as the scope of eligible taxpayers, the amount of creditable taxes (credit limitation, excess credits), and the calculation of FSI (expenses, losses), each of which may raise distinct issues under EU law. EU law issues also varied according to the type of credit method (direct, indirect, imputation).

Research of the decisions of the CJEU reveals eight lines of case law that relate, directly or indirectly, to the credit method for relieving double taxation. For the purposes of the discussion, these will be referred to, in a simplified way, as: (1) the *Avoir Fiscal/Saint Gobain* line of case law, which is foundational case law on equal treatment in direct taxation and which affects relief for double taxation; (2) the *Gilly* or 'disparity' line of case law; (3) the *FII* or 'equivalence' line of case law; (4) the *Schumacker/De Groot* or 'calculation' line of case law; (5) the *Amurta* or 'neutralization' line of case law; (6) the *Gerritse/Scorpio* or deductible expenses line of case law (which connects to the 'neutralization' line); (7) the *Marks and Spencer* or losses line of case law; and (8) the *Manninen* or the ill-fated imputation method line of case law.

The themes, or doctrines, used to unify each line of case law (e.g., the 'disparity' line, the 'equivalence' line, etc.) have each been separately discussed in tax law literature,[63] to different extents and from different angles. Building upon this, this

---

Selected Remarks from an EU Perspective, in Base Erosion and Profit Shifting (BEPS): Impact for European and International Tax Policy 319 (Robert Danon ed., Schulthess Verlag 2016) (underscoring that, while 'a highly desirable development', bringing positive steps in terms of international tax coordination, the BEPS Project should be implemented in ways that are compatible with EU law and support 'a globally fair tax system', warning against the risks that certain proposed measures such as subject-to-tax clauses and switch-over clauses may amount to a form of 'hidden tax protectionism' if over-implemented).

62. *Properly*, Oxford English Dictionary (Oxford University Press 3d ed. 2007), www.oed.com/view/Entry/152669 (last visited 7 Jun. 2018).

63. *See*, e.g., Sjoerd Douma, *The Three Ds of Direct Tax Jurisdiction: Disparity, Discrimination and Double Taxation*, 46(11) Eur. Tax'n 522 (2006); Georg Kofler, *Indirect Credit Versus Exemption: Double Taxation Relief for Intercompany Distributions*, 66(2) Bull. Int'l Tax'n 77 (2012); Georg Kofler, *Tax Treaty 'Neutralization' of Source State Discrimination under the EU Fundamental*

research seeks to bring the main conclusions from all together and analyse them specifically through the lens of the credit method, in order to derive guidance, or constraints, on its design within the framework of EU law.

1.5. RESEARCH METHODS

This research is conducted in the field of law. It uses the methods that are traditional to 'doctrinal legal research'. In an effort to define this, one study on 'doctrinal legal research' cited, among others, the following descriptions:[64]

> 'Research which provides a systematic exposition of the rules governing a particular legal category, analyses the relationship between rules, explains areas of difficulty and, perhaps, predicts future developments.'[65]
>
> 'To a large extent, it is the doctrinal aspect of law that makes legal research distinctive and provides an often under-recognised parallel to "discovery" in the physical sciences. Doctrinal research, at its best, involves rigorous analysis and creative synthesis, the making of connections between seemingly disparate doctrinal strands, and the challenge of extracting general principles from an inchoate mass of primary materials. The very notion of "legal reasoning" is a subtle and sophisticated jurisprudential concept, a unique blend of deduction and induction, that has engaged legal scholars for generations, and is a key to understanding the mystique of the legal system's simultaneous achievement of constancy and change [...].'[66]

The authors of the study, Hutchinson and Duncan, found that, at a minimum, the method of doctrinal legal research comprises a two-step process, namely: (1) 'locating the sources of the law' and (2) 'interpreting and analysing the text'.[67]

Freedoms?, 65(12) Bull. Int'l Tax'n 684 (2011); Axel Cordewener, *Cross-Border Loss Compensation and EU Fundamental Freedoms: The 'Final Losses' Doctrine Is Still Alive!*, 27(5) EC Tax Rev. 230 (2018); *see also supra* note 30.

64. Terry Hutchinson & Nigel Duncan, *Defining and Describing What We Do: Doctrinal Legal Research*, 17(1) Deakin L. Rev. 83, 102–104 (2012) (the authors compiled and studied various definitions and descriptions of the methods of doctrinal legal research, such as the 'Consultative Group on Research and Education in Law, Law and Learning: Report to the Social Sciences and the Humanities Research Council of Canada (Information Division of the Social Sciences and Humanities Research Council of Canada, 1983)' and 'Martha Minow, Dean of Harvard Law School, ... outlining the types of intellectual contribution resulting from legal scholarship' in 'Martha Minow, "Archetypal Legal Scholarship – A Field Guide", in *AALS Workshop for New Law Teachers* (AALS, 2006), 34-5 <http://www.aals.org/documents/2006nlt/nltworkbook06 .pdf>.', among others). For Minow's work, *see also* Martha Minow, *Archetypal Legal Scholarship: A Field Guide*, 63 J. Legal Educ. 65 (2013).
65. Terry Hutchinson & Nigel Duncan, *Defining and Describing What We Do: Doctrinal Legal Research*, 17(1) Deakin L. Rev. 83, 101–102 (2012) (quoting 'Dennis Pearce, Enid Campbell and Don Harding ("Pearce Committee"), *Australian Law Schools: A Discipline Assessment for the Commonwealth Tertiary Education Commission* (Australian Government Publishing Service, 1987) cited in Terry Hutchinson, *Researching and Writing in Law* (Reuters Thomson, 3rd ed, 2010) 7').
66. *Id.*, at 105 (quoting 'Council of Australian Law Deans, *CALD Statement on the Nature of Research* (May and October 2005), 3 <http://cald.anu.edu.au/docs/cald%20statement%20on%20the%20nature%20of/o201egal%20research%20-%202005.pdf>'; for the URL, *see also* https://cald.asn.au/wp-content/uploads/2017/11/cald-statement-on-the-nature-of-legal-research-20051.pdf).
67. Terry Hutchinson & Nigel Duncan, *Defining and Describing What We Do: Doctrinal Legal Research*, 17(1) Deakin L. Rev. 83, 110 (2012).

The research for this project undertakes both steps. First, in locating the sources of the law, it undertakes an extensive search of the primary sources of law, defined as encompassing treaties, legislation, regulation, case law and constitutions.[68] For EU law materials, these are available via its official database *EUR-Lex* and the *Official Journal of the European Union*. For research on the historical development of the credit method, the aim was to rely on the official historical reports to the greatest extent possible, such as those of the League of Nations and US Congressional records. Secondary sources, such as commentaries and articles published in law journals, are used as a complement to the primary sources, for identifying other legal issues that arise in practice and the dominant debates among legal experts, and as part of the literature review of existing scholarship on the topic.

As regards the second step, in order to interpret and analyse the texts, this work relies on what could be referred to as the standard methods of statutory interpretation (or sometimes as the 'classical canon of interpretation' (emphasis omitted))[69] and approaches to legal reasoning. The methods of interpretation used are those employed by judges, lawyers and legal academics alike, and include a textual (or grammatical), contextual, teleological (or purposive) and historical interpretation.[70] The starting point is often the textual interpretation, which is the 'semantic, linguistic, and grammatical analysis of a legal provision' and pays attention to the 'possibilities of variation within the relevant linguistic usage-including legal usage, other professional usage or the popular vernacular'.[71] Contextual interpretation seeks to support the search for meaning of ambiguous terms by referencing 'other related provisions or concepts in which the same word or term appears'.[72] Teleological interpretation often

68. *See*, e.g., Harvard Law School Library, *Legal Research Strategy, Primary Sources for Legal Research* (last updated 4 Dec. 2018), https://guides.library.harvard.edu/law/researchstrategy/primarysources (last visited 10 May 2019); United States, Library of Congress, *Law Library, Guide to Secondary Legal Resources* (last updated 2015), http://www.loc.gov/law/help/secondary-rsrcs.php (last visited 10 May 2019).
69. Winfried Brugger, *Concretization of Law and Statutory Interpretation*, 11 Tul. Eur. & Civ. L.F. 207, 232–233 (1996).
70. *See*, e.g., United States, Congressional Research Service, *Statutory Interpretation: General Principles and Recent Trends* (CRS Report 97-589, September 2014), https://www.everycrsreport.com/reports/97-589.html#_Toc407006254 (last visited 11 May 2019); Winfried Brugger, *Concretization of Law and Statutory Interpretation*, 11 Tul. Eur. & Civ. L.F. 207 (1996) (this article includes an overview of all four methods of interpretation); Vienna Convention on the Law of Treaties (23 May 1969), Article 31(1) (relevant for the interpretation of tax treaties); United Kingdom, Supreme Court, [2015] UKSC 44, *Anson v. Commissioners for Her Majesty's Revenue and Customs*, 1 Jul. 2015, at paras 54–59; Canada, Tax Court of Canada, 2016 TCC 131, *Société Générale Valeurs Mobilières Inc. v. The Queen*, 26 May 2016, aff'd 2017 FCA 3, at paras 9–12 (both of these cases, *Anson* and *Société générale valeurs mobilières inc.*, interpreted the credit method in the tax treaty in question and offer two examples of an interpretation relying methodically on a textual, contextual and purposive analysis, citing the Vienna Convention on the Law of Treaties).
71. Winfried Brugger, *Concretization of Law and Statutory Interpretation*, 11 Tul. Eur. & Civ. L.F. 207, 234–235 (1996).
72. *Id.*, at 237–238 (note also that the context may be narrow, looking only at the words and paragraphs surrounding the text in question, or may be broad, encompassing 'all legal provisions that are valid within the particular legal order and in some manner concern the problem to be solved or to the term or concept used in the pertinent norm').

involves researching what was written or stated by lawmakers in order to discern the purpose of a law.[73] Similarly, historical interpretation, 'in its broadest sense', 'aims at elucidating the will of past lawmakers'.[74] This is particularly relevant in the study of the texts of laws providing earlier versions of the credit method in Chapter 2.

The approach to legal reasoning could be described as 'abductive' because it has recourse to both inductive and deductive legal reasoning.[75] For example, in the analysis and synthesis of case law, the legal reasoning is inductive in that it uses a process of inference 'from the specific cases to a more general rule':

> 'Where the source of the rule is case law rather than legislation, "the lawyer will have to examine several cases to find a major premise which underlies them all". So the lawyer will have to "reason from particular case decisions to a general proposition".'[76]

In analysing the cases decided by the CJEU, the aim is to determine what general rules can be inferred that could be relevant for the credit method. In other instances, the reasoning can also be described as 'deductive':

> 'Legal reasoning is often deductive because the general rules are "given", for example through legislation. The lawyer researcher examines the legislative provision, examines the situation and then decides if the situation comes within the rule.'[77]

To the extent that certain general rules can be derived from the analysis of CJEU case law, the aim will be to apply them to more concrete questions, when considering how those rules could affect specific components of the credit method.

Moreover, in order to make convincing inferences, this requires reasoning 'by analogy' and 'by distinguishing'.[78] This involves studying the 'attributes or relations between cases' in order to identify the extent to which they are similar or different. Similar cases may be grouped together for the purpose of inferring general rules. Then, in applying general rules to new questions or concrete cases, it is often assessed whether the new situation is sufficiently similar such that it 'comes within the rule'.

In sum, the 'crux of the doctrinal method' has been described as 'the location and analysis of the primary documents of the law in order to establish the nature and parameters of the law'.[79] That is precisely what this research aims to achieve for the

73. *Id.*, at 242.
74. *Id.*, at 240. For distinctions between 'intentionalism' and 'purposivism', *see*, e.g., Jonathan R. Siegel, *The Inexorable Radicalization of Textualism*, 158(1) U. Pa. L. Rev. 117, 117–178 (2009).
75. Jane Frecknall-Hughes, *Research Methods in Taxation History*, 3(1) Rev. Behav. Econ. 5, 10 and 17 (2016); Mark Saunders, Philip Lewis & Adrian Thornhill, *Research Methods for Business Students* (Prentice Hall 5th ed. 2009).
76. Terry Hutchinson & Nigel Duncan, *Defining and Describing What We Do: Doctrinal Legal Research*, 17(1) Deakin L. Rev. 83, 111 (2012) (citing 'John H Farrar, *Legal Reasoning* (Thomson Reuters 2010)' at '91').
77. *Id.*
78. Peter Nash Swisher, *Teaching Legal Reasoning in Law School*, 74(3) L. Libr. J. 534, 537 (1981).
79. Terry Hutchinson & Nigel Duncan, *Defining and Describing What We Do: Doctrinal Legal Research*, 17(1) Deakin L. Rev. 83, 113 (2012).

foreign tax credit - i.e., to draw the EU law boundaries within which MSs are manoeuvring as they (re)design the credit method.

1.6. RESEARCH STRUCTURE

For the reasons explained here, the research is essentially divided into two parts: the credit method analysis and the EU law analysis. The starting point is to define the object of study itself, the credit method. The aim is to develop a basic conceptual framework for examining the credit method. To do so, a first step is to identify its most fundamental constituent parts - in other words, its lowest common denominator or most essential components, without which it would not be considered a credit method. From this, it is possible to distinguish what defines the credit method from what features *design* the credit method - or, in other words, the variable and optional components that allow states to tailor the credit method. This way, the conclusions derived from studying EU law have a framework: they can be categorized according to how EU law affects these design components.

For carrying out this step, first, a useful starting point for understanding a concept is to look at its origins. Therefore, this study of the credit method begins with an overview of its historical legal development. It is presented in chronological order to trace the evolution of the credit method, some of the challenges it faced and how its design was adapted in response. This chronological approach helps sort out which aspects of the credit method are historical contingencies and which are core aspects that have held stable over time. In addition, this offers insight into the reasons put forward for the credit method. In this way, one of the benefits of studying the historical legal development is to explore the rationale or rationales for a given law or legal concept, which may inform interpretation (e.g., when references are made to the object and purpose of a provision, or when teleological and historical methods of interpretation are used) and may inform design (e.g., whether the emphasis is placed on the rationale to *eliminate* double taxation, or to *mitigate* double taxation, or to facilitate international trade, each calls for slightly different features).

For each historical iteration of the credit method presented, simplified examples of its functioning will be offered. In this way, Chapter 2 doubles up as the explanation of the credit method. Second, interim conclusions are presented that derive from its history the key findings regarding the core components of the credit method versus the variable design components. At that stage, a selection of some of the most important reoccurring design components can be made. Third, these findings will be compared with, or checked against, some existing definitions of the credit method and what key components various authors and experts have highlighted. From this compilation, it is possible to devise the definition and selection of components that will be used for the purposes of this book.

As for the scope of the EU law analysis, the focus is predominantly on the case law of the CJEU interpreting the EU fundamental freedoms. The reason for this is that, to date, most of the impact of EU law on direct taxation matters stems from the 'negative tax integration' process, e.g., from the MSs striking down certain elements of direct tax laws that are found by the CJEU to be directly or indirectly discriminatory or to be non-discriminatory restrictions on free movement in the internal market.[80] After the main focus on the influence of primary EU law, there is a brief overview of secondary EU law on direct tax matters, to present any rules relevant to the credit method that MSs have managed to agree upon, with unanimous consent,[81] such as those in the Parent-Subsidiary Directive[82] and of course the ATAD I.

Each of the aforementioned lines of case law (listed in Section 1.4.) developed now well-established 'doctrines' that shape direct tax laws in the EU in significant, sometimes unexpected, ways. This structure, by arranging the cases into groups of similar subject matter, helps to create an easy-to-follow organization to trace the judicial lineage of key doctrines. Otherwise, it may be difficult to understand the findings for the credit method in an isolated way, without situating them in their context of the EU law doctrine or idea from which they stem. Also, this structure, by placing in the foreground pivotal ways in which EU law has shaped direct tax matters, renders clearer the tensions between the tax sovereignty of the MSs and an EU internal market. For each line of case law, the findings of the CJEU are discussed with the aim to selectively extract the aspects that are relevant for the credit method, covering both 'direct' credits and 'indirect' credits. In addition to the eight lines of case law studied, for the sake of completeness, a final 'miscellaneous' section will include any other relevant cases or issues that fit less neatly into a settled line of case law.

As regards the conceptual level of analysis, it corresponds to the legal lens through which the credit method is being viewed. When EU-level policymakers and legislators draft texts, be it Directives, Recommendations or research studies, the task is to keep it relevant for a diverse group of EU MSs. When the CJEU examines an issue under the preliminary ruling procedure, it does not interpret the national law itself, but rather the EU law in question. This analysis operates at a similar level. This calls for looking at the credit method more conceptually, hovering above jurisdiction-specific details, and focusing on the EU law issues.

In sum, as a starting point, of course, the two topics of the credit method and EU law are introduced, before delving into the analysis that threads them together. This

80. For more details, *see* Chapter 3; Ben J.M. Terra & Peter J. Wattel, *European Tax Law* Section 3.1.2 (Wolters Kluwer 6th ed. 2012); Peter J. Wattel, *Chapter 3: General EU Law Concepts and Tax Law, in* 1 *Terra/Wattel European Tax Law* 39, 45 et seq. Section 3.1.2 (Peter J. Wattel, Otto Marres & Hein Vermeulen eds, Wolters Kluwer 7th ed. 2019); Marjaana Helminen, *Chapter 1: EU Tax Law as Part of the Legal System, in EU Tax Law: Direct Taxation* (IBFD 2018 ed. 2018); Pasquale Pistone & Rita Szudoczky, *Chapter 2: The Coordination of Tax Policies in the EU, in Introduction to European Tax Law on Direct Taxation* 35, 36–39 (Michael Lang et al. eds, Linde 5th ed. 2018).

81. Article 115 TFEU (EU secondary law adopted in the field of direct taxation can only take the form of a directive and must be justified as 'directly affect[ing] the establishment or functioning of the internal market').

82. Council Directive 2011/96/EU of 30 November 2011 on the Common System of Taxation Applicable in the Case of Parent Companies and Subsidiaries of Different Member States, OJ L 345, 8–16 (29 Dec. 2011); Council Directive 2014/86/EU of 8 July 2014 amending Directive 2011/96/EU on the Common System of Taxation Applicable in the Case of Parent Companies and Subsidiaries of Different Member States, OJ L 219, 40–41 (25 Jul. 2014) (Parent-Subsidiary Directive).

leads to the following general structure: Chapter 2 defines the main object of study, the credit method; Chapter 3 introduces the aspects of EU law that affect direct taxes; Chapter 4 then fuses the two, serving as the core Chapter; Section 4.1. reviews the relationship between the credit method and the EU 'internal market', which has been a somewhat contentious one in academic literature; Section 4.2. analyses the credit method, first and primarily, from a primary EU law perspective, namely through the case law of the CJEU interpreting the EU Treaties; Section 4.3. complements this with a synopsis of the credit method from a secondary EU law perspective, namely through the EU legislative acts (in this case, Directives); Chapter 5 organizes the findings of the previous chapters into how they influence the design of the credit method, considering the fundamental structural components of the credit method outlined in Chapter 2. More specifically, for each design feature of the credit method (e.g., for the credit limitation), it aims to inventory whether EU law has said anything about that particular feature - i.e., to assess whether MSs are constrained in how they design a given component or whether they have freedom in its design - to sketch out more clearly the contours within which MSs are manoeuvring as they balance their 'post-BEPS' obligations.

CHAPTER 2

The Credit Method

2.1. HISTORICAL LEGAL DEVELOPMENT

2.1.1. Unilateral Measures (Circa 1880s–1920s): The Laboratory for Early Experiments with the Credit Method

2.1.1.1. Some Preliminary Remarks

Accounts of the historical legal development of international tax law tend to begin with the commonly chronicled 'evils' of 'double taxation' – a phenomenon which, it was feared, began threatening international economic exchanges most acutely after the First World War, as tax burdens increased due to the strained public revenues of war-laden states. This resulted in a push for coordination between states to develop bilateral or multilateral model provisions to relieve double taxation. The main protagonists were experts called upon by taxpayers and governments alike, meeting under the auspices of organizations such as the International Chamber of Commerce (ICC) and the League of Nations, to strategize how best to confront what was perceived to be a real menace to both peace and prosperity.

During their deliberations, numerous possibilities were initially debated. Over time, the options were whittled down to two main methods, which have become the most commonly used solutions today – namely, the credit method and the exemption method. As mentioned in the introduction, generally speaking (since it will be elaborated below), while the exemption method seeks to avoid double taxation by refraining from taxing income that taxpayers earn abroad, the credit method takes all income (domestic and foreign) into account to determine the total tax liability and then grants relief by allowing foreign taxes to reduce one-for-one the taxes owed. The latter is the focus here. Although the exemption method and other options are also touched upon (as the process of defining something can be aided by comparing and contrasting it with what it is not), this chapter recounts the development of the credit method.

Research indicates that, prior to these deliberations, the credit method – or first prototypes of the credit method – began to take shape in a diversity of forms as a *unilateral* measure (i.e., jurisdictions were acting on their own behalf by making alterations to their own laws to remedy the issue). The credit method then became concretized in its current version, regarded as standard today, through discussions on how to draft the aforementioned model *bilateral* (or multilateral) measures. Thus, following the order of these general stages of development, the subsections of this study on the historical legal development (Section 2.1.) is accordingly divided into the first phase of unilateral measures (discussed here, in Section 2.1.1.) before turning to the bilateral measures (Section 2.1.2.).

Very early on, via these unilateral measures, there was a clear distinction between what can be referred to as a 'direct' credit and an 'indirect' credit. These labels indicate the main difference between these two credits. Either a foreign state taxes the income that is directly attributable to and earned by a taxpayer itself there (e.g., through its own exertions and operations in a foreign state, by working for a foreign employer or carrying out taxable business activities in a neighbouring country) or a foreign state taxes the income that is attributable to a separate taxable entity in its territory, which the taxpayer owns, in part or in whole (e.g., by holding shares in a foreign company). While a 'direct' credit gives relief for the taxes levied on the income that the taxpayer itself generated abroad, the 'indirect' credit considers when, and under what circumstances, to extend relief to taxes that are levied on a separate taxable entity owned by the taxpayer. As it is a separate taxable entity, its profits may be taxed both at the level of the entity itself (e.g., under the foreign state's corporate income tax (CIT) laws) and then again in the hands of the taxpayer, who is seen as a distinct person from a tax law perspective. Although these are two distinct taxpayers from a legal standpoint, the 'indirect' credit recognizes that it is economically the same profits and, therefore, in certain cases, grants relief for this 'economic' double taxation, by also crediting the portion of the underlying taxes paid by the entity that could be deemed to be paid by the taxpayer. Given their distinctiveness, the 'direct' and 'indirect' credit therefore have their own dedicated subsections (in Sections 2.1.1.2. and 2.1.1.3. respectively). After their more detailed study, the lessons that can be derived from the historical development of these unilateral measures are presented (in Section 2.1.1.4.).

2.1.1.2. Credit for Taxes Paid to Another Jurisdiction: The Emergence of a 'Direct' Credit

Preliminary remarks

The enactment of the credit method by the US in the Revenue Act of 1918, which entered into force in 1919,[83] could be described as the beginning, or birth, of credit method in its modern form. At least, it is accurate to label this moment as the most important historical event in the life of the credit method, in that it was the catalyst for

83. United States, Revenue Act of 1918, Sixty-Fifth Congress, Session III, Chapter 18, Public Law 65-254 (US Government Printing Office 1919).

its recognition on the international scene,[84] and it seemed to be the most influential in shaping the mould for the design of the credit method that has now become the standard, as will become apparent throughout this section.

Research of the historical development uncovers at least three instances of credit methods that preceded the one enacted in the US. These developments occurred in the UK. The first was rather straightforward, while the second two had unique features as compared to the credit method often used today. Their main characteristics will be described here to allow for a comparison.

1894 relief in the UK

First, in 1894, the UK offered a form of relief for double taxation that resembled a 'direct' credit, but only for estate duties[85] - not yet for income taxes - paid in a 'British possession' (in Section 20 of the Finance Act 1894). The law read as follows:

> '20. -(1) Where the Commissioners are satisfied, that in a British possession to which this section applies, duty is payable by reason of a death in respect of any property situate in such possession and passing on such death, they shall allow a sum equal to the amount of that duty to be deducted from the Estate duty payable in respect of that property on the same death.'[86]

An analysis of the wording offers insight into the basic functioning of a credit method. From the wording, two steps can be discerned. First, the 'Estate duty payable' in the UK would have to be calculated, and, second, the duty 'payable' in a British possession could be deducted from this first amount. The opening phrase 'Where the Commissioners are satisfied' indicates a procedural step, as it implies an obligation to furnish some proof of the amount of taxes. The word 'payable' is used, which is open to interpretation. This implies that it is not a requirement that the tax is already 'paid', but that the tax liability be legally established in such a way that one can prove it. This leaves open the question as to what happens if the taxes ultimately paid differ from the tax liability initially payable (e.g., if a factual circumstance changes in the meantime, a correction is made, etc.). Another notable observation is that, based on a textual analysis alone, the full amount ('a sum equal to the amount of that duty') was permitted as a deduction, without any clearly specified limit or maximum (this is an important question, as later developments of the credit method reveal). In particular, the wording does not specify what would occur in cases where duties payable to a

84. *See*, e.g., *infra* note 100 and note 566.
85. Robert Willis, *Great Britain's Part in the Development of Double Taxation Relief*, 1965(4) Brit. Tax Rev. 270, 271 (1965) ('The next landmark in the double taxation field in Britain was also concerned with death duties. I doubt whether it was recognised as a landmark at the time, but it was in fact the first introduction into the British tax system of relief for double taxation by way of credit. In 1894 the British estate duty was introduced and provision was made in the legislation for duty charged in other countries of the British Empire on property situated in those countries to be deducted-that is, allowed as a credit-against the British duty on the same property').
86. Government of Ireland, Irish Statute Book, Statutes of the United Kingdom of Great Britain and Ireland, Finance Act 1894, http://www.irishstatutebook.ie/eli/1894/act/30/section/20/enacted/en/html (last visited 28 Aug. 2018) (hereinafter 'United Kingdom, Finance Act 1894').

British possession are higher than the estate duty. Given that the wording promises a 'sum equal to' the duty, this could be read as a commitment to cover the full amount of duties payable in the British possession, such that, even where those duties are higher, the UK would somehow compensate for this. The logical follow-up question would be *how* to do so, e.g., whether this would require allowing any excess amount owed to the British possessions to offset other duties or taxes owed to the UK or whether this would require a reimbursement for the excess taxes owed to the British possession (this question of what to do with an 'excess' of creditable taxes is also an important question, as later developments reveal). As the wording applied only to duties levied on the same property ('that property') and same taxable event ('same death'), this could seem to prevent the possibility of offsetting any excessive amount against duties payable on other property. Literature from the early 1900s clarifies that the credit (referred to as an 'allowance'), as a general rule, was strictly limited to the amount payable in the UK.[87] Finally, based on the wording, there was also a limited territorial scope, as only duties levied by certain British possessions could be deducted; that being the case, this was not a true 'foreign' (internationally oriented) tax credit but rather an internal colonial empire measure. In sum, the features of this credit method provision, stemming from its text, include: a two-step calculation (calculating the taxes owed to the credit-granting state, followed by determining the amount to be deducted from this); procedural considerations (e.g., proof required and to whom and how to submit it); the status of the foreign taxes as paid or payable; questions regarding the amount of creditable taxes, or limits thereon, and how to address 'excess' foreign taxes; and the territorial scope of taxes covered.

The straightforward wording of this legal provision already offers an early example of the nucleus of the credit method: where both jurisdictions exercise taxation rights in respect of the same thing, one jurisdiction allows the taxes that it would collect (or collected) to be reduced by an amount equal to the tax claim in the other jurisdiction. A simple example (Example No. 1) imagining instead that these were income taxes, the subject of this research, can help illustrate this core idea.

Example No. 1: The Basic Functioning of a Credit Method

Facts: During the relevant tax year in question, an individual taxpayer, resident in State R, operates a business through a sole proprietorship. The taxpayer earns income from business in State R and also from business in the neighbouring country, State F. Both states tax the income, as State R takes into account all the income of all its residents and as State F taxes income generated in its territory.

87. Robert Dymond, *The Death Duties: Comprising Estate, Legacy and Succession Duties with Decided Cases, Forms, Notes on Practice and the Text of the Statutes* 97–98 and 170 (Solicitors' Law Stationery Society 1920) ('The allowance is not in any case to exceed the amount of Estate Duty payable on the same property in this country, except that where Settlement Estate Duty was chargeable on the same property the balance over and above the Estate Duty might have been allowed against the Settlement Estate Duty. Orders in Council have been made applying this provision to most of the larger British Possessions (a list of which is given on page 170) …').

Profits in State R:	100	Profits in State F:	50
Tax rate in State R:	20%	Tax rate in State F:	20%
Total worldwide income (WWI):		150	
Taxes due in State F:		50 × 20% = 10	
Taxes due in State R:		150 × 20% = 30 minus foreign tax credit (FTC) of 10 = 20	
Result: Total taxes paid by taxpayer:		30	

(Note: As regards all Examples, unless otherwise specified, assumptions and simplifications are made: e.g., assuming the same rules for calculating the tax base, profits instead of losses, no foreign exchange rate differences, etc.)

1916 relief in the UK

Second, in 1916, the UK introduced (in Section 43 of the Finance Act 1916 titled 'Relief in respect of Colonial income tax')[88] what could be described as a form of credit, specifically for 'income tax'[89] levied by the British Dominions. The law read as follows:

> '43. If any person who has paid, by deduction or otherwise, United Kingdom income tax for the current income tax year on any part of his income at a rate exceeding three shillings and sixpence proves to the satisfaction of the Special Commissioners that he has also paid any Colonial income tax in respect of the same part of his income, he shall be entitled to repayment of a part of the United Kingdom income tax paid by him equal to the difference between the amount so paid and the amount he would have paid if the tax had been charged at the rate of three shillings and sixpence, or, if that difference exceeds the amount of tax on that part of his income at the rate of the Colonial income tax, equal to that amount.'

This relief was offered as a temporary concession, due to a sudden heightened concern over 'double taxation' resulting from the dual pressures of: (1) the Finance Act of 1914, which expanded the tax jurisdiction of the UK (from one which taxed income only once remitted to, or 'bought into', the UK to one which taxed 'all income derived from abroad'); and (2) 'the increases in taxation throughout the empire during the war period'.[90] Responding to these pressures, legislators enacted this provision, but

88. United Kingdom, Finance Act 1916, Section 43, http://www.legislation.gov.uk/ukpga/1916/24/pdfs/ukpga_19160024_en.pdf (last visited 28 Aug. 2018) (hereinafter 'United Kingdom, Finance Act 1916').
89. United Kingdom, Finance Act 1916, Section 43 (the Section also included the following definitions: 'In this section the expression "United Kingdom income tax" means income tax charged under the Income Tax Acts; and the expression "Colonial income tax" means income tax charged under any law in force in any British possession or any tax so charged which appears to the Special Commissioners to correspond to United Kingdom income tax').
90. Alzada Comstock, *British Income Tax Reform*, 10(3) Am. Econ. Rev. 488, 500–501 (1920). *See also* Peter Harris, *An Historic View of the Principle and Options for Double Tax Relief*, 1999(6) Brit. Tax Rev. 469, 474 (1999) (explaining the measure's temporary nature); Philip Baker, *Some*

deliberately with a limited temporal scope, expressed in the wording 'for the current income tax year'. Once again, it also had a limited territorial scope, i.e., only to the benefit of the empire for 'Colonial income tax', according to the wording.

Comparing the 1894 Estate duty relief with this 1916 relief offers insight into different design or drafting questions that can arise. For example, as compared to the 1894 provision, this 1916 provision uses the word 'paid', instead of 'payable'. Moreover, the wording implied that only *after* taxes were fully paid to the *two* jurisdictions in question could the taxpayer then claim relief in the form of a 'repayment'. Such an approach, if it were applied that way, would be harsher on the taxpayer from a cash-flow perspective since the taxpayer would bear both taxes upfront until the amount of the relief is later ascertained and repaid. Such an approach would ensure that only actual, or effective, double taxation is counteracted. However, as the 1894 provision shows, there are less burdensome approaches to achieving this. First, it could cover both taxes 'paid' and 'payable', ideally with appropriate proof that they are legally due. In this case, as indicated above, legislators should consider any procedures needed in cases of subsequent readjustments (if the amount ultimately 'paid' differs from what was declared 'payable'). Second, even if it covers only taxes 'paid', relief in the form of a credit against taxes due can be deducted at the moment of *calculating* the tax liability owed to the credit-granting state (collecting only the final amount due *after* the FTC has been subtracted, rather than collecting the full amount followed by a repayment or reimbursement of the FTC). In addition to the status of the foreign taxes (as paid or payable), comparing the two indicates that the question of what kinds of foreign taxes are eligible for relief arises, as the 1894 relief was for estate duties and the 1916 relief was for income taxes.

One distinctive feature of the 1916 provision is that this was considered only a 'partial relief',[91] as the example demonstrates below. The wording sets a clear limit (of 'three shillings and sixpence') that, according to Harris and Baker, equated to 17.5%;[92] more precisely, it applied 'so as not to reduce United Kingdom income tax below a fixed flat maximum rate, *i.e.* 17.5 per cent'.[93] In other words, the amount of the credit was dictated by the requirement to ensure that the amount the UK collected in tax revenue equalled at least 17.5% of the income.[94]

Aspects of United Kingdom Double Taxation Relief, 52(10) Bull. Int'l Fiscal Documentation 445, 447 (1998) (explaining this 'purely temporary measure ... granted for any "colonial" income tax' and the limit on its amount.); John F. Avery Jones, *Chapter I: Sir Josiah Stamp and Double Income Tax, in* 6 *Studies in the History of Tax Law* 1, 3 (John Tiley ed., Hart Publishing 2013).

91. Alzada Comstock, *British Income Tax Reform*, 10(3) Am. Econ. Rev. 488, 500–501 (1920).
92. *See*, e.g., Peter Harris, *An Historic View of the Principle and Options for Double Tax Relief*, 1999(6) Brit. Tax Rev. 469, 474 (1999). *See also* Philip Baker, *Some Aspects of United Kingdom Double Taxation Relief*, 52(10) Bull. Int'l Fiscal Documentation 445, 447 (1998).
93. Peter Harris, *An Historic View of the Principle and Options for Double Tax Relief*, 1999(6) Brit. Tax Rev. 469, 474 (1999).
94. *See also* Philip Baker, *Some Aspects of United Kingdom Double Taxation Relief*, 52(10) Bull. Int'l Fiscal Documentation 445, 447 (1998) (this limits the credit, but based on Baker's description, this can be distinguished from the type of foreign tax credit limitations (or maximum creditable amounts) used today: 'First, the United Kingdom enacted domestic law provisions for "dominion income tax relief". [...] Since the relief operated by reference to the rate of tax, the issue of

Another feature that emerges from the wording is that the source of the income and the residence of the taxpayer did not play a key role. It applied to 'any person who has paid ... United Kingdom income tax'.[95] There is no mention of residence, domicile, citizenship, or nationality in this Section of the law. According to Harris:

> 'This provision applied irrespective of source of income, in particular, irrespective of whether income was sourced in the United Kingdom or a Dominion. The only criterion for relief was that income was taxed both in the United Kingdom and in a Dominion and, accordingly, residence was also irrelevant.'[96]

This is a remarkable feature, considering the extent to which modern understandings of international taxation and relief mechanisms revolve around the source-residence distinction.

Example No. 2: Relief Limited by Reference to a Rate – The 1916 Relief in the UK

Facts: During the relevant tax year in question, an individual taxpayer, resident in the UK, operated a sole proprietorship and earned income from business in the UK and also from business in the neighbouring Dominion, State D.

Profits in UK:	100	Profits in State D:	50
Effective tax rate in UK:	20%	Effective tax rate in State D:	20%

Total worldwide income (WWI):	150
Taxes due in State D:	50 × 20% = 10
Taxes due in UK:	150 × 20% = 30

Credit limit: 'If any person [*in this case, the individual*] who has paid ... United Kingdom income tax for the current income tax year on **any part of his income** at a rate exceeding three shillings and sixpence [*at this time, in 1916, "three shillings and sixpence" = approximately 17.5%; and yes, this criterion is fulfilled because the hypothetical rate of 20% exceeds 17.5%*] proves to the satisfaction of the Special Commissioners that he has also paid any Colonial income tax [*yes, the 10 paid to State D*] in respect of the **same part** of his income [*referring, it seems, to the 50 taxed by both jurisdictions*], he shall be entitled to repayment of a **part of the United Kingdom income tax** paid by him **equal to the difference between** the amount so paid [*10 on the income of 50*] and the amount he would have paid if the tax had been charged at the rate of three shillings and sixpence

a limitation of foreign tax credit and the different bases for computation of the taxable amounts in the two countries did not arise').

95. *See supra* note 88 (citing United Kingdom, Finance Act 1916, Section 43).
96. *See*, e.g., Peter Harris, *An Historic View of the Principle and Options for Double Tax Relief*, 1999(6) Brit. Tax Rev. 469, 474 (1999).

> [*i.e., 17.5% of 50, or 8.75, and then take the difference between the 10 paid and this 8.75, to get the repayment of 1.25*] … .' (emphasis added; *see* Section 43 of the Finance Act 1916 at *supra* note 89).
>
> Result: Total taxes paid by the individual: 10 + 30 – 1.25 = 38.75
>
> Note: the relief of 1.25 amounts to 2.5% of 50, which is the amount by which the rate of 20% exceeds the rate of 17.5%.[97]

1920 relief in the UK

In 1920, after the First World War, this relief was re-evaluated by the UK's Royal Commission on the Income Tax and reintroduced in an adapted form (in Section 27 of the Finance Act 1920 titled 'Relief in respect of Dominion income tax')[98] as the 'Dominion Relief' system.[99] Notably, in the meantime, the US had enacted its credit method; however, although US law was taken into account, as records of the Royal Commission indicate,[100] the UK designed quite a different approach.

97. For a contemporaneous example, *see* Herbert E. Seed & Alfred W. Rawlinson, *Double Income Tax Relief: The Law and Practice Regarding Relief from Double Taxation* 2 (Sir Isaac Pitman & Sons 1925), in Legal Treatises, 1800–1926 (Making of Modern Law Print Editions) ('Section 43, Finance Act, 1916 - Partial Relief. The first legal enactment affording Colonial income tax relief was Section 43 of the Finance Act, 1916 (incorporated in the Income Tax Act, 1918, as Section 55 and now superseded by Section 27 of the Finance Act, 1920). That measure provided for an allowance in respect of Colonial income tax paid, on that part of a taxpayer's income which was doubly taxed, at the rate of the Colonial income tax suffered, subject to the limitation that the rate at which the relief was granted could not be greater than the excess of the rate of United Kingdom income tax which had been borne by the taxpayer, for the current income tax year, over 3s 6d in the £ [≈17.5%]. Thus, if a person were liable to British income tax at 5s in the £ [≈25%], the maximum relief obtainable would be at 1s 6d [≈7.5%], whatever rate of Colonial tax he may have had to pay. Where a person was liable to pay British tax at only 3s 6d in the £, or at some lower rate, he obtained no relief at all in respect of Colonial income tax').
98. United Kingdom, Finance Act 1920, Section 27, http://www.legislation.gov.uk/ukpga/1920/18/pdfs/ukpga_19200018_en.pdf (last visited 28 Aug. 2018).
99. *See*, e.g., Peter Harris, *An Historic View of the Principle and Options for Double Tax Relief*, 1999(6) Brit. Tax Rev. 469, 474–476 (1999). The UK Dominion relief system has been characterized differently by different sources. For example, at the League of Nations, it was labelled as 'Method III - Allocation of Relief'. *See* League of Nations, *Double Taxation and Tax Evasion, Report and Resolutions Submitted by the Technical Experts to the Financial Committee of the League of Nations* (1925), *in* 4 *Legislative History of United States Tax Conventions*, 4057, 4098 (United States, Joint Committee on Internal Revenue Taxation, US Government Printing Office 1962). It was also characterized as an 'Adjustment of tax rates by both states'. *See* Ke Chin Wang, *International Double Taxation of Income: Relief Through International Agreement 1921-1945*, 59(1) Harv. L. Rev. 73, 74 (1945). In the detailed historical account of Peter Harris, cited here, it is described as functioning like a tax credit. *See also* Michael J. Graetz & Michael M. O'Hear, *The 'Original Intent' of U.S. International Taxation*, 46(5) Duke L.J. 1021, 1022 n.3 (1997).
100. *See*, e.g., John F. Avery Jones, *Chapter I: Sir Josiah Stamp and Double Income Tax*, *in* 6 *Studies in the History of Tax Law* 1, 5 (John Tiley ed., Hart Publishing 2013); Alzada Comstock, *British Income Tax Reform*, 10(3) Am. Econ. Rev. 488, 501–502 (1920).

The first paragraph of Section 27 of the Finance Act 1920 read as follows:

> '27. – (1) If any person who has paid, by deduction or otherwise, or is liable to pay, United Kingdom income tax for any year of assessment on any part of his income proves to the satisfaction of the Special Commissioners that he has paid Dominion income tax for that year in respect of the same part of his income, he shall be entitled to relief from United Kingdom income tax paid or payable by him on that part of his income at a rate thereon to be determined as follows: –
>
> (a) if the Dominion rate of tax does not exceed one-half of the appropriate rate of United Kingdom tax, the rate at which relief is to be given shall be the Dominion rate of tax:
> (b) In any other case the rate at which relief is to be given shall be, one-half of the appropriate rate of United Kingdom tax. [...].'

What led to the 'urgency' to act, as mentioned above regarding the temporary relief of 1916, was the sudden increased tax burden (*see supra* note 90). In fact, it was not the first time the issue of double taxation was raised, but it was the first time that action was taken after previous failed attempts (such as in 1861 after the introduction of an income tax in India); this time, what made the difference was 'excessively high combined rates of tax'.[101] Rates were reaching levels that, if double taxation persisted, 'foreign business[es] might be sold' or 'evasion would be encouraged'.[102]

Another reason for taking action was 'particularly in view of (i) the distortion of competition for UK residents when other countries were giving relief to their residents' – among others, the US 1918 FTC was cited, and it was characterized as 'a deliberate policy of encouraging the investment of American capital abroad'[103] – and '(ii) the likely result of further capital not being invested in the Dominions (and to a lesser extent into the UK) if such investment suffered double taxation'.[104]

Notably, once again, the scope was territorially limited to the empire. As for the rationale, the justification for this was based on the shared interests and 'well-being of

101. John F. Avery Jones, *Chapter I: Sir Josiah Stamp and Double Income Tax, in* 6 *Studies in the History of Tax Law* 1, 3 n.8 (John Tiley ed., Hart Publishing 2013) (the 'Royal Commission's evidence lists the occasions that double taxation had been previously discussed, starting with a petition debated in the House of Commons in 1861 following the introduction of income tax in India'), at 2 n.3 (for examples of the prevailing rates in the UK and some other countries such as Australia, Canada, and Japan), at 2 & n.5 (Sir Josiah Stamp is quoted by Avery Jones as follows: 'Taxation is now rapidly developing from a merely unpleasant incident into a dominating feature of daily life, and those features which hitherto have been of little interest, because they have been too small to matter, now become of great importance.' And 'There would probably have never been any society "for the abolition of double taxation within the Empire" ... if income taxes had remained in the region of 8d [3.3%] ... (This was the rate in 1899-90)', citing 'J Stamp, *The Fundamental Principles of Taxation* (London, Macmillan, 1921, revised 1936) ("Fundamental Principles") 2, available at http://www.archive.org/stream/fundamentalprinoostamgoog#page/n8/mode/2up)') and at 3 n.6 (for two concrete examples described in the 'Minutes of Evidence' to demonstrate the detrimental impact of the increased tax burden on individuals and businesses).
102. John F. Avery Jones, *Chapter I: Sir Josiah Stamp and Double Income Tax, in* 6 *Studies in the History of Tax Law* 1, 3 n.10 (John Tiley ed., Hart Publishing 2013).
103. *Id.*, at 4.
104. *Id.*, at 3-4.

the British empire'; given this common purpose, it was unacceptable if double taxation led to certain taxpayers shouldering disproportionately more of what should be a shared burden, borne collectively on behalf of the empire.[105] In this way, relief for double taxation was linked to ideas of fairness based on solidarity. Such concerns did not exist vis-à-vis foreign states, so the case for remedying double taxation outside of the 'empire' was less strong and less urgent; instead, this was deemed better accomplished on a bilateral basis.[106]

Summing up these rationales for relief, in addition to the fair-share-to-the-'well-being of the empire' rationale, there were concerns over potentially excessive burdens of tax (in turn, stifling business and fuelling evasion) and concerns over competitive disadvantages. These reasons to find solutions to double taxation were both absolute and relative in nature, in that they related to the *absolute* overall burden befalling the taxpayer and the *relative* burden vis-à-vis other countries. Yet, apparently, these concerns were not compelling enough to make the relief more international, as it remained confined to the Dominions.

As compared to the 1916 version, the 1920 limit on the amount that could be credited changed both in terms of the rate and in terms of how it was calculated. First, the relevant rate was no longer 17.5%, but rather was half of whatever the applicable UK tax rate would be. Second, the rate was no longer concerned with ensuring a minimum amount of tax revenue, but rather with the tax rates that applied to the taxpayer's income. More precisely, the amount of relief would be, at a maximum, half

105. *See*, e.g., Philip Baker, *Some Aspects of United Kingdom Double Taxation Relief*, 52(10) Bull. Int'l Fiscal Documentation 445, 447 (1998) ('In particular, it drew a sharp distinction between double income taxation within the British Empire and with foreign countries. Within the Empire, the Commission concluded that there were a number of considerations which made the removal of double taxation an urgent necessity: "the sharing of common burdens, the common interest in the well-being of every part of the Empire, and the desire for free circulation of capital within the Empire".[26] With respect to foreign states, however, these elements were lacking', citing at n.26 'Para. 79 of the Report'); Alzada Comstock, *British Income Tax Reform*, 10(3) Am. Econ. Rev. 488, 500–501 (1920) ('It was represented to the Royal Commission that although the war represented a common effort by the empire without distinction, certain individuals within the empire who come to the mother country from the colonies for purposes of health, trade, education of children, and similar reasons, are in a sense singled out to pay twice over to the cost of the war. The commission recognized the inequities involved, and recommends the adoption of machinery for doing away with double taxation within the empire'); John F. Avery Jones, *Chapter I: Sir Josiah Stamp and Double Income Tax, in* 6 *Studies in the History of Tax Law* 1, 13 (John Tiley ed., Hart Publishing 2013) ('The Sub-committee concluded early on that the "inequity in requiring a taxpayer to make two contributions of Income Tax towards what must certainly in part be a common purpose, viz, the well-being of the British Empire; and that this inequity should be remedied". This should be done by charging only the higher of the two countries' rates of tax. Note that the argument is stated in terms of the purpose being the well-being of the Empire so that it could, and would be, argued that no relief was necessary elsewhere, even though all the conclusion set out were equally applicable to foreign investment anywhere').
106. *See supra* note 105.

of the UK tax rate and was granted for the part of the taxpayer's income on which Dominion income tax was 'paid'.[107] As explained succinctly by Baker:

> 'If the dominion rate of tax did not exceed one half of the appropriate rate of United Kingdom tax then the rate applicable in the United Kingdom was reduced by the dominion rate of tax. If the dominion rate exceeded this limit, then United Kingdom tax was reduced to one-half of its normal rate.'[108]

In this latter case, it was expected - but not obligatory - that the Dominion in question would offer relief for the part in excess. Though it was not obligatory, Harris reports that '[t]his limited reciprocity was provided by most Dominions by 1922'.[109]

Similar to the 1916 relief, the application of this 1920 relief was not conditioned on the source of the income, nor the residence of the taxpayer.[110] The relief was coordinated in such a way that the UK generally took the primary or lead role and the Dominion took a secondary reciprocal role. This led to a feature of essentially sharing the responsibility and burden for the relief between the two jurisdictions. The fact that the UK exercised colonial power over the Dominions likely helped make this arrangement more feasible.[111]

As compared to the 1916 version, the 1920 version provided more details in the law, growing from one paragraph to eight paragraphs.[112] As regards the eligible taxes, both versions specified that it applied to income taxes (and the 'super-tax' in 1920) and defined the terms 'United Kingdom income tax' and 'Colonial income tax' (or 'Dominion income tax' in 1920). The 1920 wording seemed to tighten a requirement according to which relief would be granted for the Dominion income tax only 'if that tax appears to the Special Commissioners to correspond with United Kingdom income tax or super-tax'.[113] If so, this would potentially require a selection of what features of a tax

107. *See*, e.g., Peter Harris, *An Historic View of the Principle and Options for Double Tax Relief*, 1999(6) Brit. Tax Rev. 469, 476 (1999) (It 'was limited according to a fraction of the taxpayer's tax rate', in this case 'up to one half of the United Kingdom tax rate applicable to income subject to Dominion income tax').
108. Philip Baker, *Some Aspects of United Kingdom Double Taxation Relief*, 52(10) Bull. Int'l Fiscal Documentation 445, 447 (1998).
109. *See*, e.g., Peter Harris, *An Historic View of the Principle and Options for Double Tax Relief*, 1999(6) Brit. Tax Rev. 469, 476 (1999).
110. *Id.*, at 474 and 476; John F. Avery Jones, *Chapter I: Sir Josiah Stamp and Double Income Tax*, *in* 6 *Studies in the History of Tax Law* 1, 14–15 (John Tiley ed., Hart Publishing 2013); Robert Willis, *Great Britain's Part in the Development of Double Taxation Relief*, 1965(4) Brit. Tax Rev. 270, 273 (1965); Herbert E. Seed & Alfred W. Rawlinson, *Double Income Tax Relief: The Law and Practice Regarding Relief from Double Taxation* 6 (Sir Isaac Pitman & Sons 1925), in Legal Treatises, 1800–1926 (Making of Modern Law Print Editions).
111. League of Nations, Economic and Financial Commission, *Report on Double Taxation, Submitted to the Financial Committee by Professors Bruins, Einaudi, Seligman, and Sir Josiah Stamp* (1923), *in* 4 *Legislative History of United States Tax Conventions*, 4003, 4051 (United States, Joint Committee on Internal Revenue Taxation, US Government Printing Office 1962) (hereinafter 'League of Nations, 1923 Report').
112. United Kingdom, Finance Act 1920, Section 27, http://www.legislation.gov.uk/ukpga/1920/18/pdfs/ukpga_19200018_en.pdf (last visited 28 Aug. 2018).
113. In particular, due to the removal of the word 'or'; for the difference, *compare* United Kingdom, Finance Act 1916, Section 43 ('the expression "Colonial income tax" means income tax charged under any law in force in any British possession or any tax so charged which appears to the

create the relevant correspondence and, using that framework, a comparability analysis in each case. In this way, the scope of eligible taxes would be becoming a more prominent feature. On a related point, regarding the potential interpretation and effects of words such as 'payable' versus 'paid', the drafters of the 1920 provision seem to have taken more explicit note, by employing the wording 'paid, by deduction or otherwise, or is liable to pay' UK taxes and 'paid' Dominion taxes.

As can be seen, again, the essential conditions for the application of the provision were: (1) satisfactory proof that the taxpayer paid eligible Dominion taxes and (2) either legally owed or paid UK taxes. As a result, unlike what is common today, it did not technically revolve around the source of the income or the residence of the taxpayer.

As for details regarding the calculation, five other issues (at least) were explicitly addressed. First, it stated that 'no deduction shall be made on account of the payment of Dominion income tax in estimating income for the purposes of United Kingdom income tax, [...]'.[114] In other words, it dealt with the tax base: the pre-tax amount of the income prior to the levy of any Dominion tax – or if such tax was already levied, then by adding that amount back in – should be used as the tax base in order to determine the amount of UK tax and then, from there, the amount of any relief.[115] This could be described as a form of 'gross-up'.[116] It can be particularly relevant to specify this in the law, as discussed below with regard to the 'indirect' credit (*see infra* note 300).

Special Commissioners to correspond to United Kingdom income tax') and United Kingdom, Finance Act 1920, Section 27(8) ('The expression "Dominion income tax" means any income tax or super-tax charged under any law in force in any Dominion, if that tax appears to the Special Commissioners to correspond with United Kingdom income tax or super-tax').

114. United Kingdom, Finance Act 1920, Section 27(4), http://www.legislation.gov.uk/ukpga/1920/18/pdfs/ukpga_19200018_en.pdf (last visited 28 Aug. 2018).

115. From a 1925 legal treatise, two reasons emerge for specifying this in the law: (1) relief in the UK previously was granted only by means of allowing foreign taxes to be deducted from the tax base. Therefore, the aim was to clarify that taxpayers should not obtain both a deduction from the tax base and the relief in respect of the rates of taxes due; (2) the relief in the UK applied not only to Dominion taxes paid directly by a taxpayer but also to taxes paid by a company in which a taxpayer held shares, upon receipt of dividends, for the part of those company taxes attributable to the dividends received – i.e., what is contemporarily commonly referred to as an 'indirect' credit, as discussed in further detail under Section 2.1.1.3. For further details and legal questions with respect to this 'addition' under Section 27(4), *see* Herbert E. Seed & Alfred W. Rawlinson, *Double Income Tax Relief: The Law and Practice Regarding Relief from Double Taxation* 11–12 (Sir Isaac Pitman & Sons 1925), in Legal Treatises, 1800–1926 (Making of Modern Law Print Editions).

116. *See*, e.g., Peter Harris, *An Historic View of the Principle and Options for Double Tax Relief*, 1999(6) Brit. Tax Rev. 469, 476 (1999). *See also* Richard E. Andersen, *Foreign Tax Credits*, 1.02[2] (Warren, Gorham & Lamont, Thomson Reuters Tax and Accounting, with updates through May 2019) (when discussing the direct foreign tax credit in the US, Section 901 of the internal revenue code, as it read in 2019, he explains the relevance of this: 'In order to produce the correct mathematical result, the tentative U.S. tax is computed on a taxable income base that is not reduced by the foreign taxes paid. This results in a theoretical aggregate tax burden to the two taxing jurisdictions (assuming equivalent tax rates) that equals the tax that would be owed to the United States if the same amount of its taxable income were exclusively U.S.-source and exempt from the foreign country's tax regime').

Second, the limitation was calculated on what Harris describes as a 'slice by slice' basis.[117] There are two ways to understand this term. One way to understand this term is that the limitation on the amount of the credit was calculated separately for each item of income.[118] Another way to understand this term raises a question that is relevant for income tax systems that apply progressive tax rates.[119] The question is: should the income that is taxed abroad be attributed entirely to the lowest tax bracket (a 'bottom slice rule'), entirely to the highest tax bracket (a 'top slice' rule), or attributed pro rata to all tax brackets?[120] In this case, Harris seems to refer to the first understanding (i.e., a type of per-item-of-income limitation), citing a 1925 legal treatise that provides examples illustrating that '[d]ifferent *sources* of income arising in the same Dominion but charged to different rates of Dominion income tax are dealt with separately …'.[121] It suggests that, for each item of income earned from a Dominion, the rate of Dominion tax that applied to that particular item of income would be determined and tested against the one-half-of-the-UK-rate limit.

Third, the law acknowledged the potential issues that may arise from differences in timing. To do so, it authorized the Commissioners of Inland Revenue to issue regulations 'in particular' for 'prescribing the year which in relation to any Dominion

117. *See*, e.g., Peter Harris, *An Historic View of the Principle and Options for Double Tax Relief*, 1999(6) Brit. Tax Rev. 469, 476 (1999).
118. *See*, e.g., Peter Harris & David Oliver, *International Commercial Tax* 272 (Cambridge University Press 2010) (using a straightforward example, the authors depict a foreign tax credit that is calculated separately for different types of income, i.e., one calculation for income from rent earned in a foreign country and another calculation for interest income from the same foreign country. They refer to this approach as 'a *slice-by-slice* or *item-by-item* limitation on credit'); Peter Harris, *Corporate Tax Law: Structure, Policy and Practice* 327–385 (Cambridge University Press online publication date March 2013), https://doi.org/10.1017/CBO9781139519922.007 (last visited 15 Aug. 2018) ('The UK has traditionally adopted a foreign tax credit approach to foreign tax relief.[14] The credit is limited on a slice-by-slice basis, with the income from a foreign PE constituting a single slice. […] Because this is still a slice-by-slice approach, there is no provision for transfer of excess credits between members of a corporate group').
119. *See*, e.g., Peter Harris & David Oliver, *International Commercial Tax* 271 (Cambridge University Press 2010) (the authors give an example, using the term 'slicing rule', which depicts an issue under a progressive tax rate system. 'As with the exemption system, the situation becomes more complicated if Beth is subject to progressive rates in Country B. Here Country B will have to adopt a slicing rule for the same reason as a slicing rule is required where the exemption with progression method is used (see above). Assume that Country B taxes Beth at 20 per cent on her first 100 and 40 per cent thereafter. In order to work out the limitation on credit, Country B must decide whether Beth's Country A source income is the bottom slice of her income, the top slice, or should be considered pro-rata with her Country B source income. A bottom slice rule would consider the Country A income as Beth's lowest taxed income, i.e. as that taxed at 20 per cent, and so would put the greatest limit on the foreign tax credit available for Country A tax, i.e. 20. A top slice rule would be most favourable to Beth as it would consider the Country A source income as the highest taxed part of Beth's income and so maximise Beth's foreign tax credit, i.e. a limit of 40. A pro rata rule would produce a credit limit of 30 (for the same reasons as discussed above with respect to exemption with progression)').
120. *See*, e.g., Peter Harris & David Oliver, *International Commercial Tax* 271 (Cambridge University Press 2010).
121. Herbert E. Seed & Alfred W. Rawlinson, *Double Income Tax Relief: The Law and Practice Regarding Relief from Double Taxation* 33–34 (Sir Isaac Pitman & Sons 1925), in Legal Treatises 1800–1926 (Making of Modern Law Print Editions); Peter Harris, *An Historic View of the Principle and Options for Double Tax Relief*, 1999(6) Brit. Tax Rev. 469, 476 n.26 (1999) (citing 'Seed and Rawlinson (1925), … at pp. 33-34').

income tax is, for the purposes of relief under this section, to be taken as corresponding to the year of assessment for the purposes of United Kingdom income tax'.[122]

Fourth, the law anticipated that, of course, other unforeseen issues may arise and, similarly, authorized the possibility for making regulations and 'arrangements with the Government of any Dominion' 'as may be necessary to enable the appropriate relief to be granted'.[123] For example, although not foreseen in the law, through the experience of operating this system of relief, a complication was reported to have arisen with the calculation of the income. In some instances, the amount of income would be calculated differently for the purposes of the Dominion tax and for the purposes of the UK tax.[124]

Fifth, similar to the US system enacted in 1918/1919, '[s]hareholders were entitled to both a direct and underlying foreign tax credit irrespective of level of shareholding', a topic explained further below (when studying and comparing the UK approach with the US approach).[125]

Example No. 3: The 1920 Relief in the UK

Facts: During the relevant tax year in question, an individual taxpayer, resident in the UK, operated a sole proprietorship, and earned income from business in the UK and also from business in the neighbouring Dominion, State D.

122. United Kingdom, Finance Act 1920, Section 27(7)(b). *See also* Herbert E. Seed & Alfred W. Rawlinson, *Double Income Tax Relief: The Law and Practice Regarding Relief from Double Taxation* 18 (Sir Isaac Pitman & Sons 1925), in Legal Treatises, 1800–1926 (Making of Modern Law Print Editions) ('The usual practice is to treat the Dominion fiscal year ending in the United Kingdom income tax year to which the claim relates, as being equivalent to that United Kingdom income tax year [...]').
123. United Kingdom, Finance Act 1920, Section 27(7)(a).
124. *See,* e.g., League of Nations, *Double Taxation and Tax Evasion, Report and Resolutions Submitted by the Technical Experts to the Financial Committee of the League of Nations* (1925), *in* 4 *Legislative History of United States Tax Conventions,* 4057, 4099–4100 (United States, Joint Committee on Internal Revenue Taxation, US Government Printing Office 1962) (hereinafter 'League of Nations, 1925 Report') (Appendix: Note by M. Léon-Dufour on the Various Methods Suggested for Remedying Double Taxation and Their Graphical Representation: 'The above remarks are quite general and illustrate the method of relief in its most simple form. They disregard many details which complicate the problem considerably. Under the scheme, the relief in respect of any income is to be computed by reference to the respective rates of tax and without regard to any variation in amount between the United Kingdom and the Dominion assessments for the year of claim; and, as pointed out in the report of the Royal Commission, the same source of income may be assessed at very different figures according to United Kingdom legislation and according to Dominion legislation. The taxation of dividends on shares also gives rise to complications. As a matter of fact, neither the economists nor the Government experts think that the system adopted within the British Empire can be brought into general use for international purposes'); Herbert E. Seed & Alfred W. Rawlinson, *Double Income Tax Relief: The Law and Practice Regarding Relief from Double Taxation* 6 (Sir Isaac Pitman & Sons 1925), in Legal Treatises, 1800–1926 (Making of Modern Law Print Editions) (discussing the term 'income').
125. *See,* e.g., Peter Harris, *An Historic View of the Principle and Options for Double Tax Relief,* 1999(6) Brit. Tax Rev. 469, 476 (1999).

Profits in UK:	100	Profits in State D:	50
Effective tax rate in UK:[126]	20%	Effective tax rate in State D:[127]	20%

Total income (WWI):	150
Taxes due in State D:	50 × 20% = 10
Taxes due in UK:	150 × 20% = 30

Credit limit: '27. - (1) If any person [*in this case, the individual taxpayer*] who has paid, by deduction or otherwise, or is liable to pay, United Kingdom income tax for any year of assessment on any part of his income proves to the satisfaction of the Special Commissioners that he has paid Dominion income tax [*10*] for that year in respect of the same part of his income [*50*], he shall be entitled to relief from United Kingdom income tax paid or payable by him on that part of his income [*50*] at a rate thereon to be determined as follows:-

(a) if the Dominion rate of tax [*20%*] does not exceed one-half of the appropriate rate of United Kingdom tax [*half of 20% = 10%*], the rate at which relief is to be given shall be the Dominion rate of tax [*20%*]: [*conditions not fulfilled, letter a does not apply*]
(b) In any other case the rate at which relief is to be given shall be, one-half of the appropriate rate of United Kingdom tax [*10%*]. [...].' (emphasis added; *see* Section 27 of the Finance Act 1920 at *supra* note 98)

= Relief at a rate of 10% on 50.

Taxes paid in UK: (100 × 20%) + (50 × 10%) = 25, or (150 × 20%) – (50 × 10%) = 25

If the Dominion offered relief for the excess (10%), then taxes paid in State D: 5

In a first step, both the UK and State D would tax the 50 of income at 20%, leading to (10 + 10 =) 20 of taxes in total (ETR of 40% on 50). Under this system, the second charge of 20% (10) is relinquished in the amount of 10% (5) by the UK and in the amount of 10% (5) by State D, leaving only 10 in taxes in

126. For further details on how the rates used for relief were arrived at, *see*, e.g., Herbert E. Seed & Alfred W. Rawlinson, *Double Income Tax Relief: The Law and Practice Regarding Relief from Double Taxation* 6 and 19–21 (Sir Isaac Pitman & Sons 1925), in Legal Treatises, 1800–1926 (Making of Modern Law Print Editions).
127. United Kingdom, Finance Act 1920, Section 27(8)(b) (according to the definition, it is not the nominal or statutory rate of tax used but the effective rate of tax: 'The expression "Dominion rate of tax" means the rate determined by dividing the amount of Dominion income tax paid for the year by the amount of the income in respect of which the Dominion income tax is charged for that year, except that where the Dominion income tax is charged on an amount other than the ascertained amount of the actual profits the Dominion rate of tax for the purposes of this section shall be determined by the Special Commissioners').

total (ETR of 20% on the 50, thus equal to one layer of tax, though shared between the two states).

The result of this system is that the total relief granted by the two states is equal to the lower of the two tax rates.[128] Viewed differently, the taxpayer, after relief, pays the higher of the two tax rates.

1918 relief in the US

In the meantime, in the US, the Revenue Act of 1918 devised a much broader credit relief system, which was perceived as an act of unprecedented generosity.[129] This credit 'for the first time anywhere in the world' applied without territorial restriction, granting a credit for foreign taxes paid to any foreign government on income earned abroad.[130] This really concentrated attention on the fact that 'taxes paid abroad would reduce American tax revenue dollar for dollar' and 'the United States was assuming sole responsibility for the costs of reducing the double taxation of its residents and citizens'.[131] The reference to 'sole responsibility' highlights the unilateral nature of this, i.e., that the US was granting a credit irrespective of any reciprocity or agreement with the foreign state in question. At the time of its proposal and adoption, even its author, Thomas Sewall Adams considered it 'striking' and expected it to be rejected 'because the press of wartime financing made tax relief generally inappropriate in 1918'.[132] Another renowned economist and agenda-setter in international tax policy, Edwin Seligman, is reported to have said that 'the United States is making a present of the revenue to other countries'.[133]

Regarding the rationale, the reasons for the adoption of the credit method in the US are well documented, including the views of Thomas Sewall Adams who proposed the 1918 US FTC, which offers deeper insight into its role.[134] As war financing strained government revenues, the resulting trend of increasing tax rates was often cited as a

128. League of Nations, 1925 Report, at 4098–4100 (Appendix: Note by M. Léon-Dufour on the Various Methods Suggested for Remedying Double Taxation and Their Graphical Representation).
129. Michael J. Graetz & Michael M. O'Hear, *The 'Original Intent' of U.S. International Taxation*, 46(5) Duke L.J. 1021, 1045–1046 (1997); *see also*, e.g., League of Nations, 1923 Report, at *infra* note 563 and note 566.
130. Michael J. Graetz & Michael M. O'Hear, *The 'Original Intent' of U.S. International Taxation*, 46(5) Duke L.J. 1021, 1022 (1997); *see also* Elisabeth A. Owens, *The Foreign Tax Credit: A Study of the Credit for Foreign Taxes under United States Income Tax Law* 20 (Harvard Law School 1961), but later territorial restrictions emerged, *see*, e.g., United States, Internal Revenue Code, Section 901(j) (according to which, the foreign tax credit is denied for taxes paid to certain governments, such as those with which US does not want diplomatic ties).
131. Michael J. Graetz & Michael M. O'Hear, *The 'Original Intent' of U.S. International Taxation*, 46(5) Duke L.J. 1021, 1045 (1997).
132. *Id.*, at 1045–1046.
133. *Id.*, at 1045–1046.
134. *See*, e.g., Michael J. Graetz & Michael M. O'Hear, *The 'Original Intent' of U.S. International Taxation*, 46(5) Duke L.J. 1021 (1997); Reuven S. Avi-Yonah, *All of a Piece Throughout: The Four Ages of U.S. International Taxation*, 25(2) Va. Tax Rev. 313 (2005); Jacob S. Seidman, *Seidman's Legislative History of Federal Income Tax Laws: 1938-1861* (Prentice-Hall, Inc. 1938).

key factor in spurring discussions of double taxation and the need for relief.[135] Related to this was the concern that excessive tax burdens would not only reduce compliance (on which the income tax system relies) but even encourage avoidance and evasion.[136] From the perspective of Adams and, as discussed below (in Section 2.1.2.3.), from the perspective of experts at the League of Nations, double taxation and tax evasion were linked problems.[137]

For Adams, this was also strongly linked to an idea of fairness. The income tax itself was 'sold to the American people on fairness grounds',[138] embodied in its progressive tax rates; so it is incumbent upon legislators to maintain its fairness. This can be compromised in a number of different ways, if, for example, rates rise too high, or the system grows needlessly complex, or similarly situated taxpayers are differently treated. Based on these ideas, Adams pitched 'double taxation' as a form of injustice or discrimination.[139] In a study by Michael J. Graetz and Michael M. O'Hear, Adams is quoted as saying:

> 'There is something in the legislative mind which recognizes that if one taxpayer is being taxed twice while the majority of men similarly situated are being taxed only once, by the same tax, something wrong or inequitable is being done which, other things being equal, the legislator should correct if he can.'[140]

The authors also clarify that Adams, as well as Seligman, made a distinction between situations in which double taxation was problematic (or 'unjust') and when it was not: they were less focused on the economic double taxation that arises from a 'classical' corporate taxation system or layers of taxation within the same state, from the federal and sub-federal levels, but rather on international double taxation ('concurrent taxation of the same income by different nations'), as '*discrimination:* the person who chooses to live in one country and earn money in another is singled out for a double dose of taxes'.[141]

135. *See*, e.g., Elisabeth A. Owens, *The Foreign Tax Credit: A Study of the Credit for Foreign Taxes under United States Income Tax Law* 20 (Harvard Law School 1961); Michael J. Graetz & Michael M. O'Hear, *The 'Original Intent' of U.S. International Taxation*, 46(5) Duke L.J. 1021, 1051 (1997) (citing Adams regarding tax rate increases) and at 1044 (citing tax increases in connection with financing the war efforts) and at 1045 (citing examples of tax rates around 1918 and the risk of it becoming, absent relief, 'potentially confiscatory'). For more on the war financing, *see*, e.g., Daniel C. Roper, *The War Revenue Act of 1917*, 75 Annals Am. Acad. Pol. & Soc. Sci. 159 (1918).
136. *See* Michael J. Graetz & Michael M. O'Hear, *The 'Original Intent' of U.S. International Taxation*, 46(5) Duke L.J. 1021, 1049 (1997) (citing concerns that, at high enough rates, taxes could become 'unenforceable') and at 1100 n.310.
137. *Id.*, at 1039; League of Nations, 1925 Report, at 4087 (as discussed at *infra* note 504, the discussions at the League of Nations also stated the connection between double taxation and tax evasion, as the name of the report evinces).
138. Michael J. Graetz & Michael M. O'Hear, *The 'Original Intent' of U.S. International Taxation*, 46(5) Duke L.J. 1021, 1043 (1997).
139. *Id.*, at 1047 and 1048.
140. *Id.*, at 1048 (citing a 1929 work by Adams with the title '*International and Interstate Aspects of Double Taxation*').
141. *Id.*, at 1047 n.108.

This indicates different aspects of and perceptions of 'double taxation'. Perspectives may differ as to the 'double' element that is most relevant, be it two taxes on the income in general, or two different jurisdictions taxing the income. Looking at these perceptions of 'double taxation' (*supra* note 140 and note 141), what they seem to have in common is the 'same tax' and the 'same income' (i.e., there is not an emphasis on, for example, a simultaneous levy of value-added tax and income tax), indicating the importance of the similarity of the tax base, as a component of this understanding of 'double taxation'. Incidentally, it appears that a broader notion of double taxation was addressed in the state of Wisconsin at the time, which granted a tax credit that 'permitted taxpayers to offset their personal property taxes against income taxes'.[142] This design of the credit method allows an offset of two different (potentially incomparable) taxes levied on (seemingly) two different tax bases. This could indicate that the concern in this case was less (or not solely) about juridical double taxation, but rather about the overall burden. Alternatively, there was possibly some other local Wisconsin-specific reason for allowing such an offset.

Although the increased wartime burden is what made Adams' proposal politically feasible (it was seemingly the main mover for legislators and affected businesses and other taxpayers), it seems that the inventor himself was rather concerned about this 'discrimination' component. Moreover, in his view, the state of residence of the taxpayer was responsible for this discrimination. The reasoning seemed to be that taxation of locally sourced streams of income in the state of source was natural and inevitable; this is a right that states of residence themselves do not relinquish, yet those same states of residence refused (at that time) to take into account that their, albeit justified, taxation of all income attached to their resident taxpayers is what causes their residents to be taxed twice (or more).[143] Thus, the person often credited with inventing the FTC, Adams, is on record as a proponent of a balance between source and residence; it appears that he intended the credit method, in combination with properly designed source rules, as a means to cede priority to source taxation, in a way that offered relief for double taxation while ensuring residence as a backstop measure. By backstop, it meant that the credit came equipped with an anti-avoidance or anti-evasion function since '[i]f the taxpayer evaded taxation abroad he would be caught at home'.[144] As a secondary consideration, albeit less emphasized, 'Adams also saw value in residence-based taxation as a means to protect progressive income tax rates ... .'[145] Historical accounts of Adam's deliberate consideration of this balance offer some measure of how far the current perception of the credit method departs from its original role and rationale:

142. *Id.*, at 1046 n.103.
143. More precisely, for details and quotes from Adams, *see id.*, at 1048.
144. *Id.*, at 1038–1039 & 1039 n.73.
145. *Id.*, at 1039–1040. In agreement with this view of Adams, *see*, e.g., J. Clifton Fleming Jr., Robert J. Peroni & Stephen E. Shay, *Fairness in International Taxation: The Ability-to-Pay Case for Taxing Worldwide Income*, 5(4) Fla. Tax. Rev. 299 (2001).

> 'Thus, modern claims that the U.S. international tax regime gives primacy to residence-based taxation should be understood as a repudiation-not a continuation-of its original intent.'[146]

In addition to the above concerns of excessive burdens, potential discrimination and the balance of taxation rights, with built-in backstops, there were some other intertwined economic and political, or diplomatic, rationales, attributed to Adams, Mitchell B. Carroll, and members of the Congress. Cross-border investment was viewed as not only in the 'national self-interest' but also in the interests of post-war reconstruction and peace, as it enhances 'economic well-being' on both sides;[147] depending on the precise rationale pursued, such investment should either be actively *encouraged* or supported, an approach that could reflect a rationale favouring the competitiveness of US businesses, or at least it should *not* be hampered, an approach that could reflect some sort of neutrality or same treatment rationale. Ultimately, according to Graetz and O'Hear, the FTC fit in 'with the spirit' of the time and of the 1918 Act, as the period 1918–1919 was characterized by 'a number of initiatives ... to encourage investment abroad', with ideas of peace and stability in mind as well as promoting American exports, etc.[148]

These understandings of why double taxation should be counteracted shape how policymakers set about to do it. Clearly, there were many intersecting considerations. The debates related to the rationale and how it has evolved over time will be returned to below, as subsequent periods of the historical development bring other considerations into the picture.

The discussion now turns to the design of the 1918 US FTC, where the above considerations of its author are reflected. This shows some of the interlinkages between rationale and design. For example, as discussed below, the FTC offers a 'dollar for dollar' credit;[149] in this way, it strives to eliminate double taxation, rather than

146. Michael J. Graetz & Michael M. O'Hear, *The 'Original Intent' of U.S. International Taxation*, 46(5) Duke L.J. 1021, 1040–1041 (1997) (e.g., 'Edwin Seligman described the American approach as the "extreme converse" of purely residence-based taxation'). *See also* Thomas Sewall Adams, *Introduction, in Double Taxation Relief: Discussion of Conventions Drafted at International Conference of Experts, 1927, and Other Measures*, Trade Information Bulletin No. 523 (Mitchell B. Carroll ed., US Government Printing Office 1928) (Adams himself wrote: 'Source taxation is recognized as of coordinate or greater importance than taxation at residence. The obligation of each State to protect its own nationals and residents by appropriate credits against double taxation traceable to defects in its own legislation is perhaps for the first time tacitly acknowledged').
147. Michael J. Graetz & Michael M. O'Hear, *The 'Original Intent' of U.S. International Taxation*, 46(5) Duke L.J. 1021, 1049 (1997) (listing 'other factors' such as 'a need to encourage private investments by Americans in Europe', potential 'practical benefits' of relief, 'competitiveness of American business abroad' among others. Indeed, '[c]ertain members of Congress also depicted the FTC "as a method to encourage foreign trade and to prevent revenue loss through incorporation of foreign subsidiaries or expatriation"'), at 1050 (citing Mitchell Carroll), and at 1051 (citing statements by Adams at the League of Nations and describing US interests 'to rebuild post-war Europe', all of which reflect various economic and political reasons in favour of double taxation relief).
148. *Id.*, at 1053–1054.
149. *Id.*, at 1045.

merely mitigate it. First, this reflects a desire to rectify the aforementioned discrimination, since by the US fully giving up each dollar of its overlapping taxation to the extent of each corresponding 'dollar' of foreign taxes (as opposed to, e.g., a credit of up to 0.80 cents per dollar of tax, or other possible limits, such as those seen in the UK relief at the time), it can potentially re-equalize the overall tax burden (no more, no less) between two similarly situated US taxpayers, one with only domestic-source income (DSI) and one with both DSI and FSI. Second, this reflects one way of giving first priority to source taxation (as balanced against the other aforementioned considerations). At this time, the US was not asking source states to reduce their amounts of taxation collected at source - such negotiations would come later, under bilateral tax treaties - nor asking the other states to share some of the costs of relief, as under the UK Dominion relief system.

As regards the FTC for individuals, Section 222 of the Revenue Act of 1918 read as follows:

> 'CREDIT FOR TAXES. SEC. 222.
>
> (a) That the tax computed under Part II of this title shall be credited with: (1) In the case of a citizen of the United States, the amount of any income, war-profits and excess-profits taxes paid during the taxable year to any foreign country, upon income derived from sources therein, or to any possession of the United States; and (2) In the case of a resident of the United States, the amount of any such taxes paid during the taxable year to any possession of the United States; and (3) In the case of an alien resident of the United States who is a citizen or subject of a foreign country, the amount of any such taxes paid during the taxable year to such country, upon income derived from sources therein, if such country, in imposing such taxes, allows a similar credit to citizens of the United States residing in such country; and (4) In the case of any such individual who is a member of a partnership or a beneficiary of an estate or trust, his proportionate share of such taxes of the partnership or the estate or trust paid during the taxable year to a foreign country or to any possession of the United States, as the case may be.
>
> (b) If accrued taxes when paid differ from the amounts claimed as credits by the taxpayer, or if any tax paid is refunded in whole or in part, the taxpayer shall notify the Commissioner who shall redetermine the amount of the tax due under Part II of this title for the year or years affected, and the amount of tax due upon such redetermination, if any, shall be paid by the taxpayer upon notice and demand by the collector, or the amount of tax overpaid, if any, shall be credited or refunded to the taxpayer in accordance with the provisions of section 252. In the case of such a tax accrued but not paid, the Commissioner as a condition precedent to the allowance of this credit may require the taxpayer to give a bond with sureties satisfactory to and to be approved by the Commissioner in such penal sum as the Commissioner may require, conditioned for the payment by the taxpayer of any amount of tax found due upon any such redetermination; and the bond herein prescribed shall contain such further conditions as the Commissioner may require.
>
> (c) These credits shall be allowed only if the taxpayer furnishes evidence satisfactory to the Commissioner showing the amount of income derived from sources within such foreign country or such possession of the United States, and all other information necessary for the computation of such credits.'

As regards the FTC for corporations, Section 238 of the Revenue Act of 1918 read as follows:

> 'CREDIT FOR TAXES. SEC. 238.
>
> (a) That in the case of a domestic corporation the total taxes imposed, for the taxable year by this title and by Title III shall be credited with the amount of any income, war-profits and excess-profits taxes paid during the taxable year to any foreign country, upon income derived from sources therein, or to any possession of the United States. If accrued taxes when paid differ from the amounts claimed as credits by the corporation, or if any tax paid is refunded in whole or in part, the corporation shall at once notify the Commissioner who shall redetermine the amount of the taxes due under this title and under Title III for the year or years affected, and the amount of taxes due upon such redetermination, if any, shall be paid by the corporation upon notice and demand by the collector, or the amount of taxes overpaid, if any, shall be credited or refunded to the corporation in accordance with the provisions of section 252. In the case of such a tax accrued but not paid, the Commissioner as a condition precedent to the allowance of this credit may require the corporation to give a bond with sureties satisfactory to and to be approved by him in such penal sum as he may require, conditioned for the payment by the taxpayer of any amount of taxes found due upon any such redetermination; and the bond herein prescribed shall contain such further conditions as the Commissioner may require.
>
> (b) This credit shall be allowed only if the taxpayer furnishes evidence satisfactory to the Commissioner showing the amount of income derived from sources within such foreign country or such possession of the United States, as the case may be, and all other information necessary for the computation of such credit.
>
> (c) If a domestic corporation makes a return for a fiscal year beginning in 1917 and ending in 1918, only that proportion of this credit shall be allowed which the part of such period within the calendar year 1918 bears to the entire period.'

When analysing the wording of the law, the following conditions emerge. It specifies who is entitled to a credit, what taxes are creditable, rules in case of a 'redetermination' of taxes, and a procedural condition (it is worth noting that the Revenue Act of 1918 also introduced an 'indirect credit', but this merits a separate discussion, which will be carried out below in Section 2.1.1.3.).

As regards the 'who', or the eligible taxpayers, it lists 'a *citizen* of the United States',[150] 'a *resident* of the United States',[151] a special case for 'an *alien resident* of the United States who is a citizen or subject of a foreign country',[152] 'any such individual who is a member of a partnership or a beneficiary of an estate or trust'[153] and a

150. United States, Revenue Act of 1918, Sixty-Fifth Congress, Session III, Chapter 18, Public Law 65-254, Section 222(a)(1) (US Government Printing Office 1919).
151. United States, Revenue Act of 1918, Sixty-Fifth Congress, Session III, Chapter 18, Public Law 65-254, Section 222(a)(2) (US Government Printing Office 1919).
152. United States, Revenue Act of 1918, Sixty-Fifth Congress, Session III, Chapter 18, Public Law 65-254, Section 222(a)(3) (US Government Printing Office 1919).
153. United States, Revenue Act of 1918, Sixty-Fifth Congress, Session III, Chapter 18, Public Law 65-254, Section 222(a)(4) (US Government Printing Office 1919).

'*domestic* corporation'[154] (emphasis added). In this way, residence and citizenship of the taxpayer became central.

As regards the eligible taxes, it applies to 'any income, war-profits and excess-profits taxes' and 'paid to ... any foreign country, *upon income derived from sources therein*' (emphasis added).[155] In this way, the source of the income also became central. Moreover, it applied to 'income' taxes, the interpretation of which was the subject of numerous revenue rulings of the Internal Revenue Service and cases in the US.[156] According to Elisabeth A. Owens, the 'Basic Doctrine' takes as its starting point that 'a foreign tax must fall within the United States concept of an income tax' and, thus, does not follow the foreign characterization.[157] This determination has been composed of a series of tests that included *inter alia*: whether the levy is a 'tax' (as opposed to, e.g., fees or royalties for concessions);[158] if so, whether it is a tax on 'income', 'according to United States standards of what constitutes income',[159] which essentially enquires into the tax base on which the foreign tax was levied;[160] and the purpose of the tax (i.e., the purpose is 'to reach income' and does 'not, therefore, include a tax laid on or occasioned by particular events, such as transactions, sales, or the privilege of doing business').[161] Regulations were eventually issued, which now explain that the 'predominant character of a foreign tax is that of an income tax in the U.S. sense' if it is 'likely to reach net gain', which must satisfy 'each of the realization,[162] gross receipts,[163] and net income requirements[164]'.[165]

154. United States, Revenue Act of 1918, Sixty-Fifth Congress, Session III, Chapter 18, Public Law 65-254, Section 238(a) (US Government Printing Office 1919).
155. United States, Revenue Act of 1918, Sixty-Fifth Congress, Session III, Chapter 18, Public Law 65-254, Section 222(a)(1) and Section 238(a) (US Government Printing Office 1919). It also included taxes paid 'to any possession of the United States'.
156. Elisabeth A. Owens, *The Foreign Tax Credit: A Study of the Credit for Foreign Taxes under United States Income Tax Law* 25–88 (Harvard Law School 1961). *See also*, e.g., David F. Nitschke, *New Developments in the Foreign Tax Credit: The Treasury Department Attempts to Define an Income Tax*, 2(1) Nw. J. Int'l L. & Bus. 28 (1980).
157. Elisabeth A. Owens, *The Foreign Tax Credit: A Study of the Credit for Foreign Taxes under United States Income Tax Law* 29–30 (Harvard Law School 1961).
158. *Id.*, at 30–32.
159. *Id.*, at 30.
160. *Id.*, at 33–34 and 85 ('determined very largely by the character of the foreign tax base ... if the tax base was net income or profits ...').
161. *Id.*, at 30.
162. United States, Code of Federal Regulations, Section 1.901-2 (Income, War Profits or Excess Profits Tax Paid or Accrued) ('(i) In general. A foreign tax satisfies the realization requirement if, judged on the basis of its predominant character, it is imposed – (A) Upon or subsequent to the occurrence of events ("realization events") that would result in the realization of income under the income tax provisions of the Internal Revenue Code; [...]').
163. *Id.* ('(i) In general. A foreign tax satisfies the gross receipts requirement if, judged on the basis of its predominant character, it is imposed on the basis of – (A)Gross receipts; or (B)Gross receipts computed under a method that is likely to produce an amount that is not greater than fair market value. [...]').
164. *Id.* ('(i)In general. A foreign tax satisfies the net income requirement if, judged on the basis of its predominant character, the base of the tax is computed by reducing gross receipts (including gross receipts as computed under paragraph (b)(3)(i)(B) of this section) to permit – (A) Recovery of the significant costs and expenses (including significant capital expenditures) attributable, under reasonable principles, to such gross receipts; or (B) Recovery of such

Regarding the redetermination of taxes, this refers to situations where the amount of taxes paid abroad ultimately changes ('[i]f accrued taxes when paid differ from the amounts claimed as credits by the taxpayer, or if any tax paid is refunded in whole or in part') and obliged the taxpayer to report such changes so that the credit could be readjusted accordingly.[166] Via this corrective procedural mechanism, it applies strictly to only taxes actually paid. What this indicates about the credit method is that it aims to relieve actual double taxation, as opposed to 'potential' double taxation,[167] a feature which distinguishes it from the exemption method.

Relating to both the eligible taxes and the redetermination requirement, there was also a timing component for the eligible taxes, as it applies to those 'paid during the taxable year'. Considerations of the time period for which credits were available featured in both the UK[168] and the US statutory provisions (indeed, this was even more visible in the 1920 UK Dominion Relief, since, as mentioned above, it expressly authorized regulations where there was a need to determine a correspondence between the taxable year in the UK and that in the Dominion). This follows from the emphasis on actual double taxation: as soon as a relief method seeks to be calibrated to the actual taxation in the other jurisdiction, there is a need to match the income and the taxes attributable to it as much as possible between the different jurisdictions.[169]

Finally, as for the procedural condition, similar to the relief in the UK, the taxpayer must provide satisfactory evidence of the income and taxes paid abroad.[170]

One notable feature that is missing is that, in the US, by contrast with the UK, there was *no limitation* on the amount of the credit. This contributed to its generosity. One feature that is similar to UK is that the wording of the US provisions also implied a two-step process.[171]

---

significant costs and expenses computed under a method that is likely to produce an amount that approximates, or is greater than, recovery of such significant costs and expenses. [...]').

165. *Id.*
166. United States, Revenue Act of 1918, Sixty-Fifth Congress, Session III, Chapter 18, Public Law 65-254, Section 222(a)(b) and Section 238(a) (US Government Printing Office 1919).
167. For this distinction, *see* Klaus Vogel, *Introduction, in Klaus Vogel on Double Taxation Conventions* 2, m.no. 46a (Kluwer Law International 3d ed. 1997); Klaus Vogel & Alexander Rust, *Introduction, in* 1 *Klaus Vogel on Double Taxation Conventions* 1, m.no. 55 (Ekkehart Reimer & Alexander Rust eds, Kluwer Law International 4th ed. 2015); Peter Harris, *An Historic View of the Principle and Options for Double Tax Relief*, 1999(6) Brit. Tax Rev. 469, 479 (1999) (Peter Harris makes a distinction between 'notional' or 'dependent', and discusses how this has an impact on the design of relief); Błażej Kuźniacki, *The Need to Avoid Double Economic Taxation Triggered by CFC Rules under Tax Treaties, and the Way to Achieve It*, 43(12) Intertax 758, 767 (2015) (Błażej Kuźniacki refers to 'virtual' double taxation).
168. United Kingdom, Finance Act 1916, Section 43 ('for the current income tax year') and United Kingdom, Finance Act 1920, Section 27 ('for that year').
169. *See*, e.g., Peter Harris, *An Historic View of the Principle and Options for Double Tax Relief*, 1999(6) Brit. Tax Rev. 469, 479–480 (1999).
170. United States, Revenue Act of 1918, Sixty-Fifth Congress, Session III, Chapter 18, Public Law 65-254, Section 222(c) for individuals, Section 238(b) for domestic corporations (US Government Printing Office 1919).
171. This is seen, namely, in the wording for the direct credit which states that 'the tax computed under Part II of this title [tax owed on the basis of the US tax laws] shall be credited with [the foreign taxes] ...' and, for the indirect credit which states that '... the total taxes imposed, for

In a first step, the US income taxes would be calculated on the basis of the US tax code, which essentially took into account the worldwide income of an eligible taxpayer (e.g., resident or citizen). Regarding the income – or the tax base – for this purpose, the US income taxes would be calculated on the basis of 'net income',[172] meaning that, from the revenue the taxpayer had earned throughout the tax year, certain expenses could be subtracted, or deducted. One expense was explicitly not allowed to be deducted however: the taxpayer did not have the right to deduct any foreign 'income, war-profits and excess-profits taxes allowed as a credit under Section 222'.[173] In other words, it was not possible to treat the foreign taxes both as a deductible expense (reducing the tax base) and as an FTC (reducing the taxes due). Indeed, the credit was an alternative to the deduction.[174] This emphasized one core feature, namely that the relief operated at the stage of the taxes due (as opposed to the earlier stage of calculating the tax base). Adding the foreign taxes back in (or disallowing their deduction) can be referred to as a 'gross-up' (a term used especially in the context of indirect credits, but which could also describe the treatment of taxes paid in other contexts too).[175]

After this, in a second step, an amount equal to all eligible foreign taxes could be deducted from the US income taxes. As there was no limit, the amount of foreign taxes could be fully deducted even if it was higher than the amount the US would have levied on the same income.[176] Higher foreign taxes were not an unlikely scenario. Elisabeth A. Owens cites an example given in the Hearings before the Senate Committee on Finance in 1921, according to which the US CIT rate was 12% while that of the UK was 'approximately 27%', with the result that the deduction of UK taxes in the full amount

the taxable year by this title and by Title III [tax owed on the basis of the US tax laws] shall be credited with [the foreign taxes] ...'.

172. United States, Revenue Act of 1918, Sixty-Fifth Congress, Session III, Chapter 18, Public Law 65-254, Section 212 in connection with Section 213 and Section 214 (US Government Printing Office 1919).

173. United States, Revenue Act of 1918, Sixty-Fifth Congress, Session III, Chapter 18, Public Law 65-254, Section 214(a)(3) (US Government Printing Office 1919).

174. In fact, a deduction for foreign income taxes from the tax base was the only form of relief that was available in the United States prior to enactment of the credit. *See*, e.g., National Foreign Trade Council, *The NFTC Foreign Income Project: International Tax Policy for the 21st Century – Part Two: Relief of International Double Taxation* 149 (Fred F. Murray ed.-in-chief, National Foreign Trade Council 2001), http://www.nftc.org/default/tax/fip/NFTC1a%20Volume1_part2Chap1-5.pdf (last visited 26 Apr. 2019); Elisabeth A. Owens, *The Foreign Tax Credit: A Study of the Credit for Foreign Taxes under United States Income Tax Law* 20 (Harvard Law School 1961). Regarding the option to either deduct foreign taxes or take a foreign tax credit, this is still possible. *See*, e.g., US, Internal Revenue Code, Section 27, Section 901(a) ('If the taxpayer chooses to have the benefits of this subpart ...') and Section 164(a) (as amended through 22 Dec. 2017).

175. *See*, e.g., *Gross Up*, *Black's Law Dictionary* (9th ed. 2009) (it defines 'gross up' in the context of estate and gift taxes as 'To add back to a decedent's gross estate the gift taxes paid by the decedent or the decedent's estate on gifts made by the decedent or the decedent's spouse during the three-year period preceding the decedent's death').

176. Elisabeth A. Owens, *The Foreign Tax Credit: A Study of the Credit for Foreign Taxes under United States Income Tax Law* 198 et seq. (Harvard Law School 1961); Michael J. Graetz & Michael M. O'Hear, *The 'Original Intent' of U.S. International Taxation*, 46(5) Duke L.J. 1021, 1054–1056 (1997).

could entirely wipe out any US tax liability – both the taxes that the US would otherwise collect on the FSI and taxes on its own DSI.[177]

Example No. 4: No Deduction for Foreign Taxes (or a 'Gross-Up') in the Direct Credit Context

Facts: During the relevant tax year in question, an individual taxpayer, resident in State R, operates a business through a sole proprietorship. The taxpayer earns income from business in State R and also from business in the neighbouring country, State F.

Situation in State F

Tax rate in State F	20%
Revenues	125
Expenses	25
Profits in State F	100
Taxes due in State F	20
After-tax profits available to taxpayer	80

Situation in State R

Tax rate in State R	30%
Revenues	125
Expenses	25
Profits in State R	100

Credit Method in State R

To calculate WWI:

After-tax profits available to taxpayer	80
Gross-up = add back in foreign taxes[178]	20
Profits taken into account from State F	100

177. Elisabeth A. Owens, *The Foreign Tax Credit: A Study of the Credit for Foreign Taxes under United States Income Tax Law* 198 & n.3 (Harvard Law School 1961) (citing '*Hearings Before Senate Committee on Finance on H.R. 8245*, 67th Cong., 1st Sess. 73-74 (1921)').

178. This example merely illustrates that, even though from the taxpayer's perspective, the taxpayer has in hand only the after-tax amount from State F, it is nevertheless the full pre-tax amount of 100 that is used in the computation for the credit method. In practice, in the 'direct' credit context, a separate step to add back in foreign taxes is often not explicit; the taxpayer simply reports its pre-tax income from the foreign state; i.e., the 100 in this case. An explicit add-back, or 'gross-up', is needed more in the 'indirect' credit context, as Example No. 13 in the next subsection, Section 2.1.1.3., illustrates.

Profits in State R	100
WWI	200
Taxes due in State R on WWI (200 × 30%)	60
Creditable Amount: *Unlimited Credit = No limit (MCA), thus Creditable Amount = Taxes paid to State F*	20
Taxes paid to State R = *Taxes due in State R on WWI – Creditable Amount*	40

Example No. 5.1: The Effects of an Unlimited Foreign Tax Credit

Profits in State R	100	Profits in State F	100
Tax rate in State R	10%	Tax rate in State F	20%

WWI	200
Taxes due in State F (100 × 20%)	20
Taxes due in State R on WWI (200 × 10%)	20
-Portion of taxes due in State R that are attributable to domestic profits	10
-Portion of taxes due in State R that are attributable to foreign profits	10
Creditable Amount: *Unlimited Credit = No limit (MCA), thus Creditable Amount = Taxes paid to State F*	20

Result

Taxes paid to State F	20
Taxes paid to State R = *Taxes due in State R on WWI – Creditable Amount*	0
Total taxes paid by Taxpayer	20

The effect of this hypothetical unlimited foreign tax credit is that State R fully eliminates any taxes that it would collect on the income that is double taxed, namely the foreign-source income (i.e., the 100 generated in State F) and, in this case, State R fully eliminates the 10 of taxes that it would otherwise collect on its own domestic-source income (i.e., the 100 generated in State R). The total amount that the taxpayer ends up paying is equal to 20, which is the amount the taxpayer *would have paid* if the taxpayer had generated *all 200* of its income *in State R* (200 x 10%). Yet, because the credit in State R wipes out the full tax liability there, State R does not collect any taxes; the taxes paid go entirely to State F, despite the fact that 100 was earned in each state.

Moreover, if taken to its logical extreme, assuming State F's rate were even higher, e.g., 30%, then State R, under a full unlimited credit method, would even somehow compensate for the excess (e.g., reimburse it, allow it to be carried forward) in order to grant a credit that is equal to the full 30 paid abroad. In that case, State R would eliminate its taxes on the foreign-source income, give up its taxes on the domestic-source income and owe the excess.

***Compare* Example No. 5.2. below.**

1921 relief in the US: introduction of a credit limitation

The Revenue Act of 1921 amended this issue. The 1921 reform set a limitation on the credit, or MCA, that capped the amount of the credit at the proportion of US taxes that corresponded to the FSI (as demonstrated below, in Example No. 5.2). The Act stated:

> '... and in no other case shall the amount of credit taken under this subdivision exceed the same proportion of the tax, against which such credit is taken, which the taxpayer's net income (computed without deduction for any income, war-profits and excess-profits taxes imposed by any foreign country or possession of the United States) from sources without the United States bears to his entire net income (computed without such deduction) for the same taxable year'.[179]

In other words, out of the US taxes payable on the worldwide income, a fraction would apply to determine how much relates to the FSI. The rest would relate to the US DSI. Notably, this fraction applied to all FSI ('from sources without the United States'), meaning that it did not make a distinction between different foreign countries, but rather pooled together all the FSI and the corresponding foreign taxes. This has been referred to as an 'over-all limitation'.[180] One way to express the fraction can be as follows:

179. United States, Revenue Act of 1921, Sixty-Seventh Congress, Session I, Chapter 136, Public Law 67-98, Section 222(a)(5) for individuals and Section 238(a) for corporations (US Government Printing Office 1921) (the latter stated '... *Provided,* [t]hat the amount of credit taken under this subdivision shall in no case exceed the same proportion of the taxes, against which such credit is taken, which the taxpayer's net income (computed without deduction for any income, war-profits, and excess-profits taxes imposed by any foreign country or possession of the United States) from sources without the United States bears to its entire net income (computed without such deduction) for the same taxable year').
180. Elisabeth A. Owens, *The Foreign Tax Credit: A Study of the Credit for Foreign Taxes under United States Income Tax Law* 198 (Harvard Law School 1961).

Credit limitation (MCA) = Total taxes on worldwide income × (foreign-source income/worldwide income)

$$MCA = TT_{WWI} \times (FSI/WWI)$$

Example No. 5.2: Credit Limitation (Maximum Creditable Amount (MCA))

Profits in State R	100	Profits in State F	100	
Tax rate in State R	10%	Tax rate in State F	20%	
WWI				200
Taxes due in State F (100 × 20%)				20
Taxes due in State R on WWI (200 × 10%)				20
- Portion of taxes due in State R that are attributable to domestic profits				10
- Portion of taxes due in State R that are attributable to foreign profits				10
Creditable Amount: *MCA in State R = State R's taxes attributable to foreign profits = Taxes due in State R on WWI × (Profits in State F/WWI)*				10
Result				
Taxes paid to State F				20
Taxes paid to State R = *Taxes due in State R on WWI – Creditable Amount*				10
Total taxes paid by Taxpayer				30

The result is, as regards the 100 of income that is taxed by both states (the foreign-source income earned in State F), Taxpayer ends up paying the higher of the two states' tax rates, i.e., 20 of taxes on that 100. State R eliminated the 10 of taxes it would have levied on the 100 earned in State F, but State R continues to collect the 10 of taxes attributable to the 100 of income generated domestically.

There were a handful of reasons for implementing a credit limitation. As alluded to (at *supra* note 177), changes in tax rates played a role. The effects of this unlimited credit on US tax revenue were not initially noticed as high war tax rates prevailed;[181] however, the rates in the US were reduced, while rates in European countries remained high:

181. Michael J. Graetz & Michael M. O'Hear, *The 'Original Intent' of U.S. International Taxation*, 46(5) Duke L.J. 1021, 1055 (1997).

> 'The repeal of the U.S. excess profits tax in 1921 made such a limit even more compelling. Contemporary critics derided the limitless FTC as an instance of unjustified "prodigality" on the part of the American government.'[182]

Another reason was that 'an unlimited credit could function as a US subsidy of a foreign treasury'.[183] Yet another reason was a concern over potential 'abuse'.[184] From testimony provided by Adams to the Senate Finance Committee, Graetz and O'Hear cite:

> '[The unlimited FTC] is subject to this ... rather grave abuse: If the foreign taxes are higher than our rate of taxes, that credit may wipe out taxes which fairly belong to this country ... . [W]e know of instances where big corporations whose income was derived largely from this country have had their tax wiped out, so far as this country is concerned, because the English tax rates are three times as high as ours.'[185]

As this above quote shows, there was a concern of 'taxes which fairly belong to this country'. This was most acute when foreign taxes ended up entirely preventing the US from collecting any revenue on its own domestically produced income (as for the use of the term 'abuse', it is not clear whether corporations were deliberately exploiting this or whether it was simply circumstantial). Thus, '[t]he fundamental purpose of the 1921 foreign tax credit limitation was to protect the ability of the U.S. to collect tax on U.S. source income'.[186]

The Revenue Act of 1921 addressed two key issues that arose under the credit method. In addition to the credit limitation (one key issue), it also addressed the need for clear source rules (another key issue).[187] As mentioned, unlike the UK Dominion Tax Relief, the US FTC revolved around residence and source. The credit limitation deepened this distinction since the very reason for its implementation was to distinguish between US taxes that corresponded to DSI, which the US should rightfully be able to collect, and the US taxes that corresponded to FSI, which the US was willing to reduce or even entirely forego, ceding to the tax claim of the source country.

As the above formula shows, the amount of FSI has a direct impact on the MCA. Given its placement in the numerator of the fraction, as FSI *increases*, the fraction is larger and thus the credit is larger; as FSI *decreases*, the fraction is smaller and thus the credit is smaller. Source rules were crucial for determining both the amount of the FTC for residents and the US-source income on which non-residents could be taxed, thus becoming a 'central organizing feature of the American international tax system'.[188] Examples of the source rules include: for interest income, the source was the place of

182. *Id.*, at 1056.
183. Gloria Teixeira & David Williams, *The Impact of the Unilateral Tax Credit in the US, UK and Other Tax Systems*, 23(11) Intertax 573, 576 (1995).
184. Michael J. Graetz & Michael M. O'Hear, *The 'Original Intent' of U.S. International Taxation*, 46(5) Duke L.J. 1021, 1055 (1997).
185. *Id.*, at 1055.
186. *Id.*, at 1056.
187. *Id.*, at 1057-1059.
188. *Id.*, at 1057.

residence of the debtor;[189] for dividends, the source was the place of residence of the payor; for rental and royalty income from tangible property, the source was the place where the property was situated; for income from intellectual property, the source was the place where it was used.[190] From this, it can be seen that the task was no longer to identify the amount of income that had been taxed by two jurisdictions (as in the UK, *see supra* note 95, note 96 and note 110) but to identify the 'source' of the income as 'foreign', as defined by the US code (a more formalistic approach).

As regards the main key change in 1921, i.e., the credit limitation (or MCA), this was not the end of the story. Indeed, the credit limitation became arguably the most dynamic and impactful feature of the credit method, with multiple different design considerations. It therefore merits a longer discussion here.

Subsequent developments in the credit limitation: different designs, trade-offs, and rationales

Over the years, the US has adjusted the credit limitation multiple times.[191] In 1918, the credit was unlimited. In 1921, it was limited but calculated on a global or 'over-all' basis. In 1932, Congress added a per-country limitation and, until 1954, both limits applied such that 'the amount of tax credit was limited to the lesser of the overall limitation or the sum of the per-country limitations'.[192] From 1954, only the per-country limitation applied.[193] From 1960, taxpayers could opt for either the per-country limitation or the overall limitation.[194] In 1976, the US returned to its 1921 overall limitation.[195] By 1986, the US had ventured into new territory, by adding per-basket

189. *Id.*, at 1057–1058 (there were different points of view regarding the source of interest income. While the Attorney General preferred that the source of interest income be at the residence of the creditor, Thomas S. Adams preferred that the source be at the residence of the debtor, or payer of the interest. Among the reasons cited for Adams' preference was that it 'would strengthen source-based taxation' and provide a foreign tax credit for 'American lenders in Europe').
190. *Id.*, at 1058–1059 & n.149; *see* United States, Revenue Act of 1918, Sixty-Fifth Congress, Session III, Chapter 18, Public Law 65-254, Section 217 (US Government Printing Office 1919).
191. Regarding other changes to the MCA, *see*, e.g., Elisabeth A. Owens, *The Foreign Tax Credit: A Study of the Credit for Foreign Taxes under United States Income Tax Law* 198–202 (Harvard Law School 1961); Michael J. Graetz & Michael M. O'Hear, *The 'Original Intent' of U.S. International Taxation*, 46(5) Duke L.J. 1021, 1056 n.141 (1997); John P. Steines Jr., *The Foreign Tax Credit at Ninety-Five Bionic Centenarian*, 66(4) Tax L. Rev. 545, 549–550, 551 et seq. (2013).
192. United States, House of Representatives, Committee on Ways and Means, General Tax Reform, Panel Discussions, Ninety-Third Congress, Session I, 1727 (US Government Printing Office 1973); Elisabeth A. Owens, *The Foreign Tax Credit: A Study of the Credit for Foreign Taxes under United States Income Tax Law* 199 (Harvard Law School 1961). *See also* United States, Senate, Committee on Finance, Overall Limitation on Foreign Tax Credit, Report No. 1393, Eighty-Sixth Congress, Session II, 3–4 (1960), https://www.finance.senate.gov/imo/media/doc/Rpt86-1393.pdf.
193. *See*, e.g., Elisabeth A. Owens, *The Foreign Tax Credit: A Study of the Credit for Foreign Taxes under United States Income Tax Law* 200 (Harvard Law School 1961).
194. *See*, e.g., Michael J. Graetz & Michael M. O'Hear, *The 'Original Intent' of U.S. International Taxation*, 46(5) Duke L.J. 1021, 1056 n.141 (1997).
195. *See*, e.g., *id.*, at 1056 n.141.

limitations,[196] which calculated the amount of the credit separately for different types of FSI (e.g., financial services income, shipping income, etc.), reaching nine baskets for a period of time. In a 2004 reform, effective since 2007, the US maintained the per-basket approach but reduced the baskets from nine to two, namely one for 'passive category income' and one for 'general category income'.[197] In the 2017 reform (referring only to the limitation, and leaving aside other changes), two further baskets were added, namely one for foreign branch income and one made especially for the new GILTI regime.[198]

As a result, the US has been proven to be an interesting laboratory for experimenting with calculating the FTC, from which much can be learned about the effects of the different limitations, their respective trade-offs and different justifications for and against them.[199] The following tables (*see* Example No. 6 below) offer simple numerical examples of credit limitations, to compare and contrast their operation and effects.

196. *Id.*
197. *See*, e.g., John P. Steines Jr., *The Foreign Tax Credit at Ninety-Five Bionic Centenarian*, 66(4) Tax L. Rev. 545, 549–550, 551 et seq. (2013).
198. United States, The Act to Provide for Reconciliation Pursuant to Titles II and V of the Concurrent Resolution on the Budget for Fiscal Year 2018, Pub. L. No. 115-97, signed 22 Dec. 2017, in effect from 1 Jan. 2018 (Tax Cuts and Jobs Act) (for foreign branch income, *see* Section 904(d)(1)(B) and for the GILTI tax, *see* Section 951A).
199. *See*, e.g., Elisabeth A. Owens, *The Foreign Tax Credit: A Study of the Credit for Foreign Taxes under United States Income Tax Law* 19 n.29 (Harvard Law School 1961) (citing H.R. 10087, 86th Cong., 2d Sess. (1960), for a debate on per-country versus overall credit limitations).

Example No. 6: The Effects of Different Credit Limitations

Credit Calculation – illustrating the MCA

Scenario: 1 Foreign State, 1 Type of Income, Same Tax Rates		**Scenario: 1 Foreign State, 1 Type of Income, Different Tax Rates**	
Facts: An individual taxpayer (T.P.) operates a sole proprietorship, and earns income from business in State R and also from business in the neighbouring country, State F.		Facts: same, but with different tax rates.	
Profits in State R:	100	Profits in State R:	100
Tax rate in State R:	20%	Tax rate in State R:	20%
Profits in State F:	50	Profits in State F:	50
Tax rate in State F:	20%	Tax rate in State F:	25%
WWI:	150	WWI:	150
Taxes due in State F:	50 × 20% = 10	Taxes due in State F:	50 × 25% = 12.5
Taxes due in State R:	150 × 20% = 30	Taxes due in State R:	150 × 20% = 30
FTC in State R:	lesser of foreign taxes [10] or MCA [30 × (50/150) = 10] = 10	FTC in State R:	lesser of foreign taxes [12.5] or MCA [30 × (50/150) = 10] = 10
Result:		Result:	
Taxes paid to State F:	10	Taxes paid to State F:	12.5
Taxes paid to State R:	30 – 10 = 20	Taxes paid to State R:	30 – 10 = 20
Total taxes paid by T.P.:	30	Total taxes paid by T.P.:	32.5
			(→ Excess credit: 2.5)

Effect: Because 10 is the maximum amount that can be credited in State R, and T.P. paid 10 to State F, the taxpayer is then able to credit all taxes paid to State F. The effect is that T.P. ends up paying, overall, the same amount of taxes as any other resident of State R who earns the same amount of income domestically (taxes of 30 on a net income of 150), with the procedural difference that T.P. paid some of those taxes to State F (10) and some to State R (20).	Effect: Because 10 is the maximum amount that can be credited in State R, and T.P. paid 12.5 to State F, T.P. is no longer able to credit all taxes paid to State F. An amount of foreign taxes of 2.5 cannot be credited against the taxes due in State R. The effect is that T.P. ends up paying, overall, more taxes as compared to a resident of State R who earns the same amount of income domestically. This is because State R would have only levied 10 on this amount of income (50), while State F levied 12.5 on this amount of income. State R allows a credit for 10, therefore agreeing not to collect any taxes on this amount of income, but will not reimburse T.P. for higher taxes paid to a foreign country, based on the rationale that, otherwise, it would lead to a reduction in the taxes State R collects on its own domestic-source income (DSI). While the US, for example, allows this 'excess credit' to be carried forward or carried backward,[200] there are different approaches for how to treat this 'excess' amount of 2.5, as addressed in the next subsection.

200. *See*, e.g., United States, Internal Revenue Code, Section 904(c); United States, Code of Federal Regulations, Section 1.904-2.

Credit Calculation – illustrating Different Approaches to the MCA

Different Options include	Examples of MCA Formula
Option 1: Overall/Global MCA	$MCA = TT_{WWI} \times (FSI_{F1+F2}/WWI)$
Option 2: Per-Country MCA	$MCA_{F1} = TT_{WWI} \times (FSI_{F1}/WWI)$
	$MCA_{F2} = TT_{WWI} \times (FSI_{F2}/WWI)$
Option 3: Per-Category (Basket) MCA	$MCA_{F\ business\ income} = TT_{WWI} \times (FSI_{F1\ +\ F2\ business\ income}/WWI)$
	$MCA_{F\ dividends} = TT_{WWI} \times (FSI_{F1\ +\ F2\ dividends}/WWI)$
Option 4: Per-Country Per-Category MCA	$MCA_{F1\ business\ income} = TT_{WWI} \times (FSI_{F1\ business\ income}/WWI)$
	$MCA_{F1\ dividends} = TT_{WWI} \times (FSI_{F1\ dividends}/WWI)$
	$MCA_{F2\ business\ income} = TT_{WWI} \times (FSI_{F2\ business\ income}/WWI)$
	$MCA_{F2\ dividends} = TT_{WWI} \times (FSI_{F2\ dividends}/WWI)$

Scenario: 2 Foreign States, 1 Type of Income

Facts: An individual taxpayer (T.P.) operates a sole proprietorship, and earns income from business in State R and also from business in two neighbouring countries, State F1 and State F2.

Profits in State R:	100	Tax rate in State R:	20%
Profits in State F1:	50	Tax rate in State F1:	15%
Profits in State F2:	50	Tax rate in State F2:	25%
WWI:	200		
Taxes due in State R:	200 × 20% = 40		
Taxes due in State F1:	50 × 15% = 7.5		
Taxes due in State F2:	50 × 25% = 12.5		

Option 1: Overall MCA

$MCA = TT_{WWI} \times (FSI_{F1+F2}/WWI)$

$MCA = 40 \times (100/200) = 20$

FTC in State R:

lesser of foreign taxes [7.5 + 12.5 = 20] or MCA [20] = 20

Result:

Taxes paid to State F1 & State F2: 20

Taxes paid to State R: 40 – 20 = 20

Total taxes paid by T.P.: 40

Option 2: Per-Country MCA

$MCA_{F1} = TT_{WWI} \times (FSI_{F1}/WWI)$

$MCA_{F2} = TT_{WWI} \times (FSI_{F2}/WWI)$

$MCA_{F1} = 40 \times (50/200) = 10$

$MCA_{F2} = 40 \times (50/200) = 10$

FTC in State R for F1 taxes:

lesser of foreign taxes [7.5] or MCA [10] = 7.5

FTC in State R for F2 taxes:

lesser of foreign taxes [12.5] or MCA [10] = 10
(thus not all 12.5 can be credited → 2.5 excess)

Result:

Taxes paid to State F1: 7.5

Taxes paid to State F2: 12.5

Taxes paid to State R: 40 – 7.5 – 10 = 22.5

Total taxes paid by T.P.: 7.5 + 12.5 + 22.5 = 42.5

Scenario: 2 Foreign States, 2 Types of Income

Facts: An individual taxpayer (T.P.) operates a sole proprietorship, and earns income from business in State R and from business in two neighbouring countries, State F1 and State F2. T.P. also decided to buy some shares in FCo1, a company resident in State F1, and some shares in FCo2, a company resident in State F2. T.P. receives dividends from these shareholdings.

Profits in State R:	100	Tax rate in State R:	20%
Profits in State F1:	50	Tax rate in State F1:	15%
Dividends from State F1:	25	WHT tax on dividends from State F1:	15%
Profits in State F2:	50	Tax rate in State F2:	25%
Dividends from State F2:	25	WHT tax on dividends from State F2:	15%

WWI:	100 + 50 + 25 + 50 + 25 = 250
FSI:	(50 + 25) + (50 + 25) = 150
Taxes due in State R:	250 × 20% = 50
Taxes due in State F1:	50 × 15% = 7.5
WHT tax due in State F1:	25 × 15% = 3.75
Taxes due in State F2:	50 × 25% = 12.5
WHT tax due in State F2:	25 × 15% = 3.75
Option 1: Overall MCA	**Option 2: Per-Country MCA**
$MCA = TT_{WWI} \times (FSI_{F1+F2}/WWI)$	$MCA_{F1} = TT_{WWI} \times (FSI_{F1\text{: business income + dividends}}/WWI)$ $MCA_{F2} = TT_{WWI} \times (FSI_{F2\text{: business income + dividends}}/WWI)$
MCA = 50 × (150/250) = 30	MCA_{F1} = 50 × (75/250) = 15 MCA_{F2} = 50 × (75/250) = 15
FTC in State R: lesser of foreign taxes [(7.5 + 3.75) + (12.5 + 3.75) = 27.5] or MCA [30] = 27.5	FTC in State R for F1 taxes: lesser of foreign taxes [7.5 + 3.75 = 11.25] or MCA [15] = 11.25 FTC in State R for F2 taxes: lesser of foreign taxes [12.5 + 3.75 = 16.25] or MCA [15] = 15 (thus not all 16.25 can be credited → 1.25 excess)
Result:	Result:
Taxes paid to State F1 & State F2: 27.5	Taxes paid to State F1: 11.25 Taxes paid to State F2: 16.25
Taxes paid to State R: 50 – 27.5 = 22.5	

Total taxes paid by T.P.: 50

Option 3: Per-Category MCA

$MCA_{F \text{ business income}} = TT_{WWI} \times (FSI_{F1 + F2 \text{ business income}}/WWI)$

$MCA_{F \text{ dividends}} = TT_{WWI} \times (FSI_{F1 + F2 \text{ dividends}}/WWI)$

$MCA_{F1 + F2 \text{ business income}} = 50 \times (100/250) = 20$

$MCA_{F1 + F2 \text{ dividends}} = 50 \times (50/250) = 10$

FTC in State R for business income:
lesser of foreign taxes [7.5 + 12.5 = 20] or MCA [20] = 20

FTC in State R for dividend income:
lesser of foreign taxes [3.75 + 3.75 = 7.5] or MCA [10] = 7.5

Taxes paid to State R: 50 – 11.25 – 15 = 23.75

Total taxes paid by T.P.: 11.25 + 16.25 + 23.75 = 51.25

Option 4: Per-Country Per-Category MCA

$MCA_{F1 \text{ business income}} = TT_{WWI} \times (FSI_{F1 \text{ business income}}/WWI)$

$MCA_{F1 \text{ dividends}} = TT_{WWI} \times (FSI_{F1 \text{ dividends}}/WWI)$

$MCA_{F2 \text{ business income}} = TT_{WWI} \times (FSI_{F2 \text{ business income}}/WWI)$

$MCA_{F2 \text{ dividends}} = TT_{WWI} \times (FSI_{F2 \text{ dividends}}/WWI)$

$MCA_{F1 \text{ business income}} = 50 \times (50/250) = 10$

$MCA_{F1 \text{ dividends}} = 50 \times (25/250) = 5$

$MCA_{F2 \text{ business income}} = 50 \times (50/250) = 10$

$MCA_{F2 \text{ dividends}} = 50 \times (25/250) = 5$

FTC in State R for F1 taxes on business income:
lesser of foreign taxes [7.5] or MCA [10] = 7.5

FTC in State R for F1 taxes on dividends:
lesser of foreign taxes [3.75] or MCA [5] = 3.75

FTC in State R for F2 taxes on business income:
lesser of foreign taxes [12.5] or MCA [10] = 10

FTC in State R for F2 taxes on dividends:
lesser of foreign taxes [3.75] or MCA [5] = 3.75

Result: MCA = 20, thus all foreign taxes paid on business income (20) can be credited MCA = 10, thus all foreign taxes paid on dividends (7.5) can be credited Taxes paid to State R: 50 – 20 – 7.5 = 22.5 Total taxes paid by T.P.: 20 + 7.5 + 22.5 = 50	Result: MCA = 10, thus all taxes paid to State F1 business income (7.5) can be credited MCA = 5, thus all taxes (WHT) paid to State F1 dividends (3.75) can be credited MCA = 10, thus *not* all taxes paid to State F2 business income (12.5) can be credited → excess 2.5 MCA = 5, thus all taxes (WHT) paid to State F2 dividends (3.75) can be credited Taxes paid to State R: 50 – 7.5 – 10 – 3.75 – 3.75 = 25 Total taxes paid by T.P.: 7.5 + 12.5 + 3.75 + 3.75 + 25 = 52.5

Results of Examples Compared

	Option 1 Global/Overall	Option 2 Per-Country	Option 3 Per-Category	Option 4 Per-Country Per-Category
WWI	250	250	250	250
State R TT_{WWI}	50	50	50	50
State R $TT_{-credit(s)}$	22.5	23.75	22.5	25
TT paid by T.P.	50	51.25	50	52.5

Regarding the rationales related to a credit limitation, there are two sets of rationales to consider: (1) those guiding whether or not to impose any limit and (2) if so, those guiding which type of limit to impose. To understand these rationales and trade-offs, they are first briefly overviewed, accompanied by some examples to illustrate them more concretely, and followed by some observations on the broader underlying compromises or concerns at stake.

As regards the first set of rationales, the main reason for placing a limit on the creditable amount - that is, the reason for switching from an unlimited credit to imposing some form of limit, whichever it may be - was to preserve the ability of the credit-granting state to collect taxes on domestically sourced income (as discussed at *supra* note 186). Other reasons (*see supra* notes 181–183) included the risk of potentially overgenerously subsidizing foreign treasuries and the change in the US tax rate relative to those of other states (the higher the tax rates in other states, the more expensive - even untenable - an unlimited credit could become).

As regards the second set of rationales, once it is decided to limit the amount of the credit, reasons were put forward for choosing between the different types of limits. Based on a report that compiled the various US Congressional discussions on this topic,[201] the main reason for choosing between either an overall limit or other narrower limits, such as a per-country limit, seems to be related to the phenomenon of 'averaging' or 'cross-crediting'.[202] This phenomenon - which is most pronounced under an overall limitation - is illustrated in Example No. 7, No. 8 and No. 9 below.

Over time there were arguments both in favour of and against 'averaging', which led to various tweaks to the limit in the US. One reason for curbing 'averaging' was on fairness grounds, understood as the idea that similarly situated taxpayers should receive similar treatment. In some cases, an overall limitation failed to achieve this similar treatment, due to 'averaging' - in particular, where a taxpayer earned income from more than one foreign state, at least one of which had a comparably low tax rate (*see* Example No. 7).[203] Another reason for restricting 'averaging' related to concerns over the incentives it created for taxpayers to invest overseas merely in order to deliberately inflate the amount of the credit (*see* Example No. 8).[204] Reasons for supporting 'averaging' ranged from simplicity and administrative ease (the greater the number of limitation calculations, the greater the complexity and thus compliance

201. National Foreign Trade Council, *The NFTC Foreign Income Project: International Tax Policy for the 21st Century - Part Two: Relief of International Double Taxation* (Fred F. Murray ed.-in-chief, National Foreign Trade Council 2001), http://www.nftc.org/default/tax/fip/NFTC1a%20Volume1_part2Chap1-5.pdf (last visited 26 Apr. 2019) (hereinafter 'National Foreign Trade Council Report (2001)').

202. *See*, e.g., National Foreign Trade Council Report (2001), at 160, at 172–174 (citing the 1960 legislative history).

203. *Id.*, at 170–171.

204. *Id.*, at 178, 183 ('... the separate foreign tax credit limitation for certain nonbusiness interest income. That limitation was enacted out of concern that prior law improperly encouraged the movement of U.S. capital abroad, the opposite of the concern expressed in 1954'), at 184 ('The 1986 Act marked the acme of Congressional concern that the foreign tax credit limitation rules were providing inappropriate incentives to U.S. taxpayers to make marginal investments overseas') and at 202.

burden),[205] to better reflecting the reality of many international business operations (sometimes viewed in a more integrated or consolidated way),[206] to reducing the chance that foreign losses reduce DSI (*see* Example No. 9).[207]

Example No. 7: An Overall Limitation – Averaging and 'Fairness' Concerns[208]

Facts: Taxpayer 1, Taxpayer 2 and Taxpayer 3 reside in State R and earn a total income of 10,000. Taxpayer 1 generates 8,000 in State R and 2,000 in State F1. Taxpayer 3 generates 8,000 in State R and 2,000 in another foreign state, State F2. Taxpayer 2 generates 6,000 in State R, the other income in both foreign states, namely 2,000 in State F1 and 2,000 in State F2. The tax rate in State R is 20%, in State F1 is 30% and no taxes are levied on the income in State F2.

	Taxpayer 1	**Taxpayer 2**	**Taxpayer 3**
Income			
State F1	2,000	2,000	-
State F2	-	2,000	2,000
State R	8,000	6,000	8,000
Total (WWI)	10,000	10,000	10,000
Taxes			
State F1 (30%)	600	600	-
State F2	-	0	0
State R (20%, TT_{WWI})	2,000	2,000	2,000
Credit in State R			
MCA = TT_{WWI} × (FSI_{F1+F2}/WWI)	400	800	400
Credit = lower of MCA or foreign taxes	400	600	0
Excess	200	0	0
Taxes due to State R	1,600	1,400	2,000
Total taxes paid by taxpayer	2,200	2,000	2,000

205. *Id.*, at 202, at 219–220, at 235; Fadi Shaheen, *How Reform-Friendly Are U.S. Tax Treaties?*, 41(3) Brook. J. Int'l L. 1243, 1262–1264, 1263 n.77 (2016).
206. *See*, e.g., National Foreign Trade Council Report (2001), at 172–175.
207. *Id.*, at 173, 175.
208. This is based on the example found in the Legislative History of the Revenue Act of 1932. *See* National Foreign Trade Council Report (2001), at 170–171; United States, *Legislative History of the Revenue Act of 1932: P.L. 72-154: 47 Stat. 169: June 6, 1932*, House Report 708 on H.R. 10236, 23–34 (1932).

This example (Example No. 7) is an adapted version of the one found in the 1932 legislative history and cited in the Report of the National Foreign Trade Council.[209] According to the 1932 legislative history, this 'gives preferential treatment to some taxpayers deriving income from more than one foreign country'.[210] The Congressional Report makes two observations as to how this amounts to different treatment:

(1) Taxpayer 2 'who has paid no more foreign tax than [Taxpayer 1]' is able to take a much larger credit than Taxpayer 1 and
(2) 'Although [Taxpayer 2] and [Taxpayer 3] have each received [2,000] income from [State F2] free of any tax, [Taxpayer 2], in effect, pays no tax to the United States upon this income, while [Taxpayer 3] pays the full United States tax thereon.'[211]

It concludes that: 'It seems clear that the amount of income received by [Taxpayer 2] from [State F2] should have no bearing upon the amount of credit to be allowed for the tax paid to [State F1].'[212] Thus, these arguments speak against an overall limitation and in support of a per-country limitation.

Example No. 8: An Overall Limitation – Potential Incentives to Inflate FTC

Facts: Taxpayer *MNE Inc.* is a multinational enterprise that earns an annual income of 10,000, of which 6,000 is earned in its state of residence, State R, and 4,000 is earned abroad in a foreign state, State F1. This is compared with a second scenario, as explained below. The tax rate in State R is 20% and in State F1 is 30%. In a neighbouring foreign state, State F2, the tax rate is 10%.

Taxpayer *MNE Inc.*

Scenario 1		**Scenario 2**	
Income		**Income**	
State F1	4,000	State F1	4,000
State R	6,000	State F2	4,000
Total (WWI)	10,000	State R	2,000
		Total (WWI)	10,000

209. National Foreign Trade Council Report (2001), at 170–171; United States, *Legislative History of the Revenue Act of 1932: P.L. 72-154: 47 Stat. 169: June 6, 1932,* House Report 708 on H.R. 10236, 23–24 (1932).
210. United States, *Legislative History of the Revenue Act of 1932: P.L. 72-154: 47 Stat. 169: June 6, 1932,* House Report 708 on H.R. 10236, 23–24 (1932). *See also* National Foreign Trade Council Report (2001), at 170–171.
211. United States, *Legislative History of the Revenue Act of 1932: P.L. 72-154: 47 Stat. 169: June 6, 1932,* House Report 708 on H.R. 10236, 23–24 (1932). *See also* National Foreign Trade Council Report (2001), at 170–171.
212. United States, *Legislative History of the Revenue Act of 1932: P.L. 72-154: 47 Stat. 169: June 6, 1932,* House Report 708 on H.R. 10236, 23–24 (1932).

Taxes		**Taxes**	
State F1 (30%)	1,200	State F1 (30%)	1,200
State R (20%, TT_{WWI})	2,000	State F2 (10%)	400
		State R (20%, TT_{WWI})	2,000
Credit in State R		**Credit in State R**	
MCA = TT_{WWI} × (FSI/WWI)	800	MCA = TT_{WWI} × (FSI/WWI)	1,600
Credit = lower of MCA or foreign taxes	800	Credit = lower of MCA or foreign taxes	1,600
Excess	400	Excess	0
Taxes due to State R	1,200	Taxes due to State R	400
Total taxes paid by taxpayer	2,400	Total taxes paid by taxpayer	2,000

Under scenario 1: On the 4,000 of income earned in State F1, *MNE Inc.* has already paid taxes of 1,200 to State F1. Next, *MNE Inc.* reports all of its income (10,000) to its state of residence, State R, and owes 2,000 in taxes to State R (10,000 × 20%). However, for the portion of its income that is subject to double taxation, namely the 4,000 of foreign-source income that was already taxed by State F1, it can claim a foreign tax credit against the taxes due in State R. Of the 2,000 in taxes owed to State R, 1,200 corresponds to the domestic-source income and 800 corresponds to the foreign-source income. Therefore, *MNE Inc.* can claim up to 800 as a foreign tax credit against the 2,000 owed to State R. Due to the higher rate of 30% levied in State F1, this means that *MNE Inc.* cannot claim the full 1,200 paid to State F1. There is an excess of 400. In this case, therefore, *MNE Inc.* ends up paying 1,200 to State R and 1,200 to State F1, with a total tax bill of 2,400.

Under scenario 2: There is another foreign state, State F2, where the tax rate is 10%. If 4,000 of the domestic-source income could somehow be sourced instead in State F2, the result would change. In calculating the amount of foreign tax credit to claim, of the 2,000 owed to State R, 1,600 correspond to the domestic-source income and 400 correspond to the foreign-source income. Therefore, *MNE Inc.* can claim up to 1,600 as a foreign tax credit against the 2,000 owed to State

R. *MNE Inc.* can now claim the full 1,600 paid to State F1 and State F2. In this case, therefore, *MNE Inc.* ends up with a total tax bill of 2,000. State R however collects only 400 in this case instead of 1,200. Either this 4,000 earned in State F2 was genuinely earned there, in which case this is arguably the intended result of State R's credit method, or this 4,000 was artificially converted to foreign-source income, in which case State R is arguably deprived of 800 in taxes that it should be able to collect on what is in reality domestic-source income.

Due to the concerns regarding the overall limitation demonstrated in Example No. 7 and Example No. 8, at various points in time, the US Congress enacted different types of limits for the MCA, be it per-country limitations or per-category-of-income (also known as baskets) limitations (*see supra* notes 191–198). However, it was brought to the attention of members of the US Congress that devising these narrower limitations did not always fully resolve the downsides of 'averaging'. Taxpayers in turn devised ways of achieving the effect of 'averaging', or otherwise manipulating the amount of the FTC, despite the limitations.

There were three main ways to achieve this. Taxpayers may try to convert DSI into FSI (as under Scenario 2 of Example No. 8), or to convert income from one type (e.g., business income) to another (e.g., passive investment income), or to establish 'mixer' companies. These tactics cannot all be addressed by a narrower credit limitation. For example, what a per-country limitation could address is the incentive to convert FSI from a higher tax state (e.g., State F1, where the rate is 30%, in Example No. 8) to FSI from a lower tax state (e.g., State F2, where the rate is 10%, in Example No. 8). Indeed, looking again at Example No. 8, and imagining a third hypothetical scenario, the taxpayer could have achieved a similar outcome, i.e., that the creditable amount would cover all foreign taxes, if it had shifted 2,000 from State F1 to State F2 – unsurprising, as this would have lowered its overall foreign tax bill. Arguably, from the standpoint of the revenue-generating impact on the US Treasury, this foreign-to-foreign shift is not problematic (because the MCA would remain capped at 800 and thus the tax collected would be the same). However, from the standpoint of the fairness, or same treatment, issue (as seen in Example No. 7 and seen in the two observations from the 1932 legislative history, *supra* note 209), this could be considered problematic. A per-country limitation could counteract this behaviour (i.e., shifting income from one foreign state to another for FTC purposes). However, by itself, a per-country limitation cannot prevent manipulation of the credit by shifting income from domestic sources to foreign sources (e.g., by transferring income-generating assets, such as shareholdings or loan-receivables, to a permanent establishment (PE) or a hybrid entity located abroad). It also cannot prevent manipulation of the credit by changing the character of the income (e.g., from a type of income that is taxed at a higher rate in a given foreign state, to a type of income that benefits from a lower tax rate in that foreign state). To offer a generic example of these types of concerns, the members of the US Congress learned that, in a circular fashion, US-source income could be paid out, in deductible payments to a foreign affiliate, thus avoiding US tax, then simply repatriated back as

FSI, with the right to an FTC attached.[213] For this reason, the legislators became particularly concerned with 'mobile' income – that is, income for which the source is rather easily manipulated.[214] Thus, rather than a limitation based solely on the geographic source of the income, such as a per-country limitation, what was needed was a limitation based on the type of income and/or the amount of tax borne by that income.[215] This was the main reason for creating a separate credit limitation category, or basket, for passive income (which is often 'mobile' and may be taxed at lower rates).

The third aforementioned strategy is that of the 'mixer' company. As a preliminary remark, this strategy is particularly relevant for the 'indirect' credit method, which is explained below (in Section 2.1.1.3.). Nevertheless, it is briefly mentioned here for the sake of completeness in this overview, capturing the main ways of circumventing the aim of credit limitations – limitations which are relevant for the 'direct' and 'indirect' credit alike – and the main design-adaptations in response. That said, another way in which taxpayers could, in certain cases, create the effect of averaging was by establishing a foreign holding company, sometimes referred to as a 'mixer' company,[216] to which they pass all FSI so that the foreign tax borne by the various income streams could be aggregated together.[217]

A credit limitation alone is not well equipped to counteract this. Instead, some of these tactics – such as the conversion of US-source income and 'mixer' companies – called for look-through rules.[218] The idea is that a taxpayer should not be able to

213. *See*, e.g., National Foreign Trade Council Report (2001), at 176–178.
214. *Id.*, at 178.
215. *Id.*, at 176–178 and at 202–206 (this is also the reason for the 'high-tax kick-out' in the US, according to which passive income that is taxed at a higher rate, for which the threshold has to be clearly defined, is not included in passive-income category, to ensure that this category serves its purpose of preventing certain negative incentives prompted by 'averaging').
216. *See*, e.g., National Foreign Trade Council Report (2001), at 250; Peter Harris, *An Historic View of the Principle and Options for Double Tax Relief*, 1999(6) Brit. Tax Rev. 469, 487 (1999); Otto Marres (update of 6th ed.), *Chapter 16: Division of Tax Jurisdiction; Double Tax Relief Mechanisms; Tax Treaty Issues*, *in* 1 *Terra/Wattel European Tax Law* 695, 699 and 705 (Peter J. Wattel, Otto Marres & Hein Vermeulen eds, Wolters Kluwer 7th ed. 2019).
217. *See*, e.g., National Foreign Trade Council Report (2001), at 172–173, 175 (this aggregation-of-foreign-tax treatment was possible under 'foreign base corporation' rules in the US). *See also*, e.g., Peter Harris, *An Historic View of the Principle and Options for Double Tax Relief*, 1999(6) Brit. Tax Rev. 469, 487 (1999) (this was also sometimes possible under rules for the indirect tax credit).
218. *See*, e.g., National Foreign Trade Council Report (2001), at 202 ('Additionally, for the various separate limitations to operate as intended, elaborate look-through … rules are required […]') and at 208–209 ('It is also generally agreed that look-through rules are necessary to prevent taxpayers from circumventing separate limitations by using a foreign holding company') and at 250 (at the time of this report, the UK granted a direct credit and an indirect credit. 'In computing the allowable credit, the United Kingdom has adopted a strict source-by-source, item-by-item credit limitation.' However, the UK did not have look-through rules and, thus, the limitations were circumvented in some cases: 'Before March 31, 2001, look-through rules did not exist to require a dividend passed through a chain of corporations to retain its underlying source. For this reason, many U.K. companies found it advantageous to hold their foreign subsidiaries through a "mixer" entity located in a low-tax jurisdiction such as the Netherlands. In this way, low-taxed and high-taxed dividends from different subsidiaries were blended before their source was ultimately determined at the mixer company level. Thus, rate averaging with respect to foreign dividends was easily accomplished under the U.K. indirect credit rules

artificially change the source of the income and the character of the income (e.g., converting it from 'active' business income to 'passive' investment income) by merely channelling it through other entities. The taxpayer, to accomplish this, generally acquires some degree of control over the foreign entities in question. Thus, in cases where the taxpayer owns or controls entities abroad and receives passive income (such as dividends, interest and royalties), look-through rules may be needed in order to trace the underlying source of the income and the character of the income; this helps to determine into which credit limitation category or basket that income should fall.[219] In sum, to reinforce the credit limitations, look-through rules were added: (i) to thwart certain types of manipulation of the FTC; (ii) in turn, to ensure that, when a narrower credit limitation (such as a per-category/basket-of-income limitation) is applied, the foreign income and foreign taxes are properly attributed to the correct category of the credit limitation; and (iii) in these ways, to also better align how credit limitation rules apply under the 'indirect' credit with how they apply under the 'direct' credit.[220]

However, focusing exclusively on such manipulation tactics overlooks other important aspects of the functioning of the credit method. There are important trade-offs to consider in the design of the credit limitation. While narrower limitations may prevent, or reduce the scope for, 'averaging' and manipulation of the FTC, the resulting multiplication of different credit limitations (e.g., as occurred in the US in the 1980s when it leapt to nine different credit limitation baskets, *see supra* note 196) comes at the expense of simplicity and administrability. Each limitation requires its own separate calculation and requires tracing the relevant income and taxes to its respective limitation category. The complexity of calculating the FTC increases enormously. Thus, these trade-offs should be carefully considered.

Example No. 9: Overall Limitation Versus Per-country Limitation – Effect of Losses

Facts: Taxpayer *MNE Inc.* is a multinational enterprise that operates businesses in its state of residence, State R, and two foreign states, State F1 and State F2. This year, it made profits in State R and State F1, but suffered losses in State F2. The

prior to March 31, 2001'). For more on the origins and the trend towards complexity in the US look-through rules, *see*, e.g., Charles I. Kingson, *The Foreign Tax Credit and Its Critics*, 9(1) Am. J. Tax Pol'y 1 (1991).

219. *See*, e.g., United States, Internal Revenue Code, Section 904(d)(3) and (4).

220. National Foreign Trade Council Report (2001), at 208–209 (to further elaborate, the third reason mentioned in the above text for look-through rules was explained as follows: 'In Congress' view, a dividend received by a 10-percent shareholder of a CFC, for example, should not automatically be treated as 100-percent passive income. Look-through rules reduce disparities that might otherwise occur between the amount of income subject to a particular limitation when a taxpayer earns income abroad directly (as through a foreign branch), and the amount of income subject to a particular limitation when a taxpayer earns income abroad through a CFC.' The report cites the '1986 Bluebook', which was published by the Joint Committee on Taxation of the US Congress in order to offer a 'General Explanation Of The Tax Reform Act of 1986'. The report also explains that, to the extent possible, legislators sought to align the look-through rules for foreign tax credit purposes and those used for controlled foreign company, or Subpart F, purposes).

tax rate in all three states is 20% (the tax rate is assumed to be the same in order to better isolate the effects of the losses).

Taxpayer MNE

Scenario 1 – overall limitation		**Scenario 2 – per-country limitation**	
Income		**Income**	
State F1	3,000	State F1	3,000
State F2	–3,000	State F2	–3,000
State R	4,000	State R	4,000
Total (WWI)	4,000	Total (WWI)	4,000
Taxes		**Taxes**	
State F1	600	State F1	600
State F2	0	State F2	0
State R (TT_{WWI})	800	State R (TT_{WWI})	800
Credit in State R		**Credit in State R**	
MCA = TT_{WWI} × (FSI/WWI)	0	MCA = TT_{WWI} × (FSI_{F1}/WWI)	600
Credit = lower of MCA or foreign taxes	0	Credit = lower of MCA or foreign taxes	600
Excess	600	Excess	0
		MCA = TT_{WWI} × (FSI_{F2}/WWI)	0
		Credit = lower of MCA or foreign taxes	0
		Excess	0
Taxes due to State R	800	Taxes due to State R	200
Total taxes paid by taxpayer	1,400	Total taxes paid by taxpayer	800

To compare the effects of the losses:

US taxes on domestic-source income:

800

Under the overall limitation, the US collects:

800

Under the per-country limitation, the US collects:

200

In effect, under the per-country limitation, the US could not collect the following on domestic-source income:

600

In effect, this represents 3,000 (i.e., 3,000 × 20% = 600) of domestic-source income on which the US could not collect taxes, as though the 3,000 of foreign losses in State F2 directly reduced the 4,000 of domestic income.

Another important difference that arose between the options for designing the credit limitation became visible in the case of foreign losses. As Example No. 9 demonstrates, under an overall limitation, the foreign *losses* first reduce, or cancel out, other *foreign profits*, before they have any impact on DSI.[221] Any impact on domestic profits occurs only if there is an overall foreign loss, meaning the total foreign losses were greater than the total foreign profits such that the FSI amounts overall to a negative result. By comparison, under a per-country limitation, the foreign losses can more immediately reduce the amount of taxes the US is able to collect on the DSI. For this reason, for the credit-granting country, this can be disadvantageous.

For the taxpayer, the effect of averaging and blending together all FSI, which is generally favourable in profit-making circumstances, is generally less favourable in a loss-making situation. Thus, in circumstances where foreign losses are generated, the per-country limitation is more favourable for the taxpayer (total taxes paid of 800), as compared to the overall limitation (total taxes paid of 1,400). From a cash-flow perspective, clearly the per-country limitation tends to be less burdensome on taxpayers suffering foreign losses.

Indeed, at one point during the multiple developments of credit limitations in the US, legislators recognized this downside of the overall limitation in the case of losses. In particular, they expressed concern that this would hinder taxpayers from expanding their business abroad into other foreign states since losses could be generated during the initial start-up phase in the new foreign market.[222] This was recorded as a reason for repealing the overall limitation in 1954:

221. *See*, e.g., National Foreign Trade Council Report (2001), at 175.
222. *Id.*, at 182.

> 'The credit which is now allowed for foreign taxes is subject to two limitations. The per country limitation restricts the foreign tax which may be claimed as a credit to an amount bearing the same proportion to the taxpayer's total tax liability as the income from the foreign country bears to the total income of the taxpayer. The overall limitation applies a similar formula with respect to the aggregate foreign taxes allowed as a credit. As a practical matter, however, the overall limitation is operative only when a taxpayer earns income in one foreign country and incurs a loss in another. The effect of the limitation is unfortunate because it discourages a company operating profitably in one foreign country from going into another country where it may expect to operate at a loss for a few years. Consequently the House has removed the overall limitation.'[223]

Arguably, by itself, this may be too narrow a view or concern on which to base the entire policy of the FTC limitation: it places more weight on the circumstances of initial foreign start-up losses than on other circumstances, i.e., the hopefully greater number of circumstances and longer periods of time where profits are generated. This could risk rule-making for special cases, potentially a minority of cases or at least short-term cases (as the quote above implies in specifying 'a few years'), rather than for the average scenario. However, the explanation for highlighting this concern, in this case, is that the US was changing from a lower-of-the-two-limits approach, which indeed resulted in the overall limitation being 'operative only when a taxpayer earns income in one foreign country and incurs a loss in another'.

To recap the respective disadvantages, there is a disadvantage for the credit-granting state in the case of foreign losses under the per-country limitation – which, to some extent, could be seen as counteracting the main aim of a credit limitation to preserve the ability to collect taxes on DSI. There is a disadvantage for the taxpayer in the case of foreign losses under the overall limitation. Importantly, however, both disadvantages are in principle temporary, assuming profits are generated in future years (and assuming the taxpayer can use the 'excess', *see infra* note 249). Generally speaking, it is a cash-flow disadvantage and the question is on which party, the taxpayer or the treasury, the cash-flow disadvantage falls first.

In any case, the choice of the credit limitation alone is not a watertight way of controlling the impact of foreign losses on DSI. It is also a factual question of the scale of the foreign losses. Regardless of which limitation is chosen, for the credit-granting state, the risk remains that foreign losses can affect the amount of taxes it can collect on DSI. If there is an overall foreign loss (where total foreign losses exceed total foreign profits), some effect on DSI occurs, even under the overall limitation.[224]

In response to these issues, US legislators adapted. As another approach to the issue of foreign losses, legislators in the US managed to create an effect similar to the overall limitation (i.e., of foreign losses first reducing foreign profits before reducing domestic profits) even under a credit method that contained separate limitations. To do so, they devised loss-allocation, or loss-ordering, rules. In brief, if foreign losses within

223. United States, *Internal Revenue Acts of the United States: The Revenue Act of 1954 with Legislative Histories and Congressional Documents* 106 (Bernard D. Reams Jr., ed.). *See also* National Foreign Trade Council Report (2001), at 182.

224. *See*, e.g., National Foreign Trade Council Report (2001), at 175–176.

one credit limitation category exceed the foreign profits in that category, those losses first reduce foreign profits in other credit limitation categories, before they can reduce domestic profits.[225] Put differently, foreign losses are first allocated to the foreign income in the same credit limitation category; if the losses overflow that limitation category, they are then allocated pro rata to foreign income in all other limitation categories. In later years, when income is earned, this is essentially 'recaptured':

> 'The separate limitation loss recharacterization rule provides that income subsequently earned in the same limitation as the separate limitation loss will be recharacterized as income of the same limitation reduced by the loss in an earlier year. The separate limitation recharacterization will continue each year until the entire separate limitation loss has been recaptured.'[226]

To the extent that foreign losses were greater than all the foreign income and thus reduced some of the DSI, then the foreign profits earned in future years are recaptured and, in this case, recharacterized as DSI to the extent they previously reduced DSI.

Ideally, in order to be symmetric and coherent, the same treatment should occur if domestic losses reduce FSI. In the US, though, such a proposal failed multiple times[227] before it eventually succeeded:[228]

> 'Finally, many proposals have been advanced for an overall domestic loss recapture rule that mirrors the OFL [overall foreign loss] recapture rule of section 904(f), but revenue considerations have thwarted their enactment. While domestic loss recapture would add to the foreign tax credit limitation's complexity, there is little policy disagreement that current year reductions in foreign-source income by U.S. losses should later be reversed just as current year reductions in U.S.-source income by foreign losses are later reversed under section 904(f). Domestic loss recapture would ensure that foreign as well as U.S.-source income is, over time, computed separately, that is, without reduction by losses in the other category.'[229]

There are trade-offs. The combination of multiple separate limitations, coupled with the loss-ordering and re-characterization rules, could be described as an approach that is more burdensome from the perspective of the taxpayer and that is more favourable to the credit-granting state in both the profit-making scenario (by avoiding averaging) and the loss-making scenario (by avoiding to the extent possible that foreign losses affect taxes on domestic income). On the one hand, it adheres more closely to the overarching objective of a credit limitation - namely, to safeguard the taxation of DSI - due to a stricter delimitation between FSI and DSI over time. On the other hand, the notable downside of this approach is that it significantly increases the

225. *Id.*, at 178–179, at 218, at 231–233.
226. *Id.*, at 218.
227. *Id.*, at 233.
228. United States, Internal Revenue Code, Section 904(g) (Recharacterization of Overall Domestic Loss); United States, Code of Federal Regulations, Section 1.904(g)-2 (Recapture of Overall Domestic Losses); United States, Department of the Treasury, Internal Revenue Service, Treatment of Overall Foreign and Domestic Losses, TD 9595, 77(121) US Federal Register 37576 (22 Jun. 2012) (according to the final regulations, 'the recapture of overall domestic losses ... was enacted as part of the American Jobs Creation Act of 2004 (AJCA)').
229. National Foreign Trade Council Report (2001), at 231.

complexity of the record-keeping and calculations for the credit method. Thus, not all states would strike the same balance between this accuracy and simplicity in terms of administrability and the compliance burden.[230]

Indeed, even in the US, this balance was struck differently at different times. At another point in its development, the US legislators' approach fell on the other end of the spectrum of taxpayer-friendliness, with the competitiveness of US businesses abroad in mind. In particular, the US allowed the taxpayer the choice – though irrevocable, once opted – between the overall limitation and the per-country limitation. The reasoning was that taxpayers should be able to choose the approach that best fits the structure of their business: either they view their 'foreign business as a single operation', in which case an overall limitation is fitting, including its attendant 'averaging' which was viewed as suitable for businesses that operate in an integrated way, or they view their 'businesses in various foreign countries as separate ventures' (such as 'when a company begins in a different foreign country a business which is risky and which is likely to result in losses at least for an initial period of years'), in which case a per-country approach is fitting.[231] Under such an approach, the taxpayer could opt and then fully assume the upsides and downsides of its choice, and the government likewise.

There is another widely known rationale connected to the credit limitation, but it emerged decades later. During the earlier formative years of the credit method, one aspect was not yet fully appreciated (or at least, it appears, was less publicly debated), namely the effects on investment incentives. For example, according to Graetz and O'Hear:

> 'The fundamental purpose of the 1921 foreign tax credit limitation was to protect the ability of the U.S. to collect tax on U.S. source income, but the limitation on the foreign tax credit also has had a number of effects on the investment decisions of U.S. residents. Generally, under such a limitation, if a foreign country's tax rate is higher than the U.S. rate, a U.S. investor will prefer a domestic investment to a foreign investment with an identical pre-tax rate of return. For an investor who has already made some foreign investments, however, the limitation's averaging of foreign taxes of high-tax and low-tax countries might create advantages for investments in low-tax countries (to average against the high-tax foreign country's taxes as a way of offsetting U.S. tax) or indifference about investments in high tax countries (because, due to investments in low tax countries, the limitation may not be reached). The limitation enacted in 1921 clearly eliminated the pure neutrality as between foreign and domestic investments with the same pre-tax rates of returns that had existed under the unlimited earlier version of the FTC.'

This identifies some ways in which credit limitations can affect the relative attractiveness of different investments and therefore may induce more of a given investment over others.

230. *Id.*, at 252–253 (at the time of the report, Japan, for example, did not have such loss-allocation rules as a part of its foreign tax credit regime) and at 257–258 (at the time of the report, Canada, for example, did not have such loss-allocation rules as a part of its foreign tax credit regime).
231. *Id.*, at 172–173 (citing the 1960 legislative history).

The use of this lens for viewing and assessing international taxation, and especially the methods for relief of double taxation, became prominent in the 1960s. At this time, a new term emerged, 'capital export neutrality', which came to dominate the debate about the credit method. An opposition was created between 'capital export neutrality' and 'capital import neutrality'.

Peggy B. Musgrave, who is credited with coining the term, defines 'capital export neutrality' (CEN) as follows:

> 'A term introduced and developed in the 1960s to describe a situation in which the overall burden of taxation on capital owned by resident entities of a given country is the same whether that capital is invested abroad or at home.'[232]

Musgrave defines 'Capital import neutrality' (CIN) as follows:

> 'A condition in which the same effective tax rate applies to all capital income earned within a given country, regardless of the investor's country of residence.'[233]

In other words, under CIN, the investment of an investor in a given state should be taxed the same regardless of whether the investor is a resident or a foreigner. From a 'fairness' or equal treatment standpoint, this means that the investments or business activities of all investors in a given state, regardless of their residence, can compete on equal terms, from a tax perspective. This considers the host state, or source or market state, perspective. To achieve full CIN would require that only the host state taxes the investments in its territory, all at the same effective rate, and would therefore require that all states of residence of the investors exempt the returns of these investments from any additional home state taxation. For this reason, CIN and the exemption method are often coupled together in international taxation discourse.[234]

Under CEN, in other words, an investor in its state of residence should be taxed the same regardless of whether the investor's capital is invested at home or abroad; taxes should not affect or distort this decision. From a 'fairness' or equal treatment standpoint, this means that all residents of a given state are taxed the same regardless of where they invest their capital, or regardless of the source of their income (domestic or foreign). From an 'efficiency' standpoint, '[t]ypically, economists regard CEN as essential for worldwide economic efficiency, because the location of investments would be unaffected by capital income taxes'.[235] The idea is that investors would

232. Peggy B. Musgrave, *Capital Export Neutrality, in The Encyclopedia of Taxation & Tax Policy* 45-46 (Joseph J. Cordes, Robert D. Ebel & Jane G. Gravelle eds, Urban Institute Press 2d ed. 2005).
233. Peggy B. Musgrave, *Capital Import Neutrality, in The Encyclopedia of Taxation & Tax Policy* 50-51 (Joseph J. Cordes, Robert D. Ebel & Jane G. Gravelle eds, Urban Institute Press 2d ed. 2005).
234. *See*, e.g., Peggy B. Musgrave, *Capital Import Neutrality, in The Encyclopedia of Taxation & Tax Policy* 50-51 (Joseph J. Cordes, Robert D. Ebel & Jane G. Gravelle eds, Urban Institute Press 2d ed. 2005).
235. Michael J. Graetz, *The David R. Tillinghast Lecture Taxing International Income: Inadequate Principles, Outdated Concepts, and Unsatisfactory Policy*, 54(3) Tax L. Rev. 261, 270-271 (2001). *See also* Peggy B. Musgrave, *Capital Export Neutrality, in The Encyclopedia of Taxation & Tax Policy* 45-46 (Joseph J. Cordes, Robert D. Ebel & Jane G. Gravelle eds, Urban Institute Press 2d ed. 2005).

employ their capital wherever in the world it can be put to the most productive use, as taxes would not distort that decision. This is focused on the residence, or home, state perspective. Theoretically, the credit method is one way to achieve this. For this reason, CEN and the credit method, or FTC, are often coupled together in international taxation discourse.[236]

Example No. 10: Capital Export Neutrality (CEN) and the Credit Method

To illustrate the relationship, imagine two taxpayers, Taxpayer 1 and Taxpayer 2, who are both residents of State R. Taxpayer 1 earns a total income of 200 from within State R, and Taxpayer 2 earns a total of 200, half of which is from State R and the other half is from State F.

Scenario 1: assume the tax rate in State R is 20% and the tax rate in State F is 15%.

In this case, Taxpayer 1 pays taxes of 40 (20% × 200) to State R.

Taxpayer 2 first pays taxes of 15 to State F on its income of 100 earned there. Second, Taxpayer 2 calculates its tax liability of 40, on the basis of its worldwide income of 200, in State R, then subtracts a foreign tax credit of 15 and thus pays 25 to State R.

The credit method leads to the result that Taxpayer 2 has the same tax burden of 40 (15 to State F and 25 to State R) as Taxpayer 1. In this way, both residents are taxed the same, regardless of whether they earn their income at home or abroad. This is aligned with CEN.

Scenario 2: assume the tax rate in State R is 20% and the tax rate in State F is 25%.

Again, Taxpayer 1 pays 40 on an income of 200 to State R.

Taxpayer 2 pays 25 to State F on its income of 100 earned there. State R would collect only 20 on an income of 100. However, if State R applies a credit limitation and therefore grants a credit in the amount of 20, then Taxpayer 2 ends up paying 20 (40–20) to State R and 25 to State F, for a total tax burden of 45.

Taxpayer 2 would therefore not have the same burden as Taxpayer 1 on the same amount of worldwide income of 200. In this case, CEN would not be achieved. However, if State R grants a credit for the full 25 of taxes levied in State F, then

236. *See*, e.g., Peggy B. Musgrave, *Capital Export Neutrality*, *in The Encyclopedia of Taxation & Tax Policy* 45–46 (Joseph J. Cordes, Robert D. Ebel & Jane G. Gravelle eds, Urban Institute Press 2d ed. 2005); Michael J. Graetz, *The David R. Tillinghast Lecture Taxing International Income: Inadequate Principles, Outdated Concepts, and Unsatisfactory Policy*, 54(3) Tax L. Rev. 261, 270–271 (2001); J. Clifton Fleming Jr., Robert J. Peroni & Stephen E. Shay, *Fairness in International Taxation: The Ability-to-Pay Case for Taxing Worldwide Income*, 5(4) Fla. Tax. Rev. 299 (2001); Nancy H. Kaufman, *Equity Considerations in International Taxation*, 26(4) Brook. J. Int'l L. 1465 (2001).

Taxpayer 2 ends up paying 15 (40–25) to State R and 25 to State F, for a total tax burden of 40. In this case, this 'full' credit would support CEN.

As the example illustrates, to maintain CEN when the foreign tax rate is higher (scenario 2) would require an unlimited FTC. As the historical development illustrates, an unlimited FTC existed for only a short period of time between the Revenue Act of 1918 and the Revenue Act of 1921, for the reasons discussed above. The concept of CEN, since its emergence in the 1960s, has not convinced legislators to return to an unlimited FTC. The credit method remains a compromise and balancing act of different objectives. For example, Elisabeth A. Owens detected, broadly speaking, a balance between 'tax equity', 'tax neutrality' and relief for double taxation. She observed that:

- as regards equity, the aim is 'equitable tax treatment' of US taxpayers regardless from where they derive their income, to uphold 'the principle that taxpayers with an equal amount of income should bear an equal tax burden', and the credit method helps achieve this;[237]
- as regards neutrality, although not employing the term 'capital export neutrality', she describes this now well-known characteristic of the credit method that seeks to render investors' decisions as to whether to employ their capital at home or abroad neutral from a tax standpoint;[238]
- yet, the credit method does not go so far as to require the US to reimburse in effect foreign taxes when the amount levied abroad is higher; once the US has essentially eliminated the taxes it would collect on the income, it is no longer contributing to double taxation of the income in question.[239] Similar to the idea expressed repeatedly by the CJEU (discussed in Chapter 4), states are not required 'to go beyond the cancelling of national income tax payable'.[240]

In sum, there were two design questions that legislators faced: the first was whether to limit the amount of the FTC at all, and the second was, if so, how the limit should be calculated. As can be seen, in grappling with these questions, the competing rationales and trade-offs became clearer over time.

Regarding the first question, i.e., whether to place any limit on the amount of the credit, there was one prevailing reason to place some form of limit on the credit method, as opposed to maintaining an unlimited credit, namely to preserve the ability of the credit-granting state to collect taxes on domestically sourced income. From the historical development, it seemed that a balance was sought: on the one hand, the credit-granting state assumed its right to assess its residents on their worldwide income based on a personal connection, with the underlying idea that income taxation is

237. Elisabeth A. Owens, *The Foreign Tax Credit: A Study of the Credit for Foreign Taxes under United States Income Tax Law* 84 and 87–88 (Harvard Law School 1961).
238. *Id.*, at 84.
239. *Id.*, at 84–85 n.178.
240. CJEU, Case C-262/09, *Meilicke*, 30 Jun. 2011, ECLI:EU:C:2011:438, at para. 33; CJEU, Case C-47/12, *Kronos International Inc.*, 11 Sep. 2014, ECLI:EU:C:2014:2200, at para. 83.

justified on fairness grounds – fairness which is achieved in part by aiming to tax similarly situated residents in a similar way;[241] on the other hand, it conceded that, when income is earned abroad, the states where the income is earned have an equally convincing claim. Thus ceding priority to the 'source' state through the grant of a credit recognizes this (*see*, e.g., *supra* note 143); yet, this concession should be made only for the income earned there and *not* to the extent that it impedes the ability of the credit-granting state to collect taxes on income sourced in its own territory (*see*, e.g., *supra* note 186). This reasoning is implicitly tied to fundamental questions of jurisdiction to tax and the connecting factors that establish it. These factors feature prominently in the debates prompted by international coordination that unfold in the League of Nations reports (discussed below in Section 2.1.2.). Other aforementioned reasons for a credit limitation include the risks of subsidizing foreign treasuries and the costs of high foreign tax rates relative to the credit-granting state's rates. These are more pragmatic, revenue-related concerns. Although arguably less principle-based, revenue-related concerns can command strong support, especially when the state faces greater budgetary needs, and legitimacy, if and to the extent that one assumes or accepts that a main role of taxes is to raise revenue for a well-functioning society, e.g., for the basic functions of government and the provision of public goods.[242] Finally, as for rationales *not* to use a credit limitation, the main one was the pursuit of CEN, which (setting aside potential debates) ended up being more persuasive in theory than in practice.

Regarding the second question, i.e., how the limit should be calculated: On the one hand, the continuous changes to the credit limitation could indicate that 'no consensus has ever been reached on a theoretically "correct" limitation formulation'.[243] On the other hand, the US Joint Committee on Taxation has suggested that the

241. *See*, e.g., National Foreign Trade Council Report (2001), at 153, 165, 169–171, 176, 179, 181; *supra* note 145; *infra* note 562 (where the experts in the 1923 League of Nations report express a preference for 'the principle of personal faculty at the place of residence'). *See also*, e.g., J. Clifton Fleming Jr., Robert J. Peroni & Stephen E. Shay, *Fairness in International Taxation: The Ability-to-Pay Case for Taxing Worldwide Income*, 5(4) Fla. Tax. Rev. 299 (2001).

242. *See*, e.g., *Tax*, *Black's Law Dictionary* (9th ed. 2009) (the definition in *Black's Law Dictionary* includes raising public revenue as a defining feature of a 'tax': 'tax, *n.* (14c) A charge, usu. monetary, imposed by the government on persons, entities, transactions, or property to yield public revenue. – Most broadly, the term embraces all governmental impositions on the person, property, privileges, occupations, and enjoyment of the people, and includes duties, imposts, and excises. Although a tax is often thought of as being pecuniary in nature, it is not necessarily payable in money. […]' 'Taxes are the enforced proportional contributions from persons and property, levied by the state by virtue of its sovereignty for the support of government and for all public needs. This definition of taxes, often referred to as "Cooley's definition," has been quoted and indorsed, or approved, expressly or otherwise, by many different courts. While this definition of taxes characterizes them as "contributions," other definitions refer to them as "imposts," "duty or impost," "charges," "burdens," or "exactions"; but these variations in phraseology are of no practical importance.' 1 Thomas M. Cooley, *The Law of Taxation* § 1, at 61–63 (Clark A. Nichols ed., 4th ed. 1924)). *See*, in general, for more on the historical evolution of justifications for taxation, Klaus Vogel, *The Justification for Taxation: A Forgotten Question*, 33 Am. J. Juris. 19 (1988).

243. National Foreign Trade Council Report (2001), at 201 and at 233–234.

'theoretically purest' form of limitation 'would function on an item-by-item' or 'transaction-by-transaction' basis:[244]

> 'The U.S. foreign tax credit limitation provisions historically have included rules that restrict cross-crediting in order to preserve the U.S tax base. In its most restrictive (or theoretically purest) form, the limitation would function on an item-by-item basis, so that foreign tax imposed on any item of income could offset only the U.S. tax on that item. Historically, however, the actual limitation rules have operated instead with respect to more administrable groupings of similar items of income.'[245]

Whether a per-item limitation is the most theoretically sound depends on one's view of 'double taxation', the problem that the credit method was designed to address. The above quote implies a certain view of 'double taxation'. An example, adapted from the National Foreign Tax Council report, can illustrate this point:

> Facts: Taxpayer *MNE Inc.* is a large international enterprise, resident in State R, that generates income of 1,000 in a foreign state, State F1, and 1,000 in another foreign state, State F2. The tax rate in State R is 20%, in State F1 is 30% and in State F2 is 15%.
>
> Taxpayer *MNE Inc.* pays taxes of 300 to State F1 and 150 to State F2, for a total of 450 on an income of 2,000. State R would levy taxes of 400 on 2,000, before the deduction of an FTC.
>
> One view of double taxation could be that: 'The foreign tax on the taxpayer's [2,000] of total foreign-source income is therefore [450], reflecting an effective foreign tax rate of [22.5%] percent. Because the [450] of foreign tax exceeds the pre-credit [State R] tax of [400] on the [2,000] of income, international double taxation would result if residual [State R] tax were imposed on this [2,000] of income if this [2,000] is viewed in the aggregate. Under the overall limitation,

244. Fadi Shaheen, *How Reform-Friendly Are U.S. Tax Treaties?*, 41(3) Brook. J. Int'l L. 1243, 1263 (2016) ('This transactional credit approach is clearly a legitimate dollar-for-dollar credit approach, and arguably even the most theoretically correct one') and at 1263 n.77 (Shaheen cites John P. Steines and the US Joint Committee on Taxation: '*See* STEINES, *supra* note 27, at 390 ("In theory, the limitation arguably should apply separately to each item of foreign source income, on a transaction-by-transaction basis. But that approach, which would prevent averaging ('cross-crediting') high taxes on one transaction with low taxes on another and thereby maximize U.S. residual tax, would be hopelessly impractical to administer."); STAFF OF THE J. COMM. ON TAXATION, 111TH CONG., JCS-4-09, DESCRIPTION OF REVENUE PROVISIONS CONTAINED IN THE PRESIDENT'S FISCAL YEAR 2010 BUDGET PROPOSAL, PART THREE: PROVISIONS RELATED TO THE TAXATION OF CROSS-BORDER INCOME AND INVESTMENT 76 (Comm. Print 2009) ("The U.S. foreign tax credit limitation provisions historically have included rules that restrict cross-crediting in order to preserve the U.S. tax base. In its most restrictive (or theoretically purest) form, the limitation would function on an item-by-item basis, so that foreign tax imposed on any item of income could offset only the U.S. tax on that item. Historically, however, the actual limitation rules have operated instead with respect to more administrable groupings of similar items of income")').

245. United States, Joint Committee on Taxation, *Description of Revenue Provisions Contained in the President's Fiscal Year 2010 Budget Proposal, Part Three: Provisions Related to the Taxation of Cross-Border Income and Investment*, JCS-4-09 (US Government Printing Office 2009).

> such residual U.S. taxation is avoided and therefore the overall limitation seems most appropriate if foreign-source income is properly defined as all foreign-source income in the aggregate.'[246]
>
> Another view of double taxation could be that: 'If foreign-source income were properly defined country-by-country, activity-by-activity, or item-by-item, then the other limitation formulations would seem most appropriate. In the above example, the [State F2] income of [1,000], viewed in isolation on a country-by-country basis, would not be double taxed if [50] of [State R] tax were imposed on it because it bears only [150] of foreign tax.'[247]

The quote of US Joint Committee on Taxation implies the latter view of double taxation, which is based on a strict correspondence between the foreign tax and the income on which it was directly imposed. From this viewpoint, strictly speaking, it is a given item of income and its related foreign taxes that have to be taken into account together for the purposes of relief of double taxation, whereas taxes on *other* items of income did *not* burden that specific item of income and thus did *not* contribute to the double taxation on that item of income. However, the administrative difficulty, if not impossibility, in achieving this on an item-by-item basis was recognized by the legislators.

As can be seen, each approach came with various trade-offs, whose costs and benefits were weighed against whichever rationale seemed to be prevailing at the time. Ultimately, as the quote of the US Joint Committee on Taxation suggests and as discussions during the tug of war between the positive and negative effects of 'averaging' suggest, choices between different types of limitations are tied to the classic compromises inherent in income taxation in general, namely between the most precisely targeted designs versus simplicity and administrability – the difficulty of which has not been lost on tax policy experts for centuries.[248]

Subsequent developments in the credit limitation: the question of 'excess' foreign taxes

Having decided upon and maintained a credit limitation, albeit regularly reformulated, since the Revenue Act of 1921, there was a follow-up question that legislators needed to answer. In cases where the amount of foreign taxes exceeds the amount that can be credited in the US, due to a credit limitation, legislators must decide how to treat this excess amount.

246. National Foreign Trade Council Report (2001), at 235.
247. *Id.*
248. *See*, e.g., Adam Smith, *Wealth of Nations* (W. Strahan and T. Cadell 1776) (who proposed four canons of taxation, namely equity, certainty, convenience, and economy); James Edward Meade, *The Structure and Reform of Direct Taxation: Report of a Committee Chaired by J.E. Meade* (Allen and Unwin 1978) (which includes 'Simplicity and costs of administration' among 'The Characteristics of a Good Tax Structure'); James Mirrlees et al., *Tax by Design*, Institute for Fiscal Studies (Oxford University Press 2011) (in which the balance between equity and efficiency under 'optimal tax theory' observes aims such as neutrality, simplicity and stability).

The same question arose under the UK's system of relief in 1920, for taxes levied by the Dominions that exceeded the tax rate threshold (i.e., 'one half of the appropriate rate of United Kingdom tax') (*supra* notes 107–109). The answer of the UK was that this 'excess' could not be used in the UK, but rather in the Dominions, if the latter agreed to grant reciprocal relief for the excess.

The answer of the US was, and still is, that this excess is carried backward or carried forward to be used against the taxes due in previous or future tax periods to the extent possible. In discussing the trade-offs, the National Foreign Tax Council report opined that:

> '... the carryback of foreign tax credits creates complexity and greater administrative burdens than the carryforward of foreign tax credits. Shortening the carryback period and lengthening the carryforward period could reduce some of this complexity, though at the cost of taxpayer loss of the time value of money'.[249]

Under current US law, a credit carrybackward for the unused foreign income tax is permitted for one year and a credit carryforward is permitted for the subsequent ten years.[250]

Overall, the options for the treatment of this excess include, outside of the rarer or special cases where the states concerned negotiate a form of coordinated reciprocal relief (as under the 1920 UK Dominion relief system), that the excess may be carried forward or backward or both (as in the US), that the excess may be cross-credited against similar taxes,[251] that the excess can be permitted as a deduction from the tax base,[252] or that the excess is simply lost and may not be used.

249. National Foreign Trade Council Report (2001), at 227.

250. United States, Internal Revenue Code, Section 904(c) ('(c) Carryback and carryover of excess tax paid

Any amount by which all taxes paid or accrued to foreign countries or possessions of the United States for any taxable year for which the taxpayer chooses to have the benefits of this subpart exceed the limitation under subsection (a) shall be deemed taxes paid or accrued to foreign countries or possessions of the United States in the first preceding taxable year and in any of the first 10 succeeding taxable years, in that order and to the extent not deemed taxes paid or accrued in a prior taxable year [...]').

251. *See*, e.g., *supra* note 87 (this may have been permissible in some cases under the 1894 UK relief).

252. For the option of deductibility, *see*, e.g., United Kingdom, Finance Act 1920, Section 27(4)(b); Herbert E. Seed & Alfred W. Rawlinson, *Double Income Tax Relief: The Law and Practice Regarding Relief from Double Taxation* 13 (Sir Isaac Pitman & Sons 1925), in Legal Treatises, 1800–1926 (Making of Modern Law Print Editions). *See also*, e.g., Luxembourg, Loi Modifiée du 4 Décembre 1967 Concernant l'Impôt sur le Revenue (LIR) (as amended, 'Texte Coordonné au 1er Janvier 2020', updated as of 14 May 2019), Article 13 (Income Tax Code). *See also*, e.g., Luxembourg, Le Gouvernement du Grand-Duché de Luxembourg, Guichet.lu, *Foreign Tax Credit Method*, https://guichet.public.lu/en/entreprises/fiscalite/developpement-restructuration/activite-etranger/imputation-impot-etranger.html (last visited 15 Aug. 2018) ('The surplus foreign tax (the uncredited portion) may nonetheless be offset against the taxable amount payable by the company in Luxembourg' (emphasis omitted)).

2.1.1.3. *Credit for Underlying Taxes Paid on Distributed Profits: The Emergence of an 'Indirect' Credit*

Preliminary remarks

In addition to the credit mechanism discussed so far, the Revenue Act of 1918 also offered an indirect (or 'deemed')[253] credit to shareholders. This is the type of credit that is required under the CFC rules of the EU ATAD. However, the 1918 version was not the first to exist. Some version of this type of relief can be traced back to 1881 in the UK. The version that evolved in the UK is what is sometimes referred to as an 'imputation' credit method. This is the type of credit that ended up attacked under a long line of CJEU case law (discussed in Section 4.2.8.). The two approaches ('indirect' and 'imputation') achieve ultimately the same goal, yet one is designed in a way that is more in line with EU law, while the other has faced numerous EU law challenges. To offer a deeper understanding of these two approaches, this section explores how they evolved, their underlying rationale and fundamental features, before finally turning to some more detailed design issues that arose during their historical development.

1881 relief in the UK

Traditionally, in the UK, an 'imputation' credit system was used. Under this system, according to Harris, 'companies were treated as conduits on distribution' meaning that 'United Kingdom companies passed relief granted to them to their shareholders on distribution.'[254] As mentioned, some version of this type of relief in the UK dates back to a case in 1881, *Gilbertson v. Fergusson*, making it the earliest relief in the UK. Notably, though, under the rule established by this case, the relief was limited to the underlying *UK* taxes, rather than foreign taxes.[255] This more limited scope in its design was driven by its rationale, as becomes clearer below.

This early relief, under the rule of *Gilbertson v. Fergusson*, was offered in particular constellations where there was a UK source of the underlying profits that were distributed by the non-resident corporation to a UK person (in other words, where a foreign source or entity was sandwiched between a UK source and UK taxpayers). To offer an example, a bank headquartered in Turkey with a branch in London generates profits from its activities both in Turkey and in the UK. This is, roughly, the fact pattern of the 1881 case.[256] Some of those profits are taxed in Turkey, while some of the profits

253. United States, Revenue Act of 1918, Sixty-Fifth Congress, Session III, Chapter 18, Public Law 65-254, Section 240(c) (US Government Printing Office 1919).

254. Peter Harris, *An Historic View of the Principle and Options for Double Tax Relief*, 1999(6) Brit. Tax Rev. 469, 476 (1999).

255. *Id.*, at 481–482 (discussing *Gilbertson v. Fergusson* and explaining that 'The rule stood for almost sixty years until it was overruled in 1945 (the year in which treaty double tax relief first became available) by the House of Lords in *Canadian Eagle v. R.*'); J.D.B. Oliver, *The Rule in Gilbertson v Fergusson: 140 Years of Relief for Underlying Tax*, 2007(3) Brit. Tax Rev. 293, 293 (2007) (Oliver describes the rule as '[r]elief from double taxation in relation to UK tax paid on UK source profits by a non-resident company paying dividends to UK resident shareholders').

256. J.D.B. Oliver, *The Rule in Gilbertson v Fergusson: 140 Years of Relief for Underlying Tax*, 2007(3) Brit. Tax Rev. 293, 293–294 (2007) (it involved the Imperial Ottoman Bank and profits that it distributed to UK shareholders in the 1870s; one factor that may have complicated the

have been taxed in the 'hands' of the UK branch. Eventually, when the Turkish bank pays a portion of its profits out in the form of a dividend to its UK shareholders, the question arises as to how much of the dividend can be traced back to profits already taxed in the UK and how much of the dividend can be traced back to profits taxed only in Turkey.

The aim of the relief system in the UK was to avoid taxing the UK shareholders on the portion of the dividends from profits that had *already* been taxed *in the UK*. The UK should not tax the profits generated there twice. J.D.B. Oliver cites the following from the decision:

> 'Now it may be true that there are no specific words in this statute which point out that the Government are not to receive the tax twice over, but it would be so clearly unjust and obviously contrary to the statute that the Government should have the tax payable twice over by the same person in respect of the same thing, that I would say it was a necessary implication that that could not be right.'[257]

The judge then reiterated that income tax should be levied only on the portion of dividends stemming from profits generated in Turkey and, as regards the portion stemming from profits generated in England, should be levied only once.[258] The decision's wording 'by the *same person* in respect of the same thing' (emphasis added) seems indicative of a perception of a more integrated relationship between the profits generated by the business and those then distributed to shareholders.

To resolve this 'unjust' treatment, the UK would tax the dividends, but offer a 'dividend tax credit' for any underlying UK tax. As regards the details of the calculation, the judge stated: 'Whether it is properly worked out by the rule of three sum stated in the case I know not and do not care. That is a matter for an accountant more than for a court of law.'[259]

Regarding the rationale that emerges from this case, there is a strict territorial component: no double taxation should be caused by the UK government on UK-sourced income. Yet, whereas the UK government should *not* take twice from the same

analysis of the source of the underlying profits is that, only a few years prior, it had been a UK bank, the Ottoman Bank of London, but transferred its headquarters to Turkey 'from 1863 onwards').

257. *Id.*, at 295 (citing Judge Brett L.J. in '(1881) 1 TC 501 at 518' and explaining that 'On appeal to the Court of Appeal the court unanimously affirmed the decision of the Divisional Court').

258. *Id.* (citing Judge Brett L.J. in '(1881) 1 TC 501 at 518').

259. J.D.B. Oliver, *The Rule in Gilbertson v Fergusson: 140 Years of Relief for Underlying Tax*, 2007(3) Brit. Tax Rev. 293, 295 & n.11 (2007) (citing Judge Brett L.J. in '(1881) 1 TC 501 at 518' and explaining in n.11: 'The "rule of three sum" referred to was the calculation used in the alternative assessment of both branch profits and the dividend which was discharged by the Divisional Court. As described above it calculated the amount representing the UK profits as being that proportion of the UK tax profits which the dividend paid to the UK resident shareholders bore to the total dividend. This assumed a full distribution of the UK profits and did not attempt to calculate the overall percentage of profits which had been distributed and then apportion that percentage of UK profits between the dividends to resident and non-resident shareholders'). *See also* Peter Harris, *An Historic View of the Principle and Options for Double Tax Relief*, 1999(6) Brit. Tax Rev. 469, 481–482 (1999) ('It appears the early approach for identifying the profits out of which a dividend was paid was to assume that a dividend was paid proportionately out of current year United Kingdom and foreign source profits').

thing, the UK *could* tax dividends paid from business profits arising in Turkey, irrespective of whether the Turkish government had already levied taxes on those same profits. So the possibility that the profits are taxed twice, first by Turkey, then by the UK, was not considered problematic. In other words, this was more about the proper take of the UK government and less about economic double taxation more broadly.

1918 relief in the US

The US took a different approach in its Revenue Act of 1918, in some ways broader while in others narrower. The Act stated:

> 'For the purposes of section 238 a domestic corporation which owns a majority of the voting stock of a foreign corporation shall **be deemed to have paid the same proportion of** any **income**, war-profits and excess-profits **taxes paid** (but not including taxes accrued) by such foreign corporation during the taxable year to any foreign country or to any possession of the United States upon income derived from sources without the United States, **which the amount of** any **dividends** (not deductible under section 234) **received** by such domestic corporation from such foreign corporation during the taxable year **bears to the total taxable income of such foreign corporation** upon or with respect to which such taxes were paid: *Provided*, That in no such case shall the amount of the credit for such taxes exceed the amount of such dividends (not deductible under section 234) received by such domestic corporation during the taxable year' (emphasis added in bold).[260]

Regarding the eligible taxpayers, it was narrower. The rule of *Gilbertson v. Fergusson* applied without distinction to all UK resident shareholders (thus including natural persons) and seemed to make 'no distinction between portfolio and direct investors'.[261] According to the wording in the US statutory provision, the credit is offered only to 'domestic corporations'; shareholders that are natural persons cannot claim it. Moreover, the US domestic corporation must hold 'a majority of the voting stock of a foreign corporation'. This has both a quantitative threshold (i.e., the 'majority' of stock) and a qualitative aspect (i.e., the type of stock is 'voting' stock). These differences in scope – the differences as to the types of shareholders covered and the quantitative threshold of ownership – can be explained by the broader differences in the model of corporate taxation existing in the two states (integrated versus 'classical', discussed at *infra* note 291 and note 293).

Regarding the qualitative requirement, both states encountered some similar questions. Both in the UK and in the US, a question arose regarding preference shares or stock. For this purpose, Elisabeth A. Owens distinguished between: (1) the type of stock to fulfil the ownership requirements and (2) the type of stock on which the dividends are paid to fulfil the rationale for relief.[262]

260. United States, Revenue Act of 1918, Sixty-Fifth Congress, Session III, Chapter 18, Public Law 65-254, Section 240(c) (US Government Printing Office 1919).
261. J.D.B. Oliver, *The Rule in Gilbertson v Fergusson: 140 Years of Relief for Underlying Tax*, 2007(3) Brit. Tax Rev. 293, 296 (2007).
262. Elisabeth A. Owens, *The Foreign Tax Credit: A Study of the Credit for Foreign Taxes under United States Income Tax Law* 95–99 (Harvard Law School 1961).

On the first point, regarding the ownership requirements, as mentioned above, by contrast with the UK, the US had precise specifications (i.e., the majority of voting stock; it was later reduced to 10%). According to Owens, while the reason for some form of ownership threshold was clear, i.e., for administrative feasibility,[263] neither the Congressional materials related to the Revenue Act of 1918 nor those related to subsequent changes to the indirect credit in the Revenue Act of 1951 gave a reason for the relevance of 'voting' rights. It did not seem related to the rationale of the indirect FTC in an evident or direct way, in her view,[264] and could give rise to additional questions such as 'whether shares with limited voting rights constitute voting stock, or whether 10% ownership is to be based on the value of the shares or on their number'.[265] Still, the qualitative requirement to own 'voting' stock persisted in the US until the 2017 tax reform, when the US finally broadened the definition of a 'United States shareholder' to 'any U.S. person who owns 10 percent or more of the *total value of shares of all classes of stock* of a foreign corporation' (emphasis added). The rationale is informative: the aim is to prevent strategies that could be used to manipulate whether a taxpayer meets the criteria, by, e.g., 'diluting the voting power ... through the issuance of different classes of stock'.[266] Although the details are not relevant here, the scope of application of the credit method also changed, as the US replaced the Section 902 indirect credit with an exemption for dividends, amended accordingly the indirect credit provisions under the CFC regime, while essentially expanding the role of the credit with the introduction of the GILTI regime.[267]

---

263. *Id.*, at 95-96.
264. *Id.*, at 96 (Owens surmised that 'voting stock' may have been adopted merely due to the fact that the section for the indirect credit was located near the sections for 'filing consolidated returns' which were based on 'a unity of interest in the affiliated corporations, as proven by ownership of voting stock').
265. *Id.* (the only indication she found as to the interpretation by the IRS was in 'Schedule B of Form 1118', which indicated that the IRS was interested in the number, rather than value, of shares and interested in those 'with full voting rights').
266. *See* United States, Committee on the Budget of the United States Senate, *Reconciliation Recommendations Pursuant to H. Con. Res. 71*, One-Hundred-Fifteenth Congress, Session I, 383 (US Government Printing Office 2017) (in this case, the Committee was concerned with taxpayers avoiding the status of 'United States shareholder' for the purposes of avoiding US CFC rules. However, it does not require a great stretch of the imagination to assume that taxpayers can also employ similar strategies in order to bring themselves within the scope of eligibility for benefits such as indirect foreign tax credits that are based on the percentage of 'voting stock').
267. *See* United States, An Act to Provide for Reconciliation Pursuant to Titles II and V of the Concurrent Resolution on the Budget for Fiscal Year 2018, One-Hundred-Fifteenth Congress, Session I, Public Law 115-97 (US Government Printing Office 22 Dec. 2017) (Tax Cuts and Jobs Act) (prior to the 2017 changes, Section 960(a) made reference to the rules under Section 902. As Section 902 was repealed by Pub. L. 115-97, title I, § 14301(a), Section 960 had to be adapted accordingly. Post-2017, under Section 960(a), in the case of a CFC inclusion, 'such domestic corporation shall be deemed to have paid so much of such foreign corporation's foreign income taxes as are properly attributable to such item of income'. Section 960(d) was also added, by Pub. L. No. 115-97, §14201(b), to grant a partial (80%) deemed-paid foreign tax credit with respect to GILTI inclusions); IRS, Internal Revenue Manual, at Section 4.61.10.2 (26 Mar. 2020) ('IRC 902 was repealed by the TCJA for tax years beginning after 2017, but is still effective for pre-2018 distributions to U.S. shareholders with 10% or greater voting interests in the distributor foreign corporation').

On the second point, the relevance of the type of stock for the purposes of the *ownership requirements* can be distinguished from the question as to whether relief should be granted for all dividends received on any type of stock. In the UK, in a 1937 case, *Barnes v. Hely Hutchinson*, the scope of relief was narrowed: an individual taxpayer was denied relief, in part, because 'the dividend was a preference dividend and not an ordinary dividend', on the grounds that the 'preference shareholder who receives his full dividend has suffered nothing directly or indirectly'.[268] In the US, the eligible shareholder 'may credit such taxes attributable to the dividends it receives, regardless of the nature of the stock on which it receives dividends', i.e., whether 'paid on common or preferred stock'.[269] Nevertheless, Owens argued that, in light of the rationale, the type of stock could matter. Shareholders of common stock are sure to 'pay' indirectly the foreign taxes, whereas in some cases shareholders of preferred stock are not: 'Under most circumstances, the amount of dividends it will receive is unrelated to the foreign corporate tax burden.'[270] In other words, one main rationale for the indirect FTC is that the shareholder indirectly pays the underlying taxes of the subsidiary because those underlying taxes reduce the amount of dividends the shareholder receives. Yet, in the case of preferred shares that guarantee a fixed return, this link is weakened. Owens also cited the example of British law, reflected also in the US-UK tax treaty at that time (signed 16 April 1945, since terminated and replaced), which 'allows an indirect credit only for dividends on common stock and for dividends on participating preferred stock insofar as the latter exceed the fixed rate to which the shares are entitled'.[271]

As soon as a state, as the US did, establishes specific ownership requirements (especially a quantitative threshold), an additional question becomes more pronounced, namely the time and duration of the ownership. The US Treasury eventually specified that the ownership requirements must be met at the time of receipt of the dividends.[272] Prior to this, Owens offered insight into some possible considerations:

> 'The Code and Regulations are silent on the question of the point of time at which the requisite degree of ownership is required. [...] Since the limitation of § 902(a)

268. J.D.B. Oliver, *The Rule in Gilbertson v Fergusson: 140 Years of Relief for Underlying Tax*, 2007(3) Brit. Tax Rev. 293, 296–297 (2007) (according to Oliver, the House of Lords distinguished the facts of this 1937 case from *Gilbertson v. Fergusson* both because of the 'preference dividends' and because of the fact that 'the UK tax had not been paid directly by the company [resident in India] paying the dividend but by the UK resident companies in which it held shares').
269. Elisabeth A. Owens, *The Foreign Tax Credit: A Study of the Credit for Foreign Taxes under United States Income Tax Law* 97 (Harvard Law School 1961).
270. *Id.*
271. *Id.*
272. *See*, e.g., United States, Department of the Treasury, Internal Revenue Service, Computation of Foreign Taxes Deemed Paid Under Section 902 Pursuant to a Pooling Mechanism for Undistributed Earnings and Foreign Taxes, TD 8708, 62(4) US Federal Register 923 (7 Jan. 1997); United States, Code of Federal Regulations, Section 1.902-1 (Credit for Domestic Corporate Shareholder of a Foreign Corporation for Foreign Income Taxes Paid by the Foreign Corporation, as amended in 2009); Ronald A. Worley, *The Indirect Foreign Tax Credit: A Policy Analysis of Section 902*, 13(2) Intl Tax & Bus Law 176, 185 (1996) (citing *inter alia* 'Treas. Reg. § 1.902-1(b) (as amended in 1979)').

> by requiring a minimum amount of stock ownership is purely a matter of administrative convenience, it could be argued that ownership of 10% or more of the voting stock at any time during the taxable year is sufficient to qualify the shareholder with respect to all dividends whether paid before or after it attains or relinquishes the minimum amount. On the other hand, this rule would result in a lack of uniformity in application of the 10% ownership requirement. It appears that the Service may require that the requisite degree of ownership exists at the time the dividend is paid as the result of which the domestic corporation is claiming the credit.'[273]

Finally, one question regarding the ownership requirements is whether the indirect tax credit should be granted not only for the taxes paid by the directly owned subsidiary but also for the taxes paid by sub-subsidiaries. If the credit is founded on the aforementioned rationale, namely that the shareholders are viewed as having indirectly paid the taxes that have been levied on the same underlying profits, it follows that sub-subsidiaries should be covered, as this same concern exists at other levels of ownership. The US eventually embarked on this expansion, in 1942, so that the US domestic corporation would be deemed to have paid taxes by its subsidiary and by its sub-subsidiary.[274] In that case, the ownership requirements in sub-subsidiaries must also be established, thus invoking the same questions of threshold, type and time or duration of ownership.[275] Theoretically, this same concern exists at every level of ownership; in practice, the US, for reasons of administrative practicality, eventually stopped at a maximum of six sub-tiers of subsidiaries.

While the scope of relief under the US indirect FTC was narrower than that of the UK regarding eligible taxpayers, it was arguably broader regarding eligible taxes from a territorial perspective. Relief under *Gilbertson v. Fergusson* in the UK was limited to underlying UK taxes, whereas in the US it was offered for eligible underlying taxes paid 'to any foreign country or to any possession of the United States'.

One way to view an indirect credit, as compared to a direct credit, is that it in effect expands the list of eligible taxes. In other words, under certain conditions, a credit could be obtained not only for foreign taxes that a US corporation paid directly to a foreign government but also for foreign taxes that its foreign subsidiary paid to a foreign government. As one of the shareholders - and thus owners - of the foreign subsidiary, the US domestic corporation would be considered to have indirectly paid a proportion of the taxes of its foreign subsidiary.

Determining this proportion is the crux of an indirect tax credit. The proportion of the *taxes* corresponds to the proportion of the underlying *profits* of the foreign subsidiary that are distributed to the US domestic corporation. In other words, the proportion of the overall taxes paid on the foreign subsidiary's profits which can be attributed to the amount of profits distributed to the shareholder can be 'deemed' paid

273. Elisabeth A. Owens, *The Foreign Tax Credit: A Study of the Credit for Foreign Taxes under United States Income Tax Law* 95 n.17 (Harvard Law School 1961).
274. *Id.*, at 20-21.
275. *See*, e.g., Hugh J. Ault & Brian J. Arnold, *Comparative Income Taxation: A Structural Analysis* 357-386 pt. 4 *International Taxation* (Kluwer Law International 2d ed. 2004) (discussed 'Tier limitations'); Elisabeth A. Owens, *The Foreign Tax Credit: A Study of the Credit for Foreign Taxes under United States Income Tax Law* 131-147 (Harvard Law School 1961).

by the shareholder, despite the fact that it was formally legally paid by the foreign subsidiary – hence, the terms 'deemed' or 'indirect' credit.[276] Based on the statutory wording, one way to express this would be in the following formula:

Indirect FTC = Eligible Foreign Taxes Paid × (Dividends/'Total Taxable Income').

Example No. 11: Layers of Taxation of Corporate Distributions

To better understand the rationale for extending the credit method to 'indirectly'-paid taxes, the counterfactual of a cross-border scenario in the absence of double taxation relief can help illustrate the potential problem being addressed.

A foreign subsidiary and a corporate shareholder in that subsidiary are two separate legal entities and, thus, in general, legally speaking, two separate taxpayers. Three possible layers of taxation can occur.

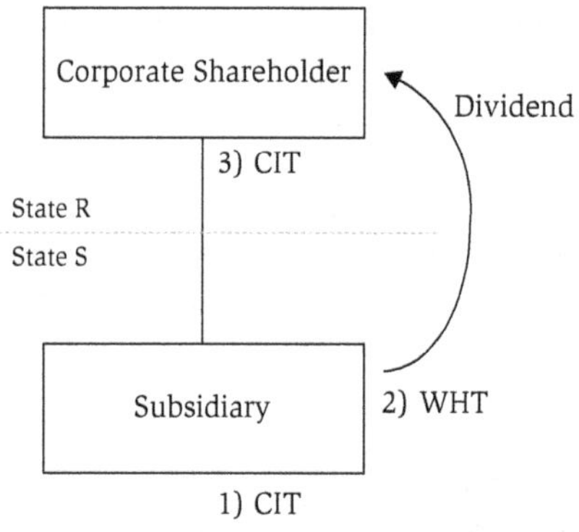

In the absence of double taxation relief, generally 3 layers of tax can occur:

Layer 1)
Subsidiary generates profits in State S.
The profits of Subsidiary are charged CIT in State S.

Layer 2)
The after-tax profits are distributed to Parent.
Subsidiary deducts WHT from dividends at source.
Explanation: State S levies a tax on Parent as a non-resident; State S requires Subsidiary to deduct WHT before income leaves territory; it is levied on and reduces the amount distributed to Parent.

Layer 3)
Dividends arrive and form part of the income taxable at the level of Parent.
The profits of Parent are charged CIT in State R.

Facts: To illustrate this in numbers, assume the parent company above in State R owns 100%, and thus is the sole shareholder, in a subsidiary in State S. The subsidiary generates profits of 100. The corporate income tax rate in State S is 20% and in State R is 35%. In addition, State S levies a withholding tax of 10% on outbound distributions of profits.

276. These terms can be used interchangeably. *See*, e.g., United States, Revenue Act of 1918, Sixty-Fifth Congress, Session III, Chapter 18, Public Law 65-254, Section 240(c) (US Government Printing Office 1919) (uses the term 'deemed'); Elisabeth A. Owens, *The Foreign Tax Credit: A Study of the Credit for Foreign Taxes under United States Income Tax Law* 92 (Harvard Law School 1961) (for a use of the term 'indirect credit'); Peter Harris, *An Historic View of the Principle and Options for Double Tax Relief*, 1999(6) Brit. Tax Rev. 469, 476 (1999) (sometimes uses the term 'underlying foreign tax credit').

(1) First, as the subsidiary generates profits (100), it will be subject to corporate income tax in its state of residence, State S (20%). The after-tax profits (80) are then available for distribution to its shareholders.
(2) Second, upon distribution, State S may levy a withholding tax on the distribution (10%), seeing as it is income now going to a distinct taxpayer, i.e., the parent company in State R, which from the perspective of State S is considered a non-resident that earned income sourced in its territory and thus also owing some contribution (8) to the state that gave rise to its income.
(3) Third, the income is received by the parent company in State R (80 of dividends, on which a withholding tax of 8 was levied). The dividends are considered part of its overall worldwide income that will be subject to corporate income tax in its residence state (35% and assuming State R does not allow a deduction for the withholding tax, then 28 of taxes are due).

This amounts to three layers of taxes on the same original 100 of profits (100 minus 20 minus 8 minus 28, leaving 44 left and total taxes paid of 56).

Although these two entities are *legally* distinct, and although there is a different reasonable justification for the tax at each layer when considered separately, taken together it is *economically* the same profits potentially being overburdened (thus potentially hindering cross-border inter-company investment).

In Example No. 11 above, both the direct credit and the indirect credit have a role to play to offer relief in such cases. As explained in Example No. 12, distinctions can be made between 'juridical' and 'economic' double taxation. This distinction, which has now become widespread,[277] was not as common, if used at all, at the time, however,[278] but rather seems to have emerged circa 1961.[279] The 'direct' credit addresses the former; the 'indirect' credit addresses the latter.

277. *See*, e.g., OECD, *Model Tax Convention on Income and on Capital 2017: Condensed Version* Introduction, para. 1 and Commentary on Articles 23 A and 23 B, paras 1–2 (OECD Publishing 2017); CJEU, Case C-128/08, *Damseaux*, 16 Jul. 2009, ECLI:EU:C:2009:471; CJEU, Case C-194/06, *Orange European Smallcap Fund*, 24 May 2008, ECLI:EU:C:2008:289, at para. 31; Opinion of AG Kokott in Case C-540/07, *Commission v. Italy*, 16 Jul. 2009, ECLI:EU:C:2009:463, at para. 45.

278. *See*, e.g., Elisabeth A. Owens, *The Foreign Tax Credit: A Study of the Credit for Foreign Taxes under United States Income Tax Law* (Harvard Law School 1961) (these terms are not used in her book when discussing the Section 901 and Section 902 credits).

279. *See* League of Nations, Fiscal Committee, *London and Mexico Model Tax Conventions: Commentary and Text* (1946), *in* 4 *Legislative History of United States Tax Conventions* 4319, 4319 and 4328 (United States, Joint Committee on Internal Revenue Taxation, US Government Printing Office 1962) (Forward and Introduction: this report offered a description of 'international double taxation' and listed three instances of it, though without expressly using term 'juridical'); Organisation for European Economic Co-operation, *Fourth Report of the Fiscal*

Example No. 12: Layers of Taxation of Corporate Distributions – Relief under the Credit Method

Scenario 1: direct credit method (no indirect credit method)

Profits generated by Subsidiary: 100
State S CIT: 20% × 100 = 20

After-tax profits distributed to Parent: 80
State S WHT: 10% × 80 = 8

State R tax liability: 35% × 80 = 28
minus direct credit: –8
= taxes paid: 20

Total taxes on initial 100 of profits: 20 + 8 + 20 = 48

Juridical double taxation and the **direct credit**: The WHT (of 10%, or 8), which was levied on the distribution as it left the territory of State S, constituted a tax levied on the parent company, as a non-resident taxpayer of State S. Thus, it was a tax paid *directly* by the parent company out of the profit distribution (of 80) owed to it. In State R, as the full amount is technically income of the parent company, resident there, it is included in the tax base and subject to corporate income tax (of 35%, or 28). This amounts to two different taxes, one levied by State S and one by State R, on the same legal entity, thus considered **'juridical' double taxation**. To remedy this, under the **direct credit**, State R would grant a foreign tax credit to the parent company for the WHT levied in State S.

Scenario 2: direct credit method and indirect credit method (1918 version)

Profits generated by Subsidiary: 100
State S CIT: 20% × 100 = 20

After-tax profits distributed to Parent: 80
State S WHT: 10% × 80 = 8

Eligible Foreign Taxes Paid × Dividends/'Total Taxable Income' = Indirect FTC *(see notes below)*
20 × 80/100 = 16

State R tax liability: 35% × 80 = 28
minus credit for taxes directly paid and deemed indirectly paid: –8 and –16
= taxes paid: 4

Committee of the OEEC on the Elimination of Double Taxation (August 1961), *in* 4 *Legislative History of United States Tax Conventions*, 4619 (United States, Joint Committee on Internal Revenue Taxation, US Government Printing Office 1962) (in this report, an explicit and unambiguous distinction between 'juridical double taxation' and 'economic double taxation' is made in 'Commentaries on Articles XXIII and XXIV concerning the methods for avoidance of double taxation').

Total taxes on initial 100 of profits: 20 + 8 + 4 = 32

Economic double taxation and the **indirect credit**: The corporate income taxes paid by the subsidiary in State S are paid by that subsidiary out of its own profits. The profits generated by the subsidiary and the profits distributed to the parent are nevertheless the same profits, economically speaking, and thus levying corporate income tax twice constitutes **'economic' double taxation**. Under the US law, the parent company seeks to determine how much of the underlying corporate income taxes that were paid by the subsidiary can be attributed to the dividends ultimately received by the parent company, and thus 'deemed' paid by the parent. The above formula is based on the above statutory wording of the Revenue Act of 1918. For that reason, two **important notes** must be made here:

- The denominator 'Total Taxable Income' changed under subsequent developments, discussed below (*see*, e.g., Example No. 14: it would eventually become 20 × 80/80 = 20).
- A 'Gross-Up' was not provided for in the law at this stage, but this too changed under subsequent developments, discussed below.

This example makes simplifications, such as implicitly assuming the income is the same under US law and under foreign law. In practice, of course, such simplifications cannot be presumed. Such simplifications mask the complications that can arise from the legal interpretation of each term in the formula, such as 'total taxable income'.

In particular, by using the 'total taxable income' in the denominator, notice how the result of the calculation does not allow a credit for the full 20 of underlying foreign taxes paid, but for only 16 out of 20 of the underlying foreign taxes paid. On the one hand, this could be considered a strange result, since the parent company is the 100% owner and sole shareholder of this subsidiary, to which the subsidiary distributed *all* of its profits. On the other hand, this could be considered the appropriate result, since only 80 is received in the US and 16 is the amount of taxes that corresponds to 80, whereas the full 20 corresponds to the full 100 not entirely received in the US.[280]

How exactly to calculate the indirect FTC gave rise to questions in the US. In such a case (as in Example No. 12), with a 100% shareholder receiving a full distribution, the question is: should the calculation lead to a result where the full taxes of 20 are creditable or should it allow a credit only for 16 corresponding to the 80 received as dividends in the US, thereby denying a credit for the portion of underlying taxes on the 100 that corresponds to the 20 of taxes paid to the foreign government?

The answer is arguably the 20 of taxes on 100 of income. However, under the 1918 version in the US, it was not considered a given. So whether one agrees depends on the rationale of the indirect credit, the rationale of this fraction and whether there is a 'gross-up'. While the main rationales for the indirect credit were largely understood,

280. For a more detailed exploration of these issues, *see*, e.g., Elisabeth A. Owens, *The Foreign Tax Credit: A Study of the Credit for Foreign Taxes under United States Income Tax Law* (Harvard Law School 1961), as will be presented at *infra* note 311.

details regarding the fraction and the 'gross-up' were clarified later in the development of the indirect credit in the US. Thus, both are addressed below in subsequent subsections (*see infra* note 300 and note 311), in order to piece together how the answer to this question evolved over time.

As for the rationale of the indirect credit, two (or three) related rationales help explain its functioning. First, '[t]he rationale is that a corporate shareholder in a foreign corporation "pays" the foreign taxes imposed on the foreign corporation through a reduction in its dividend income' (footnote omitted).[281] This is an economic rationale. Its importance is often underlined by stressing that, with this in mind, allowing multiple layers of taxation at each corporate level leads to a potential burden on cross-border corporate investment.[282] This could induce corporations to consolidate corporate structures to as few layers of ownership as possible and to as few countries as possible. This could also induce more debt financing than equity financing since equity financing risks multiple layers of taxation, whereas debt financing (due to the fact that payments, e.g., interest, on debt are generally tax deductible) will be taxed once.[283] Related to these points, one rationale is expressed as the desire to eliminate or mitigate economic double taxation (though, as mentioned above, this exact phrase may have emerged later).

Second, in some cases, 'a foreign subsidiary is much like a foreign branch of an American corporation' and thus the two should be treated the same with respect to their foreign taxes.[284] This is a rationale based on equal treatment, namely equal treatment between different legal forms of cross-border investment, e.g., either via a branch (or PE) or via a subsidiary. To understand this, assume that only a direct credit is granted, and no indirect credit is available. If a domestic corporation decides to expand its business across the border, it can either directly establish itself in the neighbouring state through a branch or incorporate a subsidiary, a new separate legal entity abroad. If it establishes a branch, as part of the same legal entity, the US domestic corporation directly pays any taxes owed on its branch profits to the foreign government and thus all of these taxes are eligible for a direct credit in the US. If it establishes

281. *Id.*, at 93.

282. *See*, e.g., Parent-Subsidiary Directive, preamble, discussed in Section 3.2. and the numerous CJEU cases that address this issue in Section 4.2.3., Section 4.2.5., and Section 4.2.8.

283. These two potential impacts on business decisions do not appear to be among the main motives cited for implementing the indirect credit in the US, but are other related general considerations. The debt versus equity financing issue is discussed by Terra/Wattel, for example. *See* Ben J.M. Terra & Peter J. Wattel, *European Tax Law* 222, Section 4.2.3 (Wolters Kluwer 6th ed. 2012).

284. Jacob S. Seidman, *Seidman's Legislative History of Federal Income Tax Laws: 1938-1861*, 872–873 (Prentice-Hall, Inc. 1938) (according to the Congressional Discussion in the Senate, where 'a domestic corporation which owns a majority of the voting stock of a foreign subsidiary, from which subsidiary the domestic corporation receives taxable dividends. In such a case a foreign subsidiary is much like a foreign branch of an American corporation. If the American corporation owned a foreign branch, it would include the earnings or profits of such branch in its total income, but it would also be entitled to deduct from the tax based upon such income any income or profits taxes paid to foreign countries by the branch in question. Without special legislation, however, no credit can be obtained where the branch is incorporated under foreign laws'). *See also* Elisabeth A. Owens, *The Foreign Tax Credit: A Study of the Credit for Foreign Taxes under United States Income Tax Law* 92 (Harvard Law School 1961).

a subsidiary, a distinct legal entity, this subsidiary is a taxpayer resident in the other state that pays taxes on the profits it generates there. The US domestic corporation is a non-resident taxpayer. The taxes paid by the subsidiary are not eligible for a direct credit. If the branch and the subsidiary generate the same amount of profits in the foreign state and pay the same amount of taxes to the foreign government, in the case of the branch all of those taxes are eligible for a direct credit in the US and in the case of the subsidiary none are eligible for a direct credit. As a result, in addition to making this choice between legal forms for business reasons, this adds an important tax consideration. The indirect credit attempts to bring more parity to this situation, to treat the two more equally from a tax perspective. Another way this rationale is sometimes phrased is, thus, to treat the subsidiary and the parent in a more integrated way, as one taxpayer,[285] just as the branch is considered one and the same with its head office. This objective is not fully achieved, due to a timing difference, since the indirect credit can be claimed only upon receipt of dividends (potentially long after taxes were paid on the profits generated), whereas the direct credit can be claimed as the tax liabilities arise on an annual basis. That said, one can argue this objective need not or cannot be fully achieved since there are some objective differences between a foreign branch and a foreign subsidiary, so the indirect credit need only strive to *approximate* the tax treatment to the extent possible. Indeed, one of the main differences between a foreign branch and a foreign subsidiary was the ability to defer US taxation, which the subsidiary could generally achieve by simply not distributing or repatriating profits to its US parent until desired, which can lead to an economic benefit (hence the eventual emergence of CFC rules). According to a Congressional Discussion on the indirect credit, '[s]ince the foreign subsidiary may not send back to the American parent company all of its profits or earnings, it follows that the American parent company should not obtain a credit for all the income and profits taxes paid to foreign countries by the European subsidiary'.[286] As will emerge from the subsequent discussions, the extent to which the indirect credit achieves its objective, how close or how far it strays, depends on how it is designed.

1920 relief in the UK

As explained (*supra* note 255), as early as 1881, the UK offered some form of relief for underlying taxes paid on distributed profits. The Finance Act 1920 also granted this type of relief to Dominion income taxes and adapted it to the half-rate Dominion relief system (discussed at *supra* note 98).[287] What is noticeable when reading Section 27 of the Finance Act 1920 is that the section contains and largely intertwines both the rules granting relief with respect to taxes paid on the underlying profits giving rise to

285. Elisabeth A. Owens, *The Foreign Tax Credit: A Study of the Credit for Foreign Taxes under United States Income Tax Law* 116–117 (Harvard Law School 1961).
286. Jacob S. Seidman, *Seidman's Legislative History of Federal Income Tax Laws: 1938-1861*, 872–873 (Prentice-Hall, Inc. 1938).
287. *See*, e.g., Peter Harris, *An Historic View of the Principle and Options for Double Tax Relief*, 1999(6) Brit. Tax Rev. 469, 476 & n.28 and 477–478 (1999) (offering insight into how this relief evolved and operated at different times, such as under treaties in 1945).

dividends and rules granting relief for taxes 'directly' paid by taxpayers.[288] This drafting seems to indicate that this underlying relief was essentially part and parcel of one unified credit system. In other words, the two credits (direct versus indirect/imputed) did not appear to be perceived as truly distinct, like they were in the US (where they were contained in two separate legal provisions, with different eligibility requirements). As a result, the scope and rules for the two types of credit were largely aligned. This made sense in light of the UK's more unified conceptualization of the corporate-shareholder relationship.

Comparison of relief: imputation credit system versus indirect credit system

A comparison of the two systems of relief (in the UK versus in the US) will lay the groundwork for understanding the legal and factual patterns featuring in the more detailed analysis of CJEU case law regarding these two approaches. To offer an overview, there were four major differences in total: two differences regarding the scope of the relief for the underlying income taxes, namely: (1) the required shareholding threshold and (2) the eligible taxpayers, a third difference regarding the overall approach, namely that (3) the UK had a more integrated corporate-shareholder taxation system, and a fourth difference regarding the operation or calculation, namely (4) the 'gross-up'. Regarding this fourth difference, however, the lack of a 'gross-up' was more of a historical oversight by the US, rather than a characteristic difference between the two systems. This section addresses the broader characteristic differences in the calculation; the 'gross-up' is discussed in the subsequent section.

First, as discussed above, in the UK, the credit for underlying taxes applied regardless of the size of the shareholding, while in the US it applied only for 'a majority of the voting stock of a foreign corporation'[289]. Second, in the UK, it was available to both individuals and corporate shareholders,[290] while in the US it was available only to corporate shareholders. Clearly, the scope in the US was more restricted. The discussion now turns to explanations for this.

These first two differences in scope can be explained by the third difference mentioned above, namely the fact that the UK operated a more 'integrated' approach to the taxation of corporations and their owners; i.e., corporations were not considered as 'final taxpayer subjects' distinct from their shareholders.[291] Indeed, the starting point

288. *See*, e.g., United Kingdom, Finance Act 1920, Sections 27(3), 27(4)(a), 27(5); Herbert E. Seed & Alfred W. Rawlinson, *Double Income Tax Relief: The Law and Practice Regarding Relief from Double Taxation* 8–16 and 28 (Sir Isaac Pitman & Sons 1925), in Legal Treatises, 1800-1926 (Making of Modern Law Print Editions).
289. United States, Revenue Act of 1918, Sixty-Fifth Congress, Session III, Chapter 18, Public Law 65-254, Section 240(c) (US Government Printing Office 1919).
290. *See*, e.g., Peter Harris, *An Historic View of the Principle and Options for Double Tax Relief*, 1999(6) Brit. Tax Rev. 469, 481 (1999); Herbert E. Seed & Alfred W. Rawlinson, *Double Income Tax Relief: The Law and Practice Regarding Relief from Double Taxation* 6 and 51 (Sir Isaac Pitman & Sons 1925), in Legal Treatises, 1800-1926 (Making of Modern Law Print Editions).
291. *See*, e.g., Peter Harris, *An Historic View of the Principle and Options for Double Tax Relief*, 1999(6) Brit. Tax Rev. 469, 475 (1999). In general, *see also* Michael J. Graetz & Alvin C. Warren Jr., *Dividend Taxation in Europe: When the ECJ Makes Tax Policy*, 44(6) Common Mkt. L. Rev. 1577, 1579–1580 (2007).

for these particular instances of double taxation is how countries conceptualize the relationship between corporations and their shareholders and then translate that into income tax treatment. Thus, the issue mainly arises with the taxation of dividends or, more broadly speaking, corporate profits that are distributed (as opposed to interest, royalties, and other types of payments).[292] Labels such as 'classical systems' and 'integration systems' are used for the different conceptualizations.[293] To compare, while 'imputation' credit systems such as that in the UK often seek to integrate personal income tax and CIT, the indirect credit system in the US sought to remedy issues within CIT, such as the difference of tax treatment between branches and subsidiaries and the multiple layers of taxation of corporate profits, yet while still viewing corporations as distinct from their individual shareholders, i.e., the natural persons that ultimately owned it (thus maintaining a more 'classical' system).

Regarding the calculations, the two systems can be effectively equivalent in terms of their result,[294] namely to attribute to the shareholders their proportionate share of the taxes levied on the underlying corporate profits, when a distribution occurs.[295] Some subtle differences arise in their operation, or their means, to achieve this result. These differences give insight into the slightly different terminology that is often employed to distinguish between the two, e.g., an 'indirect' credit for the US approach and an 'imputation' credit system for the UK approach.

292. But *see* US, Internal Revenue Code of 1954, Section 902(d), https://www.govinfo.gov/content/pkg/STATUTE-68/pdf/STATUTE-68A-Pg1.pdf (under a now-abolished Section 902(d) IRC, originally enacted in the 1954 Code, an indirect credit was granted with respect to royalties under certain conditions). For more details, *see* Elisabeth A. Owens, *The Foreign Tax Credit: A Study of the Credit for Foreign Taxes under United States Income Tax Law* 148 (Harvard Law School 1961).

293. 'Integrated' systems are often contrasted with the 'classical' corporate tax system, wherein corporations and shareholders are two distinct taxpayers, such that profits generated by a corporation are fully taxable at the level of the corporation and the after-tax profits distributed to the shareholders are considered distinct and taxable separately in the hands of the shareholders. *See*, e.g., Hugh J. Ault & Brian J. Arnold, *Comparative Income Taxation: A Structural Analysis* 273 (Kluwer Law International 2d ed. 2004) ('In the last fifty years, the two predominant corporate tax systems have been the classical system which taxes the company on its income and then taxes the shareholder separately on distributions received from the company, and the imputation system which gives the shareholder a credit for corporate tax paid, thus eliminating in whole or part the double taxation of dividends'); Ben J.M. Terra & Peter J. Wattel, *European Tax Law* 222, Section 4.2.3 (Wolters Kluwer 6th ed. 2012) ('The main distinction is between on the one hand classical systems, under which corporation tax and individual income tax ignore each other's existence (leading to economic double taxation of distributed profits), and on the other hand integration systems, which, by contrast, impute (credit) the corporation tax paid by the distributing company to (against) the individual income tax of the shareholders receiving the distribution (taking away the economic double taxation). Schedular systems are somewhere in between classical and imputation systems').

294. *See*, e.g., Peter Harris, *An Historic View of the Principle and Options for Double Tax Relief*, 1999(6) Brit. Tax Rev. 469, 481–482 (1999) ('The process involved in imputing foreign tax paid by a non-resident company under an underlying foreign tax credit system is the same as the imputation of corporation tax (domestic or foreign) paid by a resident company to its shareholders under an imputation system. [...] This equivalence of an underlying foreign tax credit system with an imputation system is well demonstrated by the original United Kingdom imputation system').

295. *Id.*, at 469, 481 (on the 'purpose of an underlying foreign tax credit system').

To better understand how the 'imputation' approach functions in general (thus, setting aside the specificities of the UK's approach), Terra and Wattel offer a clear and concise description:

> 'The most sophisticated (and therefore the most intricate) integration systems are imputation systems. They provide for full or partial imputation of the corporate income tax into the income tax payable by the shareholder. The shareholder may credit against his income tax all or part of the corporation tax attributable to the profits out of which the dividend was paid. In effect, in an imputation system, the corporation tax functions as a withholding tax creditable against the individual income tax. The credit available is called an imputation credit (*avoir fiscal, Anrechnung, credito d'imposto*). It may be expressed as a percentage of the net dividend received by the shareholder (this may amount to either partial or full imputation, depending on the percentage chosen), or as a percentage of the underlying corporate income tax (partial imputation), or it may be equal to the underlying corporate income tax (full imputation).
>
> The imputation credit may be regarded as a cheque with which the shareholder can pay (part of) his income tax due on the dividend received. It is, therefore, taxable income.'[296]

As regards its operation in practice, an imputation system often includes the following steps. First, it will determine the amount of the credit, often in one of two ways: either designating a given percentage, or fraction, of the dividend to be the credit or using a formula. An example of such a formula could be:

'corporate tax to be imputed to shareholder' = ('corporate tax before dividend'/ 'corporate cash before dividend') × 'declared dividend'[297] (in other words, multiplying the effective CIT by the dividend paid out).

An example of a fraction could be:

Corporate income tax rate/(1-Corporate income tax rate).[298]

As mentioned, the amount of the percentage or fraction affects whether the credit allows for a full imputation or a partial imputation of the underlying CIT. Second, this credit amount, so determined, is added to the dividend upon distribution (a type of gross-up of the dividend income). Third, the taxes of the shareholder are determined based on this grossed-up amount and, fourth, the credit (the initial percentage/fraction of the dividend) counts towards the taxes so determined. Similar to Terra and Wattel, Graetz and Warren also describe it in the following way: 'Under shareholder-credit integration, the corporate tax is essentially converted into a withholding tax that is creditable against the shareholder tax due on dividends.'[299]

296. Ben J.M. Terra & Peter J. Wattel, *European Tax Law* 227, Section 4.2.3.4 (Wolters Kluwer 6th ed. 2012).
297. Michael J. Graetz & Alvin C. Warren Jr., *Integration of Corporate and Shareholder Taxes*, 69(3) Nat'l Tax J. 677, 682–683 (2016).
298. *See infra* note 1718 (this fraction was used in CJEU cases discussed below, such as *Manninen* and *Accor*).
299. Michael J. Graetz & Alvin C. Warren Jr., *Integration of Corporate and Shareholder Taxes*, 69(3) Nat'l Tax J. 677, 681 (2016).

To compare the two, both the imputation credit system and the indirect FTC system provide relief *to the shareholder* for the (underlying) CIT paid by the subsidiary. To contrast the two, one way of viewing the difference is that, under the *imputation* credit system, it is the *subsidiary's country* providing the relief to the shareholder or rather the relief could be seen as emanating from the subsidiary (to the extent that the credit is viewed as 'attached' to the dividend and paid out or passed up from the subsidiary), whereas under the *indirect* FTC system, it is the *shareholder's country* providing the relief (the net dividend is received by the shareholder, who may then calculate and claim a credit for any underlying taxes of the subsidiary it can be deemed to have paid).

Moreover, often these imputation credit systems operate only in the *domestic* context. One reason is that if the imputation credit system were extended to cross-border situations, then the subsidiary country would be effectively reimbursing a foreign shareholder, over which it was not exercising full taxation powers (other than perhaps a WHT at source). Another way to explain it could be: the subsidiary state has collected CIT at the level of the subsidiary, but then, upon distribution, the subsidiary state is effectively giving some of that CIT collected to the shareholder, for the shareholder to use against his/her/its own taxes. If it is a foreign shareholder, then the subsidiary state is giving up its own CIT and transferring it to a foreign shareholder. Under the indirect FTC system, the taxation of the shareholder and the obligation to grant relief are aligned.

Subsequent developments in the indirect credit calculation: 'gross-up'

As mentioned, there was a fourth difference detected between the UK and US regimes, beyond the general differences of approach or perspective (as 'integrated' or 'classical'). This fourth difference will direct the analysis towards some technical details of the calculation of indirect or imputation credits. In the UK, there was a form of 'gross-up' involved in the calculation,[300] whereas in the US, no 'gross-up' was stipulated under the first version of the indirect credit. To understand why this is significant, the discussion turns to the role and rationale of the 'gross-up' here.

When describing above the UK Dominion tax relief and the US *direct* tax credit, the amount of the Dominion/foreign taxes should not be left out of (or must be added back into) the income that is taken into account in the UK/US, so that the tax base for determining the UK/US taxes against which the Dominion/foreign tax credit will be taken corresponds, to the extent possible, to the tax base used to calculate the Dominion/foreign taxes (*see supra* note 114 and note 173 and Example No. 4). In the case of an *indirect* credit, this requires the shareholder to include the dividend received in its tax base and, in addition, to calculate and then add to the dividend the amount of taxes 'deemed' paid with respect to that dividend.[301]

300. *See*, e.g., United Kingdom, Finance Act 1920, Section 27(4).
301. *See*, e.g., United States, Internal Revenue Code, Section 78 (Gross Up for Deemed Paid Foreign Tax Credit, as amended through 22 Dec. 2017 by Public Law 115-97 'TCJA') ('If a domestic corporation chooses to have the benefits of subpart A of part III of subchapter N (relating to foreign tax credit) for any taxable year, an amount equal to the taxes deemed to be paid by such

Example No. 13: A 'Gross-Up' in the Indirect Credit Context

Facts: A parent company in State R is the 100% sole shareholder of its subsidiary company in State S. Assume a 20% tax rate in State S and a 25% tax rate in State R. In State S, the subsidiary generates 1,000 on which it pays corporate taxes of 200 to State S. The subsidiary then distributes a dividend of 400 to its parent company. Assume also that the figures in State R and in State S are the same.

Subsidiary profits: 1,000

Subsidiary CIT paid to State S: 200

Dividend distributed by Subsidiary to Parent: 400

Step 1:

Determine the amount of CIT paid by Subsidiary that can be 'deemed' paid by Parent because it is the CIT attributable to the dividends distributed:

200 × (400/800) = 100.

Step 2:

Determine the income that must be recognized by Parent in its tax return:

Dividend + CIT 'Deemed' Paid on Dividend: 400 + gross-up of 100 = 500.

Step 3:

Determine tax liability of Parent for the 'grossed-up' tax base of 500: 500 × 25% = 125. From this tax liability, an indirect credit can be deducted of 100 (barring any particular credit limitations, etc.).

There are a number of reasons for the 'gross-up'.[302] First, without it, the foreign taxes would be used twice, first as a deduction reducing the tax base in the UK/US and second as a credit against taxes due in the UK/US. Second, if the aim is to eliminate double taxation by reducing the taxes due on a one-for-one-unit (e.g., dollar-for-dollar) basis, then mathematically this alignment or correspondence between the tax bases is needed (or at least should be strived for to the extent practically feasible) to make that possible.[303] Otherwise, rather than one-for-one, it becomes a partial credit.[304] Third, it

corporation [...] for such taxable year shall be treated [...] as a dividend received by such domestic corporation from the foreign corporation').

302. For a concise explanation of the gross-up, *see*, e.g., United States, Senate, Committee on Finance, Eighty-Seventh Congress, Session II, *Brief Summary of Provisions in H.R. 10650 the 'Revenue Act of 1962'*, 8 (US Government Printing Office 1962) (it explains, albeit briefly, why the US implemented it); National Foreign Trade Council Report (2001), at 192–193 (for more explanation with further sources for reference).

303. *See*, e.g., United States, Joint Committee on Taxation, *General Explanation of The Tax Reform Act of 1986 (H.R. 3838, 99th Congress; Public Law 99-514)*, 858 (US Government Printing Office 1987) (1986 Bluebook) (the 1986 Bluebook described the function of the gross-up in the following way: 'Under present and prior law, the amount of foreign tax thus eligible for the

may be argued that the lack of a 'gross-up' is contrary to the rationale of the indirect tax credit.

If a main rationale (*see supra* note 284) is to equalize the tax treatment of taxpayers that invest abroad directly via a branch and taxpayers that invest abroad 'indirectly' via a subsidiary, in order to reduce tax distortions in business decisions or in order to treat a parent company and its subsidiary as more integrated (so that the situation of a head office and its foreign branch, viewed as the same taxpayer, can be transposed to some extent to the situation of a parent company and its foreign subsidiary, under certain circumstances, such as majority ownership), then evidently the calculations for the direct credit, which is offered in the case of branches, and the indirect credit, which is offered in the case of subsidiaries, need to be aligned. According to Elisabeth A. Owens:

> 'If the tax treatment of foreign corporations and foreign branches is to be equalized, which is the objective of correcting the § 902 [indirect credit] calculation, "grossing up" is the only proper method of correction because "grossing up" is, in effect, required for branches which receive a full credit and no deduction for foreign creditable taxes. The treatment cannot be fully equalized by allowing a full credit and no deduction for branch taxes while granting a deduction and a partial credit for subsidiary taxes.'[305]

If the rationale is to eliminate (as accurately as possible) economic double taxation, this too offers support for using the 'gross-up' amount. Otherwise, the combination of a reduction in the *tax base* by the foreign taxes *plus* a reduction in *taxes due* by the foreign taxes may go beyond this objective, or too far, because it may result in a 'tax saving' on income earned through foreign subsidiaries.

The US experience illustrates this issue.[306] Unlike the direct credit, no 'gross-up' was required for the indirect credit, until years later under Section 78 of the Revenue Act of 1962.[307] With both a deduction and a credit, this systematically lowered the overall rate to which the taxpayer was subject in the US. Rather than being subject to the US statutory rate, the taxpayer became subject to 'the effective United States rate (United States rate as reduced by effect of deduction)'; as a result, depending on the foreign tax rate, the 'taxpayer paid the higher of the foreign rate' or this lower effective US tax rate.[308] Based on a US corporate tax rate of 52%,[309] Elisabeth A. Owens calculated that the taxpayer's overall rate could end up as low as 34% or, even under

---

indirect credit is also "grossed-up" and included in the U.S. corporate shareholder's income to treat the shareholder as if it had received its proportionate share of pre-tax profits and paid its proportionate share of foreign tax').

304. Elisabeth A. Owens, *The Foreign Tax Credit: A Study of the Credit for Foreign Taxes under United States Income Tax Law* 118 n.63 (Harvard Law School 1961).
305. *Id.*, at 118 n.63.
306. *Id.*, at 113 & n.57.
307. United States, Senate, Committee on Finance, Eighty-Seventh Congress, Session II, *Brief Summary of Provisions in H.R. 10650 the 'Revenue Act of 1962'* (US Government Printing Office 1962); Gordon Nicholson, *Gross-Up and the Tax Credit*, 16(1) Tax Executive 31 (1963).
308. Elisabeth A. Owens, *The Foreign Tax Credit: A Study of the Credit for Foreign Taxes under United States Income Tax Law* 113 n.57 (Harvard Law School 1961).
309. *See id.*, at 114 n.58 (regarding the assumptions used for the US corporate tax rate at that time).

the *American Chicle* fraction (explained below), 45.24%, thus achieving a 'tax saving' that could amount to 'a 13% reduction from the tax rate of 52%' (in cases where the foreign tax rate was 26%).[310]

Subsequent developments in the indirect credit calculation: interaction between the apportionment fraction and 'gross-up'

This 'tax saving' issue was exacerbated by ambiguities in the US statutory language. Depending on how the terms in the fraction were interpreted, this could either increase or decrease the tax saving or this could potentially create altogether other distortions or inequities.

For example, under the statutory language of the Revenue Act of 1918, the proportion of the foreign subsidiary's taxes that the US parent was 'deemed to have paid' was apportioned by the fraction: dividends received over 'total taxable income of such foreign corporation'.[311] The term 'total taxable income' was not defined, and the question arose as to whether this should be total taxable income under US law or whether this should be the total taxable income under foreign law. It had to be clarified in case law: 'in *United Dyewood Corporation v. Bowers*, decided under the Revenue Act of 1918 [...] "total taxable income" was held to be the sum used *by the foreign government* as its tax base' (emphasis added; footnote omitted).[312]

To offer a comparison, under the statutory language of the Revenue Act of 1921, the 'deemed' credit was apportioned by the fraction: dividends received over 'the accumulated profits of such foreign corporation'.[313] This time, the term was defined directly in the statute as 'the amount of its gains, profits, or income in excess of the income, war-profits, and excess-profits taxes imposed upon or with respect to such profits or income'.[314] In other words, it was the total 'gains, profits, or income' minus the related foreign taxes. To consider the possible effects of the different terms and their interpretation, vis-à-vis the 'gross-up' (or lack thereof), an example can help illustrate the possible tax savings or other results.

---

310. *Id.*, at 113 & n.57 (it is noteworthy that these were her findings even after the US Commissioner had tried to correct for the tax savings by succeeding in the *American Chicle* case to apply an additional fraction to reduce the credit; before that case, the tax savings could be even greater), 116 (explaining the 13% reduction) and 126 (further elaborating on the 26% rate).
311. United States, Revenue Act of 1918, Sixty-Fifth Congress, Session III, Chapter 18, Public Law 65-254, Section 240(c) (US Government Printing Office 1919).
312. Elisabeth A. Owens, *The Foreign Tax Credit: A Study of the Credit for Foreign Taxes under United States Income Tax Law* 109–110 (Harvard Law School 1961) (citing '*United Dyewood Corporation v. Bowers*, 44 F. 2d 399, 402 (S.D. N.Y. 1930)').
313. United States, Revenue Act of 1921, Sixty-Seventh Congress, Session I, Chapter 136, Public Law 67-98, Section 238(e) (US Government Printing Office 1921). The rationale for this change of wording was neither in the book of Elisabeth A. Owens nor in the Congressional Report.
314. United States, Revenue Act of 1921, Sixty-Seventh Congress, Session I, Chapter 136, Public Law 67-98, Section 238(e) (US Government Printing Office 1921).

Example No. 14: Interpretation Issues in the Apportionment Fraction

Facts: A parent company in State R is the 100% sole shareholder of its subsidiary company in State S. Assume a 20% tax rate in State S and a 25% tax rate in State R. In State S, the subsidiary generates 100 on which it pays corporate taxes of 20 to State S. The subsidiary then distributes everything to its parent company. Assume also that the figures in State R and in State S are the same.

Under the Revenue Act of 1918 + *United Dyewood Corporation v. Bowers*

Indirect FTC = Eligible Foreign Taxes Paid × Dividends/ Total Taxable Income

Indirect FTC = 20 × 80/100.

Indirect FTC = 16.

Under the Revenue Act of 1921

Indirect FTC = Eligible Foreign Taxes Paid × Dividends/Accumulated Profits

'Accumulated Profits' = profits – foreign tax imposed on the profits

= 100 – 20 = 80

Indirect FTC = 20 × 80/80.

Indirect FTC = 20.

Regarding the issue of possible tax savings, when the above calculations are combined with the absence of any 'gross-up', it is clear that the second calculation exacerbates the issue. The following allows for a comparison:

- Potential US tax savings = (amount of foreign taxes *not* included in the tax base, due to the absence of a 'gross-up' × fictive US tax rate) + credit
- Potential US tax savings = (20 × 25%) + 16 = 5 + 16 = 21
- Potential US tax savings = (20 × 25%) + 20 = 5 + 20 = 25

Upon recognizing this effect of the definition of 'accumulated profits' in the Revenue Act of 1921, the US Commissioner sought to remedy this. There are two ways to address the issue: either increase the US tax base (so that it is not reduced by the foreign taxes, i.e., apply a 'gross-up') or reduce the credit. The US Commissioner argued for the latter, namely that the credit should be reduced further. Eventually, years later in 1942, a case on this issue, *American Chicle Co. v. United States*, made its way to the US Supreme Court.[315] The Supreme Court upheld the position of the Commissioner. The result was to apply an additional fraction to the foreign taxes paid to reduce the credit, ideally to the extent of the deduction of those foreign taxes (hereinafter 'the additional limiting fraction').

315. Elisabeth A. Owens, *The Foreign Tax Credit: A Study of the Credit for Foreign Taxes under United States Income Tax Law* 104–105 (Harvard Law School 1961) (citing '316 U.S. 450 (1942)').

Example No. 15: The Additional Limiting Fraction

Same facts: A parent company in State R is the 100% sole shareholder of its subsidiary company in State S. Assume a 20% tax rate in State S and a 25% tax rate in State R. In State S, the subsidiary generates 100 on which it pays corporate taxes of 20 to State S. The subsidiary then distributes everything to its parent company. Assume also that the figures under State R and under State S are the same.

Indirect FTC = Eligible Foreign Taxes Paid × (Dividend/Accumulated Profits)
× (Accumulated Profits/Total Profits)

Indirect FTC = 20 × (80/80) × (80/100)

Indirect FTC = 16

Notice that the formula can be simplified by cancelling out the similar terms in the two fractions:[316]

Indirect FTC = Foreign Tax Paid × (Dividend/~~Accumulated Profits~~)
× (~~Accumulated Profits~~/Total Profits)

Indirect FTC = Foreign Tax Paid × (Dividend/Total Profits)

As can be seen, applying this additional fraction leads to the same result as the formula using the term 'total taxable income' under the Revenue Act of 1918. However, this is, in part, because of the simplifying assumptions made (i.e., that the figures under foreign law and State R law are the same). Recall that the term 'total taxable income' under the Revenue Act of 1918 was interpreted by the *United Dyewood Corporation v. Bowers* case as referring to the taxable income under the *foreign state's* laws. Against that background, whether the result of the 'total taxable income' fraction would be the same, in practice, as that of this '*American Chicle*' fraction would depend on the interpretation of the term 'total profits' in the additional '*American Chicle*'-limiting fraction, e.g., whether it refers to the sum under US law or under foreign law.

Did the US Commissioner achieve the goal? According to Elisabeth A. Owens, the tax savings was not eliminated. In fact, the aforementioned possibility to achieve up to a 13% reduction from the normal statutory tax rate (*supra* note 310) was calculated fully taking into account the additional limiting fraction of the *American Chicle* case.[317]

One simple way to calculate the tax savings that remain *in spite of* the additional limiting fraction is to compare '[t]he value of the deduction in reducing the United States tax', which is a benefit for the taxpayer, with 'the reduction in credit because of the *American Chicle* fraction',[318] which counteracts some of that benefit. In the above

316. *Id.*, at 105.
317. *Id.*, at 113–118 (*see* in particular 113 n.57).
318. *Id.*, at 113.

example, since the full 100 are *not* taken into account in the tax base of State R (as the dividend of 80 is not 'grossed up'), the tax base in State R is reduced by the foreign taxes paid of 20 and, as a result, the amount of State R taxes that the taxpayer is spared is: 20 multiplied by the tax rate of State R, or 20 × 25% = 5. To counteract this, the credit is reduced, which means that part of the foreign taxes is no longer credited in State R. The value of this reduction 'is the *foreign tax rate* times the foreign tax paid':[319] 20 × 20% = 4. In the end, this part of the tax base, 20, is excluded from the State R tax base, leading to the advantage of 5, and is taxed fully *only* in State S, leading to a cost (which is no longer offset by a credit) of 4, so an overall benefit of 1 remains. Some amount of benefit, or tax savings, will remain as long as the foreign tax rate is less than the tax rate in State R.[320]

Is the 'gross-up' a better solution? To answer this, first start with the more fundamental question asked above (*supra* note 280, repeated again here for convenience, in italics): *In such a case, with a 100% shareholder receiving a full distribution, the question is: should the calculation lead to a result where the full taxes of 20 are creditable or should it allow a credit only for 16 corresponding to the 80 received as dividends in the US, thereby denying a credit for the portion of taxes on the 100 that corresponds to the 20 of taxes paid to the foreign government?* As mentioned above, the answer depends on the rationale of the indirect credit and the rationale of this fraction. Also, as mentioned above, there are two possible responses at first glance. *On the one hand, a credit for only 16 (instead of the full 20) could be considered a strange result since the parent company is the 100% owner and sole shareholder of this subsidiary, to which it distributed all of its profits.* After all, one rationale of the indirect credit is to treat the two taxpayers as more integrated or to equalize the treatment with that of a foreign branch. *On the other hand, this could be considered the appropriate result since only 80 is received in the US and 16 is the amount of taxes that corresponds to 80, whereas the full 20 corresponds to the full 100 not entirely received in the US.* After all, there was no 'gross-up' in the US law, meaning only the after-tax profits were assessed there. Indeed, as long as no 'gross-up' was provided for under US law, the US Commissioner's response (of tacking on an additional fraction to reduce the credit) would appear to be one reasonable way to approach the problem of the tax savings. However, as shown above, not only did the Commissioner's additional fraction fail to fully eliminate the potential tax savings but also, as Elisabeth A. Owens argues, it is not aligned with the rationale of the indirect credit. On this latter point, one possible counterargument that she considered is that, because only the after-tax profits are received as dividends in the US, meaning only this amount (net of the amount of profits used to pay the tax) is actually subject to US tax, it follows that the US would not tax the amount *not* so received, i.e., 'foreign profits used to pay foreign taxes ... never received by the parent corporation'.[321] She then put forward her response:

---

319. *Id.*
320. For more details on the algebraic expression of this tax saving, Elisabeth A. Owens, *The Foreign Tax Credit: A Study of the Credit for Foreign Taxes under United States Income Tax Law* 113–118 (Harvard Law School 1961).
321. *Id.*, at 116–117.

> 'The defect in this line of argument is that it is based on a premise which would eliminate the justification for the section 902(a) credit itself. The argument is based on the assumption that the foreign subsidiary and the United States parent corporation are totally separate entities and that the income and taxes of one are unrelated to the income and taxes of the other. If this premise were accepted, there would be no reason for granting an indirect credit; if the profits of the subsidiary as earned are outside the United States tax jurisdiction and are not treated as if taxed by the United States, there is no reason for granting a credit for foreign taxes imposed on these profits. The indirect credit is based on the opposite premise that the foreign and the domestic corporation are one integrated taxpayer; the foreign taxes creditable under section 902(a) are treated as if they were taxes imposed on income of the United States corporation. [...] When an actual withholding tax is imposed, it is accepted without question that if the tax is to be credited it cannot also be deducted. This is exactly the issue which is involved in the section 902(a) calculation.'[322]

Her arguments rely on the rationale of the indirect tax credit according to which the profits, and thus the taxes imposed thereon, of the subsidiary are considered – economically at least – to also be those of the parent corporation. And, in the last part of the arguments, she touches upon the rationale based on an equality of treatment between taxpayers benefiting from the direct credit (e.g., with a foreign branch) and those not benefiting (as discussed at *supra* note 284 and note 305).

What also follows from considering the profits of the subsidiary to be the profits of the parent is a 'gross-up', i.e., the same profits that were the tax base for the subsidiary are the tax base for the parent. This also helps achieve a parity of result with the direct credit since the full amount of the taxable income (before foreign income taxes, i.e., with a form of 'gross-up') is the tax base in that case. Ultimately, in the Revenue Act of 1962, the US legislators decided that the 'gross-up' was the better solution for the indirect credit. The Committee on Finance of the US Senate explained that the current situation results in an 'overallowance for these foreign taxes paid', the 'gross-up' will correct this, and it better 'corresponds to the treatment of individuals who take credit'.[323]

Subsequent developments in the indirect credit calculation: apportionment fraction

In addition to its interaction with the 'gross-up', the apportionment fraction is not free from its own design and interpretation issues, as seen above in Example No. 14. To consider these issues, the rationale for the fraction (dividends/accumulated profits) is a helpful starting point.

The rationale – or perhaps more precisely, the function or aim – is to calculate the proportion of foreign taxes paid by the subsidiary that are 'deemed' to be paid by the parent corporation, by determining the proportion of the foreign taxes related to the dividends received by the parent. Thus, this apportionment would be necessary only when: (1) less than the full amount of the subsidiary's profits is distributed and/or (2)

322. *Id.*
323. United States, Senate, Committee on Finance, Eighty-Seventh Congress, Session II, *Brief Summary of Provisions in H.R. 10650 the 'Revenue Act of 1962'*, 8 (US Government Printing Office 1962) (regarding 'The gross-up of foreign dividends (sec. 11)').

there is more than one shareholder.[324] After all, it is an 'apportionment' fraction. If it is accepted that the rationale(s) of the indirect 'deemed' credit is based on the idea that the profits of the subsidiary should be considered the profits of the parent (under certain conditions of ownership and upon receipt of profit distributions) and, correspondingly, the taxes imposed on those profits are considered indirectly paid by the parent, then what follows is that, when the parent is the 100% sole shareholder of the subsidiary entitled to all of the profits, all of the foreign taxes should be creditable; this occurs only when the fraction is 1/1.[325] What this means is that the amounts in the numerator and in the denominator should be aligned.

However, the terms that constitute the numerator (i.e., dividends) and denominator (e.g., 'total taxable income' in 1918, 'accumulated profits' in 1921) of this apportionment fraction may not lend themselves to a consistent and clear interpretation. The denominator was particularly problematic (*see*, e.g., Example No. 14 and *supra* notes 311-313). Even after US legislators decided to more clearly define the term 'accumulated profits' directly in the law,[326] one of the key components of the definition - 'gains, profits or income of the foreign corporation' - remained undefined. Accordingly, six different ways to interpret the statutory language 'gains, profits or income of the foreign corporation' were possible, argued Elisabeth A. Owens:

> '1. "Taxable income" of the foreign corporation as computed under foreign law.
> 2. "Taxable income" of the foreign corporation as computed under United States law.
> 3. Book income or profits of the foreign corporation as computed under foreign account practice.
> 4. Book income or profits of the foreign corporation as computed under United States accounting practice.
> 5. "Earnings and profits" of the foreign corporation as computed under foreign tax law.
> 6. "Earnings and profits" of the foreign corporation as computed under United States tax law.'[327]

This list points to two sets of questions. The first overarching question that arises under the credit method is whether FSI used in the fraction should be based on the sums as determined *under foreign law* or *under the credit-granting state's law*. Next, as is well known, the income calculated according to tax laws (taxable income) or the income calculated according to accounting rules (book income) may, and often do, differ. In addition, there was the term 'earnings and profits' (E&P), a specific US tax concept that was (and still is) used to determine whether a distribution can be

324. Elisabeth A. Owens, *The Foreign Tax Credit: A Study of the Credit for Foreign Taxes under United States Income Tax Law* 104 (Harvard Law School 1961).
325. *Id.*, at 122.
326. United States, Revenue Act of 1921, Sixty-Seventh Congress, Session I, Chapter 136, Public Law 67-98, Section 238(e) (US Government Printing Office 1921) ('the amount of its gains, profits, or income in excess of the income, war-profits, and excess-profits taxes imposed upon or with respect to such profits or income').
327. Elisabeth A. Owens, *The Foreign Tax Credit: A Study of the Credit for Foreign Taxes under United States Income Tax Law* 120 (Harvard Law School 1961).

considered a dividend and its 'taxable status'.[328] Which of the above figures or standards (taxable income, book income, E&P) should be used? Or should another standard be used?

These questions have received different answers over time. Given how central the answers to these questions are to the functioning of the credit method, the following paragraphs trace the legal debates over these questions. Although oriented around the legislative developments in the US, this discussion intentionally teases out arguments and proposals that could be more widely relevant, beyond the US, for other jurisdictions grappling with the credit method.

From the above list (of six possible statutory constructions), although no definitive answer had been given at that time, Elisabeth A. Owens reasoned by process of elimination, based on what little information could be garnered at the time,[329] that 'construction 6 [was] the most reasonable interpretation of the statutory language'.[330] Owens argued that construction 1 (taxable income as computed under foreign law) was excluded.[331] This view was seemingly the exact opposite of what a US Court had previously held to be the figure for the denominator; however, that court decision was rendered based on the previous wording ('total taxable income') of the Revenue Act of 1918 (*see*, e.g., *supra* note 312). By contrast, others argued that the term 'accumulated profits' still refers to 'taxable income under foreign law less the foreign tax imposed thereon' since there was no evidence that Congress had intended to change it.[332]

The starting point for Owens' opinion was that, in her view, a case, *Untermyer v. Com.*, had already clarified the term 'dividends', which is in the numerator: when dividends are received from a foreign corporation, the taxable amount is to be computed in the same way as for a domestic corporation, which in turn is based on the rules regarding 'earnings and profits'.[333] The next step of reasoning is that, once it is determined that the numerator ('dividends') is based on a certain standard, then it logically follows that the denominator ('accumulated profits') should be based on the same standard. Otherwise, 'illogical' results follow.

For example, if 'dividends' is related to the 'earnings and profits' as computed under the law of the state of residence, State R, while 'accumulated profits' in the

328. *Id.*, at 121; *Earnings and Profits, Black's Law Dictionary* (9th ed. 2009) (the term 'earnings and profits' is defined as follows: '*Corporations*. In corporate taxation, the measure of a corporation's economic capacity to make a shareholder distribution that is not a return of capital. – The distribution will be dividend income to the shareholders to the extent of the corporation's current and accumulated earnings and profits'). For more on the term 'earnings and profits', *see also infra* note 349.

329. Elisabeth A. Owens, *The Foreign Tax Credit: A Study of the Credit for Foreign Taxes under United States Income Tax Law* 120–125 (Harvard Law School 1961) (relying *inter alia* on 'an early ruling of the Service', on case law interpreting the 'quantity which is taxable as a "dividend" when received as a distribution from a foreign corporation', and on what construction would seem to be 'most reasonable' and would avoid 'illogical consequences').

330. *Id.*, at 122.

331. *Id.*, at 123–124.

332. *Id.*, at 122–123 n.73 (citing and summarizing an argument by Gallagher).

333. *Id.*, at 121; Marcus Schoenfeld, *Some Definitional Problems in the Deemed Paid Foreign Tax Credit of Section 902: 'Dividends' and 'Accumulated Profits'*, 18(3) Tax L. Rev. 401, 411 (1963) (summarizing the arguments of Elisabeth A. Owens).

fraction refers to 'taxable income under foreign law less the foreign tax imposed thereon', it could lead to strange results. If the facts are the same as above (in Example No. 14 and Example No. 15) – i.e., the foreign subsidiary distributes everything to its sole shareholder in State R, the foreign taxes paid by the subsidiary are 20 and the dividend received is 80 – *except that* the taxable income *under foreign law* is lower, e.g., 75, then the indirect credit calculation would be: 20 × 80/75 = 21.33, i.e., a 'tax credit greater than the tax paid'.[334] If for whatever reason the foreign figure were higher than 80, e.g., 90, then the credit is less than the foreign taxes paid. In both cases, the lack of correspondence between the sum used in the numerator and that in the denominator leads to an 'improper amount of tax credit'.[335] The problem is far from a theoretical possibility. It is not uncommon for the sums arrived at under the six aforementioned possibilities to differ, as case law evidences (*see* footnote for examples).[336]

In response, another scholar put forward a different solution. Schoenfeld agrees that both the numerator and the denominator are 'to be determined under United States principles of law', but is *not* convinced that accumulated profits 'are identical to the earnings and profits'.[337] The keyword is identical. Regarding the point of agreement, Schoenfeld reasons that 'since an American statute is being construed, under basic principles of conflicts of laws, American concepts are used to construe that American statute'.[338] In support of this, he also cites the *Untermyer* case, regarding an American shareholder in a Canadian corporation, which held that American law standards should be used: 'while Canadian law applied to the corporation, American law applied to the shareholder; therefore the character of the distribution in the hands of the

334. Elisabeth A. Owens, *The Foreign Tax Credit: A Study of the Credit for Foreign Taxes under United States Income Tax Law* 122 (Harvard Law School 1961).
335. *Id.*, at 122.
336. To offer just three examples, first, *see*, e.g., Elisabeth A. Owens, *The Foreign Tax Credit: A Study of the Credit for Foreign Taxes under United States Income Tax Law* 123 (Harvard Law School 1961) (*The United Fruit Co. v. Hasset* case, in 1938, in an excerpt quoted by Owens, offers an example of the taxable income differing in the two states: a foreign subsidiary reported a 'taxable income under the laws of Great Britain of $397,475.09' and a 'profit of $76,476.71 from casual capital gains not included in taxable income under British law' yet for US purposes 'Internal Revenue adjusted the foreign subsidiary's income to a United States income tax basis and determined that the total profits of the foreign subsidiary for 1938 were $434,879.49, including the $76,476.71 of capital gains'); second, *see*, e.g., Philip Baker, *Some Aspects of United Kingdom Double Taxation Relief*, 52(10) Bull. Int'l Fiscal Documentation 445, 450 (1998) (the *Yates v. CGA* case, regarding a direct credit calculation (rather than an indirect credit), in 1979 in the UK, offers an example of how much the commercial profits according to accounting rules can differ from taxable income: a 'company's commercial profit before tax for the accounting period ending 31 December 1979 was GBP 25,577, and its taxable profits for UK corporation tax purposes (after adding back certain non-allowable deductions, such as depreciation) was GBP 40,995'); third, *see*, e.g., Philip Baker, *Some Aspects of United Kingdom Double Taxation Relief*, 52(10) Bull. Int'l Fiscal Documentation 445, 452 (1998) (the 'Notes to Clauses to the autumn Finance Bill in 1945' in the UK offers an example for calculating the limit of the credit in which it explicitly assumes divergent rules for taxable income in the US and in the UK: 'Suppose the trader's United States profits are assessed at GBP 1,000 in the United States, tax (at 40 per cent) GBP 400; and suppose that the United Kingdom measure of the same profits is GBP 900 tax (at 9 shillings) GBP 405; [...]').
337. Marcus Schoenfeld, *Some Definitional Problems in the Deemed Paid Foreign Tax Credit of Section 902: 'Dividends' and 'Accumulated Profits'*, 18(3) Tax L. Rev. 401, 411 (1963).
338. *Id.*, at 412 and 420.

shareholder was determined under American law'.[339] However, this does not render it impossible to use foreign concepts: 'if the foreign concept were incorporated by reference into American law, it would then become an "American concept"'.[340] In support of this, the previous term 'total taxable income', used under the Revenue Act of 1918, was held to refer to the taxable income under foreign law.

Regarding the point of disagreement, Schoenfeld challenged both the starting point of Owens' reasoning and her six possibilities for interpreting the definition of 'accumulated profits'. As for her starting point, according to Schoenfeld, another case, *Steel Improvement and Forge Co*, seems to endorse a *different* understanding of the term 'dividends' than that which Owens relied on.[341] The precise details are too US-specific to serve the purpose here, which is to gather more widely relevant considerations for how best to design this fraction. Suffice it to say that, if Owens' starting point (that the numerator 'dividends' relates to the concept 'earnings and profits') is challenged, then her conclusion (that the denominator 'accumulated profits' relates to the concept 'earnings and profits') no longer follows. What is *not* challenged, however, is her argumentation that: ideally, whatever concept is used for 'dividends' should be used also for the denominator, to avoid the above-mentioned 'improper' amounts of credit (*supra* note 335). This is reasoning that can be considered by any jurisdiction contemplating the design of the fraction.

More importantly, Schoenfeld argued that there are *other* possibilities for the denominator of the fraction, beyond the six possible interpretations that Owens listed. Indeed, rather than tying 'accumulated profits' to one specific already-existing US tax concept, the term could be viewed as 'an independent concept' or 'separate term of art'.[342] One argument is that, since this specific US concept of 'earnings and profits' is apparently a complex one characterized by detailed rules, he emphasized the insurmountable practical difficulties if the exact same rules for 'earnings and profits' were applied to a foreign corporation.[343] Building more broadly upon this point, another argument is that, '[s]econd, much confusion may be avoided by remembering that a foreign corporation is not a domestic corporation, and therefore there is no reason to treat it as if it were'.[344] What follows is that:

> 'Identical concepts need not be used; analogous concepts will suffice. The use of independent analogous concepts avoids forcing square pegs into round holes.'[345]

As a proposal, he put forward his definition of 'accumulated profits', which would be one that:

> 'is close to "earnings and profits," but because of practical problems cannot be identical thereto. It is an adjusted book income, as is "earnings and profits," with

339. *Id.*, at 408 (summarizing the case '21 B.T.A. 906 (1931), aff'd per curiam, 59 F.2d 1004 (2d Cir. 1932), cert. denied, 287 U.S. 647 (1932)').
340. *Id.*, at 412 (1963).
341. *Id.*, at 403 and 411.
342. *Id.*, at 416.
343. *Id.*, at 412–415.
344. *Id.*, at 420.
345. *Id.*

adjustments made much as they would be for "earnings and profits," but without requiring hypothetical elections'.[346]

And flexibility is needed:

'these similar concepts should serve as guides for defining new terms of art. Applying a rule of reason will determine what variances should exist'.[347]

In sum, Schoenfeld sought to offer a pragmatic solution that is aligned as much as possible with the US rules while allowing divergences where reasonable and necessary to take into account the inherent differences between domestic and foreign subsidiaries.

Another approach to finding a solution would be to orient the calculation around the two main aims of the indirect FTC. A discussion of such an approach could resonate beyond the borders of US tax law specificities since jurisdictions that implement an indirect credit will likely share a similar rationale (or rationales) for doing so.

For example, Worley identified the two main aims of the indirect FTC as: (1) 'relief from international double taxation' and (2) the aim that 'domestic corporations that conduct their offshore operations through foreign subsidiaries should face the same overall tax consequences as corporations that operate directly in foreign countries through branches'.[348] In light of these aims, in his view, it is absurd to base the denominator of the fraction on the US-specific concept of 'earnings and profits' (or any similar concept). It diverges, sometimes too far, from the 'taxable income' that gives rise to the problem of double taxation in the first place. Consequently, it may lead to situations where the indirect FTC cannot achieve its first aim of relief for double taxation.

To explain, 'earnings and profits' often begins from 'taxable income' but then is subject to various adjustments.[349] For example, it may be the case that interest income earned on a government bond or municipal bond would be tax exempt and thus would be excluded from 'taxable income', but because such interest is a cash flow received by the corporation, it would be added back in for computing the 'earnings and profits' that could be available for distribution. Due to the numerous special add-ins and subtractions, it is not only difficult to compute but also 'an inept yardstick by which to measure the amount of foreign taxable income that has been repatriated in a distribution from a foreign corporation',[350] in part, because 'earnings and profits' can be divorced from taxable income or even from the overall success of corporation.[351] According to Worley, the amount that should be considered is that which was 'subjected to foreign taxation'; in fact, there are cases where, despite there being foreign taxable income,

346. Marcus Schoenfeld, *Some Definitional Problems in the Deemed Paid Foreign Tax Credit of Section 902: 'Dividends' and 'Accumulated Profits'*, 18(3) Tax L. Rev. 401, 421 (1963).
347. *Id.*
348. Ronald A. Worley, *The Indirect Foreign Tax Credit: A Policy Analysis of Section 902*, 13(2) Intl Tax & Bus Law 176, 197 (1996) (citing the 1986 Bluebook).
349. *Id.*, at 199–202.
350. *Id.*, at 203.
351. *Id.*, at 203 n.180.

there is a deficit from the US perspective in E&P.[352] As a consequence of the disconnect between 'earnings and profits' and 'taxable income', there are situations of a permanent loss or indefinite deferral of any FTC, even when taxable dividends are distributed.[353] Thus, using this figure clearly does not meet the first aim in Worley's view.

Instead, for the indirect tax credit, policymakers could take inspiration from the rules used to compute the direct FTC in the case of taxes paid by foreign branches. This tends to be a figure more closely correlated with 'taxable income'.[354] If so, such an approach would serve to align the indirect tax credit calculation more with its objective of relief for international double taxation and, simultaneously, with the second objective of equalizing the tax consequences of investing abroad via a branch versus via a subsidiary.

Alternatively, Worley developed a more detailed proposal, suggesting (as one component of a broader packaged-proposal, other aspects of which are discussed below, in the subsection on timing issues) that the amount could be that as determined under foreign law. More specifically, this figure should *not* be 'processed' via the US 'earnings and profits mechanism' in order to determine 'accumulated profits' for the apportionment fraction, but rather it could be 'determined under foreign law'.[355] He referred to it, straightforwardly, as the 'undistributed net income of the subsidiary for that taxable year', which is equal to the 'net amount after foreign taxes paid'.[356] In addition to better adhering to the aims, Worley predicts this would bring significant simplifications.

Debates over whether to adopt the domestic law computation or the foreign law computation have proven more widely relevant. They arose not only in the US, but also in the UK, and not only for the indirect credit, but also for the direct credit. By comparison, in the UK context, doubts over 'whether in computing the limit on foreign tax credit one uses the foreign, source country's measure of taxable income ... or whether one applies the UK measure of taxable income' remained as recently as 1998.[357]

In an article discussing the direct tax credit in the UK, Baker weighed arguments both for and against both approaches. Some arguments advanced in favour of adopting the sum as calculated under foreign-source rules included, *inter alia*, that it would be

352. *Id.*, at 203 n.179.
353. *Id.*, at 179 and 204–205.
354. *Id.*, at 198–199 & n.154.
355. *Id.*, at 215–216 & n.255 & n.257 (he acknowledges concerns regarding the potential differences between income determination under foreign law as compared to under US law, but in his view, such differences can be addressed. If the differences are minimal, they may simply be 'disregarded as they are under the existing provisions with respect to the direct foreign tax credit'. If the differences are significant, they may be taken into account in the assessment of 'whether the foreign taxes qualify as creditable taxes').
356. Ronald A. Worley, *The Indirect Foreign Tax Credit: A Policy Analysis of Section 902*, 13(2) Intl Tax & Bus Law 176, 215–216 (1996).
357. Philip Baker, *Some Aspects of United Kingdom Double Taxation Relief*, 52(10) Bull. Int'l Fiscal Documentation 445, 445–446 (1998).

more in line with 'the rationale of double taxation relief' and with much sought-after 'simplicity'.[358]

Regarding the argument based on 'the rationale of double taxation relief', what underpins it is the desire 'to ensure that international trade and investment is not deterred by double taxation'.[359] In other words, it peels back another layer, figuratively speaking: the rationale for the credit method is double taxation relief and, underneath this, the rationale for double taxation relief is to *not* deter international trade and investment. Where the foreign taxes are *un*able to be credited in full in the UK, this results in 'a higher amount than if all the income arose from sources in the United Kingdom'.[360] The concern that seems to be implied, though it is not explicitly stated, is that, when the overall burden is higher, this could deter international trade and investment. The perspective adopted here, rather than looking only at what the UK collects on the income in question, looks at the overall tax burden on the taxpayer, taking into account both states.

To support the argument, the particularly striking example of the *Yates v. GCA International Limited* case is analysed, where the taxable income in Venezuela was significantly higher than the amount considered taxable in the UK, leading in turn to a significant amount of foreign taxes that were unable to be credited.[361] In addition to this case, to offer further context, Baker reported an increasing number of instances where foreign WHTs could not be entirely credited, since foreign states often levied taxes on the gross amount of income, especially in cases of 'interest, royalties or technical service fees',[362] whereas the UK would use the net amount of income.

In sum, calculating the credit limitation on the basis of the income as computed under residence state rules can be considered problematic when there are significant differences from the amount of taxable income that the foreign state used (e.g., gross basis versus net basis). When this divergence becomes large enough, a significant amount of the foreign taxes may not be able to be credited in the state of residence. If it is accepted that 'the rationale of double taxation relief' is 'to ensure that international trade and investment is not deterred by double taxation', then taxpayers may argue that such situations go against this rationale.

358. *Id.*, at 453-454.
359. *Id.*
360. Philip Baker, *Some Aspects of United Kingdom Double Taxation Relief*, 52(10) Bull. Int'l Fiscal Documentation 453 (1998).
361. More precisely, in Venezuela, on a payment of USD 209,300 for services, '90 per cent of the gross receipts was deemed to be GCA's net profit from the contract' on which a tax of 30% was levied, amounting to a tax equal to 'GBP 22,353'. In the UK, the total taxable income was GBP 40,995 on which a tax of 52%, amounting to corporate tax of GBP 21,317. Importantly, this is the total taxable income, i.e., *before* determining how much of this net income corresponded to this Venezuelan service contract. Ultimately, only 'approximately 2.675 per cent of the turnover for that year derived from work performed in Venezuela', resulting therefore in a correspondingly small amount of the total Venezuelan taxes that could actually be credited. For further details, *see* Philip Baker, *Some Aspects of United Kingdom Double Taxation Relief*, 52(10) Bull. Int'l Fiscal Documentation 445, 450-451 (1998).
362. Philip Baker, *Some Aspects of United Kingdom Double Taxation Relief*, 52(10) Bull. Int'l Fiscal Documentation 445, 446 (1998).

As a counterargument, this concern relies upon the overall burden on the taxpayer, a result in which both states are implicated. The potential deterrent effect results from a combination of, e.g., Venezuela's taxation of (90% of) the gross amount of a contractual payment for services deemed only partly carried out in Venezuela and the UK's taxation of only the net amount of the company's overall income, which appeared to be significantly reduced by expenses. Thus, one could argue that in such an extreme case, it is not necessarily the relief mechanism of the UK at fault. It could be argued that Venezuela was perhaps the main perpetrator of the excessive taxation in this case and shared some responsibility for relief. Indeed, a variation on this theme arises again in the CJEU case law discussions (e.g., under Section 4.2.5. and Section 4.2.6.).

Regarding 'simplicity', similar to Worley, Baker states that adopting the foreign sum for the purposes of the credit limitation is a simpler approach, as this amount will already be 'known in order to calculate the amount of foreign tax'.[363] When the 'UK measure of profits' has to be used, the FSI has to be recomputed on the basis of domestic laws, which inevitably requires rules for allocating expenses between domestic and FSI. Either expenses can be allocated proportionately or 'a direct attribution of expenses may be necessary and may be extremely difficult'.[364] This argument invokes both practical considerations, concerning the administrability of the credit method and potential compliance struggles, and principled ones, concerning a central tenet of well-designed tax systems.[365]

On the other hand, Baker acknowledges that the rationale for the credit limitation is to ensure that high foreign tax rates do not have the effect of reducing the amount of taxes the 'State granting relief' collects on its own DSI. Though, he suggests that the 'State granting relief' could limit the relief to its domestic tax rate applied to the foreign sum of income and, in this way, it 'is not left totally unprotected'.[366] Nevertheless, he recognizes the coexistence of rationales and the 'conflict' between them.

As for the indirect credit in the US, later legislative and regulatory enactments indicate that the understanding of the denominator of the apportionment fraction continued to give rise to uncertainties.[367] That the question regularly arose is evidence of its importance in practice. First and foremost, it plays an important role since the larger the denominator, the smaller the fraction and thus the smaller the amount of foreign taxes that are deemed creditable, whereas the smaller the denominator, the larger the fraction and thus the larger the amount of foreign taxes that are deemed creditable. Thus, the uncertainties, combined with possible incentives to increase the

363. *Id.*, at 454.
364. *Id.*
365. *See*, e.g., *supra* note 248.
366. Philip Baker, *Some Aspects of United Kingdom Double Taxation Relief*, 52(10) Bull. Int'l Fiscal Documentation 445, 454 (1998).
367. *See*, e.g., James P. Fuller, *The Deemed Paid Foreign Tax Credit*, 1(2) Int'l Tax J. 105, 106–108 (1975); James P. Fuller, Frederick R. Chilton Jr. & Ronald B. Schrotenboer, *The Foreign Tax Credit*, 5(3) Hastings Int'l & Comp. L. Rev. 633, 642 (1982) (citing multiple cases and revenue rulings interpreting 'accumulated profits'); the Tax Reform Act of 1986 introduced yet another term for the denominator, i.e., 'post-1986 undistributed earnings'.

credit, generate tax planning opportunities.[368] In addition, as seen above, where the basis of sums used in the numerator diverge from those used in the denominator, it can lead to 'inappropriate' amounts of FTC (*see supra* note 334 and note 335); or where the sums used for calculating the credit diverge from those used to calculate the foreign taxes abroad, it can lead to a credit much smaller than foreign taxes paid (*see*, e.g., *supra* note 361) or to the credit being 'permanently lost' (*see supra* note 353). Moreover, as long as it remains unclear precisely which figures should be used or what standards should be adopted for computing the denominator (or, for that matter, for any part of the statutory formula for an FTC), this can result in inconsistent - and therefore unfair or unequal - treatment between taxpayers, since taxpayers will proceed with claiming their FTCs based on their different interpretations of the rules of computation, meaning taxpayers with otherwise equivalent facts could wind up with different amounts of FTCs.[369]

Subsequent developments in the indirect credit calculation: timing issues

Even if the credit-granting state clearly establishes the sums to be used in the apportionment fraction, there is yet another question that arises. In view of the 'equalization' aim of an indirect FTC, this leaves unaddressed one crucial difference between foreign branches and foreign subsidiaries, namely the timing difference. The income of foreign branches is included on an ongoing basis, whereas the income distributed by foreign subsidiaries is included only upon receipt of a distribution, leading to a 'substantial benefit of tax deferral'.[370] If the underlying rationale for equalization is that business decisions should ideally be *un*distorted by differences in tax treatment, this tax deferral continues to create a distortion and ideally should also be mitigated.[371]

Moreover, what creates this possibility of tax deferral is that there are two distinct taxable events in the case of a foreign subsidiary and its shareholder. First, the subsidiary generally pays CIT on the profits that it generates on an ongoing (e.g., annual) basis. Second, the subsidiary distributes some (or all) of those profits at a later date, possibly after accumulating profits for many years, which are then potentially taxable for the shareholder. The need to reconcile these two taxable events leads to a number of timing and attribution-related questions.

In her study of the US rules and legislative developments, Owens listed four points under the 'Method of Calculation' of the indirect credit, namely: (1) the 'Attribution of dividends to annual profits of foreign corporation', (2) 'Allocations

368. *See*, e.g., James P. Fuller, *The Deemed Paid Foreign Tax Credit*, 1(2) Int'l Tax J. 105, 108 (1975); James P. Fuller, Frederick R. Chilton Jr. & Ronald B. Schrotenboer, *The Foreign Tax Credit*, 5(3) Hastings Int'l & Comp. L. Rev. 633, 642 (1982).
369. *See*, e.g., Elisabeth A. Owens, *The Foreign Tax Credit: A Study of the Credit for Foreign Taxes under United States Income Tax Law* 122 (Harvard Law School 1961) (Owens mentions in n.73 the possible issue of 'a lack of uniformity in enforcement').
370. Ronald A. Worley, *The Indirect Foreign Tax Credit: A Policy Analysis of Section 902*, 13(2) Intl Tax & Bus Law 176, 179 & n.22, 196, and 185 & n.61 (1996) (hence the motivation for CFC rules for the cases where this benefit was deemed particularly inappropriate).
371. *Id.*, at 176, 211.

needed for calculation of the credit', (3) the 'Annual calculation of section 902(a) [indirect] tax credit' and (4) 'Credit for foreign tax paid "on or with respect to" profits of a given year'.[372] Three out of four - points (1), (3) and (4) - are related to timing issues.[373]

The first issue, namely the attribution of dividends to the annual profits of the foreign corporation, refers to the need to 'trace the source of the dividends to the foreign accumulated profits of a particular year or years'.[374] As a general approximation, one way of resolving this involves a rule that deems dividends to be paid out of profits in a certain order.

Harris uses different terminology, but is essentially discussing the same issues. He calls this an 'ordering rule'.[375] More precisely, Harris suggests that this issue requires a two-pronged approach: (1) a 'recording' mechanism, i.e., a system in place for maintaining records of the underlying corporate profits and their tax treatment and (2) an 'ordering rule'. Notably, Harris discusses this from the perspective of an 'imputation' credit system, but explains that these two features are design variables that are common to both 'imputation' and 'indirect' credit systems.[376]

The first feature ('recording the corporate tax') refers, in its simplest sense, to the requirement to carefully record the amount of foreign profits and corporate taxes paid with respect to those profits. Generally speaking, this may range from item-by-item approaches, i.e., recording each item of foreign income with its foreign taxes, to pooling approaches, i.e., 'recording foreign profits with their foreign tax agreement according to pools of certain types of profits', e.g., 'by type of income (*e.g.* passive income, active income), by tax rate suffered, by location or by date'.[377] It would also be possible to allow for pooling of 'all profits of the foreign subsidiary and all foreign tax paid with respect thereto'.[378] The second feature ('an ordering rule') requires that 'the system must specify which profits are considered distributed first'.[379] Options for ordering rules include attributing dividends to foreign profits on a pro rata basis, on a

372. Elisabeth A. Owens, *The Foreign Tax Credit: A Study of the Credit for Foreign Taxes under United States Income Tax Law* 89 (Harvard Law School 1961).
373. *Id.*, at 104 (the second point, i.e., 'Allocations needed for calculation of the credit', is essentially that of the 'apportionment fraction', already discussed above. Indeed, the formula of the underlying foreign tax multiplied by the fraction of the dividend over the 'accumulated profits' (usually the distributable after-tax profits) is the central calculation of the indirect credit, which serves to determine the amount of foreign taxes 'deemed' paid by the shareholder. It simultaneously serves to '[apportion the] creditable tax among shareholders' and to '[reduce the] amount of tax creditable because less than [the] entire accumulated profits of one year are distributed'. In addition, under this heading, Owens refers to the special calculation distortions discussed in connection with the US Supreme Court *American Chicle* case, discussed already at length, at *supra* note 315).
374. *Id.*, at 102.
375. Peter Harris, *An Historic View of the Principle and Options for Double Tax Relief*, 1999(6) Brit. Tax Rev. 469, 482–486 (1999).
376. *Id.*, at 482.
377. *Id.*, at 483–485.
378. *Id.*, at 485.
379. *Id.*

first-in-first-out (FIFO) basis, a last-in-first-out (LIFO) basis, or even on a lowest-taxed-profits-out-first basis.[380] In essence, these two features ask whether the foreign income of the subsidiary and its related taxes should be subdivided by type (or some other characteristic) and/or by time.

These two aspects are interrelated. For example, if the credit-granting state opts for recording and calculating the taxes on an annual basis, or what can also be referred to as a 'layers of earnings' method[381] – that is, if it seeks to trace the dividends to the underlying profits earned and taxes paid by the foreign subsidiary in each given year – then a choice regarding some sort of ordering rule, most likely between FIFO or LIFO, becomes almost inevitable. By comparison, if a state opts for a pooling approach, which pools all profits and all taxes of the foreign subsidiary together (regardless of the tax years in question), this may incorporate an 'inherent pro-rata ordering rule', as it assumes that the dividends are 'distributed proportionately' from the different types of income earned and from the different income tax years of the foreign subsidiary.[382] Example No. 16 below offers some insight into how the two compare.

The US used both approaches. The US applied a LIFO rule for the purposes of attributing the dividends to a given taxable year,[383] meaning the dividend was deemed to first derive from the profits of the most recent year, e.g., year 3, then from year 2, then year 1. Later, with the 1986 tax reform, the US adopted a 'pooling' approach.[384] Under such an approach, generally speaking, all undistributed accumulated profits are aggregated together, as though in one big pot, so to speak, and all the related taxes are likewise aggregated together, such that whenever dividends are distributed, they are considered to carry out with them a proportionate amount of the accumulated profits and of the related taxes, irrespective of the years in which they were accumulated or paid.

Under this same heading (i.e., 'Attribution of dividends to annual profits of foreign corporation'), Owens also asks another timing question regarding, in essence, the cut-off date for the accumulated profits to take into account. More specifically, since dividends can be paid at different points of time in the year, one question that could arise is 'whether a dividend should be attributed to the profits of the corporation's entire taxable year in which the dividend is paid or only to those profits earned up to the date the dividend is paid'.[385] This problem was one of US statutory interpretation, due to the language used at that time: 'Section 902(c)(1) provides that dividends shall be treated as having been paid from the "most recently accumulated"

380. *Id.*
381. Ronald A. Worley, *The Indirect Foreign Tax Credit: A Policy Analysis of Section 902*, 13(2) Intl Tax & Bus Law 176, 185 and 190–192 (1996).
382. Peter Harris, *An Historic View of the Principle and Options for Double Tax Relief*, 1999(6) Brit. Tax Rev. 469, 485 (1999).
383. Elisabeth A. Owens, *The Foreign Tax Credit: A Study of the Credit for Foreign Taxes under United States Income Tax Law* 102 (Harvard Law School 1961).
384. United States, Joint Committee on Taxation, *General Explanation of The Tax Reform Act of 1986 (H.R. 3838, 99th Congress; Public Law 99-514)*, 868–870 (US Government Printing Office 1987) (1986 Bluebook).
385. Elisabeth A. Owens, *The Foreign Tax Credit: A Study of the Credit for Foreign Taxes under United States Income Tax Law* 103 (Harvard Law School 1961).

gains, profits, or earnings.'[386] Thus, it was a search for the precise meaning of 'most recently accumulated' profits under the previous US LIFO ordering rule.

Nevertheless, it seems to be an issue that could arise more generally (beyond just the US). To address it, different approaches are: (1) to attribute the dividend to the entire taxable year in which the dividends were paid, (2) to attribute the dividend to the accumulated profits up to the point of distribution, or (3) to attribute the dividend to the 'profits for the last full taxable year'. Whether, in practice, the dividends stem from the current year's profits or from previous years may depend on the precise details of the shareholders' decision and any company law rules governing such decisions. Therefore, another approach would be possible, namely that the accumulated profits used for the purpose of the indirect credit should reflect the reality of what the shareholders actually decided, assuming the information is by law recorded in official minutes of meetings. The risk is that this could allow too much room to manoeuvre to taxpayers and result in taxpayers obtaining different tax treatment. Owens suggests that 'a uniform rule' be adopted, to avoid 'discriminatory treatment among taxpayers'.[387] Whichever approach is adopted is fine ('since all that is involved is the determination of what year's foreign taxes will be creditable on the distribution of a dividend, and if they are not creditable at one time they will be creditable at another'), as long as it is uniformly applied.[388]

Regarding the other timing issue identified by Owens (the 'Annual Calculation of Section 902(a) [Indirect] Tax Credit'),[389] in cases where the subsidiary accumulates profits over the course of multiple years and, then, distributes a dividend that encompasses profits from this multi-year period, the question arises as to whether one calculation should be made that aggregates the profits and related taxes of the multiple years together, or whether a calculation should be made for each year with the results then summed together. To illustrate, Owens' example (modified to disregard the *American Chicle* case) shows how this affects the result.

Example No. 16: Aggregate Calculation Versus Annual Calculation

Facts: Assume that, after three years of profit generation, a dividend of 2,000 is distributed to the sole shareholder. The taxes paid to the foreign state varied over the years (the reasons for which are not important, e.g., it could be due to changes in the tax rate or special rules applying to the tax base). The numbers are as follows:

386. *Id.*
387. *Id.*
388. *Id.*
389. Elisabeth A. Owens, *The Foreign Tax Credit: A Study of the Credit for Foreign Taxes under United States Income Tax Law* 106–107 (Harvard Law School 1961).

Year	Total Profits	Tax Paid	After-Tax Profit	Portion of Dividend Paid Out of Year's Profit (LIFO)
Y3	2,000	1,000	1,000	1,000
Y2	1,000	300	700	700
Y1	500	100	400	300
Total	**3,500**	**1,400**	**2,100**	**2,000**

Option 1: Aggregate Calculation

$$1{,}400 \text{ (aggregate taxes)} \times \frac{2{,}000 \text{ (dividend)}}{2{,}100 \text{ (aggregate distributable profits)}} = \mathbf{1{,}333.33}$$

Option 2: Annual Calculation

$$1{,}000 \text{ (Y3)} \times \frac{1{,}000}{1{,}000} = 1{,}000$$

$$300 \text{ (Y2)} \times \frac{700}{700} = 300$$

$$100 \text{ (Y1)} \times \frac{300}{400} = 75$$

Total: 1,375

Source: Modified version of an example from Elisabeth A. Owens, *The Foreign Tax Credit: A Study of the Credit for Foreign Taxes under United States Income Tax Law* 106–107 (Harvard Law School 1961) (with calculations modified to disregard the *American Chicle* case and slightly rearranged in its presentation).

According to Owens, the US Tax Court decided on the latter approach, namely a separate calculation for each year.[390] The underlying idea is that:

> 'The credit is calculated just as if the corporation had distributed its profits currently rather than accumulating them over several years. Averaging of the foreign tax rates over the years involved is thus precluded. In this respect, the taxpayer receiving an indirect credit under section 902 is not given a tax advantage over a taxpayer crediting foreign taxes which he has paid directly. The direct credit

390. *Id.* (citing *General Foods Corp.* '4 TC 209 (1944), *acq.*, 1946-1 CB 2.').

is taken on an annual basis and this kind of averaging of the foreign tax rates is impossible.'[391]

The former approach (Option 1) would be more aligned with a 'pooling' approach. As can be seen, depending on how much weight is given to the rationale (for the indirect tax credit) of equalizing the treatment between foreign subsidiaries and foreign branches, this can influence the design choice between an annual calculation versus a 'pooling'/aggregate calculation.

Regarding the last timing issue ('Credit for foreign tax paid "on or with respect to" profits of a given year'),[392] this refers to the connection – or rather the potential disconnect – between the foreign profits and the foreign taxes paid on those profits. Often the two are aligned, in that the tax base upon which the foreign taxes are assessed and paid is that of the profits generated in the tax year in question. However, they may diverge. Similar to the timing issue that can arise under a direct credit, a foreign state may calculate the taxes due in a given year based on the profits of a different year, or perhaps 'on the average income of two or more years'.[393]

For example, in the context of the direct credit under the OECD/UN Model, Rust listed this as the 'crediting period' issue, described as 'the period in respect of which foreign tax should be allowed as a credit'. Difficulties can arise if, for example, prepayments of taxes are required or where 'tax on income for a current year is calculated with reference to the income figure established for the preceding year' (emphasis omitted).[394]

This is equally relevant in the context of an indirect credit because, once a dividend is distributed and is deemed attributable to the profits of a given tax year, the remaining variable needed for the equation is the foreign taxes to take into account. If a tax is assessed and falls due at the end of a given year (Y2), though the tax is based on the income of the previous year (Y1), it is plausible to argue that the tax assessed in said year (Y2) is 'paid on' the income of said year (Y2). Indeed, two judgments cited by Rust reached this conclusion.[395] Both Rust[396] and Owens[397] argue that this result

391. Elisabeth A. Owens, *The Foreign Tax Credit: A Study of the Credit for Foreign Taxes under United States Income Tax Law* 107 (Harvard Law School 1961).

392. *Id.*, at 107–108.

393. *Id.*

394. Alexander Rust, *Article 23 A Exemption Method and Article 23 B Credit Method*, *in 2 Klaus Vogel on Double Taxation Conventions* 1581, m.no. 49 (Ekkehart Reimer & Alexander Rust eds, Kluwer Law International 4th ed. 2015).

395. *Id.* ('In some States, tax on income for a current year is calculated with reference to the income figure established for the preceding year. Paragraph 61 OECD MC Comm. on Article 23 fails to indicate the assessment period in respect of which credit should then be allowed. According to the UK House of Lords and the German Bundesfinanzhof, such a tax should be "attributed" to income derived in the year of assessment while income derived in the preceding year is not more than a basis of charge. A differing view would indeed cause difficulties if the foreign State were to switch from imposing tax with reference to the preceding year to imposing tax with reference to the current year or vice versa' (emphasis omitted; footnotes omitted)).

396. Alexander Rust, *Article 23 A Exemption Method and Article 23 B Credit Method*, *in 2 Klaus Vogel on Double Taxation Conventions* 1581, m.no. 49 (Ekkehart Reimer & Alexander Rust eds, Kluwer Law International 4th ed. 2015) ('However, the House of Lords and the German Bundesfinanzhof failed to consider that the DTCs' rule on maximum deductions (credit

undermines the proper functioning of the credit method (thus both direct and indirect credit methods). Under both the MCA and the apportionment fraction, if the amount of the foreign taxes paid are divorced from the amount of income on which they were levied, this may result in amounts of creditable taxes (or limits thereof) that are effectively disassociated with the reality of the taxpayer's actual earnings over time.

For example, taking an extreme case to more clearly illustrate the disconnect, assume a taxpayer earned foreign profits of 1,000 in year 1 and only 100 in year 2 in a foreign state with a 20% flat tax rate. If the foreign state assesses the taxes for year 2 on the basis of the profits of year 1 (1,000), the taxpayer would pay taxes of 200 for year 2. If the state granting relief also applies a tax rate of 20% and takes into account the tax base of 100 generated in year 2, rather than the base upon which the foreign taxes were actually levied, the state granting relief would levy a maximum of 20 in taxes on this FSI of 100, leaving the vast majority of the foreign taxes (180) uncreditable in this year. This is clearly not the intended result.[398]

Subsequent developments in the indirect credit calculation: comparison of annual approach versus pooling approach

Having reviewed various timing issues, one main observation that can be derived is that: the extent to which the aforementioned timing questions arise is largely impacted by the decision as to whether the indirect credit will be calculated according to an annual approach or a pooling approach. The US legislative history allows for a comparison of the relative merits and weaknesses of these two main approaches, to which the discussion now turns.

If the legislators of the credit-granting state opt for an annual approach (or 'layers of earnings' method)[399] to the indirect FTC, this entails all of the above timing issues. This is because, by definition, it requires a calculation of the credit for each tax year of

limitations), particularly where income figures vary from year to year, cannot be implemented adequately unless the foreign tax can be applied against income derived in the assessment period concerned. If not, the credit allowed would often be futile. On account of this symmetry of income and taxes, the existence of which treaties presuppose, any tax calculated on the basis of the preceding year's income must, contrary to UK case law and the views of the German tax authorities, be "attributed" to the preceding year. The wordings of both original versions of the MC ("is attributable to"; "correspondant à") support this conclusion' (emphasis omitted)).

397. Elisabeth A. Owens, *The Foreign Tax Credit: A Study of the Credit for Foreign Taxes under United States Income Tax Law* 108 (Harvard Law School 1961).

398. In support of this, *see*, e.g., OECD Commentary, at para. 32.8 and at para. 61 (the Commentary indicates its support that 'timing mismatches' and similar issues should not prevent proper relief). However, as Rust, at *supra* note 396, explains, it does not provide much guidance in that respect, e.g., neither specifying the 'crediting period' nor the exchange rate conversion date. Therefore, states have to devise solutions. The US, for example, eventually created a distinction between base and timing differences and implemented clearer rules on exchange rate issues. *See*, e.g., United States, Internal Revenue Code, Section 986 and Section 905; United States, Department of the Treasury, Internal Revenue Service, Guidance Related to the Foreign Tax Credit, Including Guidance Implementing Changes Made by the Tax Cuts and Jobs Act, TD 9882, 84(242) Federal Register 69022, 69098 (17 Dec. 2019), https://www.govinfo.gov/content/pkg/FR-2019-12-17/pdf/2019-24848.pdf (Section 1.904-6, Allocation and Apportionment of Taxes).

399. Ronald A. Worley, *The Indirect Foreign Tax Credit: A Policy Analysis of Section 902*, 13(2) Intl Tax & Bus Law 176, 185 and 190 et seq. (1996).

the foreign subsidiary, and therefore an attribution of the dividends to the underlying profits and related taxes of each given tax year. As a result, it requires a more detailed recording mechanism, an ordering rule and a more careful assessment of truly which profits 'on or with respect to' the taxes were levied if the tax years of the two states diverge, and so on. In addition, the rules governing foreign losses have a more pronounced impact.

For many years, the US followed this annual 'layers of earnings' method. In doing so, it attributed the dividends to the accumulated 'earnings and profits' of the foreign subsidiary on a LIFO basis, meaning in 'reverse chronological order'. The rationale for this particular ordering rule (LIFO) seemed to be merely that it was adopted from the same rule used in the domestic context for dividends distributed out of 'earnings and profits'.[400]

This 'layers of earnings' method requires rules for carryforward or carrybackward of deficits of the foreign subsidiary. The US decided to require a carryback of any foreign deficit. If the foreign state in which the subsidiary was established also required a carryback, then there would be alignment between the figures used in the two states. However, if the foreign state did not require a carryback, then there would be a disconnect between the underlying profits/losses that the US would take into account for the purposes of the indirect credit and the amount of foreign taxes levied on the actual underlying profits taken into account in the foreign state. This disconnect had the consequence of stranding otherwise creditable foreign taxes. For example, the carryback of the deficit could potentially reduce to zero the underlying profits recorded for a previous year, yet the amount of foreign taxes would stay the same (if the foreign state did not simultaneously require a carryback and reduce the foreign taxes it collected accordingly). The problem was that, in the future, profits could not be considered distributed from that year (as there would be none, from the US perspective) and thus neither could the associated foreign taxes, leaving them permanently stranded. Put differently, it could potentially lead to a 'permanent loss of the indirect foreign tax credit for taxes paid in the prior year'[401] because '[i]f a deficit in earnings and profits eliminates the accumulated profits of the corporation from a prior year, a distribution will not be "sourced" to such year for purposes of the indirect foreign tax credit'.[402] One way to avoid this issue would be to align the carryback or carryforward for the purposes of the credit with the rules for a carryback or carryforward in the foreign state.[403]

Due to the issues experienced under this approach, US legislators transitioned to a 'pooling' approach in the 1986 tax reform.[404] Because this pooling approach

400. *Id.*, at 191 and 211 n.229.
401. *Id.*, at 191.
402. *Id.*
403. *See*, e.g., Ronald A. Worley, *The Indirect Foreign Tax Credit: A Policy Analysis of Section 902*, 13(2) Intl Tax & Bus Law 176, 218–219 & n.268 (1996).
404. *See*, e.g., United States, Joint Committee on Taxation, *General Explanation of The Tax Reform Act of 1986 (H.R. 3838, 99th Congress; Public Law 99-514)*, 868 et seq. (US Government Printing Office 1987) (1986 Bluebook); Ronald A. Worley, *The Indirect Foreign Tax Credit: A Policy Analysis of Section 902*, 13(2) Intl Tax & Bus Law 176, 185 and 192–193 (1996).

aggregates the foreign taxes paid and the undistributed earnings over time, it follows that many of the aforementioned timing issues are resolved or reduced in severity. Two main reasons were provided for moving to the 'pooling' approach: (1) 'to alleviate the situation described above in which deemed-paid foreign tax credits were lost as a result of a deficit in a foreign corporation's earnings and profits' and (2) to thwart a strategy referred to as the 'rhythm method' of distributing dividends.[405]

Regarding the loss or deficit issue, US legislators observed that '[i]n a branch situation in which foreign income is taxed currently, this loss of foreign tax credits generally would not occur', thereby recalling that the equivalence between the two forms of establishment abroad is one of the rationales for the indirect FTC.[406] The 'pooling' approach alleviates this issue since the deficit enters into the general pool of earnings accumulated over years and thus its impact is more evenly spread, reducing the risk that it directly decreases the distributable profits linked to creditable foreign taxes of one given year (interestingly, while this 'pooling' approach partially facilitates this 'equivalence' rationale in loss-making situations, in profit-making situations, it arguably does not: an *annual* calculation was found by the US Tax Court in 1944 to be more in line with this 'equivalence' rationale, as seen at *supra* note 391). According to Worley, under the 'pooling' approach, the issue of 'lost' FTCs was certainly reduced, but not entirely resolved (the 'lock-in' is at least no longer permanent).[407]

Regarding the 'rhythm method' tactic, the LIFO ordering rule seemed to be a main contributing factor. According to the US Joint Committee on Taxation explanation:

> 'It was frequently advantageous under prior law for foreign subsidiaries, where possible, to accumulate their earnings in years in which their effective foreign tax rate was low and distribute their earnings to U.S. parent corporations in years in which their effective foreign tax rate was high, rather than distributing their earnings on an annual basis with more constant dividends. Since, for purposes of computing the foreign taxes attributable to a dividend, the dividend was deemed distributed out of the subsidiary's earnings and profits for the current year first, drawing with it the foreign taxes with respect to those earnings, and then was treated as being derived from each preceding year, the distribution of dividends only in high tax years yielded a higher foreign tax credit than the average foreign taxes actually paid by that foreign subsidiary over a period of years. This result did not and does not occur in the case of a direct branch operation, since all branch income is subject to U.S. tax currently and foreign taxes eligible for the credit are taken into account currently.'[408]

The pooling approach circumscribes a taxpayer's ability to increase the FTC in this way, as it results in averaging the different amounts of taxes paid over the years.

---

405. United States, Joint Committee on Taxation, *General Explanation of The Tax Reform Act of 1986 (H.R. 3838, 99th Congress; Public Law 99-514)*, 869–870 (US Government Printing Office 1987) (1986 Bluebook).
406. *Id.*, at 869.
407. Ronald A. Worley, *The Indirect Foreign Tax Credit: A Policy Analysis of Section 902*, 13(2) Intl Tax & Bus Law 176, 204–205 & n.191 (1996).
408. United States, Joint Committee on Taxation, *General Explanation of The Tax Reform Act of 1986 (H.R. 3838, 99th Congress; Public Law 99-514)*, 869 (US Government Printing Office 1987) (1986 Bluebook).

While that is one solution, it seems that another possible solution to such strategies would be a different ordering rule, such as an ordering rule on a lowest-taxed-profits-out-first basis.[409]

Despite these improvements, Worley contended that, although the US Congressional explanations paid tribute to the aim of approximating or equalizing the tax treatment of a foreign subsidiary as compared to a direct foreign branch operation, the pooling approach fails this aim because it still leaves fully intact the benefits of deferral achieved by operating through a foreign subsidiary. To diminish this 'deferral' difference, Worley proposed that the taxation of, and the indirect tax credit for, dividends from foreign subsidiaries could be designed in a way 'which is similar to the taxation of accumulation distributions applicable to trusts' in the US,[410] a solution he referred to as the international 'throwback model'. Under this model, dividends from foreign subsidiaries would continue to be taxed only upon receipt of a distribution (so there would *not* be an automatic inclusion of income), but it would be 'designed to approximate the tax consequences that *would have applied* to the distributee *if the income had been distributed immediately*' (emphasis added).[411] To accomplish this, there are three main components to his 'throwback' model.

First, as previously mentioned, the FSI to be taken into account for the purposes of calculating the indirect FTC would be the 'undistributed net income of the subsidiary for that taxable year', which is the 'net amount after foreign taxes paid', and is essentially aligned with foreign taxable income (rather than the ill-suited 'earnings and profits' measure, in his view, as discussed above).[412] Second, and more importantly for the timing concerns, the dividends should be deemed to be distributed out of underlying profits of the subsidiary on a FIFO basis – 'in effect, "thrown back" to the earliest taxable years in which the foreign corporation had any undistributed net income'.[413] Thus, the model is based on an 'annual determination' of foreign taxable income and related foreign taxes.[414] Correspondingly, for the calculation of the US taxes against which the foreign taxes may be credited, there would also be a 'throwback':

> 'A distribution from a foreign corporation is thrown back to the taxable years of the U.S. corporation *in which the foreign subsidiary received the undistributed net income* which is now being distributed. The grossed up amount of undistributed net income is added to the U.S. tax base of the domestic corporation *for the taxable years during which it was accumulated by the foreign subsidiary* and is taxable to

409. Peter Harris, *An Historic View of the Principle and Options for Double Tax Relief*, 1999(6) Brit. Tax Rev. 469, 485 (1999).
410. Ronald A. Worley, *The Indirect Foreign Tax Credit: A Policy Analysis of Section 902*, 13(2) Intl Tax & Bus Law 176, 207 (1996).
411. *Id.*, at 211.
412. *Id.*, at 215 and 218–219 & n.268 (likewise, regarding losses: the author seems to suggest that the treatment of losses should follow how such losses are treated under foreign law. The aim is, again, to align the taxable income taken into account in the two countries, in order to avoid permanent loss or indefinite deferral of indirect foreign tax credits).
413. *Id.*, at 216.
414. *Id.*, at 211 and 215.

> the U.S. corporation at the tax rates that were applicable to it *for such years'* (emphasis added; footnotes omitted).[415]

This is notable, as the entire indirect FTC is normally taken against the US tax liability of the domestic corporation in the year in which the dividends are received by the domestic corporation (even if the dividends and deemed taxes stem from underlying profits of multiple tax years of the foreign subsidiary). By contrast, this proposal seems to suggest reopening or recalculating previous tax years of the domestic corporation and adjusting the US tax liability accordingly, as though the underlying foreign profits of each year had been directly included or distributed to the domestic corporation in the year they were earned by the foreign subsidiary. This is coherent with the rationale, as it is closer to what would happen in the case of a foreign branch operation. Both the annual-determination component and the throwback component of the design aimed to approximate the tax treatment of foreign branches, which themselves would be taxed on an ongoing annual basis. In this way, it was also designed to prevent 'a domestic corporation from taking advantage of variations in the U.S. tax rates by timing the distributions from its foreign subsidiaries to fall into taxable years in which it is paying U.S. taxes at a relatively low rate', a strategy which would not be available to a US taxpayer with a foreign branch.[416] Third, an interest charge is added to the tax liability of the US taxpayer in order to more definitively eliminate the benefit of the deferral[417] by 'tak[ing] account of the time value of money'.[418]

Given that this proposal is based on an annual determination, it would, evidently, require grappling with all aforementioned timing issues. However, according to the author, it brings simplifications in another way, namely by using the 'undistributed net income' aligned with sums used in the state of the subsidiary, including a suggestion that the use of deficits could also be aligned with the rules in that state.[419] This eschews the need to recompute everything in line with the rules of the credit-granting state. In the view of the author, this would bring welcome simplifications and, even more importantly, is superior from the perspective of the rationale of relief for double taxation because it avoids problematic mismatches (e.g., those leading to a permanent loss of an FTC). Moreover, although it entails answering the timing questions, this is a necessary compromise in order to achieve the other main rationale of the indirect FTC, as expressed by Congress, namely more equal treatment of branches and subsidiaries. One question is whether it entails procedural difficulties, to the extent it requires reopening tax assessments of previous years.

With the above, three general approaches to timing issues have been presented – (1) an annual determination coupled with a LIFO ordering rule, (2) an annual determination coupled with a FIFO ordering rule and (3) a pooling of all foreign

415. *Id.*, at 217.
416. *Id.*, at 217 n.264.
417. *Id.*, at 217–218 ('the U.S. tax liability with respect to the portion of any distribution that is thrown back to a preceding taxable year is assessed a nondeductible interest charge for the period of time between the taxable year in which the income was received by the foreign subsidiary and the taxable year in which it is distributed to the U.S. corporation [...]').
418. *Id.*, at 221.
419. *Id.*, at 215–216, 218–219 & n.268.

earnings and related taxes (with an inherent pro-rate ordering rule) – along with their respective trade-offs and questions, such as their interaction with timing issues, losses or deficits at the level of the subsidiary, FTC planning opportunities and the rationale of equalizing the tax treatment of branches and subsidiaries.

Other combinations of approaches are, of course, possible.[420] Harris in his study, *An Historic View of the Principle and Options for Double Tax Relief*, lists further possibilities. As mentioned, in addition to these two overarching approaches to the timing (annual or pooling across tax years), there could also be subdivisions according to the type or other characteristics of income. It is possible to design pools, *inter alia*, on the basis of types of income, such as active or passive, or on the basis of the tax burden, such as high-taxed or low-taxed income, or by location or source, such as income from certain states, e.g., considered tax havens.[421] Theoretically, it could be further and further subdivided until it becomes as exact as an item-by-item-of-income approach.

In order to 'protect the integrity' of such subdivisions, 'look through' rules are needed. This inevitably brings complexity and entails a heavy administrative burden, especially if all dividends must 'take their character from the profits from which they are distributed'.[422] For this reason, generally, looking through the dividends is best reserved for situations of 'control', such as for corporations that are considered CFCs.[423]

Look-through rules may be required if a credit-granting state aims to apply the same credit limitation rules applicable to a direct tax credit, such as a per-item or per-category-of-income credit limitation, also to the indirect tax credit. In order to avoid some complexity, the US sought to contain it to situations of control. Thus, it created a distinct credit limitation category or basket for 'noncontrolled section 902 corporations': if the US domestic corporation held the requisite ownership requirements in the foreign subsidiary to qualify for an indirect tax credit (under the previous Section 902),[424] but the foreign subsidiary was *not* a CFC (meaning it was *not* more than 50% owned by US persons), then the dividends from this 'noncontrolled' foreign subsidiary and the deemed-paid taxes fell in their own credit limitation category. In this case, the credit limitation applied on a 'corporation-by-corporation' basis, calculating the indirect tax credit for each non-controlled foreign subsidiary separately. Importantly, it

420. Moreover, the approach in the US continues to evolve. *See*, e.g., the changes in its 2017 tax reform, under the 'Tax Cuts and Jobs Act', *supra* note 267; IRS, Internal Revenue Manual, at Section 4.61.10.2.1 ('The pooling regime and indirect credits with respect to dividends from eligible foreign corporations under IRC 902 has been repealed for tax years of foreign corporations beginning after 12/31/2017 and tax years of U.S. shareholders within which such taxable years of foreign corporations end.').

421. Peter Harris, *An Historic View of the Principle and Options for Double Tax Relief*, 1999(6) Brit. Tax Rev. 469, 483–485 (1999).

422. *Id.* For further discussion of the complexity of look-through rules in the US context, *see*, e.g., Charles I. Kingson, *The Foreign Tax Credit and Its Critics*, 9(1) Am. J. Tax Pol'y 1, 3–15 (1991).

423. Peter Harris, *An Historic View of the Principle and Options for Double Tax Relief*, 1999(6) Brit. Tax Rev. 469, 483–484 (1999).

424. As mentioned at *supra* note 267, Section 902 was repealed by the 2017 tax reform, commonly referred to as the Tax Cuts and Jobs Act (TCJA).

would not require always looking through the dividends to the character of the income giving rise to the dividends.[425] In sum, as can be seen here, similar issues and design questions arise under both the direct credit and the indirect credit as regards the credit limitation and look-through rules (as discussed at *supra* note 218).

Classification of income

To the extent any such subdivisions by type of income (etc.) apply, the classification of income, evidently, takes on added importance. In any case, though, the classification of income takes on added importance under the indirect FTC. An indirect credit is granted, in particular, for dividends because they - coming out of *after-tax* profits of the subsidiary - can be said to have suffered some of the taxation of the subsidiary. In light of this, if income such as interest were received by a shareholder (assuming it is an arm's-length amount), an indirect tax credit would not be needed, to the extent that the interest income was deductible from the taxable income at the level of the subsidiary and, thus, could *not* be said to have suffered income taxation at that level.

Thus, the indirect credit is granted only upon receipt of certain distributions of profits out of corporate earnings taxed abroad (usually 'dividends'), or upon attribution of (or deemed distributions of) other types of covered income to the shareholder, e.g., in the case of CFC rules. What exactly constitutes the eligible previously taxed distributions of profits, though, is not always straightforward.

For example, one issue that arose in the US was whether 'liquidating distributions' should be considered a dividend for the purposes of the indirect credit.[426] Owens discussed the *Freeport Sulphur* case, where the US Court of Claims rejected this. She agreed with this outcome, reasoning the following: given that the purpose of the indirect credit is to grant relief to a parent company on the grounds that the dividend 'has already borne a corporate income tax',[427] it is reasonable to exclude income that is more in the nature of capital gains from liquidation because, although the shares may derive their value in part from the accumulated profits of the subsidiary, which have borne corporate tax, the gains are also 'a function of several other factors, e.g., when the shareholder purchased his stock and the market factors affecting the sale price of the capital equipment or stock-in-trade at the time of dissolution'. Not only was this theoretically sound, in her view, but also practical, since the foreign tax on corporate profits 'becomes more remote and more difficult to estimate'.[428] In the EU, it seems that the MSs reached a similar conclusion, as under the Parent-Subsidiary Directive (discussed further in Section 4.3.), the benefit of relief from double taxation on the distribution of profits excludes the cases 'when the subsidiary is liquidated'.[429] Indeed, the use of terms such as 'dividends' in the indirect credit will inevitably entail the

425. United States, Joint Committee on Taxation, *General Explanation of The Tax Reform Act of 1986 (H.R. 3838, 99th Congress; Public Law 99-514)*, 867–868 (US Government Printing Office 1987) (1986 Bluebook).
426. Elisabeth A. Owens, *The Foreign Tax Credit: A Study of the Credit for Foreign Taxes under United States Income Tax Law* 99–101 (Harvard Law School 1961).
427. *Id.*, at 99.
428. *Id.*, at 100.
429. *See infra* note 829, Parent-Subsidiary Directive, Article 4(1).

standard interpretation issues in this field (e.g., the treatment of redemptions of shares, the debt versus equity conundrum, the treatment of income that is recharacterized as dividends, etc.).

2.1.1.4. Interim Conclusions: Lessons from Unilateral Measures

A study of the origins of the credit method offers rich insight into various ways it has been designed, various technical issues it has confronted and various rationales that have been put forward.

The above followed the chronological development of some of the first instances of the credit method. As early as the 1880s, the UK began to experiment with offering an 'indirect' tax credit for the underlying taxes paid on income distributed to UK shareholders, following the 1881 *Gilbertson v. Fergusson* case, though, it was a limited form of relief, offered *only* for the underlying *UK* taxes rather than foreign taxes (*see supra* note 255). In 1894, the UK offered relief that resembled a 'direct' tax credit, though only for estate duties (*see supra* note 86, Section 20 of the Finance Act 1894). In 1916, the UK introduced a temporary form of credit relief specifically for income taxes. However, it was only a partial credit, as it was designed with a cap to ensure a minimum of 17.5% in UK taxes, and restricted geographically to relief for double taxation stemming from its colonies (*see supra* note 88, Section 43 of the Finance Act 1916). In 1920, the UK amended its credit, to expand the relief, now granting up to a maximum of 50% of the UK tax rate, though still restricted to '[r]elief in respect of Dominion income tax'; however, to encourage more relief, the UK uniquely devised its credit system to encourage or put pressure on its 'Dominions' to share the responsibility for relief (*see supra* note 98, Section 27 of the Finance Act 1920). As can be seen, at that time, none of the UK efforts were truly international in scope. In 1918, the US stepped into the credit method spotlight, surprising the world with enacting a full 'dollar-for-dollar' FTC, without any limit on the amount of foreign taxes that could be credited (*see supra* note 83 and note 129, the Revenue Act of 1918). So it was neither partial, nor capped, nor geographically restricted. At this time, the US also enacted an 'indirect' tax credit (*see supra* note 253). In 1921, the US amended its FTC, to introduce a credit limitation. It would continue to offer a dollar-for-dollar FTC but only up to a maximum of what the US would levy on the FSI (*see supra* note 179, the Revenue Act of 1921). Thereafter, for decades, the US experimented with different types of credit limitations and confronted numerous challenges in the computation of the credit method (especially the indirect credit method), all of which, as seen above, offer insight into various design options and how they were adapted over time.

From these early unilateral measures, already a detailed checklist can be compiled of questions and design elements that have to be considered under the credit method. The following summarizes what features were shared in common, as a first step towards isolating the core of the credit method from its variable components.

Regarding the various forms of a 'direct' credit presented above:

- One common feature was the basic operation or calculation of the credit. Each version involved a minimum of two steps, beginning with, first, determining the tax liability in the state granting relief (or using the tax liability to determine the effective tax rate (ETR), as in the UK in 1916/1920) and, second, deducting from that amount part, or all, of the taxes paid, or legally payable, to another jurisdiction (or the rate of relief).
- Another common feature was the procedural step of requiring some sort of proof of taxes legally payable or paid to the other jurisdiction.
- Related to this, another common feature was that, thus far, all versions offered relief for *actual* double taxation, based on taxes effectively paid or legally payable, as opposed to *potential* double taxation or relief for nominal tax rates or notional taxes.[430] This was particularly emphasized in the US legal provisions: in addition to requiring the aforementioned proof ('only if the taxpayer furnishes evidence satisfactory') that the foreign taxes had been paid or accrued, the US implemented a procedural 'redetermination' mechanism in case the foreign taxes ultimately paid differed or were readjusted in the future. The rules even mentioned the possibility of requiring a taxpayer to provide a form of financial guarantee or collateral as a protection against potential future changes in the amount of foreign taxes and, thus, the credit (*see supra* note 166). The relief in the UK in Section 27(3) of the Finance Act 1920 also provided for subsequent adjustments to the relief in certain cases.
- All shared in common a specification of which taxes were eligible for the credit; i.e., all specified whether they addressed 'income taxes' or other special taxes such as a 'super-tax' or a 'excess-profits tax' or 'Estate duties' (*see* especially *supra* note 156).
- One crucial difference regards eligible taxpayers. In the 1916 and 1920 versions of the UK relief, technically it was applicable to *all* taxpayers; it was not based on the residence of the taxpayer and source of the income, since the only requirement was that the income was taxed twice (by the UK and by a Dominion). In the 1918 US version, it was expressly applicable only to citizens and residents; the concepts of residence and source therefore became pivotal.
- All shared in common indications of the status of the foreign taxes, i.e., whether they were 'paid', 'payable', etc., though they adopted slightly different word choices: 'payable' (1894 UK relief), as compared to 'paid' (1916 UK relief), refined to 'has paid ... or is liable to pay' (1920 UK relief), or 'paid or accrued' coupled with a readjustment mechanism for later changes in the amount of foreign taxes (1918 US relief).
- Another question that they all share in common is the need to determine the amount of foreign taxes that can be credited, as seen with wording such as 'a sum equal to' (*see,* e.g., *supra* note 87 regarding the 1894 UK relief), and whether this refers to the full amount of foreign taxes, even when the foreign

430. At this stage, tax sparing and tax matching credits had not yet emerged, it seems, but rather appeared in the OEEC documents on bilateral measures, discussed below in Section 2.1.2.3. There is the question as to whether and to what extent they are a true credit method.

taxes are higher, or whether there is a credit limitation. Although they shared this question, the answer varied. An unlimited credit was seen, albeit only briefly, in the US (1918 US relief). All, in the end, incorporated some form of limitation.

- Yet even if all ended up with a limitation, no limitations looked alike at this stage. There were key differences in how to calculate them. There was a form of limitation based on ensuring a minimum taxation amount of 17.5% (1916 UK relief, *see* Example 2). There was a form of limitation based not on the amount of foreign taxes per se, but rather on a maximum tax rate, namely half of the applicable tax rate (1920 UK relief, *see* Example 3). Then there were a series of experiments with different credit limitations conducted in the US: e.g., overall, per country, per basket, and sometimes with options to choose between different types of limits (*see supra* note 191 et seq. and *see* Example 6).
- On a related point, if there is a limitation, then cases will inevitably arise where it is not possible to credit all of the foreign taxes. This gives rise to the question of how to treat the 'excess'. One option is that any excess simply cannot be used or compensated for in any case. It is merely a consequence of different tax amounts in the two jurisdictions and, thus, lost. Another option is that the excess could be cross-credited, by being offset against other similar taxes. This seemed to be the approach of the 1894 UK relief (e.g., 'the balance over and above the Estate Duty might have been allowed against the Settlement Estate Duty', *see supra* note 87). Other options include allowing any excess to be carried forward as an FTC to future years or carried back to past years (as was the case in the future amendments made to the US credit limitation, *see supra* note 200 and note 250) or any excess can be allowed to be deducted as an expense in the current year (*see supra* note 252). In sum, the ways to treat excess credits include: lost, cross-credited, carried forward, carried backward, deducted. The UK took a different approach under the 'Dominion Relief' system, through a form of 'limited reciprocity', encouraging the Dominion to relieve any excess above the UK's 50%-rate-limit (1920 UK relief, *see supra* note 109).
- Various technical issues arose where the provisions differed. For example, some issues especially dealt with by the legal provisions of the 1920 UK relief were: (1) the need to 'gross-up' the FSI (*see supra* note 116); (2) a 'slice-by-slice' approach, namely a separate calculation for each 'slice' or item of income (alternatively, this term can also invoke the progressive tax rate issue, namely the need to attribute the FSI either to the 'top-slice', the 'bottom-slice', or proportionately to all income brackets) (*see supra* note 117); (3) potential timing issues (*see supra* note 122); (4) the need for authorizing regulations in order to address any future unforeseen issues that arise, such as calculation issues where tax bases diverge (*see supra* note 123). Only later did the US legal provisions more explicitly address these issues.

Reviewing again the provisions as a composite whole, the overall differences in approach are striking:

Scope	*1918 US Relief*	*1916 and 1920 UK Relief*
Who is entitled to a credit	Residents and citizens (→ centrality of residence)	In essence, anyone who owed taxes both to the UK and to a 'possession' or 'Dominion'
What taxes are creditable	Income 'taxes paid ... to any foreign country' (→ centrality of source)	Income taxes paid to 'possessions' or 'Dominions'
The amount of taxes creditable	Dollar-for-dollar; unlimited in 1918, but quickly amended in 1921	Partial relief mechanism (1916 UK relief); maximum 50% of UK tax rate (1920 UK relief)

- Given the numerous structural features in common, the UK showed some possible viable alternative approaches for the credit method. Yet, as subsequent developments showed (discussed in Section 2.1.2.), especially from the discussions convened by international organizations, such as the League of Nations, on a bilateral model, these two UK approaches are now seen in retrospect as not being standard credit methods;[431] the US approach eventually emerged as the standard.

As regards the various rationales used for implementing these various forms of credit relief:

- The increase in taxation resulting from wars and concerns over excessive burdens of taxation was repeatedly cited as the driving (political) factor (*see supra* note 90 and note 135).
- As regards relief with a restricted geographical scope, this was justified by the 'well being' of the common political unit (e.g., the empire) (*see supra* note 105).
- As regards the FTC enacted by the US, a multitude of rationales were put forward: in addition to concerns over the excessive burdens of double (or multiple) taxation, there were ideas of fairness or non-discrimination (*see supra* note 140 and note 141); there were desires to strike a balance between

431. As support for view that the first UK approaches were not the standard credit as it is known today, *see*, e.g., Philip Baker, *Some Aspects of United Kingdom Double Taxation Relief*, 52(10) Bull. Int'l Fiscal Documentation 445, 447 (1998) ('An effective consequence of the acceptance of the recommendations of the Royal Commission was that relief from double income taxation by an ordinary tax credit was not a feature of the UK tax system prior to the Second World War'); League of Nations, 1923 Report, at *infra* note 555, and League of Nations, 1925 Report, at 4098 (the experts treated it as a distinct form of relief, referred to as 'the method of division of the tax', or Method III 'Allocation of Relief').

the taxation claims at the place of source and residence (*see supra* note 143); there were concerns over a balance between relief for double taxation and the prevention of tax evasion (*see supra* note 137 and note 144).

- There were some mentions of the need to facilitate, or at least not stifle, international trade. In turn, reducing burdens on the flow of international trade and investment could be beneficial both for reasons of national self-interest, such as the competitiveness of US companies on the global stage, and for reasons of global well-being, such as post-war reconstruction efforts (*see supra* note 147 and note 359).
- Eventually, certain economic concepts and the incentive effects of methods for relief of double taxation became prominent in policy discussions, especially 'capital export neutrality' (CEN) and 'capital import neutrality' (CIN) (*see supra* notes 232–233).
- In addition to the rationales for the credit as a whole, there are also distinct rationales for specific components of the credit method. The most notable example is that of the credit limitation (*see supra* notes 181–183, note 186, notes 201–239, Example No. 6–No. 9). Sometimes there are tensions between the rationales, such as between the aim to facilitate international trade and the aim to preserve the ability of the credit-granting state to collect taxes on DSI (*see supra* note 366).

Credit Limitations

Overview of Rationales, Advantages and Disadvantages

(for more details, *see supra* notes 181–183, note 186, notes 201–239, Example No. 6–No. 9)

Note: The comparative advantages and disadvantages of the types of limitations are generally only relevant in so far as there is income from more than one foreign source. If a taxpayer earns only one source of income from only one foreign state, the differences between the credit limitations will likely not have an impact. Also, of course, the precise extent to which any advantages or disadvantages manifest themselves depends on the relative tax rates and amount of income in all states concerned.

Unlimited credit	- May achieve CEN - May go beyond elimination of double taxation on FSI (where foreign taxes are higher) - Revenue concerns may arise depending on the tax rate differences between credit-granting state and foreign states (where foreign taxes are higher)

Credit limitation	- Preserves ability of credit-granting state to collect taxes on DSI - Compromises CEN: may achieve it where foreign taxes are the same or lower; undermines it where foreign taxes are higher
Credit limitation - overall	- Greater simplicity, administrative ease and less compliance burden - Averaging is possible - Has been perceived as more favourable to the objective of competitiveness abroad - More advantageous for the taxpayer in profit-making situations (i.e., with more than one source of FSI, especially if some is taxed at lower rates and others at higher rates) - Concerns over less equitable treatment, as it may favour taxpayers with positive income in more than one foreign state (Example No. 7) - Concerns over distortions, as it may incentivize foreign investments to inflate the size of the credit (Example No. 8) - Foreign losses: may result in lower FTC for taxpayer if foreign losses reduce taxed foreign profits, thus comparative cash-flow disadvantage (degree and duration of disadvantage depends on rules for 'excess' credits) - Foreign losses: may better preserve credit-granting state taxes on DSI (Example No. 9)
Credit limitation - per-country	- Comparatively less simplicity, administrative ease and greater compliance burden as compared to overall limitation - Averaging is reduced (could occur only, e.g., between differently taxed items of income from the same foreign state) - Potentially less favourable to the objective of competitiveness abroad - Less advantageous for the taxpayer in profit-making situations (i.e., with profit in more than one foreign state with differing tax rates, some comparatively lower and higher) as compared to overall limitation - Reduces concerns over distortions, as there is less room to manoeuvre, yet does not prevent conversion of DSI to FSI - requires look-through rules

	- Foreign losses: protects FTC for taxpayer with respect to a given foreign state (i.e., where profits were earned in said state, but losses were generated in another foreign state), thus comparative cash-flow advantage - Foreign losses: less likely to preserve credit-granting state taxes on DSI (Example 9) (one solution: loss-allocation and recharacterization rules)
Credit limitation – per-item	- Most precise and most protective of credit-granting state's ability to collect taxes on DSI (in profit-making circumstances) - Less favourable to the objective of competitiveness abroad - Potential for high complexity, compromising simplicity and administrative ease and increasing compliance burden - Likely eliminates distortions – but requires look-through rules - Foreign losses: protects FTC for taxpayer with respect to a given item of positive income (i.e., where profits were earned in said state, but losses were generated in another foreign state), thus comparative cash-flow advantage - Foreign losses: less likely to preserve credit-granting state taxes on DSI (Example 9) (one solution: loss-allocation and recharacterization rules)
Credit limitation – per-category/ basket	- Can strike a balance, depending on how the categories are designed, between the respective rationales, advantages and disadvantages of an overall limitation as compared to per-country/per-item limitations

From the study of the different 'indirect' credits presented above, some common considerations can be derived:

- First, as indirect credits are geared towards relief of double (or cumulative) taxation on distributions of profits to owners or shareholders, one consideration is whether the indirect credit should specify a required ownership or shareholding threshold. Under the 1881 and 1920 UK relief system, the imputation/indirect credit was granted irrespective of the size of the shareholding, whereas under the 1918 US relief system, the indirect credit was granted in the case of a majority shareholding. One could argue that, in principle, the relief should be granted irrespective of ownership (i.e., double taxation of distributed profits occurs regardless of the level of ownership, so likewise the relief should apply regardless of the level of ownership); this case is even stronger in 'integrated' corporate tax systems. Requiring a certain level of ownership seemed to be based on practical reasons of administrability.

- Related to this point, the question also arose whether the type of shares held - e.g., voting stock, or common stock versus preference shares - should be relevant. Questions regarding the type of shares arose both for the question of the ownership qualifications and for the question of whether the amount of foreign taxes deemed attached to the dividends should be adjusted (*see*, e.g., *supra* note 262).
- Second, there are additional considerations regarding the scope of distributions covered, since an indirect FTC is relevant only for distributions of profits, such as dividends, which (unlike deductible payments such as interest) formed part of the income tax base subject to tax at the level of the distributing entity. Thus, the classification of income distributions, or inclusions, becomes relevant since the shareholder can only be deemed to have indirectly 'paid' underlying taxes on certain types of underlying income.
- Third, another consideration is the scope of eligible taxpayers. Under the 1881 and 1920 UK relief systems, both individuals and corporations were eligible, whereas under the 1918 US relief system, only corporations were eligible.
- Fourth, the UK had a more integrated corporate-shareholder taxation system, which likely influenced its broader scope regarding the ownership requirements. An indirect credit can be more narrowly framed as a means to relieve economic double taxation among the layers of corporate ownership (while still viewing the ultimate natural person owners or shareholders as distinct from the legal entities they own), or be more broadly framed as a means to integrate corporations and their owners at all levels. The latter is what generally underlies 'imputation' credit systems, which repeatedly appeared in the CJEU case law (as discussed in Section 4.2.8.). In this way, it is possible to see a link between the ultimate aim or rationale of the system and how it is designed to achieve it. To be precise, although an indirect credit and an imputation credit embody different conceptions of the corporate-shareholder relationship (often referred to as a distinction between a 'classical' versus integrated corporate tax system), according to Harris, the design *questions* are largely (if not, exactly) the same;[432] however, the *answers* to those questions will likely differ.

432. Peter Harris, *An Historic View of the Principle and Options for Double Tax Relief*, 1999(6) Brit. Tax Rev. 469, 481–482 (1999) (discussing their 'equivalence') and at 482–483 (e.g., two features they have in common include the aforementioned process for 'recording the corporate tax' and 'an ordering rule'; a third feature mentioned more specifically for an imputation method is an 'adjustment mechanism'. The third, i.e., 'adjustment mechanism', in the context of an imputation credit, refers to the fact that 'the credit available to shareholders with a distribution must be adjusted so that it reflects the corporation tax allocated to the profits considered distributed'). Based on this description, perhaps the 'adjustment mechanism' is to

- Fifth, technical issues arose regarding the calculation of an indirect tax credit. Debates especially arose regarding the lack of a 'gross-up' in the US, regarding the 'apportionment fraction', especially over the denominator (*see supra* note 324, note 327 and note 367, Example No. 14 and Example No. 15), and regarding timing issues:
  - As regards the 'gross-up', history seems to have come down definitively on the side of the 'gross-up' as a necessary component.
  - As regards the denominator of the apportionment fraction, there are two intersecting axes to consider: (1) the content of the figure and (2) as determined under which laws (domestic versus foreign). As for the content, the question is whether it should be based on an accounting figure, on the taxable income as determined under the tax laws, or on a concept such as 'earnings and profits' used to determine the amount of income available for distribution. And, the question is whether it should be determined based on the accounting rules or tax rules, etc., as determined under the laws of the credit-granting state or those of the state where the distributing entity is located. Some of the arguments in favour of or against different approaches, unsurprisingly, revolved around the rationale(s), which are summarized just below.
  - As regards the timing issues, a first general choice is that between an annual determination of the indirect tax credit (looking at each tax year of the foreign subsidiary separately) or a pooling approach (aggregating together all foreign taxes of the subsidiary and all profits on which they were levied over the years). Under an annual approach, because it seeks to match the dividends to the underlying profits and the taxes levied thereon in a more precise way, this requires rules: (1) to determine the 'attribution of dividends to annual profits of foreign corporation', which in turn requires (1a) a 'recording' mechanism and (1b) an 'ordering rule' (e.g., LIFO, FIFO). This attribution may also be affected by (1c) the date of distribution of the dividends, for which it should be dictated whether to: (i) attribute the dividend to the entire taxable year in which the dividends were paid, (ii) attribute the dividend to the accumulated profits up to the point of distribution, or (iii) attribute the dividend to the 'profits for the last full taxable year' (*supra* note 387). In addition, an annual approach entails (2) a year-by-year 'annual calculation of the [indirect] tax credit' (as in Example No. 16, Option 2). Moreover, in cases where the tax years of the credit-granting state and the foreign state diverge, it requires ascertaining whether (3) the foreign tax has been paid 'on or with respect to' profits of a given year (*see supra* note 392). The 'pooling' approach alleviates these timing issues.

---

the imputation method what the 'apportionment fraction' is to the indirect tax credit, to the extent that they both play the role of determining the amount of tax to attribute to the distribution.

- When considering the two general options (annual versus pooling), in addition to these timing questions, other questions that must be considered include: their interaction with losses at the level of the subsidiary, including whether carryback or carryforward rules are required (*see supra* note 403) and the extent to which they permit opportunities to proactively time the distribution of dividends to inflate the FTC (*see supra* note 405 and note 408). In addition to these two overarching approaches to the timing (which either divides the profits year-by-year or, instead, pools them all together), further subdivisions, based on the type of income, for example, are possible (*see supra* note 421).

As regards the rationales for implementing forms of credit relief for underlying taxes:

- One rationale was an economic one based on the idea that the shareholder indirectly 'pays' some of the taxes (*see supra* note 281).
- Related to this rationale, another rationale was the concern over the same profits being subject to multiple layers of taxation (*see supra* note 282) (though the term 'economic double taxation' did not seem to be used initially).
- There was also an equal treatment rationale, based on the idea that taxpayers who invest abroad directly (e.g., via a branch) and those who invest abroad by incorporating a distinct legal entity (i.e., via a subsidiary) should have similar tax treatment regardless of the form of investing abroad. Underlying this rationale may also be the broader rationale that business decisions as to how best to expand operations abroad (e.g., directly as a branch or indirectly as a subsidiary) should not be distorted by taxes.
- The judges in the 1881 *Gilbertson v. Fergusson* case in the UK also put forward rationales based on what they considered to be the appropriate tax take of the UK government (i.e., the idea that it is *not* double taxation caused by two countries that is the problem, but rather it is when one and the same government causes double taxation on the same 'thing' that is unjust), which led to an imputation/indirect credit for any underlying UK taxes (*see supra* notes 257–259).
- Again, similar to the 'direct' forms of credit, these rationales and the intended function of a specific component of a credit method, e.g., the apportionment formula (*see supra* note 325), help better inform the design choices for these components.

Debates throughout this section, especially those discussed in Section 2.1.1.3., illustrated the possible interaction between these rationales and the design considerations. For example, as regards the denominator of the apportionment fraction (or, in other words, the FSI to take into account), to the extent the emphasis is placed on the rationale of equalizing the tax treatment of foreign branches and foreign subsidiaries, an argument can be made that whatever solution is found for the computation of the direct tax credit in the case of foreign branches should be equally employed for the computation of the indirect tax credit in the case of foreign subsidiaries. Arguments in favour of adopting the sums as computed under foreign law include that: (1) this approach better ensures that the foreign taxes will be creditable (by aligning the FSI for the purposes of computing the amount of creditable foreign taxes with the amount of income in the foreign state for the purposes of levying those foreign taxes) and therefore is more in line with the rationale of relief for double taxation and (2) it also promotes much-prized simplicity (since the figure computed under foreign law is already known, it need merely be plugged into the fraction, after being converted into the local currency). By contrast, arguments in favour of adopting the principles and laws of the credit-granting state include that: (1) it is the taxation of the shareholder concerned, whose income should be calculated according to the rules in its own state of residence; (2) it is the interpretation of a, e.g., US law which, 'under basic principles of conflicts of laws', calls upon US concepts for that purpose; and (3) principles of fairness/equity, if those are anchored into the income tax laws of a given state, could entail that taxpayers with DSI and those with FSI are subject to similar rules for the calculation of the tax base.

As regards both the direct and indirect credit, many arguments are invoked in the name of relief for double taxation. Yet given what a broad banner this is, the arguments can point in different directions in terms of design, depending on how one defines 'double taxation' or understands the relevance of 'double taxation'. For example, if the relevant ramification of double taxation is that it creates barriers to international trade and investment and, for this reason, it must be relieved or arguably eliminated, then one could reasonably focus on the overall burden that befalls a taxpayer with cross-border activities. After all, if it is more expensive overall to conduct business in a foreign country, this may deter the investor. Such concern could be used to justify design components, such as: (1) a 'full' (unlimited) FTC and/or (2) the computation of the FSI, for the purposes of the credit, on the basis of the sums as computed under foreign law. Alternatively, if the import of double taxation stems from the fact that it leads to burdens deemed excessive, as seemed to be the main concern in the post-war period, then the aim is merely to offer a sufficient amount of relief to bring the overall burden down to more reasonable levels, so that international investment and trade can continue, but not necessarily with the aim of guaranteeing taxpayers that there will never be any higher costs entailed by investing abroad. For example, if, based on its definition, 'double taxation' is deemed to occur when same income is taxed twice, then double taxation does not technically occur to the extent taxable income diverges. If a state taxes interest income, but the other state considers that type of interest not taxable, then technically this interest income is taxed only once. In other cases, both states may consider the same income taxable, yet they tax entirely different amounts of that income, e.g., due to different expense rules. If against a given amount of business income, a state would allow interest expenses directly attributable to the income to be deducted, whereas the other state requires interest expenses to be proportionately allocated, or a state would allow only 50% of the costs for a business dinner (or car or laptop, etc.), whereas the other would allow a full deduction, the result could be that, from a taxable income of, e.g., 100, one state taxes only, e.g., 50 while the other taxes, e.g., 80. Technically, double taxation occurs only to the extent of the lower of the two amounts, i.e., 50 (as this state does not tax the difference, the 80-50 = 30 taxed by the other state), and thus a credit computed on the basis of 50 technically relieves 'double taxation', as the credit-granting state ends up in effect relinquishing its ability to collect taxes on that income. In this case, any qualms with the result may have to be taken up with the expense allocation rules themselves, challenging their appropriateness (rather than the credit method per se). This understanding can justify designing a credit method, computed on the basis of the credit-granting state's rules and equipped with a per-item limitation. However, it would be rare, or even odd, for a state to design its relief rules on the basis of one singular rationale alone; rather, it is often a compromise with other rationales and aims. In sum, depending on the rationale and on how it is interpreted and balanced against other potentially equally important goals, arguments can be advanced for different interpretations or approaches to how the credit method should be designed.

2.1.2. Bilateral Measures (Circa 1920s–1960s): Coming to a Common Understanding of the Credit Method

2.1.2.1. Some Preliminary Remarks

The historical legal development thus far has shown that the origins of the credit method seem to be rooted in 'unilateral' relief offered by states, in particular the US and the UK. That is, legislators of a given state took action independently, without the involvement of other states, to implement relief for double taxation within their own domestic tax laws. As the existence of double - or triple or more - taxation stems from the overlapping tax claims of two - or more - jurisdictions, another way to bring about relief is through bilateral - or multilateral - coordination among the jurisdictions concerned. Indeed, around the same time as policymakers in the US and UK were giving shape to different forms of a credit method in their national laws, they also began to join discussions with representatives from other states, who increasingly shared concerns over double taxation. The models for bilateral double taxation relief that eventually emerged were arguably the biggest influence on the spread of the credit method (in particular, a US-style credit method), as this section shows.

The steps towards bilateral measures occurred in two phases. Although the multistate cooperation that began in 1919 with the ICC[433] and in 1921 with the League

433. International Chambers of Commerce, *History*, https://iccwbo.org/about-us/who-we-are/history/ (last visited 9 Oct. 2018) (in 1919, the International Chamber of Commerce was founded by representatives of various business interests 'in the aftermath of the First World War when no world system of rules governed trade, investment, finance or commercial relations' with a mission to set global standards 'to promote international trade and investment', referring to themselves as 'the merchants of peace'); International Chamber of Commerce, *Avoidance of Double Taxation: Exemption Versus Tax-Credit Method*, Resolution of ICC Council and Report of Commission on Taxation (February 1955). For more on the resolutions and role of the ICC during this period, *see* Michael J. Graetz & Michael M. O'Hear, *The 'Original Intent' of U.S. International Taxation*, 46(5) Duke L.J. 1021, 1066–1074 (1997) (the ICC

of Nations[434] is often cited, this, however, was the second phase. Prior to this, at the earliest stages, dating back to approximately the mid-1800s, examples of bilateral cooperation on certain tax matters began to take root in the form of treaties, especially intra- and inter-jurisdictions of the ever-evolving Central European Empires.[435] During this first phase, the coordination occurred predominantly between 'federally related or closely allied' jurisdictions.[436] It laid solid foundations for the drafting of tax treaties.

Then, in the second phase, during the period after the First World War, cooperation broadened to one that was more internationally oriented. Indeed, the stated objective of specially formed committees at the ICC and at the League of Nations was, in essence, to explore solutions to reduce double taxation in a more uniform way on an international scale.[437] Multiple meetings and reports later, the first model conventions were published,[438] becoming the blueprint for the now more than three

---

established a Double Taxation Committee and passed various influential resolutions and reports that petitioned governments to convene to find agreement and that proposed solutions for governments to consider. Some of the experts involved, such as T.S. Adams, the previously cited founder of the 1918 US foreign tax credit, were established thought leaders and policymakers, likely contributing to the visibility and credibility of the ICC's work).

434. League of Nations, 1923 Report, at 4010 ('The Financial Committee of the League of Nations, which has entrusted with the study of double taxation, decided in September 1921 to ask certain economists to prepare a report on the matter'). *See also* Klaus Vogel & Alexander Rust, *Introduction, in* 1 *Klaus Vogel on Double Taxation Conventions* 1, m.no. 21 (Ekkehart Reimer & Alexander Rust eds, Kluwer Law International 4th ed. 2015) ('Efforts of the League of Nations contributed substantially to an assimilation of the existing bilateral treaties and to the development of uniform model treaties. In 1921, the Financial Committee of the League of Nations commissioned four experts on public finance, Bruins (Rotterdam), Einaudi (Turin), Seligman (New York) and Stomp [*sic*] (London), to prepare a report on questions regarding double taxation, which was submitted in final form in 1923').
435. *See*, e.g., Klaus Vogel & Alexander Rust, *Introduction, in* 1 *Klaus Vogel on Double Taxation Conventions* 1, m.no. 20 & n.38 (Ekkehart Reimer & Alexander Rust eds, Kluwer Law International 4th ed. 2015) (citing 'Conventions were entered between Prussia and Saxony regarding direct taxes on 16 April 1869; between Austria and Hungary regarding the taxation of business enterprises on 18 December 1869/7 January 1870; between Austria and Prussia regarding avoidance of double taxation on 21 June 1899'). For a detailed discussion on the treaties between the German states, *see* Johann Hattingh, *On the Origins of Model Tax Conventions: Nineteenth-Century German Tax Treaties and Laws Concerned with Avoidance of Double Tax, in* 6 *Studies in the History of Tax Law* 31 (John Tiley ed., Hart Publishing 2013). For a detailed discussion on the 1872 agreement between Great Britain and Switzerland (Canton of Vaud) for the prevention of double taxation in respect of death duties, *see* Sunita Jogarajan, *The Conclusion and Termination of the 'First' Double Taxation Treaty*, 2012(3) Brit. Tax Rev. 283 (2012).
436. *See*, e.g., Klaus Vogel & Alexander Rust, *Introduction, in* 1 *Klaus Vogel on Double Taxation Conventions* 1, m.no. 20 (Ekkehart Reimer & Alexander Rust eds, Kluwer Law International 4th ed. 2015); Johann Hattingh, *On the Origins of Model Tax Conventions: Nineteenth-Century German Tax Treaties and Laws Concerned with Avoidance of Double Tax, in* 6 *Studies in the History of Tax Law* 31, 33 (John Tiley ed., Hart Publishing 2013).
437. *See*, e.g., discussion at *supra* note 433; League of Nations, 1923 Report, at 4010.
438. *See*, e.g., Klaus Vogel & Alexander Rust, *Introduction, in* 1 *Klaus Vogel on Double Taxation Conventions* 1, m.nos 20–27 (Ekkehart Reimer & Alexander Rust eds, Kluwer Law International 4th ed. 2015) (citing the 1923 Report to the League of Nations, the 1925 Report to the League of Nations, 'four model treaties were drafted in 1926 and 1927, which were revised and adopted in 1928', a 1929 update to the 1928 models, the 1943 Mexico Model, the 1946 London Model, the transition of the League of Nations' work to the OEEC and its successor the OECD, the 1963 Model and official Commentary, and a series of updates to the Model and Commentary in 1977,

thousand bilateral tax treaties that exist today. Notably, European jurisdictions, many of which are now EU MSs, were front-and-centre throughout this process, at both the origins of bilateral tax treaties in the mid-1800s and the post-war 1920s discussions under the auspices of international organizations.[439]

The analysis now turns to these efforts and to what can be learned about the credit method, especially from the historical reports that resulted from these multilateral meetings. What emerges is that these discussions created a feedback loop. First, the discussions were informed by and influenced by existing unilateral credit mechanisms. In turn, these mechanisms, by virtue of becoming the subject of debate, were themselves influenced. In this way, eventually some convergence gradually arrived as to a general structure for the credit method, which persists to this day.

---

in 1992, and 'in 1994, 1995, 1997, 2000, 2003, 2005, 2008, 2010, 2012 (only with regard to Article 26) and 2014'; citing the development of alternative models, such as the 1971 Model for the Andean Group, the 1980 United Nations Model, updated in 2001 and in 2011; citing the US Model in 1976 and revised in 1977, 1981, 1996, and 2006; citing attempts at multilateral conventions, such as that of 1971 'the OCAM (Common African, Madagascan and Mauretanian Organisation) ... since terminated', and 'the "Nordic Convention" between Denmark, Finland, Iceland, Norway and Sweden'; citing the efforts at EU level such as a 1968 draft 'multilateral tax treaty ... which never entered into force', the Arbitration Convention that focuses primarily on transfer pricing disputes, and Directives such as the Parent-Subsidiary Directive and the Interest-Royalty Directive which, although not international conventions, can be seen as forms of multilateral cooperation albeit with a restricted scope).

439. League of Nations, 1923 Report, at 4010 (United States, Joint Committee on Internal Revenue Taxation, US Government Printing Office 1962) (the four experts were from Rotterdam, Turin, New York and London, respectively); League of Nations, 1925 Report, at 4057 (only European countries were represented, namely Belgium, Czechoslovakia, France, Great Britain, Italy, the Netherlands, Switzerland. They held five meetings from 1922 to 1925); League of Nations, *Double Taxation and Tax Evasion, Report Presented by the Committee of Technical Experts on Double Taxation and Tax Evasion* (1927), *in* 4 *Legislative History of United States Tax Conventions*, 4111, 4115 (United States, Joint Committee on Internal Revenue Taxation, US Government Printing Office 1962) (hereinafter 'League of Nations, 1927 Report') (eight out of thirteen were European. The thirteen were: Argentina, Belgium, Czechoslovakia, France, Germany, Great Britain, Italy, Japan, the Netherlands, Poland, Switzerland, the United States, and Venezuela); League of Nations, *Double Taxation and Tax Evasion, Report Presented by the General Meeting of Government Experts on Double Taxation and Tax Evasion* (1928), *in* 4 *Legislative History of United States Tax Conventions*, 4151 and 4191–4193 (United States, Joint Committee on Internal Revenue Taxation, US Government Printing Office 1962) (hereinafter 'League of Nations, 1928 Report') (Annex: Austria, Belgium, Bulgaria, China, Czechoslovakia, Danzig, Denmark, Estonia, France, Germany, Great Britain, Greece, Hungary, Irish Free State, Italy, Japan, Latvia, the Netherlands, Norway, Poland, Romania, South Africa, Spain, Sweden, Switzerland, the United States, the Union of Socialist Soviet Republics); Organisation for European Economic Co-operation, *First Report of the Fiscal Committee of the OEEC on the Elimination of Double Taxation* (September 1958), *in* 4 *Legislative History of United States Tax Conventions*, 4445 (United States, Joint Committee on Internal Revenue Taxation, US Government Printing Office 1962) (the work of the League of Nations was eventually taken up by the Organisation for European Economic Co-operation. The name alone is indicative of the role of European states in the next stages of development of the models. The 'Members countries' were Austria, Belgium, Denmark, France, Germany, Greece, Iceland, Ireland, Italy, Luxembourg, the Netherlands, Norway, Portugal, Sweden, Switzerland, Turkey, and the United Kingdom, with 'Associate Members' the United States and Canada, and a special status for Spain and Yugoslavia).

2.1.2.2. *Forerunners (Circa 1860s): Focus on Regional Integration*

As the precursor to the discussion of the international efforts (discussed in the next Section, 2.1.2.3.), here a brief discussion of the efforts to organize the earliest tax treaties gives insight into the nascent notions of double taxation (especially how this interacted with the way taxes themselves were conceptualized), the momentum that regional integration may create for solving it (evoking themes relevant to the EU) and possible solutions (especially the exemption method, which is often perceived to be the opposite of the credit method).

Johann Hattingh in his research *On the Origins of Model Tax Conventions: Nineteenth-Century German Tax Treaties and Laws Concerned with Avoidance of Double Tax* translates the key concepts from the legislation, case law and treaties concluded by German states in the 1800s, revealing that notions such as a 'permanent establishment' and a 'taxpayer's place of residence', which are crucial components of modern models and treaties, were already elaborated at that time.[440] As for the historical context, two factors combined to provide the impetus for avoiding double taxation, namely 'The Rise of Fiscal Centralism among the German States of the Nineteenth Century'[441] and the constitutional principles of 'The North German Confederation and the Prussian Drive for Integration, 1867-71'.[442]

Regarding the first factor, Hattingh explains that the rise of fiscal federalism, or centralism, came about in the early 1800s after events that fragmented German-speaking territories (notably after the Holy Roman Empire was abolished in 1806 and after the defeat of Napoleon marked by the Congress in Vienna in 1815). This led to a desire for a (re)unification, or at least deeper integration, among the German-speaking region.[443] Coordination on tax matters was one avenue towards this end.[444] A customs union (referred to as the German 'Zollverein') was established in 1834. Yet, divisions remained, as Austria did not join, and 'after the war with Prussia in 1866', Austria left the German confederation, which seemed to spark a reinvigorated effort by Prussia for integration:

440. Johann Hattingh, *On the Origins of Model Tax Conventions: Nineteenth-Century German Tax Treaties and Laws Concerned with Avoidance of Double Tax*, *in* 6 *Studies in the History of Tax Law* 31, 31 (John Tiley ed., Hart Publishing 2013).
441. *Id.*, at 32–33.
442. *Id.*, at 33 et seq.
443. *Id.*, at 33.
444. Corroborating a tendency to seek agreement on tax matters, among others, *see*, e.g., HeinOnline, World Treaty Library, Convention between Austria and Prussia (1816), Convention Between Prussia and Saxony for The Settlement of Boundaries and Claims (1819), Convention Between Saxony and Schoenburg (1835), all of which seem to relate to coordinating powers in a time of territorial transition and, though they are not tax treaties, they show the emergence of agreements being put in place either for fiscal federalism or for merely special issues of delineating tax powers.

> 'It is at this point in history that concerns about double taxation become a feature of a new political and legal imperative for harmonisation of direct taxes.'[445]

Regarding the second factor, the 1867 Constitution of the North German Federation was based on the principle of 'equality', including a 'common citizenship' with the requirement that 'nationals … of each State of the Confederation shall be treated in every other State as natives', and on 'the freedom of movement and establishment'.[446] Two quotes from Hattingh emphasize the connection between these constitutional rights and double taxation:

> 'The creation of a common citizenship and guaranteed constitutional rights of equality and freedom of movement and establishment is the origin of the German effort to eliminate double taxation' since those constitutional rights would be invoked when double taxation was argued to be an obstacle.[447]
>
> 'The 1867 Constitution did not, however, take away the fiscal sovereignty of the Member States. Instead, the various taxes imposed throughout the Federation had to be reconciled and harmonised with the positive constitutional affirmation of the individual rights of equality, freedom of movement and establishment. When these taxes presented a barrier to the realisation of these rights, legislative intervention was required.'[448]

The parallels with the EU are obvious, given the emphasis placed on an 'economic union' and 'harmonisation of laws' 'pursuant to constitutional ideals of freedom of movement and establishment', while leaving some fiscal sovereignty with the states.[449] By contrast with the EU, however, it seems that the North German Confederation imposed a comparatively stronger legislative imperative on its 'Member States' to achieve fiscal coordination.[450] If so, one reason for this may be that it was a 'confederation', thus arguably a 'stronger' form of union than that of the EU.[451]

As can be seen, the underlying rationale for avoiding double taxation was motivated by the aims of integration, fiscal centralism, equality and freedom of movement and establishment. This influenced the understanding of double taxation:

> 'What should not be lost sight of is that the question in 1869 was not whether double taxation according to some theoretical description was present; rather, the

445. Johann Hattingh, *On the Origins of Model Tax Conventions: Nineteenth-Century German Tax Treaties and Laws Concerned with Avoidance of Double Tax*, *in* 6 *Studies in the History of Tax Law* 31, 33 (John Tiley ed., Hart Publishing 2013).
446. *Id.*, at 33-34 (citing Article 3(1) of the 1867 Constitution).
447. *Id.*, at 34 and *see also* at 37 (where the author reports the case of Prussians who owned land in Saxony, suffered double taxation and entered a petition to complain in 1867, which had an influence during the legislative process).
448. *Id.*, at 34.
449. *Id.*, at 32, 34, 60.
450. *Id.*, at 33-34 (discussing 'a legally required obligation for Member States to harmonise their fiscal laws' and how efforts to 'remove barriers' caused by double taxation, in the case of 'direct taxes', 'initially took the form of a bilateral tax treaty, and later federal legislation').
451. For more on the legal system and political structure of the EU, *see*, e.g., Rita Szudoczky, *The Sources of EU Law and Their Relationships: Lessons for the Field of Taxation* Section 3.2.1 (32 Doctoral Series, IBFD 2014) ('The Union's governance structure: between a federal State and an international organization').

issue then was whether simultaneous taxes levied among the German states on the same person infringed that person's new-found freedoms of movement and establishment (much like contemporary questions under EU tax law).'[452]

The understanding of double taxation was also influenced by the different conceptualization of taxes at that time. Many taxes at that time were 'impersonal' or 'real' taxes that 'were not levied on any measure of actual income'.[453] They were viewed as distinct taxes levied on separate items, such as taxes on land or on business.[454] One consequence of this vision of taxes as 'distinct and unrelated direct taxes'[455] was that, theoretically, 'taxes on the "same income" were an objective impossibility'.[456] Thus, the notion of double taxation differed accordingly.[457]

Crucially, one consequence that followed from this vision of taxes was that the solution that seemed most appropriate was to find a distinct 'connecting factor' for each seemingly distinct tax.[458] For example, for land or property taxes, the connecting factor was the situs or place where it was located.[459] For business taxes, it was where the business operated (answering this question led to contentious case law and eventually the notion of a PE).[460] For 'taxes imposed on the person', options included nationality, citizenship, residence, etc., and consensus eventually coalesced around residence.[461] As can be seen, in this time period, the drafters sought to assign taxation rights to one of the two states. The other state was excluded from taxing the income. As a result, the credit method was not necessary.

452. Johann Hattingh, *On the Origins of Model Tax Conventions: Nineteenth-Century German Tax Treaties and Laws Concerned with Avoidance of Double Tax*, *in* 6 *Studies in the History of Tax Law* 31, 41–42 (John Tiley ed., Hart Publishing 2013).
453. *Id.*, at 38. *See also*, e.g., League of Nations, 1925 Report, at p. 4075 (these distinctions persisted, and likely evolved. Experts refrained from giving precise definitions. Among brief descriptions of 'impersonal' taxes, or 'impôts réels', the 1925 Report explained that there 'would be no point' in giving 'very detailed definitions'. It sufficed to say that these are 'charged on the income arising from specific sources and not on the income of persons as such').
454. Johann Hattingh, *On the Origins of Model Tax Conventions: Nineteenth-Century German Tax Treaties and Laws Concerned with Avoidance of Double Tax*, *in* 6 *Studies in the History of Tax Law* 31, 41 (John Tiley ed., Hart Publishing 2013).
455. *Id.*, at 39.
456. *Id.*, at 38.
457. *Id.*, at 41.
458. *Id.*, at 38–39.
459. *Id.*
460. Johann Hattingh, *On the Origins of Model Tax Conventions: Nineteenth-Century German Tax Treaties and Laws Concerned with Avoidance of Double Tax*, *in* 6 *Studies in the History of Tax Law* 31, 47, 49–53 (John Tiley ed., Hart Publishing 2013).
461. *Id.*, at 38–39, 44–46 (discussing the '13 May 1870 ... Act for the Elimination of Double Taxation', which included a change when compared to the 1869 treaty between Prussia and Saxony, i.e., 'from citizenship to residence as the main basis for exclusive taxation'. Two possible sets of reasons for this included: (1) arguments based on 'the benefits theory of taxation' and (2) arguments based on the constitutional common citizenry – 'citizenship would have been an ill-fitting norm in the federal context: the constitutional ideals of a new overarching German citizenship that guaranteed freedom of movement and establishment ... implied that a federal citizen could take up residence anywhere ...').

To offer one example, in the 1869 tax treaty between Prussia and Saxony, the connecting factors were gathered together in one place.[462] According to Article 1, taxpayers were 'subjected to direct state tax *only* in the federal state to which they belonged as subjects' (emphasis added), subject to the specific exceptions in Articles 2–4.[463] One of the exceptions, for example, was: for land and business taxes, only the state of situs and the state where 'business is exercised' could tax (Article 2).[464] It seems that, in each case, double taxation was prevented by granting an exclusive taxation right. In sum, the general rule seemed to be that the state of citizenship had the exclusive right to tax, thus excluding the other state from taxing, *except*, where specific connecting factors for income or taxable events were identified, only the state with the relevant connecting factor could tax, requiring exemption by the state of citizenship[465] (eventually 'residence' replaced citizenship as the norm).[466] Although it, in effect, required an exemption, either by the state of citizenship or by the other state, depending on the article in question, one rule (i.e., a 'sub-rule' of Article 2, translated in Hattingh's work) alluded to the fact that the exemption applied only '*insofar as* it was *already* accordingly *taxed* in the other State [ie where the land was situated or the business exercised]' and 'demonstrably imposed' (emphasis added).[467] Notably, it seemed to be based on *actual* taxation, with some sort of subject-to-tax requirement.

Finally, on the topic of defining double taxation, a question arose regarding distributions of profits. This issue of the double taxation of distributions of profits, or dividend income – i.e., both at the level of a 'limited company' and at the level of its shareholder – came before the Imperial Court, which held that technically the company and the shareholder are completely distinct taxable persons, so this is not *inadmissible*; the '1870 Imperial Double Taxation Law' allows this.[468] This seems to echo the distinction that eventually emerged under the OECD Model, discussed below (*see infra* note 542), according to which the Model predominantly targets juridical double taxation and not economic double taxation, though Hattingh warns against equating the two situations due to the previously discussed different conceptualization of taxes at that time.[469]

It was only later, beginning with reforms in 1885 through 1891 in Prussia, that the tax systems began to introduce a full 'general income tax that adjusted the liability of

462. *Id.*, at 39. This is just one of many treaties and laws that Hattingh's work translates and analyses.
463. *Id.*, at 39–40, 72–73.
464. *Id.*
465. Johann Hattingh, *On the Origins of Model Tax Conventions: Nineteenth-Century German Tax Treaties and Laws Concerned with Avoidance of Double Tax*, *in* 6 *Studies in the History of Tax Law* 31, 40 (John Tiley ed., Hart Publishing 2013).
466. *See supra* note 461. Interestingly, *Id.*, at 40 (double taxation on the basis of dual-nationality was expressly permitted: some opinions at that time believed this 'was justified since the taxpayer enjoyed twice as much security').
467. *Id.*, at 39–40.
468. *Id.*, at 57–58.
469. *Id.*, at 58.

taxpayers to their individual capacity to pay'.[470] Along with this shift in the conceptualization of certain taxes (towards general income taxes, based on ability to pay) comes a greater likelihood of overlapping tax jurisdiction and a consequent shift in the solutions seen as suitable for double taxation relief, including the credit method. This shift towards general income taxes was not contained to this region, but became rather standard internationally (as some developments discussed in Section 2.1.2.3. indicate, *see*, e.g., *infra* note 498 and note 562).

Even bearing in mind the historical context and differences, key concepts from this period remain relevant to this day: e.g., common citizenry, free movement, connecting factors such as the place of situs, a PE and residence, and different notions of double taxation. The developments in the 1800s in this part of the world indelibly left their mark, as it eventually led to the 'conclusion in 1899 of the first tax treaty between a Member State of the German Empire and another sovereign state, namely between Prussia and Austria-Hungary' and this trend was followed with other neighbouring European states.[471]

2.1.2.3. *Picking up the Baton (Circa 1920s): Focus on International Cooperation*

2.1.2.3.1. Some Preliminary Remarks

While the above-mentioned German and adjacent states had made progress, no similar degree of consistency and coordination of action had yet caught on in other places.[472]

470. *Id.*, at 62–63, 66 (in 1896 in Austria; in 1909 and 1912 in the Hungarian part of the Austro-Hungarian Empire).

471. *Id.*, at 60, 69–70 (citing various treaties). *See also* League of Nations, 1925 Report, at 4072 (citing 'All the treaties concluded between the Central European States both before and after the war' among the solutions considered as inspiration).

472. As discussed above in Section 2.1.1.2., at *supra* note 174, no relief, other than a deduction from the tax base for foreign taxes, existed in the US until 1918 and the relief from 1918 was unilateral action; the UK offered relief only for the 'well-being of the empire'. *See also*, e.g., John F. Avery Jones, *Chapter I: Sir Josiah Stamp and Double Income Tax, in* 6 *Studies in the History of Tax Law* 1, 5 n.26 (John Tiley ed., Hart Publishing 2013) (some other states reportedly developed some limited forms of unilateral relief: 'New Zealand exempted income that had paid tax in another Dominion; Newfoundland on income that arose in the UK, Canada or the US') and at 3 n.11 ('The UK was well behind most other countries in introducing such a relief. For a contemporary article, see SE Minnis, "Double Taxation in Holland, Norway, Switzerland and Italy" (1921) 3(1) Journal of Comparative Legislation and International Law 88'); S.E. Minnis, *Double Taxation in Holland, Norway, Switzerland and Italy*, 3(1) J. Comp. Legis. & Int'l L. 88, 88–92 (1921) (according to this article, the statutory double taxation relief in the Netherlands was for colonial taxes and a one-half 'abatement' for Dutch companies receiving dividends from abroad; in Norway, Norwegian residents could benefit from an exemption of 50% of their income from real property abroad and otherwise, there was a law 'empowering the Sovereign to enter into agreements with foreign States with a view to apportioning the duty on a business which is liable to taxation both in Norway and in a foreign State' which had been used only once in practice; in Switzerland, 'In general, the Federal tribunal has declined to attempt the solution of double taxation problems of an international character, and the questions with which it deals are in the main those of inter-cantonal taxation.' But, as regards cantonal double taxation, similar to the North German Confederation

Fast forward a few decades later and the First World War erupted in 1914. Increased taxes to cover the costs of war were consistently cited[473] as a factor that finally spurred more widespread action on double taxation. As mentioned, in approximately 1919, the private sector began to mobilize and recruit renowned experts, such as Thomas S. Adams, under the ICC; shortly after, the public sector followed suit under the League of Nations.[474] From that moment forward, the activity at the League of Nations precipitated a steady stream of dialogue and reports, which, despite passing to new leadership (currently under the OECD and UN), has continued almost non-stop ever since.[475]

The questions ('terms of reference') posed to the first panel of experts convened by the League of Nations already have undertones of the mood that existed at the time, by employing the phrase 'evil consequences of double taxation'. Moreover, the questions also clearly underline the international nature of the enquiry; it was no longer confined to the 'well-being' of an empire or a given political unit that desired to be federated or integrated in some way. They included the following:

---

of 1867, rules for allocating the right to tax income were developed on the basis 'of equality before the law and freedom of domicile' of the 'Federal Constitution of 1848'; in Italy, there were no explicit rules regarding double taxation, but rather an analysis of the scope of the 'income' taxes, e.g., the extent to which Italy would tax - or not - income earned from abroad, helped 'indicate to what extent the possibility of double taxation exists'; moreover, 'as between the mother-country and colonies', which is 'of relatively small importance in the case of Italy', there was 'one point of interest in connection with war profits taxation', where a refund mechanism, similar to a credit method, was in place in cases where 'war profits tax' was paid both in the colony of Eritrea and in Italy); Michael J. Graetz & Michael M. O'Hear, *The 'Original Intent' of U.S. International Taxation*, 46(5) Duke L.J. 1021, 1046 n.103 (1997) (citing other sources that discuss the laws that existed in other states, such as Belgium and Norway, among others).

473. *See* Section 2.1.1.4. 'Interim conclusions: lessons from unilateral measures'; *see supra* note 90 and note 135.

474. *See supra* note 433 and note 434.

475. *See*, e.g., League of Nations, 1923 Report (full citation, *supra* note 111), at 4003 et seq.; League of Nations, 1925 Report, at 4057 et seq. (full citation, *supra* note 124); League of Nations, 1927 Report, at 4111 et seq. (full citation, *supra* note 439); League of Nations, 1928 Report, at 4151 et seq. (full citation, *supra* note 439); League of Nations, Fiscal Committee, *London and Mexico Model Tax Conventions: Commentary and Text* (1946), *in* 4 *Legislative History of United States Tax Conventions*, 4319 (United States, Joint Committee on Internal Revenue Taxation, US Government Printing Office 1962); Organisation for European Economic Co-operation, *First Report of the Fiscal Committee of the OEEC on the Elimination of Double Taxation* (September 1958), *in* 4 *Legislative History of United States Tax Conventions*, 4445 (United States, Joint Committee on Internal Revenue Taxation, US Government Printing Office 1962) (hereinafter 'OEEC, 1958 Report'); Organisation for European Economic Co-operation, *Second Report of the Fiscal Committee of the OEEC on the Elimination of Double Taxation* (July 1959), *in* 4 *Legislative History of United States Tax Conventions*, 4511 (United States, Joint Committee on Internal Revenue Taxation, US Government Printing Office 1962) (hereinafter 'OEEC, 1959 Report'); Organisation for European Economic Co-operation, *Third Report of the Fiscal Committee of the OEEC on the Elimination of Double Taxation* (August 1960), *in* 4 *Legislative History of United States Tax Conventions*, 4565 (United States, Joint Committee on Internal Revenue Taxation, US Government Printing Office 1962) (hereinafter 'OEEC, 1960 Report'); Organisation for European Economic Co-operation, *Fourth Report of the Fiscal Committee of the OEEC on the Elimination of Double Taxation* (August 1961), *in* 4 *Legislative History of United States Tax Conventions*, 4619 (United States, Joint Committee on Internal Revenue Taxation, US Government Printing Office 1962) (hereinafter 'OEEC, 1961 Report'); *see also supra* note 438.

- 'Can any general principles be formulated as the basis for an international convention to remove the evil consequences of double taxation, or should conventions be made between particular countries, limited to their own immediate requirements?'
- 'Are the principles of existing arrangements for avoiding double taxation, either between independent nations (e.g., the Rome Convention)[476] or between the competent (portions) of a federal state, capable of application to a new international convention?'
- 'Can a remedy be found, or to what extent can a remedy be found, in an amendment of the taxation system of each individual country, independently of any international agreement?'[477]

Before studying the credit method as one possible solution (Subsection 2.1.2.3.3.), the aim here is to provide the background to the problem that sparked its existence, namely the notion of double taxation (Subsection 2.1.2.3.2.). How 'double taxation' is defined, or what about it is perceived as problematic – which creates the rationale(s) for tackling it – has an impact on the selection and design of solutions (as seen above in Section 2.1.1. throughout the different iterations of the credit method and in Section 2.1.2.2. in the context of the German confederation).[478]

2.1.2.3.2. Excursus: Coalescing Around the Problem: The Evil Consequences of Double Taxation

Although this phenomenon of double taxation is depicted above (in the 'terms of reference' of the 1923 report) as a serious enemy, double taxation is not explicitly defined in this report. Rather, the report focuses on its economic consequences (understandably, as this is what was also requested in the 'terms of reference').[479] As far as could be detected in all reports, no concrete definition of double taxation was expressly formulated until arguably in 1958 under the Organisation for European

476. League of Nations, 1925 Report, at 4071–4072 ('After the war, the new conditions resulting from the dismemberment of a number of European empires increased the difficulties arising out of the rival claims of different states. One after the other, treaties were concluded between certain of the Austro-Hungarian Succession States among themselves or between them and neighbouring States. We may mention those concluded by the German Empire with Austria [...] We must, however, make special mention of the Convention signed at Rome on June 13th, 1921, between Austria, Hungary, Italy, Poland, the Kingdom of the Serbs, Croats and Slovenes and Roumania. This instrument is the first known example of a collective convention laying down common principles to be followed by a large number of States' (footnotes omitted)).
477. League of Nations, 1923 Report, at 4006.
478. In agreement, *see also*, e.g., Peter Harris, *Chapter III: Taxation of Residents on Foreign Source Income, in United Nations Handbook on Selected Issues in Administration of Double Tax Treaties for Developing Countries* 109, 121 (Alexander Trepelkov, Harry Tonino & Dominika Halka eds, United Nations 2013) ('Effective administration of the mechanics of elimination of double taxation requires an understanding of the accepted rationale for such relief').
479. League of Nations, 1923 Report, at 4010 ('(1) What are the economic consequences of double taxation from the point of view: (a) of the equitable distribution of burdens; (b) of interference with economic intercourse and with the free flow of capital? To what extent are these consequences similar in the different types of cases commonly described as double taxation?' In particular, the experts answered mostly letter (b)).

Economic Co-operation (OEEC),[480] though some indications appeared in 1936 with a mere half-sentence[481] and in 1946[482] (as will be discussed below in this subsection).

It is surprising that establishing a common understanding of the problem would not be at least one starting point for solutions, especially those for a diverse set of states with diverse tax systems. It is hard to precisely target a problem that is not defined. Because this is a useful starting point for designing a solution, such as the credit method, the following paragraphs collect and briefly analyse what was understood about the problem of double taxation, based on the historical reports.

Because most of the reports, especially the early ones, do not explicitly define 'double taxation', the challenge is to seek the implicit understanding. This is accomplished by searching for clues based on locating where the term is used in the reports and in what context, by studying the examples used in the reports, and by carefully analysing what is written in order to read between the lines so to speak.

From the first report in 1923, *Report on Double Taxation*, two distinctions emerge. First, the 'four experts' made an explicit distinction between double taxation as a 'barrier' and double taxation as a 'burden'.[483] This distinction revolved almost entirely around timing – in particular, the timing of a given investment vis-à-vis the timing of a new tax.[484] More specifically, it related to the effect of taxes imposed either *before* or *after* an investment is made. If an investment was made and, then, either a new tax was imposed on such investments or an existing tax was increased, this becomes an unexpected additional cost from which the investor cannot escape and is therefore a 'burden'. If an investment was not yet made and a new tax was imposed, this becomes a disincentive to make the investment, or it can become a cost that the investor pushes onto the borrower in the foreign country. If the investor is blocked from or dissuaded from investing as a result of the tax, this could be a 'barrier'. According to the report:

480. OEEC, 1961 Report, Commentaries on Articles XXIII and XXIV concerning the Methods for Avoidance of Double Taxation, at 4685 (in this report, definitions are officially put forward. Two distinct definitions of 'juridical double taxation' and 'economic double taxation' are drafted).
481. League of Nations, 1936 Report, at 4258 (although not labelling it a definition as such, the report mentions that: 'The problem submitted to the experts was twofold: to ensure that a taxpayer should not be doubly taxed by two States on account of the same capital or the same income, and to ensure that no taxpayer should take advantage of different systems of fiscal law to evade his obligations').
482. League of Nations, 1946 Report, at 4327, London and Mexico Model Tax Conventions – Commentary and Text (although not labelling it a definition as such, the report explains that: 'International double taxation arises when the taxes of two or more countries overlap in such a manner that persons liable to tax in more than one country bear a higher tax burden than if they were subject to one tax jurisdiction only. The additional burden so incurred must, of course, be due not merely to differences in tax rates for the countries concerned, but to the fact that two or more jurisdictions concurrently impose taxes having the same bases and incidence without regard to the claims of the other tax jurisdictions').
483. League of Nations, 1923 Report, at 4010–4012.
484. *Id.*, at 4013–4014 (e.g., '... the older the tax the less of a true tax it is as a general rule' due to investors, who knowing the cost of the tax, factor it into their investment calculations and expectations).

> 'So far as concerns taxation in existence at the time when an investment is made, the "burden" of double taxation is a misnomer. It can only rightly be called a "burden" if a hindrance to free action is a "burden". As a matter of fact, it is rather a "barrier", and the *appearance* of double taxation is, in fact, for the most part negatived by the ordinary operation of economic forces.'[485]

> 'So, in the case of double taxation, whatever investment exists in the area when the barrier is put up suffers a burden; whatever investment thereafter from outside gets over the barrier escapes the burden. But much potential investment is kept back altogether, and this part is "barred", not "burdened". In some senses this case is only a particular illustration of a general theory relating to the effects of taxes in general ... .'[486]

Second, by means of an example of a fictive state called Morania, the experts made an implicit distinction. They indicated that some cases of double taxation are merely 'nominal' and not 'real', implying that *not* all instances where double taxation occurs from a *legal* point of view (meaning where a taxpayer is obliged to pay taxes to more than one state) have an actual *economic* impact on a cross-border investment:

> '*Nominally* the non-resident investor pays .66 units Moranian tax and his non-resident tax in addition, *i.e.*, he suffers double taxation; in *reality*, he pays *only* his home or residence tax, for he has secured or protected himself against the Moranian tax by the additional yield required before he invested' (emphasis added).[487]

By means of another example, regarding dividends, the experts offered further insight. They discussed a case whereby the dividends received by an individual shareholder are reduced because of taxes levied abroad on the corporation – that is, the dividends are reduced in comparison to what the shareholder *would have received* if there were *not* such corporate taxation – and, on this ground, the shareholder 'has a grievance' and claims 'necessary' relief for double taxation.[488] In this way, the experts detected an economic incidence of double taxation in such cases that merits relief.

This implies that they would favour indirect credit systems, imputation credit systems, or other means to relieve 'economic' double taxation. Yet, they were also prescient in foreseeing the numerous difficult practical questions that arise under such systems of relief. They asked 'How does he establish what he has suffered?' and pointed out obstacles, including that: (i) shareholders generally have 'little knowledge of the details ... of the corporation' and the amounts paid in taxes at the level of the corporation; (ii) even if the corporation can establish its income earned and taxes paid abroad, '[o]wing to the ways in which the laws of those countries compute income, it

485. *Id.*, at 4011.
486. *Id.*, at 4012.
487. *Id.*, at 4013.
488. *Id.*, at 4050–4051 ('A common case is the following. A resident in New York holds shares in, let us say, a motor company in the United States, which has two large branch businesses, one in France and the other in England. These two branch businesses are taxed on their operations to the full in France and England, and in consequence the total resources of the corporation in the United States are reduced, and the amount of income which it distributes by way of dividends to the shareholders in New York is diminished. The shareholder realises this and has a grievance. He asks for the necessary relief under method 3').

may well be that the rates of tax imposed under those laws are quite different from the rate which the total tax bears to the income computed according to United States methods'; (iii) 'the dividends ... may be either less or more than the profits made in that year'; and (iv) there is a question 'whether the tax must be regarded as wholly applicable to the dividends or as going to swell the reserves, or being proportionately divided between them'.[489]

As an interim conclusion, from the above, two related points emerge: not all cases of 'nominal' double taxation have an economic incidence; not all cases of economic double taxation amount to double taxation from a legal point of view. On the one hand, recall that under the system of double taxation relief of the German Empire, the Imperial Court held that this type of double taxation – first at the level of the limited company and second at the level of the shareholder – was *not* double taxation under the 1870 law: under the law, it was established that the jurisdiction where the limited company operated its business had the right to tax it and, from a practical point of view, had the ability to better assess the proper amount of taxation, whereas the place where the shareholder resided had the right to levy the personal tax on the income of the shareholder, and these were simply two distinct taxpayers.[490] On the other hand, the four experts make the case that there is a clear economic incidence of double taxation in such shareholder-corporation cases. The experts also point out that there are incidences of 'nominal' double taxation that have a minimal, or no, economic incidence on a cross-border investment (for a more recent discussion, *see*, e.g., Shaviro's example of being taxed twice, or even multiple times, but at extremely low rates, e.g., 1%[491]). Clearly, the legal aspects of double taxation and economic aspects do not always coincide.

Depending on the rationale for counteracting double taxation, this dissonance matters. If the rationale is to facilitate cross-border investment and trade, then arguably policymakers should direct their attention to the economic impact of taxation. Indeed, it would be more difficult to argue that only the formal legal aspects of double taxation are to be remedied at the neglect of the economic aspects. If the rationale was merely to reduce the seemingly oppressive burden of post-war levels of taxation, then policymakers should direct their attention to the threshold at which taxation is deemed excessive – at either some *absolute* threshold of, for example, 50% of the profits or some *relative* threshold of, for example, maximum the higher of the rates of the two states. This, accordingly, would influence what solutions are prioritized (e.g., reduction of tax rates, exemption of tax base, indirect credit for taxes paid, etc.) and how they

489. *Id.*, at 4050–4051.
490. *See* Johann Hattingh, *On the Origins of Model Tax Conventions: Nineteenth-Century German Tax Treaties and Laws Concerned with Avoidance of Double Tax, in* 6 *Studies in the History of Tax Law* 31 (John Tiley ed., Hart Publishing 2013), at *supra* note 468.
491. Daniel N. Shaviro, *Fixing U.S. International Taxation* 6–7 (Oxford University Press 2014).

are designed (e.g., Kane has considered an alternative approach to drafting Article 23 under which relief could be based on the overall burden[492]).

Though it appears that the distinction had not yet been articulated at this time, this juridical versus economic distinction was subliminally emerging.

In the follow-up 1925 report, *Double Taxation and Tax Evasion*, the perspective changed from one based on economics to one shaped by expertise from careers in government.[493] Seven government-appointed representatives[494] built upon the results of previous work,[495] including on the four expert economists' 1923 Report, on the Institute of International Law, on the ICC,[496] and on existing attempts to solve the problem of double taxation both in domestic laws and in international agreements.[497] In fact, the Report is entirely dedicated to a discussion and comparison of existing *solutions* to double taxation, followed by a 'resolution' on a compromise solution.

Similar to the situation that prevailed in the 1800s (discussed in Section 2.1.2.2.), there were numerous 'impôts réels', resembling the aforementioned 'impersonal taxes'. This led to 'the difficulties caused by differences in the various fiscal systems', in particular between 'impôts réels' and 'general or personal taxes'.[498] Each called for different solutions: the former an assignment of income and the latter either the credit method or a 'tax exemption' method with a maximum limit on the relief.[499] As Hattingh explained above (*see supra* note 457), the different conceptualization of taxes at that time likely meant a different conceptualization of double taxation.

Having skipped right to solutions, no explicit attempt is made to define double taxation. However, some insight can be garnered from some examples throughout the 1925 Report and from its Appendix:[500]

492. Mitchell A. Kane, *International Tax Reform, the Tragedy of the Tax Commons, and Bilateral Tax Treaties* (June 2017) (unpublished manuscript) (presented at Colloquium: Current Developments in European and International Tax Law, WU Institute for Austrian and International Tax Law and PwC Austria, Vienna, 19 Jun. 2017) (on file with author).
493. League of Nations, 1927 Report, at 4119 (the Committee of Technical Experts on Double Taxation and Tax Evasion described the 1925 Report as a study 'from an administrative and practical point of view' by 'a group of high officials of the fiscal administrations of various countries').
494. League of Nations, 1925 Report, at 4061 (the seven representatives were all from European states, namely Belgium, Czechoslovakia, France, Great Britain, Italy, the Netherlands, Switzerland).
495. *Id.*, at 4061, 4065 and 4067.
496. *Id.*, at 4067–4069.
497. *Id.*, at 4070–4072.
498. *Id.*, at 4074–4075 (e.g., in Britain only a personal tax existed and the authors noted that 'the very expression "*impôts réels*" has no precise equivalent in the English language'. A British delegate argued that this distinction was a dangerous one, implying that both kinds of taxes ultimately affect an individual: 'In the course of our discussions on this subject, Sir Percy Thompson said: "Any classification into '*impôts réels*' and '*impôts personnels*' would become positively dangerous if any attempt was made, from the mere difference of nomenclature, to draw conclusions as to the different economic effects of these taxes"').
499. *Id.*, at 4074–4075.
500. *Id.*, at 4096 (Appendix: Note by M. Léon-Dufour on the Various Methods Suggested for Remedying Double Taxation and Their Graphical Representation).

Fig.1

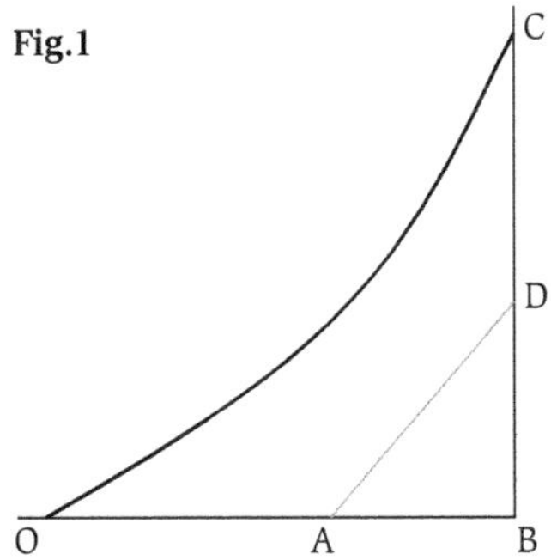

Accompanied by this graphic indication of double taxation (reproduced based on the original), the Appendix describes a classic example of taxation both on the basis of residence, by country X, and on the basis of source or origin, by country Y.[501] The figure represents the **income** of the taxpayer along the **horizontal** line, BO, of which BA is derived from country Y, and the **taxes** along the **vertical** line, BC. In this figure, 'BD represents the amount of the double taxation'.[502] In this way, the author of the Appendix shows one common *cause* of double taxation, namely an overlap of residence-based and source-based tax claims.

In addition, in other examples in the report, the experts imagine two states that both apply a personal, or general, tax to the income of the same taxpayer, and they discuss the difficulties of finding common definitions for 'fiscal domicile'. In this way, they show that double taxation occurs when states use different connecting factors (e.g., one uses nationality and the other domicile) for levying personal taxes, thus hinting at another common *cause* of double taxation, namely dual domicile (dual residence).[503]

One other notable aspect of the 1925 report is the emphasis on the link between the 'evils of double taxation' and 'tax evasion'[504] as well as other 'abuses'. By contrast with double taxation, the authors explicitly attempted to define tax evasion and delimit its scope.[505] The authors explain that, unlike 'double taxation' for which they had other reports to rely on (they had previously cited the work of the ICC, the International Law Institute, etc.), 'as far as we are aware, no enquiry has been conducted by any

501. *Id.* (the taxpayer is 'domiciled' in country X; OB represents the whole income or capital; AB is 'the part of the income or capital in another country Y, which is known as the "country of origin" to indicate that the income or capital in question is derived from abroad') The authors of the report also discuss one possible instance of 'double taxation' in connection with the limit on the relief offered under the 'deduction' (credit) method, but not much can be inferred about their understanding of 'double taxation' from this 'deduction' method example because the excess amount that cannot be credited results from some unusual features of the domestic law assumed under their example. This will be discussed at length below in this section.
502. League of Nations, 1925 Report, at 4096 (Appendix: Note by M. Léon-Dufour on the Various Methods Suggested for Remedying Double Taxation and Their Graphical Representation).
503. League of Nations, 1925 Report, at 4078–4081.
504. *Id.*, at 4087.
505. *Id.*, at 4082–4083.

international body on the subject of tax evasion'. In assessing the reasons for the reluctance to deal with the topic, they stated:

> 'We are also aware of the difficulties and objections which may be raised to all measures aimed at combating tax evasion; [...]
>
> The first criticism passed on the existing convention between France and England is that it increases the mischievous consequences of double taxation on account of the conflict of laws in respect of domicile. "The mutual interchange of information may thus, in some cases, bring, quite correctly under existing law, the whole of a personal estate under liability to taxation in both countries".
>
> To this objection, which may be made both in respect of income-tax and succession duties, it may be replied that the proposed resolutions form an indivisible whole, and that their object is to prevent both double taxation and tax evasion. The foregoing criticism will be seen to furnish a fresh proof of the close connection between these two problems.'[506]

Some concerns voiced today echo this. There are concerns that, in the rushed efforts to combat aggressive tax planning, double non-taxation, etc., under the anti-BEPS project and the ATAD, policymakers have overlooked the potential negative impact of new measures, such as new overlaps in taxation, leading to more double taxation and related disputes.[507] Back then, just as today, many hoped for a balanced approach to these two intertwined issues. One difference between then and now is that, since at least 2013, the pendulum has swung in the other direction, in that recent reports (from a successor of the League, i.e., the OECD) have centred on anti-evasion and anti-BEPS, and less on double taxation. At that time in 1925, 'public opinion in a number of countries [was] not yet ripe for the adoption of certain of the proposed measures' against tax evasion,[508] whereas now, at the time of writing, a combination of factors has shifted public opinion – e.g., a global financial crisis, the resultant austerity and budgetary pressures on citizens and governments,[509] combined with reports by media and investigative journalism[510] arguing that MNEs and wealthy

506. *Id.*, at 4085; *see also Id.*, at 4087 ('Before concluding our remarks, we think it desirable to draw attention to the connection which exists between the two problems of tax evasion and double taxation. In the course of our report, we have already noticed this fact in one of its aspects. On the one hand, conventions suggested for avoiding double taxation may contain special measures against evasion, destined to prevent any abuse arising from their application; on the other hand, the exchange of information may perhaps lead to duplication in the levying of taxes. This is tantamount to saying that, in elaborating any practical measure for dealing with one of these problems, account must also be taken of the other').

507. *See*, e.g., OECD, *BEPS: Frequently Asked Questions*, https://www.oecd.org/ctp/beps-frequently-asked-questions.pdf (last visited 11 May 2019) (among its top ten most frequently asked questions was '5. Do the BEPS measures increase the risk of double taxation?'); OECD, *Making Dispute Resolution Mechanisms More Effective, Action 14 – 2015 Final Report*, OECD/G20 Base Erosion and Profit Shifting Project (OECD Publishing 2015).

508. League of Nations, 1925 Report, at 4088.

509. Reuven S. Avi-Yonah, *The Great Recession and the International Tax Regime*, Kluwer International Tax Blog (23 Apr. 2019), http://kluwertaxblog.com/2019/04/23/the-great-recession-and-the-international-tax-regime/ (last visited 23 Apr. 2019).

510. *See*, e.g., International Consortium of Investigative Journalists, *Luxembourg Leaks: Global Companies' Secrets Exposed* (2014), https://www.icij.org/investigations/luxembourg-leaks/ (last visited 19 Dec. 2017); International Consortium of Investigative Journalists, *Panama*

individuals have not been paying a fair share due to their ability to globe-trot to lax jurisdictions and to exploit legal loopholes.

As an interim conclusion, the different conceptualization of taxes (e.g., as 'personal' or 'impersonal') seemed to call for different approaches to resolving double taxation (as also discussed in Section 2.1.2.2.). Moreover, if the rationales for combating double taxation, such as facilitating international investment and trade or reducing excessive burdens, are balanced with other aims such as the prevention of tax avoidance, evasion and abuse, the solutions for double taxation relief and their scope and design may change accordingly. This brings back to mind the earlier discussion (in Section 2.1.1.2., *see*, e.g., *supra* note 144) of T.S. Adams' view that the credit method struck this balance. As will be discussed below (in Section 2.1.2.3.3.), when discussing their version of the credit method, some concerns over 'abuse' were also highlighted by the experts in the 1925 Report, and this influenced their proposal to include not just *one* limit but rather *two* limits on the amount of relief.

In the 1927 report, the term 'double taxation' appears but it is not defined; however, based on the way or context in which it is used, it reinforces certain rationales for counteracting it. First, one rationale for counteracting double taxation is because it creates an obstacle to international investment; linked to that as a sub-rationale, the reason that international investment matters is because it is 'one of the conditions of public prosperity and world economic reconstruction'.[511] Second, double taxation is often a 'truly excessive, if not intolerable' burden, which in turn may discourage cross-border business and may push them towards tax evasion. In this way, the connection between the two problems of double taxation and tax evasion is emphasized again. Yet, it establishes a cause-and-effect relationship, with double taxation as the *cause* and tax evasion as one of the adverse *effects*, thereby ensuring that double taxation remained the priority for the time being. Similar to the 1925 report, the 1927 report also describes one cause of double taxation, namely the overlap between residence and source taxation. The relevant excerpt is as follows:

> 'Double taxation, which affects mainly undertakings and persons who exercise their trade or profession in several countries, or derive income from countries other than the one in which they reside, imposes on such taxpayers burdens which, in many cases, seem truly excessive, if not intolerable. It tends to paralyse

Papers: Exposing the Rogue Offshore Finance Industry (2016), https://panamapapers.icij.org/ (last visited 19 Dec. 2017); International Consortium of Investigative Journalists, *Paradise Papers: Secrets of the Global Elite* (2017), https://www.icij.org/investigations/paradise-papers/ (last visited 19 Dec. 2017).

511. League of Nations, 1927 Report, at 4119 ('The International Financial Conference held at Brussels in 1920 recommended that the League of Nations take up the question of double taxation.' The corresponding footnote quotes the '*Recommendations of the Brussels Conference*' which includes the sentence 'An international understanding which, while ensuring the due payment by everyone of his full share of taxation, would avoid the imposition of double taxation which is at present an obstacle to the placing of investments abroad.' They added extra emphasis: 'The Financial Committee, in its report dated June 1925, expressed its agreement with the main lines of the experts' Resolutions [on Double Taxation and Tax Evasion], but urged the importance, in any future enquiries, of taking into consideration "the disadvantage of placing any obstacles in the way of the international circulation of capital, which is one of the conditions of public prosperity and world economic reconstruction"').

> their activity and to discourage initiative and thus constitutes a serious obstacle to the development of international relations and world production.
>
> At the same time, any excessive taxation, by its very burden, brings in its train tax evasion, the nature and grave consequences of which have been emphasized on earlier occasions; the suppression of double taxation is therefore closely connected with the measures for the systematic prevention or checking of such evasion.
>
> It is for this twofold purpose that efforts will have to be made to secure international cooperation, with a view to making it possible to put a stop to an evil which has become especially acute owing to the increase in the fiscal burdens consequent upon the war; the measures advocated by the experts could not fail to bring about a reduction in, and a better distribution of, such burdens.'[512]

Not until the 1930 report did other clues on the term 'double taxation' appear. In the 1930 report, a rather provocative view was expressed. A draft resolution was submitted by a UK member of the Committee, Sir Percy Thompson, which offered his view on 'double taxation' and the true cause of the problems. His draft resolution read as follows:

> 'That the prevalent view that an undesirable economic result, *viz.*, the creation of an artificial barrier which impedes the free flow of capital into the channels in which it can be most usefully and profitably employed, is produced by *double taxation* is fallacious: that *origin taxation* is solely responsible for this undesirable economic result which would remain unaffected if all taxes based on residence were everywhere abolished and in consequence double taxation ceased to exist.'[513]

This proposal by Sir Percy Thompson is an attempt to discuss what the true underlying problem is. It displays his strong disagreement over the problem being addressed since it challenges the proposition that double taxation is the problem. Where there seems to be consensus is that the real problem is an economic one, namely the 'barrier' to the 'free flow of capital', according to his resolution. Where there is disagreement is that, in his view, its real cause is not double taxation, but origin taxation.

Then to prove his point, he closes with a counterfactual, where he seeks to isolate one of the variables (i.e., origin taxation) and to test its effect: 'if all taxes based on residence were everywhere abolished', so that only origin taxation remained in place, then 'double taxation' would cease to exist; nevertheless, now that these two variables (i.e., residence-based taxes and double taxation) are removed from the equation, the question is: do the negative economic effects (which is the true underlying concern) still remain? He implies that, yes, the 'undesirable economic result' 'would remain unaffected' since 'origin taxation' would continue to create the barriers to the free flow of capital. The Fiscal Committee decided to postpone the matter 'until its next session'.[514]

512. League of Nations, 1927 Report, at 4122–4123.
513. League of Nations, 1930 Report, at 4211.
514. *Id.*, at 4211.

In the 1931 report, the challenged mounted by Sir Percy Thompson was still not resolved. He put forward a slightly modified resolution text, in which he replaced the words 'undesirable economic result' with 'certain economic result'.[515] Some said his resolution was perhaps an observation of 'the field of theoretical economics' and asked for him to put his verbal comments in writing for the matter to be discussed more deeply in a later session. However, no subsequent reports resolved it.

In the 1936 report, the members reinvigorated the link between double taxation and tax evasion. Moreover, the report includes a first formulation of a definition of the term 'double taxation'. Regarding the link, this can be seen in 'the following resolution' by the 'Assembly of the League of Nations':

> 'The Assembly,
>
> Considering that efforts to reduce the obstacle to the international circulation of capital must not have the effect of increasing fiscal fraud;
>
> Being of opinion that double taxation is both one of the causes of fiscal fraud and at the same time a serious obstacle to the development of international economic and financial relations;
>
> And holding that only concerted action based on specific agreements for international co-operation can ensure the accurate assessment and equitable allocation of taxes;
>
> Requests the Fiscal Committee to pursue vigorously its work for the avoidance of double taxation as far as possible, and also its work on the subject of international fiscal assistance, in order to promote practical arrangements calculated, as far as possible, to put down fiscal fraud' (internal quotations omitted).[516]

After a review of the records of the Fiscal Committee, it was observed that double taxation 'occupies the chief place', overshadowing tax evasion. The idea was that this was justified since efforts against double taxation 'should proceed the application of measures for the prevention of tax evasion' because double taxation is one of the causes of tax evasion.[517] As the report explained, '[b]eing threatened by double taxation, the taxpayer tries to find a way to escape ... to resort to methods which, not only enable him to escape any excessive burden, but actually place him in a privileged position as compared with his fellow-taxpayers'.[518] Yet, they conceded, enough progress had been made on the double taxation front - citing more than 140 conventions in force at that time - that the Committee could turn its attention more to tax evasion.[519] Thereafter, they described some examples of the problem of tax

515. League of Nations, 1931 Report, at 4231–4232 ('That the prevalent view that a certain economic result - *viz.*, the creation of an artificial barrier which impedes the free flow of capital into the channels in which it can be most usefully and profitably employed - is produced by *double taxation* is fallacious; that *origin taxation* is solely responsible for this economic result which would remain unaffected if all taxes based on residence were everywhere abolished and in consequence double taxation ceased to exist').
516. League of Nations, 1936 Report, at 4257.
517. *Id.*, at 4258.
518. *Id.*
519. *Id.*

evasion,[520] remarked that it is particularly acute with 'income from moveable capital',[521] and fretted about the challenges of tackling the problem.[522] However, to offer the epilogue, according to the next report in 1937, these challenges proved too difficult to surmount and thus the members of the Fiscal Committee were not prepared 'at present' for certain measures against tax evasion.[523]

In addition to its close relationship with tax evasion, the term 'double taxation' received a first expression of its definition:

> 'The problem submitted to the experts was twofold: to ensure that a taxpayer should not be doubly taxed by two States on account of the same capital or the same income, and to ensure that no taxpayer should take advantage of different systems of fiscal law to evade his obligations.'[524]

With the wording 'a taxpayer', it seems that the effect on one and the same person paying becomes more central to the definition. If so, it was moving in a direction similar to that of the current meaning of 'juridical double taxation'.

Due to World War Two, the next report was not published until 1946. The League of Nations announced that its work would soon be undertaken by the UN.[525] This report is particularly important as it contains two updated models, one drafted in Mexico in 1943 and one drafted in London in 1946. Due to the different states (and their respective economies) represented at the meetings that drafted the Mexico Model as compared to the London model, the models offer insight into the key divide on crucial international tax topics of the time.[526] In this respect, the report acknowledged that

520. *Id.* (regarding 'The Problem raised by the Assembly', the Committee limits the scope of the study of tax evasion to: (1) income from moveable capital and (2) 'to a particular kind of fraud which is very common and hence very disturbing': '... one of the best-known methods of fraud: a taxpayer, anxious, *inter alia*, to escape from some of the burdens to which he would be liable if he collected the income from his movable capital in the country where he resides, has recourse to a country where he knows that the tax is lower and that measures of supervision do not exist of are less severe'. As regards the terminology used, it is questionable whether 'evasion' and 'fraud' are interchangeable and whether all of the examples represent what would now be deemed 'evasion' or 'fraud' or whether some represent cases of mere 'avoidance', but such questions go beyond the purposes of the discussion here).
521. *Id.* ('Such evasion is practised mainly in respect of income from movable capital ... constantly increasing ...').
522. *Id.* (what the solutions have in common is 'namely, that they disturb the circulation of capital, because they inevitably drive it to take refuge where it will be least heavily taxed'. One of the main concerns expressed by States was that, if they clamp down, the capital will flee to havens, and in fleeing will negatively impact their economic situation. They would prefer some form of 'international control'. The aim would be to 'adopt simultaneously similar methods of control for both national and international transactions' but 'Is simultaneous action possible?').
523. League of Nations, 1936 Report, at 4265–4266 (one obstacle cited was the 'difficulty of modifying legislation in order to enable governments to demand information from their nationals not needed for domestic purposes merely to suit the requirements of a foreign country'. 'To these arguments it is easy to answer that the prevention of tax evasion benefits all States ...').
524. *Id.*, at 4258.
525. *Id.*, at 4306.
526. *Id.*, at 4305–4306 ('Nevertheless, since the membership of the Mexico City and London meetings differed considerably, it is natural that the participants in the London meeting held, on various points, different views from those which inspired the Model Conventions prepared

'there persists a difference of opinion between capital-importing and capital-exporting countries as regards the taxation of interest and dividends',[527] in particular, and also 'royalties, annuities and pensions'.[528] On other matters, there seemed to be consensus, though.[529] The Committee planned to continue to discuss these topics in order to find agreement.[530]

As regards the term 'double taxation', some understanding can be gleaned from two places in the report. First, the report recognized the progress already made from the work of the League of Nations since 1923 on model conventions and the subsequent conclusion of bilateral conventions between states 'especially in the field of the prevention of international double taxation and fiscal evasion', but expressed that more progress is desired:

> 'Much remains to be done, however, especially on account of the constant increase of tax burdens and also with a view to assisting the desired revival of international trade and investment. Indeed, efforts to remove these obstacles on international economic intercourse which result from tariffs, preferences and other restrictive trade practices can be largely frustrated through the operation of tax laws ...' and efforts should be made '... with a view to solving tax problems in the interest of world rehabilitation'.[531]

Here, again, the rationale for more progress is expressed in terms of heavy or excessive burdens and in terms of reviving trade, investment and international economic intercourse, which is linked to the especially powerful motive, in a post-war period, of 'world rehabilitation'.

in Mexico'; 'The Committee is aware of the fact that the provisions contained in the 1943 Model Conventions may appear more attractive to some States – in Latin America, for instance – than those which it has agreed during its present session').

527. League of Nations, 1946 Report, at 4308 (two topics within the 'international double taxation' problems 'which seem to require prompt consideration' are: (1) 'allocation of taxable income in the case of business enterprises ...' which requires some further elaboration and (2) 'there persists a difference of opinion between capital-importing and capital-exporting countries as regards the taxation of interest and dividends').
528. *Id.*, at 4306.
529. *Id.* ('Virtually, the only clauses where there is an effective divergence between the views of the 1943 Mexico meeting and those of the 1946 London meeting are those relating to the taxation of interest, dividends, royalties, annuities and pensions').
530. *Id.* ('The Committee thinks that the work done both in Mexico and in London could be usefully reviewed by a balanced group of tax administrators and experts from both capital-importing and capital-exporting countries and from economically-advanced and less-advanced countries, when the work on international tax problems is taken over by the United Nations').
531. League of Nations, 1946 Report, at 4307–4308, at 4313–4314 (other places in the document where these associations are made include: 'A number of tax problems might be well considered under the general heading of "Trade Barriers". Experience has shown during the inter-war period that various taxes have a definite restrictive effect on international trade. These include, in addition to the whole problem of double taxation through income and similar taxes and through death duties, the following: [the list includes, inter alia, taxes on capital transfers]') and at 4315 ('In general, it is becoming increasingly evident that the conclusion by an increasing number of States of bilateral treaties along the lines of the Model Conventions of London and Mexico constitutes the most adequate means of removing the existing serious tax obstructions to the international flow of capital and foreign trade.' In these ways, it appears that the main underlying reasons that double taxation constitutes a problem are the obstacles to international trade and investment).

Second, in the 'Forward' to the Commentary and Text of the London and Mexico Model Tax Conventions, the following description of international double taxation can be found:

> 'International double taxation arises when the taxes of two or more countries overlap in such a manner that persons liable to tax in more than one country bear a higher tax burden than if they were subject to one tax jurisdiction only. The additional burden so incurred must, of course, be due not merely to differences in tax rates for the countries concerned, but to the fact that two or more jurisdictions concurrently impose taxes having the same bases and incidence without regard to the claims of the other tax jurisdictions.'[532]

This definition is much more elaborated and precise, both as to the *cause* of double taxation (or when it can be deemed to arise) – namely, the overlapping of tax jurisdictions, yet limited to an overlap 'having the same bases and incidence' – and as to its *import* – namely, the 'additional burden' due to this overlap, yet *not* one due merely to a higher rate in one of the two countries. It combines both legal elements and economic elements, being concerned with both the overlapping claims and the incidence/burden. As the analysis of the case law of the CJEU will show (in Chapter 4), this definition would seem to fit with the findings of the CJEU in double taxation cases, as it contains a seed of the idea of a 'disparity' in the meaning of EU law (for more on the meaning and evolution of this concept in CJEU cases, *see* Section 4.2.2. on the *Gilly* or 'disparity' line of case law).

In the 'Introduction' to the Commentary in the 1946 report, it explicitly states the three main 'classes' of double taxation, namely: (1) 'the co-existence of personal and impersonal tax liability';[533] (2) 'different criteria as regards personal tax liability' such as 'persons with a domicile or residence in two different countries'; and (3) 'where two or more countries regard a given kind of income or property as taxable in their respective territories…'.[534]

The work begun by the League of Nations now continued at the OEEC, founded 16 April 1948,[535] by its Fiscal Committee, established in 1956.[536] Its Members were

532. League of Nations, 1946 Report, at 4327, London and Mexico Model Tax Conventions – Commentary and Text.

533. *Id.*, at 4328, London and Mexico Model Tax Conventions – Commentary and Text ('The cases of international double taxation that may arise in connection with taxes on income and property fall into three classes. The first and most important category includes the cases due to the co-existence of personal and impersonal tax liability. Tax liability is said to be personal when it is based on the personal status of the taxpayer himself – e.g. his nationality, domicile, residence. Impersonal tax liability exists when a country taxes income earned or received within its territory regardless of the personal status of the recipient. Any person who is taxable in one country on account of his personal status and who receives income from another country or holds property therein is exposed to such double taxation. This result can be avoided only if one or both of the jurisdictions concerned limit their fiscal claims or allow a credit against their tax on account of the foreign tax').

534. League of Nations, 1946 Report, at 4328, London and Mexico Model Tax Conventions – Commentary and Text.

535. OEEC, 1958 Report, at 4453. *See also*, e.g., Klaus Vogel & Alexander Rust, *Introduction*, *in* 1 *Klaus Vogel on Double Taxation Conventions* 1, m.no. 22 (Ekkehart Reimer & Alexander Rust eds, Kluwer Law International 4th ed. 2015).

Austria, Belgium, Denmark, France, Germany, Greece, Iceland, Ireland, Italy, Luxembourg, the Netherlands, Norway, Portugal, Sweden, Switzerland, Turkey, and the UK; Associate Members were the US and Canada; and those with a special status were Spain and Yugoslavia. Considering the countries represented in all of the historical reports, especially those of the OEEC (its name alone is already an important signal), these reports seem to be a relevant source for tracing the understanding of double taxation of many EU MSs today.

During this period, the OEEC sought to update and reconcile the differences between the previous model conventions.[537] To do so, it produced four interim reports.[538]

In the first report, there was a section explicitly dedicated to the 'position of the problem', comprising a definition of 'double taxation':

> '... it was not until comparatively recent times that countries sought to settle the problems of double taxation: that is, the concurrent imposition of tax on the same subject matter by two States, by means of bilateral agreements'.[539]

Another relevant excerpt explains that:

> '... the obstacles represented by double taxation are not, in general, the result of any deliberate intention. Their effect is simply that a person doing business or investing in more than one State is arbitrarily given less favourable treatment than a person who does business or investing in one State alone'.[540]

This seems to add an element of fairness to the concerns over double taxation. Of course, how 'arbitrary' this seems depends on whether one considers these two situations, i.e., a person operating entirely within one state versus a person operating in different states, the same or different (e.g., perhaps cross-border situations, for objective reasons, justifiably incur some differences in costs).

The Committee also framed its objectives in a way that rings of a 'common market' or 'internal market' spirit, bringing back into the picture the rationales of economic integration:

> 'The Fiscal Committee is fully aware that the elimination of double taxation only constitutes a first step and that the question of co-ordination and harmonisation of

536. OEEC, 1958 Report, at 4448.
537. *Id.*, at 4460–4461 (it set itself the following ambitious aim: 'The Fiscal Committee proposes to establish a series of articles which, taken together, will finally cover all the problems which the bilateral double taxation Conventions are designed to solve and will thus constitute a Model Bilateral Convention acceptable to all Member countries. It would then be possible to envisage going further towards harmonisation ... by a single Multilateral Convention' between OEEC Members. It listed the benefits of a multilateral convention expressed in terms of the positive impact on 'trade' and 'intra-European investment').
538. OEEC, 1958 Report, at 4445; OEEC, 1959 Report, at 4511; OEEC, 1960 Report, at 4565; OEEC, 1961 Report, at 4619.
539. OEEC, 1958 Report, at 4455.
540. *Id.*, at 4456.

fiscal policies between Member countries will become increasingly important as European economic cooperation becomes closer.'[541]

The fourth and final report made the most important breakthrough, finally offering definitions in a straightforward unambiguous way. It defined 'juridical double taxation' and 'economic double taxation'. These definitions are found in the proposed Commentary on the methods for the avoidance of double taxation,[542] fittingly as that is their *raison d'etre*. Juridical double taxation occurs 'where the same income or capital is taxable in the hands of the same person by more than one State', whereas economic double taxation is 'a taxation of the same income or capital in the hands of two different persons both chargeable to tax'.[543]

In addition to the distinction between 'juridical double taxation' and 'economic double taxation', the report mentioned common causes of the two respective types. For 'international juridical double taxation', three main occurrences were listed (slightly modified and updated from the three listed in 1946), namely: (1) an overlap of residence-based taxation, (2) an overlap of what could be described as source-based taxation and (3) an overlap of residence-based and source-based taxation.[544] By comparison with the 1946 report, the terminology of 'personal' versus 'impersonal' was replaced with a distinction based on the nexus giving rise to income taxation, on the basis of either residence or, essentially, source.

For economic double taxation, the Commentary on the proposed article regarding the taxation of dividends mentioned a common cause, namely that of 'the simultaneous taxation of the company's profits in its hands and of the distributed profits in the hands of the shareholder'.[545] In the Commentary on an article regarding the taxation of interest, under the title 'International Double Taxation of Interest', another point is made that, because interest payments are usually deductible from the payer's tax base

541. *Id.*, at 4467–4468.
542. OEEC, 1961 Report, at 4685, Commentaries on Articles XXIII and XXIV concerning the Methods for Avoidance of Double Taxation.
543. *Id.*
544. *Id.* ('International juridical double taxation may arise in three cases: a) where each of two States under its domestic taxation law treats the same person as having his residence within its territory; b) where each of two States imposes tax on the same income or capital (limited tax liability in both States), e.g. where a permanent establishment in one State derives income from immovable property in another State, and neither State is the State of residence of the owner of the permanent establishment; c) where a person who has his residence in one State derives income from or owns capital in another state and both States impose tax on that income or capital'); *see supra* note 534, League of Nations, 1946 Report, at 4328, London and Mexico Model Tax Conventions – Commentary and Text.
545. OEEC, 1961 Report, at 4664, at 4666 (numerous instances in the report define economic double taxation. In the description of the tax systems, the Commentary in discussing the positions of Germany, etc. makes another important statement regarding the relationship between the conventions and economic double taxation: 'The solution proposed in paragraph 2 of the Article is based on the hypothesis that the purpose of a double taxation Convention is not to prevent the economic double taxation that occurs when a State taxes not only in the hands of the company its total industrial or commercial profits, but also, in addition, the profits distributed as dividends in the hands of the shareholder.' The report, at 4657, also contains a table that compares the laws of some states, nearly all European, on the taxation of dividends, offering insight into the various approaches to economic double taxation at that time).

as a cost, '[u]nlike dividends, interest does not suffer economic double taxation[;] that is, it is not taken both in the hands of the debtor and in the hands of the creditor'.[546] Then, there is again a hint at the underlying problem of double taxation: a 'double charge of tax can reduce considerably the interest on the money lent and so hamper the investment of capital and the development of international investment'.[547] Yet, despite acknowledgement of *both* types of double taxation - juridical and economic - the articles on the methods for the avoidance of double taxation addressed only the former and *not* the latter, as will be discussed below.

Finally, having concluded its current task, the OEEC announced yet another change in the organization, namely that it 'will shortly be reconstituted, with the participation of the United States and Canada, as the Organisation for Economic Co-operation and Development (OECD), which will have a Fiscal Committee to continue the activities of the type now undertaken'.[548]

As for interim conclusions, from the above, various reasons that have been advanced in the fight against double taxation can be considered. These include:

- the excessive burden resulting from high taxes rates, especially in periods with critical revenue needs such as war and post-war;
- the inducement this pressure creates to evade taxes;
- the desire for fiscal centralization or deeper economic integration;
- the importance of cross-border investment and trade, an objective which can be expressed in two distinct ways, either to *not* impede (or formulated positively, to remove obstacles to the free flow or movement) or to actually *encourage* or revive international trade and investment abroad;
- moreover, the importance of this is sometimes proclaimed in the name of facilitating post-war reconstruction or peaceful relations;
- the fairness aspects or discriminatory aspects of double taxation (e.g., either in *absolute* terms, in that a burden could potentially attain a level that could be seen as oppressive or unjust or confiscatory, if it leads to bankruptcy, for example, or in *relative* terms, in that it results in different treatment of a person with income from abroad).

546. OEEC, 1961 Report, at 4669.
547. *Id.*, at 4670.
548. *Id.*, at 4637 ('[...] the Recommendations relating to the avoidance of double taxation already adopted by the Council of the O.E.E.C. will be maintained and that they will apply thenceforward to the United States and Canada. These two countries will therefore directly participate in the final phase of the work of establishing a Convention with respect to taxes on income and capital'), at 4704 (after the OECD takes over from the OEEC, it states that it 'had only recently been formed at the time of preparation of this document, and had not yet published any materials relating to work being done under its auspices on model tax convention provisions. The Council of the OECD, however, at its organizational meeting on September 30, 1961, approved certain resolutions previously adopted by the OEEC relating to the elimination of double taxation through the use of tax conventions. The texts of the resolutions of the OEEC which were approved by the OECD are printed above beginning at pages 4559 and 4615 in Volume 4 of this document. The United States, being a full member of the OECD, is obliged by the terms of the resolutions to notify the OECD of the reasons why provision of the model tax convention recommended by the OECD have not been adopted in any bilateral tax convention concluded between the United States and another country which is a member of the OECD').

Various attempts to pin down more precisely when double taxation is a problem range from the dissenting opinion of Sir Percy Thompson who dismissed 'double taxation' as the problem and instead placed blame on 'origin taxation' (though it appears this did not gain momentum and was dropped) to declaring double taxation in and of itself as 'evil' on multiple occasions. There seemed to be agreement on the fact that double taxation had varying degrees of negative economic consequences. These were articulated as 'the creation of an artificial barrier which impedes the free flow of capital into the channels in which it can be most usefully and profitably employed' (Sir Percy Thompson). Another articulation was that double taxation could act either as a barrier (barring an investment from occurring) or as a burden (an extra unplanned cost for an investment), which were distinct negative consequences (1923 Report). Moreover, it is possible for double taxation to occur from a legal point of view, but with minimal economic incidence, or it can have an economic incidence, but not be seen to exist from a legal point of view.

Eventually, this legal versus economic distinction emerged as a prominent one, when it appears consensus was found on definitions of 'juridical double taxation' and 'economic double taxation'. To show just how stable these definitions have been, the current 2017 OECD Model and UN Model have maintained the exact definition of juridical double taxation and the same (and only slightly condensed) definition of economic double taxation in the Commentary on 'The Methods for Elimination of Double Taxation'.[549] In another part of the 2017 Commentary, namely its Introduction, the Commentary contains a more precise, and narrower, definition: 'International juridical double taxation can be generally defined as the imposition of comparable taxes in two (or more) States on the same taxpayer in respect of the same subject matter and for identical periods.'[550] While the first (in the Commentary on Article 23) looks at 'same person' and 'same income', this one (in the Introduction to the Commentary) looks at 'comparable taxes', 'same taxpayer', 'same subject matter' and 'identical periods'. Thus, although these definitions advance one answer to the question 'what is double taxation', they raise others, such as the interpretation of these various terms. For example, as states' concepts of income and the types of taxes imposed inevitably vary, a tax administration agent could question whether double taxation is truly arising in a given case if the agent can argue that it is not the 'same income' or not 'comparable taxes' at issue. How these terms are interpreted can either restrict or broaden the scope of the relief.

These definitions can be characterized as quite formalistic legalistic ones, by comparison with other possibilities for definitions such as that in the 1946 report based on the 'burden' and 'incidence' of taxation (for convenience, cited again in the footnote

549. OECD, *Model Tax Convention on Income and on Capital 2017: Condensed Version* Commentary on Articles 23 A and 23 B, paras 1–2 (OECD Publishing 2017) ('1. These Articles deal with the so-called juridical double taxation where the same income or capital is taxable in the hands of the same person by more than one State. 2. This case has to be distinguished especially from the so-called economic double taxation, i.e. where two different persons are taxable in respect of the same income or capital. If two States wish to solve problems of economic double taxation, they must do so in bilateral negotiations').

550. *Id.*, Introduction, para. 1.

here).[551] Even the definition of 'economic double taxation' is not as *economic* as it is *legal* (e.g., to the extent it is about 'same income', not about the actual 'burden', 'incidence' or effect).

As regards the credit method, the most evident consequence of the focus on juridical double taxation, to the exclusion of economic double taxation, is that the models' solution is thus a direct credit, without any indirect credit. What this also implies is that the models are premised on a clear separation between the income generated at the level of a corporation and the income distributed to shareholders - in other words, it assumes a 'classic' corporate tax system, as opposed to an integrated one (*see supra* note 293).[552]

There is an intersection between the definition of double taxation, the rationale (or rationales, and which one takes priority) and the design of the solution. The aim of the solution could be to merely mitigate double taxation, or the aim could be to entirely eliminate it. If the rationale is related to an excessive burden, it may suffice to merely mitigate the double taxation (to reduce it to a level that is viewed as more acceptable or bearable), and this can be accomplished in a number of ways (e.g., even simply reducing the tax rates on FSI or, in the case of the credit method, a partial credit equivalent to, say, 80% of the foreign taxes paid). If the rationale is related to cross-border investment, this alone is not so helpful or instructive: (i) since it depends on what types of investments are desired, (ii) since tax is but one of many factors weighed in certain investment decisions, and (iii) since it depends on in which direction the investments should flow (inward or outward), etc. Still, what this rationale would seem to call for is attention to the economic incidence of taxation, and not merely when double taxation formally legally occurs. As regards the credit method, this may require both a direct and indirect credit. Each component of the credit method, in turn, offers an opportunity to cater it to a particular rationale. For example, the credit limitation can be strictly applied on an item-per-item basis or more liberally applied on an overall basis. If the objective is to encourage investment abroad, there are ways to design relief to be particularly favourable (e.g., ranging from offering taxpayers the option to choose between either a per-country or overall limitation, to removing any limitation altogether, etc.). These, and other, aspects of the credit method are now the subject of the next section.

551. League of Nations, 1946 Report, at 4327, London and Mexico Model Tax Conventions - Commentary and Text ('International double taxation arises when the taxes of two or more countries overlap in such a manner that persons liable to tax in more than one country bear a higher tax burden than if they were subject to one tax jurisdiction only. The additional burden so incurred must, of course, be due not merely to differences in tax rates for the countries concerned, but to the fact that two or more jurisdictions concurrently impose taxes having the same bases and incidence without regard to the claims of the other tax jurisdictions').

552. *See*, e.g., Peter Harris, *Corporate Tax Law: Structure, Policy and Practice* 327–385 (Cambridge University Press online publication date March 2013), https://doi.org/10.1017/CBO97811395 19922.007 (last visited 15 Aug. 2018) ('The international order (and the OECD Model) was designed with the dual nature of corporate income in mind (i.e. it presumes a classical system)').

2.1.2.3.3. *Narrowing Down the Possible Solutions: A Focus on the Credit Method*

Overview of solutions initially considered in 1923

Multiple solutions to address double taxation were deliberated. In the 1923 Report, 'four possible alternatives' were expressly considered; though tacitly there were perhaps five or six. The first was labelled '*the method of deduction for income from abroad*', referring (albeit not accurately named) to the US' approach. More precisely, this approach was described as a deduction 'from the tax due from its residents [of] any tax paid by them on their income from abroad'.[553] In other words, it was the credit method by another name.

The second was labelled '*the method of exemption for income going abroad*' (notice the wording 'going abroad'). It was described as the 'extreme converse' of the first method, as it required the country of origin to exempt all income leaving its territory to go to non-resident taxpayers.[554]

The third was labelled '*the method of division of the tax*'. The governments would coordinate so that a portion of the tax went to the country of residence and a portion to the country of origin, 'to spread the burden upon the two Governments'.[555] They referenced the relationship between the British government and the Dominions. Though, it is not an exact equivalent. For example, in the Dominion relief system, relief was not based on residence and source/origin.

The fourth was labelled '*the method of classification and assignment of sources*'. Income would be classified as a specific type (e.g., 'rents of land' or 'income derived from business securities'), and the right to tax each type would be assigned to the state of origin or the state of residence. This would aim to prevent double taxation. For each type of income, one state would have the right to tax and the other state would refrain from taxing it or, basically, exempt it. This is essentially the approach (albeit not an exact equivalent) adopted by the German jurisdictions in the 1800s as described by Hattingh.[556] The experts assumed a default right of taxation for the state of residence, 'except for certain specified exemptions', yet from the text, three scenarios emerge: (1)

553. League of Nations, 1923 Report, at 4045–4046.
554. *Id.*, at 4046 ('The extreme converse, *viz.*: that the country of origin should exempt all non-residents from taxation imposed on income drawn from sources within its borders, recognises the theoretical fact that the country wanting the money cannot successfully "tax the foreigner"; it can only shut him out. It would have the effect of increasing the flow of capital from abroad and the development of less-favoured regions. This may be called *the method of exemption for income going abroad*').
555. *Id.* ('It may be possible by convention to divide specific taxes so that a portion should be borne by the country of origin and the remainder by the country of residence, *e.g.*, a Moranian having an investment in England and being liable to 5/- in the £ thereon might recover 2/6 from the British Government, and also in his own country be charged only half the normal rate of tax in relation thereto. This is an attempt to recognise both principles and to spread the burden upon the two Governments. It would leave in an unsatisfactory position issues of State loans, and is open to many of the objections, though not to the same extent, as those raised to the first proposal. This may be called *the method of division of the tax*').
556. Johann Hattingh, *On the Origins of Model Tax Conventions: Nineteenth-Century German Tax Treaties and Laws Concerned with Avoidance of Double Tax, in* 6 *Studies in the History of Tax Law* 31 (John Tiley ed., Hart Publishing 2013) (discussed above under the Section 2.1.2.2).

the state of origin would have the right to tax, for example, income from immovable property in its territory and the state of residence 'would allow the whole of the foreign tax as a deduction from its income tax on the resident in respect of such sources of income', so envisioning the credit method; (2) the residence state would have the sole and full right to tax other sources of income; and (3) in a few clearly delineated cases the state of origin would have the exclusive right to tax, which would necessarily imply an exemption in the state of residence.[557]

In discussing variations on these methods, the experts also discussed the possibility of what could be described as a revenue-sharing approach, wherein the state of residence would collect the taxes and then transfer a certain amount to the state of origin.[558] So this could be a fifth option. Enveloped within their discussion of method 4 is also an exemption by the state of residence, which despite not being *explicitly* discussed is also an option.

The experts also suggest that a universal definition of domicile and residence should be a goal.[559] Although not discussed, if one goes a step further, this shows the potential for common uniform definitions of key concepts as a means to prevent some instances of double taxation. In the EU context, Pistone once proposed the same - a common definition for 'residence' in the EU - in 2002 (*see* Section 4.1.). If all states agree on precisely when a taxpayer is deemed a resident taxpayer, then some instances of double taxation caused by more than one state claiming to be the state of residence could be prevented.

Thus, at least six options emerge from a reading of the report. The experts discussed the pros and cons of all the methods. For each method, they came across obstacles and controversies. At one point, seemingly dejected, they even raised the question: '*Must it, thus, be admitted that no solution is obtainable at the present time?*'[560] As eventually becomes clear, indeed no perfect solution is attainable, but compromises were (and are).

The analysis here now focuses on the first method, the credit method. As will be seen, the perceptions of this method changed over time, from outright rejection to one

557. League of Nations, 1923 Report, at 4046 ('By convention it might be determined to attach origin taxation specifically and wholly to particular classes of investments or embodiments of wealth, such as rents of land and of houses and mortgages on real property, but to exempt the non-resident in respect of income derived from business securities. The country of residence would allow the whole of the foreign tax as a deduction from its income tax on the resident in respect of such sources of income, but would charge other sources in full. The country of origin would retain its specific origin taxes in full. It would be necessary to give the country of residence complete power of charging all sources except for certain specified exemptions, so that the scope of its liability to remit the tax would be easily determined, and the investor, from his total income-tax demands, would be able to deduct certain specified taxes on any real property he might have. It might be desirable to impose some limit upon the power of the country of origin to levy in future specially heavy specific origin taxes, which would unduly deplete the exchequer of the country of residence. This may be called *the method of classification and assignment of sources*').

558. *Id.*, at 4054 (one solution seems to be to '... secure the principles of method 4 by combining the administrative machinery of method 2 with an aggregate collective settlement between two exchequers ...').

559. *Id.*, at 4029.

560. *Id.*, at 4053.

of the most common solutions. In the conclusions of the 1923 report, the experts unequivocally rejected the first method and found method 2, the exemption by the country of *origin*, the 'most desirable practical method'.[561] Simultaneously, they emphasized residence-based taxation ('the principle of personal faculty at the place of residence') as the inevitable sophisticated future that seemed bound to arrive, as states would industrialize and converge towards more equal economic situations, and as distinctions between debtor and creditor countries would fade.[562] The perception of the credit method at that time, which was essentially that it was generous and potentially dangerous for the credit-granting state,[563] contrasts with the perception commonly held today that the credit method favours and protects the residence state.[564] Ultimately, their preferences only partially came to pass: indeed, taxation based on ability to pay (or the personal faculty) of the taxpayer and residence-based income taxation became the norm for income taxation, gradually moving away from the previously prevalent conceptions of income taxes as 'impersonal', but the predominant solutions for double taxation eventually became a choice between either the credit method or the exemption method – *not* by the state of origin, but – by the state of residence.

League of Nations, 1923 Report[565]

In the 1923 report, the full description of the credit method (method 1) is as follows:

> 'A country might deduct from the tax due from its residents any tax paid by them on their income from abroad (analogous to the United States practice in the case of

561. *Id.*, at 4055 ('To sum up:

    (1) On the subject of income taxation in its developed form, the reciprocal exemption of the non-resident under method 2 is the most desirable practical method of avoiding the evils of double taxation and should be adopted wherever countries feel in a position to do so.
    (2) Where method 2 is repugnant owing to a reluctance to abandon the principle of origin, method 4 as modified by method 3 may be the subject of mutual conventions; but even then it is best carried out by an administrative system similar to method 2, supplemented by a collective settlement on agreed lines between the two Governments.
    (3) Where countries desire method 4, but do not care to have it carried out by combining method 2 with such an overhead government settlement, they must make the best arrangement they can under method 4, perhaps modified by method 3. But we hold out no hopes of this proving to be a smooth and practicable arrangement. It can be only approximate and not an instrument of that degree of sensitiveness and accuracy which developed communities expect').

562. *Id.*, at 4055 ('Looking forward to the future, the influence of example by others and the spirit encouraged by the operations of the League of Nations indicate the possibility of a development away from localised ideas and from the earlier stages of economic thought typified by strict adherence to the principle of origin. Moreover, as semi-developed countries become more industrialised, with the resulting attenuation of the distinctions between debtor and creditor countries, the principle of personal faculty at the place of residence will become more widely understood and appreciated and the disparity between the two principles will become less obvious, so that we may look forward to an ultimate development of national ideas on uniform lines toward method 2, if not as a more logical and theoretically defensible economic view of the principles of income taxation, at least as the most practicable solution of the difficulties of double taxation').
563. *See*, e.g., *infra* note 566.
564. *See* Section 4.1. for further discussion.
565. League of Nations, 1923 Report (full citation, *supra* note 111).

> its own citizens). This throws the whole burden of increased taxation in debtor countries upon the creditor country, and is opposed to the general practice observed by foreign Governments when issuing their loans. If this course were followed, Governments need no longer make provision for making the loans free of tax to non-resident investors, knowing that it will fall upon the exchequer of the creditor country. It is to be doubted whether such creditor countries as the United States, Great Britain and the Netherlands, having regard to their investors abroad, would ever agree permanently to put their exchequers at the mercy of all the unknown increases of taxation of foreign Governments. This may be called *the method of deduction for income from abroad.*'[566]

As for the experts' recommendation, they stated that: 'We are united in rejecting method I as being, from the point of view of the income tax proper as discussed in this section, no complete and proper solution of the matter.'[567] The main contention, which was repeatedly stated, was that method 1 places the burden of source state taxation fully on the residence state. To explain this, they offered the above-cited example of 'the general practice observed by foreign Governments when issuing their loans', which was to allow the proceeds of the loans to be tax free for non-resident investors. A credit method changes the incentives. These governments know that, if they decide to impose taxes on the loan payments, the taxes will be fully credited for the investors in their home countries, with the result that these governments can increase and collect taxes from these non-resident investors without deterring them from investing in the government loans.[568] In addition, the experts underline the distinction between a deduction of foreign taxes from the *tax base* and from the *taxes due*, again emphasizing the cost of the latter:

> 'In the British system, a deduction of foreign tax from foreign income is allowed as an expense, as shown above. The United States provision is, however, for a deduction of the foreign tax from the home tax (in case of its citizens), making a complete relief from double taxation entirely at the cost of the investor's home exchequer.'[569]

Further insight into the four experts' idea of the design of double taxation relief comes from method 3, which, since it is based on the UK's Dominion relief system, has operational similarities with the credit method:

> 'Now it is of the essence of this method that the resident shall not gain by the relief in double taxation, that is, shall not be in a better position than he would be if his income were all derived in the country where he resides. Relief is desired only to the extent of the excess over such a sum; and therefore the essence of method 3 is that the country of residence should give relief by a definite amount that has been levied in the country of origin, with, if it is desired, a maximum for that relief equal to one-half of the rate of tax levied by the country of residence.'[570]

566. *Id.*, at 4045–4046.
567. *Id.*, at 4052.
568. *Id.*, at 4045–4046.
569. *Id.*, at 4012.
570. *Id.*, at 4050.

Phrases such as 'the resident shall not gain by the relief' and emphasizing the 'amount that has been levied' indicate that this method is based on the taxes actually paid. With the word 'essence', they imply that it is a fundamental feature of this (credit) method (or methods similar to it) that the amount of relief is based on actual taxation in the other state. It should not credit more than that; otherwise, it goes beyond eliminating the 'excess' and instead favours the taxpayer with FSI. Moreover, since it mentions a 'maximum' creditable amount, the method can result in a worse position (unless the other state, like the Dominions did, credits the difference). The UK Dominion relief system was designed to result in the higher of the two jurisdictions' rates applying (as seen at *supra* note 128).

Similar to method 1, based on the US version of the credit method, method 3, inspired from the UK Dominion relief system, was also rejected. The reasons were very different. The problem with the UK's approach was *not* that it was too burdensome or risky for the residence state – quite the opposite, since the UK approach shared the obligation of relief between the two jurisdictions (as seen at *supra* note 109). Rather it was seen as unpragmatic, if not impossible, in an international context. To bring about such a sharing of the relief required certain conditions and close cooperation that seemed to exist only because it operated within a closer unit, in this case an empire. In response to the question '... why should it not be possible elsewhere?', the reasons were:

> '... that the relations existing between the Dominions and the British Government introduce factors ... of imperial allegiance and common imperial service, which induce the respective Governments to make concessions to each other. [...] Secondly, the use of a common language, the existence of a common conception of income so that divergences are of the smallest character, the easy relations that exist of a political character to enable the necessary data to be determined ....', and a 'developed civil service and a taxing department of very great intelligence and skill'.[571]

League of Nations, 1925 Report[572]

In the 1925 report, the credit method is described as follows:

> 'In the first, which may be called "the method of *total deduction*" – a method applied in principle in the United States – the country of domicile deducts from the tax due from its residents the *whole* of the tax paid by them abroad on their income.'[573]

The emphasis on 'total deduction' and 'whole of the tax paid' seems to refer to a credit method without any maximum limit on the relief, as originally conceived in 1918 in the US (slightly puzzling, because the reports are published *after* the Revenue Act of 1921 in which the US implemented an MCA, as seen at *supra* note 179). The

571. *Id.*, at 4051.
572. League of Nations, 1925 Report, at 4057 et seq.
573. *Id.*, at 4070.

Appendix[574] to the 1925 Report clarifies this. On the one hand, it referred to 'Method I. - Total Deduction' and described it as an unlimited credit. On the other hand, the Annex referred to 'Method V. - American Legislation' and described it as a credit with a maximum limitation. The hint seems to be found in the words 'in principle' above: the Appendix claims that this 'total deduction' is 'the *principle* embodied in Methods V (American Legislation) and VI (League of Nations Experts)' (emphasis added) and MCAs serve as 'correctives'.[575]

Similar to the four economists (of the 1923 report), these government experts opined that the credit method was too expensive and risky: 'The first method, which consists in refunding to the taxpayer the tax which he has paid abroad, places a country's budget at the mercy of increased taxation in another country.'[576] With this sentiment, it is clear that they were not in favour of the (unlimited) credit method approach.

In this report, after considering multiple solutions (*see* footnote for additional examples),[577] they adopted formal resolutions. As mentioned above in the discussion of double taxation, they devised two solutions according to the two main conceptions of (income) taxes existing at that time - the 'impôts réels' and 'general or personal taxes'. The authors themselves admitted difficulties in precisely defining the two categories, which explains their disclaimer that the distinction was for 'purely practical

574. *Id.*, at 4096 et seq. (Appendix: Note by M. Léon-Dufour on the Various Methods Suggested for Remedying Double Taxation and Their Graphical Representation).
575. *Id.*, at 4097 (Appendix: Note by M. Léon-Dufour on the Various Methods Suggested for Remedying Double Taxation and Their Graphical Representation).
576. *Id.*, at 4074.
577. *Id.*, at 4068 (regarding the solutions considered by the experts, the 1925 report cites other works that it took into account in adopting its resolutions, such as that of the International Chamber of Commerce and the International Law Institute. In particular, it cites the findings of the International Chamber of Commerce. The Chamber found that, as concerns 'direct taxes', 'In order to avoid double taxation, the best means would be to accept residence as a basis of the tax on income. They [the Chamber] recognise, however, that the application of this principle could not be expected to completely preclude all taxation according to its origin of income derived from landed property or even from commercial or industrial enterprises. [...].' The Chamber also recommended a universal definition of fiscal residence and the conclusion of bilateral conventions. *See* reservation made by Italy, according to which residence is better for personal taxes, but that origin is 'fairer and more equitable in the case of *impôts réels*'), at 4071-4072 (the report surveys some examples of existing double taxation relief in domestic laws and the double taxation conventions to date, up to 1924, including the first multilateral convention. *See supra* note 476 in this book. In addition to summarizing the relief offered in the US and in the UK, it summarizes the relief offered in Belgium, the Netherlands and Switzerland, revealing a range of approaches. In Belgium, it 'provided for a reduction of the rate of taxation (this may amount to three-quarters)' and what sounds similar to a credit method in some cases ('deductions from the taxation leviable ...'). In Switzerland, relief varied by canton, with the Canton of Zurich exempting two-thirds and thus taxing only one-third of 'income earned in a business situated abroad'; those of Geneva and 'Basle-Town' granted a full exemption to such income. In the Netherlands, 'the tax chargeable on the total income, including income derived from abroad, is first calculated, and then the tax which *would be due* on the latter category if it were taken alone. This second sum is then deducted from the first. The actual rate of taxation abroad is not taken into consideration').

purposes' from which 'no inference in regard to economic theory or doctrine should be drawn':[578]

- As regards the 'impôts réels', they proposed the assignment of income approach. This was based on three observations: (1) as 'origin' seemed to be of 'primary importance' for these taxes, (2) as this approach seemed to be 'most generally in use', and (3) as it 'formed the basis of numerous treaties in Central Europe and of a collective convention' (*see also,* e.g., *supra* note 453 and note 498 on similar discussions).[579]
- As regards 'personal taxes', they proposed two different types of 'deduction' methods, one of which was a credit method, based on two observations: (1) as domicile seemed to be of 'primary importance' and (2) they borrowed 'from the Dutch and American systems'.[580]

More precisely, on these grounds, for personal taxes, they adopted the following Resolutions for the methods to avoid double taxation in the state of 'domicile':

> '(1) Deduction by the State of domicile from the general income-tax of a sum which will be
>
> (a) Either the tax calculated according to the State's own scale and charged exclusively on income produced in the other countries, each of the latter being taken separately,
> (b) Or the tax actually paid abroad on the income arising abroad; this sum may be limited to the amount to be deducted in accordance with paragraph (*a*).
>
> In order to prevent a taxpayer whose entire income arises abroad from escaping all taxation in his State of domicile, the amount to be deducted on the above basis should in all cases be restricted to some fraction of the total tax chargeable in the State of domicile.'[581]

Option (1)(a) is the method inspired from the Netherlands, while option (1)(b) is the method inspired from the US.

In the Netherlands, the law provided for a deduction of the taxes that it would hypothetically levy on the FSI, from the overall taxes 'chargeable' on all of the income.[582] Crucially, it was not a deduction of the *foreign* taxes, since the amount of this deduction was *not* based on the *actual* taxes paid abroad; this method was technically indifferent to whether and how much taxes were levied abroad. Rather, it

578. *Id.*, at 4075.
579. *Id.*, at 4074-4075.
580. *Id.*
581. League of Nations, 1925 Report, at 4092-4093 (as regards the State of origin of the income, the Resolution contains the following: 'In the State of the origin of the income, only a portion of the income arising there should be taxed, the other portion being taxed in the State of domicile of the taxpayer, but at the rate applicable to his total income from every source' and 'Similar steps might be taken, or exemption might be granted, in the country of the origin of the income by means of bilateral conventions in cases where double taxation arises by reason of the existence of a general tax in the country of domicile, side by side with schedular taxes in the country of the origin').
582. *See supra* note 577.

was based *only* on the amount the Netherlands would levy on the FSI. In effect, although the experts did not use the term 'exemption' and although they seemed to equate the Netherland's approach with a credit method, the Netherland's approach is a form of exemption in its effect, which is calculated in a way similar to the credit method. Today, it is sometimes referred to, more precisely, as a 'tax exemption'.[583]

The authors suggested a credit limitation. The wording 'each of the latter being taken separately', under letter (a), seems to indicate that the income from each foreign state should be treated separately, in a separate calculation, i.e., a per-country limitation. Notably, they proposed a *double limit* on any relief in the state of domicile. Thus, as regards the credit method under option (1)(b), first, the amount of relief should be the amount of tax actually paid in the foreign state, but may be limited to the 'tax calculated according to the [domicile] State's own scale'. Second, the amount of relief should nevertheless stop at a maximum of 'a certain percentage of the tax imposed on the whole of the income', 'for example, to a fourth of the tax'. It seems this second limit would be an overall cap on all relief (not on a per-country basis).

The authors justified this based on the need to prevent certain 'abuses'. However, based on the example they used to demonstrate their point, it was not about 'abuse' in the sense of a taxpayer acting with an intent to unduly take advantage of the relief.[584] It was rather about a concern over what they would consider 'excessive relief'. It is excessive in light of their assertion that the state of domicile should be able to levy a certain minimum amount of taxes on their residents because the state of domicile offers 'the protection of the laws and ... the advantage of national institutions'.[585]

Example No. 17: Comparison of 'Tax Exemption' Method under Option 1(a) and Credit Method under Option 1(b) of the 1925 Report

Facts: Taxpayer A, resident in State A, has income of 200, of which 50 is derived from State B and 50 is derived from State C. State A applies a tax rate of 30%, State B a tax rate of 40% and State C a tax rate of 10%.

Before any relief, the amount of taxes paid by Taxpayer A would be as follows:

State A: 200 × 30% = 60

State B: 50 × 40% = 20

583. *See*, e.g., Ben J.M. Terra & Peter J. Wattel, *European Tax Law* 1021 (Wolters Kluwer 6th ed. 2012) (in the words of Terra/Wattel, 'The difference of principle between tax exemption and the credit method is that under the credit method the *foreign* tax attributable to the foreign income is deducted from the total tax due on the worldwide income, whereas under the tax exemption method the *home State* tax attributable to the foreign income is deducted (see section 4.2.2.)').

584. League of Nations, 1925 Report, at 4079 ('Take the case of a Moranian manufacturer or landowner whose total income is 100,000 crowns, 90,000 crowns of which he derives from immovable property or commercial establishments situated in Imeria. Relief in this case would, even when the maximum is applied, represent a very large sum. Our proposal is that the country of domicile should in every case limit the relief it gives to a certain percentage of the tax imposed on the whole of the income ...').

585. League of Nations, 1925 Report, at 4079.

State C: 50 × 10% = 5

Total: 85

Relief: Option (1)(a)

(Assumption: applies per-country)

Per-country limit for State B:

According to its tax rate, State A would apply 30% to the 50 from State B: 30% × 50 = 15.

- Result: Relief of 15, irrespective of the taxes of 20 in State B.

Per-country limit for State C:

According to its tax rate, State A would apply 30% to the 50 from State C: 30% × 50 = 15.

- Result: Relief of 15, irrespective of the taxes of 5 in State C.

Taxes in State A: 60 – relief of 15 – relief of 15 = 30

Taxpayer A: 30 + 20 + 5 = 55 (5 lower than if Taxpayer A earned everything in State A)

Relief Option (1)(b)

Per-country limit for State B:

The lower of either (i) the taxes actually levied in State B = 20 or (ii) the limit calculated in accordance with letter (a) = 15.

- Result: Relief of 15 for the taxes of 20 in State B.

Per-country limit for State C:

The lower of either (i) the taxes actually levied in State C = 5 or (ii) the limit calculated in accordance with letter (a) = 15.

- Result: Relief of 5 for the taxes levied in State C.

Taxes in State A: 60 – relief of 15 – relief of 5 = 40

Taxpayer A: 40 + 20 + 5 = 65 (5 higher than if Taxpayer A earned everything in State A)

Limit from second sentence

Assume it is one-fourth of 'total tax chargeable' = ¼ × 60 = 15.

If it is intended to apply as an overall cap on all relief, then it would cut the above relief by 50% (30 down to 15) and 25% (20 down to 15), respectively.

To illustrate the resolutions with examples, the authors adopted the fictive states of Morania (as used in the 1923 report) and Imeria. The relevant facts of the example, simplified and slightly adapted, assume that a taxpayer 'domiciled' in Morania earns 100,000 crowns, of which 20,000 crowns are derived from immovable property in Imeria. Morania applies a tax rate of 5% to 10,000 crowns, 10% to 20,000 crowns, 30% to 80,000 crowns and 40% to 100,000 crowns.[586]

Then, surprisingly, the facts assume that Morania would levy 40,000 crowns of general income tax on the 100,000 crowns. Thus, it is not a progressive system with increasing marginal taxes, wherein each progressively higher tax rate is imposed on each progressively higher bracket of income, but rather each rate is imposed on the entirety of the income as soon as the amount surpasses a given threshold. If so, then a criticism of this system is that the step effect is disproportionate at each threshold. At each step of income, the effect of earning 1 *more* crown could suddenly result in a taxpayer keeping *less* net income after taxes than a taxpayer 1 crown *below* the same threshold. For example, under Morania's tax system, a taxpayer that earns 79,000 crowns pays 7,900 in taxes and keeps 71,100 crowns, whereas the taxpayer that earns 80,000 crowns pays 24,000 in taxes and keeps 56,000 crowns. As for the other fictive state, Imeria, taxes are levied at a rate of either 8% (**scenario 1**) or 12% (**scenario 2**), thus either 1,600 crowns or 2,400 crowns.[587]

Regarding how the draft resolutions apply to these facts, under the scenario that Imeria has an 8% rate, 'Morania will give relief to the extent of 1,600 crowns and will only collect 38,400 crowns.' Under the scenario that Imeria has a 12% rate, 'Morania may limit the relief to that corresponding to her own rate, *i.e.*, 2,000 crowns, and may collect 38,000 crowns.'

The second scenario is of particular interest. Notice that by taking the figure of 2,000, they assume that Morania imposes 10% on the income of 20,000 crowns from abroad; i.e., Morania applies the rate that *would have* applied had the taxpayer hypothetically earned only 20,000 in its territory. This seems strange because, recalling the facts, Morania actually levied 40% on the entire income of 100,000, including – evidently – the 20,000 from Imeria.

This does not appear to be an accident, but rather indeed seems to be one possible intended application of the wording of the draft resolutions. To explain, the above wording refers to a limit based on the 'tax calculated according to the State's own scale and charged exclusively on income produced in the other countries'. Then the authors of the report cited the following problem of double taxation:

> 'As Imeria continues to enforce its 12 per cent rate, the taxpayer will have to pay 2,400 crowns as the Imerian tax and will receive relief in Morania only to the extent of 2,000 crowns. It may therefore be argued that in this case there will be *double taxation* to the extent of 400 crowns, *owing to* the *difference between the rates of taxation* in the two countries' (emphasis added).[588]

586. *Id.*, at 4078 ('Let us suppose, by way of illustration, that the rate of income-tax in Morania is 5 per cent for a total income of 10,000 crowns, 10 per cent for an income of 20,000 crowns, 30 per cent for an income of 80,000 crowns and 40 per cent for an income of 100,000 crowns').
587. *Id.*
588. League of Nations, 1925 Report, at 4079.

This comment raises questions about the credit limitation and 'double taxation'. The real underlying problem here seems less about the difference in tax rates and more about a unique combination of factors in this case (to illustrate the distinction, Scenario 3 of Example No. 18 shows a 'pure' difference-in-tax-rates case). That is, the real problem is the combination of the (unusual) income tax rate system with an MCA based on a *hypothetical* tax rate, which was *not* the rate actually applied to the doubly taxed FSI. The rate that Morania should have used to calculate its limit should have been 40% because that is the rate that Morania actually *effectively* applied to the entirety of the taxpayer's 100,000 crowns, thus also to the 20,000 crowns. In this case, the limit would be 40% of 20,000, or 8,000, ensuring that the full 2,400 collected in Imeria is deductible as an FTC. This would be the more reasonable result under this tax system. There would not even be a negative revenue effect for Morania under this approach considering that Morania collected 8,000 on that portion of the income; thus, if it allows a credit of 2,400, that leaves 5,600 in its coffers.

It can also be noted that, based on the facts of the report's example, it is slightly different from a credit limitation under which FSI is attributed to the lowest income bracket in a more standard progressive tax rate system (briefly discussed at *supra* note 117). Scenario 4 of Example No. 18 considers this issue.

Example No. 18: Alternative Morania-Imeria Scenarios – Effect of Different Tax Rates Versus Attribution of Foreign-Source Income to a Given Tax Bracket

Scenario 3

To better illustrate when the tax rate differences are relevant, assume a scenario 3 to compare the above 1925-report approach with another approach to the credit limitation. In this scenario, Imeria levies a much higher rate of 41%. Imeria would levy 8,200 on the 20,000. The limit in Morania would be based on the 40% that Morania truly levied on the income, thus 8,000. Morania would therefore allow a credit of the lower of the taxes actually levied (8,200) or the amount of its taxes attributable to the same income (8,000); thus, from the 40,000 collected, it would grant a foreign tax credit of 8,000. This would leave an excess of 200 collected in Imeria that are not credited in Morania. This can be said to be 'owing to the difference between the rates of taxation in the two countries'.

Scenario 4

To better illustrate the questions that could arise under a standard progressive tax rate system, assume a **scenario 4**, where Morania operated such a system. Adopting one view of Morania's tax rates in the 1925 report, it would thus collect:

On the first 10,000: 0%

0% × 10,000 crowns = 0

On the next portion of income from 10,000 to 20,000: 5%

5% × (20,000 – 10,000 crowns) = 500

On the next portion of income from 20,000 to 80,000: 20%

20% × (80,000 – 20,000 crowns) = 12,000

On the next portion of income from 80,000 to 100,000: 30%

30% × (100,000 – 80,000 crowns) = 6,000

On the next portion of income from 100,000 or more: 40%

40% × 0 = 0

Total: 500 + 12,000 + 6,000 = 18,500

Imeria continues to levy 12% (as in the 1925 report), i.e., taxes of 2,400, on 20,000 crowns.

If Morania had applied a standard progressive system, such that part of the income, i.e., the first 20,000 earned, was actually taxed at a lower rate (such that only taxes of 500 were collected), then such a result, i.e., where *not all* of the foreign taxes can be credited, would be more reasonable (than in the report's scenario), since Morania would *actually* collect *less* on that income than Imeria.

However, its reasonableness would nevertheless depend on whether Morania could convincingly argue that foreign-source income should always be attributable to the *lowest*-taxed bracket of income. The authors of the 1925 report seemed to believe so, and seemed to justify it based on concerns over excessive relief (as explained at *supra* note 585) and the importance of residence as a basis for taxation, as the analysis of the report's Appendix example (below) additionally shows.

Analysis in light of 'double taxation'

Considering the 1925 report's comment (at *supra* note 588), in these scenarios, it is an interesting question to ask whether this constitutes 'double taxation'.

Scenario 3's excess could be considered 'double taxation' only if the authors believe that eliminating 'double taxation' means that the amount of taxes paid by the taxpayer can never exceed the amount that should be paid to the residence state, Morania. Alternatively, it could be argued that the residence state Morania has fully eliminated double taxation since, by virtue of granting relief in the amount of 8,000, all of the double taxation that is attributable to Morania exercising its taxing rights over this income of 20,000 crowns is eliminated (brought down to 0); in this case, the problem is – not one of double taxation, but – the existence of a higher tax rate in Imeria. Such considerations and debates will arise again under the discussion of CJEU case law on the credit method (especially in Section 4.2.2.).

In Scenario 4, one could argue that if there is an objective reason to attribute foreign-source income to the lowest bracket, then it is the appropriate result since the credit-granting state will have fully eliminated the taxes that it would collect on that income. It is not immediately apparent what reasons (beyond higher revenue collection) support this. Perhaps one reason could be: since the taxpayer earned only 20,000 in Imeria, the taxpayer was presumed to be taxed at the lowest rates on Imeria's progressive scale, and, therefore, it is acceptable for Morania to treat it the same way for the purpose of double taxation relief. This justification would thus depend on what happens in the other state.

One could counterargue that, since the income is fungible (as the 20,000 is clearly included in and taxed in the same way as all the rest of the 100,000), the effective tax rate that applied to all the income was 18.5%. Therefore, to effectively eliminate double taxation, Morania should apply the credit limitation based on this effective tax rate that applied.

As can be seen, this example illustrates some considerations relevant for the question as to whether the foreign-source income should be attributed to one bracket (e.g., the highest, the lowest) or attributed proportionately to all income brackets, for the purposes of the credit limitation.

In sum, the MCA proposed by the League of Nations and that of the US system differed in two key ways: not only did the League of Nations impose two separate maximum limits but also it dictated the use of the tax rate that corresponds *only* to the FSI alone, treated separately.

The insistence on an MCA comes across clearly in the Appendix attached to the Report. An example of an unlimited FTC reads in the following way:

'METHOD I. – TOTAL DEDUCTION.

Country Y collects the tax BD on the income AB, which under its own legislation is taxable in that country. The country of domicile X first calculates the tax on the whole of the taxpayer's income OB. It then deducts BD, the amount of the tax actually collected by the country of origin, without any restriction whatever. It therefore only collects CD (Fig. 2).

Fig. 2

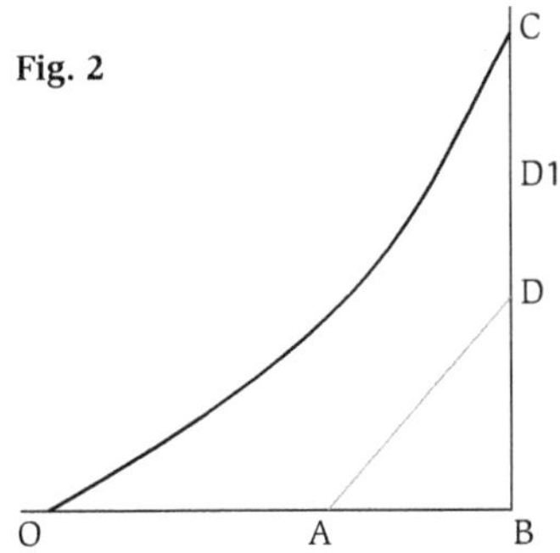

This system has the *great disadvantage* of placing the budget of the country of domicile X at the mercy of country Y. If the latter increases its scale of taxation and collects BD_1 instead of BD, country X will find the amount of its tax reduced and will only collect CD_1 instead of CD.

This system may lead to *curious results*:

(a) Take the case of two taxpayers, Peter and Paul. The former has his entire capital OA invested in X, his country of domicile; the latter, who is a richer man than Peter, has in his country X the same capital OA as his neighbour, but has in addition the capital AB invested in a foreign country Y. If the system of total deduction is adopted, without any maximum being fixed, the taxpayer Paul will pay his country of domicile the sum represented by CD_1. This is less than the amount paid by his less wealthy neighbour Peter, who, however, has the same amount of capital invested in their common country of domicile.

(b) A taxpayer invests part AB of his fortune abroad in 1924, it being assumed that his total wealth OB is the same as it was in 1923. If there is no limit to the amount of the relief, the State of domicile will remit for 1924 BD_1, *i.e.*, a sum larger than the tax on the portion of the wealth invested abroad when calculated on its own scale. In 1924, it would give up more than it collected in 1923 - an inequitable arrangement.

(c) Finally, if (Fig. 3) the scale of taxation is higher in country Y than in country X, and if the income AB is considerably larger than the income OA, it may well happen that point D appears above point C, in which case *total relief becomes impossible*, since the country of domicile collects less than the other country.

Fig. 3

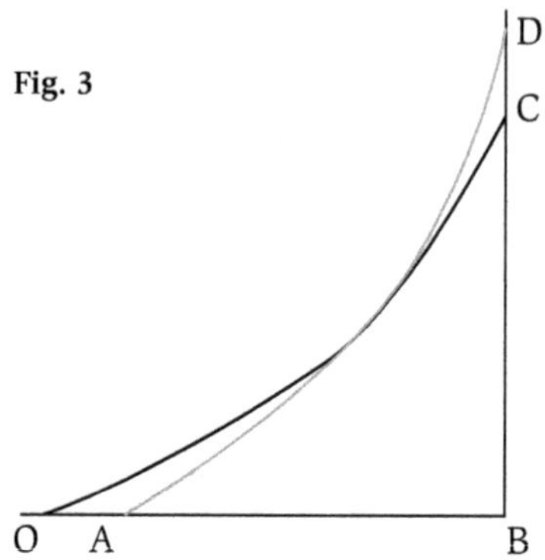

Hence both theorists and legislators themselves have been led to apply *correctives* to this system by *fixing a maximum for the relief* borne by the State of domicile. This is what was called for by the Special Committee of the International Chamber of Commerce in its 1922 draft resolution (Doc. F. 5*a*); it is also the principle embodied in Methods V (American Legislation) and VI (League of Nations Experts), which we shall consider later on' (emphasis added).[589]

The three sub-examples (letters a, b, and c) serve to illustrate three 'curious' or 'inequitable' results of a credit method without any credit limitation. All assume that the taxes collected in the foreign state are higher than those collected in the state of residence (or 'domicile'). Letters a and c offer insight into why the report suggests that a limit in some form should be imposed. Letter b (with the wording 'its own scale') seems aimed, in part, at offering insight into why the limit should additionally be based on the rate in the state of residence that *would* apply to the FSI alone (though it would not convincingly justify applying a purely hypothetical lower tax rate as in the Morania-Imeria example above, as the above-discussed alternative scenarios of Example No. 18 show).

Further insight can be garnered by pulling out the tacit assumptions. According to the example, one undesirable result is that one taxpayer, who is wealthier, with part of his capital invested abroad contributes *less* to the state of residence than his fellow compatriot, who is poorer, and invests all of his capital at home. This relies on a comparison of two resident taxpayers and their respective contributions to their state of *residence*. The result seems to cause two offences, in the view of the author of the Appendix:

(1) First, as the tone of the wording implies, it is negative that the richer taxpayer contributes less than the poorer taxpayer, which would infringe notions of

589. *Id.*, Appendix, at 4097.

fairness to the extent that income taxes are based on the ability-to-pay principle.

(2) Second, it implies that it is negative that the richer taxpayer contributes less than the poorer taxpayer, specifically, to the state of residence. It overlooks whether the richer taxpayer pays more taxes *overall*, after the taxes paid to *both* states are taken into account. There is an unexpressed underlying assumption of the duty of residents to contribute to their state of residence (or 'domicile' in this case), implying that the connection of residence leads to a stronger duty in this regard.

Another undesirable result, according to the example, is that the aim of granting (total) relief is simply rendered impossible to achieve in certain circumstances. The sub-example in letter c assumes a difference in taxes between the two states (i.e., 'higher in country Y than in country X') such that the amount of taxes collected in the foreign state (Y), on the FSI, exceeds the total amount of tax due in the state of residence (X), on all income from both domestic and foreign sources. Overall, the example places a strong emphasis on the financial sacrifice of the state of residence and on fairness between taxpayers (vis-à-vis their state of residence). And, for these reasons (*rather than* reasons related to, e.g., the right of the state of residence to preserve its ability to collect taxes on DSI, as discussed *inter alia* at *supra* note 186), it expresses deep concerns with the prospect of a full credit without any limit.

League of Nations, 1927 Report and 1928 Report

The resolutions of the 'Technical Experts' in the 1925 report were then transformed into draft wording for articles of a convention in two subsequent reports: the 1927 report and the 1928 report. In the 1927 report, the 'Committee on Double Taxation and Tax Evasion' largely agreed with the resolutions of 1925, making changes to points of detail only.[590] In the 1928 report, the opinions of government representatives on the draft texts were gathered and their meetings resulted in some amendments.[591] Comparing the wording of the draft articles on the credit method, and their commentaries, in 1927 and in 1928, they are quite close with only small changes in wording. For this reason, they are analysed side-by-side.

Within the draft convention of 1927, the credit method was found under 'Personal Taxes' (Part II of the convention)[592] in Article 10, which provided for taxation

590. League of Nations, 1927 Report, at 4122.
591. League of Nations, 1928 Report, at 4191–4193 (Austria, Belgium, Bulgaria, China, Czechoslovakia, Danzig, Denmark, Estonia, France, Germany, Great Britain, Greece, Hungary, Irish Free State, Italy, Japan, Latvia, the Netherlands, Norway, Poland, Romania, South Africa, Spain, Sweden, Switzerland, the United States, the Union of Socialist Soviet Republics).
592. League of Nations, 1927 Report, at 4127 et seq. (Part I regarding 'Impersonal Taxes', in essence, gives the prior right to tax income from immovable property to the state of situs (Article 2), for business income to the state where a permanent establishment is located (Article 5), for income from transferable securities other than shares, such as bonds, to the state of the debtor (Article 3), for income from shares to the state of the 'real centre of management of the undertaking' (Article 4), etc., and then Part II regarding 'Personal Taxes', in essence, states that only the state where the taxpayer has his or her fiscal domicile can levy a 'personal tax on total income' and,

in the state of domicile with a credit for the taxes paid abroad.[593] The draft Article 10 and its commentary accomplished two goals: first they defined the term 'residence' and then proposed the method of relief.

In the 1928 report, this was maintained with minor changes. The article was contained in what the government representatives called 'Draft Convention No. 1a'.[594] Notably, only the credit method was provided for. The 'tax exemption' method (Option (1)(a) in the 1925 report) was no longer included. However, there was an alternative. It was not in a draft article, but rather in the commentary, where one paragraph described an alternative method of avoiding double taxation which, although not labelled as such, is an 'exemption with progression' method.[595] As for the draft articles, the following table compares the relevant texts:

1925 Resolutions	*1927 Draft Convention*	*1928 Draft Convention No. 1a*
'3. The precise method of avoiding double taxation must be a matter to be worked out in detail between the States concerned, having regard to the circumstances and nature of the respective fiscal systems; but the experts indicate two methods which may be of assistance to any States which may contemplate entering into such conventions: • (1) Deduction by the State of domicile from the general income-tax of a sum which will be • (a) Either the tax calculated according to the State's own scale and charged exclusively on income produced in the other countries, each of the latter being taken separately,	'The personal tax on the total income shall be levied by the State in which the taxpayer has his fiscal domicile, *i.e.*, his normal residence, the term "residence" being understood to mean a permanent home. If the State of domicile does not impose impersonal taxes on its taxpayers domiciled therein, it shall deduct from its personal tax the lesser of the two following amounts: (a) Either the amount of the tax which would be levied exclusively on such part of the income as is taxed in the other Contracting State, or (b) The amount of the tax paid in the said State, including the personal tax when for special reasons the	'The personal tax on the total income shall be levied by the State in which the taxpayer has his fiscal domicile, *i.e.*, his normal residence, the term "residence" being understood to [text unclear] permanent home. The State of domicile shall deduct from its personal tax the lesser of the two following amounts: (a) Either the amount of the tax actually paid in the other Contracting State on income from immovable property (Article 2) and on income from industrial, commercial or agricultural undertaking (Article 5); or (b) The amount of the tax relating to the income referred to in paragraph (a) at

for this reason, where the state of origin has exercised its right to tax, the state of fiscal domicile will avoid the double taxation by means of a credit method).

593. League of Nations, 1927 Report, at 4125.
594. League of Nations, 1928 Report, at 4162–4163.
595. League of Nations, 1927 Report, at 4131 and League of Nations, 1928 Report, at 4168 ('The experts have further contemplated another method of avoiding double taxation. The tax in the State of domicile of the taxpayer would be calculated at the rate applicable to the whole of the income, but it would only be levied on that part of his income which is taxable in that country, that is to say, exclusive of the income taxed in the country of its origin. Thus a taxpayer domicile in State A drawing a total income of 100,000 francs, 20,000 of which is derived from immovable property situated in State B, would only be taxed in State A on 80,000 francs, but at the rate applicable to 100,000 francs').

1925 Resolutions	*1927 Draft Convention*	*1928 Draft Convention No. 1a*
• (b) Or the tax actually paid abroad on the income arising abroad; this sum may be limited to the amount to be deducted in accordance with paragraph (a).	State of origin has imposed such a tax on income from immovable property or from industrial, commercial or agricultural undertakings situated within its territory.	the rates in force in the State of domicile.
• In order to prevent a taxpayer whose entire income arises abroad from escaping all taxation in his State of domicile, the amount to be deducted on the above basis should in all cases be restricted to some fraction of the total tax chargeable in the State of domicile.'	These deductions shall not in total exceed *x* per cent of the total personal tax leviable in the State of domicile. When the State of domicile imposes impersonal taxes, the deductions provided for above shall not include impersonal taxes which correspond or relate to income taxed in the other Contracting State.'[596]	This deduction shall not in total exceed *x* per cent of the total personal tax leviable in the State of domicile. When the State of domicile imposes impersonal taxes, the deduction provided for above shall not include impersonal taxes which correspond or relate to income taxed in the other Contracting State.'[597]

596. League of Nations, 1927 Report, at 4125. Regarding this final paragraph, *see* League of Nations, 1927 Report, at 4130–4131 and League of Nations, 1928 Report, at 4168 (the Commentary for both drafts explains that this method of relief is relevant where the state of domicile 'only levies' general personal income taxes, but not where it also levies impersonal taxes. 'If this general tax is of a purely complementary nature, and is additional to impersonal taxes, there will be no need for relief, or at any rate such relief will have to be limited. For this reason, the last paragraph of Article 10 lays down that, if the State of domicile levies impersonal taxes, the deductions provided for under (a) or (b) in Article 10 shall not include the impersonal taxes corresponding or relating to the income taxed in the State of origin'). *See also* Georg Kofler, *Article 23B: Methods for Elimination of Double Taxation, in Global Tax Treaty Commentaries* Section 1.2.1.4.1 (Richard Vann ed.-in-chief, Pasquale Pistone et al. eds, Global Topics IBFD updated as of February 2019) ('[T]he 1928 Draft Ia assumed worldwide taxation by the residence state and then dealt primarily with double taxation relief if that state did not impose impersonal taxes but only a personal tax (under the obvious assumption that such state's impersonal taxes are "included" in the personal tax)') and at n.234 and sources cited therein ('Where, however, the personal tax in the residence state is of purely complementary nature and is additional to impersonal taxes, neither draft saw a need (or at most a limited one) for granting relief. Hence, the last paragraphs of art. 10 *1927 Draft* and art. 10 *1928 Draft Ia* laid down that if the residence state levies impersonal taxes, the credit shall not include the impersonal taxes corresponding or relating to the income taxed in the state of origin').
597. League of Nations, 1928 Report, at 4163.

1927 Commentary	*1928 Commentary*
'In order to avoid double taxation, the State of domicile, if it does not levy impersonal taxes on persons resident therein, will make a deduction from its personal tax with regard to the income taxed in the country of origin. But what should be the amount of such deduction? It is to be limited to the *lesser* of the two following amounts, *i.e.*: (a) The amount of the tax which would be paid in the State of domicile exclusively on such part of the income as is liable to taxation in the State of origin; or (b) The amount of the tax paid in the State of origin. [...] Moreover, the two deductions may not in total exceed *x* per cent of the total amount of the personal tax levied in the country of domicile. This restriction is designed to prevent a taxpayer whose whole income is derived from abroad from escaping all taxation in his country of domicile' (footnote omitted).[598]	'In order to avoid double taxation, the State of domicile will make a deduction from its personal tax with regard to the income taxed in the country of origin. But what should be the amount of such deduction? It is to be limited to the *lesser* of the two following amounts, *i.e.*: (a) Either the amount of the tax actually paid in the other Contracting State on income from immovable property (Article 2) and from industrial, commercial or agricultural undertakings (Article 5); or (b) The amount of the tax on the income referred to in paragraph (a) at the rates in force in the State of domicile. This deduction may not exceed *x* per cent of the total amount of the personal tax levied in the country of domicile. This restriction is designed to prevent a taxpayer whose whole income is derived from abroad from escaping all taxation in his country of domicile' (footnote omitted).[599]

From the text and commentary, some observations can be made regarding the scope and operation of the relief. From the start, all versions emphasize 'residence'. Residence is relevant both for the scope and for the rationales supporting the credit limitations. In this way, the personal scope is clear: a taxpayer is eligible for relief only if the taxpayer is deemed to have a 'fiscal domicile' in the state in question, defined as where the 'normal residence' is located, which in turn is where the 'permanent home' is located. Thus, these terms would have significant interpretative value, especially if taxpayers would have accommodation in more than one state. Given this personal scope, the state responsible for granting relief is, evidently, the state of this 'residence'.

As regards the eligible taxes, or the material scope, the state of residence is presumed to levy 'personal' taxes and the relief is intended to reduce this 'personal' tax

598. League of Nations, 1927 Report, at 4130-4131.
599. League of Nations, 1928 Report, at 4168.

liability. The foreign taxes that are eligible for being deducted from this 'personal' tax liability are:

- 'the tax actually paid abroad on the income arising abroad' 'in the other countries, each of the latter being taken separately' (the credit method under Option 1(b) of the 1925 report);
- the tax paid in the other state, '*including the personal tax* when for special reasons the State of origin has imposed *such* a tax *on income from immovable property* or *from industrial, commercial or agricultural undertakings* situated within its territory' (emphasis added) (the credit method drafted in the 1927 report); or
- 'the amount of the tax actually paid in the other Contracting State on *income from immovable property* (Article 2) and *on income from industrial, commercial or agricultural undertaking* (Article 5)' (emphasis added) (the credit method drafted in Convention No. 1a of the 1928 report).

As can be seen, all share in common that eligible taxes are: (1) those *actually paid*, (2) paid to a given 'other' state on income 'arising' there or from property 'situated' there (thus making the source relevant), and (3) paid on 'income' and, generally, on certain types of income in some cases, such as taxes on income from immovable property or from commercial undertakings (thus making the classification of income relevant). Moreover, under the 1927 and 1928 drafts, the distinction between 'personal' and 'impersonal' taxes played a more explicit role in the scope of eligible taxes. One way of reading the articles is that eligible taxes were the other Contracting State's taxes levied on the income in question, whether on an 'impersonal' or 'personal' basis (the assumption seems to be that they would generally be of an 'impersonal' nature, but the 1927 draft wording states '*including* the personal taxes ...' where relevant; the 1928 draft is broadly formulated to apply to 'tax actually paid' in the other state without further qualification) *except* in cases where the state of residence *itself* applies 'impersonal' taxes (*see* further explanations in the footnote at *supra* note 596).

As regards the amount, the wording for the credit limitation differs in the two draft articles:

- in 1927, the credit is limited to 'the amount of the tax which *would be* levied *exclusively* on such part of the income as is taxed in the other Contracting State' or
- in 1928, the credit is limited to '[t]he amount of the tax *relating to* the income referred to in paragraph (a) at the rates in force in the State of domicile'.

In the 1927 version, the word 'exclusively' could be interpreted as maintaining the experts' view in the 1925 report that the limit should be based on the rate that 'would' *hypothetically* apply to that income if that were the sole income of the taxpayer (thus, not necessarily based on the rate that was *actually* applied to that income). In the 1928 version, the wording seems open to more than one interpretation (due to removing the hypothetical 'would be levied' and replacing it with the more general phrase 'relating to', to dropping the word 'exclusively', and to using the plural 'rates'). The wording 'the rates in force' leaves open the question as to precisely which rate, or rates, should be used to determine the 'tax relating to the [foreign source] income'. The interests of taxpayers are at stake since an interpretation that attributes the income in question to the lowest tax rate on the progressive scale minimizes the creditable amount. However, because the example (below) in the commentary is the same in both 1927 and 1928 in all relevant respects, one cannot with certainty draw a conclusion as to whether any substantial change was intended. The example in the commentary is as follows:

> 'A taxpayer domiciled in State A draws a total income of 100,000 francs, 20,000 of which are derived from an industrial or commercial undertaking situated in State B, which, under this head, levies an impersonal tax of 4,000 francs.
>
> The tax in State A will be calculated on the total of the income (for instance, at the rate of 20 per cent), *i.e.*, 100,000 × 20 / 100 = 20,000 francs, but the fiscal authorities will deduct therefrom the sum of 4,000 francs mentioned above, so that the tax will be reduced to 20,000 – 4,000 = 16,000 francs.
>
> If, however, in the State of domicile the tax only amounts to 3,000 francs on an income of 20,000 francs, 3,000 francs will be deducted and the tax will then be reduced to 20,000 – 3,000 = 17,000 francs. A State will thus not suffer loss owing to the fact that its nationals engage in business in other States.'[600]

It is notable that both texts have a double limit: in addition to limiting the credit to the amount that the residence state would collect on the FSI, the credit is also capped at '*x* per cent of the total amount of the personal tax levied in the country of domicile'.

The final sentence of the example in the commentary hints at what the rationale for the credit limitation is: 'A State will thus not suffer loss owing to the fact that its nationals engage in business in other States.'[601] The rationale for the second (double) limit is expressed above as 'designed to prevent a taxpayer whose whole income is derived from abroad from escaping all taxation in his country of domicile', which guarantees that a taxpayer always contributes something to the state of residence. Evidently, this contribution is viewed as a duty of being a resident. This duty remains,

600. *Id.*; League of Nations, 1927 Report, at 4131 (comparing the 1927 commentary and the 1928 commentary, there were some subtle simplifications made to the example, but none which change in a substantial way how the credit limitation was calculated. The 1927 version read as follows: 'A taxpayer domiciled in State A draws a total income of 100,000 francs, 20,000 of which are derived from an industrial or commercial undertaking situated in State B, which, under this head, levies an impersonal tax of 3,000 francs and a personal tax of 1,000 francs, *i.e.*, a total of 4,000 francs.

The tax in State A, which does not levy impersonal taxes, will be calculated on the total of the income (for instance, at the rate of 20 per cent), *i.e.*, 100,000 x 20 / 100 = 20,000 francs, but the fiscal authorities will deduct therefrom the sum of 4,000 francs mentioned above, so that the tax will be reduced to 20,000 – 4,000 = 16,000 francs.

If, however, in the State of domicile the personal tax only amounts to 3,000 francs on an income of 20,000 francs, 3,000 francs will be deducted and the tax will then be reduced to 20,000 – 3,000 = 17, 000 francs. A State will thus not suffer loss owing to the fact that its nationals engage in business in other States').

601. League of Nations, 1927 Report, at 4131, and League of Nations, 1928 Report, at 4168.

even if the taxpayer does not earn any income in its state of residence. In this way, 'residence' as a connecting factor for jurisdiction to tax is again given a heavy weight.

As the table below shows, in the 1928 report, in addition to the above-cited 'Draft Convention No. 1a' (which adopted largely the same text as its 1927 counterpart), the government officials drafted two alternative model conventions 'more capable of adaptation to the fiscal systems of certain States or groups of States'.[602] The inspiration for adding these two alternative model conventions can be found in the final conclusions of the 1927 report, where it was stated that the 1927 draft model was most amenable to certain tax systems, while it could be 'abridged' for others. In particular, the 1927 draft was designed for countries that 'levy impersonal taxes and also a personal general tax' and could also be useful in the case of 'a general tax in the country of domicile, and schedular taxes in the country of origin'. In other cases, the model text could be adapted. The 1928 meeting set out to develop these abridged models. It drafted 'two new texts of model bilateral Conventions which draw no distinction between impersonal and personal taxes, the first applying particularly to relations between countries in which taxation by reference to domicile predominates, and the second to relations between countries possessing different fiscal systems'.[603]

In the first case, where both states apply taxation on the basis of residence ('domicile'), the main method of relief is a credit method. This model convention, 'Convention No. 1b', had the following structure: the general principle is that income is taxable in the state of residence (Article 1); however, priority is given to taxation at source in certain cases, such as immoveable property and PEs (Article 2).[604] In *all* cases, the state of residence has the right to tax, and thus it has the default right to tax, while in *some* specifically enumerated cases, the state of source also has a right to tax in addition to the state of residence, and thus it has a 'priority' right to tax. The obligation for relief is placed on both states, depending on the income in question. First, in the cases where both states have the right to tax under the convention, the state of residence must apply the credit method. It must credit the taxes levied 'by priority' at source, subject to a credit limitation. Second, in all cases *not* specifically enumerated in Article 2 (e.g., the taxation of income from 'transferable securities'), the state of source should *not* tax and must therefore refund any taxes it levied, upon receiving 'proper evidence', which in the end results in an exemption by the state of origin and sole taxation by the state of residence in those cases.

In cases where the two states simply have 'different fiscal systems', there are a combination of methods. First, in most cases, double taxation is avoided, it seems, by

602. League of Nations, 1928 Report, at 4159.
603. *Id.*, at 4161.
604. *Id.*, at 4170–4171 (to offer some examples, Article 2 gives priority to taxation at source for: (a) income from immovable property and from mortgages, to the place where the property is situated; (b) income from 'Industrial, Commercial or Agricultural' activities, to the place where a permanent establishment is located; (c) income in the form of fees for managers and directors, to the place where the 'real centre of management of the undertaking' is located; (d) income from salaries, to the place where 'the recipients carry on their employment', or income from public officials' salaries 'who are serving abroad', to the state that pays those salaries; (e) income in the form of 'public pensions', to the place of the 'debtor of such income').

the assignment of income approach. For example, income from immovable property is taxable in the state in which the property is situated, wages are taxable in the state where the employment is exercised, and so on,[605] whereas 'annuities or income from other claims not referred to in the previous paragraphs' (seemingly a catch-all 'other income' article)[606] is taxable in the state of residence. In these cases, what seems to be an exemption with progression method applies. Second, in the specific case of 'income from movable assets', the state of residence of the 'creditor' has the taxation right, but the state from where the income originates maintains its right to levy a tax at source. In certain cases, the state of residence must offer relief and it may choose to apply either a credit method or a form of exemption method. Where double taxation remained, the states would have to come to an agreement.

The table below sets out a comparison of their draft articles on the avoidance of double taxation:

1928 Convention No. 1a	*1928 Convention No. 1b*	*1928 Convention No. 1c*
Convention No. 1a[607] (nearly same as 1927 draft – 'to countries which levy impersonal taxes and also a personal general tax')	Convention No. 1b[608] ('to relations between countries in which taxation by reference to domicile predominates')	Convention No. 1c[609] ('to relations between countries possessing different fiscal systems')
'The personal tax on the total income shall be levied by the State in which the taxpayer has his fiscal domicile, *i.e.*, his normal residence, the term "residence" being understood to [text unclear] permanent home. The State of domicile shall deduct from its personal tax the lesser of the two following amounts:	'A. *Deductions* On reporting his or its total income from all sources, any person or company domiciled in the territory of one of the Contracting States shall be granted relief in respect of taxes payable in the other Contracting State on income taxable under Article 2 by priority in such other Contracting State.	'If, under the provisions of this Convention, either of the Contracting States has surrendered any taxable element of income or wealth, it shall retain the right to apply to the entire taxable property not exempted the rate of its general tax on income or total wealth corresponding to the whole of the income or total wealth of the taxpayer.'

605. *Id.*, at 4173–4175 (it essentially followed the same rules as in Article 2 of Convention No. 1b, cited at *supra* note 604).
606. *Id.*, at 4174 (Article 8).
607. *Id.*, at 4161–4163.
608. *Id.*, at 4170–4172.
609. *Id.*, at 4173–4175.

1928 Convention No. 1a	*1928 Convention No. 1b*	*1928 Convention No. 1c*
(a) Either the amount of the tax actually paid in the other Contracting State on income from immovable property (Article 2) and on income from industrial, commercial or agricultural undertaking (Article 5); or (b) The amount of the tax relating to the income referred to in paragraph (a) at the rates in force in the State of domicile. This deduction shall not in total exceed *x* per cent of the total personal tax leviable in the State of domicile. When the State of domicile imposes impersonal taxes, the deduction provided for above shall not include impersonal taxes which correspond or relate to income taxed in the other Contracting State.'	For this purpose the State of domicile shall deduct from its tax on the total income the lesser of the two following amounts: (a) The tax imposed by the other Contracting State on income taxable by priority therein; or (b) An amount which represents the same proportion of the tax payable on the total income as the income taxable by priority bears to the total income. B. *Refunds* The State which has collected an origin tax on revenues not enumerated under Article 2 shall refund the amount on production of proper evidence.'	As regards the taxation of income from movable assets by both States: 'In this case the State of domicile which, in addition to its ordinary direct tax, levies a special tax on income originating in the other State, shall refrain from levying that tax or shall deduct therefrom the tax paid in the other State. In order to avoid or to mitigate the effects of such double taxation as is not, under the various fiscal systems, prevented by the provision of the previous sub-paragraph, the Contracting States shall come to an agreement, if necessary, to allow either the remission, in respect of the tax levied by the State of domicile, of the whole or part of the tax deducted by the State of origin, or a refund, upon production of proper evidence by the State of origin, of the whole or part of the tax collected by it by means of deductions.'

As regards the credit method, 'Convention No. 1c' merely mentions the credit method as an option, without further elaboration, thus precluding any meaningful comparisons, whereas 'Convention No. 1b', with its own draft text, offers some insightful points of comparison.

The credit limitation in 'Convention No. 1b' is less severe than in 'Convention No. 1a' because it does not contain wording for a double limit. Both contain the first, or main, limitation. That is, they are limited to the amount of taxes that would be collected by the state of residence on the FSI. On this point, however, the wording changed. The wording under 'Convention No. 1b' resembles more the wording used in the US.[610] While '1a' refers to the *tax rates* in the state of residence, '1b' revolves around *a proportion* of the total taxes due in the state of residence. The relevance of this change of wording is that: it spells out a formula that can be applied rather mechanically, reducing some of the guessing or potential interpretation ambiguity as regards which rates apply. The starting point is the 'tax payable on the total income' and the calculation seeks the 'proportion' of this tax that is equal to the income taxable in the other state over the total income. Presumably the starting point itself, the 'tax payable on the total income', already incorporates the progressive tax rates, if any. It is then multiplied by a ratio that is based on the relative amounts of income. This has the effect of assuming the foreign income is spread proportionately among all progressive income tax brackets. Under CJEU case law, this type of calculation was at issue under the *Schumacker/De Groot* line of case law (as discussed in Section 4.2.4.).

As regards the second limit, in '1b', no absolute ceiling was placed on the credit, up to 'x per cent of the total personal tax leviable'.[611] Good riddance to this second limit since it is rather arbitrary. While the first limit is aligned with the goal of relief for double taxation, in that the residence state should eliminate all taxes that it would have otherwise levied on the doubly taxed income, but does not have to go further than that, the second limit blatantly permits double taxation, by rendering the relief only partial, and is motivated mostly, if not solely, by protecting the coffers of the residence state (which by itself, irrespective of the worthiness of this aim, is somewhat extrinsic to a relief mechanism aim).

League of Nations, 1931 Report

As regards the methods for relief of double taxation in particular, the next main developments did not arise until the 1931 report.[612] While previous reports (in 1929 and in 1930) focused on bilateral model conventions – 'bilateral' was deemed the most

610. United States, Revenue Act of 1921, Sixty-Seventh Congress, Session I, Chapter 136, Public Law 67-98, Section 222(a)(5) for individuals and Section 238(a) for corporations (US Government Printing Office 1921) (under Section 222(a)(5), the credit limitation was worded in the following way: '... and in no other case shall the amount of credit taken under this subdivision exceed the same proportion of the tax, against which such credit is taken, which the taxpayer's net income (computed without deduction for any income, war-profits and excess-profits taxes imposed by any foreign country or possession of the United States) from sources without the United States bears to his entire net income (computed without such deduction) for the same taxable year'. Under Section 238(a), the credit limitation was worded in the following way: '... *Provided,* [t]hat the amount of credit taken under this subdivision shall in no case exceed the same proportion of the taxes, against which such credit is taken, which the taxpayer's net income (computed without deduction for any income, war-profits, and excess-profits taxes imposed by any foreign country or possession of the United States) from sources without the United States bears to its entire net income (computed without such deduction) for the same taxable year').

611. League of Nations, 1928 Report, at 4170–4172.

612. Neither the 1929 Report nor the 1930 Report contained relevant discussions regarding the methods for relief of double taxation.

practicable due to diverges between existing tax systems[613] – the 1931 report picked back up on an idea of a multilateral, or 'plurilateral', convention. However, the Committee[614] expressed serious doubts as to the feasibility of plurilateral conventions and thus could not reach a final decision.[615]

The three plurilateral drafts in the Appendix contained relief provisions, the details of which seemed to raise more questions than answers. Sometimes they diverged from the language used in draft model conventions of previous reports, employing undefined language such as the word 'rebate' or 'recoup'. While the first draft plurilateral convention contained a few preliminary sentences of clarification, there is not a dedicated commentary to accompany the other two draft conventions. For this reason, the analysis here studies the first draft, where there is potentially some value added from being able to piece together at least one plausible understanding of the wording, and shares one observation regarding the second draft. Apart from that, and as the drafts were not ultimately approved, further analysis does not seem merited here.

Regarding the first draft convention,[616] which is accompanied by a brief commentary, its Articles 13–15 offer relief. The brief commentary reads as follows:

> 'Articles 13 to 15 contain measures to avoid double taxation when the State of fiscal domicile levies an impersonal or personal tax on income which under the Convention is taxable solely in the State of origin, or when the latter levies a tax on income which under the Convention is taxable only in the State of the taxpayer's fiscal domicile.
>
> In the former case the proportion of relief will be equal to the proportion between this income and the total taxable income, so that the rate applied will be maintained. In other words the relief will be determined by the application of a rule of three. It may not, however, exceed the amount of tax paid in the country of origin of the income.
>
> In this latter case the tax paid in the country of origin will simply be refunded.

613. *See*, e.g., League of Nations, 1927 Report, at 4122 (the idea of a 'collective' convention was mentioned in the 1927 report. However, the Committee was of the opinion that, while this approach was needed for the combat against tax evasion, it was not recommendable for double taxation. 'In the matter of double taxation in particular, the fiscal systems of the various countries are so fundamentally different that it seems at present practically impossible to draft a collective convention, unless it were worded in such general terms as to be of no practical value').
614. League of Nations, 1929 Report, at 4196–4197 (after the 1928 report, a permanent Committee was established. Up until this point, they had been mostly ad hoc or temporary. This permanent Committee dedicated itself to tracking the progress of conventions concluded between states on the basis of the draft models and to studying the technical questions left open by the general meeting of government experts).
615. League of Nations, 1931 Report, at 4227–4228.
616. *Id.*, at 4232 et seq. (the first draft convention was contained in Appendix I, titled 'Draft Plurilateral Convention for the Prevention of the Double Taxation of Certain Categories of Income'), at 4237 et seq. (the second draft convention was in Appendix II, 'Draft Plurilateral Convention "A"') and at 4239 et seq. (the third draft convention was in Appendix III, 'Draft Plurilateral Convention "B"'). On Draft 'A', *see also* Georg Kofler, *Article 23B: Methods for Elimination of Double Taxation, in Global Tax Treaty Commentaries* Section 1.2.1.5 (Richard Vann ed.-in-chief, Pasquale Pistone et al. eds, Global Topics IBFD updated as of February 2019).

> The method of refunding may also be followed in the first case mentioned above.'[617]

In sum, depending on the type of income and the allocation of taxation rights for said income, the articles seem to include three types of relief.

First, it offers what appears to be a type of 'deduction', or credit, method in the state of residence ('fiscal domicile'), in cases where the state of residence taxes income that is taxable 'solely' in the state of origin. However, the commentary does not offer the clearest explanation at first glance. This will be explored further below.

Second, it requires a full refund of any taxes collected in the state of origin, in cases where the state of origin taxes income that is taxable only in the state of residence. There is a form of subject-to-tax clause, since the refund is granted only upon proof that taxes were actually paid to the state of residence (*see* Article 14 below).

Third, it provides for the apportionment of taxes or income in certain cases. For example, in the case of dual residence, an apportionment of taxes on certain kinds of income is made based on the amount of time spent in each country[618] or, in the case of enterprises operating PEs in other states, the competent authorities should agree upon apportioning the income derived from each state.

The relief provisions were drafted as follows:

> Article 13: relief from the State of fiscal domicile
>
> 'When the State of fiscal domicile of a recipient of the income referred to in Articles 2 [income from immovable property, excluding that derived from industrial, commercial or agricultural enterprises], 3 [income derived from mortgages on such property], 10 [salary of an official or public servant] and 11 [a public pension] has charged tax on any such income, the interested party may claim partial relief.
>
> The proportion of this relief shall be equal to the proportion between this income and the total income chargeable, but it may not exceed the amount of the tax payable on that income in the State of origin. The appropriate relief shall, where necessary, be given by way of repayment.
>
> The last paragraph of Article 12 [quoted below] shall apply in this case; the interested party must produce the official documents certifying that the tax has been paid in the State in which the income originates.'[619]
>
> Article 14: relief by means of refund from the state of origin
>
> 'If the State of origin of the income referred to in Articles 6 to 9 [income from public loans; earnings of frontier workers; authors' rights and income from patents; life annuities] has levied a tax on such income, the interested party may claim a refund, provided he proves that the income has been taxed in the State of his fiscal domicile. The last paragraph of Article 12 [quoted below] shall apply to claims under the present Article.'[620]

617. League of Nations, 1931 Report, at 4234.
618. *Id.*, at 4235. *See also* League of Nations, 1927 Report, at 4126, and League of Nations, 1928 Report, at 4169 and 4170–4171 (Article 11 in the 1927 Draft Convention and in the 1928 Draft Convention No. 1a and Article 1 of the 1928 Draft Convention No. 1b contained the same idea).
619. League of Nations, 1931 Report, at 4235–4236.
620. *Id.*, at 4236.

Article 15: relief for PEs abroad from the State of fiscal domicile

'If, in the case provided for at the end of the first paragraph of Article 4, the State of fiscal domicile of a company has levied a tax on the income of its permanent establishments situated in the territory of other contracting States, that company may claim partial relief from the tax. The last two paragraphs of Article 13, and also the second paragraph of Article 4, shall apply in this case.'

Article 12: relief by means of apportionment

'When a taxable natural person has a fiscal domicile in the territory of two or more of the contracting States, he may claim that the impersonal or personal tax on the income referred to in Articles 6 to 9 [income from public loans; earnings of frontier workers; authors' rights and income from patents; life annuities] shall be apportioned according to the length of his stay in each as compared with the total length of his stay in all those countries during the financial year. The appropriate relief shall, when necessary, be given by way of repayment.

The countries concerned may, if they think fit, adopt some method of apportioning the tax other than that indicated in the previous paragraph, in particular when the taxpayer has not resided during the fiscal year in a country in which he has a fiscal domicile.

The claim referred to in the first paragraph must be presented in the form prescribed by the competent authorities of each country, accompanied by vouchers, within six months after the close of the financial year, provided, however, that the time allowed for making the claim shall not be less than six months from the date of the notification to the taxpayer of the latest assessment.'[621]

Article 13 appears to be a credit method, especially since it makes reference to the tax liability abroad (stating in the text that 'it may not exceed the amount of the tax payable on that income in the State of origin' and in the commentary that it may not exceed 'the amount of tax paid in the country of origin'). Article 13 calculates what it refers to as the 'proportion of this relief', or perhaps a percentage of relief. It uses language that is similar to that of a credit limitation (MCA), by applying a ratio, or limiting fraction, that is equal to the 'proportion between this income and the total income chargeable'.[622] In other words, it seems that the ratio is between the 'origin'-source income in question and the total taxable income in the state of residence. Upon first reading, it is not immediately clear to *what* this ratio is applied: will the ratio be multiplied against the total taxes in the residence state? On this point, the commentary (*supra* note 617) merely states that 'the proportion of relief will be equal to the proportion between this income and the total taxable income, *so that the rate applied will be maintained*' (emphasis added), without specifying or demonstrating by example the meaning of this reference to the 'rate applied'. Based on a combined reading of the text and the commentary, multiplying the 'proportion of relief' against the total taxes due seems to be the most plausible reading. If so, the following example illustrates this:

621. *Id.*, at 4235.
622. *Id.*, at 4235–4236.

	Income:	*Tax Rate: %*	*Taxes Due:*
Assume in the state of origin:	40	10	4
Assume in the state of residence:	100 (total)	20	20

Calculation of the relief in the state of residence:

> Wording: 'proportion of relief' = 'the proportion between this income and the total income chargeable' = %
> Proportion of relief = 40/100 = 40%
> Amount of relief = the proportion of relief, 40%, of the taxes due = 40% × 20 = 8
> If a relief of 8 were granted, then the taxpayer would pay 12 to the residence state, and only 4 in this case to the foreign state, so that the taxpayer pays only 16 in total, which amounts to an ETR of 16% on 100. However, it then follows with a cap: 'It may not, however, exceed the amount of tax paid in the country of origin of the income.'
> Maximum amount = tax paid in foreign state = 4
> Tax due in the residence state after relief: 20 - 4 = 16
> Total taxes paid by taxpayer: 4 in state of origin + 16 in state of residence = 20

A notable feature of the text of all the above relief articles in this plurilateral proposal is that they include some specifics on the procedure. They state the obligation to furnish proof of taxes paid, as a condition for relief. The articles even prescribe some timelines (e.g., 'within six months after the close of the financial year'). Unfortunately, the wording was considerably less clear on the credit method itself.

While this first draft plurilateral convention seems to include a form of limited ('ordinary') tax credit, what is very interesting to note is that: as Kofler points out, the second draft plurilateral convention (Draft 'A') seems to provide for a full credit.[623] That is, most of the provisions of Draft 'A' seem to grant exclusive taxation rights to one state (using the wording 'shall be taxable only' in that state), sometimes to the state of 'fiscal domicile', sometimes to the other state (e.g., the state of situs or of the payment). Under its Articles 13–16, when the exclusive taxation right is granted to one of the states, the other state is given the choice between exemption and a 'rebate' of the 'full tax borne'. For example, its Article 14 states that:

> 'The relief provided for in Articles 2, 3, 11 and 12 [e.g. immovable property and income from mortgages on that property, taxable only in the state of *situs*] from the taxation of the country of the fiscal domicile of the recipient of the income shall be given either by way of exemption or *by way of a rebate* involving, if necessary, *a refund of tax*, and the following provisions shall have effect in relation to any item of income to which these articles refer:

623. Georg Kofler, *Article 23B: Methods for Elimination of Double Taxation, in Global Tax Treaty Commentaries* Section 1.2.1.5 (Richard Vann ed.-in-chief, Pasquale Pistone et al. eds, Global Topics IBFD updated as of February 2019); *see* League of Nations, 1931 Report, at 4238–4239.

(a) The exemption of any such item of income from taxation in the country of domicile of the recipient shall not operate to reduce the rate of personal tax payable in that country.
(b) The country of domicile shall be deemed to have discharged its obligations under the said articles if it recoups the taxpayer *to the extent of the full tax borne* in the country of origin.
(b) The rules laid down in the last paragraph of Article 13 [stating the procedures, such as the six-month deadline, etc.] shall apply to claims under the present article; the interested party must produce the official documents certifying that the tax has been paid in the State in which the income originates' (emphasis added).

League of Nations, 1933 Report, 1935 Report and 1936 Report

The Committee continued to produce interim reports, providing updates on the states concluding conventions and examining technical questions. For example, in 1935, there is a note about the 'constant extension of this network of Conventions' and that the 'progress achieved has been particularly remarkable in the field of direct taxes on income' - citing ten Conventions concluded since 1931, predominantly between what are currently EU countries.[624] This tendency occurred despite the Great Depression and protectionism in other areas of trade.[625]

One question that arose in some of the reports (e.g., the 1930 and 1933 reports) is related to the credit method in an ancillary (but nevertheless important) way. The Committee expressed a desire for further research and for agreement on certain 'fiscal and juridical terminology' and technical matters, such as questions related to methods of accounting[626] and 'concepts of gross income, net income, expenses, general overhead, etc.'[627] As the above debates in the US over the term 'accumulated profits' in the credit method fraction, among others, showed,[628] these questions have an obvious impact on the taxation of income and thus when they differ between states give rise to difficulties. Nevertheless, these matters now are almost unquestionably and solely relegated to the domain of domestic law. The current 2017 Commentary on Articles 23 A and 23 B of the OECD Model states that these are details of domestic law, or possibly bilateral negotiations, which models cannot address.[629]

624. League of Nations, 1935 Report, at 4249.
625. *Id.*, at 4250 ('All these Conventions, with certain differences of detail, apply the principles laid down by the model Conventions drafted in 1928 by the general meeting of Government experts').
626. League of Nations, 1930 Report, at 4209 (some questions the Committee planned to further investigate were related to accounting issues, as the following excerpts show: 'working principles and methods of accounting; their effect upon international double taxation' and 'Methods - more particularly accounting methods - of ascertaining taxable profits which could be adopted by the fiscal administrations of the various countries and which would at the same time be equitable and reasonable from the point of view of the undertakings taxed, and would as far as possible prevent international double taxation, ...').
627. League of Nations, 1933 Report, at 4243.
628. *See supra* note 326 and note 337.
629. OECD, *Model Tax Convention on Income and on Capital 2017: Condensed Version* Commentary on Articles 23 A and 23 B, paras 62-66 (OECD Publishing 2017).

League of Nations, 1946 Report: 'revision and codification' of the draft texts

The most important next developments came in the 1946 Report. A feedback loop began to emerge between the first model conventions and the actual practice of negotiating and concluding bilateral tax treaties.[630] The negotiators of existing bilateral tax treaties devised some improvements upon the model conventions and, thus, the members of the Committee embarked upon the 'work of revision and codification', seeking to incorporate the best practices into an updated model convention. Thus, the texts of the credit method in this report reflect this process.

In this context, meetings were held in Mexico City in 1940 and 1943 and in London in 1946, from which two different draft model conventions were issued, the Mexico Model Convention and the London Model Convention.[631] To offer a general outline of the models:

> 'According to the proposals embodied in the Mexico and London Model Conventions, double taxation of income and property is prevented by two sets of clauses which are mutually complementary. In the first place, a definition is given of the conditions under which each kind of income as characterised by the type of property or activity from which it is derived may be taxed in a country according to the criterion of impersonal tax liability. In the second place, it is provided that taxes so paid are to be deducted from, or credited against, the tax due by the taxpayer in the country where he has his residence or "fiscal domicile".'[632]

Thus, it relied on the credit method for the relief of double taxation. Notably, this is the first use of the term 'credit' detected among these historical reports, instead of 'deduction' or 'first method'.[633]

The updated text as a result of the 'revision and codification' process was as follows:

630. League of Nations, 1946 Report, at 4325–4326 ('The numerous tax treaties which were concluded during the decade which preceded the war contained, however, various improvements on the 1928 Model Conventions. The Fiscal Committee, for its part, had been able to carry further the work initiated by the General Meeting of Government Experts. Moreover, new trends and new problems had appeared in the field of international trade and investment. Consequently, it seemed desirable to prepare new model conventions that would reflect the technical progress achieved since 1928 and codify the views and recommendations that had been expressed by the Fiscal Committee in the course of its various sessions').

631. *See*, e.g., League of Nations, 1946 Report, at 4326.

632. *Id.*, at 4329.

633. *Id.*

Text of the Credit Method in the Mexico Model	*Text of the Credit Method in the London Model*
'Article XIII. The State where the taxpayer has his fiscal domicile shall retain the right to tax the entire income of the taxpayer whether derived from its territory or from that of the other contracting State, but shall deduct from its tax on such entire income the lesser of the two following amounts: A. The tax collected by the latter contracting State on the income which is taxable in its territory according to the preceding Articles; B. The amount which represents the same proportion in comparison with the total tax on the income that is taxable in both States as the income taxable in the other State in comparison with the total income.'[634]	'Article XIII. The State where the taxpayer has his fiscal domicile shall retain the right to tax the entire income of the taxpayer whether derived from its territory or from that of the other contracting State, but shall deduct from its tax on such entire income the lesser of the following amounts: A. The tax collected by the other contracting State on the income which is taxable in its territory according to the preceding Articles; B. The amount which represents the same proportion of the tax of the State of fiscal domicile on the entire net income of the taxpayer as the net income taxable in the other State bears to the entire net income.'[635]

From the wording, a few key features of the scope and operation are immediately apparent. The wording '[t]he State where the taxpayer has his fiscal domicile' followed by 'shall' makes it clear that the addressee is the residence state and the article contains an obligation. Related to this, similar to previous drafts (e.g., 1927, 1928), the personal scope – of the convention as a whole and of this article – revolves around the 'fiscal domicile' of the taxpayer. According to the Commentary, which is the same for both the London and Mexico drafts, the 'fiscal domicile' refers to 'the place where a person has his normal residence or permanent home'; for 'a partnership, company or other similar entity', it refers to 'the country under the laws of which it was organised' (in the Mexico Model) or to 'the country in which their real centre of management is situated' (in the London Model).[636] Thus, again, the connection with residence becomes clear. The rationale for this, in the Commentary, is that these persons should enjoy double taxation relief because fiscal domicile in a country normally entails a 'general tax liability on their total income from domestic and foreign sources'.[637]

634. League of Nations, 1946 Report, at 4386 and 4388.
635. *Id.*, at 4387 and 4389.
636. *Id.*, at 4330–4331.
637. *Id.*, at 4331.

The basic two-step operation of the credit method is clearly expressed. First, tax is calculated on the basis of 'the entire income of the taxpayer' and, second, from this, the relevant 'tax collected by the other contracting State' must be deducted.

As regards the scope of the taxes that can be deducted, a few observations can be made. First, the article applies to taxes that are levied on 'the income which is taxable ... *according to the preceding Articles*' (emphasis added).[638] Thus, there are two conditions: the taxes must be covered by the convention (i.e., be among those listed by the Contracting States in the first article) and must be levied in accordance with the convention or, to phrase it negatively, cannot be levied in violation of the convention. For example, if the other state levies more taxes than it has a right to levy under the articles of the convention, then the residence state is not obliged by Article XIII to grant a credit for that excessive part. As a corollary, however, if and to the extent that the other state has the right to tax and taxes in accordance with the convention, then the residence state *must* grant a credit for that amount. In this way, the scope of the credit is linked to other articles in the convention. This is a special feature of these bilateral measures. In addition, the word 'collected' could be interpreted as a requirement that the taxes have already been paid, as opposed to merely 'accrued' or 'payable'. The Commentary is silent on this.

As in previous bilateral drafts, the amount of taxes that can be credited is limited. The amount of the credit will be either the taxes actually paid to the other state or, at most, the amount of the residence state's taxes that correspond to the income taxable in the other state. Despite the different wording in the Mexico version and the London version on this point, both articles intend to achieve the same result, though the London version reads more clearly (it avoids the redundancy of the phrase 'in comparison with' in the Mexico version).

According to the wording (taking the example of the London version), the calculation of the credit limitation starts with the total taxes due in the state of residence ('the tax of the State of fiscal domicile on the entire net income of the taxpayer') and states that the credit is limited to a 'proportion' of these total taxes. This 'proportion' is equal to (is the 'same ... as') the income taxable in the other State over the total income taxable in the state of residence ('the net income taxable in the other State bears to the entire net income'). The Commentary confirms, though it is evident from the wording, that the MCA will operate only when the tax rate is effectively higher in the other state.[639]

638. *Id.*, at 4386–4389.

639. *Id.*, at 4349 ('It may be noted that the above-mentioned limit of deduction will operate in the country of "fiscal domicile" only when the tax schedule in the other country is so high that the effective percentage of tax in respect of the part of income taxable in its territory exceeds the tax percentage which in the country of "fiscal domicile" corresponds to the total income of the taxpayer').

$$\textbf{1946 Model MCA} = \textbf{`the tax of the State of fiscal domicile on the entire net income of the taxpayer'} \times \frac{\textbf{`the net income taxable in the other State'}}{\textbf{`the entire net income'}}$$

It is significant that the London version uses the term 'net income'.[640] This dictates to the residence state, to some extent, its tax base; at least, it excludes that the tax base is a gross amount. Such wording could play an important substantive role, since, as future cases (e.g., in 2016) would demonstrate, taxpayers may argue that the state of residence should adopt a 'gross tax base' or a tax base similar to that of the *other* state (of source/origin) if that would allow them to benefit from a larger credit.[641] These types of arguments are considered again below in the discussion of the CJEU case law (where findings are brought together from the *Gilly* or 'disparity' line of case law and the *Gerritse/Scorpio* or deductible expenses line of case law). This wording seems to be a remnant of – and thus a clear marker of the influence of – the US wording. The credit limitation in the US Revenue Act of 1921, for example, was: '... and in no other case shall the amount of credit ... exceed the same proportion of the tax, against which such credit is taken, which the taxpayer's net income ... from sources without the United States bears to his entire net income ... for the same taxable year'.[642]

League of Nations, 1946 Report: commentary on the draft texts

In the Commentary, the title for Article XIII is the 'Taxation Rights of the Country of "Fiscal Domicile"'. In this way, it highlights both the duty and rights of the state of residence: in addition to its obligation to grant the credit, it emphasizes this state's right to tax the entire income of the taxpayer. The right to do so is precisely what entails its obligation to grant relief, so the two go hand-in-hand.

Overall, there seems to be an aim to strike a balance between different responsibilities and obligations. According to the Commentary, '[r]egard is to be had, however, not only to the interests of the taxpayer but also to those of the State in which he has his fiscal domicile' and then it follows with an explanation of the credit limitation.[643] In other words, the state of residence offers its residents relief, but only to the extent that it would tax; thus, where the taxes levied in the *other* state are higher than what the state of residence would levy, the taxpayer receives a credit up to the amount the state of residence would levy, but not more. Moreover, the Commentary

640. *Id.*, at 4387 and 4389.
641. *See*, e.g., Canada, Tax Court of Canada, 2016 TCC 131, *Société Générale Valeurs Mobilières Inc. v. The Queen*, 26 May 2016, aff'd 2017 FCA 3; Canada, Federal Court of Appeal, 2017 FCA 3, *Société Générale Valeurs Mobilières Inc. v. Canada*, 10 Jan. 2017; France, Conseil d'État (Supreme Administrative Court), N° 357189, *SA Crédit Industriel et Commercial*, 7 Dec. 2015; Philip Baker, *Some Aspects of United Kingdom Double Taxation Relief*, 52(10) Bull. Int'l Fiscal Documentation 445 (1998), at *supra* note 357.
642. United States, Revenue Act of 1921, Sixty-Seventh Congress, Session I, Chapter 136, Public Law 67-98, Section 222(a)(5) (US Government Printing Office 1921) (Section 222(a)(5) applies to individuals. For the text that applies to corporations under Section 238(a), *see supra* note 179 and note 610).
643. League of Nations, 1946 Report, at 4349.

suggests that 'it may be found advantageous to [...]' set 'fixed or ceiling tax rates' that can be levied on certain types of income, such as 'income from capital', in the other state.[644] In other words, the two states could negotiate that the 'other State' agree to a fixed, hopefully lower, tax rate on certain items of income. Though the Commentary does not spell it out, this also would have the effect that the credit granted by the state of residence is lower. Another side effect could be that, if the taxes levied in the other state are lower, the taxpayer is more likely to receive a credit for all the foreign state's taxes, thereby avoiding the issues of 'excess' amounts of foreign taxes that are not creditable.

What comes across from these different parts of the Commentary is that the rationale for the credit limitation is to balance 'the interests' of the state of residence and the taxpayer (by comparison with the rationale seen in the US that a state of residence should be able to keep intact its right to levy taxes on DSI). In addition, a limit on the rates that the other state may levy is presumed to balance the interests of the state of residence and the other state. One reason for the viewpoint that this would achieve balance between the two states possibly stemmed from the perception that the credit method was a generous form of relief, which demanded a lot from the state of residence. Indeed, as previously discussed, in the 1923 report, the authors of the report went so far as to outright reject the credit method (method 1) on the grounds that it demanded too great a sacrifice from the state of residence and left its treasury vulnerable to increases in the rates of tax in the foreign state.[645] At this stage in 1946, the credit method became the main method in both the Mexico and London drafts; thus, the credit method clearly became viewed as more feasible, but it is likely that the overall impression of its generosity lingered.

The Commentary also mentioned a few other technical issues that were not written into the text of the article. It advised the negotiators of the two states to bear in mind some potential obstacles to ensuring that the taxpayer could receive the credit, namely potential timing issues and attribution issues. The term 'timing issues' is used here to refer to problems that could result from the fact that '[t]axable years and tax collection dates differ from country to country'.[646] The term 'attribution issues' is used here to refer to problems that could result from the fact that countries may have different conceptions of what a tax on dividends is (in particular, WHTs, not the underlying corporate taxes). In some cases, countries may view this as a tax on the corporation, while in other cases, countries may view this as a tax on the shareholder.[647] If the two countries want to ensure that a shareholder may receive a credit for such taxes, the two countries should specify 'that taxes which a company is required to withhold from dividends it distributes or to pay on such dividends shall be considered as having been paid by the shareholder for the purpose of this article'.[648]

644. *Id.*
645. *See*, e.g., *supra* note 566, note 568, note 569.
646. League of Nations, 1946 Report, at 4350.
647. *Id.* ('Depending on the system followed by that country in respect of the taxation of corporate income, the tax borne by such dividends may take different forms – *e.g.*, the form of a tax paid by the distributing company in its own name or that of a tax on corporate earnings').
648. League of Nations, 1946 Report, at 4349–4350.

On the topic of the taxation of dividends, another relevant issue is relief for 'economic double taxation'. The London model, not the Mexico Model, would have provided such relief. This was found in a different article, namely Article VIII, which was drafted specifically for dividends. In this case, the London model suggested the exemption method instead of the credit method. According to the Commentary:

> 'Paragraph 2 of the present article is intended to avoid the special cases of double or multiple taxation which may occur when the income distributed by a company is derived from dividends received from subsidiaries or related companies, etc. It was thought that an equitable and convenient manner of avoiding such double taxation was to exempt inter-company dividend distributions when the recipient company had a dominant participation in the management or capital of the paying company, so that the dividends tax is collected once only on the final distribution of dividends.'[649]

OEEC, 1958 Report: explicit mention of 'exemption' and 'credit'

After a brief pause, the work of the 1946 report was resumed by the OEEC Fiscal Committee, which issued four interim reports in order to study and update the model conventions.[650]

In the first report (1958), the OEEC merely announced its intention to re-evaluate and update the articles on 'the technical methods of avoiding double taxation (e.g. the exemption method and the tax credit method)'.[651] Note again the use of the term 'credit'. As mentioned above, the 1946 report seemed to contain the first mention of 'credit' among these historical reports and, in this 1958 report, this is the first time detected (as far as the writer is aware) where the two methods are referred to in such an explicit way as the 'credit method' and the 'exemption method'.

As regards the term 'credit method', it is helpful since it avoids confusion. This approach to relief for double taxation had been referred to in rather ambiguous ways over time, such as 'the method of deduction for income from abroad' or 'the deduction method' or merely 'method I', labels which could equally apply to a deduction of foreign taxes from the tax base as an expense.[652] Moreover, the standardization of the

649. *Id.*, at 4345.
650. OEEC, 1958 Report (full citation, *supra* note 475); OEEC, 1959 Report (full citation, *supra* note 475); OEEC, 1960 Report (full citation, *supra* note 475); OEEC, 1961 Report (full citation, *supra* note 475).
651. OEEC, 1958 Report, at 4459–4460 (in total, the OEEC announced seven questions that would become the focus of the Committee, three of which dealt with the taxation of passive income (dividends, interest and royalties). 'In conjunction with the study of these matters, it will also study the technical methods of avoiding double taxation (e.g. the exemption method and the tax credit method)').
652. *See*, e.g., United Kingdom, Finance Act 1894, Section 20; United Kingdom, Finance Act 1916, Section 43; United Kingdom, Finance Act 1920, Section 27 (the word 'credit' was not initially used in the laws on relief in the UK); League of Nations, 1923 Report, at 4045–4046 (In the 1923 Report for the League of Nations, it is referred to as '*the method of deduction for income from abroad*'); John F. Avery Jones, *Chapter I: Sir Josiah Stamp and Double Income Tax*, *in* 6 *Studies in the History of Tax Law* 1, 4 n.15 (John Tiley ed., Hart Publishing 2013) ('The current term "credit" will be adopted, although the expression was not then in use. There is no reference to credit in the 1920 Report or so far as the writer is aware in the evidence, it being referred to as

terminology was perhaps a sign that the credit method and, now alongside it, the exemption method were emerging as the main approaches for the models.

OEEC, 1959 Report

As of the second report (1959), the details were not yet settled on 'technical methods of avoiding double taxation (exemption method and tax credit method)'.[653] One of the reasons for the delay was explained as follows:

> 'On these questions [referring to three questions on royalties, dividends and interest, respectively], and on the fourth also [referring to the methods of avoiding double taxation], the establishment of uniform rules is made more complicated by the great disparity between national laws and regulations which has led Member countries to adopt very different solutions in the bilateral Conventions hitherto concluded between them.'[654]

As regards the interpretation of the articles of the model convention, the OEEC clarified that the wording 'shall be taxable only' is used 'wherever the State of residence is given the exclusive right to tax' and the wording 'may be taxed' is used 'wherever the State of source is given a right to tax'.[655] This ends up becoming relevant for the scope of application of the methods, as discussed under the fourth report below.

OEEC, 1960 Report

As of the third report (1960), progress was made on the study of the methods of avoiding double taxation, but the draft articles were still under discussion. Its study indicated that the method of 'exemption of foreign income' and a 'credit against tax for foreign taxes' were the 'two methods most commonly employed'.[656] It became clear that one single method could not be proposed, but instead, it would study these two 'principal forms' and draft articles for both:

> 'As regards technical methods of avoiding double taxation, the Fiscal Committee's studies are now sufficiently advanced for it to be possible to formulate concrete proposals at an early date. After a thorough study of the various forms that can be taken by the two methods most commonly employed (exemption of foreign income, credit against tax for foreign taxes), the Fiscal Committee has recognised that, in present circumstances, it would be fruitless to try to impose one single method. It considers that double taxation can be successfully countered by restricting the use of the methods to two clearly defined principal forms, based respectively on exemption and on the tax credit. But the elaboration of final

deduction which caused confusion between deducting the foreign tax from the income and deducting it from the UK tax; see below n 86'); but *see* United States, Revenue Act of 1918, Sixty-Fifth Congress, Session III, Chapter 18, Public Law 65-254 (US Government Printing Office 1919) (however, the US already labelled it a 'credit for taxes' in the Revenue Act of 1918).

653. OEEC, 1959 Report, at 4525–4526 (it clarified that, at this stage, the question of exemption and tax credit methods is 'in no way prejudged by the wording of the ten Articles proposed').
654. *Id.*, at 4526.
655. *Id.*, at 4526–4527.
656. OEEC, 1960 Report, at 4580.

> solutions depends to a certain extent on those which will be adopted in relation to the three questions referred to in the foregoing paragraph.'[657]

OEEC, 1961 Report: compromises culminating in the draft text

In the fourth report (1961),[658] the OEEC announced that it had finally settled, or struck compromises, for the remaining, most vexing issues before it.[659] It was now able to present the articles and commentaries drafted for dividends, interest and royalties and for the 'methods for avoidance of double taxation'.[660] With this accomplishment, it hoped that:

> 'By the progressive harmonization of principles, definitions, rules and methods and the constant growth of the network of Conventions, taxpayers will be guaranteed more stable taxation treatment and double taxation will be eliminated more effectively. This will also have a favourable effect on the international movement of goods, services, capital and persons.'[661]

Incidentally, this last sentence sounds reminiscent of the free movements guaranteed by the then Treaty Establishing the European Economic Community (TEEC), which had been signed just a few years before on 25 March 1957.

As regards the first set of issues, namely the taxation of dividends, interest and royalties, now sometimes referred to as 'passive' or 'investment' income,[662]

---

657. *Id.*
658. For an analysis of 'a preliminary report in March 1959 (the 1959 Report)' and 'further memoranda and reports' in 1959 and 1960, discussed at various sessions of the Fiscal Committee, that formed the background and draft proposals that 'became part of the 1961 Fourth Report of the Fiscal Committee on the Elimination of Double Taxation (articles XXIII and XXIV)' and eventually the 1963 OECD Draft, *see* Georg Kofler, *Article 23B: Methods for Elimination of Double Taxation, in Global Tax Treaty Commentaries* Section 1.2.2.1 (Richard Vann ed.-in-chief, Pasquale Pistone et al. eds, Global Topics IBFD updated as of February 2019) (as Kofler explains, the preliminary report in March 1959 laid the foundations for the draft texts and commentary eventually adopted). For the full text of the March 1959 report, *see* OEEC, Working Party No. 15 of the Fiscal Committee, *Preliminary Report on Methods for Avoidance of Double Taxation* (2 Mar. 1959), The History of Tax Treaties Data Base, https://www.taxtreatieshistory.org/data/html/FC-WP15(59)1part1E.html (last visited 3 Mar. 2019) (the draft of the credit method is found in 'Draft A').
659. OEEC, 1961 Report, at 4625 (the OEEC reiterated the difficulty, a 'long and arduous task', of drafting Articles for dividends, interest and royalties due to 'divergences between the economic interests of the States' and 'between their legislations'. It 'was the chief obstacle to be overcome' and, for this reason, 'a common solution to this problem thus marks both a success and a definite step forward, in spite of the fact that a few reservations have been entered by certain countries on the solution adopted'. The OEEC submitted three Articles for this issue, plus two Articles for the 'methods for avoidance of double taxation' and another Article for the MAP).
660. *Id.*
661. OEEC, 1961 Report, at 4630.
662. *See*, e.g., OECD, *Glossary of Tax Terms*, https://www.oecd.org/ctp/glossaryoftaxterms.htm (last visited 5 May 2018) (the term 'passive income' is defined as 'Income in respect of which, broadly speaking, the recipient does not participate in the business activity giving rise to the income, e.g. dividends, interest, rental income, royalties, etc.').

compromises were reached.[663] Most relevant, as regards the credit method, is the compromise regarding dividends and interest. For dividends and interest, an enduring feature was established, namely that of shared taxation. This shared taxation is achieved by means of allowing the state of source to tax payments of dividends or interest, but capping this right at a maximum rate (e.g., 10% for interest; 5% or 15% for dividends), and allowing the state of residence of the recipient to also tax the income, but coupled with the credit method for the taxes levied at source.[664] For royalties, the state of residence was granted the exclusive taxation right.[665] As no right to levy taxes at source was granted to the state of source, no need for a credit arose.

As regards the methods, another enduring legacy for model conventions was established. Unlike the two drafts of model conventions presented in 1946, it was no longer the credit method alone as the predominant method. Instead, two alternative methods for relief of double taxation were drafted: one for the credit method and one for the exemption method.[666] Then, and now, states are permitted to freely choose between the two under the model. One exception is that, under the model text, the credit method is always applicable in the cases of dividends and interest.[667] The rationale was not expressed in terms of risks of the mobility of this type of income, as it sometimes is today (*see*, e.g., *infra* note 1023). Rather, the rationale for insisting on the credit method in these cases of passive investment income was explained as simply what logically flows from the shared taxation compromise between residence and source-based taxation:[668]

663. In both the League of Nations, 1927 Report, and League of Nations, 1946 Report, there were debates over which state should have the right to tax income from shares. *See*, e.g., League of Nations, 1927 Report, at 4128 (the 1927 Report, Commentary on Article 4, suggested that 'income from shares or similar interests' would be taxable in the State of 'the real centre of management'. The 'British expert has expressed dissent': an exception identical to that of Article 3, paragraph 2, according to which 'the said income may be taxed in the State of domicile of the creditor', should be added here because 'The principle of taxing business profits in the State in which they are earned has been conceded in Article 5, and provision has been made in Article 10 for a deduction of the tax so charged from the personal tax in the State of domicile. In the view of the British expert it is unreasonable that the financial burden of granting relief from double taxation in respect of the additional tax on dividends should also fall on the State of domicile'); League of Nations, 1946 Report, at 4345 (this concern of the British expert becomes clearer upon reading the joint Commentary to the 1943 Mexico Draft and the 1946 London Draft, at p. 25 of the Commentary, where it explains the differences between the Mexico and London draft regarding the taxation of income from dividends and why they differ: 'According to this article, dividends were to be taxed in the country where the capital from which they were derived was invested – *i.e.*, put into productive use. The result was that in most cases dividends would have been taxable in the same country as the business profits from which they were paid out').
664. OEEC, 1961 Report, at 4632.
665. *Id.*
666. OEEC, 1961 Report, at 4634–4635.
667. Another exception is that, under few articles, the state of residence agrees to give exclusive taxation to the other state, thereby excluding itself from taxing the income, effectively obliging itself to exempt the income. It seems that this exception was perhaps solidified or clarified later, since it was not yet clear at this stage in the development of the Model on the basis of the four interim reports of the OEEC.
668. OEEC, 1961 Report, at 4635, para. 29.

'Where the right to tax is shared between the two Contracting States, as in the case of the Articles proposed for dividends and interest, the State of residence cannot be expected to use the exemption method, because that would amount to its relinquishing the tax to which it is entitled' under the compromise agreed to.[669]

In this report, the existence of different types of credit method also became clear, as it distinguished between a full credit method and an 'ordinary credit method'. It also distinguished between a full exemption method and an 'exemption with progression' method. Other variations were also discussed in the Commentary (below). The versions endorsed by the Committee were the ordinary credit method and the exemption with progression method.[670]

This denotes a convergence. From the initial four (or arguably six) methods for relief of double taxation in the initial 1923 report, the process of decades of discussion and reporting on actual trends in practice, both in domestic laws and in conventions concluded,[671] two methods were selected. Just as in the body of the Report, the Commentary too indicated that the selection of the two methods for avoidance of double taxation resulted from a study showing that in practice these were the 'two leading principles' in conventions between 'Member States'.[672] The culmination of these efforts concretized the shape and wording of model conventions today.

As regards the proposed text of the two 'Articles on the Methods for Avoidance of Double Taxation', they are as follows:[673]

Under the exemption method in Article XXIII:

'1. Where a person being a resident of a Contracting State derives income from or owns capital in the other Contracting State and that income or capital, in accordance with the provisions of this Convention, may be taxed in that other Contracting State, the first-mentioned State shall, subject to the provisions of paragraph 2 of this Article, exempt such income or capital from tax but may, in calculating tax on the remaining income or capital of that person, apply the rate of tax which would have been applicable if the exempted income or capital had not been so exempted.'

'2. Where a person being a resident of a Contracting State derives income from the other Contracting State and that income, in accordance with the provisions of Articles XX and XXI [on dividends and interest] of this Convention, may be taxed in that other Contracting State, the first-mentioned State shall allow as a deduction

669. *Id.*, at 4635.
670. *Id.*, at 4634–4635, 4690.
671. Indeed many of the OEEC reports dedicated one section of the report to updates regarding the laws passed and conventions concluded since the previous report. Moreover, the interim reports of the OEEC suggested that extensive studies had been carried out on all of the various questions it posed for the drafting of the updated articles of the model convention. From this process, the two methods were selected. *See*, e.g., OEEC, 1961 Report, at 4634 (the report describes the credit method and the exemption method as the 'most commonly used'), e.g., at 4686 (they are the 'two leading principles'), e.g., at 4690 (the report mentions that both have been adopted in conventions and some have a preference for one or the other). *See also* Georg Kofler, *Article 23B: Methods for Elimination of Double Taxation, in Global Tax Treaty Commentaries* Section 1.2.2.1 (Richard Vann ed.-in-chief, Pasquale Pistone et al. eds, Global Topics IBFD, updated as of February 2019), at *supra* note 658.
672. *See also* OEEC, 1961 Report, at 4686.
673. *Id.*, at 4649 (Annex D).

from the tax on the income of that person an amount equal to the tax paid in that other Contracting State. Such deduction shall not, however, exceed that part of the tax, as computed before the deduction is given, which is appropriate to the income derived from that other Contracting State.'[674]

Under the credit method in Article XXIV:

'Where a person being a resident of a Contracting State derives income from or owns capital in the other Contracting State and that income or capital, in accordance with the provisions of this Convention, may be taxed in that other Contracting State, the first-mentioned State shall allow:

a) as a deduction from the tax on the income of that person, an amount equal to the income tax paid in that other Contracting State;
b) as a deduction from the tax on the capital of that person, an amount equal to the capital tax paid in that other Contracting State.

The deduction in either case shall not, however, exceed that part of the income tax or capital tax, respectively, as computed before the deduction is given, which is appropriate, as the case may be, to the income derived from or the capital owned in that other Contracting State.'[675]

OEEC, 1961 Report: explanations and examples of the two main methods

First, the general explanations of the two methods offer useful overviews, before, second, enquiring into the more specific issues of their wording and application, identified in the Commentary. Although more attention is on the credit method here, both methods are discussed, for two reasons. First, states could choose between the two Articles, but, regardless of their choice, states would end up relying on both methods to some extent. Even if a state opted for the exemption method, the credit method would nevertheless apply to dividends and interest, due to the aforementioned compromise for these two forms of income.[676] If a state opted for the credit method, it would nevertheless apply the exemption method in cases, albeit few, where the articles give an exclusive taxation right to the state of source.[677] So the two methods coexist.[678] Due to this coexistence, it is valuable to also discuss the fundamentals of the exemption method with progression. Moreover, second, this allows for a comparison with the credit method that underscores some of its own fundamental characteristics.

674. *Id.*, at 4649 (for the text of the article) and at 4634–4635 (for general remarks).
675. *Id.*
676. This exception was explicitly written into the second paragraph of Article XXIII.
677. OEEC, 1961 Report, at 4686 (at paras 6–7, this Commentary on the Methods for Avoidance of Double Taxation mentions two cases: (1) in some cases, the source state fully renounces its right to tax, where an Article uses the wording 'shall be taxable only' in the 'other State' and (2) in some cases, the source state does not renounce its right to tax, where an Article uses the wording 'may be taxed'; although not yet mentioned here, the same principle will ultimately also apply to the residence state where income 'shall be taxable only' in the source state). *See, e.g.*, *infra* note 731; OECD, *Model Tax Convention on Income and on Capital 2017: Condensed Version* Article 19 (OECD Publishing 2017) (the residence state in some cases renounces its right to tax, thus granting exclusive taxation rights to the other state, under, for example, Article 19 on 'Government Service').
678. OEEC, 1961 Report, at 4690–4691.

To begin, in the 'General Remarks on the Articles Concerning Methods for Avoidance of Double Taxation', the methods are explained as follows:

- Under the exemption method, in general, 'the State responsible for preventing the double taxation leaves the income or capital in question out of account in computing the total income or capital which it is going to tax'.[679]
- Under the exemption with progression, 'the income or capital in question, although left out of account in determining the total income or capital, is nevertheless taken into account in determining the rate of tax to be applied to the remainder of the income or capital'.[680]
- Under the credit method, in general, 'such State takes such income or capital into account, but deducts from the total tax which it would otherwise charge the tax paid in the other State on the income or capital in question'.[681]
- Under the ordinary credit method, 'the deduction which the State concerned allows against the tax which it would otherwise charge is the amount of tax paid in the other State limited so as not to exceed so much of the tax in the first mentioned State as relates to the income or capital in respect of which a right to tax is given to the other State'.[682]

In the 'Commentaries on Articles XXIII and XXIV Concerning the Methods for Avoidance of Double Taxation',[683] according to its explanation of the exemption method[684] and of the credit method,[685] it succinctly summarizes that: the fundamental difference is 'that the exemption system looks at income, the credit system at tax on income'.[686]

The Commentary explains the general effects of the methods. Under the exemption method – either full or with progression – 'the level of the tax in the State of source would have no influence on the amount of tax given up by the State of residence'.[687] Under the credit method, 'the State of residence never gives up an amount of its tax greater than the tax levied in the State of source'.[688] In other words, while the exemption method applies irrespective of the amount of tax in the state of source, the opposite is the case for the credit method. Another way this distinction is sometimes expressed, though not in the Commentary, is the distinction between relief for potential, or nominal, double taxation versus relief for actual double taxation.[689]

To show the effects of the two methods, the Commentary discusses what happens when the rate of tax in the state of source is higher or is lower than the rate in

679. *Id.*, at 4634.
680. *Id.*, at 4634–4635.
681. *Id.*, at 4634.
682. *Id.*, at 4634–4635.
683. *Id.*, at 4685 et seq.
684. *Id.*, at 4686.
685. *Id.*
686. OEEC, 1961 Report, at 4687.
687. *Id.*, at 4688.
688. *Id.*, at 4690.
689. *See supra* note 167.

the state of residence. To summarize the idea that the Commentary seeks to convey (and to be a bit more comprehensive than the Commentary is), assume three scenarios: (i) the tax rates are the same in the state of residence and state of source, (ii) the tax rate is lower in the state of source and (iii) the tax rate is higher in the state of source. To consider the effects on taxpayers (setting aside the effects on the states), assume two taxpayers with the same income, with the only difference being that taxpayer R derives income only from the state of residence, whereas taxpayer F derives a portion of the income from the state of residence and a portion from the state of source:

- Under scenario (i) where the tax rates are the same, the effects of the methods are the same – that is, all else equal, the taxpayers pay the same amount of tax under both the credit method and the exemption method (assuming the state of source collects its tax).
- Under scenario (ii) where the tax rate is lower in the state of source, taxpayer F pays *less* taxes overall than taxpayer R under the exemption method (either full or with progression);[690] taxpayer F pays the same overall amount of tax as taxpayer R under the credit method.
- Under scenario (iii) where the tax rate is higher in the state of source, taxpayer F pays *more* taxes overall than taxpayer R under the exemption method (with progression)[691] and the ordinary credit method;[692] under the full credit, taxpayer F pays the same overall amount of tax as taxpayer R;[693] under the full exemption, taxpayer F may be slightly better off than taxpayer R,[694] depending on the tax rate differential.

To show the effects on both taxpayers and the state of residence, the Commentary included two tables, which are reproduced here,[695] with additional notes included inside brackets:

690. OEEC, 1961 Report, at 4688 (para. 19).
691. *Id.*, at 4688 (para. 20).
692. *Id.*, at 4689–4690 (para. 24).
693. *Id.*, at 4690 (para. 25).
694. *Id.*, at 4688 (para. 20).
695. *Id.*, at 4688–4689 (para. 21).

'Table I. **This Table Shows the Total Amount of Tax in the Different Cases Illustrated Above**

I. All income [100,000] **arising in the State of residence: ... 35,000** [facts assumed 35% tax rate on 100,000 and 30% tax rate on 80,000]		
II. Income arising in two States, viz. 80,000 in the State of residence and 20,000 in the State of source.	Tax in State of source 4,000 (*case i*) [assumed 20% tax rate]	Tax in State of source 8,000 (*case ii*) [assumed 40% tax rate]
No Convention	39,000 [35,000 + 4,000]	43,000 [35,000 + 8,000]
a) full exemption	28,000 [24,000 + 4,000]	32,000 [24,000 + 8,000]
b) exemption with progression	32,000 [28,000 + 4,000]	36,000 [28,000 + 8,000]
c) ordinary credit	35,000 [35,000 – FTC 4,000 + 4,000]	36,000 [35,000 – max. FTC 7,000 + 8,000]
d) full credit	35,000 [35,000 – FTC 4,000 + 4,000]	35,000 [35,000 – full FTC 8,000 + 8,000]'

'Table II. **This Table Shows the Amount of Tax Given up by the State of Residence**

	Tax in State of source 4,000 (*case i*)	Tax in State of source 8,000 (*case ii*)
No Convention	0	0
a) full exemption	11,000	11,000
b) exemption with progression	7,000	7,000
c) ordinary credit	4,000	7,000
d) full credit	4,000	8,000'

As for the scope, the Commentary begins by specifying the precise and limited 'scope of the articles', which is to address juridical double taxation, not economic double taxation.[696] It then specifies precisely when the articles will actually apply. For this, it differentiates between exclusive and shared taxation rights. In some cases, the

696. *Id.*, at 4685.

state of source 'renounces its right to tax' and exclusively the state of residence has the right to tax, in which case 'no question of double taxation arises'. This is signalled by the wording 'shall be taxable only' in an article of the convention. If no double taxation arises in these cases, the method article need not apply. In the cases where the taxing right is shared between the state of source and the state of residence, it implies 'the prior right of taxation in the State of source' and 'the State of residence must give relief so as to avoid double taxation'. This is signalled by the wording 'may be taxed' in an article of the convention.[697]

Although this evolution has been apparent for some time now in previous reports and draft conventions, here it is definitively established that the responsible state is the 'State of residence' and that this is an obligation. In some places in the Commentary, it is described as an 'absolute obligation'.[698]

As regards economic double taxation, the issue is consigned to bilateral negotiations. The Commentary mentions the option of offering an indirect tax credit:

> 'in respect of dividends received from companies in other States, credit, not only for the amount of tax directly levied on the dividends in those other States, but also for that part of the companies' tax which is appropriate to the dividends'.[699]

Whereas the 1946 London version provided for a solution directly in the proposed text, here it is merely a suggestion in the Commentary; also, whereas the London version proposed an exemption, here it is the indirect credit method approach.

Although there is the aforementioned fundamental difference between the credit method and the exemption method (*supra* note 686), sometimes their differences become blurred in how similarly they may operate. Two variations on the methods that exemplify this are: (1) the 'tax exemption' method and (2) the tax sparing or tax matching credit methods.

Regarding the first, another part of the Commentary (paragraph 28) refers to what could be described as a 'tax exemption' method.[700] According to the Commentary, it is a 'system where the State of residence gives up the part of its own tax appropriate to the income from the State of source – irrespective of the tax paid in the State of source' and it 'produces the same result as an exemption system with progression'.[701] It was the method in the 1925 Resolutions, option (1)(a), inspired from the Netherlands (*supra* note 581 and Example No. 17) and, as will be seen below, was the method that featured in the CJEU *De Groot* case (discussed in Section 4.2.4., *infra* note 1315). Indeed, the calculation of this 'tax exemption' is so similar to a credit method that the same findings as in *De Groot* were extended in another CJEU case, *Beker*, to the credit method.

As regards one possible rationale for using this approach, the reason this method is put forward in the Commentary is that it may help avoid issues in the calculation of

697. *Id.*, at 4686.
698. *Id.*, at 4691.
699. *Id.*, at 4695 (para. 52).
700. *Id.*, at 4690.
701. *Id.*

social benefits in the state of residence. 'If in a particular State the amount of income as determined for income tax purposes is used as a measure for other purposes, e.g. social benefits', then applying the exemption method in such a way as to fully exclude the income abroad from the tax base may alter the amount of social benefits, among other things.[702] If so, then the exemption method can be drafted in a way to take the income into account, determine the total taxes and then apply a ratio to determine the amount of those taxes to 'exempt'. For this purpose, the Commentary provides alternative proposed wording (notice the similarities with the credit method):

> 'Where a person being a resident of a Contracting State derives income from or owns capital in the other Contracting State and that income or capital, in accordance with the provisions of this Convention, may be taxed in that other Contracting State, the first-mentioned State shall, subject to the provisions of paragraph 2 of this Article, allow as a deduction from the income tax or capital tax that part of the income tax or capital tax, respectively, which is appropriate, as the case may be, to the income derived from or the capital owed in that other Contracting State.'[703]

Regarding the second variation, an example is the relief referred to as a tax 'matching credit', which gives a credit for a predetermined fixed amount. For example, it would assume a tax equal to 20% of the income and offer a 'credit' for this notional amount, irrespective of the actual amount of foreign taxes paid on the income.

As regards the rationale, under the title 'The relation in special cases between the taxation in the State of source and the ordinary credit method',[704] the Commentary discusses one potentially negative effect of the credit method, particularly in cases where the state of source intentionally decreases its taxes, for its own desired policy reasons, on certain income. Under the credit method, the state of residence will include that income in its tax base, tax it and offer the credit for the (reduced amount of) taxes levied in the state of source. The effect is that the lower rate that the state of source hoped to extend *to the taxpayer* as a benefit or incentive merely leads to a smaller credit in the state of residence, and the taxpayer nevertheless pays, overall, the amount of taxes due in the state of residence. This neutralizes or 'nullifie[s]' the benefit for the taxpayer. The Commentary mentions the example of 'tax incentive reliefs to encourage industrial output' or exemptions for 'pensions to war wounded soldiers'.[705] In cases

702. OEEC, 1961 Report, at 4692.
703. *Id.*, at 4692. *See also* the OECD, *Model Tax Convention on Income and on Capital 2017: Condensed Version* Commentary on Articles 23 A and 23 B, para. 37 (OECD Publishing 2017).
704. OEEC, 1961 Report, at 4694–4695.
705. *Id.*, at 4694. *See also* Georg Kofler, *Article 23B: Methods for Elimination of Double Taxation, in Global Tax Treaty Commentaries* Section 1.2.2.1. and Section 3.3.4 (Richard Vann ed.-in-chief, Pasquale Pistone et al. eds, Global Topics IBFD updated as of February 2019) (as can be seen, given their origins, these provisions are '(correctly) not viewed as an issue of double taxation but rather one of economic development and investment stimulation'. Indeed, 'the 1959 Report noted that, in some cases, a provision in a bilateral tax treaty may also serve purposes other than the avoidance of double taxation that the application of the credit system (and hence the imposition of a residual tax) could undermine').

such as these, 'by reason of the concessions, that other State [the state of residence] secures what may be called an uncovenanted gain for its own Exchequer'.[706]

The solutions proposed are either to apply the exemption method or to apply a 'matching credit' whereby 'the State of residence will allow as a deduction from its own tax an amount corresponding to the tax which would have been paid in the State of source if no concession had been granted by that State'.[707] To ensure 'satisfactory results', 'the State of source should be able to notify to the State of residence the amount of tax that would have been paid if no relief had been granted'.[708] It is notable here that this seems to be an early sign of a possible shift in the perception of the credit method, from a perception that it is overly (and almost dangerously) generous to a perception that it may cause some negative effects.

OEEC, 1961 Report: exemption method article, specific issues

In the Commentary on the exemption method, the discussion of the exemption (with progression) method reinforces its 'potential' nature, in that the Commentary unambiguously states that the 'State of residence *must* accordingly give exemption *whether or not* the income or capital in question *is actually taxed* in the State of source' (emphasis added).[709] The benefit of this is that it is 'practical' and avoids the 'onerous and time-consuming investigations of the actual taxation position in the State of source'.[710] Yet in the next paragraph, the Commentary notes that some states may deviate from this 'absolute obligation' 'to give exemption'.[711] What is clear, therefore, is that, in general, there is no requirement that any tax was levied in the state of source. Indeed, to require that the income was actually subject to tax before granting the exemption would go against the convention as currently worded – hence, the need to 'deviate' by adding special wording. This is an explicit confirmation that there is no implied subject-to-tax condition (without express wording to the contrary). This could result in a situation where the convention grants the right to tax to the state of source, which thus entails the state of residence's obligation to grant exemption, yet the state of source does not exercise its right to tax. If this happens, the income is taxed neither in the state of source nor in the state of residence. Ironically, a method to avoid double taxation is 'applied' in a case where no double taxation is occurring. An outcome of no taxation (sometimes referred to as 'double non-taxation') under these conditions was perfectly in line with the convention based on this model. Here the Commentary planted the seed of an issue that grows more prominent later; it was eventually addressed in 2000.[712]

706. OEEC, 1961 Report, at 4694.
707. *Id.*, at 4695.
708. *Id.*
709. OEEC, 1961 Report, at 4691 (para. 32).
710. *Id.*
711. OEEC, 1961 Report, at 4691.
712. *See*, e.g., OECD, *Model Tax Convention on Income and on Capital 2017: Condensed Version* Commentary on Articles 23 A and 23 B, paras 32.1–32.7, 56.1–56.3 (OECD Publishing 2017) (since 2000, the OECD Commentary on Articles 23 A and 23 B has contained paragraphs 32.1–32.7 to address 'conflicts of qualification' and the OECD Model has included Article 23A(4) to address 'conflicts of interpretation'). For debates on this topic, *see*, e.g., Jean-Marc

Under the exemption method, the Commentary addresses only one technical issue, namely the treatment of losses (also a theme of future CJEU case law, discussed in Section 4.2.7.). The Commentary gives express permission for a loss recapture mechanism (it states 'there should be no objection' to it).[713]

The Commentary then concludes with a brief discussion of the second paragraph of the exemption method, which, as mentioned, states that the credit method will apply in the cases of dividends and interest.[714] Again, the Commentary (paragraph 39) explains why the credit method, instead of exemption, applies for dividends and interest - namely, to respect the way taxation rights were allocated under the compromise (*see*, e.g., *supra* note 663). It then makes a prediction: it predicts that the MCA will be of 'limited significance' because 'the rate of tax in the State of residence will very often be higher than the rate in the State of source'.[715] In other words, it will usually be possible to fully credit the foreign taxes levied in the State of source.

Future developments proved the crystal ball of the OEEC not so clear on this point since numerous cases arose, including some under CJEU case law, where the MCA became a problem from the perspective of the taxpayer. Baker's 1998 article includes complaints of precisely this issue (*see supra* note 357). One possible reason that the Commentary missed the target is that this prediction seemed based solely on the 'rate of tax'. It may have been a safe prediction that the rate of tax in the residence state would 'very often' be higher than 5%, 10% or 15%. What this prediction overlooked is the difference in the *tax base* to which those rates are applied (often gross versus net).

Of course, such a problem will not arise under the full credit. The Commentary gives the option for States to decide to adopt the full credit method, 'by deleting the second sentence of the paragraph', as a solution.[716] Yet, earlier reports, i.e., the 1925 report,[717] were vehemently opposed (*see supra* note 589) and the US, which had experience with a full credit, instead adopted a credit limitation in the Revenue Act of

Déry & David A. Ward, *Canada: Interpretation of Double Taxation Conventions*, 78a Cahiers de Droit Fiscal International 259, 281–284 (IFA 1993); Alexander Rust, *The New Approach to Qualification Conflicts Has Its Limits*, 57(2) Bull. Int'l Tax'n 45 (2003); John F. Avery Jones, *Conflicts of Qualification: Comment on Prof. Vogel's and Alexander Rust's Articles*, 57(5) Bull. Int'l Tax'n 184 (2003); Michael Lang, *General Report: Double Non-taxation*, 89a Cahiers de Droit Fiscal International 73, 73, 96, 98–99 (IFA 2004).

713. OEEC, 1961 Report, at 4692 (para. 38) ('Where the State of residence allows as a deduction from the income it assesses the amount of a loss incurred in the other State, there should be no objection if, when profits are made subsequently in the other State, the amount of the exemption for the later years is restricted appropriately. States are left free in this respect ...').
714. *Id.*, at 4692–4693 (paras 39–40).
715. *Id.*, at 4693 (para. 40).
716. *Id.* (the sentence that could be deleted in order to convert the article into a full credit method is: 'The deduction in either case shall not, however, exceed that part of the income tax or capital tax, respectively, as computed before the deduction is given, which is appropriate, as the case may be, to the income derived from or the capital owned in that other Contracting State'). Similarly, *see also* OECD, *Model Tax Convention on Income and on Capital 2017: Condensed Version* Commentary on Articles 23 A and 23 B, para. 58 (OECD Publishing 2017).
717. League of Nations, 1925 Report, at 4096 et seq. (Appendix: Note by M. Léon-Dufour on the Various Methods Suggested for Remedying Double Taxation and Their Graphical Representation).

1921 (*see supra* note 179). As will be seen in Chapter 4, the MCA ended up playing a consequential role in the CJEU case law (e.g., in the *Schumacker/De Groot* line of case law and in the 'neutralization' line of case law).

OEEC, 1961 Report: credit method article, specific issues

Regarding the credit method in more detail, the Commentary lists three 'different forms':

- 'ordinary credit': 'a) The deduction given by the State of residence may be restricted so that the deduction does not exceed that part of its own tax appropriate to the income from the other State.'
- 'full credit': 'b) In some forms of the credit system the State of residence allows a deduction of the total amount of tax paid in the State of source.'
- 'c) Further variations of the credit system are possible, e.g. where the State of residence limits the deduction to an amount not exceeding the tax which it would itself have imposed on that income if the taxpayer had no other income.'[718]

The third variation, letter c), merely alters the MCA. In an income tax system based on progressive tax rates, the effect of this MCA is that the amount of tax on the FSI is calculated according to the *lowest* marginal rate on the progressive income tax scale. In other words, it assumes that the FSI is attributed to the first tranche of income, or income bracket, earned by the taxpayer, to which the lowest rate on the progressive scale applies. Recall that this is what was proposed in the 1925 Report, as illustrated in its Morania-Imeria example (at *supra* note 586 and note 587) and in the alternative scenarios in Example No. 18.[719] In a system where a state applies each progressively higher rate to each progressively higher bracket of income, then different assumptions may be possible as regards in which bracket the FSI falls. The question is what justifies this particular assumption, as opposed to assuming the FSI is attributed to the highest tranche so that the highest progressive tax rate is used to calculate the relief, or is attributed proportionately to all tranches so that the average tax rate is used to calculate the relief. However, the Commentary does not discuss it further.

The Commentary then addresses the ordinary credit method as drafted in Article XIII. Before turning to the Commentary, some initial observations can be made on the basis of comparing the wording of this 1961 draft with the 1946 drafts. Despite the different wording, the basic structure remained the same (e.g., the role of 'residence', the two-step operation, the MCA, the limitation of the credit to taxes levied in accordance with the convention, etc.). As compared with the 1946 drafts, the beginning of the article changed in two substantive ways.

First, the material scope expanded to cover both income taxes and, where relevant, 'capital taxes'. The Committee decided that the same rules could apply to

718. OEEC, 1961 Report, at 4687.

719. *See also*, e.g., *supra* notes 117 et seq. (the term 'slicing rule', e.g., 'bottom slice' rule and 'top slice' rule, has also been used in this context).

capital taxes. While the focus here remains on income taxes, this does raise the question of whether the capital taxes could be credited against income taxes, and vice versa. The Commentary addressed this. Based on the way 'the Article is drafted', the general rule is a strict relation between the type of tax, i.e., 'income tax only against income tax' and 'capital tax only against capital tax'.[720] The Commentary sought to clarify that, for example, if the state of residence does not itself have a capital tax, it does not have to grant a credit against its own income taxes for capital taxes levied in the other state. However, by deviation, under bilateral negotiations, 'two Contracting States may agree that a tax called a capital tax is of a nature closely related to income tax and may, therefore, wish to allow credit for it against income tax and vice versa', among other deviations which they are free to choose.[721] From this, there is an idea that only like taxes have to be creditable against other like taxes. In other words, it seems to imply a criterion of similarity. Naturally, this will give rise to interpretation questions regarding the nature of an income tax (or capital tax) and what characteristics are decisive for determining whether a foreign tax is sufficiently similar to an income tax (or capital tax). This touches upon the broader issue of the notion of creditable or eligible taxes, a question that continues to give rise to debates.[722]

Second, while the 1946 drafts declared that the state of residence 'shall retain the right to tax the entire income of the taxpayer' regardless from where it is derived,[723] the 1961 draft did not include this broader statement. Rather its wording stuck more narrowly to the exact scope of application of the article for the purposes of the bilateral convention, stating the conditions under which it is triggered: 'Where a person being a resident of a Contracting State derives income from ... the other Contracting State and that income ..., in accordance with the provisions of this Convention, may be taxed in that other Contracting State'. This opens up the possibility that sometimes the right to tax of the state of residence may be precluded under the convention, for example, if an exclusive right to tax is granted to the state of source for an item of income.

720. OEEC, 1961 Report, at 4694.

721. *Id.* (other suggestions of the commentary include: 'There will be cases where, because one State does not impose a capital tax or because both States impose capital taxes only on domestic assets, no double taxation of capital will arise. In such cases it is, of course, understood that the reference to capital taxation may be deleted. Furthermore, negotiating States may find it desirable, regardless of the nature of the taxes included under the Convention, to allow credit for the total amount of tax in the State of source against the total amount of tax in the State of residence. Where, however, a Convention includes both real capital taxes and capital taxes which are in their nature income taxes, the Contracting States may wish to allow credit against income tax only for the latter mentioned capital taxes. In such cases, Contracting States are free to alter the proposed Article so as to achieve the desired effect').

722. *See*, e.g., Marjaana Helminen, *General Report: The Notion of Tax and the Elimination of International Double Taxation or Double Non-taxation*, 101b Cahiers de Droit Fiscal International 17, 17–76 (IFA 2016); *supra* note 157 (for the discussion of the US interpretation of a creditable 'income' tax). On the topic of 'double taxation', *see*, e.g., *supra* note 140 (similar to the above discussion of the views of Adams and Seligman, this part of the Commentary in the 1961 Report also offers insight into the understanding of 'double taxation'. Since it implies that relief is granted only for similar taxes, then double taxation is a problem only when the two states are taxing the same thing or base).

723. *See* text of both the Mexico version and the London version at *supra* note 634 and note 635.

In addition, as compared with the 1946 drafts, the wording of the second part of the article differed as regards the MCA.[724] The 1961 version no longer specified a proportion, or ratio. Nor did it make reference to the tax rates or rate scales applicable in the state of residence. Rather, it stated that the credit ('deduction') 'shall not, however, exceed that part of the income tax ..., as computed before the deduction is given, which is *appropriate* ..., *to* the income derived from ... that other Contracting State' (emphasis added). Since the article is addressed to the state of residence, the reference to income taxes 'as computed before the deduction is given' signifies that the first step is for the state of residence to compute its own income taxes. It, then, instructs the state of residence to ascertain the 'part of the income tax' that is 'appropriate ... to' the income from the other state. The wording 'appropriate ... to' is broad, leaving more discretion to the state of residence as regards the precise calculation or way that it arrives at this amount. The Commentary, as discussed below, offers some explanation.

The Commentary presents some potential technical issues that can arise under the MCA.[725] It presents two scenarios. First, it is possible that different kinds of income are derived from the state of source, but, under its domestic law, the state of source taxes only *one* of those kinds of income. In this scenario, the Commentary instructs the state of residence to take into account *only* that one item of income actually taxed in the state of source, as the relevant FSI for determining the MCA.[726] This secures the right of the state of residence to tax fully those other items of income derived from the state of source that were not actually taxed there. By lessening the amount of FSI in the equation, this lessens the MCA.

Second, it is possible to generate *positive* FSI but suffer *losses* in the state of residence. More specifically, the Commentary addresses the scenario where the losses are 'less than the income from abroad', thus implying that there is still overall a positive result. In this scenario, 'the tax charged in *the State of residence* will *in its entirety* be appropriate to the income from the State of source, and the maximum deduction which the State of residence is to allow will consequently be the tax charged in *that State*' (emphasis added).[727] In this scenario, the only income that ends up constituting a positive tax base in the state of residence is income which was generated in the state of

724. For convenience, the wording of the second part of the article is copied again here. Under the Mexico version, the 1946 wording was that the state of residence ('domicile') 'shall deduct from its tax on such entire income the lesser of the two following amounts: A. The tax collected by the latter contracting State on the income which is taxable in its territory according to the preceding Articles; B. The amount which represents the same proportion in comparison with the total tax on the income that is taxable in both States as the income taxable in the other State in comparison with the total income'. Under the London version, the 1946 wording was that the state of residence ('domicile') 'shall deduct from its tax on such entire income the lesser of the following amounts: A. The tax collected by the other contracting State on the income which is taxable in its territory according to the preceding Articles; B. The amount which represents the same proportion of the tax of the State of fiscal domicile on the entire net income of the taxpayer as the net income taxable in the other State bears to the entire net income'.

725. OEEC, 1961 Report, at 4693 (para. 43).

726. OEEC, 1961 Report, at 4693 (in this case, 'the maximum deduction which the State of residence is to allow will be that part of its tax which is appropriate only to that item of income which is taxed in the State of source').

727. *Id.*

source, or rather a portion of what was generated there, so any taxes due in the state of residence are necessarily 'appropriate to' the income from the state of source. The state of residence will give as a credit the *entirety* of its taxes, reducing what it collects down to zero; however, the creditable taxes would likely be smaller than what was actually collected in the state of source, meaning not all source state taxes would be credited.

With these two scenarios, it seems that the Commentary sought to clarify the wording 'appropriate ... to'. Yet, despite the rather broad wording of the text, the language of the Commentary - in its instructions for both scenarios - adopts a mandatory tone (by using words such as 'will' and 'is to allow'). However, it was softened. After the OECD took over the project of the model conventions, shortly after this 1961 report, from the OEEC, some adjustments were made to these paragraphs to include much more flexible language. Under both scenarios, the Commentary states that 'other solutions are possible' and that the details are left to domestic law.[728]

Once again, another organizational transition passed the work from the OEEC to the OECD.[729] Still, the OEEC credit method article proposed in 1961 endured the test of time. It formed the basis of the first draft OECD Model Tax Convention on Income and on Capital in 1963[730] and has remained largely the same to this day. The following table allows for a comparison of the texts of Article 23B in 1961, 1963, 1977 and 2017 (with explanatory notes of changes in footnotes).[731]

728. *See*, e.g., OECD, *Model Tax Convention on Income and on Capital 2014: Full Version*, C(23)-27 and C(23)-59 (OECD Publishing 2015) (*see* the 'History' notes).

729. 4 *Legislative History of United States Tax Conventions* 4704 (United States, Joint Committee on Internal Revenue Taxation, US Government Printing Office 1962).

730. OECD, *Model Tax Convention on Income and on Capital 2014: Full Version*, I-2 and M-55 (OECD Publishing 2015); Jeffrey Owens & Mary Bennett, OECD Centre for Tax Policy and Administration, *OECD Model Tax Convention: Why It Works* (OECD Observer No. 269, October 2008), http://oecdobserver.org/news/archivestory.php/aid/2756/OECD_Model_Tax_Convention.html (last visited 2 Jan. 2019) ('By 1963 a full draft was ready though it was not until 1977 that the model Double Taxation Convention was published. The 1963 draft was essentially the consolidation of four earlier drafts, the first one of which was published in 1958. This is why we consider that the birth of the OECD model was 1 July 1958').

731. OECD, *Model Tax Convention on Income and on Capital 2014: Full Version*, M-55 (OECD Publishing 2015) (other than a renumbering of paragraphs in 1977, virtually no changes to the credit method per se occurred from 1977 through 2014. In 1977, a second paragraph was added - not to change the credit method itself - but rather in order to clarify the obligations of the state of residence where the credit method does *not* apply, namely wherever the state of residence has agreed under other articles of the convention to grant the state of source the *exclusive* taxation right. In these cases, the state of residence has precluded itself from taking the income into account in its tax base. Nevertheless, it retains the right to take the income into account for determining the tax rate that applies. In other words, the state of residence applies an exemption with progression. The wording is as follows: '2. Where in accordance with any provision of the Convention income derived or capital owned by a resident of a Contracting State is exempt from tax in that State, such State may nevertheless, in calculating the amount of tax on the remaining income or capital of such resident, take into account the exempted income or capital') and OECD, *Model Tax Convention on Income and on Capital 2017: Condensed Version* Article 23 A, Article 23 B and Commentary on Articles 23 A and 23 B, paras 11.1-11.2 (OECD Publishing 2017) (in the 2017 Model, a parenthesis was inserted: 'Where a resident of a Contracting State derives income or owns capital which may be taxed in the other Contracting State in accordance with the provisions of this Convention *(except to the extent that these provisions allow taxation by that other State solely because the income is also income*

Article 23 B Credit Method	
1961	**1963**
'Where a person being a resident of a Contracting State derives income from or owns capital in the other Contracting State and that income or capital, in accordance with the provisions of this Convention, may be taxed in that other Contracting State, the first-mentioned State shall allow: (a) as a deduction from the tax on the income of that person, an amount equal to the income tax paid in that other Contracting State; (b) as a deduction from the tax on the capital of that person, an amount equal to the capital tax paid in that other Contracting State. The deduction in either case shall not, however, exceed that part of the income tax or capital tax, respectively, as computed before the deduction is given, which is appropriate, as the case may be, to the income derived from or the capital owned in that other Contracting State.'[732]	'1. Where a resident of a Contracting State derives income or owns capital which, in accordance with the provisions of this Convention, may be taxed in the other Contracting State, the first-mentioned State shall allow: (a) as a deduction from the tax on the income of that person, an amount equal to the income tax paid in that other Contracting State; (b) as a deduction from the tax on the capital of that person, an amount equal to the capital tax paid in that other Contracting State. 2. The deduction in either case shall not, however, exceed that part of the income tax or capital tax, respectively, as computed before the deduction is given, which is appropriate, as the case may be, to the income or the capital which may be taxed in the other Contracting State.'[733]

derived by a resident of that State or because the capital is also capital owned by a resident of that State), the first-mentioned State shall allow: [...]' (emphasis added). In its Commentary, the OECD implies that this is a mere technical clarification by arguing that the change 'would logically follow from the wording of Articles 23 A and 23 B even in the absence of that phrase'). For more on the 2017 change, *see*, e.g., Georg Kofler, *Some Reflections on the 'Saving Clause'*, 44(8/9) Intertax 574 (2016); Georg Kofler, *Article 23B: Methods for Elimination of Double Taxation, in Global Tax Treaty Commentaries* (Richard Vann ed.-in-chief, Pasquale Pistone et al. eds, Global Topics IBFD updated as of February 2019).

732. OEEC, 1961 Report, at 4649 (United States, Joint Committee on Internal Revenue Taxation, US Government Printing Office 1962).

733. OECD, *Model Tax Convention on Income and on Capital 2014: Full Version*, M-55 (OECD Publishing 2015) (the 'History' notes that slight adaptations were made to the 1963 version when drafting the 1977 model convention, notably to merge the two paragraphs into one. A comparison of the wording also shows that, as regards the credit limitation, or MCA, 'The deduction' was changed to 'Such deduction' and 'appropriate ... to' was changed to 'attributable ... to').

1977	2017
'1. Where a resident of a Contracting State derives income or owns capital which, in accordance with the provisions of this Convention, may be taxed in the other Contracting State, the first-mentioned State shall allow: a) as a deduction from the tax on the income of that resident, an amount equal to the income tax paid in that other State; b) as a deduction from the tax on the capital of that resident, an amount equal to the capital tax paid in that other State. Such deduction in either case shall not, however, exceed that part of the income tax or capital tax, as computed before the deduction is given, which is attributable, as the case may be, to the income or the capital which may be taxed in that other State. 2. Where in accordance with any provision of the Convention income derived or capital owned by a resident of a Contracting State is exempt from tax in that State, such State may nevertheless, in calculating the amount of tax on the remaining income or capital of such resident, take into account the exempted income or capital.'	'1. Where a resident of a Contracting State derives income or owns capital which may be taxed in the other Contracting State in accordance with the provisions of this Convention (except to the extent that these provisions allow taxation by that other State solely because the income is also income derived by a resident of that State or because the capital is also capital owned by a resident of that State), the first-mentioned State shall allow: a) as a deduction from the tax on the income of that resident, an amount equal to the income tax paid in that other State; b) as a deduction from the tax on the capital of that resident, an amount equal to the capital tax paid in that other State. Such deduction in either case shall not, however, exceed that part of the income tax or capital tax, as computed before the deduction is given, which is attributable, as the case may be, to the income or the capital which may be taxed in that other State. 2. Where in accordance with any provision of the Convention income derived or capital owned by a resident of a Contracting State is exempt from tax in that State, such State may nevertheless, in calculating the amount of tax on the remaining income or capital of such resident, take into account the exempted income or capital.'

2.1.2.4. *Interim Conclusions: Lessons from Bilateral Measures*

By studying the historical developments of these bilateral measures, the perspective has expanded from that of the unilateral measures of the UK and the US to the efforts of multiple states - most of which were European states. This not only further developed the findings from studying the unilateral measures but also introduced some key concepts (e.g., tax exemption, tax matching credit) that are relevant for the discussions in subsequent chapters.

Following the same approach as for the unilateral measures (in Section 2.1.1.), this section traced the chronological development of the credit method in bilateral measures. It began with the efforts to coordinate the overlap of taxation rights circa the mid-1800s among the Central European jurisdictions, as these were forerunners of bilateral efforts that came later in the 1920s under international organizations.

During this mid-1800s period, the preferred approach to address double taxation was a pre-emptive one, i.e., to aim to avoid it in the first place by conferring the exclusive taxation right to one state at a time, depending on the type of income or tax in question. This preference may have been bolstered by the conception of taxes as more 'impersonal', unrelated levies (*see*, e.g., *supra* notes 453–455), rather than as one unified personal income tax (*see*, e.g., *supra* note 470, note 498, note 562). From this conception of taxes, a fitting solution was therefore to determine, for each distinct levy, which state should have the right to collect it (*see supra* note 458, e.g., for taxes related to property, the state of situs). Where the other state had the exclusive taxation right, the state of residence or citizenship had to refrain from taxing, and vice versa. Thus, it seemed to function as a full exemption, which fell on both states to varying degrees to uphold. For this reason, the credit method did not feature (seemingly, not at all) in the tools used in this region; it becomes more relevant where taxes are conceived as general 'personal' income taxes. However, the exemption method under the 1869 tax treaty between Prussia and Saxony shared at least one familiar trait, namely that it applied only if taxes were actually paid in the other state (*see supra* note 467).

More broadly speaking, the developments during this period contributed in significant ways to the structure of tax treaties (e.g., via concepts such as residence and PEs) and in relevant ways to the understanding of double taxation. On that topic, early signs of the issue of economic double taxation arose, which demonstrated one way of interpreting the issue, namely that economic double taxation was not prohibited, as the taxation of the enterprise was considered to be separate from the taxation of the individual shareholder (*see supra* note 468). This is quite different from the perception expressed in the UK in 1881 (*see*, e.g., *supra* note 254, note 257). This divergence points to distinctions that become more clearly defined later, between a more 'classical' corporate taxation system and a more 'integrated' one. As will be seen below, ultimately, both the bilateral model conventions and the CJEU's case law push states more towards the 'classical' approach. On double taxation in general, during this time period, one rationale for relief for double taxation was that of regional integration, a rationale that is not lost on EU MSs today. Notably, this end was also pursued under the banners of equality, common citizenship and free movement, as balanced against fiscal sovereignty (*see supra* note 446, but *compare* note 450) – a theme that will reappear throughout subsequent chapters.

Picking up the baton, in the 1920s, experts appointed by the ICC and by various governments convened under the League of Nations to seek international solutions to double taxation. This section then covered hundreds of pages of official reports published under the League and its successor organizations, the OEEC and the OECD. It extracted the various drafts of the credit method to examine its features.

Taking into account the interim conclusions under the unilateral measures (Section 2.1.1.4.), the study of the bilateral measures reinforced and built upon many of the design features and considerations listed. As a preliminary remark, however, the fact that a measure is unilateral or bilateral leads to an overarching difference between the two, detected above (*see,* e.g., *supra* note 638), namely that the application of the credit method in a convention is, perhaps evidently, dictated to a larger extent by the scope of the convention itself. In some cases, the scope of the credit method is accordingly expanded and, in other cases, confined. For example, on the one hand, its application is triggered whenever the other state is allocated the right to tax under the allocation rules of the convention; generally, the state of residence is then obliged to grant the credit. On the other hand, the amount of the credit is limited to the taxes levied in compliance with the rules of the convention; generally, the state of residence can then refuse to grant the credit for the taxes levied in violation of the convention.[734] In practice, the precise relationship between unilateral measures and bilateral measures, or between domestic law and tax treaty law, can differ in myriad ways depending on the legal systems in question (e.g., monist systems, dualist systems, etc.)[735] and the precise wording of the provision (e.g., the extent to which it refers to domestic law).[736]

734. *See,* e.g., Peter Harris, *Chapter III: Taxation of Residents on Foreign Source Income, in United Nations Handbook on Selected Issues in Administration of Double Tax Treaties for Developing Countries* 109, 120 et seq. (Alexander Trepelkov, Harry Tonino & Dominika Halka eds, United Nations 2013) (in explaining the structural differences between unilateral rules and tax treaty rules, Harris explains that '[i]n particular, they [unilateral foreign tax relief rules] are not confined by reference to a treaty; rather domestic law of the residence country will rule all aspects of scope of the relief. So, in applying unilateral rules a residence country must identify what is *foreign source income* for which relief is available and how that income is to be calculated (including the allocation of expenses). Contrast tax treaties, where (as mentioned above) it is the right of the source country to tax that determines the residence country's obligation to provide relief. Unilateral rules must identify when foreign taxes are sufficiently similar to domestic taxes to qualify for relief. This can be a difficult matter. Contrast tax treaties, which often clearly identify taxes to be credited (although that clarity can be blurred if the "substantially similar tax" requirement is engaged). Unilateral rules also usually provide for a nexus between the foreign tax and the foreign income in order to qualify for relief, for example, the foreign income must (according to the rules of the residence country) be seen to have a source in the foreign jurisdiction that imposes the foreign tax').

735. *See,* e.g., Brian J. Arnold, *Chapter I: An Overview of the Issues Involved in the Application of Double Tax Treaties, in United Nations Handbook on Selected Issues in Administration of Double Tax Treaties for Developing Countries* 1, 3 et seq. (Alexander Trepelkov, Harry Tonino & Dominika Halka eds, United Nations 2013).

736. *See,* e.g., John F. Avery Jones, *A Tale of Two Taxes: The Interaction Between Treaty and Unilateral Relief, in Liber Amicorum Sven-Olof Lodin* 64, 64–73 (Krister Andersson, Peter Melz

Importantly, this does not radically change *which* fundamental questions need to be answered, but may change *how* they are answered. For example, the fundamental question of what taxes are creditable must be answered and the tax treaty may provide the answer directly (e.g., if there are no unilateral relief measures) or may expand the answer (e.g., if the tax treaty covers special taxes that would not ordinarily be creditable under domestic law) or restrict the answer (e.g., if the other state levies taxes beyond what it has the right to levy under the convention).

Turning back to these questions, regarding the 'direct' credit, the following observations can be derived:

- By contrast with the unilateral measures, every single one of the drafts of the credit method for bilateral measures addressed the state of 'fiscal domicile' or residence.
- By extension, this meant that the eligible taxpayers were those that were resident in the state granting relief. As the unilateral measures in the UK demonstrated, it is feasible to design forms of a credit method that apply irrespective of residence and that do not fall entirely on the state of residence. Within the context of the British Empire, the UK would grant relief corresponding to the rate of tax levied in a 'Dominion', up to a maximum of 50% of the UK tax rate, and encouraged the Dominion to grant relief for the remainder. In the international discussions, such an approach was rejected as impractical on the grounds that, *inter alia*, such mutual concessions would only be possible in the context of a much closer legal or political union (*see supra* note 571). Moreover, the increased emphasis on residence seemed to coincide with the gradual re-envisioning of taxes on income as personal in nature, rather than 'impersonal'. Thus, similar to the US credit method, residence became central to the operation of the provision.
- The state of residence was always instructed to 'deduct from its tax' a given amount of foreign taxes, which is of course possible *only after* its own taxes have already first been calculated. In this way, the basic two-step operation – of first calculating the taxes due in the state of residence and second deducting the FTC from that amount – was inherently implied in the wording of each draft version. What this underscores is that the relief given under the credit method operates at the level of the taxes due (a feature which became even more apparent and relevant in comparison with the exemption method in the 1961 draft commentary).
- Regarding the status of the foreign taxes, unlike the unilateral measures where references to taxes 'payable' or 'accrued' were found, the wording in the various drafts for bilateral measures used 'paid', 'actually paid', 'imposed', or 'collected'. This places emphasis on the goal to offer relief for 'actual' double taxation.

& Christer Silfverberg eds, Kluwer Law International 2001); Gloria Teixeira & David Williams, *The Impact of the Unilateral Tax Credit in the US, UK and Other Tax Systems*, 23(11) Intertax 573 (1995).

- Unlike the unilateral measures, specifications regarding the proof of the taxes paid abroad or other procedural specifications were rare. Other than in a draft 'plurilateral' convention, which was not revived, and in the 1928 draft convention 'No. 1b', which merely mentions 'On reporting his or its total income from all sources ...', explicit procedural indications were left out.
- As regards the eligible taxes, in earlier versions, such as in the 1927 draft convention, the eligibility of certain taxes turned, in part, on their character as 'personal' or 'impersonal'; however, such distinctions eventually lost relevance. Shortly after, a tendency appeared in, for example, the two drafts presented in the 1946 report and the 1961 draft, to limit the FTC to taxes levied on the basis of or in compliance with the articles in the convention (*see*, e.g., *supra* note 638). Thus, the scope of eligible taxes becomes more dependent on the scope of a given model convention (which remains the case to this day). By 1961, the eligible taxes were taxes 'on income' or 'on capital' (which remains to this day). The state of residence need only allow income taxes levied in the other state to be deducted against its own income taxes (according to the 1961 Commentary, at *supra* note 720), seeming to imply a criterion of comparability or similarity (a question that also arose under unilateral relief measures, *see*, e.g., *supra* note 156 and note 157).
- Regarding the amount of the credit, while an unlimited credit was discussed, it was immediately rejected. Every version that was drafted contained some sort of credit limitation. It seemed that all experts had heeded the lessons of the 1918 US relief and, similar to the 1921 US relief, saw the need for a credit limitation.
- Regarding the design of the credit limitation (MCA), this is where the most substantial deviations occurred among the versions. The earliest drafts were the strictest. The 1925 resolutions, 1927 draft convention, 1928 draft convention 'No. 1a' all included a double limit: not only was the amount of the credit limited to the amount of taxes that the state of residence would collect on the income taxed in the other state but also limited to 'some fraction of the total tax chargeable in the State of domicile' (*see supra* note 581 and note 597). This second limit was eventually abandoned (a welcome change, *see supra* note 611).
- As regards the first limit, there were roughly three different approaches to drafting the MCA that could be detected among the different versions of the credit method. First, some focused on the 'rates' or 'scale' in the state of residence that would apply to the income in question (*see*, e.g., 1925 resolutions, 1928 draft convention 'No. 1a'). If the MCA is calculated by reference to the tax rate in the state of residence that applies to the FSI, then the interpretive question of *which tax rate* arises. Thus, the calculation risks running more directly into the dilemma of deciding between, for example, the tax rate for the lowest income bracket or for the highest income bracket. Second, some MCA wording focused on a ratio between the income taxable in the other state and that taxable in the state of residence (*see*, e.g., 1928 draft convention 'No. 1b',

the two 1946 drafts). If the MCA is calculated by limiting the credit to a proportion of the total amount of taxes, i.e., by multiplying this total by a ratio of FSI over WWI, then this mathematically treats the FSI as though it were proportionately allocated to all brackets of income. Third, the 1961 version avoided both approaches and adopted broader wording, referring to the amount of residence-state tax 'which is appropriate ... to' the income from the other state. This gives greater flexibility to the state granting the credit and, correspondingly, leaves it open to a wider range of interpretations.

- As can be seen, there was an intersection between the calculation of the credit limitation and the issue regarding under which progressive income tax bracket the FSI can be assumed to fall (e.g., 'top-slice', 'bottom-slice', etc.). In the 1925 resolutions, an assumption was made that FSI falls under the lowest income bracket. The 1927 draft convention seemed to follow this idea. The 1961 draft commentary also mentioned this as one possible option for drafting the credit method (*see supra* note 718). This assumption minimizes the amount of credit that can be claimed.
- When the credit is limited, another related issue is how to treat any potential excess amount of foreign taxes that are not creditable in the state of residence. In the 1961 draft commentary, this eventuality is mentioned, but it is deemed to have a low risk of occurring; this was due to the compromise with the state of source under which it agrees to reduce its WHTs (*see supra* note 715). This may have proved slightly too optimistic, as future developments, including case law of the CJEU, show. Although it is true that the tax rate in the state of source in these cases may often be lower than that in the state of residence, this overlooked the importance of the tax base differences (i.e., gross versus net taxation).
- Regarding what taxes are creditable, and how much, there is also a territorial component. As regards the territorial scope, under the UK measures, the scope was often limited to taxes levied in its Dominions and, under the US measures, the scope was generously extended to taxes levied in any foreign state. By virtue of their bilateral nature, the measures drafted in this context required a credit only for taxes levied in the other state. As regards the impact on the credit limitation, this would seem to permit a per-country limitation. The 1925 resolutions, upon which the first draft 1927 convention was based, used the wording 'each of the latter being taken separately', which seemed to indicate that the income from each foreign state should be treated separately, in a separate calculation, i.e., a per-country limitation. A state could ask whether a per-item limitation would also be permitted. This is relevant since, as a general rule, it can be a more restrictive approach. The wording of different drafts pointed in different directions. For example, the 1928 draft convention 'No. 1a' stated that the credit would be limited to 'the amount of the tax actually paid in the other Contracting State on *income from immovable property (Article 2)* **and** *on income from industrial, commercial or agricultural undertaking (Article 5)*' (emphasis added). On the one hand, by mentioning the specific types of

income, this could point to a per-item limitation; on the other hand, the wording seems to aggregate the income together by using 'and', thus referring to all income that is taxable in the other state in accordance with the convention. Eventually, after the first model convention was compiled together by the OECD on the basis of the 1961 draft, the Commentary was updated from 1977 onwards (paragraph 64):[737] it mentions all limitations, per-item, per-country, overall, without addressing whether the wording endorses one over the other.[738]

- The amount of the credit limitation depends upon the amount of income that is considered FSI for that purpose. A question can arise when there is a divergence between the two states as regards what constitutes taxable income. If multiple items of income are derived from the state of source, yet the state of source taxes only one of them, while the state of residence considers all of them taxable, the question is whether the amount of the credit limitation is: (1) the amount of residence-state tax that is appropriate to *all* the income derived from the other state or (2) the amount of residence-state tax that is appropriate to the income that is *taxable* in the other state (*see supra* note 726). While the wording of the 1961 draft stated that the credit is limited to 'that part of the income tax ... which is appropriate to ... the *income derived from* ... that other Contracting State' (emphasis added), which could imply the first interpretation, the 1961 draft commentary argued for the second, stating that the residence state need only take into account the item of income that was actually taxed in the other state. This reduces the credit limitation. On the one hand, this amount is all that is necessary to eliminate any actual double taxation that is occurring; on the other hand, this interpretation would not clearly stem from the wording of the provision.
- Other issues that were merely touched upon in the discussions over bilateral measures included: timing issues (*see supra* note 646) and issues relating to the calculation of FSI (*see supra* notes 626–627 and note 640). Unlike under the unilateral measures, the gross-up of FSI by foreign taxes did not receive much explicit attention (if any) in the reports. Calculation details were ultimately left to domestic law.
- As can be seen, in the end, by the 1961 report, it is the features of the US version of the credit method that predominate, namely the centrality of

737. OECD, *Model Tax Convention on Income and on Capital 2014: Full Version*, C(23)-59 (OECD Publishing 2015) (according to the 'History' notes, paragraph 64 was added in 1977).

738. As a result, views may differ on this point. *See*, e.g., Richard Vann, *Chapter 18: International Aspects of Income Tax*, *in* 2 *Tax Law Design and Drafting* 39 (Victor Thuronyi ed., International Monetary Fund 1998), https://www.imf.org/external/pubs/nft/1998/tlaw/eng/ch18.pdf (last visited 4 Nov. 2018) ('Given that tax treaties are premised on an item-by-item foreign tax credit limit, rather than on a worldwide limit aggregating all foreign income of the taxpayer, the item-by-item limit is probably easiest to use in domestic law'). For a different view, *see*, e.g., Alexander Rust, *Article 23 A Exemption Method and Article 23 B Credit Method*, *in* 2 *Klaus Vogel on Double Taxation Conventions* 1581, m.no. 57 (Ekkehart Reimer & Alexander Rust eds, Kluwer Law International 4th ed. 2015) (explaining that DTCs do not necessarily imply a per-item credit limitation).

residence and source, offering a dollar-for-dollar (unit-for-unit) credit, subject to the MCA.

As regards an 'indirect' credit, what is noticeable in the study of the bilateral measures is its general absence. The bilateral measures focused almost exclusively on the 'direct' credit method, by contrast with the unilateral measures. This is attributable to the limited scope of the bilateral measures in the model conventions. That is, eventually it was decided that the articles on the methods for double taxation relief address 'juridical double taxation', as opposed to 'economic double taxation' (*see supra* note 542). In this way, the models assume a 'classical' corporate tax system, as opposed to an 'integrated' corporate-shareholder system (*see supra* note 552). The 1946 London draft model was the only one to include a draft provision for the elimination of economic double taxation on dividends; in this case, it suggested the exemption method (*see supra* note 649). The 1961 draft commentary, on the texts eventually adopted for the first OECD model, mentioned that relief of economic double taxation is completely optional and suggested that the states could negotiate for an indirect credit (*see supra* note 699). Clearly, opinions differed on the necessity to address economic double taxation. The '1870 Imperial Double Taxation Law' did not require it (*see supra* note 468), whereas the economists authoring the 1923 report would have considered it worthwhile to address (*see supra* note 488).

In their brief discussion on the topic in the 1923 report, the economists touched upon some considerations for relief for economic double taxation. In particular, they called attention to the practical difficulties in offering relief for economic double taxation, which stemmed from:

- challenges in obtaining information about the amount of taxes levied at the corporate level;
- different approaches to the calculation of income;
- the fact that dividends may encompass profits from multiple different years, and
- ascertaining the amount of corporate tax attributable to the dividends (*see supra* note 489).

The first three points mostly reiterate and reinforce considerations listed above. To be specific, obtaining information about taxes levied abroad could be said to relate to procedural issues that arise under both direct and indirect credits, and divergent determinations of taxable income and timing issues complicate the calculations under both as well. That said, these problems are exacerbated in the case of indirect credits, due to the fact that the income and taxes have to be traced from another taxpayer. In particular, there is an extra layer of timing considerations due to the fact that, structurally, there are two distinct taxable events – the generation of profits and the distribution of profits – that have to be reconciled or realigned. Profits may be generated, and taxed, over the course of multiple tax years, before a decision is eventually made to distribute a portion of the profits to the owners or shareholders. A question immediately follows as to whether the distributed portion of the profits relates to the earliest tax year, the most recent tax year, or all tax years proportionately. As regards the fourth point mentioned in the 1923 report, this is what ties them altogether. It is the defining calculation of an indirect credit, which is an extra step as compared to a direct credit, that was referred to above as an 'apportionment' formula (*see* the interim conclusions under Section 2.1.1.4.).

The study of bilateral measures brings yet another point of added value. As this phase involved intense debates over different methods, the comparison allowed for a deeper understanding of the credit method, helping establish where its contours lie or where it begins to morph into a different method. The 1961 report, which can be seen as a culmination of the work, is particularly insightful, by allowing the comparing and contrasting of the credit method so clearly from its contemporary counterpart the exemption method. There are three general distinctions between the credit method and the exemption method that can be derived from the draft commentary:

(1) while the exemption method operates at the level of the income tax base, the credit method operates at the level of the income taxes;
(2) while the exemption method is indifferent to the level, or collection, of tax in the other state, the credit method hinges on it; and
(3) consequently, while the exemption method may offer 'relief' for even potential or nominal double taxation, the credit method offers relief for actual or effective double taxation.

Otherwise, the two methods can approach one another quite closely in either their operation or their effects in certain cases, such as under: (1) the tax exemption method and (2) tax sparing or (especially) matching credits. The tax exemption method employs a calculation that is almost indistinguishable from that of the credit method and it operates at the level of the taxes due. The difference is that, from the taxes due in the state of residence, *all* of the taxes attributable to the FSI in question are deducted, regardless of whether taxes were actually levied in the foreign state(s) or how much. In other words, here the operation is nearly identical, but the effect is different. Tax matching credits grant a credit for a predetermined amount of foreign taxes, regardless of how much was actually levied. To the extent that the credit compensates for taxes actually levied, it functions as a credit method; to the extent that the credit is granted above that amount, even where taxes were not levied, it functions as a partial exemption method. It may operate like a credit method, but its effect is different.

From the above, the credit method emerges as one of the main methods for relief of double taxation. This was far from inevitable considering it seemed nowhere to be found in the first phase of bilateral conventions, in the 1800s among European powers, and considering it competed against multiple other methods in the 1923 report and, at that time, was soundly rejected by experts. Moreover, of the different forms of credit method (or quasi or partial credit methods) in the unilateral phase, the US version ultimately took over. This was also not inevitable, considering that a UK version, i.e., its 1920 Dominion Relief System, was also on the table in the 1923 report. And, at that time, both were soundly rejected by experts. Both were considered undesirable and unfeasible for different reasons. In sum, the trajectory of the credit method could be described as: non-existent in the mid-1800s, rejected in the early 1920s, heavily relied upon in the 1946 drafts, and settled upon as alternative option in the late 1950s and in the 1960s.

One hypothesis for this trajectory - from favouring an approach granting an exclusive allocation of taxation rights in the mid-1800s to an approach incorporating the credit method in the mid-1900s - is that it was caused in part by the shift in the conceptualization of taxes from impersonal to more personal taxes.[739]

739. At least, a correlation can be detected in studying the historical developments. Given that many taxes were initially conceptualized as distinct impersonal taxes on distinct taxable events, it followed logically that the right to levy them should be granted based on a connection with the taxable event giving rise to the income or value. If the rights to each particular stream of income can be connected to one specific nexus, this system prevents an overlap of taxation from occurring in the first place and thus creates a de facto exemption or a system of refraining from taxation in the first place (one caveat is: of course, it prevents an overlap to the extent nexus/source conflicts can be avoided). When all states conceptualize the taxes in the *same* way, solutions are more readily achievable. Eventually income taxes became increasingly conceptualized as taxes on a particular individual or taxpayer, with a view on all of the relevant income, expenses and (personal) circumstances. As long as states continued to simultaneously tax on the basis of some sort of impersonal/objective nexus with their territory, while broadening their notion of personal taxes, this resulted in an overlap. To the extent that both states are seen as having legitimate claims - because convincing arguments can be made for the legitimacy of both claims (on the basis of an objective connection with the territory, on the basis of a personal connection with the state, on considerations of 'economic allegiance', etc.) - this leads to a more inevitable recalcitrant overlap. It calls for a different system. Now it becomes more likely that it has to be a system of *relief*, rather than *prevention* in the first place. To the extent that the objective connection to a territory is legitimate, asking states to renounce *all* such claims will not find agreement; indeed, this approach (i.e., asking states to exempt at origin) was endorsed in the 1923 report, but did not end up adopted. To the extent that a personal connection to a state is legitimate (because income taxes came to be seen as being levied on and directly affecting the income earned by a person and their capacity to contribute), asking states to renounce *all* such claims will not find agreement. Against this background, it is less of a surprise that the credit method came to the forefront (e.g., in the 1946 report) as a compromise. At first (e.g., 1923 report and 1925 report), the credit method was depicted as almost absurdly generous, especially in the case of an unlimited credit. Moreover, an unlimited credit did not amount to much of a compromise between the two presumably equally legitimate claims (on an objective basis versus a personal one) because, as the early reports decried, this places the entire burden of relief on the state with the personal connection. In fact, in some cases, the credit could reach amounts that entirely wipe out that state's ability to collect taxes on the income in question, thus not fully respecting its claim. In fact, the credit could reach such amounts that it could wipe out, not only the ability to collect taxes on the basis of a legitimate personal connection, but also it could even reduce, or wipe out, the ability of that state to collect taxes on 'domestic' income earned within its own territory, thereby 'violating' both of its legitimate claims to tax. Hence, in came two different forms of compromise within a system based on the credit method, namely a credit limitation in the credit-granting state coupled with a limitation in the other state on the amount of taxes that can be levied, in some cases. This trajectory seems to reflect T.S. Adams' view of the credit method as a compromise.

2.2. THE CORE OF THE CREDIT METHOD AND COMPLEMENTARY DESIGN FEATURES

From a study of the unilateral measures (Section 2.1.1.) and the bilateral measures (Section 2.1.2.), detailed lists were compiled of the features and considerations that arose throughout the historical evolution of the credit method (*see* especially Sections 2.1.1.4. and 2.1.2.4.). This section now compares and consolidates these findings in order to generate a more concise summary. The details are distilled into keywords, for easier future reference in subsequent discussions in the book. This facilitates setting up a framework for analysis.

The aim is that the framework is sufficiently comprehensive so as to be relevant across time and jurisdictions. To this end, the historical analysis sought to identify the issues that proved relevant since the origins of the credit method, thus withstanding the test of time, so to speak. To be relevant across jurisdictions requires finding the common denominators, which are sufficiently high-level to remain relevant more globally while filtering out details that seem too jurisdiction-specific.

Most importantly, it is crucial to keep in mind the aim of this compilation, namely as a support for the EU law analysis. This determines what is relevant here. As will be seen in subsequent chapters, when the CJEU is confronted with a national provision that is allegedly contrary to EU law, it is not interpreting the precise wording of that provision; rather, it is assessing the effects of that legislation and whether those effects contravene EU law. Therefore, what is relevant here is to identify the main functional components of the credit method.

As regards a 'direct' credit, the following points proved relevant:

- a basic two-step operation, such that the relief operates at the level of taxes due;
- relief for 'actual' double taxation;
- eligible taxpayers, an aspect which, in turn, relates to which state/jurisdiction is responsible for relief;
- eligible taxes:
  - type, e.g., income, capital, estate;
  - territory, e.g., dominions, all states, the other Contracting State;
  - status, e.g., paid or payable.
- the amount of creditable taxes, e.g., 'dollar-for-dollar' versus partial, unlimited versus limited:
  - if limited, type of limit, e.g., overall, per-country, per-item;
  - if limited, treatment of excess.
- foreign-source income:
  - determination of tax base, e.g., divergences in notions of taxable income, source rules, gross-up, sums based on foreign law versus sums recalculated under domestic law, allocation of expenses, losses;
  - progressive tax rate issue, e.g., 'bottom-slice', 'top-slice';
  - timing issues, e.g., divergent taxable years, exchange rate differences.
- procedural issues, e.g., proof, a redetermination mechanism.

From the above points, there were two that featured consistently throughout the evolution of the credit method. First, there is its basic two-step operation, described numerous times above, which results in the fact that the relief intervenes at the stage of the taxes due. As Harris concisely explained, since the income tax equation is, in its simplest expression, the tax base multiplied by the tax rate equals the taxes due (tax base × tax rate = tax due), relief for double taxation can occur at any of those three points, i.e., at the level of the tax base, tax rate or tax amount.[740] This distinguishes the credit method from a mere deduction of the foreign taxes from the *tax base*, i.e., a deduction method, and from a deduction of, or an exclusion of, the foreign income from the *tax base*, i.e., an exemption method.

Second, another distinguishing feature is the reliance of the credit on the actual taxes paid, or due, in the other state. Thus, it can be said to be aimed at actual double taxation, as opposed to 'potential' double taxation. This distinguishes the credit method from the tax exemption method and, technically also, a tax sparing credit or a tax matching credit method. While they both have a similar two-step operation, neither relies (fully) on the actual amount of taxes paid in the other state. In this way, certain approaches that are labelled as a credit method – such as a tax matching credit – may not actually be one in the 'purest' sense. Rather, a tax sparing credit or tax matching credit, in terms of its effect, is actually a hybrid credit-exemption method. Moreover, they serve a purpose beyond the main aim of relief for double taxation: they originate from the desire to support socially oriented or development-oriented tax reductions or exemptions in the source state (*see supra* notes 704–705). For this reason, it is not the focus of this study on the credit method. In sum, as the two aforementioned features were the components shared by all versions to varying degrees and as they help distinguish the credit method from other methods, they can be argued to form the *core of the credit method*.

If so, as a result, everything else can be considered a *variable component*, or a design feature. Questions regarding the eligible taxpayer, the eligible taxes, etc. can all be variegated without compromising its nature as a credit method. Even certain features that seem to be held as sacred today, such as the fact that the credit method is granted by the state of residence to its own residents, are not necessarily *defining* features (since it can be designed differently). For example, the system of relief implemented in 1920 in the UK vis-à-vis its 'Dominions' demonstrates that other approaches are possible, if the conditions are right (e.g., establishing a close enough cooperation between jurisdictions, usually via political or legal ties, to render the coordination of mutual concessions possible). Moreover, as seen below, in the discussion of CJEU case law, this also ends up relevant for EU MSs in cases where, for example, they must also extend relief to non-residents (discussed in Section 4.2.1.). Indeed, the centrality of residence has become the widely accepted standard, but the standard can be distinguished from the core. Recognizing this potentially frees up thinking about the design of a credit method. Thus, numerous features can be tweaked

740. Peter Harris, *An Historic View of the Principle and Options for Double Tax Relief*, 1999(6) Brit. Tax Rev. 469, 479 (1999).

according to the aims pursued and according to the understanding of 'double taxation', both of which - although also often taken for granted - can vary, as the historical developments have also shown.

Also, another observation regarding these design features is that they can be roughly categorized according to their function. First, certain design features dictate the *scope*, such as who are the eligible taxpayers (personal scope) and what are the eligible taxes (material scope), which may include the question as to whether taxes paid to *all* foreign jurisdictions or only certain jurisdictions are covered (thus, in turn, affecting the territorial scope). Second, as with all laws, there are the substantive aspects and *procedural* ones to help carry out the former, such as the need to furnish proof of taxes paid abroad, in what format and within what time frame. Third, other design features affect its *operation and effects*, namely all considerations related to its calculation, such as a potential MCA and a gross-up of the FSI by the taxes paid abroad.

This conceptualization - and compartmentalization - of the direct credit method seems to find support in literature and other sources. First, regarding the core of the credit method, *Black's Law Dictionary* contains an entry for 'tax credit' that defines it as '[a]n amount subtracted directly from one's total tax liability, dollar for dollar, as opposed to a deduction from gross income'.[741] This definition, stripped of its US-specific elements, emphasizes the two-step operation, which offers relief at the level of taxes due. The entry for 'foreign tax credit' defines it as '[a] tax credit against U.S. income taxes for a taxpayer who earns income overseas and has paid foreign taxes on that income', which emphasizes its reliance on taxes already paid to another jurisdiction.[742] The International Bureau of Fiscal Documentation (IBFD) International Tax Glossary entry for 'credit, foreign tax' defines it as 'a method of relieving international double taxation under which, in general terms, taxes imposed on foreign income may be credited against, e.g. deducted from domestic tax on that income'.[743] Apart from this main definition, the entry continues on to add other points, namely the fact that credits are granted under treaties (bilateral measures) or under domestic law (unilateral measures), that they may be 'subject to one or more limitations', that only certain types of taxes may be covered and that there is a distinction between direct and indirect credits - indicating that these are all features and points that are common, but not part of the core definition. Its entry on 'credit, direct' defines it as a '[t]erm used generally in relation to a credit for foreign taxes paid by a domestic taxpayer'.[744] Although this could imply residence as a defining feature, the entry uses the modifier 'generally', indicating that this aspect can vary. In addition, another entry, namely on the term 'reverse credit', is defined as '[a] credit granted by the source state for taxes imposed by the residence state',[745] also indicating that this 'residence' aspect can vary. Thus, the lowest common denominator, or unifying feature, remains that it is relief for taxes

741. *Tax Credit, Black's Law Dictionary* (11th ed. 2019).
742. *Foreign Tax Credit, Black's Law Dictionary* (11th ed. 2019).
743. *Credit, Foreign Tax, IBFD International Tax Glossary* (IBFD Online Tax Glossary 2018).
744. *Credit, Direct, IBFD International Tax Glossary* (IBFD Online Tax Glossary 2018).
745. *Reverse Credit, IBFD International Tax Glossary* (IBFD Online Tax Glossary 2018).

paid, or due, to another jurisdiction by means of deducting them from the taxes due in the state granting relief.

Second, regarding the variable components, a study of issues flagged under the credit method in various sources seems to bolster the selection of issues derived from the historical overview and attests to their ongoing relevance. The table below aims to show this. For example, since the comprehensive work of Elisabeth A. Owens in 1961, and her list of the 'Basic Rules of the Foreign Tax Credit',[746] treatises and practice guides, such as that by Richard Andersen on 'Foreign Tax Credits', have been published and regularly updated in the US.[747] This allows a comparison of issues identified in the historical legal developments with an up-to-date present-day list of credit method issues highlighted in that work. From a more global perspective, the Klaus Vogel Commentary on the credit method in double taxation conventions (DTCs) and, more recently, the Global Tax Treaty Commentaries include a comprehensive discussion of key issues that arise under those provisions.[748] Hugh J. Ault and Brian J. Arnold in 'Comparative Income Taxation: A Structural Analysis' listed the 'Issues in the structure of a foreign tax credit system' within the 'Mechanisms for relief of double taxation'.[749] In 2011, the annual IFA Congress examined the 'key practical issues to eliminate double taxation of business income', gathering the reports of experts from more than 30 countries and the EU. From the reports, six 'key factors of unrelieved double taxation' were identified, many of which occur under both the credit method and exemption method. This list gives insight into reoccurring problems in the design components (or resulting from their interaction with other rules).[750]

As seen in the table below, if the items from these above-cited lists (quoted below in the right column) are compared with the list of variable (design) components identified from the historical analysis above, it can be seen that they are largely aligned (which lends some credibility to the selection). And, importantly, it can be seen whether the list of variable components allows the diverse and complex key issues that arise in practice to be accounted for (which shows that the selection is sufficiently

746. Elisabeth A. Owens, *The Foreign Tax Credit: A Study of the Credit for Foreign Taxes under United States Income Tax Law* 4–15 (Harvard Law School 1961) (hereinafter, for the purposes of this section: 'Owens, *The Foreign Tax Credit*').

747. Richard E. Andersen, *Foreign Tax Credits* (Warren, Gorham & Lamont, Thomson Reuters Tax and Accounting, with updates through May 2019) (hereinafter, for the purposes of this section: 'Andersen, *Foreign Tax Credits*').

748. Alexander Rust, *Article 23 A Exemption Method and Article 23 B Credit Method, in 2 Klaus Vogel on Double Taxation Conventions* 1581, m.nos 37–60 (Ekkehart Reimer & Alexander Rust eds, Kluwer Law International 4th ed. 2015) (hereinafter, for the purposes of this section: 'Rust, *Credit Method, Klaus Vogel on Double Taxation Conventions*'); Georg Kofler, *Article 23B: Methods for Elimination of Double Taxation, in Global Tax Treaty Commentaries* (Richard Vann ed.-in-chief, Pasquale Pistone et al. eds, Global Topics IBFD updated as of February 2019).

749. *See* both Hugh J. Ault & Brian J. Arnold, *Comparative Income Taxation: A Structural Analysis* 357–386 pt. 4 *International Taxation* (Kluwer Law International 2d ed. 2004); Hugh J. Ault & Brian J. Arnold, *Comparative Income Taxation: A Structural Analysis* 446–466 (Kluwer Law International 3d ed. 2010) (hereinafter, for the purposes of this section: 'Ault & Arnold, *Comparative Income Taxation*').

750. Gauthier Blanluet & Philippe J. Durand, *General Report: Key Practical Issues to Eliminate Double Taxation of Business Income*, 96b Cahiers de Droit Fiscal International 17 (IFA 2011) (hereinafter, for the purposes of this section: 'Blanluet & Durand, IFA, *Key Practical Issues*').

comprehensive). Helpfully, this exercise also enriches the understanding of the variable components by adding further details and new questions that have arisen in practice over time (to that end, explanatory notes are provided in footnotes).

Core of the Credit Method - basic two-step operation, such that the relief operates at level of taxes due - relief for 'actual' double taxation	
Variable Components of the Credit Method	
Credit method issues identified in historical legal developments	*Credit method issues identified in literature*
Scope:	
- eligible taxpayers	'Who Is Entitled to the Credit'[751] 'Eligible Taxpayers'[752] 'Similar Credit Requirement for Resident Aliens'[753] 'term "resident" [as] defined in Article 4'[754] 'person entitled to claim a credit ... is the person who was liable to pay the foreign tax'[755] 'Access to the Direct Credit': '"Technical Taxpayer" Requirement'[756]

751. Owens, *The Foreign Tax Credit*, at 4-15.
752. Andersen, *Foreign Tax Credits* (in this treatise, after the 'Overview' in Chapter 1, the first substantive Chapter is 'Chapter 2. Eligible Taxpayers'. This term refers predominantly to 'U.S. persons' and, in specific cases, 'Foreign persons' that earn 'income effectively connected with the taxpayer's conduct of a trade or business within the United States'. 'U.S. persons' covers 'individuals', who are 'U.S. citizens' and 'resident aliens', and 'corporations'. In the case of corporate and other legal entities, the main aspect that affects the question of which taxpayer is eligible to claim the foreign tax credit is whether the entity itself is taxable or whether it is treated as a 'pass through', 'pay through' or 'fiscally transparent' entity, e.g., passing along gains, losses and likewise the related foreign taxes to the partners, shareholders or owners of the entity. The 'eligible taxpayer' is also affected by the option for certain affiliated domestic corporations to file consolidated tax returns, in which case the 'common parent' of the group generally becomes responsible for the foreign tax credit calculations and elections for the group. It may also be the case that a given entity, for example, the 'Domestic international sales corporations (DISCs)' in the US, is not subject to tax or is exempt and, for that reason, would not be eligible for a foreign tax credit).
753. Owens, *The Foreign Tax Credit*, at 4-15.
754. Rust, *Credit Method, Klaus Vogel on Double Taxation Conventions*, at m.no. 41.
755. *Id.*, at m.no. 46 (this is an element of the scope of a direct credit, as opposed to an indirect credit. This question is relevant in general and also in special cases. For example, it is relevant in 'sham' situations, e.g., with interposed companies. This question is also relevant in situations where the two states apply different tax treatment to entities, such as partnerships, and it must therefore be ascertained whether it is the partner or the partnership that pays the taxes and therefore is eligible for the credit).
756. Andersen, *Foreign Tax Credits* (in this treatise, its Chapter 5 on 'Access to the Direct Credit' covers a range of issues. The Subsections are: 5.01 Introduction, 5.02 'Technical Taxpayer'

	'Inconsistent classifications of foreign entities'[757]
- eligible taxes - type, e.g., income, capital, estate - territory, e.g., dominions, all states, the other Contracting State - status, e.g., paid or payable	'What Foreign Taxes are Creditable'[758] 'Eligible Taxes'[759] 'United States Tax Against Which Credit Is Allowed'[760] 'given against "the tax on income" and "the tax on capital"' and 'for taxes to which the treaty applies' (original emphasis omitted)[761] 'Creditable taxes'[762] 'Classes of income or capital in respect of which the credit method is envisaged'[763]

Requirement, 5.03 Satisfaction of Tax Liability, and 5.04 Special Assessment Rules. The last is US-specific, while the others cover issues of broader relevance. According to the Introduction (5.01), the chapter focuses on two requirements, namely that: '(1) the taxpayer seeking to claim the credit be the person on which the foreign tax was actually imposed (the so-called technical taxpayer requirement) and (2) the tax in question has in fact been paid or accrued'. The first could be considered a component of the 'eligible taxpayer', while the latter could be considered a component of 'eligible taxes'. In addition to covering the status of 'eligible taxes' as 'paid or accrued', its Section 5.03 on 'Satisfaction of Tax Liability' covers timing issues and procedural issues).

757. Blanluet & Durand, IFA, *Key Practical Issues*, at 46–50 (as explained in the explanatory notes to other sources in the footnotes above, this report also identified the issue that when entities are classified differently for tax purposes, e.g., as opaque or transparent, this can complicate the question of which taxpayer is eligible to claim the foreign tax credit).
758. Owens, *The Foreign Tax Credit*, at 4–15.
759. Andersen, *Foreign Tax Credits* (in this treatise, both Chapters 3 and 4 are dedicated to 'Eligible Taxes', the first to the 'General Principles' and the second to 'Specific Levies'. Some of the 'General Principles' may be of broader relevance, while the latter consists mostly of examples of specific cases of foreign levies regarding which the US IRS has issued rulings or the US courts have decided. Under the 'General Principles', the Subsections discuss: (1) the criteria for determining whether a foreign levy is a 'tax', which requires that it is compulsory and collected 'pursuant to the authority of a foreign country to levy taxes', and whether it is an 'income tax' in the US sense, excluding, e.g., 'soak-up' taxes; (2) the 'amount of creditable tax', which reiterates that the FTC is granted for taxes actually paid or accrued abroad, since it excludes taxes that will be 'refunded, credited, rebated or forgiven', 'used to grant a subsidy to the taxpayer', 'subject to further reduction ...' or again 'not compulsory'; (3) 'taxes in lieu of income taxes' that may also be creditable under certain conditions in the US; (4) explicit rules in the US for what is referred to as a 'dual capacity taxpayer', which – because taxes paid 'in exchange for a specific economic benefit' are not creditable – simply 'distinguish between the creditable portion of taxes paid and the noncreditable portion paid in exchange for a specific economic benefit'; and (5) certain specific FTC-related questions for which the US IRS refuses to issue rulings).
760. Owens, *The Foreign Tax Credit*, at 4–15 (this heading falls under eligible taxes, understood broadly, and it points out an issue that is particularly relevant for a jurisdiction that has other special taxes, such as 'the tax on accumulated earnings (section 531)' that existed at that time in the US or a municipal business tax, and thus needs to decide whether a credit is allowed against those taxes as well).
761. Rust, *Credit Method, Klaus Vogel on Double Taxation Conventions*, at m.no. 43.
762. Ault & Arnold, *Comparative Income Taxation*, at 446–466.
763. Rust, *Credit Method, Klaus Vogel on Double Taxation Conventions*, at m.no. 48 (this is an element of the scope of relief in tax treaties based on the OECD Model or UN Model, which

	'Access to the Direct Credit': 'Satisfaction of Tax Liability', meaning that the taxes must have been 'paid or accrued' (depending, e.g., on the taxpayer's method of accounting) and including questions that overlap with timing and procedural issues (below)[764]
Operation:	
- amount of creditable taxes - e.g., 'dollar-for-dollar' vs. partial, unlimited vs. limited - if limited, type of limit, e.g., overall, per-country, per-item - if limited, treatment of excess	'Limitation on the Amount of Credit'[765] 'Maximum deduction (limitation)'[766] 'Excess amounts of creditable foreign tax; losses'[767] 'Limitations on the credit'[768] 'Carryover of excess credits or limitation'[769]

underscores the interaction between the allocation rules and Article 23. In particular, the Vogel Commentary here refers to the specific case of Article 23A(2): Article 23A(1) provides the exemption method, but under Article 23A(2) the credit method nevertheless applies to interest and dividends, and sometimes other classes of income. This exception to the exemption method resulted from a historical compromise, as seen above at *supra* note 664. Thus, the interpretation of 'dividends' and 'interest' is relevant because, if income falls under one of these two categories, then the taxes levied would be creditable under credit method, rather than exempt. Although the discussion in the Vogel Commentary relates to this specific tax treaty issue, which affects the scope of taxes that are creditable on the basis of the OECD Model or UN Model, this issue could be generalized to other situations. In any situation where a state decides to grant a credit only for certain classes of income, this naturally has an impact on the scope of eligible taxes and, by extension, the amount of eligible taxes. Thus, it can be seen as pertaining to the *scope* of eligible taxes in that, rather than all income taxes, only income taxes attributable to, e.g., dividends are eligible. Alternatively, it can be seen as an issue of the *amount* of eligible or creditable taxes, because rather than all foreign-source income being taken into account, only, e.g., dividends are. In any case, if only certain classes of income give rise to a foreign tax credit, then the question of the attribution of taxes to that income usually immediately follows; in this way, the two questions - of scope and of amount - are intertwined).

764. Andersen, *Foreign Tax Credits*, at *supra* note 756.
765. Owens, *The Foreign Tax Credit*, at 4-15.
766. Rust, *Credit Method, Klaus Vogel on Double Taxation Conventions*, at m.no. 50.
767. *Id.*, at m.no. 58 (the reference to 'losses' refers to losses at home or losses from a third state and its impact on the amount of the credit, i.e., how it leads to the situation that there are no domestic taxes against which the foreign taxes can be credited. This shows that the questions regarding the amount of creditable taxes and the questions regarding the foreign-source income in the next row of the table are inherently interconnected).
768. Ault & Arnold, *Comparative Income Taxation*, at 446-466.
769. *Id.*

	'The Section 904 Limitation',[770] including 'Look-through rules',[771] 'Allocation of U.S.-source income',[772] 'Allocation of taxes', and 'Effect of the limitation' discussing the carryback and carryover rules 'Foreign tax credit limitations'[773]
– foreign-source income – calculation of tax base, e.g., gross-up, sums based on foreign law vs. sums recalculated under domestic law, allocation of expenses, losses, divergences in notions of taxable income – progressive tax rate issue, e.g., 'bottom-slice', 'top-slice'	'net income': when calculating the FSI in accordance with the rules of the state of residence, questions may arise such as 'the valuation of assets and liabilities, the allowance of business expenses and the rates of capital allowance', the allocation of deductions to FSI, etc.[774] 'determining the tax rate "attributable" to the income from abroad'[775] 'Losses incurred abroad' can be set off against domestic income[776] 'Allocation of expenses to foreign-source income'[777] 'Treatment of losses in the credit computation'[778] 'The Section 904 Limitation: Computing Foreign-Source Gross Income',[779] discussing the source rules for different types of income and the scope of income covered (e.g., interest, dividends, amounts includable from certain foreign corporations such as CFCs), the overall foreign loss rules, the overall domestic loss rules

770. Andersen, *Foreign Tax Credits* (Chapter 7 is dedicated to the history and structure of the Section 904 limitation and, therefore, many of the subtopics are quite US-specific, e.g., the details of the various legislative changes and limitation baskets used by the US over time, a specific anti-avoidance rule ('deconsolidation' rules) and other 'special cases'. In addition, Chapters 10 and 11 discuss special cases, namely 'The Oil and Gas Limitation' and 'Special Limitations').
771. *Id.* ('These "look-through" rules treat income derived through entities controlled by U.S. persons essentially as if the income were earned through a foreign branch').
772. *Id.* ('Section 904(g) was enacted to ensure that foreign corporations would not be used by U.S. taxpayers to change U.S.-source income to foreign-source income').
773. Blanluet & Durand, IFA, *Key Practical Issues*, at 41–42.
774. Rust, *Credit Method, Klaus Vogel on Double Taxation Conventions*, at m.no. 53, m.nos 51–55.
775. *Id.*, at m.no. 56.
776. *Id.*, at m.no. 59.
777. Ault & Arnold, *Comparative Income Taxation*, at 446–466.
778. *Id.*
779. Andersen, *Foreign Tax Credits* (Chapter 8, 'The Section 904 Limitation: Computing Foreign-Source Gross Income', includes the following Subsections: 8.01 Introduction, 8.02 'United States' Defined, 8.03 Interest, 8.04 Dividends, 8.05 Compensation for Services, 8.06 Rents and Royalties, 8.07 Sales of Property, 8.08 Underwriting Income, 8.09 Transportation Income, 8.10

	'The Section 904 Limitation: Computing Foreign-Source Taxable Income',[780] discussing the allocation and apportionment of deductible items 'Diverging views on taxable income', regarding 'Source of income'[781] or 'Nature or character of income'[782] 'Inconsistent allocation of deductions between domestic and foreign sources'[783] Issues regarding the ability to 'deduct foreign losses against domestic income'[784]

Space or Ocean Income, 8.11 International Communications Income, 8.12 Financial Instruments, 8.13 Amounts Includable from Certain Foreign Corporations, 8.14 Overall Foreign Loss Rules, 8.15 Overall Domestic Loss Rules).

780. Andersen, *Foreign Tax Credits* (Chapter 9, 'The Section 904 Limitation: Computing Foreign-Source Taxable Income', includes the following Subsections: 9.01 Introduction, 9.02 History, 9.03 Definitions, 9.04 Basic Allocation and Apportionment Rules, 9.05 Income Tax Treaties (regarding the impact or lack thereof on US domestic-source rules), 9.06 Allocation and Apportionment of Specific Deductions).
781. Blanluet & Durand, IFA, *Key Practical Issues*, at 30–33 (income may have connections with more than one state, e.g., if the payer is in one state, but the activities or property giving rise to it are in another state. In some cases, diverging views on the source of the income can inflate the credit and, in other cases, reduce it or lead to its refusal. If authorities of the credit-granting state do not agree that a given stream of income has a foreign source, or if they 'attribute the income to a source located in a foreign country different from the foreign country taxing the income', they may refuse to grant a credit for foreign taxes levied on such income. Alternatively, if authorities of a credit-granting state deem income to be sourced in a foreign state, yet the foreign state does not tax it, this may increase the amount of income that is deemed foreign-source and increase the credit. There is an important interaction between the type of credit limitation and source rules: source rules are much more important if the credit-granting state uses a per-country limitation).
782. *Id.* (regarding the character of the income, if the authorities of the foreign state believe the income is subject to a withholding tax (e.g., income from technical services) or to a higher withholding tax (e.g., interest subject to 10% rather than dividends qualifying for a lower or no withholding tax), whereas the authorities of the credit-granting state believe the income is, for example, business income that should not be taxable in the other state, the credit may be refused or reduced).
783. Blanluet & Durand, IFA, *Key Practical Issues*, at 33–38 ('Normally, allocation of expenses to domestic income increases the foreign tax credit limitation, i.e. the basis for imputation of the tax credit, whereas allocation of expenses to foreign income reduces the limitation …'. Diverging rules can also lead to tax planning where taxpayers seek to allocate, e.g., interest expenses, to the state with the higher tax rate).
784. *Id.*, at 38–41.

– timing issues – e.g., divergent taxable years, exchange rate differences	'Conversion of Foreign Tax Into United States Dollars'[785] 'Time at Which Credit Is Claimed'[786] 'Crediting period'[787] 'Access to the Direct Credit':[788] 'Satisfaction of Tax Liability', including issues such as the 'Determination of Taxable Year', the 'Deferral of Recognition of Taxes' in the case of 'Contested Taxes' or 'Split Taxes'[789] 'Distortions due to temporal differences in the recognition of taxable income', focusing mostly on 'Temporal differences in the recognition of taxable income between the residence country and the source country',[790] briefly mentioning 'Other timing discrepancies';[791] this can sometimes also lead to 'Deferral rules or similar principles'[792] such as CFC rules

785. Owens, *The Foreign Tax Credit*, at 4-15 (discussing both timing issues and foreign-source income calculation issues).
786. *Id.* (although the word 'time' indicates its clear relation to timing issues, this heading also shows the relationship with the status of eligible taxes as paid or payable, since what Owens explains here is the following: 'a foreign tax generally becomes creditable either in the United States tax year in which it was paid or in the year it accrued, depending upon the method of tax accounting used by the taxpayer'. She also discusses contested taxes, for which a credit 'may not be claimed until the contest is settled … the contested tax is then related back to the taxable year for which the foreign tax was in dispute and credited against the United States tax for that year').
787. Rust, *Credit Method, Klaus Vogel on Double Taxation Conventions*, at m.no. 49 (this is described as 'the period in respect of which foreign tax should be allowed as a credit'. Difficulties can arise if, for example, prepayments of taxes are required or where 'tax on income for a current year is calculated with reference to the income figure established for the preceding year' (original emphasis omitted). Similar issues are reiterated below under the discussion of timing issues under the indirect credit).
788. Andersen, *Foreign Tax Credits*, at *supra* note 756.
789. *Id.*, at 5.03[6][b] (discussing Section 909). For more on Section 909, *see*, e.g., US, Internal Revenue Service, *Foreign Tax Credit Guidance under Section 909 Related to Foreign-Initiated Adjustments*, Notice 2016-52, https://www.irs.gov/pub/irs-drop/n-16-52.pdf (according to the US IRS, 'section 909 … is intended to prevent the separation of creditable foreign taxes from related income' and it prevent this 'generally by deferring the right to claim credits until the related income is included in U.S. taxable income'. For example, 'Section 909(a) provides that, if there is a foreign tax credit splitting event with respect to a foreign income tax paid or accrued by a taxpayer, such tax will not be taken into account before the taxable year in which the related income is taken into account by the taxpayer.' *See also* Section 909(b) regarding 'a specified 10-percent owned foreign corporation' and Section 909(c) for its application to partnerships).
790. Blanluet & Durand, IFA, *Key Practical Issues*, at 44-46 (examples of timing issues include, e.g., the temporal gap between taxes levied on an accrual basis in one jurisdiction versus the time when the taxes are actually paid in the other jurisdiction, zero-coupon bonds taxed on an accrual basis versus the taxes actually paid only upon maturity, deferred taxation of capital

- procedural issues - e.g., proof, a redetermination mechanism	'Correction of Credits Previously Taken'[793] 'Administrative Requirements for Claiming Credit'[794] 'credit procedure'[795] 'Access to the Direct Credit':[796] 'Satisfaction of Tax Liability', including issues such as 'Proof of Payment' and 'Foreign Tax Redeterminations'

There were a few items on the lists of these authors that do not fall neatly within the above categories, which should be studied for the insight they bring here or for the distinctions they allow to be clarified. Owens also listed the 'Effect of Income Tax Treaties on the Credit', the 'Election of Credit', and finally the 'Indirect Credit Under Section 902 of the Code'. Rust in the Vogel Commentary also listed the 'Credit method complemented by domestic law' (at m.no. 47).

What Owens and Rust both draw attention to is the relationship between domestic law and tax treaties. As mentioned above, this is a crucial related issue. It will be invoked when analysing the CJEU neutralization line of case law (under Section 4.2.5.). While it does not change the fundamental questions that need to be answered (e.g., the question of which taxes should be eligible for the FTC), it can fundamentally alter how a given question is answered (e.g., it can expand the list of eligible taxes). In other words, this interaction is not a design component as such, but it must be kept in mind in the design process since the interaction between unilateral measures and bilateral measures has a direct impact on the ultimate scope or application of certain design components.

As regards the 'Election of Credit', this is rather a jurisdiction-specific issue: in the US, there are rules regarding whether a taxpayer may opt for either a credit or a deduction of foreign taxes from the tax base. Thus, it touches upon the relationship

gains due to roll-over relief versus immediate taxation of capital gains. 'In states such as Luxembourg, Malta or Portugal, if the foreign tax is paid before the foreign income becomes taxable in the residence state, the taxpayer has to wait until the foreign source income is recognized to credit the foreign tax. If the foreign tax is paid after the foreign income is recognized, the taxpayer is entitled within the established statutes of limitations to amend retroactively the corresponding tax returns. However, if the applicable statutes of limitations have expired at the time the foreign tax is paid or modified, the foreign tax can no longer be credited. It may, however, in certain cases be deducted as an expense in the year it is effectively incurred, as in Luxembourg').

791. *Id.*, at 46 ('For instance, in Venezuela, the taxpayer must compute the tax credit based on the exchange rate as of the date of payment of the foreign taxes. Therefore, a devaluation of the Venezuelan currency between the date of payment of the foreign taxes and the date of the filing of the tax return may adversely affect the taxpayer').
792. *Id.*, at 43–44.
793. Owens, *The Foreign Tax Credit*, at 4–15 (discussing the status of eligible taxes as paid or payable and the procedure for redetermination).
794. *Id.*
795. Rust, *Credit Method, Klaus Vogel on Double Taxation Conventions*, at m.no. 60.
796. Andersen, *Foreign Tax Credits*, at *supra* note 756.

between the credit method and other methods, another important issue which jurisdictions may have to consider but which is not strictly speaking a design feature of the credit method as such. Lastly, Owens mentions the 'Indirect Credit Under Section 902 of the Code', which brings its own additional design features, to which the discussion now turns.

As regards 'indirect' credits, the following additional considerations proved relevant:

- eligibility for an indirect FTC becomes a question of some form of ownership relationship, so this becomes an additional consideration for the scope of eligible taxpayers;
- the eligible distributions is an additional consideration since an indirect FTC may be available only for distributions of profits, usually dividends (as such income bore taxation at the level of the subsidiary, as opposed to deductible payments, such as interest) and potentially only for dividends distributed on certain types of shares, or possibly also for other specified types of income if such income is included or deemed distributed under other regimes such as CFC rules;
- the calculation presents additional considerations since it requires an apportionment fraction to determine the appropriate amount of underlying income taxes that can be attributed to the portion of profits distributed;
- timing issues present additional considerations since there are two taxable events that have to be reconciled in order for an indirect tax credit to function, i.e., the initial taxation levied on the profits generated by the subsidiary and the potential subsequent taxation when such profits are potentially later distributed or otherwise included in the income of the shareholder;
- the role of the type of corporate income taxation system (e.g., 'classical' versus integrated) is influential in determining how to answer some of the above questions.

From the above considerations (*see also* interim conclusions under Section 2.1.1.4. and Section 2.1.2.4.), the list of design features and questions for the 'indirect' credit could be organized as follows:

Indirect Credit **Additional Considerations**
Scope:

- **as regards eligible taxpayers**
  - type, e.g., individuals, corporations
  - relationship, e.g., required threshold of ownership (quantitative) and required type of ownership (qualitative, e.g., voting shares, etc.)

- **as regards the eligible distributions**
  - qualifying distributions of profits, such as dividends
  - classes of income deemed distributed to or included in income of shareholder

Operation:

- **as regards the figures to be used in the calculation,**
  - the 'gross-up', adding the deemed taxes to the dividends and including this total in the tax base
  - the 'apportionment fraction' (especially regarding the FSI represented in the denominator): (1) the content of the figure, e.g., accounting figure, taxable income, 'earnings and profits', and (2) as determined under which laws, the credit-granting state or the foreign state

- **as regards timing and other operational issues**
  - **annual determination** (per year) vs. **pooling approach** (aggregated over the years)
    - considerations: annual determination requires more detailed rules for tracing the distribution to the underlying profits and corresponding tax year ('attribution of dividends to annual profits of foreign corporation') and an 'annual calculation of the [indirect] tax credit' (e.g., Example No. 16, Option 2)
  - **a 'recording' mechanism**
    - by time, as mentioned above, e.g., annual determination or pooling approach
    - by type, e.g., category of income (e.g., active or passive), high-taxed income vs. low-taxed income, item-by-item
      - consideration: requires look-through rules
  - **an 'ordering rule'**
    - e.g., pro rata basis, a FIFO basis, a LIFO basis, a lowest-taxed-profits-out-first basis
      - consideration: possible incentives to strategically time the distribution of dividends to inflate the FTC
  - **the date of distribution of the dividends**
    - (i) attribute the dividend to the entire taxable year in which the dividends were paid, (ii) attribute the dividend to the accumulated profits up to the point of distribution, or (iii) attribute the dividend to the 'profits for the last full taxable year'
  - **in case of divergence of taxable years, verifying whether the foreign tax has been paid 'on or with respect to' profits of a given year**
  - **losses at the level of the subsidiary**
    - especially carryback or carryforward rules, based on credit-granting state rules or foreign state rules

- **the type of CIT system**
  - e.g., integrated corporate-shareholder taxation system vs. classical corporate-shareholder taxation system, which, in turn, leads to different perceptions as to how the credit is granted (e.g., either the credit is perceived as being passed up the corporate chain or the credit is calculated exclusively at the shareholder level) and as to what the answers to the above questions should be

As mentioned in Chapter 1, under the ATAD, EU MSs will have to grant an indirect credit in the case of CFC rules. These rules 'have the effect of re-attributing the income of a low-taxed controlled subsidiary to its parent company' and '[d]epending on the policy priorities of that State [the state of residence of the parent company], CFC rules may target an entire low-taxed subsidiary, specific categories of income or be limited to income which has artificially been diverted to the subsidiary'.[797] Thus, it is important to consider whether these rules raise any additional considerations. Key considerations are that, under CFC rules: (1) the scope of the indirect credit extends to other types of income (whichever income is covered by the CFC rules) and (2) the timing is shifted. Yet, both of these are largely variations on the themes above, calling upon adjustments to, for example, the 'recording' mechanism.

As regards the income, CFC rules often target only certain types of income, such as passive income and/or income that is low-taxed – i.e., income at greater risk of being diverted and improperly deferred from taxation in the shareholder state – thus adjusting the 'recording' mechanism accordingly and relying on 'look through' rules. As regards the timing, the indirect credit is generally offered only upon receipt of dividends, whereas the CFC rules involve a current attribution (or deemed distribution) of the targeted income. In some ways, this may simplify the timing considerations because, as CFC rules assume that the shareholder receives the income on an ongoing or annual basis, it eschews the need to trace dividends back to prior tax years. However, an additional timing consideration arises from the need to coordinate the two sets of rules at a later moment: when dividends are later distributed, there is the risk that the income has already been taxed in the hands of the shareholder under CFC rules and could potentially be taxed again as dividends in those same hands; thus, there should be rules to account for the income previously taxed under the CFC rules. According to the OECD, most jurisdictions that have CFC rules exclude or exempt the dividends to the extent that they stem from previously taxed income,[798] although the UK at one point used a credit mechanism for this purpose (*see infra* note 1877). This entails its own 'recording' mechanism, i.e., to record the income that has been previously included or previously deemed distributed and the income that has not been

797. Council Directive (EU) 2016/1164 of 12 July 2016 Laying Down Rules Against Tax Avoidance Practices that Directly Affect the Functioning of the Internal Market, OJ L 193, 1–14, preamble recital 12 (19 Jul. 2016).
798. OECD, *Designing Effective Controlled Foreign Company Rules, Action 3 – 2015 Final Report*, OECD/G20 Base Erosion and Profit Shifting Project, 68, para. 131 (OECD Publishing 2015).

included (e.g., because it was active business income, taxed at a sufficiently high rate). It also entails an 'ordering rule'; e.g., once a distribution is actually made, it may be treated as coming first out of the previously taxed income pool and then out of the remainder of the profits of the controlled foreign subsidiary.

Beyond these two points, though, as a general rule, the calculation of the amount of the indirect tax credit is - or should be - essentially the same. It relies on an apportionment fraction to calculate the amount of underlying taxes that are attributable to the income that is included at the level of, or deemed distributed to, the shareholder. Ideally, the figures used for the FSI should be the same. That is, if the rules for the indirect credit require, for example (and without prejudice to the other options), that the figure be the 'earnings and profits' of the foreign subsidiary calculated in accordance with the rules of the credit-granting state, the CFC rules would ideally require the same.[799]

On the debate as to whether this figure should be based on the rules of the credit-granting state or the subsidiary state (discussed in Section 2.1.1.3. and summarized in Section 2.1.1.4.), CFC rules bring in one additional argument. The rationale of CFC rules may call for the FSI to be recalculated under the laws of the credit-granting state where the shareholder resides. CFC rules tend to be based on an anti-diversion rationale, namely to prevent the inappropriate diversion of profits from the shareholder's state to the subsidiary's state merely to benefit from a lower tax rate and from the deferral of taxation that establishing a subsidiary generally allows.[800] In light of this, as the CFC rules assume that this income was improperly diverted and therefore should technically be income of the shareholder, and as income of the shareholder would have only been calculated according to the credit-granting state's rules, it would be coherent with this assumption to recalculate the income under the laws of the credit-granting state.

799. *See*, e.g., 47A C.J.S. Internal Revenue § 489 *Income from Sources Without United States – Foreign Tax Credit*, Westlaw (database updated January 2015) ('Earnings and profits generally are computed in the same manner for actual distributions as they are for subpart F inclusions').

800. For the rationale, or purpose, of the CFC rules as explained in case law of the CJEU, *see*, e.g., CJEU, Case C-196/04, *Cadbury Schweppes and Cadbury Schweppes Overseas*, 12 Sep. 2006, ECLI:EU:C:2006:544, at para. 26; CJEU, Case C-135/17, *X GmbH*, 26 Feb. 2019, ECLI:EU:C:2019:136, at para. 65 and at para. 67. For more in general on the purpose and design of CFC rules and the relationship with EU law, *see*, e.g., *CFC Legislation, Tax Treaties and EC Law* (Michael Lang et al. eds, Kluwer Law International 2004); Alexander Rust, *CFC Legislation and EC Law*, 36(11) Intertax 492 (2008); Christiana HJI Panayi, *Chapter 16: The ATAD's CFC Rule and Its Impact on the Existing Regimes of EU Member States, in The Implementation of Anti-BEPS Rules in the EU: A Comprehensive Study* 355 (Pasquale Pistone & Dennis Weber eds, IBFD 2018); Robert J. Danon, *Chapter 17: Some Observations on the Carve-Out Clause of Article 7(2)(a) of the ATAD with Regard to Third Countries, in The Implementation of Anti-BEPS Rules in the EU: A Comprehensive Study* 379 (Pasquale Pistone & Dennis Weber eds, IBFD 2018).

CHAPTER 3

EU Law and Direct Taxes

3.1. INDIRECT AND DIRECT TAXES IN THE INTERNAL MARKET

As is seen more vividly below when discussing the case law, one insightful aspect of studying the credit method in the EU law context is just how pointedly it targets the tension between the aim to establish an internal market and the sovereignty carefully guarded by EU MSs in the area of direct taxation. After the devastation of the two World Wars, what was clear at the time of the origins of the 'Communities', which over time morphed and expanded into the EU,[801] was a need for economic integration in hopes to ingrain incentives for stability and peace – to make war 'not merely unthinkable, but materially impossible', according to the famous Schuman Declaration of 9 May 1950.[802]

801. *See*, e.g., Marjaana Helminen, *Chapter 1: EU Tax Law as Part of the Legal System, in EU Tax Law: Direct Taxation* (IBFD 2018 ed. 2018) ('The founding treaties of the European Communities, i.e. the European Coal and Steel Community (ECSC), the European (Economic) Community (EEC, later EC), and the European Atomic Energy Community (Euratom), form the basis of EU law. These treaties are in force in the form as amended by the Treaty on European Union – i.e. the Treaty of Maastricht (signed in 1992; entered into force in 1993), the Treaty of Amsterdam (signed in 1997; entered into force in 1999), the Treaty of Nice (signed in 2001; entered into force in 2003) and the Treaty of Lisbon (signed in 2007; entered into force in 2009).[31] These treaties (i.e. the TEU and the TFEU) and the accession treaties of the new Member States are primary EU law'); European Parliament, European Parliamentary Research Service, Christian Salm, *Impact of the ECSC Common Assembly on the Politics, Negotiation and Content of the Rome Treaties*, PE 563.518 (March 2017).

802. European Union, The Schuman Declaration – 9 May 1950, EUROPA: Official Website of the European Union, https://europa.eu/european-union/about-eu/symbols/europe-day/schuman-declaration_en (last visited 19 Aug. 2018). *See also* Treaty Establishing the European Coal and Steel Community (ECSC Treaty), Document 11951K/TXT (Paris, 1951), 11, http://data.europa.eu/eli/treaty/ceca/sign (last visited 19 Aug. 2018) (the Treaty was signed in Paris in 1951 between Belgium, Germany, France, Italy, Luxembourg and the Netherland. Its preamble is entirely dedicated to considerations of peace through economic integration: 'CONSIDÉRANT que la paix mondiale ne peut être sauvegardée que par des efforts créateurs à la mesure des dangers qui la menacent; CONVAINCUS que la contribution qu'une Europe organisée et vivante peut apporter à la civilisation est indispensable au maintien des relations pacifiques; CONSCIENTS que l'Europe ne se construira que par des réalisations concrètes créant d'abord

What was not yet clear was the extent to which certain taxes would have an impact on this process. On the one hand, it was immediately apparent that customs duties, or import or export, and similar, taxes, that by definition are triggered at border-crossings would be a hindrance – all the more so given that the initial focus was on goods, i.e., a 'common market' for coal and steel.[803] On the other hand, income taxes, which are more personal in nature, seemed appropriately the remit of domestic tax policy and thus were presumably a less visible threat to economic exchanges.[804] Eventually, a distinction emerged between 'direct' and 'indirect' taxes,[805] which persists to this day in the Treaty on the Functioning of the European Union (TFEU) and renders legislative action at the EU level in the area of 'direct' taxes more challenging.

The TFEU contains explicit legal bases regarding customs duties (Article 28 and Article 30 TFEU) and taxes on products (Article 110 TFEU) and 'indirect taxes' (Article

---

une solidarité de fait, et par l'établissement de bases communes de développement économique; SOUCIEUX de concourir par l'expansion de leurs productions fondamentales au relèvement du niveau de vie et au progrès des œuvres de paix; RÉSOLUS à substituer aux rivalités séculaires une fusion de leurs intérêts essentiels, à fonder par l'instauration d'une communauté économique les premières assises d'une communauté plus large et plus profonde entre des peuples longtemps opposés par des divisions sanglantes, et à jeter les bases d'institutions capables d'orienter un destin désormais partagé, …').

803. *See also* Treaty Establishing the European Coal and Steel Community (ECSC Treaty), Document 11951K/TXT (Paris, 1951), Article 4, 16–17, http://data.europa.eu/eli/treaty/ceca/sign (last visited 19 Aug. 2018).

804. *See,* e.g., Peter J. Wattel, *Chapter 1: Introduction, in* 1 *Terra/Wattel European Tax Law* 3, 5 (Peter J. Wattel, Otto Marres & Hein Vermeulen eds, Wolters Kluwer 7th ed. 2019) ('Generally speaking, indirect taxes have been harmonized at EU level because they are conspicuous and direct obstacles to free trade […]'. 'Direct taxes, by contrast, are taxes on the income or wealth of (legal) persons, having a less direct and less visible effect on trade and services, although one may argue they distort trade just as much as transaction taxes […]'). For a slightly different view on the balance struck as regards direct taxes, *see,* e.g., Moris Lehner, *Limitation of the National Power of Taxation by the Fundamental Freedoms and Non-discrimination Clauses of the EC Treaty,* 9(1) EC Tax Rev. 5 (2000) ('This regulatory restraint is not due to an underestimation of the effects of direct taxes on an economic community, a common market or an internal market. Rather, the Treaty explicitly addresses the problem of direct taxes in a very important area, namely that of double taxation. However, this is done only sotto voce, in one of its last Articles (Art. 293), where it is something of an afterthought and overcautiously formulated in view of the importance of the problem. Double taxation is to be eliminated only "so far as is necessary", and only the Member States are addressed, not the bodies of the Community. A proviso in terms of a reservation of power favouring the Member States could not be more clearly formulated' (footnotes omitted)).

805. For the EU law definition of 'indirect taxation', *see,* e.g., Article 112 TFEU (it uses the language 'charges other than turnover taxes, excise duties and other forms of indirect taxation') and Article 113 TFEU (it uses the language 'turnover taxes, excise duties and other forms of indirect taxation'). *See also,* e.g., European Documentation, *Taxation in the Single Market,* 8–9 (Office for Official Publications of the European Communities 1990) ('"Direct taxation" refers to the taxes which are imposed directly on individuals or firms with the requirement that they transfer the corresponding amounts to the Treasury. It covers, for example, personal income tax, corporation tax, inheritance tax, etc. In the case of indirect taxation, the taxes are included in the price of goods or services and are therefore borne by the final consumer. However, it is the enterprise selling the goods or services which transfers the corresponding amount of tax to the Treasury. The person liable to pay the tax is not therefore the same as the person who bears the tax charge. The most common indirect taxes are VAT (value-added tax) and excise duties (special taxes on the consumption of certain goods such as tobacco, alcoholic beverages and mineral oils)').

113 TFEU) within its Chapter on 'Tax Provisions', whereas there is no explicit legal basis for other taxes, notably income (or direct) taxes. Instead, EU institutions searched for legal bases that could lend themselves to an interpretation that could be connected to income (direct) taxes within the TFEU. These are found in the TFEU's Chapter providing for an 'Approximation of Laws'. The main provision of this chapter (Article 114 TFEU) is dedicated to 'the achievement of the objectives set out in Article 26 [on the internal market]' and follows the 'ordinary legislative procedure' (decided by majority vote);[806] however, it explicitly excludes 'fiscal provisions' from its scope. The remaining possibilities for legal bases allow for EU action regarding issues that: (1) 'directly affect the establishment or functioning of the internal market' (Article 115 TFEU), (2) are 'distorting the conditions of competition in the internal market' (Article 116 and Article 117 TFEU), and (3) relate to 'the creation of European intellectual property rights' (Article 118 TFEU) – all of which have more circumscribed conditions and procedures for being enacted.

Thus far, when the EU has taken action in the domain of income taxes, it has relied on Article 115 TFEU. Three features of this article include that: it restricts the legal instruments that may be passed (only Directives, at the exclusion of regulations, decisions, recommendations and opinions),[807] it follows a 'special legislative procedure' (decided by unanimous vote), and acts taken on this basis (theoretically) must be justified 'as directly affect[ing] the establishment or functioning of the internal market'. Importantly, among the division of 'competences' between the Union and the MSs, the establishment of the internal market is designated as a 'shared' competence (as opposed to an exclusive competence of the Union).[808] In such cases, action at the level of the Union is further circumscribed by the principle of subsidiary[809] and the principle of proportionality.[810]

As a result, the customs union and value added tax are covered by Union legislation,[811] while comparatively little in the realm of income (direct) taxes is covered by Union legislation. The Directives with an impact on substantive income (direct) tax laws predominantly address very targeted issues of CIT, such as the elimination of WHTs on interest or on dividends, or the deferral of taxes on cross-border mergers and

806. For more details, *see* Article 289 and Article 294 TFEU.

807. For more on EU legal acts, *see* Article 288 TFEU.

808. For more details, *see* Treaty on European Union (TEU), Consolidated Version, Document C:2012:326:TOC, OJ C 326, 13–45, Article 5 (26 Oct. 2012) (hereinafter 'TEU'); Article 3–Article 6 TFEU.

809. Article 5(3) TEU ('Under the principle of subsidiarity, in areas which do not fall within its exclusive competence, the Union shall act only if and in so far as the objectives of the proposed action cannot be sufficiently achieved by the Member States, either at central level or at regional and local level, but can rather, by reason of the scale or effects of the proposed action, be better achieved at Union level').

810. Article 5(4) TEU ('Under the principle of proportionality, the content and form of Union action shall not exceed what is necessary to achieve the objectives of the Treaties').

811. For a consolidated version of the legislation that constitutes the customs union, *see* Regulation (EU) No. 952/2013 of the European Parliament and of the Council of 9 October 2013 Laying Down the Union Customs Code (recast), OJ L 269, 1–101 (10 Oct. 2013). For VAT, *see*, e.g., Council Directive 2006/112/EC of 28 November 2006 on the Common System of Value Added Tax, OJ L 347, 1–118 (11 Dec. 2006).

acquisitions, all under carefully prescribed conditions.[812] Otherwise, Directives focus on administrative/procedural matters, to facilitate the exchange of information and assistance in the collection of taxes (which has dramatically expanded in recent years, largely catalysed by the anti-BEPS initiatives) or to resolve disputes.[813] For now, this more piecemeal approach is inevitable since, rather than being able to act on a direct dedicated legal basis, a link to the internal market should be found and, even then, the increased risk arises that a proposal can be blocked by merely one MS, a seemingly not so uncommon phenomenon.[814] This is perhaps not surprising in a field for which (as the above has shown) the MSs have not yet agreed to include an explicit legal basis in the EU Treaties. Though, it can be noted that the concept of the internal market has readily adapted itself to the cause of legislation in the area of income (direct) taxes in those few instances where MSs decided they want to act.

As it plays such a key role, this concept of the 'internal market' is worth a brief exploration. In some version, it has appeared in all of the Treaties that have laid the foundations[815] for the EU. In the 1951 Treaty establishing the European Coal and Steel Community (*see supra* notes 801–802), the term 'common market' (*le marché commun*) was used and its legal requirements were laid down in Article 4. It legally required, within the Community, the abolishment and prohibition of:

> 'a) import and export duties, or taxes of equivalent effect, and quantitative restrictions on the circulation of products;
> b) measures or practices establishing discrimination between producers, between buyers or between users, notably in what concerns the conditions of price or the delivery and transport tariffs/fees, as well as measures or practices that create obstacles to the free choice by buyers of their suppliers;
> c) subventions or aids granted by the States or special charges imposed by them, in any form whatsoever;

812. *See*, e.g., *infra* note 829, note 830 and note 831.
813. *See*, e.g., *infra* note 834, note 835 and note 833.
814. *See*, e.g., European Commission, Proposal for a Council Directive on the Common System of Taxation Applicable to Parent Companies and Their Subsidiaries of Different Member States, COM(1969) 6 Final, OJ C 39, 7–9 (22 Mar. 1969); European Commission, Proposal for a Council Directive on the Common System of Taxation Applicable to Mergers, Divisions and Contributions of Assets Involving Companies of Different Member States, COM(1969) 5 Final, OJ C 39, 1–6 (22 Mar. 1969) (e.g., the initial proposals for the Parent-Subsidiary Directive and Merger Directives were issued in 1969 by the European Commission, but agreement could not be found on the Directives before 1990); European Commission, Proposal for a Council Directive Concerning the Harmonization of Systems of Company Taxation and of Withholding Taxes on Dividends, COM(75) 392 Final, OJ C 253, 2–8 (5 Nov. 1975) (this Directive was proposed by the Commission in 1975, but was ultimately rejected and withdrawn); European Commission, Proposal for a Council Directive on a Common Consolidated Corporate Tax Base (CCCTB), COM(2011) 121 Final (16 Mar. 2011) (this proposal was launched in 2011. Agreement was not found. It was recently relaunched in 2016. Agreement still has not been found).
815. *See*, e.g., European Union, Founding Treaties, EUR-Lex: Access to European Union Law, https://eur-lex.europa.eu/collection/eu-law/treaties/treaties-founding.html (last visited 18 Aug. 2018) (the official Europa EUR-lex website on European Union Law lists the following as 'founding treaties': Treaty Establishing the European Coal and Steel Community (1951); Treaty Establishing the European Atomic Energy Community (1957); Treaty Establishing the European Economic Community (1957); Treaty on European Union (1992)).

d) restrictive practices affecting the distribution or the exploitation of markets'.[816]

In the 1957 TEEC,[817] one of the two Treaties of Rome, the very first substantive article (following only Article 1 which officially established the European Economic Community (EEC)), began immediately with the aim of 'the establishment of a common market' and 'a progressive convergence, or approximation, of the economic policies of its Member States'.[818] To carry out these aims, it required, among others:

'a) the elimination, between Member States, of customs duties and quantitative restrictions upon entry and exit of merchandise, as well as all other measures of equivalent effect,
b) the establishment of a common customs tariff and a common commercial policy vis-a-vis third states,
c) the abolition, between Member States, of obstacles to the free circulation of persons, services and capital, [...]
f) the establishment of a regime ensuring that competition is not distorted in the common market, [...]
h) the convergence, or approximation, of national legislation to the extent necessary for the functioning of the common market'.[819]

---

816. Treaty Establishing the European Coal and Steel Community (ECSC Treaty), Document 11951K/TXT (Paris, 1951), Article 4, http://data.europa.eu/eli/treaty/ceca/sign (last visited 19 Aug. 2018) (author's translation from French).
817. Treaty Establishing the European Economic Community (TEEC), Document 11957E/TXT (Rome, 1957), http://data.europa.eu/eli/treaty/teec/sign (last visited 19 Aug. 2018) (concluded between Belgium, France, Italy, Luxembourg, the Netherlands and West Germany).
818. *Id.*, Article 2 ('La Communauté a pour mission, par l'établissement d'un marché commun et par le rapprochement progressif des politiques économiques des États membres, de promouvoir un développement harmonieux des activités économiques dans l'ensemble de la Communauté, une expansion continue et équilibrée, une stabilité accrue, un relèvement accéléré du niveau de vie, et des relations plus étroites entre les États qu'elle réunit.') (author's translation from French).
819. *Id.*, Article 3 ('*a*) l'élimination, entre les États membres, des droits de douane et des restrictions quantitatives à l'entrée et à la sortie des marchandises, ainsi que de toutes autres mesures d'effet équivalent,
b) l'établissement d'un tarif douanier commun et d'une politique commerciale commune envers les États tiers,
c) l'abolition, entre les États membres, des obstacles à la libre circulation des personnes, des services et des capitaux,
d) l'instauration d'une politique commune dans le domaine de l'agriculture,
e) l'instauration d'une politique commune dans le domaine des transports,
f) l'établissement d'un régime assurant que la concurrence n'est pas faussée dans le marché commun,
g) l'application de procédures permettant de coordonner les politiques économiques des États membres et de parer aux déséquilibres dans leurs balances des paiements,
h) le rapprochement des législations nationales dans la mesure nécessaire au fonctionnement du marché commun,
i) la création d'un Fonds social européen, en vue d'améliorer les possibilités d'emploi des travailleurs et de contribuer au relèvement de leur niveau de vie,
j) l'institution d'une Banque européenne d'investissement, destinée à faciliter l'expansion économique de la Communauté par la création de ressources nouvelles,
k) l'association des pays et territoires d'outre-mer, en vue d'accroître les échanges et de poursuivre en commun l'effort de développement économique et social') (author's translation from French).

Under the TEEC, the establishment of a common market was a carefully planned and monitored process, scheduled to occur in three distinct phases over a period of twelve years.[820] In the 1992 Treaty officially establishing the 'European Union', the 'internal market' was associated with similarly worded goals, of free movement and of undistorted competition, also based on a timetable.[821]

As for the current law, the TFEU gives insight into both what the internal market is (what it is comprised of) and what it is not (what is incompatible with it):

- As for the former, the TFEU states that '[t]he internal market shall comprise an area without internal frontiers in which the free movement of goods, persons, services and capital is ensured in accordance with the provisions of the Treaties' (Article 26(2) TFEU) and the subsequent articles set out more precisely how to achieve this 'free movement' 'in accordance with ... the Treaties'. In short, the 'free movement' provisions revolve around prohibition of discrimination and restrictions, as subsequent discussions of CJEU case law show.
- As for the latter (i.e., what is not in line with the internal market), the TFEU states that certain actions by 'undertakings' are incompatible with the internal market, namely 'all agreements between undertakings, decisions by associations of undertakings and concerted practices which may affect trade between Member States and which have as their object or effect the prevention, restriction or distortion of competition within the internal market'. This is followed by a list of examples of such practices (Article 101(1) TFEU) and 'abuse by one or more undertakings of a dominant position' (Article 102 TFEU). Moreover, certain actions by the MSs themselves are incompatible with the internal market, namely 'any aid granted by a Member State or through State resources in any form whatsoever which distorts or threatens to distort competition by favouring certain undertakings or the production of certain goods shall, in so far as it affects trade between Member States', commonly known as state aid (Article 107(1) TFEU).[822]

From the above, a few conclusions can be drawn. First, it is clear that from the origins that the founding goal was European economic integration, and this was first embodied by a common/internal market. Second, another reoccurring theme is that of

820. *Id.*, Article 8.

821. Treaty on European Union (TEU), Document 11992M/TXT (Maastricht, 1992), OJ C 191, 1–112 (29 Jul. 1992), http://data.europa.eu/eli/treaty/teu/sign (last visited 19 Aug. 2018) (the TEU was signed in Maastricht in 1992 by Belgium, Denmark, Germany, Greece, Spain, France, Ireland, Italy, Luxembourg, the Netherlands, Portugal, and the UK. Regarding the term 'internal market', it states: 'an internal market characterized by the abolition, as between Member States, of obstacles to the free movement of goods, persons, services and capital; [...] a system ensuring that competition in the internal market is not distorted; [...] the approximation of the laws of Member States to the extent required for the functioning of the common market').

822. *See also* Treaty Establishing the European Economic Community (TEEC), Document 11957E/TXT (Rome, 1957), Articles 85 et seq. and Article 92, http://data.europa.eu/eli/treaty/teec/sign (last visited 19 Aug. 2018) (these rules were already present in the 1957 Treaty).

a step-by-step, progressive process of integration, unfolding in phases. As will be seen below, the CJEU translates this idea into the phrase 'in the current state of EU law', thereby acknowledging that it can evolve. Third, although the terminology has slightly differed (from 'common market' to 'internal market' and even 'single market'), the concept seems to have continuously revolved around two general components:

(1) removing barriers to cross-border movements, by means of a customs union, by means of free circulation, by means of prohibiting certain restrictions and especially discriminatory treatment, etc.; and
(2) free and fair competition undistorted by states (e.g., protectionist measures of states, state aid) and market actors (e.g., manipulating prices, abuse of dominant market position).[823]

In what follows, an analysis of 'Positive Integration and Direct Taxes' in Section 3.2. reveals how these two components of the internal market have been invoked to address concerns of double taxation and (double) non-taxation.

Having made a basic sketch of the internal market, the foundations are laid to further explore the relationship between EU law and income (direct) taxes. Two key distinctions become inevitable here, namely that: (1) between primary and secondary EU law and (2) between 'positive' and 'negative' integration. The term 'primary EU law' is used to refer to the primary source of law on which the EU is based, namely the founding Treaties, currently the Treaty on European Union (TEU) and the TFEU.[824] The term 'secondary EU law' is used to refer to legislative acts passed by the EU institutions on the basis of the articles of primary EU law, namely regulations, Directives, among others.[825] The terms 'secondary' and 'primary' also indicate the legal hierarchy, namely that primary EU law takes precedence; secondary EU law must be passed and implemented in line with provisions of the EU Treaties. Based on these laws, the goal of further EU integration is described as occurring in, generally, two ways. First, MSs take positive steps towards further integration, under the auspices of the EU institutions and on the basis of the Treaties, by enacting secondary legislation – i.e., 'positive

823. *See also*, e.g., Peter J. Wattel, *Chapter 1: Introduction, in* 1 *Terra/Wattel European Tax Law* 3, 3 (Peter J. Wattel, Otto Marres & Hein Vermeulen eds, Wolters Kluwer 7th ed. 2019) ('An internal European market having the characteristics of a national market requires, in particular, free movement of goods, services, persons and capital irrespective of national borders (Art. 26(2) TFEU), undistorted conditions of competition within that EU market (the so-called "level playing field"; Arts. 101-109 TFEU), as well as harmonization of national laws insofar as disparities between national laws impede the functioning of the internal market (Art. 114 TFEU)').
824. *See* European Union, Summaries of EU Legislation, Glossary of Summaries, EUR-Lex: Access to European Union Law, https://eur-lex.europa.eu/summary/glossary/community_law.html (last visited 11 May 2019) (*see* the entry for 'EU law' distinguishing between 'primary' and 'secondary' law). *See supra* note 58 (citing the TFEU), note 801, note 808 and note 821 (citing the TEU).
825. *See* Article 288 TFEU.

integration', also referred to as 'policy integration'.[826] Second, MSs may have to remove, change or simply disapply certain national laws in cases where they do not comply with EU law, as a result of decisions by the CJEU or by the EU Commission – i.e., 'negative integration', also referred to as 'market integration'.[827] With these distinctions in mind, the next sections overview the relationship between EU law and income (direct) taxes in the process of positive integration, before turning to its development in the process of negative integration.

3.2. POSITIVE INTEGRATION AND DIRECT TAXES

As mentioned, due to the lack of an explicit legal basis in the Treaties for approximating laws on income (direct) taxes, the EU institutions and MSs have relied on Article 115 TFEU[828] as an implicit legal basis that allows the approximation of laws, etc., 'as directly affect the establishment or functioning of the internal market'. Thus, the concept of the 'internal market' has been employed in order to establish a legal basis for Directives in this field. This section overviews the link made between the internal market and income (direct) taxes and detects patterns in the evolution of secondary EU law on this point. To do so, it categorizes the Directives according to their function and aim, followed by some observations on how and where the internal market concept appears.

As a starting point, the Directives under the category of 'direct taxation', according to the EUR-lex search of the official website of the EU, are the following:

- Council Directive 2011/96/EU of 30 November 2011 on the common system of taxation applicable in the case of parent companies and subsidiaries of different Member States (the Parent-Subsidiary Directive);[829]

826. *See*, e.g., Ben J.M. Terra & Peter J. Wattel, *European Tax Law* 36, Section 3.1.2 (Wolters Kluwer 6th ed. 2012); Peter J. Wattel, *Chapter 1: Introduction*, *in* 1 *Terra/Wattel European Tax Law* 3, 5 (Peter J. Wattel, Otto Marres & Hein Vermeulen eds, Wolters Kluwer 7th ed. 2019).

827. *See*, e.g., Ben J.M. Terra & Peter J. Wattel, *European Tax Law* 36, Section 3.1.2 (Wolters Kluwer 6th ed. 2012); Peter J. Wattel, *Chapter 1: Introduction*, *in* 1 *Terra/Wattel European Tax Law* 3, 5 (Peter J. Wattel, Otto Marres & Hein Vermeulen eds, Wolters Kluwer 7th ed. 2019).

828. Each directive cited below lists Article 115 TFEU (or its predecessors) as its legal basis.

829. In chronological order, *see* European Commission, Proposal for a Council Directive on the Common System of Taxation Applicable to Parent Companies and Their Subsidiaries of Different Member States, COM(1969) 6 Final, OJ C 39, 7–9 (22 Mar. 1969); Council Directive 90/435/EEC of 23 July 1990 on the Common System of Taxation Applicable in the Case of Parent Companies and Subsidiaries of Different Member States, OJ L 225, 6–9 (20 Aug. 1990); Council Directive 2003/123/EC of 22 December 2003 Amending Directive 90/435/EEC on the Common System of Taxation Applicable in the Case of Parent Companies and Subsidiaries of Different Member States, OJ L 7, 41–44 (13 Jan. 2004); Council Directive 2011/96/EU of 30 November 2011 on the Common System of Taxation Applicable in the Case of Parent Companies and Subsidiaries of Different Member States, OJ L 345, 8–16 (29 Dec. 2011) (the version currently in force); Council Directive 2014/86/EU of 8 July 2014 amending Directive 2011/96/EU on the Common System of Taxation Applicable in the Case of Parent Companies and Subsidiaries of Different Member States, OJ L 219, 40–41 (25 Jul. 2014) (amended to prevent the Directive from leading to 'situations of double non-taxation' by adding an anti-hybrid payment rule); Council Directive (EU) 2015/121 of 27 January 2015 Amending Directive 2011/96/EU on the Common System of Taxation Applicable in the Case of Parent

- Council Directive 2003/49/EC of 3 June 2003 on a common system of taxation applicable to interest and royalty payments made between associated companies of different Member States (the Interest-Royalty Directive);[830]
- Council Directive 2009/133/EC of 19 October 2009 on the common system of taxation applicable to mergers, divisions, partial divisions, transfers of assets and exchanges of shares concerning companies of different Member States and to the transfer of the registered office of an SE or SCE between Member States (the Merger Directive);[831]
- The Savings Directive, which is now repealed; and[832]
- Council Directive (EU) 2017/1852 of 10 October 2017 on tax dispute resolution mechanisms in the European Union (the Tax Dispute Resolution Directive).[833]

The list of Directives under the category of 'direct taxation' and the 'prevention of tax evasion and avoidance' expands to include the following:

- Council Directive 2011/16/EU of 15 February 2011 on administrative cooperation in the field of taxation and repealing Directive 77/799/EEC,[834] which has been amended multiple times[835] since 2014 as a result of various anti-BEPS initiatives (the Administrative Cooperation Directive).

Companies and Subsidiaries of Different Member States, OJ L 21, 1–3 (28 Jan. 2015) (amended to include a 'common minimum anti-abuse rule').

830. *See* Council Directive 2003/49/EC of 3 June 2003 on a Common System of Taxation Applicable to Interest and Royalty Payments Made Between Associated Companies of Different Member States, OJ L 157, 49–54 (26 Jun. 2003).

831. In chronological order, *see* European Commission, Proposal for a Council Directive on the Common System of Taxation Applicable to Mergers, Divisions and Contributions of Assets Involving Companies of Different Member States, COM(1969) 5 Final, OJ C 39, 1–6 (22 Mar. 1969); Council Directive 90/434/EEC of 23 July 1990 on the Common System of Taxation Applicable to Mergers, Divisions, Transfers of Assets and Exchanges of Shares Concerning Companies of Different Member States, OJ L 225, 1–5 (20 Aug. 1990); Council Directive 2005/19/EC of 17 February 2005 Amending Directive 90/434/EEC 1990 on the Common System of Taxation Applicable to Mergers, Divisions, Transfers of Assets and Exchanges of Shares Concerning Companies of Different Member States, OJ L 58, 19–27 (4 Mar. 2005); Council Directive 2009/133/EC of 19 October 2009 on the Common System of Taxation Applicable to Mergers, Divisions, Partial Divisions, Transfers of Assets and Exchanges of Shares Concerning Companies of Different Member States and to the Transfer of the Registered Office of an SE or SCE Between Member States, OJ L 310, 34–46 (25 Nov. 2009) (the version currently in force).

832. Council Directive 2003/48/EC of 3 June 2003 on Taxation of Savings Income in the Form of Interest Payments, OJ L 157, 38–48 (26 Jun. 2003); Council Directive (EU) 2015/2060 of 10 November 2015 Repealing Directive 2003/48/EC on Taxation of Savings Income in the Form of Interest Payments, OJ L 301, 1–4 (18 Nov. 2015).

833. Council Directive (EU) 2017/1852 of 10 October 2017 on Tax Dispute Resolution Mechanisms in the European Union, OJ L 265, 1–14 (14 Oct. 2017).

834. In chronological order, Council Directive 77/799/EEC of 19 December 1977 Concerning Mutual Assistance by the Competent Authorities of the Member States in the Field of Direct Taxation, OJ L 336, 15–20 (27 Dec. 1977); Council Directive 2011/16/EU of 15 February 2011 on Administrative Cooperation in the Field of Taxation and Repealing Directive 77/799/EEC, OJ L 64, 1–12 (11 Mar. 2011) (the version currently in force).

835. Council Directive 2014/107/EU of 9 December 2014 Amending Directive 2011/16/EU as Regards Mandatory Automatic Exchange of Information in the Field of Taxation, OJ L 359, 1–29 (16 Dec. 2014) (implementing the 'automatic exchange of financial account information');

- Council Directive (EU) 2016/1164 of 12 July 2016 laying down rules against tax avoidance practices that directly affect the functioning of the internal market (the ATAD I).[836]
- Council Directive (EU) 2017/952 of 29 May 2017 amending Directive (EU) 2016/1164 as regards hybrid mismatches with third countries (the ATAD II).[837]

As it is closely related, Convention 90/436/EEC on the elimination of double taxation in connection with the adjustment of profits of associated enterprises (the Arbitration Convention) should also be mentioned.[838] As the title indicates, it is not a directive or other EU law instrument, but a convention that the MSs negotiated and concluded outside of (or perhaps alongside) the EU Treaties.[839] However, it should be noted that the aforementioned Tax Dispute Resolution Directive aims at directly building upon and improving this mechanism.[840]

Council Directive (EU) 2015/2376 of 8 December 2015 Amending Directive 2011/16/EU as Regards Mandatory Automatic Exchange of Information in the Field of Taxation, OJ L 332, 1–10 (18 Dec. 2015) (implementing the 'exchange of advance cross-border rulings and advance pricing arrangements'); Council Directive (EU) 2016/881 of 25 May 2016 Amending Directive 2011/16/EU as Regards Mandatory Automatic Exchange of Information in the Field of Taxation, OJ L 146, 8–21 (3 Jun. 2016) (implementing country-by-country reports); Council Directive (EU) 2016/2258 of 6 December 2016 Amending Directive 2011/16/EU as Regards Access to Anti-Money-Laundering Information by Tax Authorities, OJ L 342, 1–3 (16 Dec. 2016); Council Directive (EU) 2018/822 of 25 May 2018 Amending Directive 2011/16/EU as Regards Mandatory Automatic Exchange of Information in the Field of Taxation in Relation to Reportable Cross-Border Arrangements, OJ L 139, 1–13 (5 Jun. 2018).

836. Council Directive (EU) 2016/1164 of 12 July 2016 Laying Down Rules Against Tax Avoidance Practices that Directly Affect the Functioning of the Internal Market, OJ L 193, 1–14 (19 Jul. 2016).
837. Council Directive (EU) 2017/952 of 29 May 2017 Amending Directive (EU) 2016/1164 as Regards Hybrid Mismatches with Third Countries, OJ L 144, 1–11 (7 Jun. 2017).
838. Convention on the Elimination of Double Taxation in Connection with the Adjustment of Profits of Associated Enterprises, 90/463/EEC, OJ L 225, 10–24 (20 Aug. 1990).
839. *Id.* (although it is an independent convention, and not an EU law instrument under Article 288 TFEU, it was concluded with the following stated aim: 'desiring to give effect to Article 220 of that Treaty [the Treaty establishing the European Economic Community], by virtue of which they have undertaken to enter into negotiations with one another with a view to securing for the benefit of their nationals the elimination of double taxation').
840. Council Directive (EU) 2017/1852 of 10 October 2017 on Tax Dispute Resolution Mechanisms in the European Union, OJ L 265, 1–14, preamble recital 7 (14 Oct. 2017) ('The improved dispute resolution mechanism should build on existing systems in the Union, including the Union Arbitration Convention'). *See also*, e.g., Pasquale Pistone, *Chapter 8: The Settlement of Cross-Border Tax Disputes in the European Union in* 1 *Terra/Wattel European Tax Law* 331, 332 (Peter J. Wattel, Otto Marres & Hein Vermeulen eds, Wolters Kluwer 7th ed. 2019) ('Much has changed ever since, and for the good, giving the affected taxpayer up to four options for requesting the settlement of cross-border tax disputes within the European Union.[2] [...] In particular, they are the dispute resolution mechanisms applicable under Article 25 of the OECD Model,[3] the ones included as minimum standard (Part V) and with optional nature (Part VI) in the BEPS Multilateral Instrument (hereinafter also: BEPS MLI),[4] the EU Multilateral Arbitration Convention signed on 23 July 1990[5] and the EU Tax Arbitration Directive of 10 October 2017[6]') and at 338 ('The 2017 EU Tax Arbitration Directive does not repeal the EU Tax Arbitration Convention, but supplements it in a way that produces some partial overlaps – namely for cross-border transfer pricing disputes – and thus increases the complexity in the options available to the affected taxpayer(s). In areas falling within the scope of the EU Arbitration

As a preliminary observation, the results of this search reflect a shift in the policy of the EU. As regards earlier Directives (and the convention), the predominant focus was the elimination of double taxation. Most recent Directives appear under the category of 'prevention of tax evasion and avoidance', with the exception of Tax Dispute Resolution Directive. According to the dates of the latter Directives, they have all been enacted (or replaced and dramatically updated)[841] since the 2008–2009 financial crisis and most since 2014.

Another observation is that the Directives can be categorized into those that affect substantive tax law provisions in the MSs (e.g., the Parent-Subsidiary Directive, the Merger Directive, the Interest-Royalty Directive, and the ATAD) and those that affect procedural aspects of tax law (e.g., the Administrative Cooperation Directive and the Tax Dispute Resolution Directive, which now overlaps with and seeks to improve the, again though not a directive, Arbitration Convention).[842] Thus, there are two axes that intersect: their legal nature (substantive versus procedural) and their aim (to prevent barriers/double taxation versus to prevent avoidance/evasion).

Whether a directive is substantive or is procedural, as well as whether it aims to reduce double taxation or to combat tax evasion and avoidance, has an impact on how it was justified in the name of the internal market:

- In the category of Directives that affect the substance of tax laws with an aim to reduce double taxation or remove barriers are the Parent-Subsidiary Directive, the Merger Directive and the Interest-Royalty Directive.
- In the category of Directives that affect procedures with an aim to combat tax evasion and avoidance are the Directives concerning mutual assistance and the exchange of information.
- In the category of Directives that affect procedure with an aim to reduce double taxation is the Tax Dispute Resolution Directive.
- In the category of Directives that affect the substance of tax law with an aim to combat tax evasion and avoidance are the two ATADs.

A study of the preambles in these different categories of Directives reveals some trends as to how issues of income (direct) taxation are tied to the internal market.[843] In

Convention and Directive, associated enterprises are free to choose between the two legal instruments and bear the consequences arising in connection with their decision') and at 336 (citing Article 20 of the Convention, described as a 'sunset' clause); Jean-Philippe Van West & Christiane Zöhrer, *The EU Arbitration Convention and Directive*, *in Introduction to European Tax Law on Direct Taxation* 311 (Michael Lang et al. eds, Linde 5th ed. 2018).

841. In the case of the Administrative Cooperation Directive, to be precise, the first instance of administrative cooperation dates back to 1977, but since 2011 it has been repealed and replaced and even its replacement has been substantially amended and expanded.

842. *See supra* note 840.

843. On the relevance of the preambles, in general, *see*, e.g., Rita Szudoczky & Dennis Weber (update and elaboration of 6th ed.), *Chapter 2: Constitutional Foundations: EU Tax Competences; Treaty Basis for Tax Integration; Sources and Enactment of EU Tax Law*, *in* 1 *Terra/Wattel European Tax Law* 11, 33 (Peter J. Wattel, Otto Marres & Hein Vermeulen eds, Wolters Kluwer 7th ed. 2019) ('Legislative acts must be sufficiently reasoned and must refer to the proposals [...] (Article 296 TFEU).'); Marjaana Helminen, *Chapter 1: EU Tax Law as Part of*

the first category (substantive/double taxation), two points come into view. The Interest-Royalty Directive is the most straightforward, by immediately explaining that: '(1) In a Single Market having the characteristics of a domestic market, transactions between companies of different Member States should not be subject to less favourable tax conditions than those applicable to the same transactions carried out between companies of the same Member State' and emphasizes 'ensuring the equality of tax treatment as between national and cross-border transactions'.[844] The Parent-Subsidiary Directive and Merger Directive also mention similar concerns that 'existing tax provisions ... are generally less advantageous than those applicable to parent companies and subsidiaries of the same Member State'.[845] Thus, one first commonality that emerges clearly from all three is an underlying concern of different (worse) treatment or discrimination of the cross-border case as compared to the domestic case. In addition, the Parent-Subsidiary Directive and the Merger Directive note, with only slightly different wording, that 'existing tax provisions ... vary appreciably from one Member State to another'[846] and 'differences between these systems tend to produce distortions';[847] therefore, 'it is necessary to introduce with respect to such operations tax rules which are neutral from the point of view of competition'.[848] However, the Interest-Royalty Directive does not mention anything similar. Thus, one theme that emerges from two out of three is that of undistorted competition. In sum, these justifications resemble the two aforementioned components of the internal market that stem from the Treaties, namely: (1) free movement by removing certain restrictions, especially discrimination, and (2) free and fair competition by removing distortions.

In the second category (procedural/tax avoidance), the earliest of the Directives, the 1977 Mutual Assistance Directive, stated that the 'international nature of the problem [of tax evasion and tax avoidance] means that national measures, whose effect does not extend beyond national frontiers are insufficient' and therefore 'collaboration between administrations' is necessary. Such a statement would now seem more related to the principle of subsidiarity, though at that time it was not expressly stated as such.[849] As for the link between 'practices of tax evasion and tax avoidance' and the internal market, it warns that such practices 'are liable to bring about distortions of competition of capital movements and of conditions of competition' and

the Legal System, *in EU Tax Law: Direct Taxation* Section 1.8.1 (IBFD 2018 ed. 2018) ('The objectives of the EU founding treaties and the directives must be taken into account in EU law interpretation.' *See* CJEU case law references cited therein). For examples of the use of preambles for interpretation in CJEU cases, *see*, e.g., CJEU, 18 Sep. 2003, C-168/01, *Bosal*, ECLI:EU:C:2003:479, at para. 5, para. 22, para. 28; CJEU, Case C-498/10, *X NV*, 18 Oct. 2012, ECLI:EU:C:2012:635, at para. 45, para. 47.

844. Interest-Royalty Directive 2003, preamble recitals 1 and 4.
845. Parent-Subsidiary Directive 1990; Parent-Subsidiary Directive 2011, preamble recital 6. Similarly, *see* Merger Directive 1990; Merger Directive 2009, preamble recital 3; Interest-Royalty Directive 2003, preamble recital 1.
846. Parent-Subsidiary Directive 1990.
847. Merger Directive 1990.
848. *Id.*
849. For the origin and history of the principle of subsidiarity, *see*, e.g., European Parliament, *The Principle of Subsidiarity* (May 2018), http://www.europarl.europa.eu/factsheets/en/sheet/7/the-principle-of-subsidiarity (last visited 25 Aug. 2018).

'they therefore affect the operation of the common market'.[850] Although repealed, the Savings Directive was the next to fall in this category. This directive noted the problem that 'residents of Member States are currently often able to avoid any form of taxation in their Member State of residence on interest they receive in another Member State'[851] – an issue of non-taxation – and '[t]his situation is creating distortions in the capital movements between Member States, which are incompatible with the internal market'.[852] Thus far, at least in the earliest Directives, it seems that concerns over double taxation are linked predominantly to the removal of barriers (the first component of the internal market) and that concerns over tax evasion/avoidance are predominantly linked to distortions of competition (the second component of the internal market).

Both of these Directives have been repealed and, in their place, a much broader regime of administrative cooperation and exchange of information exists since the 2011 Administrative Cooperation Directive (as amended). In this preamble, the link is less clear; notably, its legal bases are both Article 115 TFEU and Article 113 TFEU, as it covers both direct and indirect taxes. It mentions numerous characteristics of, again, the global nature of the problem ('tremendous development of the mobility of taxpayers, of the number of cross-border transactions and of the internationalisation of financial instruments')[853] and for this reason 'it is indispensable to develop new administrative cooperation'.[854] As for the internal market, it simply states that:

> '[t]his increasing difficulty affects the functioning of taxation systems and entails double taxation, which itself incites tax fraud and tax evasion, while the powers of controls remain at national level. It thus jeopardises the functioning of the internal market'.[855]

Without phrasing it in language connected either with barriers/disadvantageous treatment or with distortions of competition, it implies that double taxation and tax fraud and evasion are *themselves* direct risks for the internal market.

In the third category (procedural/double taxation), the link is clearer. The Tax Dispute Resolution Directive claims that different interpretations or applications giving rise to disputes:

> 'can create serious tax obstacles for businesses operating across borders. They create an excessive tax burden for businesses, and are likely to cause economic distortions and inefficiencies and to have a negative impact on cross-border investment and growth'.[856]

850. Mutual Assistance Directive 1977, *supra* note 834 (to be precise, altogether in one line the recital of the preamble threw together 'budget losses' and 'violations of the principle of fair taxation' and that such practices 'are liable to bring about distortions of capital movements and of conditions of competition' and 'they therefore affect the operation of the common market'. The first two appear somewhat extraneous, without a clear basis in the Treaty at that time).
851. Savings Directive, preamble recital 5.
852. *Id.*, preamble recital 6.
853. Administrative Cooperation Directive, preamble recital 1.
854. *Id.*, preamble recital 2.
855. *Id.*, preamble recital 1.
856. Tax Dispute Resolution Directive, preamble recital 1.

In this way, it makes a clear connection with the removal of obstacles (not necessarily discriminatory ones, but obstacles as such) and distortions. It never explicitly uses the term 'internal market' in its justifications; instead, only later, at the stage of declaring itself 'in accordance with the principle of subsidiarity', the preamble considers it as given that this affects the 'proper functioning of the internal market'.[857]

In the fourth category (substantive/tax avoidance), the ATAD frames its justification with the need to prevent the fragmenting of the internal market and the need for coordinated action given the nature of the problem.[858] There are some echoes of the idea from the 1977 Mutual Assistance Directive, namely that the global reach of the problem requires global solutions; if MSs all act alone and in an uncoordinated fashion, it perversely leaves open, and potentially creates more of, the loopholes intended to be closed. This fourth category makes for a new unusual creature in the development of EU law in income (direct) taxation thus far.[859] First, some of its measures (e.g., exit taxes) will cover situations beyond those that involve evasion and avoidance (though, the most recent exchange of information amendments do this too). In particular, MSs are now concerned with the phenomenon of 'aggressive tax planning', which, even if legal, is seen as constituting unfair and distortive practices, available only to savvy MNEs. Second, by virtue of creating new tax rules – which expand rather than restrict taxation – the directive itself has the potential to create barriers (e.g., some MSs that have never had exit taxes will have to impose them in certain cases when taxpayers

857. *Id.*, preamble recital 10.

858. ATAD I, preamble recital 2 ('It is essential for the good functioning of the internal market that, as a minimum, Member States implement their commitments under BEPS and more broadly, take action to discourage tax avoidance practices and ensure fair and effective taxation in the Union in a sufficiently coherent and coordinated fashion. In a market of highly integrated economies, there is a need for common strategic approaches and coordinated action, to improve the functioning of the internal market and maximise the positive effects of the initiative against BEPS. Furthermore, only a common framework could prevent a fragmentation of the market and put an end to currently existing mismatches and market distortions').

859. Numerous authors have remarked various aspects of the novel nature of the ATAD. *See*, e.g., Pasquale Pistone, *European Tax Integration: The Need for a Traffic Light at the Crossroads of Law, Policy and Politics, in European Tax Integration: Law, Policy and Politics* (Pasquale Pistone ed., IBFD 2018), Online Books (last visited 6 Sep. 2018); Aloys Rigaut, *Anti-tax Avoidance Directive (2016/1164): New EU Policy Horizons*, 56(11) Eur. Tax'n 497, 497 (2016) (this article, written by a representative of the Council of the European Union, declares the ATAD as 'a defining moment for EU tax policy' which 'represents a new building block of EU tax policy and opens up a number of new horizons'); Daniel Gutmann et al., *The Impact of the ATAD on Domestic Systems: A Comparative Survey*, 57(1) Eur. Tax'n 2, 2 (2017) (these authors discuss the unique nature of the ATAD, stating that it 'represents a turning point in the history of EU tax legislation'. 'The historical importance of the ATAD is not only attributable to the fact that it lays down rules of substantive law that go far beyond the reach of existing directives in the field of direct taxation (which, in short, are mainly aimed at eliminating tax surcharges that adversely affect the functioning of the internal market). The ATAD's importance is also due to its very broad scope, which is defined in article 1' since 'even purely domestic situations might fall within the scope ...'); The 2014 amendment to the Parent-Subsidiary Directive was perhaps a first warning sign or step in this direction. *See*, e.g., Werner Haslehner, *Anti-hybrid Measures in the Parent Subsidiary Directive and the EU's Competence to Harmonise*, Kluwer International Tax Blog (31 Aug. 2015), http://kluwertaxblog.com/2015/08/31/anti-hybrid-measures-in-the-parent-subsidiary-directive-and-the-eus-competence-to-harmonise/ (last visited 20 Aug. 2018).

leave or some that have never had CFC rules will have to implement them for the first time). This underscores the need for its insistence in recital (5) that 'the rules should not only aim to counter tax avoidance practices but also avoid creating other obstacles to the market, such as double taxation'. And this is where the credit method (as well as dispute resolution and coordination) plays a role.

In the area of positive integration in income (direct) taxation, legislative action predominantly revolves around the elimination of double taxation or the prevention of tax evasion and avoidance, or going even further, income going untaxed for unintended or undesirable reasons such as aggressive tax planning. Regarding the legal basis, from the above, it can be seen that the link with the internal market does not have to be very explicit. In various ways, both double taxation and various forms of undesirable no/low taxation have been linked to the internal market, either because they create barriers or distort competition (thus framed using language found in the Treaties) or simply because double taxation and tax evasion or avoidance were deemed problems in their own right for the internal market. Evidently, whenever the MSs decide to act unanimously together to pass EU legislation, room to manoeuvre in creating this link has been accepted.[860] As will be discussed below, this malleability that manifests itself in this process of *positive* integration is much more constrained in the process of *negative* integration.

3.3. NEGATIVE INTEGRATION AND DIRECT TAXES

Transitioning from the 'internal market' concept in secondary EU law (e.g., in the Directives), this section briefly turns to its role in primary EU law (e.g., in the interpretation of the Treaties). Because secondary EU law is more difficult to pass in the field of direct taxation (i.e., due to the aforementioned unanimity requirement), the CJEU has played an important role - hence, the oft-cited distinction between 'positive integration' (by MSs acting together to pass legislation) versus 'negative integration' (by striking down incompatible national laws, usually as a result of the CJEU's interpretation).[861]

The CJEU can be described as a unique and powerful judicial institution. Its uniqueness stems from the 'sui generis' nature of the supranational legal order of the EU itself,[862] of which it is an integral part. Its power, or influence, stems from its

860. For more on the CJEU's reluctance to challenge Directives, *see*, e.g., Rita Szudoczky, *The Sources of EU Law and Their Relationships: Lessons for the Field of Taxation* (32 Doctoral Series, IBFD 2014).

861. *See*, e.g., Peter J. Wattel, *Chapter 1: Introduction*, *in* 1 *Terra/Wattel European Tax Law* 3, 5 (Peter J. Wattel, Otto Marres & Hein Vermeulen eds, Wolters Kluwer 7th ed. 2019) (discussing the more 'modest' role of 'Positive integration' for direct taxes, as compared to indirect taxes; '... most of the integration of direct taxes is a result of prohibitions, *i.e.* case law of the CJEU holding national tax measures incompatible with primary EU law').

862. *See*, e.g., CJEU, Case C-26/62, *Van Gend en Loos*, 5 Feb. 1963, ECLI:EU:C:1963:1 (according to the CJEU, the 'European Economic Community constitutes a new legal order of international law'. This landmark case established the 'direct effect' of EU, at that time EEC, law); CJEU, Case C-6/64, *Costa v. E.N.E.L.*, 15 Jul. 1964, ECLI:EU:C:1964:66 (phrases such as 'the EEC

position in the judicial hierarchy, from the precedence of EU law[863] and from the remedies in place for non-compliance with its decisions. What could be described as the 'judicial branch' of this supranational EU legal order is composed of the national courts and the CJEU, each with their defined roles.[864] The CJEU is the highest instance in the hierarchy for the interpretation of EU law, in order to ensure, within this union of diverse legal systems, a uniform interpretation of EU law.[865]

Two main ways in which questions of EU law reach the CJEU are via a preliminary ruling procedure (Article 267 TFEU) and an infringement procedure (Article 258 TFEU).[866] Under a preliminary ruling procedure, a domestic court of a MS may refer a question to the CJEU 'if it considers that a decision on the question is necessary to enable it to give judgment'.[867] In general, domestic courts have the option to refer a question, but domestic courts of final resort or last instance have the obligation to do so (exceptions being the doctrines of *acte clair* and *acte éclairé*).[868] This obligation aims to avoid contradictions between decisions deemed final and EU law, which could cause serious disruptions in a national legal system under doctrines of res judicata and could undermine the aim of a uniform interpretation of EU law.[869] The domestic court stays the proceedings while it awaits the decision of the CJEU on the

---

Treaty has created its own legal system' and 'its special and original nature' appear. This landmark case established the 'supremacy' or 'precedence' of EU law).

863. *See supra* note 862 (the combined effect of the *Van Gend en Loos* case and the *Costa v. E.N.E.L.* case was to establish the doctrines of the 'direct effect' and 'precedence' of EU law, which gave EU law power over national laws). *See also,* e.g., Rita Szudoczky, *How Does the European Court of Justice Treat Precedents in Its Case Law? Cartesio and Damseaux from a Different Perspective: Part I,* 37(6/7) Intertax 346, 347 (2009) (the fact that the CJEU has established such fundamental and far-reaching principles as 'direct effect' and 'precedence' via case law could be seen as evidence of its powerful role and its rule-making tendencies. According to Szudoczky, 'Case law has a great importance in EC law. It is commonplace that fundamental concepts of EC law, such as supremacy, direct effect, and Member States liability for damages caused to individuals by the breach of Community law, have all been developed by the ECJ in its case law instead of having been laid down by positive legal texts, such as the founding treaties of the EC. Having regard to the predominantly judicially developed character of EC law, [...]').
864. Article 19(1) TEU ('The Court of Justice of the European Union shall include the Court of Justice, the General Court and specialised courts. It shall ensure that in the interpretation and application of the Treaties the law is observed. Member States shall provide remedies sufficient to ensure effective legal protection in the fields covered by Union law').
865. *See,* e.g., CJEU, *Recommendations to National Courts and Tribunals in Relation to the Initiation of Preliminary Ruling Proceedings,* OJ C 257, 1–8, para. 1 (20 Jul. 2018).
866. *See,* e.g., CJEU, *Annual Report 2018: Judicial Activity* 11 (2019).
867. Article 267 TFEU.
868. *Id.*; CJEU, *Recommendations to National Courts and Tribunals in Relation to the Initiation of Preliminary Ruling Proceedings,* OJ C 257, 1–8, paras 3–6 (20 Jul. 2018). For a concise overview of *acte éclairé* and *acte clair, see,* e.g., Marjaana Helminen, *Chapter 1: EU Tax Law as Part of the Legal System, in EU Tax Law: Direct Taxation* Section 1.8.2 (IBFD 2018 ed. 2018).
869. CJEU, Case C-416/17, *Commission v. France (Précompte mobilier),* 4 Oct. 2018, ECLI:EU:C:2018:811, at paras 109–110; Opinion of AG Wathelet in Case C-416/17, *Commission v. France,* 25 Jul. 2018, ECLI:EU:C:2018:626, at para. 90 ('Comme l'a souligné l'avocat général Bot, le non-respect par les juridictions nationales dont les décisions ne sont pas susceptibles d'un recours juridictionnel de droit interne de leur obligation de renvoi conduit à priver la Cour de la mission fondamentale qui lui est assignée à l'article 19, paragraphe 1, premier alinéa, TUE, qui est d'assurer "le respect du droit dans l'interprétation et l'application des traités" (43)').

aspect of EU law relevant to the case before it.[870] The CJEU interprets the aspect of EU law in question and the domestic court is the one that actually applies the interpretation to the national measure and precise facts of the case.[871]

Under an infringement procedure, generally the Commission brings a complaint against a MS for laws or practices that it alleges are not complying with EU law. It is a multistage procedure, first beginning with exchanges of reasoned opinions between the Commission and the MS and, potentially, culminating in a case before the CJEU.[872] If it arrives before the CJEU, because it is the Commission bringing the complaint, the burden falls on the Commission to provide sufficient evidence and arguments to convince the CJEU of the infringement.

There are some notable differences between the two procedures. One is that, in an infringement procedure, there are no facts pertaining to a specific case to consider, as a result of the fact that the Commission brings a complaint about a law or practice in general, rather than, as under the preliminary ruling procedure, a domestic court posing a question on the basis of a specific case before it. This leads to another difference. Under an infringement procedure, the CJEU is essentially called upon to pronounce itself on the compatibility of that national law with EU law. By contrast, according to the CJEU, a 'preliminary ruling may be given upon the "interpretation of the Treaty"' but '[t]his provision gives the Court no jurisdiction either to apply the Treaty to a specific case or to decide upon the validity of a provision of domestic law in relation to the Treaty, as it would be possible for it to do under Article 169 [i.e. the infringement procedure]'.[873] Rather, the CJEU 'is competent to provide the national court with all criteria for the interpretation of [EU] law which may enable it to determine the issue of compatibility for the purposes of the decision in the case before it'.[874] In many cases, it seems to be a fine line (to the extent that the interpretation of the CJEU leaves little room for conclusions other than to deem the domestic law incompatible).

As regards the legal value, Article 91 of the official Rules of Procedure announces the 'binding nature of judgments and orders' which commences 'from the date of its delivery'.[875] If the interpretation of the CJEU leads to the ultimate result that a given

870. *See*, e.g., CJEU, *Recommendations to National Courts and Tribunals in Relation to the Initiation of Preliminary Ruling Proceedings*, OJ C 257, 1–8, para. 23 (20 Jul. 2018).
871. *Id.*, paras 8 and 11; CJEU, Case C-253/03, *CLT-UFA*, 23 Feb. 2006, ECLI:EU:C:2006:129, at paras 35–37.
872. Article 258 TFEU. *See also* Article 259 TFEU (for matters brought by MSs) and Article 260 TFEU (for possible penalties).
873. CJEU, Case C-6/64, *Costa v. E.N.E.L.*, 15 Jul. 1964, ECLI:EU:C:1964:66, at 592–593.
874. CJEU, Case C-55/94, *Gebhard*, 30 Nov. 1995, ECLI:EU:C:1995:411, at para. 19. *See also*, e.g., European Parliament, Jacques Malherbe, Philippe Malherbe, Isabelle Richelle, Edoardo Traversa, with the contribution of Daphné de Laveleye, *The Impact of the Rulings of the European Court of Justice in the Area of Direct Taxation 2010*, PE 457.367, IP/A/ECON/ST/2010-18, para. 19 (April 2011).
875. CJEU, *Consolidated Version of the Rules of Procedure of the Court of Justice of 25 September 2012* (1 May 2019), https://curia.europa.eu/jcms/jcms/Jo2_7031/en/ (last visited 10 Apr. 2019) (citing and consolidating the CJEU, *Rules of Procedure of the Court of Justice of 25 September 2012*, OJ L 265, 29 Sep. 2012, as amended on 18 Jun. 2013, OJ L 173, 65, 26 Jun. 2013, and on 19 Jul. 2016, OJ L 217, 69, 12 Aug. 2016, and on 9 Apr. 2019, OJ L 111, 73, 25 Apr. 2019).

national law is found to be contrary to the provision of EU law in question, then, due to the fact that EU law takes precedence, the consequence is that the contravening national law is essentially inapplicable. That is, a law on the books of a MS should cease to apply immediately, even without a formal repeal or amendment.[876] The question as to who is bound is not explicitly stated. While it can safely be assumed that the interpretation is binding on the domestic court that referred the question, i.e., binding *inter partes*, as held by the CJEU,[877] its binding effect on the courts or authorities of other EU MSs, e.g., whether cases constitute some form of 'precedent' as known in common law systems, has been debated.[878] Regardless of precisely how one characterizes it, the CJEU, the Commission, the Advocates General and the MSs recognize, or reason as though there is, a more widespread binding nature of the interpretations (by *inter alia* relying on their reasoning in past case law). For example, in a case related to the credit method (discussed in Section 4.2.8.), according to Advocate General (AG) Melchior Wathelet:

> '[...] the cases interpreted by the CJEU have a "generalised" effect within the legal order of the Union: once a provision of EU law has been interpreted by the CJEU, this interpretation applies to all jurisdictions. This interpretation specifies the meaning and the scope of the rule of Union law in question as the rule must be and

---

876. *See*, e.g., Opinion of AG Wathelet in Case C-628/15, *The Trustees of the BT Pension Scheme*, 21 Dec. 2016, ECLI:EU:C:2016:1002, at para. 84 ('It should be recalled at the outset that, in accordance with the principle of the primacy of EU law, provisions of the Treaties and directly applicable measures of the institutions have the effect, in their relations with the internal law of the Member States, merely by entering into force, of rendering automatically inapplicable any conflicting provision of national law') and at para. 85 ('As is apparent from consistent case-law, when faced with a rule of law that is incompatible with directly applicable EU law, the national court is required to disapply that national rule and to apply, among the various procedures of the internal legal order, those which are appropriate to safeguard the individual rights conferred by EU law'); CJEU, Case C-628/15, *The Trustees of the BT Pension Scheme*, 14 Sep. 2017, ECLI:EU:C:2017:687, at para. 49 (regarding the effect of FF to render national laws that are contrary 'inapplicable'), para. 50 (regarding the right to a refund), para. 54 ('Next, it must be recalled that, according to the settled case-law of the Court, both the administrative authorities and the national courts called upon, within the exercise of their respective jurisdiction, to apply provisions of EU law, are under a duty to give full effect to those provisions, if necessary refusing of their own motion to apply any conflicting provision of national law, and it is not necessary for that court to request or to await the prior setting aside of that provision of national law by legislative or other constitutional means (see, to that effect, in relation to administrative authorities, judgments of 22 June 1989, *Costanzo*, 103/88, EU:C:1989:256, paragraph 31, and of 29 April 1999, *Ciola*, C-224/97, EU:C:1999:212, paragraphs 26 and 30, and, in relation to courts, judgments of 9 March 1978, *Simmenthal*, 106/77, EU:C:1978:49, paragraph 24, and of 5 July 2016, *Ognyanov*, C-614/14, EU:C:2016:514, paragraph 34)'), and para. 56 (it is 'required to disapply the provisions of that legislation which is responsible for the treatment that is contrary to Article 63 TFEU, so as to give full effect to EU law').
877. *See*, e.g., European Parliament, European Parliamentary Research Service, Rafał Mańko, *Briefing: Preliminary Reference Procedure*, PE 608.628, 10–11 (July 2017) (citing *inter alia* the *Wünsche* case, at para. 13).
878. *Id.*; Rita Szudoczky, *How Does the European Court of Justice Treat Precedents in Its Case Law? Cartesio and Damseaux from a Different Perspective: Part I*, 37(6/7) Intertax 346, 347 (2009); Rita Szudoczky, *The Sources of EU Law and Their Relationships: Lessons for the Field of Taxation*, 26 (32 Doctoral Series, IBFD 2014).

should have always been understood and applied since the moment of its entry into force'.[879]

In this very case being commented by the AG, the Conseil d'État in France was held responsible in 2018 for its failure to refer a question to the CJEU under a preliminary ruling procedure, in part for failing to properly take into account the findings of a previous case from the UK decided in 2012 by the CJEU[880] in the Conseil d'État's process of deciding how to deal with a similar issue that arose in France.[881] In effect, the courts in France were expected to follow that previous decision. Other cases and rules invoked in support of the obligation to follow interpretations of the CJEU include *Da Costa*[882] and *Kühne & Heitz*[883] and the 'principle of sincere cooperation' under Article 4(3) TEU.[884] Moreover, the aforementioned 2012 and 2018 cases showcased concrete examples of the types of mechanisms in place to *enforce* EU law, including enforcement of previous interpretations of the CJEU, such as a 'claim for the repayment of the tax unduly levied (*San Giorgio* ...) or only a claim for damages (*Brasserie du Pêcheur and Factortame* ...)'.[885] As a result of the combination of these factors, the case law of the CJEU is undeniably an important source of EU law.[886]

In addition to the role of the CJEU, some general remarks can be made regarding the approach of the CJEU in its case law on direct (income) taxation (as it is relevant for Chapter 4). In these cases, the relevant EU law to comply with is nearly always the 'fundamental freedoms' of the TFEU,[887] namely the free movement of persons (Article 45 TFEU for workers and Article 49 TFEU for establishment), services (Article 56

879. Opinion of AG Wathelet in Case C-416/17, *Commission v. France*, 25 Jul. 2018, ECLI: EU:C:2018:626, at para. 92 (this is the author's own unofficial translation from French).
880. CJEU, Case C-35/11, *Test Claimants in the FII Group Litigation*, 13 Nov. 2012, ECLI: EU:C:2012:707.
881. CJEU, Case C-416/17, *Commission v. France (Précompte mobilier)*, 4 Oct. 2018, ECLI:EU: C:2018:811, at paras 100–114.
882. CJEU, Joined Cases C-28/62, C-29/62 and C-30/62, *Da Costa en Schaake NV, Jacob Meijer NV, Hoechst-Holland NV*, 27 Mar. 1963, ECLI:EU:C:1963:6.
883. CJEU, Case C-453/00, *Kühne & Heitz*, 13 Jan. 2004, ECLI:EU:C:2004:17.
884. *See*, e.g., European Parliament, European Parliamentary Research Service, Rafał Mańko, *Briefing: Preliminary Reference Procedure*, PE 608.628, 10–11 (July 2017); European Parliament, Jacques Malherbe, Philippe Malherbe, Isabelle Richelle, Edoardo Traversa, with the contribution of Daphné de Laveleye, *The Impact of the Rulings of the European Court of Justice in the Area of Direct Taxation 2010*, PE 457.367, IP/A/ECON/ST/2010-18, para. 19 (April 2011); Opinion of AG Wathelet in Case C-628/15, *The Trustees of the BT Pension Scheme*, 21 Dec. 2016, ECLI:EU:C:2016:1002, at paras 73, 84–85 (when discussing the consequences of a decision of the CJEU that a national provision is 'inconsistent' with EU law, the Advocate General makes reference to Article 4(3), the 'principle of sincere cooperation', and Article 19(1) TEU, the obligation 'to provide remedies sufficient to ensure effective legal protection', and mentions the need to 'disapply' the incompatible national provision); CJEU, Case C-628/15, *The Trustees of the BT Pension Scheme*, 14 Sep. 2017, ECLI:EU:C:2017:687, at para. 47 (regarding Article 4(3) TEU and Article 19 TEU).
885. CJEU, Case C-35/11, *Test Claimants in the FII Group Litigation*, 13 Nov. 2012, ECLI:EU: C:2012:707, at para. 35. For an overview, *see*, e.g., Marjaana Helminen, *Chapter 7: Legal Remedies, in EU Tax Law: Direct Taxation* (IBFD 2018 ed. 2018).
886. Rita Szudoczky, *The Sources of EU Law and Their Relationships: Lessons for the Field of Taxation*, 26 (32 Doctoral Series, IBFD 2014).
887. *See*, e.g., European Parliament, Jacques Malherbe, Philippe Malherbe, Isabelle Richelle, Edoardo Traversa, with the contribution of Daphné de Laveleye, *The Impact of the Rulings of*

TFEU), capital (Article 63 TFEU) and, albeit less common in direct taxation cases, goods (Article 28 TFEU). Free movement for essential factors of production is necessary for the EU's goal of creating an 'internal market' (Article 26 TFEU). Based on the wording of the articles, all are essentially specialized non-discrimination rules, calling for 'the abolition of any discrimination based on nationality' and prohibiting 'restrictions' on these free movements.[888] With this in mind, it is not difficult to imagine that taxes, which constitute a cost, and specifically those which more negatively affect cross-border movement as compared to a similar domestic scenario, may constitute obstacles to this free movement and, thus, the internal market.

In order to identify whether such obstacles are occurring, the CJEU's analysis generally follows a predictable pattern, assessing first whether a given case falls within the scope of EU law and which provision (e.g., which fundamental freedom) applies; second, whether there is a discrimination or restriction, often involving the comparability analysis; and finally, whether a justification for the discrimination/restriction can be accepted, including a proportionality analysis. These steps, and especially the precise role and placement of the comparability analysis,[889] are described in slightly different ways. For example, Wattel cites the *Gebhard* case for the CJEU's own general overview:

> 'It follows ... from the Court's case-law that national measures liable to hinder or make less attractive the exercise of fundamental freedoms guaranteed by the Treaty must fulfil four conditions: they must be applied in a non-discriminatory manner; they must be justified by imperative requirements in the general interest;

---

the European Court of Justice in the Area of Direct Taxation 2010, PE 457.367, IP/A/ECON/ST/2010-18, para. 22 (April 2011).

888. *See*, e.g., Article 45 TFEU ('2. Such freedom of movement shall entail the abolition of any discrimination based on nationality between workers of the Member States as regards employment, remuneration and other conditions of work and employment') and Article 49 ('Within the framework of the provisions set out below, restrictions on the freedom of establishment of nationals of a Member State in the territory of another Member State shall be prohibited [...]'). *See also*, e.g., Peter J. Wattel, *Chapter 3: General EU Law Concepts and Tax Law*, *in* 1 *Terra/Wattel European Tax Law* 39, 61 (Peter J. Wattel, Otto Marres & Hein Vermeulen eds, Wolters Kluwer 7th ed. 2019) ('The four freedoms (free movement of goods, services, persons and capital) encompass two basic rights: a right of cross-border circulation (market *access*, including the freedom to leave the State of departure unhindered) and a prohibition of discrimination on grounds of nationality or origin on the market (market *equality*)'); European Parliament, Jacques Malherbe, Philippe Malherbe, Isabelle Richelle, Edoardo Traversa, with the contribution of Daphné de Laveleye, *The Impact of the Rulings of the European Court of Justice in the Area of Direct Taxation 2010*, PE 457.367, IP/A/ECON/ST/2010-18, para. 24 (April 2011).
889. *See*, e.g., Peter J. Wattel, *Chapter 3: General EU Law Concepts and Tax Law*, *in* 1 *Terra/Wattel European Tax Law* 39, 75 (Peter J. Wattel, Otto Marres & Hein Vermeulen eds, Wolters Kluwer 7th ed. 2019); Rita Szudoczky, *The Sources of EU Law and Their Relationships: Lessons for the Field of Taxation*, 728–729 (32 Doctoral Series, IBFD 2014) (Szudoczky discusses the three main factors for comparability, and some of the inconsistencies and conceptual ambiguities); Opinion of AG Kokott in Case C-48/13, *Nordea Bank*, 13 Mar. 2014, ECLI:EU:C:2014:153, at paras 21–28 (Advocate General Kokott presents arguments for dispensing with the comparability analysis in future cases); Michael Lang, *Recent Case Law of the ECJ in Direct Taxation: Trends, Tensions and Contradictions*, 18(3) EC Tax Rev. 98 (2009).

> they must be suitable for securing the attainment of the objective which they pursue; and they must not go beyond what is necessary in order to attain it.'[890]

Wattel then specifies that '[f]or (direct) tax purposes, the Court's rule of reason may be summarized in a slightly different four-step test', or three-step test, if one combines the comparability steps. Although Wattel provides more details, including examples and debates, some excerpts to give the basic idea include:

> '(1a) A *prima facie* comparability test: does the national tax measure *prima facie* distinguish between cross-border investment/work/establishment and comparable domestic investment/establishment/work (resident/nonresident; emigrant/non-emigrant; domestic-source income/foreign-source income, etc.)? [...] If the measure falls foul of this test, the Court applies:
>
> (1b) A teleological comparability test: is there an objective difference between the cross-border and the internal case which explains the difference in tax treatment of the cross-border case? [...] It is true, however, that the Court is notorious for mixing up this step (objective comparability) and the next step (justifiability of the - discriminatory - measure); [...] If there still is a discrimination present, viewed in light of the aim of the national tax measure at issue, the Court applies:
>
> (2) A justification test: is there a mandatory requirement of public interest (a legitimate aim) justifying the discriminatory measure, *e.g.* curbing abuse, safeguarding tax base integrity, or ensuring effective fiscal supervision? If so, the Court applies:
>
> (3) A proportionality test: is the discriminatory, but justifiable tax measure effective (appropriateness subtest) and does it not restrict free movement beyond what is necessary to attain its legitimate aim (proportionality *stricto sensu*)?'[891]

Although only a basic overview, this lays some foundations for understanding which part of the CJEU's analysis is being referenced in subsequent discussions (in Chapter 4).

Crucially, the cases often begin with a well-known *competence-with-compliance* quotation[892] – that is, although the MSs retain sovereignty in the field of direct taxation,

890. CJEU, Case C-55/94, *Gebhard*, 30 Nov. 1995, ECLI:EU:C:1995:411, at para. 37; Peter J. Wattel, *Chapter 3: General EU Law Concepts and Tax Law*, *in* 1 *Terra/Wattel European Tax Law* 39, 74 (Peter J. Wattel, Otto Marres & Hein Vermeulen eds, Wolters Kluwer 7th ed. 2019).

891. Peter J. Wattel, *Chapter 3: General EU Law Concepts and Tax Law*, *in* 1 *Terra/Wattel European Tax Law* 39, 74 et seq. (Peter J. Wattel, Otto Marres & Hein Vermeulen eds, Wolters Kluwer 7th ed. 2019).

892. *See*, e.g., CJEU, Case C-270/83, *Commission v. France (Avoir Fiscal)*, 28 Jan. 1986, ECLI: EU:C:1986:37, at para. 24 (the CJEU contains a seed of this idea in its first case on income taxes where it declares that 'It must first be noted that the fact that the laws of the Member States on corporation tax have not been harmonized cannot justify the difference of treatment in this case. Although it is true that in the absence of such harmonization, a company's tax position depends on the national law applied to it, Article 52 of the EEC Treaty [freedom of establishment] prohibits the Member States from laying down in their laws conditions for the pursuit of activities by persons exercising their right of establishment which differ from those laid down for its own nationals'); CJEU, Case C-279/93, *Schumacker*, 14 Feb. 1995, ECLI:EU:C:1995:31, at para. 21 (the CJEU expresses the idea as 'Although, as Community law stands at present, direct taxation does not as such fall within the purview of the Community, the powers retained by the Member States must nevertheless be exercised consistently with Community law (see the judgment in Case C-246/89 Commission v United Kingdom [1991] ECR 1-4585, paragraph 12)',

they must exercise their power, or competence, in compliance with EU law. This recalls the main overarching compromise being balanced in this case law. Thus, what becomes apparent below in the analysis of the case law is the attempt of the CJEU to draw the line as to what it *can* accomplish and what it *cannot* accomplish in terms of furthering integration in the internal market by means of interpreting EU law, or negative integration, and where, instead, because of the division of competences in the EU, it falls upon the MSs to enact legislation, or positive integration (e.g., leading to distinctions between discrimination and disparities).

citing a case regarding fishing vessels for the source); CJEU, Case C-80/94, *Wielockx*, 11 Aug. 1995, ECLI:EU:C:1995:271, at para. 16 ('Although direct taxation falls within the competence of the Member States, the latter must none the less exercise that competence consistently with Community law and therefore avoid any overt or covert discrimination by reason of nationality'); CJEU, Case C-107/94, *Asscher*, 27 Jun. 1996, ECLI:EU:C:1996:251, at para. 36.

CHAPTER 4

The Credit Method under EU Law

4.1. THE CREDIT METHOD AND THE INTERNAL MARKET: DEBATES IN LITERATURE

At first glance, it may appear rather benign to state that the credit method - if properly designed - is one of the tools currently needed by EU MSs. It seems likely to become an increasingly present fixture in the post-BEPS/post-ATAD landscape (as discussed in Chapter 1). However, this statement could be (or have been) viewed as somewhat contentious in academic literature. This is because many tax law scholars, especially leading up to and around the turn of the century, were more closely scrutinizing the relationship between the methods to relieve double taxation and EU law, and the closely related concepts of residence and source.[893] To varying degrees, some questioned, or outright challenged,[894] the compatibility of the credit method with EU law, in

893. *See*, e.g., Peter J. Wattel, *Home Neutrality in an Internal Market*, 36(5) Eur. Tax'n 159 (1996); Paul Farmer, *EC Law and National Rules on Direct Taxation: A Phoney War?*, 7(1) EC Tax Rev. 13 (1998); Moris Lehner, *Limitation of the National Power of Taxation by the Fundamental Freedoms and Non-discrimination Clauses of the EC Treaty*, 9(1) EC Tax Rev. 5 (2000); Peter J. Wattel, *Progressive Taxation of Non-residents and Intra-EC Allocation of Personal Tax Allowances: Why Schumacker, Asscher, Gilly and Gschwind Do Not Suffice*, 40(6) Eur. Tax'n 210 (2000); John F. Avery Jones, *A Comment on 'Progressive Taxation of Non-residents and Intra-EC Allocation of Personal Tax Allowances'*, 40(8) Eur. Tax'n 375 (2000); Eric C.C.M. Kemmeren, *Principle of Origin in Tax Conventions: A Rethinking of Models* (Pijnenburg vormgevers.uitgevers 2001); Klaus Vogel, *Which Method Should the European Community Adopt for the Avoidance of Double Taxation?*, 56(1) Bull. Int'l Fiscal Documentation 4 (2002); Pasquale Pistone, *The Impact of Community Law on Tax Treaties: Issues and Solutions* 177–178, 197–201 (Kluwer Law International 2002); Ben J.M. Terra & Peter J. Wattel, *European Tax Law* 210–222 (Wolters Kluwer 6th ed. 2012); Otto Marres (update of 6th ed.), *Chapter 16: Division of Tax Jurisdiction; Double Tax Relief Mechanisms; Tax Treaty Issues*, in 1 *Terra/Wattel European Tax Law* 695, 698–709 (Peter J. Wattel, Otto Marres & Hein Vermeulen eds, Wolters Kluwer 7th ed. 2019).

894. *See*, e.g., Peter J. Wattel, *Home Neutrality in an Internal Market*, 36(5) Eur. Tax'n 159 (1996); Klaus Vogel, *Which Method Should the European Community Adopt for the Avoidance of Double Taxation?*, 56(1) Bull. Int'l Fiscal Documentation 4 (2002).

particular with the fundamental freedoms of the internal market. It is therefore only upon understanding prior debates regarding the relationship between EU law and the credit method that the above statement assumes any potential significance. Also, only then is it possible to discern any evolutions in the perceptions of and role of the credit method in the EU to date. For this reason, the aim of this section is to discuss the debates, analysing both the arguments and counterarguments, regarding the credit method in the EU.

The question 'Which Method Should the European Community Adopt for the Avoidance of Double Taxation?' was posed most directly by Klaus Vogel in 2002.[895] It was also Klaus Vogel along with Peter J. Wattel who, in answering this question, argued against the credit method.[896] Vogel wrote that applying the credit method, among EU MSs, was contrary to EU law. He predicted that this could 'lead to a verdict of the Court against the credit method'.[897] He implied that if the CJEU does *not* decide in this way, it is likely for political rather than legal reasons:

> 'Political considerations in solving such conflicts are not illegitimate for a constitutional court, which the European Court of Justice in fact is. Such courts always have to find a balance between applying the law as they see it and finding political acceptance of their decisions by their constituents. Therefore, there is little chance that the European Court of Justice will in the near future declare the credit method a violation of the rights of EU citizens.
>
> This does not necessarily mean that the credit method does not violate EC law. As was shown before, the credit method hampers investment, the provision of services and the taking up of employment in the other EU Member States, and there is no legal justification recognizable for these impediments.'[898]

To arrive at this conclusion, Vogel's reasoning in this article proceeded first with policy considerations before turning to the legal considerations. As regards the policy considerations, he explained a key difference between the credit method and the exemption method, which revolves around economic theories put forward by Richard

895. Klaus Vogel, *Which Method Should the European Community Adopt for the Avoidance of Double Taxation?*, 56(1) Bull. Int'l Fiscal Documentation 4 (2002) (in support of certain points, he cited *inter alia* Lehner, Jiménez, Kemmeren, and Kokott); Vogel also explored this topic in other works and publications, such as Klaus Vogel, *Should Europe Adopt a Uniform Method for the Avoidance of Double Taxation?*, IBFD International Tax Academy (1999); Klaus Vogel, *Taxation of Cross-Border Income, Harmonization and Tax Neutrality under European Community Law*, Foundation for European Fiscal Studies, Erasmus University Rotterdam, No. 2 (1994).

896. Peter J. Wattel, *Home Neutrality in an Internal Market*, 36(5) Eur. Tax'n 159 (1996); Klaus Vogel, *Which Method Should the European Community Adopt for the Avoidance of Double Taxation?*, 56(1) Bull. Int'l Fiscal Documentation 4 (2002).

897. Klaus Vogel, *Which Method Should the European Community Adopt for the Avoidance of Double Taxation?*, 56(1) Bull. Int'l Fiscal Documentation 4, 10 (2002) ('[I]t is very well possible that the conflict between the credit method and the EC's market freedoms will one day lead to a verdict of the Court against the credit method as a method to avoid double taxation among the EU Member States').

898. *Id.*

and Peggy Musgrave in the US in the 1960s,[899] namely that the credit method achieves CEN, while the exemption method achieves CIN.

It is worth briefly recalling the distinction between CEN and CIN (discussed above at *supra* notes 232–233) since much of the reasoning - not only of Vogel but, it seems, nearly all authors that entered this debate - follows from this or relates to it in some way. Under the credit method, a residence state will tax its residents on their worldwide income, thus both FSI and DSI, and, in a second step, from its residents' taxes due on their worldwide income, the residence state allows a credit to be deducted in the amount of foreign taxes levied on the FSI (setting aside the discussion of credit limitations for now). As a result, the resident generally pays the same amount of taxes that it would have paid if it had earned all of its income domestically. If so, CEN is achieved. That is, since the resident will pay the domestic level of taxes regardless of whether it earns income from domestic or from foreign sources, the idea is that the resident's decisions to earn income from at home or from abroad will not be affected by taxes. Under the exemption method, a residence state will tax its residents only on the income earned domestically and, generally speaking, will exclude the FSI from the tax base. On the DSI, the resident pays the domestic amount of taxes, while on the FSI, the resident pays the level of taxes levied in the foreign state. As a result, ideally, the resident pays the same amount of taxes on the income earned in the foreign state as all other taxpayers earning the same income in that same foreign state. This allows investors 'compete at equal terms in the capital market of any country'.[900] If so, CIN is achieved. In sum, CEN is achieved when an investor is taxed the same regardless of whether its capital is invested at home or abroad, whereas CIN is achieved when all investors in a given state pay the same amount of taxes on their income there.

Vogel's article was in large part a response to a wave of economic scholarship, mostly from the US, that advocated the 'superiority' of the credit method on the grounds the CEN was more likely to achieve worldwide efficiency and 'inter-individual and inter-nations equity'.[901] He suspected a biased analysis since this happened to coincide with the taxation system of the US.[902] Thus, after explaining these 'mainstream theories', he presented numerous criticisms, first, of CEN and, second, of the credit method.[903] To begin, the theories themselves, CEN and CIN, are self-contradictory, and he seemed to point out the futility of the exercise of attempting to isolate only one factor (i.e., the export of capital or the import of capital) while pretending all other factors remain constant.[904] To contradict the literature on the

899. Klaus Vogel, *Which Method Should the European Community Adopt for the Avoidance of Double Taxation?*, 56(1) Bull. Int'l Fiscal Documentation 4, 4 (2002) (citing 'Musgrave, Richard, "Criteria for Foreign Tax Credit", in *Taxation and Operations Abroad*, Symposium, 1960, at 83' and 'Richman (now Musgrave), Peggy, *Taxation of Foreign Investment Income. An Economic Analysis*, 1963').
900. *Id.*, at 5 (quoting Richard Musgrave).
901. *Id.*
902. *Id.* ('Surprisingly, therefore - or was it not so surprising? - their theories justified the United States' system of international taxation as it exists').
903. Klaus Vogel, *Which Method Should the European Community Adopt for the Avoidance of Double Taxation?*, 56(1) Bull. Int'l Fiscal Documentation 4, 5–6 (2002).
904. *Id.*, at 5 (*see*, e.g., the whisky and water analogy).

'superiority' of the credit method, he cited studies that reached opposite conclusions, namely that CEN may not be the best or only means to achieve the aforementioned equities,[905] and that source-based taxation also has some equity or fairness-based merits in its camp.[906] Moreover, he agreed with one author's characterization of CEN as 'fiscal imperialism' because 'it discriminates against investment in low-tax states, in particular developing countries'.[907] In any case, the credit method was never based on CEN in the first place, according to its 'original intent', citing Graetz and O'Hear. Second, the credit method suffers from major disadvantages, for example, by placing individuals and enterprises at a competitive disadvantage when competing abroad[908] and by being plagued with numerous complexities.[909]

On the foundations of these wide-ranging policy considerations, Vogel then built his legal case. First, one leading factor – for Vogel and others – that prompted this line of questioning was a turning point in the CJEU's case law, when it expanded from a narrower analysis that focused on the prohibition of 'discrimination' to a broader analysis of 'restrictions'.[910] Depending on just how far this prohibition of restrictions could be stretched, it could capture far more direct tax measures of EU MSs, including arguably the credit method.

According to Vogel, this expansion was pivotal because neither the credit method nor the exemption method discriminated. For this reason, in order for the credit method to be against EU law, it would have to be argued that the credit method was a 'restriction' in the meaning of the CJEU's case law. To do so, first, Vogel recalled that the supporters of the credit method tout its ability to achieve CEN, which 'is another way of stating that it counteracts and eliminates any attractiveness of investment', of work or of providing services, etc., that results from lower taxes in the other MS.[911] Second, under EU law, while MSs remain competent to set their tax rates and tax bases, EU citizens 'are at liberty to exploit the differences resulting from this diversity of tax

905. *Id.*, at 7.
906. *Id.*, at 7–8.
907. *Id.*, at 5 (citing 'Bracewell-Milnes, *The Economics of International Tax Avoidance*, 1980, at 30, 35').
908. *Id.*, at 6.
909. *Id.*, at 6–7.
910. *See*, e.g., Moris Lehner, *Limitation of the National Power of Taxation by the Fundamental Freedoms and Non-discrimination Clauses of the EC Treaty*, 9(1) EC Tax Rev. 5, 11 and 14 (2000) (Lehner's article is dedicated to this change in the CJEU's case law, a development that he criticizes. He posed the question of whether the 'imputation method' would be one of the casualties of the CJEU's expansive view on 'restrictions' as violations of the internal market) and at 9 n.65 (Lehner cited the cases wherein, at this time, this restriction-based approach could be detected: '*Rewe-Zentral-AG gegen Bundesmonopolverwaltung für Branntwein*, C-120/78 [1979] ECR 649; *Keck et Mithouard*, joined cases C-267 and C-268/91 [1993] ECR I-6097; *Säger v Dennemayer*, C-76/90 [1991] ECR I-4221; *Van Binsbergen v Bestuur van de Bedrijsvereniging voor de Metaalnijverheid*, C-33/74 [1974] ECR 1299' and also mentioned: 'the ECJ's *Daily Mail* decision'); Klaus Vogel, *Which Method Should the European Community Adopt for the Avoidance of Double Taxation?*, 56(1) Bull. Int'l Fiscal Documentation 4, 8–9 (2002) (this change in the analysis of the CJEU is one of the main grounds on which Vogel based his arguments. He cited 'Cases *Asscher*, C-107/94, *Futura*, C-250/95, *Gilly*, supra note 42, *Jessica Safir*, C-118/96, and *AMID*, C-141/99', and work by Lehner and Reimer).
911. Klaus Vogel, *Which Method Should the European Community Adopt for the Avoidance of Double Taxation?*, 56(1) Bull. Int'l Fiscal Documentation 4, 9 (2002).

systems' (within certain limits of avoiding distortive, disloyal or abusive behaviour).[912] Bringing the two together, the credit method and CEN lead to a preference for the residence state, by rendering less attractive the free movement to other MSs, and thus 'interferes with' or is 'an intrusion into' this free movement guaranteed by the 'EC Treaty'.[913] Thus, this amounts to an 'indirect interference' that violates EU law.[914]

As early as 1996,[915] Peter Wattel also argued that the credit method was contrary to EU law. Similar to Vogel, one of the preconditions for the arguments was a shift in the CJEU's case law from non-discrimination to non-restriction, or what he referred to as 'non-interference'.[916] Against this background, the starting point for Wattel's argument was '[t]he [EU] principle of national (tax) treatment', which he defined as the requirement that '[EU] source states should grant national treatment to non-resident employees, self-employed persons and companies'.[917] Based on this EU law principle, the credit method was problematic because '[a] credit system may pre-empt national treatment'.[918] To explain his concern, some relevant excerpts include:

> 'The mechanism of the credit method for the prevention of international double taxation by the home state will take away the benefits granted by the source state. Therefore, it is not the taxpayer who benefits from national tax treatment granted by the source state, but the Treasury of his home state, which will only give credit for the tax actually paid in the source state.'[919]
>
> In other words, the 'national treatment to be granted by source states to non-resident economic operators also in respect of direct taxation is rendered totally meaningless (at least to the economic operator involved) if the home state of the economic operator is a high-tax-level credit country'.[920]
>
> In even stronger language, Wattel added that the credit method 'is aimed at frustrating equal treatment of resident and non-resident taxpayers operating within one tax jurisdiction'.[921]

While this appears to be his main line of argument, his aversion to the credit method had other grounds as well. He also criticized the credit method for being 'fundamentally incoherent'[922] or 'inconsistent'. Piecing together his arguments in 1996 with his arguments in a rebuttal to Avery Jones in 2000,[923] his inconsistency argument can be explained as follows: the credit method seeks to achieve CEN – that is, neutrality as to whether its residents invest at home or abroad, or work at home or across the border (etc.). The level of tax should not influence whether a resident decides to

912. *Id.*
913. *Id.*
914. *Id.*
915. Peter J. Wattel, *Home Neutrality in an Internal Market*, 36(5) Eur. Tax'n 159 (1996).
916. *Id.*, at 161 (highlighting, for example, the *Bosman* case).
917. *Id.*, at 159 (1996).
918. *Id.*
919. *Id.*
920. Peter J. Wattel, *Home Neutrality in an Internal Market*, 36(5) Eur. Tax'n 159–160 (1996).
921. *Id.*, at 160.
922. *Id.*
923. John F. Avery Jones, *A Comment on 'Progressive Taxation of Non-residents and Intra-EC Allocation of Personal Tax Allowances'*, 40(8) Eur. Tax'n 375, 375–377, 376 (2000).

operate entirely at home or abroad. However, this works only when the tax rate in the foreign state is lower. If the tax rate in the foreign state is higher, it fails. In this case, the only way to maintain neutrality would be for the state of residence to grant a full credit, meaning a credit for all taxes levied in the foreign state, even leading to a 'refund' if those taxes are greater than what the state of residence would itself levy.[924] This would ensure that the taxpayer never – regardless of the rate in the source state – pays more taxes than what the taxpayer would have paid if all activities were carried out in the state of residence. That would be true CEN. However, states that provide an FTC tend to apply a credit limitation. For this reason (where the source tax rate is higher), 'contrary to the principle, the decision by a resident as to where to invest, where to accept a job or where to perform services *is* affected by tax-level considerations'[925] (in this case, the credit method leads to the same result as the exemption method and CIN).[926]

Wattel adds that, from an internal market perspective, it is doubtful whether tax should be considered so different from other factors that induce economic operators to choose a given market, such as a 'skilled labour force, distribution infrastructure, inflation and interest rate, buying power of the public, political stability, or climate'.[927] This implies that MSs should be able to compete to some extent on the basis of tax. However, he concedes that:

> '[t]his is definitely not to say that one should be indifferent to the distortive effects of excessive or unfair tax competition between states; it is only to say that the relative differences between the *normal* income tax levels of states usually fairly accurately reflect relative differences in economic opportunity and public services. Pre-empting such differences by the home state by taxing the possible benefit away definitely has a protectionist side: it protects credit states against the competition of other Member States'.[928]

Recalling the 'fiscal imperialism' label cited by Vogel, in a similar vein, here the credit method is depicted as a form of fiscal protectionism.[929]

In addition, in later work, Wattel criticized the 'complications' of the credit method, such as its 'administrative complexity', 'the division of the burden of proof (the taxpayer must demonstrate that, and how much, tax was paid in the source country)',[930] and a cumbersome calculation (e.g., referring to issues, as discussed in Chapter 2, such as determining the taxes attributable, applying either 'foreign tax law

924. Peter J. Wattel, *Home Neutrality in an Internal Market*, 36(5) Eur. Tax'n 159, 159 (1996).
925. *Id.*
926. Ben J.M. Terra & Peter J. Wattel, *European Tax Law* 214 (Wolters Kluwer 6th ed. 2012).
927. Peter J. Wattel, *Home Neutrality in an Internal Market*, 36(5) Eur. Tax'n 159, 161 (1996).
928. *Id.*
929. *See also* John F. Avery Jones, *A Comment on 'Progressive Taxation of Non-residents and Intra-EC Allocation of Personal Tax Allowances'*, 40(8) Eur. Tax'n 375, 375–377, 376 (2000) (Wattel explains, in his rebuttal, that 'The credit method is the worst of two worlds. It is, therefore, a disincentive to accept a job abroad or to invest abroad. The credit method is intrinsically protective of the national market and budget, and it is intrinsically restrictive of the freedom of movement'); Ben J.M. Terra & Peter J. Wattel, *European Tax Law* 220 and 222 (Wolters Kluwer 6th ed. 2012).
930. Ben J.M. Terra & Peter J. Wattel, *European Tax Law* 214 (Wolters Kluwer 6th ed. 2012).

or imposing a separate home State system of determining the foreign tax connected to the foreign source income', etc.), a problem which is exacerbated when the credit extends to the underlying taxes of subsidiaries and sub-subsidiaries.[931]

As seen above, Vogel and Wattel were outspoken critics of the credit method. Other authors also expressed hesitations or doubts. One general difference is that, in most cases, other authors concentrated more on the arguments that the exemption method, or CIN, was more in line with the EU internal market, while they appeared to strike a more cautious tone as regards the (in)compatibility of the credit method.

For example, Lehner focused his analysis on 'the distinction between the function of the fundamental freedoms on the one hand as *non-discrimination clauses* primarily based on the concept of equality, and on the other as *prohibitions of restrictions* primarily based on the concept of liberty rights'.[932] He was critical of the development from the former to the latter in the reasoning of the CJEU because he predicted that this could severely impinge on the national sovereignty of MSs in direct taxation in ways that were 'even likely to be in conflict with the fundamental values of domestic tax law systems'.[933] Relevant for this discussion, he pondered whether the 'imputation method' (by which he appears to refer to the 'credit method' more generally) could be caught by this new wide 'restriction'-net cast by the CJEU. In answering this question, he was more circumspect.

His general orientation, or his starting point, is one of caution against too expansive an interpretation of the fundamental freedoms. Various statements throughout the article are indicative:

> 'An internal market, in the sense of a market which is homogeneous in its basic structures, is an important and desirable goal. However, this goal has not yet been fully achieved. The internal market cannot be produced simply by interpreting the EC Treaty' (footnotes omitted).[934]

Implicitly there is a distinction here between what is aspirational and what was currently the legal situation. At the beginning of the article, he emphasizes the centrality of taxation to the sovereignty of MSs, the 'principle of limited powers' in the EU and the deliberate 'regulatory restraint' in the 'EC Treaty' as regards direct taxation.[935] Thus, this lens calibrated his reasoning.

He weighed an argument in favour of the credit method: 'eliminating double taxation in this way' is in line with MSs' commitment under (the former) Article 293 EC Treaty (since abolished). He weighed an argument against the credit method: 'But on the other, given a higher tax rate in the seat state, the imputation method can lead to

931. *Id.*, at 215.
932. Moris Lehner, *Limitation of the National Power of Taxation by the Fundamental Freedoms and Non-discrimination Clauses of the EC Treaty*, 9(1) EC Tax Rev. 5, 7 (2000).
933. *Id.*
934. Moris Lehner, *Limitation of the National Power of Taxation by the Fundamental Freedoms and Non-discrimination Clauses of the EC Treaty*, 9(1) EC Tax Rev. 5, 12 (2000) (internal citations omitted).
935. *Id.*, at 5.

a competitive disadvantage as against enterprises resident in the source country.'[936] In addition, Lehner discerned that certain disadvantages in a cross-border context result from 'the hitherto little-noticed fact that discrimination and restrictions are very often due to the confluence of two different national tax systems'[937] (foreshadowing similar concepts such as the 'exercise in parallel' of taxation rights and 'disparities', discussed in Section 4.2.2.). One example of this occurred with the methods to eliminate double taxation. He agreed that the credit method has its disadvantages, '[b]ut disadvantages may also result from the exemption method'.[938] Similar to other authors, Lehner also mentioned that neutrality can be brought about by either method, mentioning both CEN and CIN.[939] On balance, he concluded, with measured language, that 'the exemption method appears to be the better way for Europe to dismantle restrictions'.[940] He believed that, overall, 'the objective of competitive neutrality ... is variously sketched out by the EC Treaty' and that a 'restriction' approach by the CJEU moves in that direction, but firmly believed that the fundamental freedoms currently do not permit this ('exceeding the bounds of judicially admissible construction'). Therefore, the CJEU is not the appropriate vehicle for moving in this direction; rather, the way to proceed is via harmonization through the 'appropriate legislative actions by the Council'.[941]

As another example, Kemmeren's thesis was that EU MSs, and more broadly all countries with 'globalizing economies', need a source-based approach to taxation, or more precisely an 'origin'-based approach, and they need CIN, or more precisely capital *and labour* import neutrality (i.e., CLIN rather than merely CIN).[942] In arguing that 'CLIN best satisfies the EC Treaty', he opens with the following overview of his main arguments:

> 'As argued above, an open economy will likely incline more towards CLIN. Economies become increasingly open as a result of globalization. For the European Community, the concept of an open market economy is one of the fundamental principles. Therefore, the author finds strong support to base tax treaties on the CLIN principle. The EC Treaty certainly does not prohibit doing so. In the author's opinion, CLIN best satisfies the objectives and principles of the EC Treaty. Regarding the efficiency of the common market, tax neutrality should prevail (see 3.1.) The common market is analogous in nature to the domestic market of a single

936. *Id.*, at 11.
937. *Id.*, at 10–11.
938. *Id.*, at 14.
939. *Id.*
940. *Id.* (on this point, he cited some of his previous work, i.e., 'Lehner, StuW 1998, pp. 159ff' and some of Vogel's previous work, i.e., 'Vogel, "Should Europe adopt a uniform method for the avoidance of double taxation?", IBFD International Tax Academy, Lecture No. 1, p. 11').
941. Moris Lehner, *Limitation of the National Power of Taxation by the Fundamental Freedoms and Non-discrimination Clauses of the EC Treaty*, 9(1) EC Tax Rev. 5, 15 (2000).
942. Eric C.C.M. Kemmeren, *Principle of Origin in Tax Conventions: A Rethinking of Models* (Pijnenburg vormgevers.uitgevers 2001); Eric C.C.M. Kemmeren, *Source of Income in Globalizing Economies: Overview of the Issues and a Plea for an Origin-Based Approach*, 60(11) Bull. Int'l Tax'n 430 (2006); Eric C.C.M. Kemmeren, *Legal and Economic Principles Support an Origin and Import Neutrality-Based over a Residence and Export Neutrality-Based Tax Treaty Policy, in Tax Treaties: Building Bridges between Law and Economics* (Michael Lang et al. eds, IBFD 2010) Online Books IBFD (last visited 2 Aug. 2016).

state although, as mentioned above, a genuine internal market still does not exist. CLIN underscores in the best way possible the operation of such a market established by the Member States by creating a level playing field in them; labour and capital originating in the Member States will compete on equal terms in the labour and capital markets of any state irrespective of the worker's or investor's place of residence.'[943]

A level playing field, or competition on equal footing, is what ties CLIN and the 'European Community' together, as the *former facilitates* this within the market in question and the *latter requires* this within its 'internal market'. For each of the fundamental freedoms, he explained how CLIN ensures neutrality, and thus efficiency, better than capital and labour *export* neutrality (CLEN).[944] In searching the sources of EU laws - the 'EC Treaty', the case law of the CJEU, and Directives - he identified indications regarding its relationship with CLIN and CLEN. In the 'EC Treaty', he cited references to 'an open market economy with free competition' in Article 4 and Article 98 of the EC Treaty (currently, Article 119 and Article 120).[945] From the CJEU case law, findings show that 'the principle of origin and the territoriality principle [...] can actually be applied under the fundamental freedoms of the EC Treaty'.[946] The wording 'can be applied' seems conscientiously selected, as he concludes from the cases he reviews that the fundamental freedoms clearly allow it (e.g., 'In *Futura*, the ECJ explicitly accepted the territoriality principle'),[947] but do not require it (e.g., in *Gilly* and other cases, the CJEU accepts that MSs are 'free to choose their own system for relieving double taxation'),[948] but this does not diminish the prospect that the fundamental freedoms would be best facilitated by these principles.[949]

In favour of this prospect, some findings of the CJEU imply that 'EU citizens and economic operators can choose within the European Community the most suitable tax system for themselves and their investments and can decide which of the Member States makes the most appealing "offer" regarding the tax burden and public services'

943. Eric C.C.M. Kemmeren, *Source of Income in Globalizing Economies: Overview of the Issues and a Plea for an Origin-Based Approach*, 60(11) Bull. Int'l Tax'n 430, 442 (2006).
944. *Id.*
945. *Id.*
946. *Id.*
947. Eric C.C.M. Kemmeren, *Source of Income in Globalizing Economies: Overview of the Issues and a Plea for an Origin-Based Approach*, 60(11) Bull. Int'l Tax'n 430, 443 (2006) ('In *Futura*, the ECJ explicitly accepted the territoriality principle. The case dealt with the carry-forward of losses derived from a Luxembourg permanent establishment of a French resident company.[131] The carryforward was made subject to, inter alia, the condition that the loss be economically related to the income earned by the taxpayer in Luxembourg. Regarding this condition, the ECJ ruled that a system of calculating the basis of assessment for non-resident taxpayers which, when calculating the tax payable by them in Luxembourg, takes into account only the profits and losses arising from their Luxembourg activities is in conformity with *the tax principle of territoriality* and cannot be regarded as entailing any discrimination, overt or covert, prohibited by the E(E)C Treaty.[132]').
948. *Id.*
949. *Id.*

(footnotes omitted).[950] Vogel also relied on this argument. This was sometimes summarized as the possibility for 'jurisdiction shopping' within the EU.[951] Kemmeren cited the *Eurowings* case, decided in 1999, as a potentially relevant example.

In the *Eurowings* case, the rules for calculating the tax base of the German trade tax were disputed.[952] The trade tax is a municipal business tax.[953] To calculate the tax base, a taxpayer starts with the tax base as calculated for income tax purposes and then makes certain adjustments. As regards one such adjustment, under certain conditions, payments that had been made and deducted for income tax purposes had to be added back, or more precisely *half* of the amount of the payment had to be added back, into the tax base of the German taxpayer.[954] Consequently, this increased the tax base subject to the trade tax. The payments did *not* have 'to be added back where trade tax [was] already payable on them by the [recipient]'.[955]

This criterion gave rise to the problem. On its surface, this requirement to add back in 50 % of certain payments was triggered by a seemingly neutral criterion, i.e., in essence, when the payments were made to recipients who were *not* liable to the trade tax. In practice, this meant that payments made to German recipients that were liable to trade tax did *not* have to be added back in, whereas payments to recipients outside of Germany that, of course, were *not* subject to the German trade tax *did* have to be *added back in*.

In this case, the German company *Eurowings* leased an aircraft from an Irish company.[956] Under the Trade Tax Law, the German company had to add 50 % of the payments made to the Irish company back into its tax base, among other things.[957] The German company argued that this amounted to different treatment on the basis of whether the recipient was in Germany or in another EU MS.[958] As a result of leasing an aircraft from an Irish company, rather than a German company, Eurowings was treated less favourably.[959] The German Court asked whether this difference in treatment could be justified based on the fact that 'the lessor, an undertaking governed by Irish law, pays no tax comparable to the trade tax and enjoys "Shannon privileges" in the form of

950. Eric C.C.M. Kemmeren, *Source of Income in Globalizing Economies: Overview of the Issues and a Plea for an Origin-Based Approach*, 60(11) Bull. Int'l Tax'n 430, 442 (2006) (footnotes omitted).
951. *See*, e.g., Ben J.M. Terra & Peter J. Wattel, *European Tax Law* 46–47, 647–648, 695–697 (Wolters Kluwer 6th ed. 2012) (the basic principle was established in the *Centros* case, C-212/97, and then extended to tax cases such as *Cadbury Schweppes*, C-196/04, and *Eurowings*, C-294/97, and became most apparent in *ICI*, C-264/96); Dennis Weber, *Abuse of Law in European Tax Law: An Overview and Some Recent Trends in the Direct and Indirect Tax Case Law of the ECJ – Part 2*, 53(7) Eur. Tax'n 313, 322–324 Section 6 (2013) (tracing its development through *Centros*, C-212/97; *Inspire Art*, C-167/01; *Akrich*, C-109/01; *Barbier*, C-364/01; *De Lasteyrie*, C-9/02; *Cadbury Schweppes*, C-196/04; *Eurowings*, C-294/97).
952. CJEU, Case C-294/97, *Eurowings*, 26 Oct. 1999, ECLI:EU:C:1999:524, at para. 2.
953. *Id.*, at para. 4 ('Business tax is a non-personal tax payable by any business establishment regardless of the resources and personal situation of the taxpayer who owns it').
954. CJEU, Case C-294/97, *Eurowings*, 26 Oct. 1999, ECLI:EU:C:1999:524, at paras 3–11.
955. *Id.*, at paras 11, 18.
956. *Id.*, at para. 13.
957. *Id.*
958. CJEU, Case C-294/97, *Eurowings*, 26 Oct. 1999, ECLI:EU:C:1999:524, at para. 19.
959. *Id.*

a 10% corporation tax'.[960] The CJEU held that the freedom to provide services 'precludes national legislation on trade tax such as that at issue in the main action'.[961] The commonly cited[962] paragraphs of the judgment are paragraphs 43–45 where the CJEU reasoned:[963]

> '43 Contrary to what was argued by the Finanzamt, that difference of treatment can also not be justified by the fact that the lessor established in another Member State is there subject to lower taxation.'
>
> '44 Any tax advantage resulting for providers of services from the low taxation to which they are subject in the Member State in which they are established cannot be used by another Member State to justify less favourable treatment in tax matters given to recipients of services established in the latter State (see, as regards Article 52 of the EC Treaty (now, after amendment, Article 43 EC), *Commission* v *France,* paragraph 21, and *Asscher,* paragraph 53, both cited above).'
>
> '45 As the Commission rightly observed, such compensatory tax arrangements prejudice the very foundations of the single market.'

Finally, when studying the relevant EU Directives on direct taxation, Kemmeren found evidence of support for *residence*-based taxation in the Parent-Subsidiary Directive, the Interest-Royalty Directive and the Savings Directive.[964] Similarly, Wattel noted that secondary law, such as the Parent-Subsidiary Directive, reaffirmed that the MSs are free to choose either method.[965] However, Vogel argued that secondary law cannot be determinative since primary law takes precedence.[966]

In Kemmeren's work, the emphasis was more on the arguments in favour of CLIN, which entails the exemption method, than on a condemnation of the credit method. By comparison with Lehner, Kemmeren's general orientation leaned more towards the ideal of the internal market and away from the legal and political compromises that had been made regarding direct taxation under EU law; however, he clearly inserted similar caveats (e.g., 'although, as mentioned above, a genuine internal market still does not exist'). This can be explained by differences in the objective of their respective articles and, thus, may or may not have anything to do with any real difference in views. Lehner's article sought to critically analyse a recent

960. CJEU, Case C-294/97, *Eurowings,* 26 Oct. 1999, ECLI:EU:C:1999:524, at para. 21.
961. *Id.*, at paras 43–45.
962. *See,* e.g., Eric C.C.M. Kemmeren, *Source of Income in Globalizing Economies: Overview of the Issues and a Plea for an Origin-Based Approach,* 60(11) Bull. Int'l Tax'n 430, 443 (2006); Dennis Weber, *Abuse of Law in European Tax Law: An Overview and Some Recent Trends in the Direct and Indirect Tax Case Law of the ECJ – Part 2,* 53(7) Eur. Tax'n 313, 324 (2013); Ben J.M. Terra & Peter J. Wattel, *European Tax Law* 46–47, 647–648, 695–697 (Wolters Kluwer 6th ed. 2012); Pasquale Pistone, *The Impact of Community Law on Tax Treaties: Issues and Solutions* 197–198 (Kluwer Law International 2002).
963. CJEU, Case C-294/97, *Eurowings,* 26 Oct. 1999, ECLI:EU:C:1999:524, at para. 46.
964. Eric C.C.M. Kemmeren, *Source of Income in Globalizing Economies: Overview of the Issues and a Plea for an Origin-Based Approach,* 60(11) Bull. Int'l Tax'n 430, 444–445 (2006).
965. Peter J. Wattel, *Progressive Taxation of Non-residents and Intra-EC Allocation of Personal Tax Allowances: Why Schumacker, Asscher, Gilly and Gschwind Do Not Suffice,* 40(6) Eur. Tax'n 210, 213 (2000).
966. Klaus Vogel, *Which Method Should the European Community Adopt for the Avoidance of Double Taxation?,* 56(1) Bull. Int'l Fiscal Documentation 4, 9 (2002).

legal development and its potential legal consequences; Kemmeren sought to propose policies (specifically for tax treaties) based on economic and legal principles. This entails that he operates in the realm of first principles and what would be required in his view for an internal market to become 'analogous in nature to the domestic market of a single state'. Both authors imply that MSs have to work together.

On balance, Kemmeren concluded that 'we see conflicting trends in EC law regarding source-based taxation'. On the one hand, '[t]he ECJ's case law supports such an interpretation, or at least does not preclude it. On the other hand, the income tax directives are generally more in favour of residence-based taxation'. Nevertheless, he states that '[i]f an actual common market does not exist and 25 different income tax systems must be accepted, CLIN, source-based income taxation and an origin-based interpretation of source best satisfy the objectives and goals of the EC Treaty'.[967]

As another example of an author commenting on these topics, Pistone also reported on the trends on this topic, detecting a shift in opinion:

> 'Only a few years ago stronger taxing powers to the State of source – such as for the withholding tax on cross-border flows of income – were regarded as an obstacle to integration within the Community. However, since the Ruding Report, scholars have started to consider that a return to source-State taxation could solve the problems of compatibility with Community law, granting equal treatment to taxpayers according to their substantial situation and regardless of where they are residents.'[968]

In this context, Pistone too expressed doubts regarding the compatibility of the credit method with EU law.[969] First, CEN appears to contradict the goal of achieving an internal market.[970] Second, the *Eurowings* decision raises the question of 'whether the natural compensatory function of tax differentials for the purpose of achieving CEN is in itself compatible with equal access to the internal market'.[971] Third, the credit method 'precluded national treatment in the source-State, or rather transformed it in a matter of different tax rates and structure across EU Member States'.[972] He cautioned that, if the credit method were rendered incompatible with EU law, this would have 'far-reaching' consequences, such as on 'the structure of domestic law in many countries (such as France, Italy and Spain)' and on the ability-to-pay principle enshrined in some national constitutions.[973] Nevertheless, MSs must heed the supremacy of EU law and, fortunately, reasonable solutions were available. For example, exemption with progression could also be argued to adhere to the ability-to-pay

967. Eric C.C.M. Kemmeren, *Source of Income in Globalizing Economies: Overview of the Issues and a Plea for an Origin-Based Approach*, 60(11) Bull. Int'l Tax'n 430, 445 (2006).
968. Pasquale Pistone, *The Impact of Community Law on Tax Treaties: Issues and Solutions* 201 (Kluwer Law International 2002).
969. *Id.*, at 197–198.
970. *Id.*, at 198.
971. *Id.*
972. *Id.*
973. Pasquale Pistone, *The Impact of Community Law on Tax Treaties: Issues and Solutions* 199 (Kluwer Law International 2002).

principle.[974] Pistone observed an increasing emphasis, from the CJEU's case law and from scholars such as Wattel,[975] on the requirement of national treatment in the source state. As national treatment in the source state requires 'equal access to the market between residents and non-residents'[976] and cases such as *Schumacker* demonstrate that 'the global situation of the taxpayer can be ascertained also in other States', Pistone considered that perhaps 'the role and function of residence-based taxation should be reconsidered within the Community'.[977] To contribute to the discussion, he put forward proposals for strengthening source-based taxation and carefully considered their pros and cons.[978] Moreover, Pistone pondered whether the real problem lies at a deeper, even more fundamental layer, namely with the concept of 'residence' itself.[979] Indeed, 'residence', a domestic law concept, may be conceptually incompatible with an internal market where rights are conferred under the EU Treaties to all EU citizens. In other words, there may be a 'mismatch between the *national* concept of residence and the *supranational* rights conferred by Community law' (emphasis added).[980] Ultimately, though, '[a] complete solution to such issues seems indeed only possible when a common tax policy for the EU is established, i.e. only when Community institutions have become competent in the field of direct taxes'.[981]

To offer a summary of arguments and counterarguments:

From the above, key recurring arguments advanced by various authors regarding the credit method under EU law can be derived. Their reasoning was based on:

(i) the theory that the credit method results in CEN, which leads to a form of 'protectionism' for the 'home' market or state of residence;
(ii) the various inconveniences, as well as the 'fundamental inconsistency', of the credit method;
(iii) the notion that the principle of equality embedded within the fundamental freedoms required full 'national treatment' in the 'host' state or state of source;
(iv) the prediction that the CJEU would pursue a broad interpretation of 'restrictions' of the fundamental freedoms;
(v) the findings resulting from cases such as *Eurowings* that appeared to enjoin MSs to give a green light to tax jurisdiction shopping;[982]

974. *Id.*, at 199–200.
975. *Id.*, at 197.
976. *Id.*, at 200.
977. *Id.*
978. For details, *see* Pasquale Pistone, *The Impact of Community Law on Tax Treaties: Issues and Solutions* 201 et seq. (Kluwer Law International 2002).
979. *Id.*, at 178.
980. *Id.*
981. Pasquale Pistone, *The Impact of Community Law on Tax Treaties: Issues and Solutions* 178–179 (Kluwer Law International 2002).
982. On the relevance of *Eurowings, see,* e.g., Eric C.C.M. Kemmeren, *Source of Income in Globalizing Economies: Overview of the Issues and a Plea for an Origin-Based Approach,* 60(11) Bull. Int'l Tax'n 430, 442–443 (2006); Moris Lehner, *Limitation of the National Power of Taxation by the Fundamental Freedoms and Non-discrimination Clauses of the EC Treaty,* 9(1)

(vi) the tension between the concepts of residence and EU citizenship.[983]

It seems safe to characterize the scholarship on EU tax law from around the turn of the century as predominantly in favour of the exemption method and, in one way or another, against the credit method. However, some authors were of a different view and, even the authors most decidedly against the credit method, made some concessions. Here the discussion now turns to the concessions and counterarguments.

(i) The CEN-based arguments

The link between the credit method and CEN may not be as strong as suggested. To begin, when the credit method was first conceived, CEN was nowhere to be found among its original rationales.[984] Vogel acknowledges this (indeed, his article gave the impression that he wielded the CEN argument, not because he was so attached to the theory, but rather because proponents of the credit method were). The term 'capital export neutrality' was coined in the 1960s by the Musgraves, decades after the 'invention' of the credit method. It is true that thereafter CEN became a seemingly powerful rallying cry in favour of the credit method, once economic studies began espousing the theory that CEN would best achieve, *inter alia*, 'worldwide efficiency'. It is understandable then that there would be a backlash from those who prefer the exemption method. In this (more heated) academic climate, the distinction between the credit method based on CEN and the exemption method based on CIN seemed to be one of the most divisive sticking points of disagreement. This generates a deadlocked debate because CEN and CIN are mutually exclusive and because, as theoretical concepts, these 'neutralities' are inherently oversimplified (as economic concepts or models often must be). A singular focus on only these factors, in turn, creates the impression of a clear-cut opposition between the credit method and the exemption method. Such a categorical picture loses shades of nuance, leading to a lack of compromise and thus, as Graetz indicates, a possible lack of creative thinking for alternative solutions.[985]

Recalling that CEN was not one of the original rationales cues debaters to recall other rationales, such as the ability-to-pay principle, a compromise with source taxation and a simultaneous 'backstop' to pure source-based taxation,[986] that revive nuances. Even within the economic discipline, discussions are not settled as regards the appropriate balances to strike between concepts such as neutrality, efficiency,

EC Tax Rev. 5, 10–11 (2000); Pasquale Pistone, *The Impact of Community Law on Tax Treaties: Issues and Solutions* 197–198 (Kluwer Law International 2002).

983. *See*, e.g., Pasquale Pistone, *The Impact of Community Law on Tax Treaties: Issues and Solutions* 178 (Kluwer Law International 2002).
984. *See*, e.g., *supra* note 232 and note 233.
985. Michael J. Graetz, *The David R. Tillinghast Lecture Taxing International Income: Inadequate Principles, Outdated Concepts, and Unsatisfactory Policy*, 54(3) Tax L. Rev. 261, 269 (2001) ('We have been blinded by adherence to inadequate principles and remain wedded to outdated concepts') and at 276 (limiting the perspective to CEN and CIN 'both inhibits an adequate understanding of the normative underpinnings of international income tax policy and improperly limits serious consideration of alternative policies').
986. *See*, e.g., *supra* note 144 and note 146.

equity and fairness.[987] As Graetz added, there are entangled political and diplomatic considerations as well that realistically cannot be ignored.[988] When all factors are brought back into play, neither the exemption method nor the credit method are a perfect solution; neither come out unscathed. Compromises look not only more feasible, but necessary. For example, Graetz suggested that different types of income may call for different approaches, such as an exemption for active business income under certain conditions and an FTC, or merely a deduction, for income from portfolio investments.[989] Vogel suggested that a compromise could be 'exemption in combination with a subject-to-tax clause', thus relying on the credit method only when necessary to avoid non-taxation.[990]

Overreliance on these theories in setting international tax policy should be eschewed also because they are unrealizable in any consistent or systematic way in practice. They can be fully achieved only in a theoretical world that does not exist - as long as differences persist between countries' tax systems and as long as tax is but one factor that investors or workers (etc.) consider in their cost-benefit analysis for cross-border activity. In the real second-best world, both CEN and CIN are afflicted by their helpless contingency on the ever-changing circumstances of taxpayers and tax systems in other countries (e.g., it depends on the tax rates on a given income in other countries, or whether a taxpayer makes losses or profits in a given country or year) and the infinite permutations thereof. Graetz makes this point in the clearest way:

> 'It is by now known that it is impossible to achieve CEN and CIN simultaneously in the absence of either a worldwide government or identical income tax bases and rates in all nations.'[991]

987. *See* in general, e.g., James Mirrlees et al., *Tax by Design*, Institute for Fiscal Studies (Oxford University Press 2011); Michael J. Graetz, *The David R. Tillinghast Lecture Taxing International Income: Inadequate Principles, Outdated Concepts, and Unsatisfactory Policy*, 54(3) Tax L. Rev. 261 (2001).
988. Michael J. Graetz, *The David R. Tillinghast Lecture Taxing International Income: Inadequate Principles, Outdated Concepts, and Unsatisfactory Policy*, 54(3) Tax L. Rev. 261, 307 et seq. (2001).
989. *Id.*, at 261, 323–335 (more precisely, Graetz distinguished between income from active business earned by corporations, income from portfolio investments earned by individuals, and wages earned abroad by individuals. In his view, this distinction is relevant because which principles, e.g., efficiency and fairness, take priority differ depending on the income in question), at 331 (discussing proposals for active business income earned by corporations) at 332–334 (discussing proposals for 'portfolio income-interest, dividends, and capital gains-earned by U.S. individuals from foreign sources'), at 334 (discussing proposals for portfolio income of corporations), at 334–335 (discussing proposals for wages earned by individuals abroad, including one from 'Kees von Raad of the Netherlands').
990. Klaus Vogel, *Which Method Should the European Community Adopt for the Avoidance of Double Taxation?*, 56(1) Bull. Int'l Fiscal Documentation 4, 6 (2002). For an analysis of the subject-to-tax clause in the EU Commission's 2012 Recommendation and the switch-over clause in the 2016 Draft ATAD, *see* Pasquale Pistone, *BEPS, Capital Export Neutrality and the Risk of Hidden Tax Protectionism. Selected Remarks from an EU Perspective, in Base Erosion and Profit Shifting (BEPS): Impact for European and International Tax Policy* 319 (Robert Danon ed., Schulthess Verlag 2016).
991. Michael J. Graetz, *The David R. Tillinghast Lecture Taxing International Income: Inadequate Principles, Outdated Concepts, and Unsatisfactory Policy*, 54(3) Tax L. Rev. 261, 272 (2001).

> 'My favorite way of making this point is in terms of an irreconcilable conflict among the following three simple principles:
>
> *Principle 1*: People should pay equal taxes on their income regardless of the country that is the source of that income. In particular, U.S. taxpayers should be treated equally regardless of the source of their income.
> *Principle 2*: All investments in the United States should face the same burden regardless of whether a U.S. person or a foreign person makes the investment. In other words, U.S. and foreign-owned investments and businesses should be treated equally.
> *Principle 3*: Sovereign countries should be free to set their own tax rates and to vary them as their domestic economic situations demand.
>
> The essential difficulty is that the first two principles can hold simultaneously only when capital income is taxed at the same rate in all countries. [...] That has never happened, and it never will. Moreover, there would be no way to keep such a system in place without violating Principle 3. [...].'[992]

With this in mind, policy proposals founded predominantly on the grounds of CEN and CIN merit some scepticism. Vogel seemed to agree with Graetz on this point,[993] and Terra and Wattel also recognized the 'irreconcilable' nature of CEN and CIN.[994] Recent literature has reinforced criticisms of these neutralities. For example, Shaviro described it as '[d]rowning in' an 'Alphabet Soup' of acronyms for various neutralities that are inadequate, rely on fallacies and distract from other more important 'margins' of analysis for setting international tax policy.[995]

All the above simply serves to suggest that CEN/CIN-based arguments may be starting from a rather problematic, or limited, premise. Nevertheless, for the sake of argument, assuming CEN and CIN can be achieved, or in the individual cases where they are achieved, then one can contend with whether EU law prefers CIN over CEN. The answer turns on the arguments (iii) and (iv) discussed further below.

(ii) The inconveniences and inconsistencies arguments

In response to arguments regarding the inconveniences of the credit method, two sets of counterarguments can be put forward. First, it is possible to relativize the debate, as both methods have advantages and disadvantages. Second, in any case, there are ways to overcome some of the inconveniences that were red-flagged. In other words, certain

992. *Id.*, at 272 n.36 (2001).
993. Klaus Vogel, *Which Method Should the European Community Adopt for the Avoidance of Double Taxation?*, 56(1) Bull. Int'l Fiscal Documentation 4, 5 (2002).
994. Ben J.M. Terra & Peter J. Wattel, *European Tax Law* 210 (Wolters Kluwer 6th ed. 2012).
995. Daniel N. Shaviro, *Fixing U.S. International Taxation* 14–15 (Oxford University Press 2014) (contenders in this 'alphabet soup' or 'battle of the acronyms' include 'competing one-dimensional efficiency norms' such as 'CEN (capital export neutrality), CIN (capital import neutrality), and NN (national neutrality)' as well as 'CON (capital ownership neutrality), NON (national ownership neutrality), and GPN (global portfolio neutrality)'. 'Ostensibly, all one needs to do, in order to choose the right international tax policy, is not to consider tradeoffs (as one might have expected from the style of analysis typically deployed elsewhere) but rather to plunge into the alphabet soup, pick a single winner, and determine whether it supports worldwide taxation or exemption').

perceived inconveniences are not inherent flaws of one or the other method, but are design flaws that could be 'remedied'.

Regarding the first point, one of the reoccurring complaints against the credit method is that it entails administrative burdens, resulting from reporting obligations for all the income and taxes from abroad, and inevitably 'cumbersome' calculations.[996] In the case of natural persons, it is harder to sustain this complaint. In cases where the exemption with progression method applies, individuals are also faced with reporting obligations as regards their income earned from abroad and thus may have many of the same administrative difficulties of the credit method. In cases where the 'tax exemption' method applies (as in the Netherlands, explained in Chapter 2, and in the *De Groot* case, explained in Section 4.2.), the calculation is nearly identical to that of the credit method. In the case of legal persons that are taxable entities, it may be easier to sustain. Taxable entities subject to CIT are often subject to a flat tax rate, rather than a progressive tax rate scale. In this case, it would not be necessary for a company to report all of its worldwide income to its residence state for the residence state to be able to determine the tax rate that should apply. Clearly, then, the residence state would not need to require this reporting obligation. It is possible that the residence state would require it anyway, depending on the extent to which the residence state deems such information necessary to ensure that only the appropriate amount of income is exempt. At this point, the links between the first point and the second point are apparent: the administrative procedures can be designed to be more or less difficult, depending on the aims and compromises. In theory, if a full exemption were applied, where the residence state was indifferent to the income earned and tax situation abroad, and thus allowed taxpayers to exclude all such income from the tax base without further questions asked, then this would lead to quite a gap between the administrative requirements for the credit method and those for the exemption method. In practice, where adjustments are made to the exemption method, because the residence state compromises with the ability-to-pay principle (e.g., exemption with progression method) and, relatedly, compromises with the risk of no or low taxation (e.g., exemption with more extensive reporting obligations or, going further, exemption with a subject-to-tax clause or switch-over clause), the gap is significantly reduced.[997]

The exemption method is often seen not only as simpler but also as more advantageous. Yet, as Lehner observed, 'disadvantages may also result from the exemption method'.[998] For example, in the case of losses, the 'credit may reduce the impact of tax obstacles to the exercise of fundamental freedoms', Pistone noted in

996. *See*, e.g., Ben J.M. Terra & Peter J. Wattel, *European Tax Law* 214–215 (Wolters Kluwer 6th ed. 2012); CJEU, Case C-47/12, *Kronos International Inc.*, 11 Sep. 2014, ECLI:EU:C:2014:2200, at para. 75 (the CJEU sometimes refers to the 'administrative burden inherent in the imputation method').

997. *See also*, e.g., Gauthier Blanluet & Philippe J. Durand, *General Report: Key Practical Issues to Eliminate Double Taxation of Business Income*, 96b Cahiers de Droit Fiscal International 17, 51 (IFA 2011).

998. Moris Lehner, *Limitation of the National Power of Taxation by the Fundamental Freedoms and Non-discrimination Clauses of the EC Treaty*, 9(1) EC Tax Rev. 5, 14 (2000).

2002.[999] It was prescient since a similar issue arose later in the 2014 *Kronos* case,[1000] where the taxpayer complained of the disadvantage of the exemption method applying to dividends in a cross-border context, as compared to the 'imputation method' applying to dividends in a domestic context, in a case involving losses (as discussed in Section 4.2.3., at *infra* note 1256). There may be other cases where the credit method proves advantageous. It may depend on the design of the credit method (e.g., the credit method in the US previously allowed for generous cross-crediting, as discussed in Chapter 2, *see*, e.g., *supra* note 206 and note 231). As Terra and Wattel point out, a 'per-country' application may be restrictive, whereas an 'overall' application allows averaging.[1001] In the case of dividends, many of the disadvantages of the credit method may not transpire in practice, and the credit method can become de facto similar to an exemption, due to the effect of deferral.[1002] As can be seen, whether the exemption method or the credit method is more favourable depends to a large extent on the specific facts and circumstances and design.

As noted in Chapter 2, the credit method and the exemption method share certain fundamental design issues (e.g., allocation of expenses to FSI and DSI).[1003] As a case in point, the aforementioned 'tax exemption' shows just how close the two methods can be, even in the details of their calculation. Similarly, when discussing the pros and cons of a shift from a credit method to an exemption method, Graetz noted:

> 'In an exemption system, we would need to retain rules to distinguish foreign and domestic source income and to separate active business income from passive income. Anti-abuse rules along the lines of subpart F and the foreign personal holding company rules also would have to be retained. Look-through rules would be necessary to protect against mischaracterization of income and source.'[1004]

999. Pasquale Pistone, *The Impact of Community Law on Tax Treaties: Issues and Solutions* 198 n.77 (Kluwer Law International 2002).
1000. CJEU, Case C-47/12, *Kronos International Inc.*, 11 Sep. 2014, ECLI:EU:C:2014:2200.
1001. Ben J.M. Terra & Peter J. Wattel, *European Tax Law* 214 (Wolters Kluwer 6th ed. 2012).
1002. *See*, e.g., Robert J. Peroni, J. Clifton Fleming Jr. & Stephen E. Shay, *Getting Serious About Curtailing Deferral of U.S. Tax on Foreign Source Income*, 52(2) SMU L. Rev. 455 (1999); OECD, *Tax Sparing: A Reconsideration* (OECD Publishing 1998); Kim Brooks, *Tax Sparing: A Needed Incentive for Foreign Investment in Low-Income Countries or an Unnecessary Revenue Sacrifice?*, 34(2) Queen's L.J. 505 (Spring 2009); Deborah Toaze, *Tax Sparing: Good Intentions, Unintended Results*, 49(4) Can. Tax J. 879 (2001).
1003. *See*, e.g., OECD, *Model Tax Convention on Income and on Capital 2017: Condensed Version* Commentary on Articles 23 A and 23 B, para. 62 (OECD Publishing 2017); Peter Harris, *Chapter III: Taxation of Residents on Foreign Source Income, in United Nations Handbook on Selected Issues in Administration of Double Tax Treaties for Developing Countries* 109 (Alexander Trepelkov, Harry Tonino & Dominika Halka eds, United Nations 2013); Brian J. Arnold, *International Tax Primer* 62–63 (Wolters Kluwer 3d ed. 2016); Hugh J. Ault & Brian J. Arnold, *Comparative Income Taxation: A Structural Analysis* (Kluwer Law International 2d ed. 2004).
1004. Michael J. Graetz, *The David R. Tillinghast Lecture Taxing International Income: Inadequate Principles, Outdated Concepts, and Unsatisfactory Policy*, 54(3) Tax L. Rev. 261, 330 (2001).

In the 2011 IFA General Report, after reviewing chapters contributed from countries all around the world, the authors noted that, generally speaking, it seemed that 'complexity and sophistication are more a consequence of how the exemption or the credit systems are applied than of the system by itself'.[1005]

The idea of this counterargument is that, to the extent that the exemption method and the credit method give rise to similar inconveniences, perhaps these inconveniences are not a basis for making a blanket distinction between the two. Also, to the extent that some of the inconveniences can be minimized through design, perhaps these inconveniences are not a basis for discrediting one or the other method (often the credit method), but rather for directing more attention to the method's design and application. One may also ponder whether recent legal developments in the dramatic expansion of the exchange of information in the EU (and globally) and ongoing technological developments in processing of data could someday mitigate problems related to reporting obligations or the calculations required.

Regarding the argument that the credit method is 'fundamentally inconsistent': Terra and Wattel criticized the ordinary credit method as 'inconsistent' in that it achieves CEN only when tax rate in the state of source is lower, but it abandons this principle when the tax rate in the state of source is higher. They admit that a design feature, namely a credit carryforward, could solve the issue, but it does not work if: (1) the tax on the FSI 'is structurally higher' or (2) there is no FSI in subsequent years.[1006] Be that as it may, this seems extraneous to the question of its compatibility with EU law. Importantly, numerous authors (as cited throughout the discussion above) argue that CIN is more in line with the EU internal market. Adopting this perspective on EU law, then, the counterargument is that, in these cases, there does not appear to be any problem from an EU law perspective. Indeed, in those instances where the ordinary credit method is 'inconsistent', the very reason it is inconsistent is because factually CIN is occurring, rather than CEN. Where the source state rates are higher, the exemption method and the credit method would lead to the same result. In both cases, the taxpayers end up competing on an equal footing in the state of source, from a tax perspective, as desired. Thus, 'inconsistent' does not equal 'incompatible'. Based on this part of the authors' reasoning, an EU law problem with the ordinary credit method occurs only when the rate of tax in the state of source is lower than in the state of residence. This brings us to the next two arguments.

(iii) The national treatment argument

Regarding the notion that the principle of equality embedded within the fundamental freedoms required full 'national treatment' in the 'host' state or state of source, Avery Jones counterargued that the CJEU does not seem to require national treatment to the full extent or in the unconditional way suggested by Wattel. Rather, the CJEU explicitly recognized that residents and non-residents are, in principle, *not* comparable. Thus,

1005. Gauthier Blanluet & Philippe J. Durand, *General Report: Key Practical Issues to Eliminate Double Taxation of Business Income*, 96b Cahiers de Droit Fiscal International 17, 51 (IFA 2011).

1006. Ben J.M. Terra & Peter J. Wattel, *European Tax Law* 214 (Wolters Kluwer 6th ed. 2012).

under the CJEU's case law, there are instances where different treatment of non-residents is acceptable. In addition to establishing this, the judgment in *Schumacker* can also be read as accepting residence-based or home-state-based taxation.[1007]

As regards the *Schumacker* case (after considering its impact on 'tax credit countries'), Paul Farmer, for example, respectfully disagreed with Wattel's view:

> 'Professor Wattel considers the ruling to be wrong in law and unworkable. He argues that the principle underlying previous cases was that non-residents using their migration rights are entitled to national treatment; they are therefore by definition in a similar position to residents. Underlying Professor Wattel's criticisms is the basic proposition that the criterion of the place where a taxpayer's income is concentrated is inadequate in an increasingly integrated market in which it is common for taxpayers to receive income from different sources.'[1008]
>
> And, 'It is respectfully submitted that, given the constraints of the Court's role, its analysis in *Schumacher* was essentially sound. In recognizing that there may be relevant differences in the situations of tax residents and tax non-residents the Court applied existing principles. The right of persons exercising their Community freedoms to national treatment does not automatically place them in the same position as resident taxpayers. What it means is that they are entitled to have their situations compared and, where they are for all material purposes in the same tax position, are entitled to the same treatment. Put another way, adverse treatment of non-residents must be objectively justified.'[1009]

Although the precise contents of the national treatment obligation may vary depending on the context, the specific 'national treatment' in question for Wattel was that of the tax rates or tax burden. More specifically, regarding the credit method, Wattel argued that the credit method essentially cancels out the benefit of national treatment, specifically in the case where the tax rate in the credit-granting state is higher and the tax rate in the host state is lower. In this case, the host state is obliged to extend the national treatment to the incoming EU citizens and economic operators (i.e., it cannot subject them to a higher tax burden), but this lower tax rate does not end up benefitting these EU-free-movers, since they pay the difference to their home state under the credit method. The contention is that if the host state is obliged to extend national treatment, it should, as intended, benefit these taxpayers (not the Treasuries of the home state). It reflects a sentiment of injustice from this result.

However, generally speaking, to the extent the free movement provisions are non-discrimination norms, the CJEU is tasked with assessing whether a contested law in a given MS gives rise to discrimination or different treatment. In this assessment, the national treatment obligation of the host state is technically distinct from the equal treatment obligation of the home state. Even its critics agreed that the credit method is

1007. *See* Peter J. Wattel, *Home Neutrality in an Internal Market*, 36(5) Eur. Tax'n 159, 162 (1996) (Avery Jones commented at the end of the article). For more on their exchange of views, *see also* John F. Avery Jones, *A Comment on 'Progressive Taxation of Non-residents and Intra-EC Allocation of Personal Tax Allowances'*, 40(8) Eur. Tax'n 375, 375–377 (2000) (which includes Wattel's comments).

1008. Paul Farmer, *EC Law and National Rules on Direct Taxation: A Phoney War?*, 7(1) EC Tax Rev. 13, 17 (1998).

1009. *Id.*, at 18.

not a *discriminatory* tax treatment; it enables the home state to tax its residents the same regardless of the source of their income. As long as both states are respecting their respective EU law obligations, they pass scrutiny; otherwise, it becomes a much broader assessment and a question of choosing between policies or MSs. The above argument assumes that the 'national treatment' obligation of the host state should have a bearing on the home state's equal treatment obligations vis-à-vis its own residents and implies that the former should perhaps trump the latter. This in turn seems rooted in a notion that the 'internal market' inherently gives priority to the market jurisdiction. If based on non-discrimination reasoning alone, it would not seem possible to reach the conclusion advocated by Wattel; rather, it would depend on the question of 'restrictions' and just how extensively that concept can/should be interpreted.

(iv) The restrictions argument

Regarding whether the CJEU should pursue a broad interpretation of 'restrictions' of the fundamental freedoms, there are two counterarguments. First, although the CJEU expanded its reasoning to also prohibit restrictions, this does not go so far as to require MSs to support or favour going abroad. In debating this with Wattel, Avery Jones responded: 'It is not the purpose of free movement to *encourage* working abroad [...]' (emphasis added).[1010] On another occasion where Wattel and Avery Jones debated the topic, Avery Jones explained that:

> 'A person working in his home state and considering whether to work abroad will, if he works in a lower-tax state, pay less tax than if he worked at home under an exemption system, but the same tax under a credit system. The free movement of persons is about avoiding discouragement to working abroad, not about giving tax benefits for working abroad. [...].'[1011]

If one accepts the CEN-premise, then it could be argued that in the cases where CEN is achieved, the state of residence does not in any way impede a taxpayer from investing or working abroad; rather, to the contrary, CEN, by definition, makes this choice neutral as regards the tax rates. Yet, labelling the credit method as 'protectionist' suggests, by contrast, that, rather than being neutral, it incentivizes keeping investment at home and, by implication, disincentivizes investing abroad. This is at odds with CEN (which assumes neutrality, whereas protectionism assumes the credit method is not neutral). Under this logic, which would deem the credit method a 'protectionist' measure of the residence state, the exemption method could be deemed an inducement to invest abroad. Avery Jones' argument contains the idea that a negative obligation to abstain from mounting restrictions would not equate to a positive obligation to encourage cross-border movement. In any case, the precise incentives at play change relative to the respective tax rates, income or losses (etc.) in the states concerned. (Dis)incentives are not always synonymous with restrictions (or

1010. John F. Avery Jones, *A Comment on 'Progressive Taxation of Non-residents and Intra-EC Allocation of Personal Tax Allowances'*, 40(8) Eur. Tax'n 375, 375 (2000).
1011. Peter J. Wattel, *Home Neutrality in an Internal Market*, 36(5) Eur. Tax'n 159, 162 (1996) (*see* the text under 'John Avery Jones writes').

the lack thereof). To assume so, and if taken to the logical extreme, could capture all taxes as restrictions since taxes are bound to have incentive effects.

Second, and more importantly, the CJEU ultimately drew a line at 'disparities'. At that time, there was only a faint outline of this due to the *Gilly* case; it was far from settled at this stage. However, for one author, Paul Farmer, it was clear:

> 'In the author's view it is clear that a distinction of some sort must be made between discriminatory taxation (i.e. the imposition, as in *Schumacher, Wielockx* and *Asscher,* of a higher domestic tax burden on those exercising their freedom of movement or investment) and the restrictions which may arise from the mere exercise of tax jurisdiction or from conflicts of tax jurisdiction. To say that no fiscal restrictions are lawful would ultimately be to deny Member States the right to tax altogether! Moreover, it is submitted that, in the case of restrictions arising from double taxation, it is not for the Court to act as a referee responsible for deciding whether it is the home state or the host state which must surrender revenue. That is a matter for the Member States to resolve themselves either by harmonizing legislation adopted under Art 100 of the Treaty or in fulfilment of their duty under Art 220 to enter into negotiations with a view to securing the abolition of double taxation.'[1012]

Lehner and Wattel also suspected that later cases would reveal that not all disadvantages that may arise in a cross-border context are captured by the CJEU's restriction analysis. According to Vogel, 'as Moris Lehner correctly pointed out on several occasions, discrimination and restrictions (and, in particular, the distortion of competition brought about by the tax credit method) very often are the result of the combined action of both contracting states'.[1013] More precisely, some disadvantages result, not from the credit method itself, but from disparities between the MSs, on matters that they remain sovereign to set under EU law such as their tax rates and tax bases (as discussed below in Section 4.2.1.). Such disparities should be addressed through positive integration.

(v) The Centros/Eurowings argument[1014]

As regards the *Eurowings* case, it could be counterargued that the judgment seemed to be stretched beyond its intended finding. This was enabled by the phrase 'compensatory tax arrangements' found in paragraph 45, whose ambiguity allowed it to be taken to different contexts. The CJEU held that a MS cannot use the mere fact that tax rates are lower in another MS as a justification for different treatment of its own residents. This presupposes a measure that applies different treatment to residents based on, in

1012. Paul Farmer, *EC Law and National Rules on Direct Taxation: A Phoney War?*, 7(1) EC Tax Rev. 13, 27 (1998).

1013. Klaus Vogel, *Which Method Should the European Community Adopt for the Avoidance of Double Taxation?*, 56(1) Bull. Int'l Fiscal Documentation 4, 9 (2002) (internal citations omitted).

1014. On the relevance of *Eurowings, see,* e.g., Eric C.C.M. Kemmeren, *Source of Income in Globalizing Economies: Overview of the Issues and a Plea for an Origin-Based Approach,* 60(11) Bull. Int'l Tax'n 430, 442–443 (2006); Moris Lehner, *Limitation of the National Power of Taxation by the Fundamental Freedoms and Non-discrimination Clauses of the EC Treaty,* 9(1) EC Tax Rev. 5, 10–11 (2000); Pasquale Pistone, *The Impact of Community Law on Tax Treaties: Issues and Solutions* 197–198 (Kluwer Law International 2002).

this case, whether they obtained a service from a provider in the same MS or whether they obtained a service from a provider in another MS. The measure in question did not resemble a credit method. Crucially, the comparison was between a German company that obtained leasing services from a German provider as compared to a German company that obtained leasing services from an Irish provider. It has already been clearly established, however, that the credit method does *not* lead to different treatment; rather, one of its main purposes is to tax all residents the same regardless of whether they earn income from domestic sources or from foreign sources. So, fundamentally, the issue at stake in *Eurowings* does not even arise under the credit method.[1015]

The idea of paragraph 45, read in its context, especially with paragraph 44, is that, in the EU 'single market', MSs must accept that its residents are at liberty to obtain services from other MSs (or, by extension, to work in other MSs or invest in other MSs, etc.) and cannot treat them differently from other residents as a result of this (the credit method, in fact, seeks to achieve exactly the type of same treatment espoused, as regards the taxes levied by the state of residence). The fact that tax rates differ in other MSs (sometimes higher, sometimes lower) is a result of the fact that the 'single market' is far from complete, yet, in the meantime, residents still have a right to exercise their freedoms. Thus, to allow the non-harmonized differences of tax rates to be a justification for different treatment would paralyse what there is of a 'single market'. In a way, CJEU decisions like this one are a slight inducement for the MSs to continue to approximate their legislation in direct taxation.[1016]

(vi) The residence argument

Regarding the idea that there is a tension between residence in a MS and EU citizenship,[1017] although it is not a main argument, it is conceptually a cogent point to consider.[1018] What can be said, however, is that this argument for now belongs to the

1015. *See also*, e.g., CJEU, Case C-298/05, *Columbus Container Services*, 6 Dec. 2007, ECLI:EU:C:2007:754, at para. 48 ('Contrary to what the applicant in the main proceedings claims, it also does not follow from paragraphs 43 and 44 of the judgment in Case C-294/97 *Eurowings Luftverkehr* [1999] ECR I-7447 that the freedoms of movement guaranteed by the Treaty preclude the application of national legislation such as that in issue in the main proceedings') and at para. 49 ('Although the Court, in the *Eurowings Luftverkehr* judgment, held that a Member State cannot justify the application of a tax levy to recipients of services on the ground that the persons providing those services were subject to low taxation in another Member State, the case which led to that judgment concerned national legislation that subjected providers of services established in the Member State concerned to less favourable tax treatment than those established in other Member States. However, in the main proceedings in the present case, limited partnerships such as Columbus and partnerships established in Germany are subject, as regards their partners, to a tax treatment that is not based on such a difference in treatment').

1016. For a similar view, *see*, e.g., Dennis Weber, *Abuse of Law in European Tax Law: An Overview and Some Recent Trends in the Direct and Indirect Tax Case Law of the ECJ – Part 2*, 53(7) Eur. Tax'n 313, 322–324 Section 6 (2013).

1017. *See*, e.g., Pasquale Pistone, *The Impact of Community Law on Tax Treaties: Issues and Solutions* 178 (Kluwer Law International 2002).

1018. Indeed, this harks back to the perspective that arose under the constitutional principles of equality and free movement in the North German Confederation, *see*, e.g., *supra* note 461.

aspirational realm, worth pondering for a future with a more fully integrated internal market.[1019] At this time, this is a question that, under the EU Treaties, remains with the MSs. As Pistone acknowledged, the balance of competences between EU institutions and MSs in the field of direct taxation would have to be adjusted for solutions on this point.[1020] Thus, this issue does not yet have a bearing on whether the credit method is currently legally contrary to EU law. More importantly, even if this argument were accepted – and thus distinctions in tax law could no longer be based on 'residence' – the credit method does not necessarily have to be based on 'residence', contrary to popular belief – as seen in Chapter 2 (*see supra* note 98 and note 110), as seen in the arguments of Wattel (*see infra* note 1311), and as seen in cases such as *Avoir Fiscal* and *Saint Gobain* (*see* Section 4.2.1.).[1021]

(vii) Other concessions

In addition to the above, the authors, even those who argued against the credit method, made certain concessions. Most authors recognized, either explicitly or very implicitly, the role of the credit method as a 'backstop' to source-based taxation:

- According to Pistone, 'as long as significant tax rate differentials are maintained on the international scenario between industrialised countries and both developing countries and tax havens, residence-based taxation should remain applicable. Other solutions would in fact merely produce outwards flows from industrialised countries. A different scenario exists (or will be achieved insofar as EU tax havens will be removed) within the Community, so that different conclusions could be reached'.[1022]
- Terra and Wattel observed the widespread role of the credit method in the case of passive investment income due to its international mobility and the difficulty of detecting its source.[1023] The authors cite the relevance of the credit

1019. In that connection, Pistone and more recently Pitrone suggest one interim solution for the current internal market, namely whether a uniform definition of 'residence' among EU MSs could be a step forward. Federica Pitrone, *Tax Residence of Individuals Within the European Union: Finding New Solutions to Old Problems*, 8(3) World Tax J. 357 (2016).

1020. Pasquale Pistone, *The Impact of Community Law on Tax Treaties: Issues and Solutions* 178–179 (Kluwer Law International 2002) ('A complete solution to such issues seems indeed only possible when a common tax policy for the EU is established, i.e. only when Community institutions have become competent in the field of direct taxes').

1021. Along similar lines, *see*, e.g., Martti Nieminen, *Debate on the CCCTB: Destination-with-Credit Formula: A Simple Add-On that Would Make the CCCTB More Resilient in the Face of Tax Competition and Tax Planning*, 47(5) Intertax 490 (2019) (in order to make the CCCTB proposal more robust against tax rate competition, the author proposes a 'destination-with-credit formula', under which 'the Member State(s) of sales would be obligated to grant a computational credit for foreign taxes paid based on the other attributes of the baseline formula (labour and assets)'. In other words, this would also be a credit system applied by the state of sales, rather than the state of residence of the taxpayer).

1022. Pasquale Pistone, *The Impact of Community Law on Tax Treaties: Issues and Solutions* 201 (Kluwer Law International 2002).

1023. Ben J.M. Terra & Peter J. Wattel, *European Tax Law* 218 (Wolters Kluwer 6th ed. 2012); Otto Marres (update of 6th ed.), *Chapter 16: Division of Tax Jurisdiction; Double Tax Relief Mechanisms; Tax Treaty Issues*, in 1 *Terra/Wattel European Tax Law* 695, 703 (Peter J. Wattel, Otto Marres & Hein Vermeulen eds, Wolters Kluwer 7th ed. 2019).

method in the case of some aggressive tax planning or harmful tax competition.[1024]
- In discussing a 'drawback' of the exemption method, they wrote, 'it may encourage resident taxpayers to invest in foreign, relatively low-tax countries instead of investing at home. On a before-tax basis, such investments may well be sub-optimal from a capital productivity viewpoint'.[1025] It 'may also invite resident taxpayers to divert domestic income to foreign tax havens (tax avoidance)'.[1026]
- In this context, Vogel suggested exemption with a subject-to-tax clause.[1027] What this means is, of course, recognition of some role for the credit method.[1028]

Returning to Vogel's question, 'Which Method Should the European Community Adopt for the Avoidance of Double Taxation?', in answering this question, the degree of pushback against the credit method varied - from denouncing to doubting, from those who positioned themselves more as pro-exemption-method to those who were openly anti-credit-method. Some argued that the exemption method seemed more in line with the internal market (e.g., Kemmeren, Lehner, Pistone); others argued that not only is the exemption method more in line, but also the credit method is negative for, if not contrary to, the internal market (e.g., Wattel and Vogel). For others, the credit method did not pose a problem or was neutral from the perspective of EU law (e.g., Avery Jones and Farmer).

It is one thing to argue that the exemption method would be ideal for an internal market, and it is another thing to argue that the credit method is actually contrary to the internal market. The former is oriented towards the aspirational aspects, the latter towards the legal ones. In other words, it seems that the opinions varied depending on whether the starting point was a somewhat normative aspirational perspective, assuming a fully functioning and frictionless marketplace that the internal market ought to be or strives to be, or a more positivistic legal perspective, considering only the internal market that exists, in its current state, with its various compromises or

1024. Ben J.M. Terra & Peter J. Wattel, *European Tax Law* 218 (Wolters Kluwer 6th ed. 2012); Otto Marres (update of 6th ed.), *Chapter 16: Division of Tax Jurisdiction; Double Tax Relief Mechanisms; Tax Treaty Issues*, in 1 *Terra/Wattel European Tax Law* 695, 703 (Peter J. Wattel, Otto Marres & Hein Vermeulen eds, Wolters Kluwer 7th ed. 2019).

1025. Ben J.M. Terra & Peter J. Wattel, *European Tax Law* 216 (Wolters Kluwer 6th ed. 2012); Otto Marres (update of 6th ed.), *Chapter 16: Division of Tax Jurisdiction; Double Tax Relief Mechanisms; Tax Treaty Issues*, in 1 *Terra/Wattel European Tax Law* 695, 702 (Peter J. Wattel, Otto Marres & Hein Vermeulen eds, Wolters Kluwer 7th ed. 2019).

1026. Ben J.M. Terra & Peter J. Wattel, *European Tax Law* 217 (Wolters Kluwer 6th ed. 2012); Otto Marres (update of 6th ed.), *Chapter 16: Division of Tax Jurisdiction; Double Tax Relief Mechanisms; Tax Treaty Issues*, in 1 *Terra/Wattel European Tax Law* 695, 703 (Peter J. Wattel, Otto Marres & Hein Vermeulen eds, Wolters Kluwer 7th ed. 2019).

1027. Klaus Vogel, *Which Method Should the European Community Adopt for the Avoidance of Double Taxation?*, 56(1) Bull. Int'l Fiscal Documentation 4, 6 (2002).

1028. *See supra* note 144 and note 146 (recalling the discussions under the historical developments in Chapter 2, it seems that the role of the credit method is simply coming back full circle to, and being reinforced in, one of its original intents).

caveats,[1029] or somewhere in between. Also, as mentioned, there was a pivot in the case law around that time. Given the ambiguity, reasonable people took reasonably different views. Thus, a related point that cannot be overlooked is that EU law is 'dynamic' or evolving.[1030] This emanates not only from the Treaties themselves (e.g., an ever closer Union)[1031] but also from the CJEU case law[1032] (e.g., regularly referring to the 'current state' of EU law).

Regarding the legal aspects, the answers rely predominantly on the premise an author holds regarding what is understood to be a restriction of the fundamental freedoms and what the internal market (in direct taxation) requires. On these points, some changes have brought clarifications in the meantime, such as: (1) a clearer emergence of the 'disparities' concept, discussed in Section 4.2.2. below;[1033] (2) a declaration by the CJEU that the exemption method and the credit method are 'equivalent', under certain conditions, discussed in Section 4.2.3. below; and (3) a heightening of concerns over 'double non-taxation' and BEPS on the EU agenda, such that they were translated into hard law (e.g., in amendments to the Parent-Subsidiary Directive, in the ATAD, etc.) and gave rise to State Aid investigations. This last point brings more to centre stage some of the aforementioned concessions regarding the credit method (e.g., in the context of passive income, aggressive tax planning, harmful tax competition) and may have led to a recalibration in the perceptions of what the internal market requires. What this could mean for the credit method is that it is not contrary as initially thought, but rather complementary. CJEU case law has continued to further refine the relationship between the credit method and EU law[1034] and,

---

1029. Regarding compromises and caveats, *see*, e.g., Peter J. Wattel, *Commentary on Chapter 12: Anathema to the Internal Market*, *in European Tax Integration: Law, Policy and Politics* (Pasquale Pistone ed., IBFD 2018) (Wattel argues, *inter alia*, that there is '(No) internal market in respect of direct taxation').

1030. *See*, e.g., Servaas van Thiel, *EU Case Law on Income Tax* 3–4 (IBFD 2001).

1031. To be precise, *see*, e.g., Vaughne Miller, *'Ever Closer Union' in the EU Treaties and Court of Justice Case Law* (UK House of Commons Library, Briefing Paper 16 Nov. 2015), https://researchbriefings.parliament.uk/ResearchBriefing/Summary/CBP-7230 (last visited 10 Jul. 2018).

1032. *See*, e.g., Servaas van Thiel, *EU Case Law on Income Tax* 3–9 (IBFD 2001).

1033. *See*, e.g., *infra* note 1152 in Section 4.2.2.

1034. To list some examples, *see*, e.g., CJEU, Case C-385/00, *de Groot*, 12 Dec. 2002, ECLI:EU:C:2002:750; CJEU, Case C-319/02, *Manninen*, 7 Sep. 2004, ECLI:EU:C:2004:484; CJEU, Case C-513/04, *Kerckhaert and Morres*, 14 Nov. 2006, ECLI:EU:C:2006:713; CJEU, Case C-446/04, *Test Claimants in the FII Group Litigation*, 12 Dec. 2006, ECLI:EU:C:2006:774; CJEU, Case C-170/05, *Denkavit Internationaal and Denkavit France*, 14 Dec. 2006, ECLI:EU:C:2006:783; CJEU, Case C-292/04, *Meilicke*, 6 Mar. 2007, ECLI:EU:C:2007:132; CJEU, Case C-379/05, *Amurta*, 8 Nov. 2007, ECLI:EU:C:2007:655; CJEU, Case C-298/05, *Columbus Container Services*, 6 Dec. 2007, ECLI:EU:C:2007:754; CJEU, Case C-194/06, *Orange European Smallcap Fund*, 24 May 2008, ECLI:EU:C:2008:289; CJEU, Case C-67/08, *Block*, 12 Feb. 2009, ECLI:EU:C:2009:92; CJEU, Case C-521/07, *Commission v. Netherlands*, 11 Jun. 2009, ECLI:EU:C:2009:360; CJEU, Case C-128/08, *Damseaux*, 16 Jul. 2009, ECLI:EU:C:2009:471; CJEU, Case C-540/07, *Commission v. Italy*, 19 Nov. 2009, ECLI:EU:C:2009:717; CJEU, Case C-262/09, *Meilicke*, 30 Jun. 2011, ECLI:EU:C:2011:438; CJEU, Joined Cases C-436/08 and C-437/08, *Haribo Lakritzen Hans Riegel BetriebsgmbH and Österreichische Salinen AG*, 10 Feb. 2011, ECLI:EU:C:2011:61; CJEU, Case C-310/09, *Accor*, 15 Sep. 2011, ECLI:EU:C:2011:581; CJEU, Case C-35/11, *Test Claimants in the FII Group Litigation*, 13 Nov. 2012, ECLI:EU:C:2012:707; CJEU, Case C-168/11, *Beker*, 28 Feb. 2013, ECLI:EU:C:2013:117; CJEU,

indeed, it has found that, in the current state of EU law, the credit method is not a violation. Of course, this does not mean that there are no constraints on its design. Against this background and to explore this further, the subsequent sections turn to the analysis of this case law.

4.2. THE CREDIT METHOD UNDER EU PRIMARY LAW

4.2.1. The *Avoir Fiscal/Saint Gobain* or Relief for Non-residents Line of Case Law

The discussion of CJEU case law on direct taxation begins with two landmark cases, namely the *Commission v. France (Avoir Fiscal)*[1035] case and the *Saint Gobain*[1036] case. There are three reasons for this. The first is that *Avoir Fiscal* is commonly considered the foundational case for the fundamental freedoms in the field of direct taxation,[1037] and *Saint Gobain* reinforced and expanded its findings that are relevant to granting relief. Until *Avoir Fiscal*, it was uncertain what, if any, impact fundamental freedoms could have on direct taxation.[1038] After all, direct taxation remained (and remains) a 'competence' of the MSs, so this touched upon constitutional-esque questions regarding the division of competences between the EU institutions and MSs under the EU Treaties. The CJEU, in *Avoir Fiscal*, endowed the fundamental freedoms with a rather strong power over direct taxation, as they could even have an impact on the very building blocks of direct taxation such as the distinction between residents and non-residents. This seemed to have opened the flood gates, so to speak, as hundreds of cases have come before the CJEU since.

Related to the first reason, the second is that starting with these cases therefore aids the structure of this chapter, as they introduce some of the most important reoccurring themes of the CJEU's case law on direct taxation, upon which subsequent sections build. The third reason is that, conveniently, these two cases both happen to

---

Case C-48/13, *Nordea Bank*, 17 Jul. 2014, ECLI:EU:C:2014:2087; CJEU, Case C-47/12, *Kronos International Inc.*, 11 Sep. 2014, ECLI:EU:C:2014:2200; CJEU, Joined Cases C-10/14, C-14/14 and C-17/14, *J. B. G. T. Miljoen, X, and Société Générale SA*, 17 Sep. 2015, ECLI:EU:C:2015:608; CJEU, Case C-176/15, *Riskin and Timmermans*, 30 Jun. 2016, ECLI:EU:C:2016:488; CJEU, Case C-28/17, *NN*, 4 Jul. 2018, ECLI:EU:C:2018:526; CJEU, Case C-416/17, *Commission v. France (Précompte mobilier)*, 4 Oct. 2018, ECLI:EU:C:2018:811. In addition to CJEU case law, *see* EFTA, Case E-1/04, *Fokus Bank v. Norway*, 23 Nov. 2004; EFTA, Case E-7/07, *Seabrokers v. Norway*, 7 May 2008.

1035. CJEU, Case C-270/83, *Commission v. France (Avoir Fiscal)*, 28 Jan. 1986, ECLI:EU:C:1986:37.

1036. CJEU, Case C-307/97, *Saint Gobain*, 21 Sep. 1999, ECLI:EU:C:1999:438 (note that the paragraphs cited here are based on the official PDF version of the judgment, http://curia.europa.eu/juris/showPdf.jsf;jsessionid=8AB852819DAE7B6DC03815F6D97C7E35?text=&docid=44717&pageIndex=0&doclang=EN&mode=lst&dir=&occ=first&part=1&cid=10791363 (last visited 10 Aug. 2018), and in some cases, the numbering of the paragraphs appears to differ from the HTML version on the Curia website).

1037. *See*, e.g., Werner Haslehner, *'Avoir Fiscal' and Its Legacy after Thirty Years of Direct Tax Jurisprudence of the Court of Justice*, 44(5) Intertax 374, 374 (2016).

1038. *See*, e.g., Servaas van Thiel, *EU Case Law on Income Tax* xi (IBFD 2001); Werner Haslehner, *'Avoir Fiscal' and Its Legacy after Thirty Years of Direct Tax Jurisprudence of the Court of Justice*, 44(5) Intertax 374, 374 (2016).

deal explicitly with the credit method – in particular, an 'imputation' credit. Although they do not delve into the details of its design, these cases are indeed the first in the series that start to thread EU law and the credit method together.

As regards the design of the credit method, their main impact is to affect its scope of application in EU MSs. On that point, the responsibility to provide relief for double taxation normally falls on the state of residence of the taxpayer, as indicated in the *Schumacker* line of case law (discussed in Section 4.2.4.) and the *ACT Test Claimants* 'imputation' case (discussed in Section 4.2.8.). Yet, the cases in this subsection, *Commission v. France (Avoir Fiscal)* and *Saint Gobain*, indicated that EU MSs may nevertheless have the obligation to extend relief to *non-resident* taxpayers.

To begin, the 1986 *Commission v. France (Avoir Fiscal)*[1039] case, a landmark for 'direct taxation' in EU law, addressed a tax credit. In particular, this case discussed an 'imputation credit' offered in France, referred to as the '*avoir fiscal*'. The goal of the tax credit was to mitigate the economic double taxation ('cumulative taxation') of profit distributions, first subject to corporation tax at a rate of 50% and second to either personal income tax or again corporation tax in the hands of the shareholder.[1040] As regards the operation of the tax credit, the law offered the shareholders a 'tax credit' equal to one-half of the amount actually paid by the distributing company.

Notably, the benefit could be enjoyed only by those 'persons who have their habitual residence or registered office in France'.[1041] This covered, therefore, subsidiaries set up in France by companies of other EU MSs, but excluded branches, or agencies or PEs set up in France by companies of other EU MSs. Thus, the comparison was between French companies or subsidiaries of non-resident companies versus other 'secondary' establishments in France (i.e., branches, agencies or PEs of non-resident companies). The Commission seized on the fact that, while the former had their seat or registered office in France, the latter of course did not.[1042] To demonstrate the difference in treatment, an example of the Commission can be depicted as follows:[1043]

Subsidiary	**Permanent Establishment**
Assume: receives distribution of 100 from a French company	Assume: receives distribution of 100 from a French company
Tax credit: 50% of 100 = 50	Tax credit: not eligible
Taxable income: 100 + tax credit of 50 = 150	Taxable income: 100

1039. CJEU, Case C-270/83, *Commission v. France (Avoir Fiscal)*, 28 Jan. 1986, ECLI:EU:C:1986:37.
1040. *Id.*, at 286 and at 299–300, para. 3.
1041. *Id.*, at 287 (more precisely, it could be granted to 'persons who have their habitual residence or registered office in France' under 'Article 158 ter of the Code général des Impôts' or to 'persons resident in the territory of States which have concluded an agreement with France for the purpose of avoiding double taxation' under certain conditions under 'Article 242 quater of the code général des impôts') and at 300, para. 4.
1042. *Id.*, at 289.
1043. *Id.*

Tax: 150 × 50% = 75 CIT *minus* tax credit of 50 = 25 CIT due	Tax: 100 × 50% = 50 CIT due

The Commission brought an infringement procedure[1044] against France on the grounds that subjecting the two situations to different tax treatment amounted to discrimination on the basis of a company's registered office being in another EU MS, in violation of the freedom of establishment. Indeed, dividends distributed by French companies to branches of non-resident companies in France were not able to benefit from the tax credit in the same way as French recipients, *even though* the dividends formed part of the branches' taxable income in France in the same way as French recipients.

The arguments of the French government included that the different treatment does not amount to discrimination because it applies to situations that are objectively different.[1045] For a number of reasons, companies and subsidiaries are simply *not comparable* with secondary establishments such as branches and agencies. The former are distinct legal entities, while the latter are not. The former are residents and the latter are not, a widespread legitimate distinction in direct taxation that is necessary, non-discriminatory and not based on nationality.[1046] From these more fundamental differences, a number of subtle differences follow, such as the fact that only subsidiaries are subject to the fees for incorporation, while PEs are not. In short, branches and agencies benefit from other advantages that subsidiaries do not benefit from,[1047] and thus any disadvantage from not getting a credit 'must be viewed in the overall context' of all relevant tax provisions.[1048] In any case, if the company from another MS does not like the fact that its branch cannot get the tax credit, this does not prevent its establishment in France; this non-resident EU company can still establish itself in France and simply opt for a subsidiary instead of a secondary establishment.[1049]

1044. CJEU, Case C-270/83, *Commission v. France (Avoir Fiscal)*, 28 Jan. 1986, ECLI:EU:C:1986:37, at 300–301, paras 6–7 (the Commission infringement was limited to insurance companies in France, but the issue was more broadly relevant: 'The Commission has added that although it has restricted its action to the insurance sector because it has received complaints only in regard to that sector, all the Member States, and in particular France, must nonetheless draw all the appropriate conclusions from the Court's judgment, even in regard to other sectors') and at 289–290 (the reason for the complaints from insurance companies seems to stem from the fact that the problem was more pronounced in the insurance sector, entailing a 'double disadvantage', according to the Commission, due to rules under certain EU Directives that regulated the insurance industry at that time).
1045. *Id.*, at 291 and at 302, para. 12.
1046. *Id.*, at 291 and at 303–304, para. 17.
1047. *Id.*, at 291–292 ('The fact that a secondary establishment does not have separate legal personality enables it to operate under more favourable conditions than subsidiaries inasmuch as it can make use of the capital and certain operating facilities of the non-resident company and inasmuch as it benefits from the reputation of that company and the guarantee of solvency which it provides'), at 292 ('Secondary establishments are not liable to the fees which companies incorporated under French law, including subsidiary companies, must pay at the time of incorporation, increase in capital, transformation etc.') and at 303–304, para. 17.
1048. *Id.*, at 291 and at 303–304, para. 17.
1049. *Id.*, at 305, para. 22.

Furthermore, France reminded the Commission and the CJEU that 'direct taxation is within the jurisdiction of the Member States'[1050] and problems arise from the lack of harmonization at the Community level on the question of direct taxation. France also put forward the need to prevent tax evasion (which likely should have been translated as 'tax avoidance' throughout)[1051] since it argued that extending the tax credit to secondary establishments may induce foreign companies to attribute all of their French shareholdings to their secondary establishments in France in order to take advantage of the tax credit in cases where the tax credit would otherwise not be available to them.[1052]

The Commission argued that this treatment is discriminatory because the tax credit is based on where a company's registered office is located, which is tantamount to a company's 'nationality'.[1053] The French tax law subjects branches and agencies to the *same* tax base and tax rate as companies (i.e., a form of territorial tax base, taxed at 50%), yet a different criterion is used for offering the tax credit (i.e., that of being incorporated under French law). Thus, the two are taxed the same, but only one (i.e., French companies) benefits from a tax credit. Also, by putting certain secondary forms of establishment at a disadvantage, the French legislation has the effect of forcing foreign companies to choose the legal form of a subsidiary, incorporated under French law, rather than allowing those companies to freely choose the form of establishment, as either a subsidiary or an agency or a branch.[1054] Comparing the French government's argument and the Commission's argument on this point, it becomes clear that this was a crucial open question as to the precise substantive rights granted by the freedom of establishment. To make it more contentious, on this point, the AG sided with France.[1055] Furthermore, the fact that 'Community' law is not harmonized on a

1050. *Id.*, at 290–291.

1051. In agreement, *see*, e.g., Werner Haslehner, *'Avoir Fiscal' and Its Legacy after Thirty Years of Direct Tax Jurisprudence of the Court of Justice*, 44(5) Intertax 374, 375 n.8 (2016).

1052. CJEU, Case C-270/83, *Commission v. France (Avoir Fiscal)*, 28 Jan. 1986, ECLI:EU:C:1986:37, at 294. *See also*, e.g., Paul Farmer, *EC Law and National Rules on Direct Taxation: A Phoney War?*, 7(1) EC Tax Rev. 13, 23 (1998) (describing France's argument); OECD, *Model Tax Convention on Income and on Capital 2017: Condensed Version* Commentary on Article 24(3), para. 50 (OECD Publishing 2017) (where an almost identical argument is presented).

1053. CJEU, Case C-270/83, *Commission v. France (Avoir Fiscal)*, 28 Jan. 1986, ECLI:EU:C:1986:37, at 294.

1054. *Id.*, at 294 and at 305, para. 22 (at this time, it was not yet known with certainty whether this was a problem. Arguably, different treatment of different forms of establishment did not necessarily mean that establishment *as such* was restricted. The CJEU clarified this at para. 22 of the judgment).

1055. Opinion of AG Mancini in Case C-270/83, *Commission v. France (Avoir Fiscal)*, 16 Oct. 1985, ECLI:EU:C:1985:413, at 283, para. 11 ('The French Government contended that that argument was without foundation and I share its opinion. Discrimination and restrictions on establishment are different phenomena and it does not necessarily follow that a measure likely to give rise to the one will also contribute to the other. Thus, the discouragement of agencies and branches may be an aspect of the discriminatory treatment of foreign companies but does not affect their right to establish themselves in France. According to Article 52, that right includes the abolition of restrictions on "the setting up of agencies, branches or subsidiaries". In my opinion, those words cannot be interpreted as meaning that the three forms of secondary establishment must be subject to absolutely identical rules whether in regard to taxation or to anything else').

particular matter does not release MSs from their obligation to ensure that their laws are non-discriminatory. In response to France's argument about tax evasion (or tax avoidance), the Commission explained that this risk was inexistent, considering that distributions of dividends from France to a foreign subsidiary would be subject to only a limited WHT at source, whereas distributions of dividends from France to a PE in France of a foreign company would be fully subject to French CIT at the rate of 50% and, even with the tax credit, would often pay more than the limited WHT at source.[1056]

The CJEU accepted the arguments of the Commission. It agreed that the 'registered office ... serves as the connecting factor with the legal system of a particular State, like nationality in the case of natural persons'.[1057] As regards comparability, since French law placed both subsidiaries and PEs 'on the same footing for the purposes of taxing their profits', France had thus placed them in an objectively comparable situation.[1058] Just like French companies, branches of non-resident companies were subject to CIT on their income earned in France; in fact, because France applies a form of 'territorial' CIT system, the two were even more comparable in that respect.[1059]

1056. CJEU, Case C-270/83, *Commission v. France (Avoir Fiscal)*, 28 Jan. 1986, ECLI:EU:C:1986:37, at 295.

1057. *Id.*, at 304, para. 18. For a more recent formulation of the idea, which is now settled case law, *see*, e.g., CJEU, Case C-446/04, *Test Claimants in the FII Group Litigation*, 12 Dec. 2006, ECLI:EU:C:2006:774, at para. 40 ('In the case of companies, it should be borne in mind that their registered office for the purposes of Article 48 EC serves, in the same way as nationality in the case of individuals, as the connecting factor with the legal system of a State. Acceptance of the proposition that the Member State in which a company seeks to establish itself may freely apply different treatment merely by reason of its registered office being situated in another Member State would deprive Article 43 EC of all meaning (see, to that effect, Case 270/83 *Commission* v *France* [1986] ECR 273, paragraph 18; Case C-330/91 *Commerzbank* [1993] ECR I4017, paragraph 13; *Metallgesellschaft and Others*, paragraph 42; and *Marks & Spencer*, paragraph 37). Freedom of establishment thus aims to guarantee the benefit of national treatment in the host Member State, by prohibiting any discrimination based on the place in which companies have their seat (see, to that effect, *Commission* v *France*, paragraph 14, and *SaintGobain ZN*, paragraph 35)').

1058. CJEU, Case C-270/83, *Commission v. France (Avoir Fiscal)*, 28 Jan. 1986, ECLI:EU:C:1986:37, at 304–305, paras 19–20 ('Even if the possibility cannot altogether be excluded that a distinction based on the location of the registered office of a company or the place of residence of a natural person may, under certain conditions, be justified in an area such as tax law, it must be observed in this case that French tax law does not distinguish, for the purpose of determining the income liable to corporation tax, between companies having their registered office in France and branches and agencies situated in France of companies whose registered office is abroad. By virtue of Article 209 of the code général des impôts, both are liable to taxation on profits made in undertakings carried on in France, to the exclusion of profits which are made abroad or which France is entitled to tax under the terms of a double taxation agreement.' 'Since the rules at issue place companies whose registered office is in France and branches and agencies situated in France of companies whose registered office is abroad on the same footing for the purposes of taxing their profits, those rules, cannot, without giving rise to discrimination, treat them differently in regard to the grant of an advantage related to taxation, such as shareholders' tax credits. By treating the two forms of establishment in the same way for the purposes of taxing their profits, the French legislature has in fact admitted that there is no objective difference between their positions in regard to the detailed rules and conditions relating to that taxation which could justify different treatment').

1059. *Id.*, at 298 (the Commission made this point in the following way: 'In France however a resident company, by virtue of the principle of territoriality, is taxed only on its profits made in France and not on those of its secondary establishments abroad and consequently its tax

After comparability was established, all other arguments were succinctly rejected. The argument regarding the other advantages that a PE might benefit from as compared to a subsidiary was dismissed. This could not justify the refusal of the tax credit, seemingly because such advantages were hypothetical (implied by the wording 'any advantages which branches and agencies *may* enjoy ...' and '*[e]ven if* such advantages actually exist ...' (emphasis added)) and unrelated to the specific tax disadvantage at issue.[1060] In addition, the CJEU hinted that the freedom of establishment guarantees both the right of establishment *as such* and the right to freely choose the *form* of establishment: 'The second sentence of the first paragraph of Article 52 expressly leaves traders free to choose the appropriate legal form in which to pursue their activities in another Member State and that freedom of choice must not be limited by discriminatory tax provisions.'[1061] As regards the argument regarding tax evasion (or tax avoidance), the CJEU held that 'the risk of tax avoidance cannot be relied upon in this context. Article 52 of the EEC Treaty does not permit any derogation from the fundamental principle of freedom of establishment on such a ground'.[1062] This last argument is a prime example of how the CJEU case law may evolve over time. The need to prevent tax abuse, avoidance and evasion has since become one of the possible justifications that MSs may put forward before the CJEU.[1063]

The CJEU's approach to 'comparability' (i.e., based on being taxed in the same way) is a long-lasting remnant of this case that has reappeared in subsequent direct taxation cases, reformulated in slightly different ways. It has been described as a form

---

position, from the point of view of the determination of its taxable income is no different from that of a secondary establishment of a nonresident company'). For further details, *see* Opinion of AG Mancini in Case C-270/83, *Commission v. France (Avoir Fiscal)*, 16 Oct. 1985, ECLI:EU:C:1985:413, at 282, para. 10.

1060. CJEU, Case C-270/83, *Commission v. France (Avoir Fiscal)*, 28 Jan. 1986, ECLI:EU:C:1986:37, at 305, para. 21.

1061. *Id.*, at 305, para. 22. *See*, e.g., Opinion of AG Mischo in Case C-307/97, *Saint Gobain*, 2 Mar. 1999, ECLI:EU:C:1999:110, at para. 24. *See also*, e.g., CJEU, Case C-253/03, *CLT-UFA*, 23 Feb. 2006, ECLI:EU:C:2006:129 (in this case, the CJEU clearly confirmed this aspect of the freedom of establishment that it also entails the free choice between the different forms of establishment); Werner Haslehner, *'Avoir Fiscal' and Its Legacy after Thirty Years of Direct Tax Jurisprudence of the Court of Justice*, 44(5) Intertax 374, 383–385 (2016) (Haslehner describes the evolution of 'The Freedom to Choose Between Types of Establishment (Neutrality of Legal Forms)' and also describes the limits on this freedom: 'The opposite, however, is not true: A company pursuing activities in another Member State through a subsidiary cannot claim the same treatment as a branch. In that respect, the vertical comparison trumps the horizontal comparison and, as the subsidiary is itself a resident, it cannot claim discrimination when treated less favourably than a non-resident. Such *reverse discrimination* is generally understood to be unaffected by the fundamental freedoms.[66]' Moreover, it seems limited to only corporate investors, not to individuals who set up establishments in the host state, and it is limited to the host state perspective, as cases such as *Bosal*, *Columbus Container Services*, and *X Holding* have shown that, from the home state – of state of origin – perspective, outward investments via subsidiaries or PEs are not comparable).

1062. CJEU, Case C-270/83, *Commission v. France (Avoir Fiscal)*, 28 Jan. 1986, ECLI:EU:C:1986:37, at 306, para. 25.

1063. *See*, e.g., Ben J.M. Terra & Peter J. Wattel, *European Tax Law* 914 (Wolters Kluwer 6th ed. 2012); Werner Haslehner, *'Avoir Fiscal' and Its Legacy after Thirty Years of Direct Tax Jurisprudence of the Court of Justice*, 44(5) Intertax 374, 391 (2016).

of 'legal' comparability rather than a 'factual' comparability.[1064] Indeed, the CJEU dismissed nearly all other differences between branches and subsidiaries as irrelevant (e.g., the fact that branches do not make dividend distributions to the head office, the fact that subsidiaries pay special fees for incorporation). Some of the differences were factual, while some were legal. The only factor or attribute that the CJEU considered relevant was the legal treatment under the tax law. Perhaps this approach could therefore be described as a tax-law-based or 'tax legal' comparability. The lens of analysis of the CJEU, in this case, seemed exclusively focused on the specific tax law referred to it and whether that tax law, from an isolated perspective, is discriminatory. Through this zoomed-in lens, the comparability analysis filtered out and ignored other company law issues, other factual circumstances or even other tax law issues that may serve to compare and contrast the situations. Some indication as to how the CJEU narrowed its lens of analysis is visible in paragraph 10 of the judgment:

> 'Since some uncertainty as to the precise subject matter of this action has become visible during the proceedings, it must once again be pointed out that the action is concerned with disparity in the treatment in regard to the shareholders' tax credit of, on the one hand, insurance companies whose registered office is in France, including subsidiaries set up in France by foreign companies, and, on the other, of branches and agencies established in France by insurance companies whose registered office is in another Member State. The action does not therefore deal generally with every difference in treatment between, on the one hand, companies as independent legal entities and, on the other, branches and agencies without separate legal personality. Finally, it must be particularly emphasized that the action does not concern differences which may exist in the rules regarding taxation applicable to branches and agencies, on the one hand, and, on the other hand, subsidiaries of companies whose registered office is in another Member State where those branches and agencies or those subsidiaries transfer to the company which owns them profits made in the undertakings carried on by them in France.'

This approach has also been described in other ways. For example, Paul Farmer referred to it as a 'source-by-source analysis': if a resident company and a PE of a non-resident company are taxed in the same way on dividends (or on a given source of income), denying a tax benefit 'to one inevitably entailed discrimination in relation to that source of income'.[1065] Werner Haslehner has likened it to a 'principle of consistency'.[1066] In this way, Haslehner explains, the CJEU acknowledges the sovereignty of MSs to design their tax systems and the factors serving as a basis for their taxation, as

1064. *See*, e.g., Michael Lang, *Recent Case Law of the ECJ in Direct Taxation: Trends, Tensions and Contradictions*, 18(3) EC Tax Rev. 98, 101 (2009).

1065. Paul Farmer, *EC Law and National Rules on Direct Taxation: A Phoney War?*, 7(1) EC Tax Rev. 13, 23 (1998).

1066. Werner Haslehner, *'Avoir Fiscal' and Its Legacy after Thirty Years of Direct Tax Jurisprudence of the Court of Justice*, 44(5) Intertax 374, 381 (2016) (citing articles by 'See, e.g., Axel Cordewener et al., *The Tax Treatment of Foreign Losses: Ritter, M&S and the Way Ahead (Part Two)*, Eur. Tax. 218 (223) (2004); J. Englisch, *The European Treaties' Implications for Direct Taxes*, 33 Intertax 310 (328) (2005)').

long as the MSs apply it consistently.[1067] As subsequent sections reveal, this underlying principle gave way to a more expansive approach through other cases, as Haslehner also observed, 'the Court further extended its comparability approach to hold non-residents comparable to residents in all circumstances in which they are subject to tax on the particular type of income to which a benefit in question was directly connected'. In other words, the same taxation was no longer the required yardstick for comparability but merely the act of the state exercising its jurisdiction to tax over the non-resident.[1068] For this reason, Terra and Wattel have referred to this as a 'subject-to-tax' approach.[1069]

Given the comparability (and given the CJEU's indication that the freedom of establishment also guaranteed the right to freely choose the legal form of establishment), the tax credit had to be granted to PEs, located in France, of companies from other EU MSs. Consequently, in cases where a MS taxes a non-resident company established in its territory in the same way as a resident company, the freedom of establishment requires that the non-resident is treated in the same way as residents as regards relief pertaining to that taxation.

Similar to the *Avoir Fiscal* case, the main topics of the *Saint Gobain* case[1070] included comparability in the case of companies, the freedom of establishment and relief for double taxation. Rather than a domestic imputation credit, the *Saint Gobain* case discussed a domestic 'indirect tax credit' and relief under tax treaties.

Regarding the facts, a French company, Saint Gobain SA, established a branch in Germany.[1071] For this reason, Saint Gobain SA was deemed to have a PE under German tax law; thus, the French company was subject to limited tax liability in Germany on the income generated by its PE, including any income resulting from assets that its PE exploited in Germany.[1072] Among its assets, this PE held (together with other companies) shares in various companies (e.g., in the US, in Switzerland and others).[1073] By contrast with *Avoir Fiscal*, which concerned shareholdings in domestic companies,

1067. Werner Haslehner, *'Avoir Fiscal' and Its Legacy after Thirty Years of Direct Tax Jurisprudence of the Court of Justice*, 44(5) Intertax 374, 381–383 (2016); Werner Haslehner, *'Consistency' and Fundamental Freedoms: The Case of Direct Taxation*, 50(3) Common Mkt. L. Rev. 737, 738–740 (2013).

1068. Werner Haslehner, *'Avoir Fiscal' and Its Legacy after Thirty Years of Direct Tax Jurisprudence of the Court of Justice*, 44(5) Intertax 374, 381–382 (2016).

1069. Ben J.M. Terra & Peter J. Wattel, *European Tax Law* 892–894 (Wolters Kluwer 6th ed. 2012); Peter J. Wattel, *Chapter 14: Conceptual Background of the CJEU Case Law in Direct Tax Matters in* 1 *Terra/Wattel European Tax Law* 611, 626–630 (Peter J. Wattel, Otto Marres & Hein Vermeulen eds, Wolters Kluwer 7th ed. 2019).

1070. CJEU, Case C-307/97, *Saint Gobain*, 21 Sep. 1999, ECLI:EU:C:1999:438.

1071. *Id.*, at para. 3.

1072. *Id.*, at paras 5–7.

1073. *Id.*, at paras 9–14 (more precisely, the PE held 10.2% of the shares in a company in the United States and over 98% in two companies in Germany. These two German companies in turn held shares in companies in Italy (24.8%), in Switzerland (33.34%), and in Austria (46.67%). Under a group taxation regime, the PE formed a group with the two German companies, which involved the transfer of the profits and losses of those German companies to the PE. The profits that were deemed transferred to and directly attributable to the PE included dividends from these shareholdings).

Saint Gobain concerned shareholdings in domestic and foreign companies, both EU and non-EU.[1074]

As for the contested issue, Germany refused to allow Saint Gobain three forms of tax relief, 'designed to prevent dividends which are received in Germany by companies with shareholdings in foreign companies and which have already been taxed abroad from being taxed again in Germany'.[1075] First, Germany refused the exemption granted under the Germany-US DTC and under the Germany-Switzerland DTC.[1076] Second, Germany refused to grant the indirect credit offered under domestic law.[1077] Third, the shareholding in the US company was included in the tax base subject to capital tax, and Germany refused to grant the relief, referred to as the 'capital tax concession', provided for under domestic law.[1078] German tax authorities explained that these benefits were only granted to German companies subject to unlimited tax liability in Germany. Saint Gobain considered it contrary to the freedom of establishment to be excluded from these benefits.[1079]

The CJEU reiterated the finding of *Avoir Fiscal* that a company's registered seat serves as a proxy for the company's nationality.[1080] Under the freedom of establishment, Germany must accord the same treatment to companies registered in other EU MSs, in effect other EU nationals, that it accords to its own nationals.[1081] The CJEU observed that, by denying tax relief to PEs of non-resident companies, they are placed at a disadvantage compared to German companies, which 'makes it less attractive for those companies to have intercorporate holdings through German branches, ... which thus restricts the freedom to choose the most appropriate legal form'.[1082]

The CJEU then analysed whether the difference in treatment was justified.[1083] The German government argued that PEs of non-resident companies are objectively different from companies resident in Germany, as the first are subject to limited tax liability and the second to unlimited tax liability.[1084] Further anchoring its reasoning in *Avoir Fiscal*, the CJEU responded that they are nevertheless comparable by virtue of the fact that PEs of both non-resident companies and resident companies are subject to tax on dividends received from shares in foreign companies.[1085] The difference in treatment applies only as regards the grant of the tax relief in question.

Germany put forward other arguments - i.e., the difference in treatment is justified, first, by the need to prevent a reduction in tax revenue; second, by certain

1074. Opinion of AG Mischo in Case C-307/97, *Saint Gobain*, 2 Mar. 1999, ECLI:EU:C:1999:110, at para. 26.
1075. CJEU, Case C-307/97, *Saint Gobain*, 21 Sep. 1999, ECLI:EU:C:1999:438, at para. 15.
1076. *Id.*, at paras 16–19.
1077. *Id.*, at paras 20–21.
1078. *Id.*, at paras 22–23.
1079. *Id.*, at para. 23.
1080. *Id.*, at para. 36.
1081. *Id.*, at para. 35.
1082. *Id.*, at paras 39, 43.
1083. *Id.*, at para. 45.
1084. *Id.*, at paras 46–47.
1085. *Id.*, at paras 47–48 ('Shareholdings in foreign subsidiaries and sub-subsidiaries in Germany are liable to tax there irrespective of whether they are held by resident company or by a non-resident company').

advantages that PEs have over resident subsidiaries; third, by the division of competences in the EC Treaty; and fourth, supported by Sweden, by the fact that the reciprocity and balance struck in tax treaties would be 'disturbed' if their benefits have to be extended beyond their agreed-upon scope - each rejected. These are briefly addressed here, to the extent they help explain certain foundational aspects of the CJEU's reasoning that reoccur in other cases discussed below.

Regarding the first argument, the CJEU dismissed the justification based on the need to prevent a reduction in tax revenue because it is not listed in the Treaty as a ground and cannot be regarded as a matter of 'overriding general interest'.[1086] The import of this is twofold: first, it shows the emergence of case-law-based justifications (as opposed to those explicitly listed in the EC/EU Treaties) and, second, it shows that one such justification, often pitched by MSs, namely the concern over a reduction in tax revenue, is rejected outright by the CJEU.

Second, according to Germany, PEs have an advantage regarding the transfer of profits to the non-resident parent company,[1087] since as opposed to being transferred in the form of dividends, which Germany can tax by means of a WHT at source, profits of a PE are automatically attributable to the non-resident company without any WHT at source.[1088] Again, reiterating *Avoir Fiscal*, the CJEU held that the discriminatory treatment cannot be justified or compensated for by other (unrelated) advantages.[1089] In rejecting Germany's argument, what the CJEU does here is imply which attributes it

---

1086. *Id.*, at paras 50–51 (the German government pointed out that, in the case of resident subsidiaries, Germany has the right to tax any subsequent distributions of dividends that the subsidiary makes. Thus, the relief offered to resident subsidiaries when they receive dividends is, in part, compensated for by Germany's right to subsequently levy a tax when they later distribute any dividends. In the case of a PE of a non-resident company, Germany has no right to tax any subsequent distributions of dividends by the non-resident company. Thus, the revenue lost from extending relief to the PE upon receipt of dividends is not compensated for by taxation at a later moment of distribution).

1087. *Id.*, at para. 52.

1088. *Id.*, at para. 53.

1089. *Id.*, at para. 54. For more on possible counterarguments, *see*, e.g., Opinion of AG Mischo in Case C-307/97, *Saint Gobain*, 2 Mar. 1999, ECLI:EU:C:1999:110, at paras 65–69; João Félix Pinto Nogueira, *Chapter 29: Portugal: PE and Non-discrimination Regarding Domestic Relief for Double Economic Taxation, in Tax Treaty Case Law Around the Globe 2014* 293, Section 29.4 (Eric C.C.M. Kemmeren et al. eds, IBFD/Linde 2015) (although the CJEU did not further elaborate this point, arguments were brought forward by the Advocate General (AG). Regarding the above-mentioned withholding tax advantage for PEs, it could be rejected as both hypothetical and unrelated (AG, at paras 65–69). First, it could be argued that this is merely a *hypothetical* advantage because it is not guaranteed that a subsidiary will redistribute the dividends received, as it could reinvest the capital (Pinto Nogueira, at Section 29.4), or it could redistribute only a portion. In the particular case of Germany, the split-rate system that applied upon distribution of dividends made it harder to establish whether arithmetically there would actually be any advantage: 'the proportion of the dividend of the subsidiary which is distributed to the parent company is taxed at a lower rate (36%) than the rate applied to the dividend transferred to the parent company by the branch (50%)', leading to an advantage for the subsidiary, rather than the PE (AG, at para. 67). Second, it could be argued that this is unrelated if one considers that the withholding tax is levied on a different taxable event (i.e., upon redistribution of the dividends) and on a different taxable person (i.e., the WHT levied on the ultimate parent, not the subsidiary benefiting from the relief at issue in this case) (AG, at para. 69). In other words, Germany sought to create a connection between the

deems (ir)relevant to the comparison. Once the comparability is established from the viewpoint of the specific aspect of taxation in question – namely dividends *received* and subject to corporation tax in the MS – then the mere formal status as a branch or a subsidiary, or as a resident or a non-resident, becomes irrelevant, regardless of the fact that other aspects of company law or tax law may differentiate the two.

Lastly, the German government sought to rely on, as a justification, a constitutional-type argument based on the division of competences in the Treaty (at that time, the EC Treaty), namely that direct taxation ('taxation of income and profits') is a competence of the MSs, that 'the conclusion of bilateral treaties with a non-member country does not come within the sphere of Community competence' and that there is an 'absence of Community harmonization' on these matters.[1090] The Swedish government added an argument that emphasized the special nature of tax treaties, which should make them more immune from these attacks.[1091] In response, the CJEU reasoned that even if MSs are free to conclude tax treaties 'to determine the connecting factors for the purposes of *allocating* powers of taxation as between themselves' (emphasis added),[1092] MSs must nevertheless respect EU law '[a]s far as the *exercise* of the power of taxation so allocated is concerned' (emphasis added).[1093] In this way, the CJEU created a distinction between the allocation of taxation rights under DTCs and the exercise of taxation rights under DTCs.[1094] By extending the benefits, such as an exemption, contained within DTCs concluded with non-MSs, a MS ensures that the taxation rights are *exercised* in accordance with EU law. And, in doing so, the *allocation* agreed upon in the DTC is not undermined in any way. A decision by Germany to extend a treaty exemption to non-resident taxpayers will not affect the rights or obligations of the non-MSs under the DTCs.[1095] Indeed, DTCs do not prevent such an extension, nor do DTCs prevent a MS from, for example, unilaterally exempting income on the basis of its domestic law.[1096] From this reasoning, it follows that the fact that the benefit in question is provided for in a DTC with a non-MS does not shelter it from EU law responsibilities. Thus, even in the case of DTCs with non-MSs, 'the national treatment principle requires the Member State which is party to the treaty to grant to permanent establishments of non-resident companies the advantages provided for by that treaty on the same conditions as those which apply to resident companies'.[1097] Germany was therefore obliged to unilaterally extend the benefits of the exemption

---

relief it grants to a subsidiary in its territory upon receipt of dividends from a sub-subsidiary and the withholding tax that it can levy when (or if) that subsidiary (potentially) redistributes profits to its shareholder).

1090. CJEU, Case C-307/97, *Saint Gobain*, 21 Sep. 1999, ECLI:EU:C:1999:438, at para. 54 (namely 'that double-taxation treaties are based on the principle of reciprocity and that the balance inherent in such treaties would be disturbed if the benefit of their provisions was extended to companies established in Member States which were not parties to them').

1091. *Id.*, at para. 56.

1092. *Id.*, at para. 57.

1093. *Id.*, at para. 58.

1094. *See also*, e.g., CJEU, Case C-290/04, *FKP Scorpio Konzertproduktionen*, 3 Oct. 2006, ECLI:EU:C:2006:630, at paras 54–55 (reiterating this distinction and citing other cases for it).

1095. CJEU, Case C-307/97, *Saint Gobain*, 21 Sep. 1999, ECLI:EU:C:1999:438, at para. 60.

1096. *Id.*, at para. 61.

1097. *Id.*, at para. 59.

under the DTCs, in addition to the indirect tax credit under domestic law and the exemption for capital tax under domestic law.

Although these outcomes (from *Avoir Fiscal* and *Saint Gobain*) are now widely known and taken for granted in EU tax law circles, in the initial stages, granting an indirect tax credit (or an exemption) for dividends received by PEs of non-resident companies was not necessarily an obvious or inevitable outcome.[1098] The outcome in these cases followed from two factors, namely the existence of a non-discrimination norm (the freedom of establishment) and how the comparability was established when applying it. That is, in the absence of a non-discrimination rule, states may be reluctant to grant these benefits, and, even in the presence of a non-discrimination rule, it depends on how it is interpreted.

For example, the OECD Model contains Article 24(3), which states that the taxation of PEs of non-resident companies cannot be 'less favourably levied' than that of resident companies. On the one hand, on this legal basis, the same outcome was reached in, for example, a 2013 case decided in Portugal regarding a provision nearly identical to Article 24(3) OECD Model in the Portugal-Brazil DTC.[1099] Moreover, on an indirectly related side note, in the *Royal Bank of Scotland* case, the CJEU even referred to the non-discrimination article in the 1953 Greece-UK DTC as evidence that Greece regarded the PE of a non-resident UK company as comparable.[1100] On the other hand, the OECD Commentary does not seem to take a definitive stance on whether this non-discrimination rule also obliges relief such as indirect tax credits or exemptions for the economic double taxation of dividends. In the Commentary (2017), it presents arguments in favour (in paragraph 49) and arguments against this (in paragraph 50), which nearly mirror the debates that took place between the parties in both the *Avoir Fiscal* and *Saint Gobain* cases. While the CJEU was convinced by the arguments in favour, perhaps not all courts applying such rules will be. For example, Alexander Rust in the *Klaus Vogel on Double Taxation Conventions* argues in favour, yet cites the cases and differing opinions on this issue.[1101] Some MSs at the time of *Avoir Fiscal* had already reasoned that the relief should be extended, as evidenced by the Commission's

1098. *See*, e.g., Adolfo J. Martín Jiménez, Francicso Alfredo García Prats & José M. Calderón Carrero, *Triangular Cases, Tax Treaties and EC Law: The Saint-Gobain Decision of the ECJ*, 55(6) Bull. Int'l Tax'n 241, 244 (2001) (the authors explain that many EU MSs under domestic law 'follow the international tax pattern, thus denying PEs access to the domestic tax measures that mitigate the international double taxation suffered by resident companies'. In this connection, the authors illustrated the issue with the example of Spain's laws).

1099. *See*, e.g., João Félix Pinto Nogueira, *Chapter 29: Portugal: PE and Non-discrimination Regarding Domestic Relief for Double Economic Taxation, in Tax Treaty Case Law Around the Globe 2014* 293 (Eric C.C.M. Kemmeren et al. eds, IBFD/Linde 2015) (citing 'PT: Arbitration Committee, 26 Nov. 2013, 154/201').

1100. CJEU, Case C-311/97, *Royal Bank of Scotland*, 29 Apr. 1999, ECLI:EU:C:1999:216, at para. 6 and para. 31 (as this is an early tax treaty, from 1953, it deviates from the OECD Model, but contains the general principle of the non-discrimination article. To see the wording, *see* the United Kingdom, HM Revenue & Customs, *Collection: Tax Treaties, Greece: Tax Treaties* (15 Aug. 2008), = https://assets.publishing.service.gov.uk/government/uploads/system/uploads/attachment_data/file/498354/1953-greece-dtc_-_in_force.pdf (last visited 26 Feb. 2019)).

1101. Alexander Rust, *Article 24 in Klaus Vogel on Double Taxation Conventions* (Ekkehart Reimer & Alexander Rust eds, Kluwer 4th ed. 2015), at m.nos 71–72 and m.no. 78.

description in *Avoir Fiscal* of '*Legislation of the Member States on this subject*'.[1102] Evidently that was not the case for France and for Germany. Only after the decision of *Avoir Fiscal*, and as *Saint Gobain* was making its way through the courts, did the German legislature suspect an infringement of the freedom of establishment; thus, it changed its law for tax periods after 1994.[1103] That said, in the EU, after these two cases, the fate of the (indirect) credit method in these cases is sealed.

A question that then arises is whether the same finding would apply to a direct credit. The OECD Commentary suggests that these are reoccurring questions for many states. The question was not addressed in the *Saint Gobain* case because, although Germany refused the indirect credit, Germany did grant a direct credit to the PE.[1104] The reasons for this were not explained. When discussing the grant of a direct credit to a PE of a non-resident company (e.g., for a WHT levied at source on dividends or on interest attributable to a PE), the Commentary on Article 24(3) of the OECD Model makes a distinction between a credit granted under domestic law and one granted under a DTC. It argues that a state should extend a direct credit for WHTs 'when such credit is granted to resident enterprises *under domestic laws*' (emphasis added).[1105] As for extending the grant of a credit that is offered *under a DTC*, it is more complicated.[1106] It seems that most of the states agree to offer relief, but not all.[1107]

If the states do so, then the question arises as to the amount of the credit to grant because there are potentially two DTCs involved: (1) that between the third state (from which the dividends, interest, etc., arise) and the state in which the PE is situated and (2) that between the third state and the state of residence of the enterprise of which the PE forms part. A problem arises if the two DTCs contain different rates of WHT on the streams of income in question. As noted in Chapter 2 (*see*, e.g., *supra* note 638), the direct credit obligation under DTCs is capped at the amount that may be levied in accordance with the DTC. In the *Saint Gobain* case, for example, the DTCs in question would be, *inter alia*, the DTC between Switzerland and Germany[1108] (where the PE is situated) and the DTC between Switzerland and France[1109] (where the head office of the PE is situated). As there was a 33.34% shareholding in a Swiss company, it would

1102. CJEU, Case C-270/83, *Commission v. France (Avoir Fiscal)*, 28 Jan. 1986, ECLI:EU:C:1986:37, at 298.
1103. CJEU, Case C-307/97, *Saint Gobain*, 21 Sep. 1999, ECLI:EU:C:1999:438, at paras 25–29.
1104. *Id.*, at para. 20.
1105. OECD, *Model Tax Convention on Income and on Capital 2017: Condensed Version* Commentary on Article 24, para. 67 (OECD Publishing 2017).
1106. *Id.*, para. 68.
1107. *Id.*, para. 70.
1108. CJEU, Case C-307/97, *Saint Gobaïn*, 21 Sep. 1999, ECLI:EU:C:1999:438, at para. 18 (the case cited 'the Convention concluded on 11 August 1971 between the Federal Republic of Germany and the Swiss Confederation for the avoidance of double taxation with respect to taxes on income and capital, as amended by the Protocol of 30 November 1978 (BGBl. 1972 II, p. 1022; 1980 II, p. 750), provides, in the version which was in force in relation to taxes collected before 1990').
1109. France-Switzerland Income and Capital Tax Treaty (1966) (as amended through 1969), IBFD Tax Treaties Database (accessed 27 Feb. 2019) (this DTC was not cited in the CJEU case as it was not relevant for its decision; it is selected for the sake of a hypothetical example, as it is the DTC that was closest to 1988, the relevant tax year in the facts of the *Saint Gobain* case).

have been possible under the Switzerland-Germany DTC to levy a 15% WHT at source and under the Switzerland-France DTC to levy a 5% WHT at source. Thus, the question that arises is whether Germany takes into account the 15% rate or the 5% rate for determining the extent of its obligation to grant the credit. The solution mentioned in the Commentary on Article 24 of the OECD Model is summarized in the *Klaus Vogel on Double Taxation Conventions* treatise as follows:

> 'The credit obligation contained in the DTC PE State/third State, however, may be more favourable than the credit according to domestic law. This is regularly the case with respect to a tax sparing provision contained in a tax treaty between the PE State and a third State.[175] The treaty credit obligation is subject to two limitations: First, the PE State is not required to grant a credit to the PE that is higher than the credit granted to domestic enterprises. Second, the credit may not exceed the amount of tax that the third State may levy under the DTC residence State/third State (no. 70 OECD MC Comm. on Article 24).'[1110]

As regards EU law, the same questions can be asked as to whether the direct credit must be granted and, if so, how much. MSs should, based on the CJEU's interpretation of the relevant non-discrimination rule of EU law (the freedom of establishment), also extend a direct credit to PEs of non-resident EU companies.[1111] Indeed, nothing in the reasoning of the CJEU in these cases seems affected by the type of method (e.g., direct or indirect credit), nor whether it is found in domestic law or in a tax treaty. The reasoning applied equally to an imputation credit in France, under its domestic law, as well as an exemption, indirect credit and capital tax relief in Germany, under its domestic law and/or its tax treaties. The decisive factor was, in essence, whether the PE of the non-resident company was taxed the same as resident companies, or subsidiaries, on the income (or capital) in question; if so, any related relief granted to resident companies should be extended to those PEs. A brief distinction may be merited here because, as discussed below (in Section 4.2.2.), the *Gilly* line of case law, and the *Kerckhaert and Morres* case in particular, suggests that the fundamental freedoms do not require direct credits to be granted; however, that line of case law addresses the residence state and a credit granted to its own residents, whereas these cases deal with the state of non-residence, or the host state, which affects the comparison and thus the outcome, as will become more apparent below.

Having argued that the CJEU's reasoning also applies to a *direct* credit for PEs of non-resident companies, questions arise regarding the *amount* of the credit. This becomes relevant because, as mentioned above, there are three states involved – i.e., the MS of the PE, the MS of the company to which the PE belongs, and the state of source of the income, which is attributable to the PE – and such 'triangular' scenarios often confront challenges due to the bilateral nature of tax treaties. According to the

1110. Alexander Rust, *Article 24 in Klaus Vogel on Double Taxation Conventions* (Ekkehart Reimer & Alexander Rust eds, Kluwer 4th ed. 2015), at m.no. 77.

1111. In agreement, *see*, e.g., Adolfo J. Martín Jiménez, Francisco Alfredo García Prats & José M. Calderón Carrero, *Triangular Cases, Tax Treaties and EC Law: The Saint-Gobain Decision of the ECJ*, 55(6) Bull. Int'l Tax'n 241, 243–244 (2001).

decision, the CJEU was concerned with the host state, Germany, extending the same treatment to the PE as compared to its residents:

> 'In the case of a double-taxation treaty concluded between a Member State and a non-member country, the national treatment principle requires the Member State *which is party to the treaty* to grant to permanent establishments of non-resident companies the advantages provided for *by that treaty* on the same conditions as those which apply to resident companies' (emphasis added).[1112]

In both this paragraph and the following paragraph of the judgment, the CJEU refers to the DTCs between Germany and the third state. Thus, this could be read as obliging Germany to grant the amount of credit permitted under German domestic law as modified by the Germany-Switzerland (PE state-third state) DTC, as though the PE were a subsidiary/resident in Germany. The decision is less clear about the impact, if any, of the France-Switzerland (head office state-third state) DTC.

One can consider different constellations to test the implications for the PE in such a situation. First, a few preliminary notes are in order. Presumably, from the third state perspective, from which the dividends (interest, etc., as the case may be) originate, the relevant DTC is that with the state where the 'resident' company is located (e.g., Switzerland-France DTC). The reason is that, as a general rule, a PE is not a 'resident' for treaty purposes, and thus the third state would likely not consider the DTC with the PE state (e.g., Switzerland-Germany) applicable in determining the limit on its WHT under the dividends article. Yet, from the PE state's perspective (e.g., Germany), under EU law as interpreted in *Saint Gobain*, it is precisely this DTC that is relevant (e.g., Switzerland-Germany). Another DTC is also potentially relevant, namely the PE state-residence state DTC (e.g., Germany-France DTC) since the PE could invoke the non-discrimination rule of Article 24(3) of that DTC. Similarly, the non-discrimination rule embodied in the freedom of establishment applies in the relationship between France, where the head office is located, and Germany, where the French company's ability to establish itself and choose the legal form of establishment (e.g., a PE, subsidiary, etc.) is affected by how Germany taxes the PE in question.[1113] Against the background of these preliminary considerations, some basic examples can illustrate the issue of determining the amount of the credit:

1112. CJEU, Case C-307/97, *Saint Gobain*, 21 Sep. 1999, ECLI:EU:C:1999:438, at para. 59.

1113. For a more detailed analysis of non-discrimination rules, *see* Werner Haslehner, *'Avoir Fiscal' and Its Legacy after Thirty Years of Direct Tax Jurisprudence of the Court of Justice*, 44(5) Intertax 374, 383–386 (2016) (and the sources cited therein, notably in footnotes nn.57–58); Kasper Dziurdz & Christoph Marchgraber eds, *Non-discrimination in European and Tax Treaty Law: Open Issues and Recent Challenges* (Linde 2015); Adolfo J. Martín Jiménez, Francisco Alfredo García Prats & José M. Calderón Carrero, *Triangular Cases, Tax Treaties and EC Law: The Saint-Gobain Decision of the ECJ*, 55(6) Bull. Int'l Tax'n 241, 243–244 and 251 (2001).

Constellation 1	Constellation 2
DTC third state-PE state	DTC third state-PE state
= 15% withholding tax on dividends	= 5% withholding tax on dividends
DTC third state-R State	DTC third state-R State
= 5% withholding tax on dividends	= 15% withholding tax on dividends
Third state levied 5%	Third state levied 15%
PE state: limit on credit obligation	PE state: limit on credit obligation
= 5% or 15%?	= 15% or 5%?

The first constellation involves the following considerations. Assuming the credit rules are based on the amount of foreign taxes actually paid, then the PE state would grant 5%. Otherwise, if the PE state grants the 15% rate, despite only 5% being levied in the third state, this would amount to a form of 'tax matching credit' (*see supra* note 704), leading to a more favourable combined tax burden than for residents/subsidiaries. This could be described as a form of 'reverse discrimination', which, although not prohibited by the EU fundamental freedoms,[1114] is arguably not what EU law requires. A similar question regarding the amount of the credit arose under the imputation credit line of case law (as discussed in Section 4.2.8.), and the findings indicate that, if the purpose of the credit that is granted to residents is to eliminate (in the 'imputation' cases, economic) double taxation of the taxes *actually* paid at the level of the distributing company (in other words, the reason the shareholder credit was fixed at 3/7ths was based on the amount of CIT due in that MS), then granting a credit for the foreign taxes *actually* paid (rather than extending the exact same 3/7ths amount to foreign-source dividends) is what is needed for re-establishing equal treatment. Likewise, if a direct credit that is granted to resident companies is contingent upon the taxes actually paid abroad, the same should apply to PEs of non-resident companies.

The second constellation involves the following considerations. In this scenario, a difficulty arises because resident enterprises would be granted a 5% credit (and this would correspond to the fact that the source state levied only 5%). However, 15% was actually levied, in the case of the PE. If the credit is limited to the 5%, the PE remains at a disadvantage as regards its overall effective burden as compared to resident companies. If the 15% is credited, the PE obtains the same overall effective burden as compared to resident companies. There are two possible readings of the judgment. A literal reading would be that the obligations of the PE state are limited to those that would apply under its domestic law, up to the limit established in the DTC to which it is party, i.e., the third state-PE state DTC. This is the limit that would apply to its resident companies.[1115] A second reading, argued by Hans van den Hurk, would be that

1114. *See*, e.g., Marjaana Helminen, *Chapter 2: Non-discrimination and Basic Freedoms, in EU Tax Law: Direct Taxation* Section 2.1.2 (IBFD 2018 ed. 2018).

1115. *See*, e.g., Eric C.C.M. Kemmeren & Hans-Peter Peeters, *Avoidance of Double Taxation and Its Interaction with European Triangular Arrangements*, 19(1) EC Tax Rev. 4, 16 (2010) (the

the PE state should credit the higher amount, namely the 15% actually levied in the third state, since 'national treatment' requires equalizing to the extent possible the effective tax burden between non-residents, i.e., the PEs of non-resident companies receiving dividends from the third state, and residents, i.e., the subsidiaries or companies receiving dividends from the third state.[1116] Based on this view, a freedom-of-establishment-friendly approach would thus be to oblige the PE state to credit the taxes effectively levied at source on the dividends (interest, etc., as the case may be), subject to the higher of the two limits in the two DTCs in question (as opposed to the lower of the two limits suggested by the OECD in the context of Article 24). The first approach would ensure a legal (and potentially hypothetical) equal treatment (assuming the PE *were* a subsidiary, what limit *would have* applied), while the second approach would ensure an effective equal treatment (seeking to ensure that the tax burden on the PE is not more than that on a subsidiary). Although the latter (or similar solutions that achieve actual equal treatment)[1117] are more aligned with the true underlying aim of the fundamental freedoms, the wording of the decision's national treatment obligation seems to require only the extension of benefits granted to its own

---

analysis of Kemmeren and Peeters seems to suggest that a credit based on the rate under the third state-PE state DTC is what is technically required by the PE state under the *Saint Gobain* judgment. As they explain based on their examples, 'State P grants a 10% tax credit for withholding tax on interest of state S, in accordance with the P-S DTC. With the application of this tax credit, state P must be considered to satisfy the *Saint-Gobain* ruling, because a resident of state P would have received the same tax credit. However, state S has levied 15%, in accordance with the R-S DTC, which is not reduced directly on the basis of the P-S DTC, because the PE does not qualify as a treaty resident under the P-S DTC.' They hypothesize that, in some cases, the source state may have to help the PE state in the effort to eliminate the unfavourable treatment of the PE. This is only, of course, if the source state is also an EU MS).

1116. Hans van den Hurk, *Did the ECJ's Decision in Saint-Gobain Change International Tax Law?*, 55(4) Bull. Int'l Tax'n 152, 157 (2001) (when discussing the *Saint Gobain* decision, the author explains that 'the ECJ ruled that a Member State which is one of the contracting states to a treaty is, by virtue of the principle of "national treatment", obliged to offer the same treaty advantages under the same conditions to permanent establishments as to fully resident companies (finding 58 of the ECJ). This finding is interpreted (by this author) as meaning that Member State B, in the above example, must grant a tax credit for the foreign tax paid by the permanent establishment (through withholding) in such a way that the permanent establishment is not taxed more heavily than a fully resident company in B. This means that the higher withholding tax (20%) must be credited, even if the tax credit for the profits of fully taxable companies is normally limited to 10%. In this case, the permanent establishment is compensated for the higher foreign tax by a higher domestic tax credit in B. The most important argument for this conclusion is Art. 43 of the EC Treaty, which obliges the Member States to give "national treatment". This leads to the conclusion that the effective tax rate on a permanent establishment must be equal to that on a resident corporation. In the author's opinion, this is necessary even if, as a result, the country concerned loses tax revenues. The Member State is, after all, one of the contracting parties to the tax treaty and could and should have taken measures').

1117. *See*, e.g., Eric C.C.M. Kemmeren & Hans-Peter Peeters, *Avoidance of Double Taxation and Its Interaction with European Triangular Arrangements*, 19(1) EC Tax Rev. 4, 16–18 (2010) (the authors argue that, under some circumstances, source states, which are EU MSs, should also play a role in supporting the aim of equal treatment of PEs in these *Saint Gobain* types of circumstances); Adolfo J. Martín Jiménez, Francicso Alfredo García Prats & José M. Calderón Carrero, *Triangular Cases, Tax Treaties and EC Law: The Saint-Gobain Decision of the ECJ*, 55(6) Bull. Int'l Tax'n 241, 247–250 (2001) (the authors argue for a 'full extension of the PE state's treaty network to PEs', involving the cooperation of source states in this aim).

nationals by its own laws or treaties, i.e., extending the treaty benefits of DTCs to which the PE state is a party.

Interim Summary

Since the *Avoir Fiscal* and *Saint Gobain* cases, it has become clear that, under EU law, PEs (e.g., branches or agencies) established by companies of other EU MSs – because they are taxed in essentially the same way as nationally incorporated companies – must also receive the same relief with respect to that taxation. Moreover, this refers to both relief offered on the basis of domestic law and that offered on the basis of tax treaties.

The relationship between residence and the FTC is one that is generally taken for granted. As the historical development in Chapter 2 showed, the expectation that the state of residence is responsible for offering an FTC, or other relief, for foreign taxes eventually became the standard. Accordingly, the status of a 'resident' is usually one of the conditions that a taxpayer must satisfy in order to obtain an FTC. This is often explained by the fact that the residence of a taxpayer is commonly accompanied by taxation of the worldwide income of that taxpayer.[1118] It seems generally agreed that the exercise of full tax jurisdiction over a taxpayer's income entails a corresponding obligation to offer relief for the portions of income that come from foreign sources on which taxes were already levied abroad.[1119] Consequently, what underlies the relationship between residence and the FTC is a relationship between full taxation and an FTC.

This (underlying) connection is essentially what the comparability analysis reveals in these two cases. It exposes and pushes further this connection between how a state taxes certain income and what obligations follow from that. While *non*-EU MSs *may* have the option of drawing solid boundaries around their obligation to offer relief that trace a more formal distinction between residence versus non-residence (as some parts of the above-cited OECD Commentary allude to),[1120] EU MSs *must* examine more closely the substance of the tax treatment in question. If the tax treatment is in substance similar to that of residents, then the relief should be extended as well.[1121]

1118. *See*, e.g., Elisabeth A. Owens, *The Foreign Tax Credit: A Study of the Credit for Foreign Taxes under United States Income Tax Law* 2–3 (Harvard Law School 1961).

1119. *See*, e.g., OECD, *Model Tax Convention on Income and on Capital 2017: Condensed Version* Article 4(1) (OECD Publishing 2017) (this is also the concept on which the OECD Model is based. Under the definition of Article 4(1), residence is determined based on which state can subject the taxpayer to unlimited tax liability).

1120. *See*, e.g., OECD, *Model Tax Convention on Income and on Capital 2017: Condensed Version* Article 24(3) (OECD Publishing 2017) (the word 'may' is used here because this depends on whether there are provisions similar to Article 24(3) OECD Model in their tax treaties and how they interpret and apply those provisions).

1121. This is confirmed in numerous other cases. *See*, e.g., CJEU, Case C-311/97, *Royal Bank of Scotland*, 29 Apr. 1999, ECLI:EU:C:1999:216, at para. 28 ('As far as the method of determining the taxable base is concerned, the Greek tax legislation does not establish, as between companies having their seat in Greece and companies which, whilst having their seat in another Member State, have a permanent establishment in Greece, any distinction such as to justify a difference of treatment between the two categories of companies. ... [T]ax is calculated, in the case of both Greek and foreign companies, on net income or profits after deduction of the part thereof corresponding to non-taxable receipts, ... ') and para. 29 ('It is true that companies having their seat in Greece are taxed there on the basis of their world-wide income (unlimited tax liability) whereas foreign companies carrying on business

This tends to be the case where a MS is the host state, or state of establishment, of a PE of a non-resident company from another EU MS.

As a result, the (personal) scope of the credit method is broadened under the EU fundamental freedoms. Not only residents but also in some cases non-residents must be granted a tax credit. The CJEU ruled on this explicitly in the case of an imputation credit (*Avoir Fiscal*) and an indirect credit (*Saint Gobain*), but the same reasoning should also apply to a direct credit. However, although relief will be extended to these PEs of non-resident companies on the grounds of this 'national treatment' obligation, 'national treatment' might not always be achieved in effect: as Constellation 2 above illustrated, if the credit limitation is based on the tax rates (e.g., for dividends, interest, etc.) under the DTC between the source state and the PE state, but the tax rates under the DTC between the source state and the residence state of the company are higher, PEs of non-resident companies may be treated *legally* the same, but nevertheless face a higher effective tax burden than resident companies. In addition, these two cases lay the foundations for one of the main approaches to the comparability analysis - which could be expressed as a *same-taxation-same-relief* reasoning (subsequently expanded to a 'subject-to-tax' approach) - that will frequently reappear.[1122]

4.2.2. The *Gilly* or 'Disparity' Line of Case Law

Considering the goal of achieving an EU internal market, the decisions in this line of case law[1123] were initially surprising, or perhaps disappointing, for some EU law observers. To begin, two earlier cases in this line will be briefly explained - the *Gilly* case[1124] and the *Kerckhaert and Morres* case[1125] - as they lay out the most important findings of the CJEU as regards the relationship between EU law, (juridical) double taxation, and the credit method, which have been confirmed and further clarified by future case law.

in that State through a permanent establishment are subject to tax there only on the basis of profits which the permanent establishment earns there (limited tax liability). However, that circumstance, ... is not such as to prevent the two categories of companies from being considered, all other things being equal, as being in a comparable situation as regards the method of determining the taxable base').

1122. *See*, e.g., CJEU, Case C-311/97, *Royal Bank of Scotland*, 29 Apr. 1999, ECLI:EU:C:1999:216; CJEU, Case C-253/03, *CLT-UFA*, 23 Feb. 2006, ECLI:EU:C:2006:129. For the cases where the comparability analysis was expanded to a 'subject-to-tax' approach, *see*, e.g., the cases on outgoing dividends discussed in the 'neutralization' line of case law under Section 4.2.5.

1123. *See*, e.g., CJEU, Case C-336/96, *Gilly*, 12 May 1998, ECLI:EU:C:1998:221; CJEU, Case C-403/03, *Schempp*, 12 Jul. 2005, ECLI:EU:C:2005:446; CJEU, Case C-513/03, *van Hilten-van der Heijden*, 23 Feb. 2006, ECLI:EU:C:2006:131; CJEU, Case C-513/04, *Kerckhaert and Morres*, 14 Nov. 2006, ECLI:EU:C:2006:713; CJEU, Case C-194/06, *Orange European Smallcap Fund*, 24 May 2008, ECLI:EU:C:2008:289; CJEU, Case C-67/08, *Block*, 12 Feb. 2009, ECLI:EU:C:2009:92; CJEU, Case C-128/08, *Damseaux*, 16 Jul. 2009, ECLI:EU:C:2009:471; CJEU, Case C-96/08, *CIBA*, 15 Apr. 2010, ECLI:EU:C:2010:185; CJEU, Case C-157/10, *Banco Bilbao Vizcaya Argentaria SA*, 8 Dec. 2011, ECLI:EU:C:2011:813; CJEU, Case C-540/11, *Levy and Sebbag*, 19 Sep. 2012, ECLI:EU:C:2012:581; CJEU, Case C-194/15, *Véronique Baudinet*, 4 Feb. 2016, ECLI:EU:C:2016:81.

1124. CJEU, Case C-336/96, *Gilly*, 12 May 1998, ECLI:EU:C:1998:221.

1125. CJEU, Case C-513/04, *Kerckhaert and Morres*, 14 Nov. 2006, ECLI:EU:C:2006:713.

In 1998, the CJEU decided on the case of Mr and Mrs Gilly,[1126] a couple that lived in France near the border with Germany. Mrs Gilly regularly commuted to Germany where she worked as a teacher. Under the France-Germany DTC, both states had a right to tax her income. Germany taxed her income earned from employment there, and, as a resident of France, France would tax her worldwide income and then offer a credit for the taxes paid in Germany.

According to the DTC, the tax credit in France is equal to 'the amount of the French tax on the relevant income'.[1127] France used a rather standard way to calculate the credit:[1128]

$$\text{Maximum amount of credit} = \text{Net income taxed in Germany} \times \frac{\text{Tax payable on the total net income taxable in France}}{\text{Total net income taxable in France}}$$

Simple fictive numbers can be used to demonstrate the issue. Assume Mrs Gilly earns 200 in total worldwide income, 100 of which comes from her teaching employment in Germany. Assume Germany levies 30% on the 100 of employment income (30) and France levies 20% on the 200 of worldwide income (40). France agrees to offer a credit, using the above formula (20 = 100 × (40/200)). The goal of the formula is for France to determine how much of its total taxes of 40 correspond to the 100 of income that was double taxed. Out of the 40, France levies a tax of 20 on the 100 of income from Germany.

The difference in treatment, argued Mrs Gilly, arises from the fact that the tax credit provided in France (20) is less than the actual taxes paid in Germany (30), thereby allowing some of the alleged double taxation to remain and penalizing those who have exercised their freedom of movement.[1129] It is true that, if Mrs Gilly had exercised her employment in France and thus earned all 200 there, the total taxes paid would be 40 (ETR 20%), whereas by exercising her employment in Germany, she pays 30 to Germany and then 20 to France (40 total minus the credit of 20) amounting in total to taxes paid of 50 (ETR 25%). However, if France granted this larger 'full' credit (30), this would reduce the amount of income taxes it collected on domestically earned income (of the 40 of total taxes, 20 corresponds to 100 of income from Germany and 20 to 100 of income from France). One of the questions was whether this credit method should be deemed incompatible with the free movement of workers by virtue of resulting in higher taxation.[1130]

The CJEU reasoned, first, that the objective of DTCs is 'to prevent the same income from being taxed in each of the two States' but does not go so far as 'to ensure

1126. CJEU, Case C-336/96, *Gilly*, 12 May 1998, ECLI:EU:C:1998:221.
1127. *Id.*, at para. 8.
1128. *Id.*, at para. 9.
1129. *Id.*, at paras 42–45.
1130. *Id.*, at para. 13 (*see* question 6).

that the tax to which the taxpayer is subject in one State is no higher than that to which he or she would be subject in the other'.[1131] Second, the unfavourable tax treatment results from 'the differences between the tax scales of the Member States concerned, and, in the absence of any Community legislation in the field, the determination of those scales is a matter for the Member States'.[1132]

In other words, it is not the credit mechanism itself that is at fault for the different treatment. Both states tax the 100, Germany in the amount of 30 and France in the amount of 20. For its part, France reduces its 20 down to 0 under the credit method. The excess amount of 10 results from a higher tax rate in Germany. In the absence of harmonization at the EU level, it is perfectly acceptable for two states to decide to have different tax rates; it is clearly within their national competence to do so. Thus, the CJEU decided that the free movement of workers does not preclude this provision since the unfavourable tax treatment of Mrs Gilly in this case does not result from discriminatory treatment by France but rather from the different tax rates in two different MSs. What is of particular relevance for the credit method is that, implicitly, the CJEU decision accepted that EU MSs can use a credit limitation, also referred to as an MCA (*see supra* note 179 and Example No. 5).

Years later, in 2006, the CJEU decided on the case of Mr Kerckhaert and Ms Morres,[1133] both resident in Belgium and receiving dividends from a company in France. The taxpayers brought an action against the Belgian Tax Authority because it refused to allow them a credit for the 15% of foreign taxes withheld on dividends received from France, despite the fact that Belgium agreed to provide this credit under the France-Belgium DTC. However, the Belgian legislature had changed the national law. According to the Belgian Tax Code, all dividends became subject to a 25% tax rate, without an FTC. The taxpayers argued that denying their right to the credit resulted in a heavier tax burden imposed on dividends from France as compared to dividends from Belgium, thus infringing the free movement of capital.[1134]

As for the reasoning of the CJEU, since its decision in *Gilly*, a handful of decisions in the meantime (e.g., *Verkooijen*,[1135] *Lenz*,[1136] *Manninen*[1137]) had established that there is *no* objective difference between a taxpayer that receives dividends from companies established *in other MSs* and a taxpayer that receives dividends from companies established *in its own MS* (i.e., they are comparable, as discussed in Section 4.2.5.); therefore, different treatment on this basis infringes the fundamental freedoms.[1138] However, in this case, Belgian law treated all dividends the same in that all dividends were taxed at an identical rate of 25%.[1139] On that account, the CJEU decided

1131. *Id.*, at para. 46.
1132. *Id.*, at para. 47.
1133. CJEU, Case C-513/04, *Kerckhaert and Morres*, 14 Nov. 2006, ECLI:EU:C:2006:713.
1134. *Id.*, at para. 13.
1135. CJEU, Case C-35/98, *Verkooijen*, 6 Jun. 2000, ECLI:EU:C:2000:294.
1136. CJEU, Case C-315/02, *Anneliese Lenz*, 15 Jul. 2004, ECLI:EU:C:2004:446.
1137. CJEU, Case C-319/02, *Manninen*, 7 Sep. 2004, ECLI:EU:C:2004:484.
1138. CJEU, Case C-513/04, *Kerckhaert and Morres*, 14 Nov. 2006, ECLI:EU:C:2006:713, at para. 16.
1139. *Id.*, at para. 17.

that there is no difference in treatment.[1140] Instead, any unfavourable consequences that could arise from the Belgian law in question resulted from the 'exercise in parallel by two Member States of their fiscal sovereignty'.[1141] The Court recalled established principles about the 'current state' of 'Community law' regarding the lack of harmonization at the EU level in direct taxation and that MSs remain competent in this area, including in determining the allocation criteria for taxation with a view to eliminating double taxation under international agreements.[1142]

The CJEU decided that, in light of the above considerations, the free movement of capital does not preclude the Belgian law which makes dividends subject to the same uniform rate, 'without providing for the possibility of setting off tax levied by deduction at source in [an]other Member State' (i.e., without providing a credit for foreign taxes).[1143]

By contrast with the *Gilly* case, where at least double taxation was relieved (with the contention revolving around whether the credit was large enough), in the *Kerckhaert and Morres* case, Belgium completely eliminated its credit method and did not offer any relief from double taxation.[1144] Considering the EU's goal to construct an internal market and the view of many scholars that higher costs for cross-border EU scenarios (due to less favourable tax treatment) is a blatant obstacle standing in the way of fully realizing this goal,[1145] these findings were frustrating yet instructive. They illuminated the tension between the goal of achieving a border-less internal market and the tax sovereignty confined to national borders.

As was highlighted in subsequently decided cases – especially the *Damseaux* case[1146] – what the cases in this line of decisions have in common is the problem of 'juridical double taxation'.[1147] Juridical double taxation is defined by the OECD as 'the imposition of comparable taxes in two (or more) States on the same taxpayer in respect of the same subject matter and for identical periods' (as also discussed in Chapter

1140. But *see*, e.g., Georg Kofler, *Chapter 7: Double Taxation and European Law – Analysis of the Jurisprudence, in Double Taxation Within the European Union* 97, 118 (Alexander Rust ed., Kluwer 2011) (Kofler notes that discrimination can also arise if the *same* treatment is given to situations which are objectively *different*, and he cites where the CJEU seems to dismiss the issue).
1141. CJEU, Case C-513/04, *Kerckhaert and Morres*, 14 Nov. 2006, ECLI:EU:C:2006:713, at para. 20.
1142. *Id.*, at paras 21–23.
1143. *Id.*, at para. 24.
1144. Though, Belgium may have allowed a deduction of the foreign taxes from the tax base, according to Kofler. *See* Georg Kofler, *Chapter 7: Double Taxation and European Law – Analysis of the Jurisprudence, in Double Taxation Within the European Union* 97, 116 (Alexander Rust ed., Kluwer 2011).
1145. *See*, e.g., Opinion of AG Ruiz-Jarabo Colomer in Case C-376/03, *D*, 26 Oct. 2004, ECLI:EU:C:2004:663, at para. 85 ('[...] the establishment of a single market through attainment of the fundamental freedoms of movement, since the fact that a taxable event might be taxed twice is the most serious obstacle there can be to people and their capital crossing internal borders').
1146. CJEU, Case C-128/08, *Damseaux*, 16 Jul. 2009, ECLI:EU:C:2009:471.
1147. *Id.*, at para. 11, para. 23, para. 26, and para. 35 (although this term was not explicitly mentioned in the *Gilly* case and *Kerckhaert and Morres* case, it was included in both the questions of the referring court and in the decision of the CJEU in *Damseaux*). *See also* CJEU, Case C-194/06, *Orange European Smallcap Fund*, 24 May 2008, ECLI:EU:C:2008:289, at para. 31.

2),[1148] a definition cited by EU institutions.[1149] Thus, by definition, juridical double taxation occurs as a result of *more than one* state having jurisdiction over the same taxpayer.[1150] In other words, it materializes when two (or more) states are simply rightfully exerting their sovereign right to tax a given taxpayer – i.e., 'the exercise in parallel by two Member States of their fiscal sovereignty' – making it difficult to pinpoint *one* of the MSs' laws as giving rise to a discrimination or restriction. It is often contrasted with 'economic double taxation', which occurs 'where two different persons are taxable in respect of the same income or capital'.[1151] The relevance of this distinction for the credit method becomes even more evident in the next set of cases below (in Section 4.2.3.).

In these cases of international 'juridical double taxation', what is absolutely key is the CJEU's (proclaimed) inability to impute discriminatory treatment to either of the MSs. This has lead scholars to make a distinction between discrimination, disparities and, in some cases, dislocations.[1152] Disparities result from the inevitable variations, such as tax rates and tax base, between states' tax systems;[1153] dislocations result from inevitable variations in criteria used by different states to assert jurisdiction over parts of the tax base that may overlap and cause double taxation, in the absence of coordination;[1154] discrimination results from the rules of one tax jurisdiction that applies 'different rules to comparable situations' or applies 'the same rule to different situations'.[1155] Through this lens, according to the CJEU case law, the credit method *in itself* is not discriminatory, even where its calculation leads to the result that *not* all of the taxes levied in the source state can be credited (often referred to as an 'excess credit' situation), since that results from a disparity (different tax rates).

The cases also have in common the repeated notion that EU law in its 'current state' does not provide any criteria as grounds on which to allocate taxation rights

1148. OECD, *Model Tax Convention on Income and on Capital 2017: Condensed Version* Introduction, para. 1 (OECD Publishing 2017).

1149. *See*, e.g., European Commission, Communication from the Commission to the European Parliament, the Council and the European Economic and Social Committee, Double Taxation in the Single Market, COM(2011) 712 Final, 4 (11 Nov. 2011).

1150. OECD, *Model Tax Convention on Income and on Capital 2017: Condensed Version* Commentary on Articles 23 A and 23 B, para. 3 (OECD Publishing 2017) (note, for example, that all three scenarios – i.e., (1) residence-residence or 'concurrent full liability to tax', (3) residence-source, and (3) source-source or 'concurrent limited tax liability' – involve two states).

1151. OECD, *Model Tax Convention on Income and on Capital 2017: Condensed Version* Commentary on Articles 23 A and 23 B, para. 2 (OECD Publishing 2017).

1152. *See*, e.g., Peter J. Wattel, *Chapter 3: General EU Law Concepts and Tax Law*, *in* 1 *Terra/Wattel European Tax Law* 39, 86 et seq. (Peter J. Wattel, Otto Marres & Hein Vermeulen eds, Wolters Kluwer 7th ed. 2019); Sjoerd Douma, *The Three Ds of Direct Tax Jurisdiction: Disparity, Discrimination and Double Taxation*, 46(11) Eur. Tax'n 522 (2006); Rita Szudoczky, *The Sources of EU Law and Their Relationships: Lessons for the Field of Taxation*, 525 (32 Doctoral Series, IBFD 2014) (the author explains that, while the concept of disparity 'appeared in *Gilly*, the textbook case on disparities is *Schempp* where the Court clarified that the fundamental freedoms cannot remedy disadvantages originating from disparities').

1153. *See*, e.g., Opinion of AG Geelhoed in Case C-374/04, *Test Claimants in Class IV of the ACT Group Litigation*, 23 Feb. 2006, ECLI:EU:C:2006:139, at paras 37, 43–47.

1154. *Id.*, at paras 37, 48–54.

1155. *Id.*, at paras 55–56.

between MSs.[1156] According to the CJEU, nothing in EU law dictates which MS is responsible for relieving the double taxation. Its reference to the 'current state' of EU law seems to suggest that EU law could evolve in ways that touch upon more aspects of direct taxation, e.g., as more secondary EU law is enacted, and perhaps some criteria may emerge from this process that will empower and guide the CJEU in these double taxation situations. Scholars have put forward ideas,[1157] yet the CJEU for the time declares itself powerless in the face of the exercise in parallel of fiscal sovereignty or disparities.[1158]

This perceived powerlessness applies not just vis-à-vis domestic tax law but also vis-à-vis DTCs. Following the *Kerckhaert and Morres* case,[1159] some observers asked whether Belgium had committed a 'treaty override' (by abolishing the credit under its domestic law that was provided for in the DTC) and, in particular, whether that would matter under EU law. Some arguments which were put forward – such as whether the CJEU's recognition that the 'abolition of double taxation within the European Community is one of the objectives of the Treaty'[1160] combined with the EU MSs' duty of 'sincere cooperation' to 'refrain from any measure which could jeopardise the attainment of the Union's objectives'[1161] – could lead to the conclusion that it is against EU law to disregard DTC obligations.[1162] In this particular Belgian DTC, though, the credit method article made the availability of the credit dependent on Belgian national

1156. CJEU, Case C-128/08, *Damseaux*, 16 Jul. 2009, ECLI:EU:C:2009:471, at para. 33 and para. 35; CJEU, Case C-298/05, *Columbus Container Services*, 6 Dec. 2007, ECLI:EU:C:2007:754, at para. 45 ('Community law, in its current state and in a situation such as that in the main proceedings, does not lay down any general criteria for the attribution of areas of competence between the Member States in relation to the elimination of double taxation within the European Community. Consequently, apart from Council Directive 90/435/EEC of 23 July 1990 on the common system of taxation applicable in the case of parent companies and subsidiaries of different Member States (OJ 1990 L 225, p. 6), the Convention of 23 July 1990 on the elimination of double taxation in connection with the adjustment of profits of associated enterprises (OJ 1990 L 225, p. 10) and Council Directive 2003/48/EC of 3 June 2003 on taxation of savings income in the form of interest payments (OJ 2003 L 157, p. 38), no uniform or harmonisation measure designed to eliminate double taxation has as yet been adopted at Community law level (see *Kerckhaert and Morres*, paragraph 22)').

1157. *See*, e.g., Joachim Englisch, *The European Treaties' Implications for Direct Taxes*, 33(8/9) Intertax 310, 323 et seq. (2005) (in the analysis under Section D: Abolition of International Double Taxation); Georg Kofler, *Chapter 7: Double Taxation and European Law – Analysis of the Jurisprudence, in Double Taxation Within the European Union* 97 (Alexander Rust ed., Kluwer 2011); Alexander Rust, *Chapter 8: How European Union Law Could Solve Double Taxation, in Double Taxation Within the European Union* 137 (Alexander Rust ed., Kluwer Law International 2011); Peter J. Wattel, *Chapter 9: Passing the Buck Around – Who Is Responsible for Double Taxation? – Comments on Profs. Kofler and Rust's Analysis, in Double Taxation Within the European Union* 157 (Alexander Rust ed., Kluwer 2011).

1158. *See*, e.g., CJEU, Case C-513/04, *Kerckhaert and Morres*, 14 Nov. 2006, ECLI:EU:C:2006:713, at para. 20 and paras 22–24; CJEU, Case C-96/08, *CIBA*, 15 Apr. 2010, ECLI:EU:C:2010:185, at paras 27–29.

1159. CJEU, Case C-513/04, *Kerckhaert and Morres*, 14 Nov. 2006, ECLI:EU:C:2006:713.

1160. *See*, e.g., Article 352 TFEU (former Article 220 EC Treaty; now abolished); CJEU, Case C-128/08, *Damseaux*, 16 Jul. 2009, ECLI:EU:C:2009:471, at para. 28; CJEU, Case C-336/96, *Gilly*, 12 May 1998, ECLI:EU:C:1998:221, at para. 16.

1161. Article 4(3) TEU.

1162. *See*, e.g., Eric C.C.M. Kemmeren & Hans-Peter Peeters, *Avoidance of Double Taxation and Its Interaction with European Triangular Arrangements*, 19(1) EC Tax Rev. 4, 12 (2010).

law.[1163] Thus, it was presumably understood *not* to be a 'treaty override'. In any case, the following year, in 2007, in the *Columbus Containers Services* case,[1164] Germany's (alleged) treaty override was accepted,[1165] and in 2009, in the *Damseaux* case, which dealt with the exact same Belgian DTC, the CJEU stated that it 'does not have jurisdiction ... to rule on a possible infringement, by a contracting Member State, of provisions of bilateral [tax] conventions',[1166] further anchoring MSs' sovereignty in the relief of (juridical) double taxation.

As regards the *Columbus Container Services* case, what is particularly relevant about this case is that the complaint more explicitly challenged the compatibility of the credit method *as such* with EU law. Whereas the complaint in the *Gilly* case was essentially about too small a credit (or an excess credit situation) and the complaint in *Kerckhaert and Morres* case was about the abolition of the right to any credit, the complaint in the *Columbus Container Services* case was about whether it was compatible to switch from the exemption method to the credit method. In this context, the CJEU was called upon to answer some questions that scholars had been pondering around the turn of the century regarding whether the CJEU's at-that-time newly evolving non-discriminatory restriction analysis would engulf the credit method (*see* Section 4.1.).

As for the facts, the taxpayers, who all resided in Germany, operated a partnership in Belgium.[1167] The partnership qualified as a 'coordination center' in Belgium, which allowed it to benefit from a more favourable tax base calculation there.[1168] Under the tax treaty between Belgium and Germany, Belgium had the right to tax the profits attributable to the partnership in Belgium and Germany agreed to exempt the profits. Under Germany's domestic law, changes had been made under a law referred to as 'the Foreign Transaction Tax Law (Gesetz über die Besteuerung bei Auslandsbeziehungen (Außensteuergesetz)), as amended by the Law on combating abuse and harmonising taxation (Missbrauchsbekämpfungs- und Steuerbereinigungsgesetz) of 21 December 1993' in order to, basically, extend similar treatment that applied under Germany's CFC rules to other entities abroad such as partnerships. Thus, after this

1163. Belgium-France Income Tax Treaty (1964) (as amended through 1971), IBFD Tax Treaty Database (unofficial translation) (Article 19(A)(1) states that '[a]n individual resident in Belgium who receives dividends which are subject to the tax system described in paragraphs 2 and 3 of Article 15 may, instead of crediting the lump-sum amount of foreign tax referred to above, apply the tax credit, *at the rate and in the manner provided for the Belgian law for dividends*, from such income, on condition that he requests this in writing at the latest within the time limit laid down for the lodging of the annual tax return' and the aforementioned 'lump-sum' credit was also 'deducted *under the conditions laid down in Belgian law*' (emphasis added)).

1164. CJEU, Case C-298/05, *Columbus Container Services*, 6 Dec. 2007, ECLI:EU:C:2007:754.

1165. *Id.*, at para. 46 ('Although the Member States have, within the framework of their powers referred to in paragraph 27 of this judgment, entered into numerous bilateral conventions designed to eliminate or to mitigate those negative effects, the fact none the less remains that the Court has no jurisdiction, under Article 234 EC, to rule on the possible infringement of the provisions of such conventions by a contracting Member State').

1166. CJEU, Case C-128/08, *Damseaux*, 16 Jul. 2009, ECLI:EU:C:2009:471, at paras 19–22.

1167. CJEU, Case C-298/05, *Columbus Container Services*, 6 Dec. 2007, ECLI:EU:C:2007:754, at paras 13–14.

1168. *Id.*, at para. 12.

change, if a partnership earned certain types of passive income and this income was taxed at 'too low' a rate, i.e., less than 30 %, in the other state, then Germany would no longer exempt the income, but instead would tax the income and relieve double taxation by granting an FTC.[1169]

The taxpayers argued that, by replacing the exemption method with the credit method, Germany's law was incompatible with the freedom of establishment because it 'has the effect of rendering the cross-border establishments ... less attractive'. The resulting 'withdrawal of the tax advantage', i.e., a lower tax rate in Belgium, 'which the latter enjoyed infringes unjustifiably the freedom of establishment guaranteed by the EC Treaty'.[1170] Moreover, the taxpayers complained that Germany had 'no justification for not applying the provisions of the Bilateral Tax Convention' to exempt the income, thus implying that this override of the treaty could also be an issue under EU law.[1171] The German Court had doubts since '[t]he additional taxation to which those provisions make foreign income subject would, it believes, be likely to dissuade German residents from investing in a Member State other than the Federal Republic of Germany', and for this reason asked the CJEU whether a switch from the exemption to the credit method was compatible with EU law.[1172] This potentially 'dissuasive' aspect was unclear at this stage of EU case law.

On this point, the CJEU recalled its case law on the scope of the freedom of establishment, which showed how its interpretation had expanded. First, in addition to what the wording of Article 43 EC (now Article 49 TFEU) explicitly states as to requiring equal treatment in the host state, the freedom of establishment must also address the MS of origin and prohibit it from 'hindering the establishment in another Member State of one of its nationals'[1173] – the reason being that, otherwise, the freedom of establishment could be deprived of its meaning and role, if such a back door to potentially discriminatory or restrictive measures were left open. Second, in addition to tackling discriminatory measures, the freedom of establishment has also been interpreted as tackling measures that 'prohibit, impede or render less attractive' the act of setting up an establishment in another EU MS.[1174] Having said that, the question then is: what types of measures are caught under this broader umbrella?

The CJEU began by clarifying that 'the effect of rendering the pursuit of Columbus' activities more expensive than if that taxation had been carried out using the exemption method provided for in the Bilateral Tax Convention ... does not necessarily mean that those provisions constitute a restriction on the freedom of establishment within the meaning of Article 43 EC'.[1175] In other words, it is not merely a 'more expensive' element that matters, since that could go so far as to imply that MSs cannot have higher tax rates than other MSs. Rather, as the next steps of the CJEU's

1169. *Id.*, at paras 3–12.
1170. *Id.*, at para. 22.
1171. *Id.*, at para. 23.
1172. *Id.*, at para. 24.
1173. *Id.*, at paras 33–34.
1174. *Id.*
1175. CJEU, Case C-298/05, *Columbus Container Services*, 6 Dec. 2007, ECLI:EU:C:2007:754, at para. 38.

reasoning suggest, in this case, there must also be some different-treatment element that can be detected. The CJEU observed that this 'set-off method' in Germany is similar to the method in Belgium that was scrutinized in the *Kerckhaert and Morres* case and that such 'legislation merely subjects, in Germany, the profits made by such partnerships to the same tax rate as profits made by partnerships established in Germany'.[1176] In this way, the CJEU underlined the comparison it considered relevant and the effect of the credit method:

> '[s]ince partnerships such as Columbus do not suffer any tax disadvantage in comparison with partnerships established in Germany, there is no discrimination resulting from a difference in treatment between those two categories of partnerships'.[1177]

Related to the topic of which comparison is the relevant one to make, an argument regarding the free choice of legal form of establishment was invoked - an issue that was central to *Avoir Fiscal* and *Saint Gobain* (*see* Section 4.2.1.) - namely that the credit method could lead to a distortion as to whether a German resident can freely establish itself abroad as a partnership versus as a subsidiary.[1178] The assumption underlying this argument was that if the German taxpayers in question would have established themselves by means of a subsidiary in Belgium, then only Belgium would be able to tax said subsidiary at the rate applicable in Belgium, i.e., a lower rate, whereas by virtue of establishing themselves by means of a partnership in Belgium, their residence state Germany could take into account the income and, through the credit method, increase the taxation up to the higher rate applicable in Germany. The CJEU rejected this argument:

> 'In this respect, it must be recalled that the fiscal autonomy referred to in paragraphs 44 and 51 of this judgment also means that the Member States are at liberty to determine the conditions and the level of taxation for different types of establishments chosen by national companies or partnerships operating abroad, on condition that those companies or partnerships are not treated in a manner that is discriminatory in comparison with comparable national establishments.'[1179]

The CJEU did not elaborate on this point, but a comparison between the two sets of cases clarifies a distinction implicitly made. Unlike in *Avoir Fiscal* and *Saint Gobain*, where, as host states, the 'national treatment' obligation of the freedom of establishment applied, this case was based on the perspective of a home state, where the relevant question was whether it hinders the establishment of its residents abroad. The above-cited 'fiscal autonomy' of the MS is impacted differently depending on the perspective, i.e., either as the host state or the home state. In the former case, the MS as a host state fully chooses its tax base and tax rate, etc.; however, it must (merely) extend, or apply, those choices to non-resident taxpayers that establish themselves there in a way that treats those non-residents in a consistent and equal way to

1176. *Id.*, at para. 39.
1177. *Id.*, at para. 40.
1178. *Id.*, at paras 50-54.
1179. *Id.*, at para. 53.

residents. Such an extension leaves intact the MS's overall design choices, but may merely broaden the scope to taxpayers of other EU MSs in certain cases. In the home state, the comparison is different. It is no longer the treatment of its residents as compared to non-residents coming in (host state perspective) but rather the treatment of its residents going out, or extending their activities abroad into other EU MSs, meaning that the comparison is between its residents whose activities do not cross the border and its residents whose activities do cross the border. Thus, in the home state case, this MS is fully free to set its tax base, tax rates and its tax treatment of different legal entities, as long as it ensures that it treats those two categories of residents equally, i.e., residents who exercise their fundamental freedoms by undertaking cross-border activities with those who stay fully in the home state. If so, then the home state has fulfilled its EU law obligations of not hindering their establishment or operations abroad.

From this perspective, then, the credit method is compatible, since generally speaking, it serves to tax residents in the same way regardless of whether they earn income from at home or from abroad. Where the tax rate in the home state is higher, as in the *Columbus Container Services* case, the credit method generally equalizes the tax rate that applies to the two situations. Where the tax rate in the other MS is higher, as in the *Gilly* case, the credit method eliminates the tax liability owed to the home state on the income from the other MS and thus any excess amount that cannot be credited results from the higher rate in the other MS.

As regards whether it is relevant if the switch-over to the credit method under domestic law contravenes the exemption method in the tax treaty, the CJEU declared that it has no jurisdiction to rule on this matter. The CJEU's role is to interpret whether a MS's laws comply with EU law, and not whether the domestic law of a MS is compatible with its own tax treaties. The latter is a distinct legal issue that, according to the AG, falls outside the scope of EU law.[1180]

The taxpayers invoked the *Eurowings* case (discussed above under Section 4.1.), among their various arguments. However, the CJEU distinguished the national legislation at issue, i.e., the credit method, from the *Eurowings* case. The legislation challenged in *Eurowings* actually led to a different treatment on the basis of where a service recipient was established and, in that case, such a difference in treatment cannot be justified merely because the service recipient is subject to lower taxation.[1181] By contrast, the credit method does not, as mentioned before, even lead to a relevant difference of treatment in the first place.

From all of the above cases, the CJEU now considers these points so settled that it subjected a similar case in 2016[1182] to a 'reasoned order', i.e., an expedited procedure that is possible under the rules of procedure of the Court only 'where the reply to such a question may be clearly deduced from existing case-law or where the answer to the

1180. *Id.*, at paras 46–47.
1181. *Id.*, at paras 48–49.
1182. CJEU, Case C-194/15, *Véronique Baudinet*, 4 Feb. 2016, ECLI:EU:C:2016:81 (at the time of writing, the order is available on the InfoCuria database only in French and in Italian, so this discussion contains this author's translations from French).

question referred for a preliminary ruling admits of no reasonable doubt'.[1183] As a result of its succinctness, it offers a clear summary of the key points of this line of case law.

As for the facts, briefly stated, in *Véronique Baudinet*, individuals from Italy received dividends from France. On the basis of the 1989 tax treaty between France and Italy, France levied a WHT of 15% and Italy agreed to the credit method.[1184] From their taxes due in Italy, the individuals deducted the entire amount of the French WHT.[1185] However, under Italian law, certain types of income, such as profit distributions from companies, were not fully taken into account in the tax base; rather only 40% of that income was included in the tax base.[1186] For this reason, the tax authorities reduced the credit, as it should correspond only to the amount of income actually included in the tax base in Italy.[1187] The individuals complained that, since the WHT in France could not be fully credited in Italy, this caused holding shares in a company in France to be less favourable than holding shares in a company in Italy, thus dissuading individuals from holding shares in companies in another EU MS and thus infringing the free movement of capital.[1188]

The order, decided on the basis of the free movement of capital and the freedom of establishment,[1189] reiterated that MSs have the sovereign right to design their income tax system, such as their tax base and tax rates,[1190] and that EU law in its current state does not prescribe general criteria for the repartition of competences between MSs for the elimination of double taxation within the EU.[1191] As a consequence, in some cases, more than one state will tax dividends if the states both legitimately exercise their fiscal competence to tax.[1192] In such cases, there is nothing in EU law that dictates that the state of residence is obliged to prevent such disadvantages from these overlapping taxation rights.[1193] To demand otherwise would lead to a situation where the state of residence is obliged to adapt its tax system in response to the tax systems of all other MSs (e.g., if another MS decides to, for example, double its tax rate on outgoing dividends, the state of residence alone would be stuck with the bill, so to speak, and its ability to collect taxes could be subject to the whims of other MSs' legislators, compromising its own sovereignty in this area). As the CJEU had implied in *Damseaux*,

1183. CJEU, Case C-194/15, *Véronique Baudinet*, 4 Feb. 2016, ECLI:EU:C:2016:81, at para. 19; CJEU, *Consolidated Version of the Rules of Procedure of the Court of Justice of 25 September 2012* (1 May 2019), https://curia.europa.eu/jcms/jcms/Jo2_7031/en/ (last visited 10 Apr. 2019) (citing and consolidating the CJEU, *Rules of Procedure of the Court of Justice of 25 September 2012*, OJ L 265, 29 Sep. 2012, as amended on 18 Jun. 2013, OJ L 173, 65, 26 Jun. 2013, and on 19 Jul. 2016, OJ L 217, 69, 12 Aug. 2016, and on 9 Apr. 2019, OJ L 111, 73, 25 Apr. 2019).
1184. CJEU, Case C-194/15, *Véronique Baudinet*, 4 Feb. 2016, ECLI:EU:C:2016:81, at paras 9–10.
1185. *Id.*, at para. 13.
1186. *Id.*, at paras 3–8.
1187. *Id.*, at para. 14.
1188. *Id.*, at para. 16.
1189. *Id.*, at paras 21–29 (for the reasons relating to the scope and applicability of the fundamental freedoms).
1190. *Id.*, at para. 30.
1191. *Id.*, at para. 33.
1192. *Id.*, at para. 31.
1193. *Id.*, at para. 33.

it cannot via the judicial process make such decisions on the attribution of taxation powers on behalf of MSs:

> 'In a situation where both the Member State in which the dividends are paid and the Member State in which the shareholder resides are liable to tax those dividends, to consider that it is necessarily for the Member State of residence to prevent that double taxation would amount to granting a priority with respect to the taxation of that type of income to the Member State in which the dividends are paid.'[1194]

What the EU law in question is mainly equipped to address is discrimination. To the extent that higher taxation on a cross-border situation is merely an incidental disadvantage that can result from the MSs' competence in the field of taxation, and not from a discriminatory measure imputable to either MS, such disadvantages are generally not addressed by the TFEU.[1195] In this case, because Italy taxed all dividends in the same way, regardless of whether they were distributed by a company in Italy or in France, the CJEU did not find any discrimination.[1196] Thus the disadvantage in question, i.e., overall higher combined tax costs, is not caused by Italy or its credit method alone, but by the fact that both states tax, i.e., the exercise in parallel of their rightful fiscal competence left intact under EU law.[1197] Rather than being problematic, it seems that Italy, to the extent possible, did indeed eliminate any double taxation caused by its own tax system: on 40% of the income, the dividends were simply not taxed at all in Italy, as they were entirely left out of the tax base; thus, Italy did not cause double taxation on that portion of the dividends; on the remaining 60%, it granted a credit corresponding to the taxes it would have levied on that portion. One potential small novelty shown in this case is that a mixed system, i.e., combining a form of partial exemption with a credit method, is compatible with EU law. As of 25 February 2021, the CJEU confirmed a number of its holdings in this line of case law in the *Société Générale SA* case, frequently citing this *Baudinet* case as well as the *Gilly* case and the 'parallel exercise of tax jurisdiction'.[1198]

Interim Summary

While the *Avoir Fiscal* and *Saint Gobain* cases could be described as revealing the potency of the fundamental freedoms, this *Gilly* or 'disparity' line of case law could be described as revealing the limits of the fundamental freedoms. In this line of case law, another perspective was analysed. Rather than the perspective of the host state, or the state of establishment (as under the *Avoir Fiscal* and *Saint Gobain* cases), the perspective was that of the home state, or state of residence. Accordingly, the relevant comparison changed. These cases were brought by resident taxpayers who earned

1194. CJEU, Case C-128/08, *Damseaux*, 16 Jul. 2009, ECLI:EU:C:2009:471, at para. 32.
1195. CJEU, Case C-194/15, *Véronique Baudinet*, 4 Feb. 2016, ECLI:EU:C:2016:81, at para. 32.
1196. *Id.*, at para. 34.
1197. *Id.*, at para. 35.
1198. CJEU, Case C-403/19, *Société Générale SA*, 25 Feb. 2021, ECLI:EU:C:2021:136, at paras 26, 27, 28, 29 (citing the *Baudinet* case), para. 39 (citing *Gilly*), and paras 20, 22, 28, 40, 41 (citing the 'parallel exercise of tax jurisdiction').

income from abroad, as a result of, for example, crossing the border to work and thus earning employment income from another EU MS or holding shares in a company abroad and thus earning dividends from another EU MS. Hence, the comparison was between residents who earned all of their taxable income within the MS and residents who earned taxable income from other EU MSs. The problem arose from the fact that, as a result of earning income in another MS, the resident in question would be subject to income tax by more than one MS. Consequently, these cases confronted international juridical double taxation.

In such cases, the CJEU found itself unable to effectively wield the fundamental freedoms against this. It regularly repeated the reasons for its restraint. Direct taxation remains in the sovereignty of MSs. This freedom encompasses their right to design their tax base, set their tax rates, etc. and, according to the CJEU, no criteria can be deduced from EU law for prioritizing certain connecting factors (e.g., source, residence) for exercising tax jurisdiction over others. MSs are free to design their income tax systems, as long as they are not discriminatory or restrictive in light of the fundamental freedoms, which is generally assessed based on different treatment of comparable situations. If two MSs are both exercising their legitimate right to tax the income of the same taxpayer in a non-discriminatory way, although this leads to double taxation and although this may mount a barrier to cross-border activities, it is a barrier that the CJEU cannot forcefully dismantle with the fundamental freedoms. Rather, as long as direct taxation remains in the competence of EU MSs, in this 'current state' of EU law, certain overlaps of tax jurisdiction simply require the MSs to act together, to decide to coordinate their respective tax jurisdiction. Not all aims can be effectively or appropriately achieved through the EU judiciary. From this, key concepts emerged: while the fundamental freedoms cover discrimination, they do not cover 'disparities' or 'the exercise in parallel by two Member States of their fiscal sovereignty', or to that some add 'dislocations' (*see supra* note 1152).

As regards the credit method, since juridical double taxation was involved, it was the direct credit that was concerned. The CJEU held that, from the state of residence perspective, an income tax measure passed its scrutiny under the fundamental freedoms if it treated all residents the same who found themselves in a comparable domestic and cross-border situation.

On this basis, it was acceptable to have no credit method (or relief) whatsoever. In the *Kerckhaert and Morres* case, the MS abolished its tax credit, yet it taxed its residents at a uniform 25% rate on dividends, regardless of whether the dividends were generated in the MS in question or in other MSs.

In the *Gilly* case, a credit method applied; however, the amount of the tax credit in the MS of residence was lower than the amount of taxes actually paid in the other MS. This problem was not attributed to the credit method, but rather resulted from the fact that the other MS applied higher tax rates to the income in question than did the MS of residence. The other MS retains sovereignty under EU to set its tax rates, a right with which the CJEU cannot interfere. The MS of residence eliminated the taxes it collected on the income by means of the FTC, but could not be obliged under EU law to grant a credit larger than the amount of taxes that it would otherwise collect on the doubly taxed part of the income. To oblige this would force the MS of residence to reduce taxes that it collects on its own domestically generated income and, in effect, force it to adapt its tax system to that of another MS; this, the CJEU deemed too great an intrusion into a MS's competence in the area of direct taxation. As a result, an 'ordinary' direct credit method, i.e., limited by an MCA which corresponds to 'the fraction of its national tax corresponding to the income from abroad',[1199] is accepted by the CJEU.

In the *Columbus Container Services* case, the exemption method was 'overridden' by the credit method. This made the cross-border case more 'expensive' than it previously was under the exemption method. However, it did not make the cross-border case more expensive, and thus less favourably treated, than the comparable domestic case. Indeed, the CJEU observed that the credit method merely has the effect of taxing the comparable cross-border case at the same rate as the domestic case. This finding that, from the perspective of the MS of residence, the credit method is not discriminatory is perhaps not surprising if one recalls from Chapter 2 that the equal treatment of residents' income regardless of whether it is foreign source or domestic source is often one of the main justifications for a credit method. Comparing the *Columbus Container Services* case and the *Gilly* case, it can be seen that the credit method generally leads to the higher of the two MSs' taxes being collected, an outcome that is acceptable to the CJEU in light of MSs' sovereignty to set their tax rates.

This distinction between disparities and discrimination prompts one question, not explicitly addressed by the case law: although 'excess' credit situations and international juridical double taxation situations are often attributable to disparities, could discrimination be found in credit method cases where a MS levies a WHT on, e.g., interest and dividends at a rate of 30%, and domestically this WHT is fully creditable against the final tax liability on dividends and interest, whereas in the cross-border situation the foreign WHTs on interest and dividends are only creditable up to the MCA? Could this be seen as discriminatory different treatment, resulting from granting what equates to a full credit in the domestic context while enforcing an MCA in the cross-border context? As the answer to this question relies on a combination of this line of case law, the neutralization line of case law (discussed in Section 4.2.5.) and the deductible expenses line of case law (discussed in Section 4.2.6.), a more extensive response is elaborated in the conclusions (discussed in Chapter 5). In short, the answer is: from the perspective of the CJEU, this is unlikely a problem of the credit method that is imputable to the credit-granting MS, but rather a problem of the WHT, imputable to the MS in its role as the state of the payer or distributing entity.

As regards whether the relief is provided in domestic law or in a tax treaty, and the interaction between the two, according to the *Damseaux* case and *Columbus Container Services* case, this is for the national court to determine in light of its own legal system. The CJEU's analysis will then proceed from the result of that interpretation by the national court and assess that resulting legal situation in light of EU law.[1200]

1199. CJEU, Case C-336/96, *Gilly*, 12 May 1998, ECLI:EU:C:1998:221, at para. 48.
1200. *See also*, e.g., Michael Lang, *Double Taxation Conventions in the Case Law of the CJEU*, 46(3) Intertax 181, 184 (2018).

Finally, because the CJEU accepted that Germany could unilaterally switch from the exemption method to the credit method, the *Columbus Containers Services* case also offered a first indication that the credit method and exemption method were potentially equally compatible under EU law. This equivalence between the credit and exemption method is the topic of the next section (Section 4.2.3.).

4.2.3. The *FII* or 'Equivalence' Line of Case Law

The fact patterns in this series of cases, essentially, revolved around the different tax treatment of dividends as regards the method to relieve double taxation.[1201] On a preliminary terminological note, both indirect credit methods and imputation credit methods are referred to in the cases, but, for the purposes of the issue examined in this line of case law, they can be viewed as synonymous terms; the distinctive features of imputation method systems will be expanded upon below (in Section 4.2.8.).[1202] One

1201. CJEU, Case C-446/04, *Test Claimants in the FII Group Litigation*, 12 Dec. 2006, ECLI:EU:C:2006:774; CJEU, Joined Cases C-436/08 and C-437/08, *Haribo Lakritzen Hans Riegel BetriebsgmbH and Österreichische Salinen AG*, 10 Feb. 2011, ECLI:EU:C:2011:61; CJEU, Case C-35/11, *Test Claimants in the FII Group Litigation*, 13 Nov. 2012, ECLI:EU:C:2012:707; CJEU, Case C-47/12, *Kronos International Inc.*, 11 Sep. 2014, ECLI:EU:C:2014:2200.

1202. *See*, e.g., CJEU, Case C-47/12, *Kronos International Inc.*, 11 Sep. 2014, ECLI:EU:C:2014:2200, at paras 58–62 (as for the issue discussed here, it concerns the perspective of the state of residence and, in particular, the treatment immediately upon receipt of dividends from abroad. At this moment, the indirect credit and imputation credit can play a similar role. Where they tend to differ in treatment is at the moment of redistribution by that same resident recipient, because at that moment an imputation credit can often be passed up in some way to the next shareholder, whereas this is not a feature of a typical 'indirect credit'. For example, the *Kronos* case delineates the scope of the issue in the following way:

> '58 Kronos contends that, because of the refund of tax paid by the company distributing the dividends, investment in a resident company is more advantageous than investment in a non-resident company in a situation where the company receiving the dividends makes losses.
>
> 59 It further submits that the imputation regime would not be equivalent to the exemption regime if account were also taken of the taxation of the dividends in Germany when redistributed to shareholders.
>
> 60 In this context, it should be recalled first of all that the referring court alone can determine the subject-matter of the questions which it proposes to refer to the Court (judgment in *Kersbergen-Lap and Dams-Schipper*, C154/05, EU:C:2006:449, paragraph 21).
>
> 61 By its second question, the referring court asks the Court not about the effects of the tax treatment of the dividends distributed by the resident and non-resident companies on the shareholders of the company receiving them if they are redistributed to those shareholders, but only about the effects of the tax treatment of the dividends so far as concerns the company receiving them.
>
> 62 The request for a preliminary ruling does not contain an indication that the shareholders' situation was considered relevant by the referring court, information relating to the tax treatment of any dividends redistributed by the company receiving them, or information regarding the effects that application of the exemption and imputation methods at the level of that company has on the tax situation of its shareholders').

of the key questions was whether a MS violated EU law if it offered resident taxpayers an exemption for dividends received from resident companies and, instead, offered an indirect credit for foreign taxes on dividends received from abroad.[1203] Although the exemption method and the indirect/imputation credit method serve the same goal – to relieve double taxation – they use different means to this end, often with different economic results. Previous case law, such as *Verkooijen*,[1204] *Lenz*,[1205] and *Manninen*[1206] (especially the *Manninen* case[1207] as regards credit mechanisms),[1208] had already established that the state of residence of a taxpayer should consider dividends from domestic sources and dividends from foreign sources comparable[1209] and, therefore:

> 'where a Member State has a system for preventing or mitigating the imposition of a series of charges to tax or *economic* double taxation as regards dividends paid to residents by resident companies, it must treat dividends paid to residents by non-resident companies *in the same way*' (emphasis added).[1210]

This statement underscores a decisive difference with the 'disparity' case law: while the former addressed 'juridical double taxation', this case law addressed 'economic double taxation'. This is relevant for two interrelated reasons. First, for the CJEU, it seems that it is structurally easier to detect discrimination by a MS of residence in cases of economic double taxation than in cases of juridical double taxation (*see*, e.g., the discussion above in Section 4.2.2. regarding 'parallel exercise'). If a state proves that it is capable of eliminating the cumulative tax burden on distributions of profits that it causes within its own borders, presumably it can also do so across borders. Measures to mitigate or eliminate economic double taxation can apply exclusively within a national market (e.g., allowing an exemption, or dividends-received deduction, for dividends paid from a domestic subsidiary to a domestic parent company) and can also be extended to cross-border situations (e.g., the Parent-Subsidiary Directive obliged all MSs to do so), whereas the measures at issue in CJEU cases to mitigate or eliminate juridical double taxation were by definition[1211] for the cross-border situation (e.g., the residence state applies the credit method or exemption

1203. *See*, e.g., CJEU, Case C-446/04, *Test Claimants in the FII Group Litigation*, 12 Dec. 2006, ECLI:EU:C:2006:774, at para. 31.
1204. CJEU, Case C-35/98, *Verkooijen*, 6 Jun. 2000, ECLI:EU:C:2000:294.
1205. CJEU, Case C-315/02, *Anneliese Lenz*, 15 Jul. 2004, ECLI:EU:C:2004:446.
1206. CJEU, Case C-319/02, *Manninen*, 7 Sep. 2004, ECLI:EU:C:2004:484.
1207. *Id.*, at para. 8 (to offer a brief explanation, this case addressed an imputation system designed to relieve economic double taxation by granting shareholders a tax credit 'equal to 29/71sts of the amount of the dividends' to take into account that corporate income tax was already levied on the Finnish corporations at 29%).
1208. CJEU, Case C-446/04, *Test Claimants in the FII Group Litigation*, 12 Dec. 2006, ECLI:EU: C:2006:774, at para. 64, para. 184, para. 215, para. 216 (the CJEU cited mentioned these three cases at least four times).
1209. *See*, e.g., CJEU, Case C-319/02, *Manninen*, 7 Sep. 2004, ECLI:EU:C:2004:484, at paras 32–37 (regarding comparability in light of the objective pursued by the legislation).
1210. CJEU, Case C-446/04, *Test Claimants in the FII Group Litigation*, 12 Dec. 2006, ECLI:EU: C:2006:774, at para. 72.
1211. If the commonly cited definition, as formulated in the OECD Model, and which has also been cited by EU institutions, is used. *See supra* note 1148 and note 1149.

method to *FSI*) caused by more than one tax jurisdiction.[1212] Second, the way that the CJEU has proceeded in these cases is, in part, to reason that, since the objective of the legislation is to relieve economic double taxation, from this perspective (i.e., in light of the objective of the legislation), dividends from domestic sources and from foreign sources are the same, because both are liable to a series of double, or multiple, tax levies (i.e., both suffer from economic double taxation).

The above-cited statement (at *supra* note 1210) also makes reference to the 'same way', or equal treatment. The most crucial finding of this case law is that, in principle, the indirect credit method and the exemption method are equivalent in this regard.[1213] The foundational case for this was the *Test Claimants in the FII Group Litigation* case.[1214] It was not without controversy, considering the AG and the CJEU had different views as to how to answer the (first) question posed by the UK Court.

As regards the UK legislation under scrutiny, it applied the following system: for dividends received by a UK resident company from shareholdings in UK resident subsidiaries, the exemption method applied, whereas for dividends received from abroad, the credit method applied. More specifically, for dividends received from 'portfolio' shareholdings of less than 10% in companies outside of the UK, only a direct credit for WHTs was granted. For dividends received from more substantial shareholdings of 10% or more in companies outside of the UK, an indirect credit was also granted

1212. Though it is possible that juridical double taxation occurs in internal situations, what is addressed here is cross-border or international situations. *See*, e.g., *Double Taxation, IBFD International Tax Glossary* (Julie Rogers-Glabush ed., IBFD 7th ed. 2015) ('Juridical double taxation may be described as the imposition of comparable taxes by two (or more) tax jurisdictions on the same taxpayer in respect of the same taxable income or capital. [...] Double taxation may be domestic, i.e. where taxes are imposed within a sovereign state by different taxing authorities (e.g. by different members of a federation), or international [...]. Juridical double taxation is most commonly encountered in an international context [...]'); European Commission, Communication from the Commission to the European Parliament, the Council and the European Economic and Social Committee, Double Taxation in the Single Market, COM(2011) 712 Final, 4 (11 Nov. 2011) ('Double taxation, in the sense discussed here, may be described as the imposition of comparable taxes by two (or more) tax jurisdictions in respect of the same taxable income or capital[10]. Although double taxation can also occur in purely domestic situations, in particular as far as it concerns economic double taxation, this Communication focuses on cross-border situations only'); Opinion of AG Kokott in Case C-540/07, *Commission v. Italy*, 16 Jul. 2009, ECLI:EU:C:2009:463, at paras 44–47.

1213. CJEU, Case C-446/04, *Test Claimants in the FII Group Litigation*, 12 Dec. 2006, ECLI:EU:C:2006:774, at paras 48–57.

1214. *Id.*, at para. 31 (in particular, it was prompted by the first question posed by the UK national court to the CJEU. There were multiple questions posed regarding various aspects of the UK's dividend relief system, some of which go beyond the discussion here and are instead reserved for the discussion under the 'imputation' line of case law (in Section 4.2.8). The first question was posed as follows: 'Is it contrary to Article 43 or [Article] 56 EC for a Member State to keep in force and apply measures which exempt from corporation tax dividends received by a company resident in that Member State ("the resident company") from other resident companies and which subject dividends received by the resident company from companies resident in other Member States ("nonresident companies") to corporation tax (after giving double taxation relief for any withholding tax payable on the dividend and, under certain conditions, for the underlying tax paid by the non-resident companies on their profits in their country of residence)?').

'for the underlying foreign corporation tax on the profits out of which the dividends were paid'.[1215]

AG Geelhoed began his reasoning by reiterating his view that a restriction or disadvantageous tax treatment that stems from the fact that tax systems remain 'national' – i.e., that stems 'purely from disparities or the division of tax jurisdiction between two or more Member States' tax systems, or from the coexistence of national tax administrations' – does not infringe the fundamental freedoms in question.[1216] Rather, the restriction must stem from some discriminatory component of the legislation in question.[1217] From the perspective of the home state, this essentially means that the MS should not treat FSI less favourably than DSI.[1218] As regards the credit method, it is perfectly possible for it to be designed in line with EU law.[1219] This includes the design feature of an MCA because, although it could restrict 'in one sense' investment in another state:

> 'this is a good example of a restriction flowing purely from disparities between national tax systems, with which Article 43 EC is not concerned. Likewise, while the fact that taxpayers receiving foreign-source dividends may, in the case of a credit system, be under an obligation to complete additional formalities in order to prove the amount of foreign corporation tax paid in order to qualify for the credit, this is what I have termed a "quasi-restriction" resulting inevitably from the fact that tax administrations are at present national' (footnotes omitted).[1220]
>
> From this, he concluded that '[i]n sum, there is in principle no problem under Article 43 EC with the application of a credit system of double economic taxation relief'.[1221]

Up until this point, this reasoning echoes the 'disparity' line of case law, also decided from a residence, or home, state perspective. However, the particularity of this case was the *coexistence* of two different methods, i.e., applying an exemption method for the domestic dividends and a credit method for foreign dividends, and its relevance for the home state's non-discrimination obligation. According to the AG, '[t]he answer to this question depends on whether this distinction has the effect that the UK treats foreign-source dividends less favourably than domestic-source dividends'.[1222]

1215. Opinion of AG Geelhoed in Case C-446/04, *Test Claimants in the FII Group Litigation*, 6 Apr. 2006, ECLI:EU:C:2006:240, at para. 41; CJEU, Case C-446/04, *Test Claimants in the FII Group Litigation*, 12 Dec. 2006, ECLI:EU:C:2006:774, at para. 33.
1216. Opinion of AG Geelhoed in Case C-446/04, *Test Claimants in the FII Group Litigation*, 6 Apr. 2006, ECLI:EU:C:2006:240, at paras 38–39.
1217. *Id.*, at para. 39.
1218. *Id.*, at para. 40 ('In the case of a Member State exercising worldwide (home State) tax jurisdiction, as I noted in my Opinion in *Test Claimants in the ACT Group Litigation*, this principle means essentially that such a State must treat foreign-source income of its residents consistently with the way it has divided its tax base. Insofar as it has divided its tax base to include this foreign-source income – i.e., by treating it as taxable income – it must not discriminate between foreign-source and domestic income.[39] In particular, its legislation should not treat foreign-source income less favourably than domestic-source income').
1219. *Id.*, at para. 44.
1220. *Id.*, at para. 45.
1221. *Id.*, at para. 46.
1222. *Id.*, at para. 47.

Regarding the substantial shareholdings for which an indirect credit was granted, the AG observed that, while certain administrative or procedural differences (e.g., the fact that a credit method may require proof of the taxes paid abroad) are not relevant, there is one relevant difference. Under the exemption method, any tax benefits that are provided to the subsidiary are preserved for, or 'passed on', to the parent as well, since no additional tax is levied on the parent, whereas under the credit method, any tax benefits that are provided to the subsidiary cannot be 'passed on' to the parent because the amount of tax is 'topped up' to the parent's level. This could lead, in effect, to a reduced burden on the domestic dividends under an exemption method, as compared to the foreign dividends under a credit method. As a corollary, this may lead to situations where the tax burden on the foreign-source dividends is higher - i.e., less favourable - than that on the domestic-source dividends.[1223]

Regarding the portfolio shareholdings for which only a direct credit was granted, the AG held that this was clearly discriminatory.[1224] In the case of domestic dividends, even for portfolio shareholdings, an exemption was granted, meaning that no further UK tax was levied upon receipt of the dividends and thus economic double taxation was relieved. In the case of foreign dividends, UK tax was levied upon receipt of the dividends, yet no relief for economic double taxation was offered. It relieved only the juridical double taxation on the shareholder stemming from any possible WHT levied on the dividends.

For these reasons, the AG concluded that the answer to the first question should be that the UK legislation, regarding both the substantial shareholdings for which an indirect credit was granted and the portfolio shareholdings for which only a direct credit was granted, should be found contrary to the freedom of establishment and the free movement of capital.[1225]

The CJEU did not exactly follow the opinion of the AG. It agreed that the freedom of establishment and the free movement of capital require that the two sets of dividends (domestic-sourced and foreign-sourced) must be treated 'in the same way' under a MS's system to eliminate double taxation.[1226] For the portfolio dividends, the CJEU agreed that the legislation did not achieve this and thus was contrary to the free movement of capital.[1227] For the substantial shareholdings, a MS's legislation that applies exemption for domestic-sourced dividends and an indirect credit for foreign-sourced dividends is acceptable.[1228] However, the CJEU qualified this assertion of 'equivalence' in two ways:

1223. *Id.*, at paras 49–50.
1224. *Id.*, at para. 53.
1225. *Id.*, at para. 56.
1226. CJEU, Case C-446/04, *Test Claimants in the FII Group Litigation*, 12 Dec. 2006, ECLI:EU:C:2006:774, at para. 72.
1227. *Id.*, at paras 71–74.
1228. *Id.*, at paras 57, 60, 72–73.

(1) the tax rate *of the state of residence in question* that applies to the foreign-sourced dividends should not be higher than the tax rate that applies to domestic-sourced dividends;[1229] and
(2) 'the tax credit is at least equal to the amount paid in the Member State of the company making the distribution, up to the limit of the amount of the tax charged in the Member State of the company receiving the distribution'.[1230]

This makes it acceptable under EU law for the state of residence of the recipient to apply a credit limitation (or MCA), meaning the state of residence can give a credit for the foreign taxes up to the amount of tax that it would domestically levy on the foreign-source dividends, cap the credit at this threshold and does not have to 'repay the difference',[1231] thus confirming a similar finding in *Gilly* (*see* Section 4.2.2. for an example) but extending it to the indirect credit. Considering the relationship between the first and second conditions stipulated by the CJEU, it is the cause that counts, namely whether there is a discriminatory component or a mere disparity – that is, the state of residence cannot apply a higher tax rate to foreign-source dividends, but a higher rate can occur and be acceptable *if* this higher rate results from the fact that the tax rate *of the other state* is higher. Finally, the CJEU's stipulation that 'the tax credit is at least equal to the amount paid in' the other MS implies that the credit should be a unit-for-unit (e.g., EUR-for-EUR) credit and thus would exclude a partial credit (e.g., for every EUR of foreign taxes, only 0.90 cents is credited, as seems to be the case in Hungary,[1232] or for every USD of creditable foreign taxes, only 0.80 cents is credited, as under the US GILTI rules 80% partial credit[1233]).

As regards the type of credit, as seen above, the CJEU specified that, when addressing these cases of economic double taxation, it is not sufficient for the state of residence of the recipient to offer a credit merely for WHTs levied by the state of source (or rather the state of the distributing entity), as this would merely relieve juridical double taxation on the recipient. The state of residence must offer a credit for the underlying CITs paid by the distributor of the dividends, as this would relieve economic double taxation on the same profits.[1234] In other words, this case law requires an 'indirect credit', not a 'direct credit'.

1229. *Id.*, at para. 49.
1230. *Id.*, at para. 73 ('... provided that the rate of tax applied to foreign-sourced dividends is no higher than the rate of tax applied to nationally-sourced dividends and that the tax credit is at least equal to the amount paid in the Member State of the company making the distribution, up to the limit of the amount of the tax charged in the Member State of the company receiving the distribution').
1231. *Id.*, at paras 50–52.
1232. *See*, e.g., Levente Torma, *Hungary: Individual Taxation*, Country Analyses IBFD Section 7 (last visited 4 Jul. 2018); Levente Torma, *Hungary: Corporate Taxation*, Country Analyses IBFD Section 7 (last visited 4 Jul. 2018).
1233. *See*, e.g., United States, Department of the Treasury, Internal Revenue Service, Guidance Related to the Foreign Tax Credit, Including Guidance Implementing Changes Made by the Tax Cuts and Jobs Act, REG-105600-18, 83(235) Federal Register 63200, 63216 (7 Dec. 2018).
1234. CJEU, Case C-446/04, *Test Claimants in the FII Group Litigation*, 12 Dec. 2006, ECLI:EU:C:2006:774, at para. 63.

This assertion of 'equivalence' created a conundrum for the CJEU since the legal reasoning became intertwined with highly variable, factually contingent arithmetic considerations. From a legal standpoint, the CJEU has to balance the fundamental freedoms with the division of competences under the TFEU. Similar to the choice of tax base and tax rate, the choice between the credit method and exemption method forms part of the MSs' national sovereignty in direct tax matters.[1235] Yet, the latter tend to get presented to the CJEU since, unlike the tax base and tax rate, which *may* have a cross-border impact, double taxation relief mechanisms by their nature often address cross-border situations. As a result, it very well embodies the aforementioned tension between EU law and national sovereignty in tax matters. Indeed, the choice between exemption and credit is fundamental in direct tax matters and is inherently tied to other crucial policy issues and principles, such as the ability-to-pay principle sometimes anchored in constitutions.[1236] Rather than going so far as to impose one method over the other, the CJEU takes the less far-reaching approach of recalling that MSs have the freedom to choose (division of competences) so long as they respect the equal treatment, or non-discrimination, rules (fundamental freedoms). The challenge stems from the precise meaning to be given to the legal requirement of equal treatment, since, in these cases, determining under what circumstances these two methods fulfilled this legal obligation became linked to numerical considerations, such as comparisons of tax burdens, and thus became entangled in calculations.

In theory, all things equal, this equivalence exists, as can be shown with a simple example (Example No. 19).

Example No. 19: Equivalence in Theory Between Exemption and Indirect Credit

	Indirect credit	Exemption
Profits of 100%-owned subsidiary	100	100
Taxes paid by subsidiary Assume: 20% CIT in MS 2	20	20
Profits distributed to parent in MS 1	80	80

1235. *Id.*, at para. 47 ('As regards the question whether a Member State may operate an exemption system for nationally-sourced dividends when it applies an imputation system to foreign-sourced dividends, it must be stated that it is for each Member State to organise, in compliance with Community law, its system for taxing distributed profits and, in particular, to define the tax base and the tax rate which apply to the company making the distribution and/or the shareholder receiving them, in so far as they are liable to tax in that Member State').
1236. *See*, e.g., Germany, Grundgesetz (Constitution), Article 3(1).

	Indirect credit	Exemption
Taxes paid by parent **Assume: 20% CIT in MS 1**	0 (after credit) Calculation: Tax base: 80 + 20 (gross-up) = 100 Tax rate: 20% Tax: 20 Credit for underlying CIT on subsidiary: 20 Final liability in MS 1: 20–20 = 0	0 (exempt)
Total tax burden	20	20

In reality, given that direct taxation is under the control of the MSs, the inevitable differences in tax rates and tax bases will alter this. In fact, tax rates may diverge even *within* one and the same MS. When the CJEU demands that the tax rate on foreign-source dividends *not* be *higher* than that on domestic-source dividends, then it matters whether this refers to nominal tax rates or ETRs. For example, as the UK claimants pointed out in *Test Claimants in the FII Group Litigation (FII I)*,[1237] the aggregate taxes levied on their profits in the domestic context can end up lower under the exemption method (as compared to the credit method), due to the possibility that a UK subsidiary may not pay the full nominal rate of UK tax (e.g., 20%), but instead may pay a lower effective rate of tax (e.g., 15%, which can occur if the UK subsidiary benefited from other special reliefs that reduce the tax base). For this reason, the same case came before the CJEU a second time.[1238]

In the second *Test Claimants in the FII Group Litigation (FII II)*,[1239] the CJEU added more qualifications to its assertion of equivalence. The equivalence 'will be compromised' if the domestic subsidiary is subject to: (1) a nominal tax rate[1240] or (2) an effective level of tax[1241] that is lower (e.g., 15%) than the nominal tax rate (e.g., 20%) that applies to the parent. What happens in these cases is that, in the purely domestic scenario (where exemption is granted), because the profits are taxed only once at the level of the domestic subsidiary at the lower nominal or effective rate (15%) and then exempted upon receipt by the parent, the rate that ultimately applies is the lower one (15%). In the cross-border scenario (where an indirect credit is granted), the

1237. CJEU, Case C-446/04, *Test Claimants in the FII Group Litigation*, 12 Dec. 2006, ECLI:EU:C:2006:774, at para. 54.
1238. CJEU, Case C-35/11, *Test Claimants in the FII Group Litigation*, 13 Nov. 2012, ECLI:EU:C:2012:707.
1239. *Id.*
1240. CJEU, Case C-35/11, *Test Claimants in the FII Group Litigation*, 13 Nov. 2012, ECLI:EU:C:2012:707, at para. 44.
1241. *Id.*, at para. 46.

profits are taxed at the level of the subsidiary at whatever the foreign rate is (assume it is also a lower ETR of 15%) and then included in the tax base of the parent, taxed presumably at the nominal rate (20%), with an FTC deducted from the overall taxes owed (20%-15%, such that after the credit, 5% is paid to the state of residence and 15% was already paid to the foreign state). The consequence is that the amount of tax levied on the distributed profits will be lower in the domestic scenario under the exemption method (a total of 15%) than in the comparable cross-border scenario under the credit method (a total of 20%), i.e., the cross-border scenario will be less favourably taxed.

Example No. 20: Equivalence Between Exemption and Indirect Credit Compromised

	Indirect credit (cross-border)	**Exemption (domestic)**
Profits of 100%-owned subsidiary	100	100
Taxes paid by subsidiary Assume: 20% CIT in MS 1 & 2, but 15% ETR	15	15
Profits distributed to parent in MS 1	85	85
Taxes paid by parent Assume: 20% CIT in MS 1	5 (after credit) Calculation: Tax base: 85 + 15 (gross-up) = 100 Tax rate: 20% Tax: 20 Credit for underlying CIT on subsidiary: 15 Final liability in MS 1: 20–15 = 5	0 (exempt)
Total tax burden	20	15

Thus, CJEU conceded one difference, potentially undermining its assertion of equivalence: 'Unlike the exemption method, the imputation method therefore does not enable the benefit of the corporation tax reductions granted at an earlier stage to the company paying dividends to be passed on to the corporate shareholder.'[1242] However, if the difference between the nominal rate and the effective rate that applies to the

1242. *Id.*, at para. 48.

subsidiary occurs only in exceptional cases, this is not a problem (i.e., 'the exemption and imputation methods do not immediately cease to be equivalent').[1243] Upon closer inspection, it was discovered that, in the UK, apparently this occurred 'in the majority of cases'.[1244] For this reason, in the UK's case, the two methods did not ensure equal tax treatment.[1245]

Surprisingly, the CJEU then offered a rather striking possible solution for the UK's dilemma:[1246] it proposed that a more proportionate (less restrictive) measure would be to apply the credit method on the basis of the nominal rate, rather than the ETR.[1247] This would be a departure from a main characteristic of the credit method, which is to credit taxes that were actually *effectively* paid. One result would be that, in cases where the taxes effectively paid by the subsidiary are lower than the nominal rate, this amounts to a sort of tax 'matching' credit (i.e., a credit granted for a *notional* amount of taxes that were *not* actually paid, the notional amount being equal to the difference between the amount based on the nominal rate and the amount actually paid based on the ETR), which may, in turn, amount to a partial exemption.[1248]

The reasoning for this, in paragraphs 60 and 61 of the judgment, is likewise striking:

> 'The tax exemption to which a resident company receiving nationally-sourced dividends is entitled is granted irrespective of the effective level of taxation to which the profits out of which the dividends have been paid were subject. That exemption, in so far as it is intended to avoid economic double taxation of distributed profits, is thus based on the assumption that those profits were taxed at the nominal rate of tax in the hands of the company paying dividends. It thus resembles grant of a tax credit calculated by reference to that nominal rate of tax.'[1249]

This second part of the paragraph is questionable since the exemption method is not technically based on any particular rate. In fact, as paragraph 61 states, the exemption method 'is granted irrespective of the effective level of taxation' levied on the subsidiary. By extension, the exemption method may apply irrespective of whether *any* taxes were levied at all (unless there is a special subject-to-tax or switch-over or anti-avoidance measure). Notably, the quote from the CJEU focuses on a domestic participation exemption. It is true that in the domestic context, it would seem more likely that an inter-company participation exemption is based on an assumption that taxes on the distributed profits were already paid to the state Treasury in question by the domestic subsidiary. However, as the UK case exemplified, the UK granted an

1243. *Id.*, at para. 50.
1244. *Id.*, at para. 51.
1245. *Id.*, at para. 52.
1246. *Id.*, at paras 60–62.
1247. *Id.*, at para. 62.
1248. On the point that a matching credit is similar to a partial exemption, *see*, e.g., Alexander Rust, *Article 23 A Exemption Method and Article 23 B Credit Method*, *in 2 Klaus Vogel on Double Taxation Conventions* 1581, m.no. 65 (Ekkehart Reimer & Alexander Rust eds, Kluwer Law International 4th ed. 2015).
1249. CJEU, Case C-35/11, *Test Claimants in the FII Group Litigation*, 13 Nov. 2012, ECLI:EU:C:2012:707, at para. 61.

exemption in the domestic context, despite the fact that many local subsidiaries apparently paid lower ETRs. Thus, it can be argued that, in the cross-border context and potentially also the domestic context, the exemption method neither takes into account the nominal tax rate nor the ETR. Yet the CJEU then continues and implies that what clearly follows from its statement (i.e., that the exemption method applies irrespective of the *effective* level of taxation) is that 'exemption ... is thus based on the assumption that those profits were taxed at the *nominal* rate of tax in the hands of the company paying dividends' (emphasis added). That the exemption method ignores the effective rate of tax does not necessarily entail that it cares about the nominal rate of tax. However, the CJEU emphasizes the purpose. If the purpose is to eliminate economic double taxation, indeed for this purpose to be fulfilled, granting an exemption would implicitly assume that the profits suffered such double taxation (otherwise, there is arguably no need to eliminate inexistent economic double taxation). Still, this possibly assumes *some* taxation occurred, but not necessarily at the nominal rate applicable; one may not care at all about what precise rate applied and the method may be decided upon with full awareness that the ETR and/or nominal rate of the subsidiary may be lower.[1250]

What the CJEU seemed to want to express was: to the extent that subsidiaries abroad also benefit from lower ETRs than their nominal tax rate in the foreign state, the benefit of those lower taxes can be, at least partially, if not fully, pushed up to the parent if the credit is granted based on the nominal rate. In other words, the CJEU was stating the obvious that a partial exemption will be closer to full exemption. Perhaps it was seeking a way to avoid going so far as to simply require the full exemption method to be extended in order to uphold its equivalence reasoning.

Returning to the aforementioned conundrum (touched upon just above at *supra* note 1235), for a MS to assess its compliance with the *FII I* and *II* cases (assuming of course that it has a similar system for relief), a myriad of numerical possibilities arises as soon as a state tries to imagine all possible ETRs that may result from diverse combinations of national tax laws (e.g., those affecting the tax base, special regimes for research and development, etc.), before even taking into account the methods themselves. Given the theoretical equivalence (illustrated in Example No. 19), one can wonder whether it is an issue of the method per se or rather an issue of these other (arguably extrinsic) circumstances. Based on these decisions of the CJEU, the EU law compatibility of a given national law to some extent hinges upon other factual and legal

1250. To compare with another example of a participation exemption at EU level, *see*, e.g., Georg Kofler, *Indirect Credit Versus Exemption: Double Taxation Relief for Intercompany Distributions*, 66(2) Bull. Int'l Tax'n 77, 87 (2012) (what Kofler explains about the Parent-Subsidiary Directive may also support this idea that the nominal rate is not necessarily assumed. 'Neither of the two methods is tied to prerequisites other than a minimum holding percentage (article 3(1)) and, optionally, a holding period of two years (article 3(2)), and Member States are, hence, barred from introducing additional requirements, such as, for example, that a shareholding must be considered as a "fixed financial asset",[132] the existence of a tax treaty,[133] or a certain level of taxation of the subsidiary's income.[134] As for the last point, technically, article 2 of the Directive, *inter alia*, requires that a company has to be subject to one of the taxes listed in article 2(1)(c) "without the possibility of an option or of being exempt", a condition whose interpretation is heavily discussed and may perhaps only exclude companies that are fully exempt from taxation[135]').

circumstances that can change on a case-by-case basis, such that in one instance it is compatible and in the next it is not. This volatility risk was reduced by the CJEU's condition that a MS should check whether the differences (e.g., lower ETR of its subsidiaries) are widespread or exceptional.[1251]

Another important clarification in this line of case law results from the *Haribo & Salinen* (joined) cases in Austria. In this case, it was underlined that the indirect credit method may lead to a disadvantage in certain loss situations. For example, a taxpayer suffers a loss in its home state (-100), in a year in which it receives profits distributed from abroad (20). Under the credit method, the income is included in the tax base, in order to calculate the total tax liability and then to offer an FTC against that liability. In this case, though, no taxes are levied when there is a loss (-80). There are two possible disadvantages:

(1) no FTC can be given because there are no domestic taxes against which it can be offset, and
(2) any potential loss carryforward (LCF) has now been reduced (from –100 to –80).[1252]

Under the exemption method, the FSI is generally not included in the tax base, so it does not affect the losses. According to the CJEU, to maintain equivalence between exemption and credit in these circumstances, the MS should allow a credit carryforward into future years.[1253] This credit carryforward is only relevant for indirect credits (for underlying CIT), *not* for direct credits (for WHTs at source). In fact, according to the CJEU, a MS is not even required to provide any direct credit for WHTs.[1254]

1251. CJEU, Case C-35/11, *Test Claimants in the FII Group Litigation*, 13 Nov. 2012, ECLI:EU:C:2012:707, at para. 50.

1252. *See*, e.g., CJEU, Joined Cases C-436/08 and C-437/08, *Haribo Lakritzen Hans Riegel BetriebsgmbH and Österreichische Salinen AG*, 10 Feb. 2011, ECLI:EU:C:2011:61, at paras 27–28, 173; Veronika Daurer & Nicole Tüchler, *Foreign Tax Credit: Is a Carry-Forward Obligatory?*, 66(10) Bull. Int'l Tax'n 563, 563 and 566, Section 1 (2012).

1253. CJEU, Joined Cases C-436/08 and C-437/08, *Haribo Lakritzen Hans Riegel BetriebsgmbH and Österreichische Salinen AG*, 10 Feb. 2011, ECLI:EU:C:2011:61, at para. 159 ('Where national legislation, such as that at issue in the main proceedings, does not provide for the credit for the corporation tax paid in the State where the company distributing the dividends is established to be carried forward, foreign-sourced dividends suffer, in a system such as that at issue in the main proceedings, higher taxation than that resulting from application of the exemption method for nationally-sourced dividends') and para. 160 ('[...] Article 63 TFEU must be considered to preclude such legislation') and para. 163 ('However, as is clear from paragraph 158 of the present judgment, national legislation which, for dividends from non-residents companies, does not allow the credit for the tax paid abroad to be carried forward, whilst exempting nationally-sourced dividends from corporation tax, does not prevent economic double taxation in respect of the foreign-sourced dividends').

1254. CJEU, Joined Cases C-436/08 and C-437/08, *Haribo Lakritzen Hans Riegel BetriebsgmbH and Österreichische Salinen AG*, 10 Feb. 2011, ECLI:EU:C:2011:61, at para. 166 ('Second, with regard to whether, when applying the imputation method, account must be taken of the tax withheld at source in the State of the company making the distribution, it should be noted that such tax creates the conditions for juridical double taxation unless a credit is granted for it in the State where the company receiving the dividends concerned is established') and para. 171 ('Accordingly, Article 63 cannot be interpreted as obliging a Member State to provide, in its tax

Although the cases discussed thus far spotlight the challenges of the indirect credit method, the exemption method is not free from its own challenges.[1255] The intense scrutiny of the indirect credit method stems logically from the fact that, in these cases, it was the method that applied to the cross-border scenario, which under EU law should not be treated less favourably. For that reason, the potentially 'unfavourable' aspects of the credit method were put under the microscope. The 2014 *Kronos* case[1256] examined the reverse situation where the exemption method applied to cross-border cases and an indirect credit (imputation) method applied to domestic cases. Here, of course, a taxpayer complained of a disadvantage of the exemption method as compared to the 'imputation' method.[1257]

The disadvantage that the taxpayer, Kronos, complained of concerned losses. In scenarios where the shareholder company had suffered losses, the exemption method had no effect, as simply no income was taken into account.[1258] In such loss scenarios, the 'imputation' method had the effect that the amount of losses was reduced, as the income was taken into account, thereby reducing any future LCF (or backward), yet this was accompanied by, in some cases, a partial or full refund of the tax credit corresponding to the dividends (i.e., a tax credit for the underlying taxes paid by the subsidiary):[1259]

> 'Kronos contends that, because of the refund of tax paid by the company distributing the dividends, investment in a resident company is more advantageous than investment in a non-resident company in a situation where the company receiving the dividends makes losses.'[1260]

---

legislation, that a credit is to be granted for the withholding tax levied on dividends in another Member State in order to prevent the juridical double taxation – resulting from the parallel exercise by the Member States concerned of their respective powers of taxation – of the dividends received by a company established in the first Member State (see, to this effect, Case C-513/04 Kerckhaert and Morres [2006] ECR I-10967, paragraphs 22 to 24)').

1255. *See*, e.g., Gauthier Blanluet & Philippe J. Durand, *General Report: Key Practical Issues to Eliminate Double Taxation of Business Income*, 96b Cahiers de Droit Fiscal International 17 (IFA 2011); Georg Kofler, *Indirect Credit Versus Exemption: Double Taxation Relief for Intercompany Distributions*, 66(2) Bull. Int'l Tax'n 77 (2012).

1256. CJEU, Case C-47/12, *Kronos International Inc.*, 11 Sep. 2014, ECLI:EU:C:2014:2200.

1257. *Id.*, at paras 58, 71–82 (for a discussion of advantages and disadvantages of the methods).

1258. *Id.*, at para. 73 ('On the other hand, dividends distributed by a company resident in another Member State or in a third State were exempt from tax in Germany and were not taken into account when determining the amount of tax of the company receiving them. Therefore, they had no effect either on the basis of assessment of the company receiving them or on any losses that it might be able to carry forward or back').

1259. *Id.*, at para. 72 ('In a situation such as that at issue in the main proceedings, where the company receiving the dividends had in addition made losses, the dividend paid by a resident company was taken into account when determining the amount of tax of the company receiving it, which meant that the losses were partially or fully set off and, therefore, were reduced or were precluded from being carried forward to a subsequent year or back to a previous one. When the income from the dividends paid by resident companies did not exceed the losses recorded by the company receiving them, the tax payable by the latter was nil and the tax credit in respect of the tax on the dividends distributed by the German subsidiary was refunded').

1260. *Id.*, at para. 58.

By contrast, in the joined *Haribo & Salinen* cases discussed above, the taxpayers complained that the credit method gave rise to disadvantages in the case of losses. Comparing these two complaints reveals how contingent the effects of the methods (and whether they are perceived as advantageous or disadvantageous) are on the particular facts and circumstances, such as whether the taxpayer is in a profit-making situation or a loss-making situation, the time at which the credit is granted, and the tax rates in the respective states.

The reasoning of the CJEU in the *Kronos* case can be broken into five points. First, the CJEU applied its findings in the two *FII* cases by analogy to this one. As a general rule, a MS is free to design its regime for preventing economic double taxation of dividends in this way: because the CJEU accepted the application of the exemption method in the domestic scenario and the indirect credit method in the cross-border scenario, in principle the reverse is also acceptable.[1261]

Second, upon weighing the advantages and disadvantages, the CJEU was not convinced that the exemption method was more disadvantageous than the 'imputation' method. The CJEU observed that, because under the exemption method, the profits do not affect the tax base of the recipient, it left intact the recipient's ability to bring forward and use in that tax period any previously recorded losses.[1262] Likewise, it avoided the negative consequences of reducing any potential current losses that the receiving company 'might be able to carry forward or back' to other tax periods.[1263] Moreover, 'the exemption method, in some circumstances, enabled the benefit of lower taxation in the State of the company distributing the dividends to be preserved',[1264] and the exemption method 'spared the entire administrative burden inherent in the imputation method'.[1265]

Third, the CJEU conceded that the 'imputation system' did have one relevant advantage, namely that the refund granted to domestic companies under Germany's 'imputation' system resulted in a 'tax-flow advantage'.[1266] Furthermore, the CJEU conceded that, in past cases, it had ruled that a cash-flow advantage that is granted to domestic situations, while being denied to comparable cross-border situations, infringes the free movement of capital.[1267] The issue of cash-flow advantages was also relevant under the imputation method line of case law, as will be discussed below (in Section 4.2.8.). However, in the *Kronos* case, the 'comparable' characteristic was lacking, according to the CJEU, because there was an 'objective difference' between the dividends in the domestic case and those in the cross-border case.

On this point, fourth, the main reason for this objective difference was that the cross-border dividends are not taxed at all – that is, Germany does *not* exercise its

1261. *Id.*, at paras 66–67.
1262. *Id.*, at para. 76.
1263. *Id.*, at para. 73.
1264. *Id.*, at para. 74.
1265. *Id.*, at para. 75.
1266. *Id.*, at para. 79.
1267. *Id.*, at para. 80.

jurisdiction to tax over them.[1268] This could be seen as a corollary of the *same-taxation-same-relief*, or 'subject-to-tax', comparability assessment that evolved from the *Avoir Fiscal* and *Saint Gobain* cases (discussed in Section 4.2.1.). In this connection, the CJEU made various pronouncements regarding the relationship between the fundamental freedoms and the fiscal sovereignty that remains with the MSs and how this affects the methods for relief:

> 'The Court has already held that the free movement of capital, enshrined in Article 63(1) TFEU, cannot have the effect of requiring Member States to go beyond the cancelling of national income tax payable by a shareholder in respect of foreign-sourced dividends received and to reimburse a sum whose origin is in the tax system of another Member State (see, by analogy, judgment in *Test Claimants in the FII Group Litigation*, EU:C:2006:774, paragraph 52), if the first Member State is not to see its fiscal autonomy limited by the exercise of the fiscal power of the other Member State (see, in particular, judgment in *Meilicke and Others*, C-262/09, EU:C:2011:438, paragraph 33 and the case-law cited).'[1269]

> 'Consequently, in a situation where the Member State does not exercise its powers of taxation over the incoming dividends - either by taxing them or by taking them into account in a different way - as regards the company receiving them, its obligations, as the Member State of residence of the company receiving the dividends, do not go so far as to require it offset the tax burden resulting from the exercise of the tax powers of another Member State or of a third State.'[1270]

Thus, although the outcome was the same (namely 'equivalence'), the reasoning was different.

Fifth, related to this, the CJEU reasoned that the advantages and disadvantages were 'logical complements':

> 'Second, the refund requested by Kronos constitutes, in the context of the imputation method, the logical complement of taking the dividends into account and of the previous reduction of the losses that can be carried forward. Without such a refund, the taking of the dividends into account and the reduction of the losses of the company receiving them are liable to result in economic double taxation of those dividends in subsequent tax years when the results of the company receiving the dividends are positive (see, to this effect, judgment in *Cobelfret*, C-138/07, EU:C:2009:82, paragraphs 39 and 40, and order in *KBC Bank and Beleggen, Risicokapitaal, Beheer*, C-439/07 and C-499/07, EU:C:2009:339, paragraphs 39 and 40).
>
> By contrast, in the context of the exemption method, as the losses are not reduced, there is no risk of economic double taxation of the dividends received. The lack of a refund is counterbalanced by not taking the dividends into account when determining the basis of assessment.'[1271]

In this way, the CJEU gave further reinforcement to and insight into its view that a logically coherent design for an 'imputation' credit and an indirect credit system,

1268. *Id.*, at paras 81–82.
1269. *Id.*, at para. 83.
1270. *Id.*, at para. 85.
1271. *Id.*, at paras 87–88.

given the aim of relief for economic double taxation, necessitates either a credit carryforward (as suggested in *Haribo & Salinen*) or, as Germany's alternative design shows, a refund of the tax credit in the tax year in question. In addition, the CJEU reiterated the equivalence, subject to certain conditions, of the two approaches[1272] from its now clearly settled case law.

Interim Summary

By comparison with the *Gilly* or 'disparity' line of case law, which addressed juridical double taxation and thus the direct credit method, this line of case law addressed economic double taxation and thus the indirect credit method and 'imputation' credit method. Hence, the facts revolved around distributions of profits or dividends. It was, similar to the *Gilly* line, reasoned from the state of residence perspective, or more precisely the state of residence of the parent company or shareholder. The comparison was, thus predictably, between the tax treatment of parent companies receiving dividends from domestic sources and of parent companies receiving dividends from foreign sources. Importantly, in these cases, the *main* issue was *not* that of a MS granting relief to the domestic stream of dividends while denying relief for the cross-border receipt of dividends, but rather that the MS offered a different *type* of relief in the two cases – in most cases, an exemption for dividends from domestic sources and an indirect credit for dividends from foreign sources. As the domestic and cross-border situations were deemed comparable, especially 'in the light of the objective of preventing the imposition of a series of charges to tax',[1273] to which both streams of dividends are potentially subjected, the two merited the same treatment. In interpreting this 'same' treatment requirement, the CJEU declared that, in principle, an exemption and an indirect credit achieved this in essentially the same way. It was clearly not the only inevitable outcome since the AG and the CJEU in *FII I* came to (partially) different conclusions on this point.

There were additional conditions placed on this 'equivalence'. These conditions are relevant for their potential impact on the design of MSs' relief systems, with some implications for an indirect credit in particular. First, in terms of instructions for MSs, what can be derived from this case law is that if a MS grants an exemption to domestic dividends, then it is not sufficient to grant only a direct credit for WHTs on dividends from abroad. The MS must grant an indirect credit for the underlying corporate taxes paid by the subsidiary abroad. Second, if a MS grants an exemption to domestic dividends and an indirect credit to foreign dividends, the state of residence of the recipient must ensure that the tax rate it levies on the foreign dividends is not higher than that levied on domestic dividends.

Third, the credit should be at least equal to the amount of taxes levied in the other state, so the MS should strive to fully credit unit-for-unit (e.g., EUR-for-EUR) the

1272. *Id.*, at paras 66–67.
1273. CJEU, Case C-446/04, *Test Claimants in the FII Group Litigation*, 12 Dec. 2006, ECLI-:EU:C:2006:774, at para. 87.

foreign taxes. This seems to preclude a partial credit, as mentioned above. However, it is acceptable to restrict this to the MCA, where the foreign taxes are greater than what the state of residence would levy on the income in question. The state of residence eliminates the taxes that it would levy on the FSI without going further than this. To the extent that higher taxes on the foreign dividends merely stem from a higher tax rate in the state of the subsidiary, there is not a different or discriminatory treatment caused by the state of residence of the recipient. Thus, considering both the 'disparity' line of case law and this 'equivalence' line of case law, an MCA is compatible with EU law both in the case of a direct credit and in the case of an indirect credit.

Fourth, the 'equivalence' between the exemption method (for domestic dividends) and the indirect credit method (for foreign dividends) is 'compromised' if domestic subsidiaries are taxed at a lower nominal rate or ETR – in particular, on a widespread basis and not merely in exceptional cases. Thus, to avoid any incompatibility, a MS must essentially review, and if needed redesign, its tax system – i.e., the rules potentially affecting the tax base and other special regimes – so that the rate that applies to domestic subsidiaries is not – or is only very exceptionally – lower than that of parent companies. Otherwise, if domestic subsidiaries regularly benefit from lower taxes, then in this case, the CJEU (surprisingly) made its own design suggestion, namely that a more proportionate way to design the credit method would be to grant a credit on the basis of the nominal tax rate in the foreign state, rather than basing it strictly on the taxes effectively paid abroad. This would be similar to a matching credit, which in some cases amounts to a partial exemption.

Fifth, in a situation where the recipient of the dividends has suffered losses domestically, yet earned dividends from abroad, the credit method may entail two disadvantages, namely that: (1) the taxpayer is not able to benefit from the relief because no taxes are levied in the state of residence on an overall negative result against which an FTC can be deducted and (2) this may lead to a reduction of the taxpayer's LCF because the current losses are reduced by the amount of the positive income (i.e., the dividends) that is incorporated into the tax base. In such cases, to ensure 'equivalence', a MS must grant a credit carryforward. Alternatively, in the *Kronos* case, Germany's legislation resolved such loss scenarios by simply granting a full or partial refund of the tax credit attached to the dividends in the tax year in question (although in the *Kronos* case it was an 'imputation' method only for domestically sourced dividends, it is not unimaginable to extend such a system to other EU MSs, if it were needed). Otherwise, to avoid these various constraints or counterbalancing measures, a MS would have to apply only one of the methods exclusively, either an exemption for both domestic and cross-border cases or an indirect credit for both domestic and cross-border cases.

4.2.4. The *Schumacker/De Groot* or 'Calculation' Line of Case Law[1274]

In 1995, in the (in)famous *Schumacker* case,[1275] the CJEU established the general rule that the state of residence is responsible for granting tax-related benefits that take into account a given taxpayer's personal and family circumstances (e.g., adjustments for married couples, child tax credits, etc.). More notably, it also established the exception, i.e., under what circumstances the state of source (or, more precisely, the state of non-residence where employment is exercised, etc.) takes on this responsibility.

As regards the facts, Mr Schumacker commuted across the border into Germany for work and earned all his income there. As a result, no income was earned in his state of residence, Belgium. In addition, the income was not taxable in Belgium due to the DTC under which Germany could tax the income from employment and Belgium agreed to exempt it.[1276] Consequently, there was no tax base or tax liability in Belgium for the purposes of calculating adjustments to the progressive rate for married couples, or deducting special allowances or credits for personal and family circumstances.[1277] Germany also did not provide such benefits to Mr Schumacker. Similar to many states, Germany subjected residents to unlimited tax liability, taking into account their overall ability to pay, along with the accompanying personal benefits, while it subjected non-residents to limited tax liability, only on income deemed earned within the territory. In comparison to his colleagues who were residents in Germany, Mr Schumacker who was a non-resident faced a heavier tax burden since neither state made allowances for his personal situation. In his view, he suffered disadvantageous treatment by virtue of exercising the free movement of workers.

The CJEU reasoned that, normally, residents and non-residents are *not* comparable from the perspective of direct tax law,[1278] but in *exceptional* circumstances, they become comparable, such as when the taxpayer earns nearly all income (90% or more) and pays nearly all taxes (e.g., automatically deducted at source by the employer) in the state of *non*-residence[1279] without sufficient income in its state of residence. In such a case, the CJEU ordered Germany (the state where the income was earned) to extend

1274. CJEU, Case C-279/93, *Schumacker*, 14 Feb. 1995, ECLI:EU:C:1995:31; CJEU, Case C-385/00, *de Groot*, 12 Dec. 2002, ECLI:EU:C:2002:750; CJEU, Case C-527/06, *Renneberg*, 16 Oct. 2008, ECLI:EU:C:2008:566; CJEU, Case C-168/11, *Beker*, 28 Feb. 2013, ECLI:EU:C:2013:117; CJEU, Case C-303/12, *Guido Imfeld and Nathalie Garcet*, 12 Dec. 2013, ECLI:EU:C:2013:822.

1275. CJEU, Case C-279/93, *Schumacker*, 14 Feb. 1995, ECLI:EU:C:1995:31.

1276. *Id.*, at paras 16, 19 (according to the case, 'the said income is also only taxable in the Federal Republic of Germany, in accordance with the Double Taxation Agreement between the Federal Republic of Germany and the Kingdom of Belgium', concluded on 11 Apr. 1967. In the case of Belgium, under domestic law, it generally levied taxes on the basis of worldwide income but, under the Belgium-Germany DTC, Belgium was obliged to exempt the income earned in Germany).

1277. *Id.*, at paras 16, 19, 41 (the state of residence, Belgium, was unable to provide these personal benefits for related legal and factual reasons, namely because only the state of employment, Germany, had the right to tax the income under the DTC (*see*, e.g., question 3 posed by the national court) and because 'the tax payable there [in Belgium] is insufficient').

1278. *Id.*, at paras 31, 34–35.

1279. *Id.*, at paras 33, 36, 37.

the same treatment (e.g., tax-related family benefits) to Mr Schumacker (a *non*-resident, cross-border worker) as it gives to its own residents. In one of its less precisely formulated paragraphs, the CJEU stated that the (indirect) discrimination arose from the fact that his personal circumstances were taken into account *nowhere* ('neither in the State of residence nor in the State of employment')[1280] and, for this reason, this is often cited as the CJEU's rule that ensures personal circumstances are taken into account *somewhere*.[1281]

Similar to previous cases, the decision related to a matter at the core of MSs' direct tax sovereignty. In income (or direct) tax law, the distinction based on residence is a fundamental factor of connection with a given territory that determines a state's jurisdiction to tax a person. However, by contrast with previous cases (such as in the 'disparity' line of case law), the CJEU found itself able to prescribe which state was responsible (namely, the state of residence, as a general rule). To reach this conclusion, the CJEU made reference to, *inter alia*, the OECD Model.[1282] The assumption is that, since taxpayers' 'financial and personal' interests are centred in the state of residence, this state can better assess their personal needs and circumstances,[1283] and the CJEU used this as a consideration for allocating responsibility to a given MS. In this way, the CJEU was able to find a criterion, though not necessarily from EU law. Such seeming inconsistencies give rise to suspicions of result-driven reasoning and exacerbate some scholars' perplexity at the CJEU's professed inability to find solutions in other cases (most notably, in the 'disparity' line of case law).[1284] However, also by contrast with previous cases, discrimination could be found in the *Schumacker* case,[1285] since the different treatment could be attributed entirely to Germany's income tax law provisions, unlike in the 'disparity' credit method cases where the different treatment arose from two MSs' diverging laws.

Another consideration that seemed to factor into the analysis of the CJEU is that, in this case, the DTC required Belgium, the state of residence, to exempt Mr Schumacker's employment income that was taxable in Germany. One question that arises is whether the outcome would have been different had the credit method applied instead

1280. *Id.*, at para. 38.
1281. *See*, e.g., Otto Marres (update of 6th ed.), *Chapter 16: Division of Tax Jurisdiction; Double Tax Relief Mechanisms; Tax Treaty Issues, in* 1 *Terra/Wattel European Tax Law* 695, 712 (Peter J. Wattel, Otto Marres & Hein Vermeulen eds, Wolters Kluwer 7th ed. 2019); Luc De Broe & Thomas Gernay, *Belgium: The Imfeld & Garcet Case and the Levy Case, in ECJ Recent Developments in Direct Taxation 2012* 9, 16 (Michael Lang et al. eds, Linde 2013) (i.e., 'somewhere and only once').
1282. CJEU, Case C-279/93, *Schumacker*, 14 Feb. 1995, ECLI:EU:C:1995:31, at para. 32.
1283. *Id.*
1284. *See*, e.g., *supra* note 1157.
1285. CJEU, Case C-279/93, *Schumacker*, 14 Feb. 1995, ECLI:EU:C:1995:31, at paras 26–29, 36–38 (according to the CJEU, first, it could be indirectly linked to nationality. Second, fault could be assigned to one MS's laws. Regarding the first, discrimination on nationality is prohibited. However, Germany did not deny the benefits on the basis of his Belgian nationality. Rather, it was on the basis of non-residence in Germany. However, since non-resident persons are usually non-nationals, this distinction may lead to an indirect, or covert, form of discrimination on the basis of nationality, according to the CJEU. Regarding the second, it was Germany's laws that denied the benefits to non-residents, while granting it to residents, leading to a different treatment).

of the exemption method.[1286] If the credit method had applied, then presumably Belgium would have been able to tax the worldwide income of Mr Schumacker, thus offering the prospect of taking into account personal and family circumstances, before granting a credit for taxes paid in Germany.

On this question, the *Gilly* case[1287] (discussed above in Section 4.2.2.) could be interpreted as an indication that, where the credit method applies, the *Schumacker* rule does not. Indeed, there were some similarities in the fact patterns (i.e., frontier workers earning employment income in Germany) and Mrs Gilly also raised an issue regarding her personal and family circumstances.[1288] However, based on the way the paragraphs of the judgment expressed the issue, the precise connection being made between the personal and family circumstances and the credit method was not clear. The argument was framed as follows:

> 'because Mrs Gilly's personal and family circumstances are not taken into account in Germany, whereas they are taken into account in France when calculating the tax on the total income, the tax credit accorded in the State of residence is lower than the amount of tax actually paid in the State of employment, taking account of the rebates and reductions accorded in the first State'.[1289]

Thus, since Mrs Gilly was openly acknowledging that her personal and family circumstances were indeed taken into account in France, it was not the same as in *Schumacker* where the personal and family circumstances were not taken into account anywhere. It was not a *nowhere-somewhere* situation. Rather, the argument seemed to be that the very fact that personal and family circumstances were taken into account in France, but not in Germany, lowered the amount of the credit. It is true that when the tax base for the income in question is lower in the state of residence (due to allocating expenses, either personal or professional, to the FSI), the amount of credit will be lower (as elaborated below in Section 4.2.6.). However, Mrs Gilly referred to the effect on the 'tax on total income'. This indicates that perhaps the Gilly couple was invoking a calculation issue, similar to the issues that will be discussed below under *De Groot* and *Beker*. Wattel suspected that this was the case and thus the CJEU may have misunderstood the complaint.[1290] The CJEU did not enter into further detail or explanation. It simply stated that 'it is common ground' – thus implying that all parties agreed – that the cause of the lower credit was solely the different tax rate scales in France and in Germany,[1291] i.e., a 'disparity'. As regards the *Schumacker* issue, the CJEU reasoned that *Schumacker* rule did not apply: the state of non-residence, Germany, was *not* obliged to take into account Mrs Gilly's personal and family circumstances since Mrs

1286. *See*, e.g., Paul Farmer, *EC Law and National Rules on Direct Taxation: A Phoney War?*, 7(1) EC Tax Rev. 13, 14 (1998).
1287. CJEU, Case C-336/96, *Gilly*, 12 May 1998, ECLI:EU:C:1998:221.
1288. *Id.*, at paras 43–44.
1289. *Id.*, at para. 44.
1290. Peter J. Wattel, *Progressive Taxation of Non-residents and Intra-EC Allocation of Personal Tax Allowances: Why Schumacker, Asscher, Gilly and Gschwind Do Not Suffice*, 40(6) Eur. Tax'n 210, 216 and 218–220 (2000).
1291. CJEU, Case C-336/96, *Gilly*, 12 May 1998, ECLI:EU:C:1998:221, at para. 47; Opinion of AG Ruiz-Jarabo Colomer in Case C-336/96, *Gilly*, 20 Nov. 1997, ECLI:EU:C:1997:556, at para. 61.

Gilly was treated as having taxable income in her state of residence, France, based on which her personal and family circumstances were indeed taken into account. According to the CJEU, her income was 'aggregated within the basis for assessing the personal income tax payable by her tax household in France, where she is therefore entitled to the tax advantages, rebates and deductions provided for in the French legislation'.[1292] Whether this was rendered possible due specifically to the credit method is left open, since two reasons were cited as to why her income was 'aggregated' in France - namely because: (1) the taxable unit in France was her 'tax household' as a whole[1293] and (2) the income was 'aggregated' under the operation of the credit method[1294] - and the CJEU did not make an explicit attribution to one or the other reason.[1295] One could potentially induce it from the reasoning, though.

If so, the follow-up question is: *should* it matter - for the purpose of determining the obligations of the state of *non*-residence in a *Schumacker* situation - whether the state of residence applies the exemption method or the credit method? It is true that when the state of residence applies the exemption method, and in particular a form of exemption method where the FSI is *not* included in the tax base at all in the state of residence, then it is much clearer that the state of residence is unable to take into account the corresponding personal and family circumstances. In a *Schumacker* situation, this shifts the obligation to the state of non-residence. It is true that when the state of residence applies a credit method, it does, in a first step, include the FSI in the tax base. If the *Gilly* case is a confirmation that the credit method thus deems the state of residence capable of fully granting personal and family circumstances and the state of non-residence is therefore released from any obligation to do so, even under *Schumacker* circumstances, did the CJEU get it right? According to Paul Farmer, the credit method in the state of residence should not necessarily change the *Schumacker* outcome: it is possible to transpose the reasoning to credit-granting residence states and he provided examples to illustrate this point.[1296]

To dispel the claim that the credit method would invariably resolve the dilemma in *Schumacker*, it suffices to show one example of a *Schumacker*-type situation where, despite applying the credit method, the state of residence remains unable to fully provide the personal and family circumstances of the taxpayer in question. If so, then the existence of the credit method in the state of residence should not be viewed, as a general rule, as a *Schumacker*-proof scenario.

To illustrate this, assume a hypothetical set of facts combining aspects of the *Schumacker* and *Gilly* cases. A taxpayer, who resides and has a family in MS R, earns all of her income of 100,000 in MS S. MS S applies a higher tax rate to the income, 30%, than MS R, 20%. In MS R, the taxpayer is entitled to 10,000 in deductions for personal and family circumstances. In this case, MS S would levy taxes of 30,000 (= 100,000 ×

1292. CJEU, Case C-336/96, *Gilly*, 12 May 1998, ECLI:EU:C:1998:221, at paras 49–50.
1293. Opinion of AG Ruiz-Jarabo Colomer in Case C-336/96, *Gilly*, 20 Nov. 1997, ECLI:EU:C:1997:556, at para. 59.
1294. CJEU, Case C-336/96, *Gilly*, 12 May 1998, ECLI:EU:C:1998:221, at para. 42.
1295. *Id.*, at paras 49–50.
1296. Paul Farmer, *EC Law and National Rules on Direct Taxation: A Phoney War?*, 7(1) EC Tax Rev. 13, 14 (1998).

30%). Under the credit method, MS R would include the income of 100,000 in its tax base, and it would grant deductions for personal and family circumstances of 10,000, for a net taxable income of 90,000. On this, taxes of 18,000 (= 90,000 × 20%) would be due. It would grant a credit for the 30,000 levied in MS S but up to the limit that MS R would itself levy on this income, namely up to 18,000. Thus, MS R grants a credit of 18,000, thereby eliminating the tax liability there and collecting 0 in taxes. There is an excess of 12,000 that could not be credited. To the extent that this excess credit is merely a reflection of the difference in tax rates between the MSs, this is perfectly acceptable under EU law (as discussed under the 'disparity' line of case law under Section 4.2.2. and the 'equivalence' line of case law under Section 4.2.3.). To the extent that this excess credit represents a loss of personal benefits, it would be problematic.

There are different ways to test for this. To answer the first question, namely to what extent an excess credit is attributable solely to a difference in tax rates, one approach proposed by Farmer is simply to take the gross FSI (gross, meaning before any deductions for personal circumstances) and multiply it by the difference in the tax rates: 100,000 × (30%–20%) = 10,000. This isolates the tax rate variable, by setting aside differences in the tax base. Thus, of the excess of 12,000, much of it, up to 10,000, can be attributed to a difference in the tax rates in the two MSs. The 2,000 must be explained by some other factor then. This is explained by a difference in the tax base, and the only difference in the tax base was the 10,000 of personal and family circumstances. As a result, the personal and family circumstances are not fully taken into account; while they were entirely deducted from the tax base in a first step, they are partially cancelled out at the level of the taxes due in a second step. They were inadvertently neutralized in the amount of the tax rate in the state of residence, 20%, multiplied by the personal and family circumstances, 10,000, which explains the remaining 2,000 of the 12,000-excess credit. To make this more visible, compare the following scenarios, adapted from Farmer's examples (in Example No. 21).

Example No. 21: The Credit Method in *Schumacker* Scenarios[1297]

MS R tax rate < MS S tax rate		
Scenario 1	Scenario 2	Scenario 3
Income from MS R: 0	Income from MS R: 9,000	Income from MS R: 10,000
Income from MS S: 100,000	Income from MS S: 100,000	Income from MS S: 100,000
Tax in MS S, 30%: 30,000	Tax in MS S, 30%: 30,000	Tax in MS S, 30%: 30,000

1297. For additional further elaborated and very practical examples, which depict the UK's three-step approach to calculating the foreign tax credit, *see* the originals on which this modified example is based in Paul Farmer's article. Paul Farmer, *EC Law and National Rules on Direct Taxation: A Phoney War?*, 7(1) EC Tax Rev. 13, 15–17 (1998).

MS R tax rate < MS S tax rate		
Scenario 1	Scenario 2	Scenario 3
Tax in MS R, 20%: 100,000 subtract 10,000 for personal and family circumstances = 90,000 tax base × 20% = 18,000 Tax credit: the lesser of the taxes levied in MS S, 30,000, or the MCA = 18,000 Excess credit: 12,000	Tax in MS R, 20%: 109,000 subtract 10,000 for personal and family circumstances = 99,000 tax base × 20% = 19,800 Tax credit: the lesser of the taxes levied in MS S, 30,000, or the MCA = 19,800 Excess credit: 10,200	Tax in MS R, 20%: 110,000 subtract 10,000 for personal and family circumstances = 100,000 tax base × 20% = 20,000 Tax credit: the lesser of the taxes levied in MS S, 30,000, or the MCA = 20,000 Excess credit: 10,000

In all three scenarios, the income earned in the state of non-residence is more than 90% of the total income and little is earned in the state of residence, thereby qualifying as *Schumacker* scenarios. Also, in all three scenarios, there is an excess credit. This is important because it is particularly in these cases where the risk is greatest that the personal and family circumstances are not fully granted in the state of residence. By comparison, in other cases, the credit method can ensure that the personal and family circumstances are granted, and this tends to happen when the tax rate in the state of residence is *higher* than in the state of source, such that '[t]he additional state A [state of residence] tax on [the taxpayer's] income is sufficient to ensure that the deduction of his personal reliefs does not produce excess credit'.[1298] Thus, an excess credit can be seen as a warning signal.

When more closely inspecting it in the above scenarios, the excess credit can be explained by the difference in tax rates up to the amount of 10,000 (= (30%-20%) × 100,000). In the second scenario, it is notable that the extra 200 happens to coincide with the 1,000 of personal and family circumstances that could not be deducted from the income generated in the state of residence (= 9,000 earned in the state of residence – deduction of 10,000 for personal and family circumstances = –1,000, and 1,000 × 20% = 200). In the third scenario, it is notable that the excess credit can be fully attributed to a difference in the tax rates between the two MSs. At this point, the personal and family circumstances are fully granted in MS R.

Based on the above, the objective is to take the explanatory power of these examples one step further, thus building upon Farmer's work, to extract some general indicators and ratios that MSs can use to determine when, even under a credit method

1298. Paul Farmer, *EC Law and National Rules on Direct Taxation: A Phoney War?*, 7(1) EC Tax Rev. 13, 16 (1998).

scenario, the *Schumacker* doctrine should technically apply. The question that the tax authorities in the two MSs ask themselves is under what circumstances the state of non-residence is obliged to provide the personal and family circumstances instead of the state of residence. The existence of the credit method alone should not suffice because the core issue is, arguably, *not* merely whether the state of residence is able to take into account the income, but more precisely whether the state of residence is able to take into account the income in a manner that enables it to also fully provide the personal and family circumstances.[1299] As the examples demonstrate, the two are not always aligned. It varies depending on numerous factors, such as the tax rates in the two MSs, the amount of income in the respective states, and the amount of the personal allowances in question.

In this respect, the third scenario (of Example No. 21) is particularly informative because it shows the break-even point. The difference in this scenario is that there is income of 10,000 earned in the state of residence against which the entire 10,000 of deductions for personal and family circumstances can be used. From this, it can be derived that what seems to matter most is that there is sufficient income in the state of residence to fully absorb the personal and family circumstances to which the taxpayer is entitled in that state. To the extent that the taxable income generated in the state of residence is inferior to these personal deductions, there will likely be an excess credit, part of which is attributable to a portion of the personal deductions being lost. From this, the following ratios can be derived:

$$\frac{\text{Amount of domestic-source income (DSI)}}{\text{Amount of deductions for personal and family circumstances in MS R}} \geq 1$$

MS R can absorb the personal and family circumstances.

$$\frac{\text{Amount of domestic-source income (DSI)}}{\text{Amount of deductions for personal and family circumstances in MS R}} < 1$$

MS R cannot absorb the personal and family circumstances in full → MS S must do so.

In other words, the ratio of the income generated in the state of residence to the amount of personal deductions should be superior to 1 in order for it to take into account in full the personal deductions.

Now broadening the perspective to include the income generated in the other MS, where the net global income (namely, net of the deductions for personal and family circumstances) equals, or is greater than, the gross FSI, holding all else equal, the residence state *is* in a position to fully absorb the personal and family circumstances;

1299. *Id.*

thus, the obligation need not be transferred to the state of non-residence. This can be expressed with the following ratios:

$$\frac{\text{Net global income (= FSI + DSI – deductions for personal circumstances and family circumstances in MS R)}}{\text{Gross FSI (i.e., without any deductions for personal and family circumstances)}} \geq 1$$

MS R can absorb the personal and family circumstances.

$$\frac{\text{Net global income (= FSI + DSI – deductions for personal circumstances and family circumstances in MS R)}}{\text{Gross FSI (i.e., without any deductions for personal and family circumstances)}} < 1$$

MS R cannot absorb the personal and family circumstances in full → MS S must do so.

In other words, if it is greater than 1, the state of residence can absorb the personal and family circumstances; if it is less than 1, the state of residence cannot do so in full and thus the state of non-residence must do so.

In seeking different indicators for detecting a *Schumacker*-type problem, another is the amount of the tax credit. Once the amount of the tax credit reaches at least the amount that the state of residence would levy on the gross income from the other state, then the state of residence has granted the largest credit possible within the limits of the MCA. Any excess credit beyond that amount is explained by the differences in the tax rates. One way to translate this into an indicator would be:

- if FTC < (gross FSI × tax rate MS R), then there is a *Schumacker* issue. That is, if the credit would be below the product of the gross FSI (gross, meaning without personal deductions) multiplied by the tax rate in MS R, then part of the excess credit may represent lost personal deductions;
- if FTC ≥ (gross FSI × tax rate MS R), then there is no *Schumacker* issue. That is, if the credit would be equal to or greater than the product of the gross FSI (gross, meaning without personal deductions) multiplied by the tax rate in MS R, then the excess credit represents mere tax rate differences, and presumably MS R managed to fully provide for the personal and family circumstances of the taxpayer.

In sum, in these cases where there is an excess credit, and where part of it represents lost personal deductions, yet the state of residence has done all it can within the exercise of its respective taxation powers over the income in question, what this means is that the state of residence is unable – given its current tax rate and tax base structure, which remains within its sovereignty to set under EU law – to fully grant the personal and family circumstances. The *Schumacker* doctrine would thus dictate a switch to the state of non-residence, which should grant the personal and family circumstances.

If so, the question arises as to the implications for the MS of residence. The *Schumacker* case directly addresses the state of *non*-residence; the CJEU did not instruct the state of residence on how to adapt itself to the fact that the state of non-residence now takes into account the personal and family circumstances of the taxpayer. This is likely due to the fact that, in that case, the state of residence, Belgium, applied the exemption method to the income. No adjustment would be needed, assuming that Belgium disregarded the income in any case under the exemption method. By contrast, if the credit method applies, there is greater dependence on what happens in the other state. Thus, some adaptations may be needed.

First, the question arises as to whether the state of residence should now refuse to grant any personal deductions, knowing that they are now taken into account in the other MS. Second, if the answer to the first question is yes, then the question arises as to whether an adjustment should be made to the amount of the credit, to prevent it from cancelling out the *Schumacker*-mandated benefits in the other MS. Some examples can demonstrate the relevance of these questions.

Example No. 22: The Impact, If Any, of the *Schumacker* Situation on the Credit Method in MS R

Alternative 1	
Scenario 1	Scenario 2
Income from MS R: 0 Income from MS S: 100,000	Income from MS R: 0 Income from MS S: 100,000
Assume *Schumacker* applies: MS S must take into account personal and family circumstances. Tax in MS S, 30%: 100,000 – 10,000 = 90,000 × 30% = 27,000	**Assume *Schumacker* applies: MS S must take into account personal and family circumstances.** Tax in MS S, 20%: 100,000 – 10,000 = 90,000 × 20% = 18,000
Assume MS R decides to fully disregard personal and family circumstances, knowing that MS S now has the obligation. Tax in MS R, 20%: 100,000 × 20% = 20,000 Tax credit: the lesser of the taxes levied in MS S, 27,000, or the MCA, 20,000 = 20,000	**Assume MS R decides to fully disregard personal and family circumstances, knowing that MS S now has the obligation.** Tax in MS R, 20%: 100,000 × 20% = 20,000 Tax credit: the lesser of the taxes levied in MS S, 18,000, or the MCA, 20,000 = 18,000

Excess credit: 7,000 *Total taxes paid: 27,000*	20,000 – 18,000 = 2,000 paid to MS R *Total taxes paid: 20,000*

Regarding the first question (whether or not to continue to grant personal relief), Farmer's starting point is that 'it would in principle be lawful for state A [the state of residence] to refuse to grant reliefs on the ground that responsibility for granting reliefs had been transferred to state B'.[1300] If so, then a problem may arise, which becomes particularly evident in the second scenario under Alternative 1. Where the taxes levied in MS S are less than the amount levied in MS R, then because the credit method in MS R 'taxes' the difference, according to Farmer MS R is rendering ineffective MS S' attempt to remedy its own different treatment in accordance with the *Schumacker* judgment. Here, because the example assumes the two states tax at the same 20% rate, clearly none of the difference (the 2,000 paid to MS R) can be explained by a difference in the tax rates; rather, it is explained solely by the difference in the tax base and the sole difference in that respect stems from MS S' grant of personal and family circumstances (2,000 = 10,000 × 20%).

As Farmer assumes that a MS may answer yes to the first question (i.e., MS R may refuse to grant relief), this gives rise to the second question as to whether an adjustment is needed. Farmer explains why and how such an adjustment should occur:

> 'it is submitted that, by virtue of its duty of cooperation under Art 5 of the Treaty, state A would be prohibited from frustrating state B's efforts to eliminate the discrimination by collecting the revenue surrendered by state B. It must therefore grant a credit for the tax surrendered as if it had been paid'.[1301]

Regarding the 'how', applying his solution to the above example gives the following result:[1302]

Tax in MS S, 20%: 100,000 – 10,000 = 90,000 × 20% = 18,000
Tax in MS R, 20%: 100,000 × 20% = 20,000
Tax credit: the lesser of the taxes levied in MS S, 18,000, or the MCA, 20,000
= 18,000
+ Notional tax credit for the amount given up by MS S: 10,000 × 20%
= 2,000
= 20,000
Excess credit: 0

1300. *Id.*
1301. *Id.*
1302. Paul Farmer, *EC Law and National Rules on Direct Taxation: A Phoney War?*, 7(1) EC Tax Rev. 13, 16–17 (1998).

In this way, the extra 2,000 charged by MS R is reduced to 0, thus leaving intact all personal benefits granted by MS S. To make the results of his solution more visible, assume a small tax rate difference:[1303]

Tax in MS S, 21%: 100,000 – 10,000 = 90,000 × 21% = 18,900
Tax in MS R, 20%: 100,000 × 20% = 20,000
Tax credit: the lesser of the taxes levied in MS S, 18,900, or the MCA, 20,000
= 18,900
+ Notional tax credit for the amount given up by MS S: 10,000 × 21%
= 2,100
= 21,000, but again the MCA kicks in to limit it to 20,000
Excess credit: 1,000

Here, the excess credit can be explained fully in terms of the tax rate difference (1,000 = (21%-20%) × 100,000). The result is the same as under the exemption method.[1304] The notional credit thus fully eliminates any excess credit attributable to a cancelling out of personal reliefs. Another indicator that this stems from a tax rate difference is a comparison between the taxes paid in this case, namely 18,900, with the taxes that would have been paid if this were a purely domestic scenario in MS R, namely 18,000 (= (100,000 – 10,000) × 20%). The difference, 900, is equal to the difference in tax rates, namely 1% × 90,000.

As regards the 'why', Farmer states that it would be 'inappropriate' for MS R to undo the benefits that MS S is obliged to extend to the taxpayer, and he invokes the principle of loyalty as a ground for urging MS R to adapt accordingly.[1305]

From these concerns, at first glance, the case law of the CJEU appears to contain a contradiction or unforeseen discrepancy. On the one hand, under the 'disparity' line and the 'equivalence' line of case law, the credit method is clearly permitted, and the mere fact that, for example, in cases where the tax rate in the other MS is lower, this method has the effect of bringing up the rate that applies to the income to the higher rate applicable in MS R is not an infringement of the fundamental freedoms. On the other hand, in this case, the CJEU established this *Schumacker* doctrine to aid taxpayers who exercise their fundamental freedoms, yet the benefits of the *Schumacker* case that are granted in MS S could in certain circumstances be (partially) cancelled out if MS R applies the credit method. Albeit rather incongruous, it may be the case that this is perfectly in line with the current state of EU law since distinct obligations arise depending on whether a MS is in the position of residence or of source, and these obligations are not always aligned; thus, it may merely be yet another instance of the limits of the fundamental freedoms. The *Schumacker* decision appears to address only the MS of non-residence and not the MS of residence. Moreover, this gap between the EU law obligations of MS S and MS R is perhaps unsurprising, as this would not be the

1303. *Id.*
1304. *Id.*
1305. *Id.*

first and only such tension created in the CJEU's case law: for example, a similar one arises in the 'neutralization' line of case law (discussed below in Section 4.2.5.).

Alternatively, these *Schumacker* scenarios may be treated as special, exceptional scenarios. Indeed, normally the credit method is acceptable because, from the standpoint of the state of residence, MS R, the credit method tends to treat all residents the same regardless of whether they earn domestic or FSI. However, in a *Schumacker* situation, it could be argued that there is an objective difference between the average resident and the *Schumacker*-resident. From the standpoint of the state of *non*-residence, MS S, the CJEU deems a non-resident taxpayer earning (nearly) all of its income in MS S and little to no income in its state of residence to be in a situation comparable to residents of *MS S*. As a corollary, from the standpoint of MS R, this resident is arguably no longer comparable to other residents in this state. If so, MS R may have to adjust to its tax treatment of this resident, to avoid discrimination arising from applying the same treatment to what is now revealed to be an objectively different situation. This could serve as another ground on which to support Farmer's proposed solution.

Example No. 23: The Impact, If Any, of the *Schumacker* Situation on the Credit Method in MS R

Alternative 2	
Scenario 1	Scenario 2
Income from MS R: 0 Income from MS S: 100,000	Income from MS R: 0 Income from MS S: 100,000
Assume *Schumacker* applies: MS S must take into account personal and family circumstances. Tax in MS S, 30%: 100,000 – 10,000 = 90,000 × 30% = 27,000	**Assume *Schumacker* applies: MS S must take into account personal and family circumstances.** Tax in MS S, 20%: 100,000 – 10,000 = 90,000 × 20% = 18,000
Assume MS R nevertheless takes into account personal deductions. Tax in MS R, 20%: 100,000 – 10,000 = 90,000 × 20% = 18,000	**Assume MS R nevertheless takes into account personal deductions.** Tax in MS R, 20%: 100,000 – 10,000 = 90,000 × 20% = 18,000
Tax credit: the lesser of the taxes levied in MS S, 27,000, or the MCA, 18,000 = 18,000 Excess credit: 9,000	Tax credit: the lesser of the taxes levied in MS S, 18,000, or the MCA, 18,000 = 18,000 Excess credit: 0

Total taxes paid: 27,000 (more than in a purely domestic MS R scenario due to higher tax rate in MS S)	*Total taxes paid: 18,000 (same as in a purely domestic MS R scenario)*

Returning to the first question (i.e., whether MS R should continue to grant personal benefits and allowances), although MS S is obliged to grant personal deductions, the response of MS R is not specified in the decision. Another response could also be that a state of residence, which includes the income in its tax base under its credit method, nevertheless continues to grant its own personal deductions. If so, as shown in the second scenario above, under Alternative 2, this seems to reduce the risk that the credit method in MS R inadvertently cancels out the benefits granted in MS S. However, this would rely on the assumption that the obligation transfers *in full* and *unconditionally* to MS S (irrespective of what happens in MS R, on the grounds that MS R will not be able to fully take into account the personal and family circumstances, even if it tries).[1306] And, it helps that there is 0 income earned in MS R in this case (as in *Schumacker*). A counterargument to this approach would be that this may in turn risk a 'double dip' or a double deduction of personal benefits (where the taxpayer deducts personal and family circumstances twice in two different MSs); so it can be argued that family and personal circumstances must be *fully* taken into account *somewhere*, but not twice. This risk is especially pronounced under a tax base exemption method. Yet, here, under the credit method, both states are assumed to be taxing the full amount of the income. To the extent the income is fully included in a tax base twice, a deduction for personal benefits twice does not necessarily lead to any unwarranted or excessive advantage for the taxpayer.[1307] The taxpayer still tends to end up paying the higher of the two rates. This double-deduction question was invoked in the context of the credit method in, for example, the *Centro Equestre da Lezíria Grande*[1308] and *Brisal and KBC Finance Ireland*[1309] cases (discussed below under Section 4.2.6.) and the *NN*[1310] case (discussed below under Section 4.2.7.). Thus, in those discussions, there will be further clarification and an example will be used to distinguish problematic scenarios of double deductions from legitimate ones.

However, a deliberate simplification was made in the examples' scenarios, in order to more clearly isolate the effects of tax rate differences versus a neutralization of personal reliefs. That is, the examples assume that both states grant the same personal

1306. But, *see*, e.g., CJEU, Case C-527/06, *Renneberg*, 16 Oct. 2008, ECLI:EU:C:2008:566, at para. 63, cited at *infra* note 1340 (given the wording in the *Renneberg* decision, it is unclear whether this assumption can hold). *See also*, e.g., Opinion of AG Mengozzi in Case C-527/06, *Renneberg*, 9 Jul. 2008, ECLI:EU:C:2008:362, at para. 53, but *compare* paras 84, 85, 89.

1307. In agreement, *see*, e.g., John F. Avery Jones, *A Comment on 'Progressive Taxation of Non-residents and Intra-EC Allocation of Personal Tax Allowances'*, 40(8) Eur. Tax'n 375, 375 (2000) ('Giving the full allowance in the host State saves all this computation and if the home State applies the tax credit system the result is that taxpayer does not benefit twice').

1308. CJEU, Case C-345/04, *Centro Equestre da Lezíria Grande*, 15 Feb. 2007, ECLI:EU:C:2007:96.

1309. CJEU, Case C-18/15, *Brisal and KBC Finance Ireland*, 13 Jul. 2016, ECLI:EU:C:2016:549.

1310. CJEU, Case C-28/17, *NN*, 4 Jul. 2018, ECLI:EU:C:2018:526.

and family benefits (i.e., both would happen to grant a deduction of 10,000 from the tax base), which in reality is likely a rare case, as personal and family benefits vary between states, both in amount and in the manner they are granted. Generally speaking, differences in the design of those regimes should not matter from the CJEU's perspective, as those details in principle remain within the sovereignty of the MSs. Rather the CJEU concerned itself with ensuring that a taxpayer is not denied personal and family circumstances by virtue of exercising its free movement rights under EU law. Thus, similar to mere differences in tax rates, mere differences in the precise amounts of personal and family benefits would seem to fall under the disparity category. The more relevant benchmark is whether MS R grants the same benefits as it grants to all residents and/or whether MS S grants the same benefits as it grants to all its residents. If both do so, then both are likely acting in line with EU law and this could eschew the need for the notional credit advocated by Farmer. However, the potential downside is that differences in the amount of relief offered by the two MSs will have a greater influence on the final result, whereas the notional credit better guarantees that, once MS S is obliged to extend its benefits to non-residents, the MS S benefits remain intact. Thus, to further consider the relative merits and effects of these two possible responses of MS R, it is worthwhile to test a few additional iterations of the above examples to observe how changes in the amount of personal deductions could play a role.

Example No. 24: Possible Responses of MS R to a *Schumacker* Situation

Facts: 100,000 generated in MS S, 0 in MS R, but MS R applies credit method

	MS S	MS R	MS S	MS R	MS S	MS R	MS S	MS R
Gross Income:	100,000	100,000	100,000	100,000	100,000	100,000	100,000	100,000
Personal Reliefs:	0	-5,000	0	-5,000	0	-10,000	0	-10,000
Net Income:	100,000	95,000	100,000	95,000	100,000	90,000	100,000	90,000
Tax Rate:	20%	20%	21%	20%	21%	20%	30%	20%
Tax Liability:	**20,000**	**19,000**	**21,000**	**19,000**	**21,000**	**18,000**	**30,000**	**18,000**
Credit:		19,000		19,000		18,000		18,000
Excess Credit:		1,000		2,000		3,000		12,000
Total Taxes Paid:		20,000		21,000		21,000		30,000
	Note: none of the excess is attributable to tax rate differences; thus, it is attributable to a loss of personal reliefs		Note: 1,000 of the excess is attributable to tax rate differences, the rest is attributable to a loss of personal reliefs		Note: 1,000 of the excess is attributable to tax rate differences, the rest is attributable to a loss of personal reliefs		Note: 10,000 of the excess is attributable to tax rate differences, 2,000 is attributable to a loss of personal reliefs	

MS S must grant relief, should MS R also?

	MS S	MS R	MS S	MS R	MS S	MS R	MS S	MS R
Gross Income:	100,000	100,000	100,000	100,000	100,000	100,000	100,000	100,000
Personal Reliefs:	-10,000	-5,000	-10,000	-5,000	-5,000	-10,000	-5,000	-10,000
Net Income:	90,000	95,000	90,000	95,000	95,000	90,000	95,000	90,000
Tax Rate:	20%	20%	21%	20%	21%	20%	30%	20%
Tax Liability:	**18,000**	**19,000**	**18,900**	**19,000**	**19,950**	**18,000**	**28,500**	**18,000**
Credit:		18,000		18,900		18,000		18,000
Paid to MS R:		1,000		100		0		0
Excess Credit:		0		0		1,950		10,500
Total Taxes Paid:		19,000		19,000		19,950		28,500

MS S must grant relief, should MS R refuse and instead grant a notional credit?

	MS S	MS R	MS S	MS R	MS S	MS R	MS S	MS R
Gross Income:	100,000	100,000	100,000	100,000	100,000	100,000	100,000	100,000
Personal Reliefs:	-10,000	0	-10,000	0	-5,000	0	-5,000	0
Net Income:	90,000	100,000	90,000	100,000	95,000	100,000	95,000	100,000
Tax Rate:	20%	20%	21%	20%	21%	20%	30%	20%
Tax Liability:	**18,000**	**20,000**	**18,900**	**20,000**	**19,950**	**20,000**	**28,500**	**20,000**
Credit for MS S tax:		18,000		18,900		19,950		28,500
(+)Notional credit:		2,000		2,100		1,050		1,500
		20,000		21,000		21,000		30,000
MCA:		20,000		20,000		20,000		20,000
Credit granted:		20,000		20,000		20,000		20,000
Paid to MS R:		0		0		0		0
Excess Credit:		0		0		0		8,500
Total Taxes Paid:		18,000		18,900		19,950		28,500

The above are solutions, or responses, which could be described as a 'second-best solution' from the viewpoint of Wattel for the second-best world in which the CJEU and MSs are operating. A third ideal-world possibility was discussed by Wattel in his 'plea in favour of fractional taxation'.[1311] This becomes clearer after the discussion of the next case, *De Groot*, to which the analysis now turns.

1311. Peter J. Wattel, *Progressive Taxation of Non-residents and Intra-EC Allocation of Personal Tax Allowances: Why Schumacker, Asscher, Gilly and Gschwind Do Not Suffice*, 40(6) Eur. Tax'n 210, 222 (2000) (he attributes the term and initial expression of the idea to Kees van Raad, written in Dutch).

In addition to the open questions discussed above, the now-established *Schumacker* doctrine has had (perhaps unexpected) reverberations in other cases.[1312] Its findings affect not only the taxation of non-residents but also the way in which a state of residence calculates relief for double taxation of its own residents. This became apparent in the *De Groot* case[1313] and, most relevant for the credit method, the *Beker* case.[1314]

In the *De Groot* case, the Netherlands calculated its exemption method in the following way (a way that closely resembles an MCA under the credit method):

- it calculated a resident's (theoretical) tax liability on the basis of its total worldwide taxable income (in order to determine where the taxpayer's true ability to pay falls on the progressive income tax rate scale), and
- it reduced this amount by multiplying the tax liability by a ratio of the gross FSI over the gross worldwide taxable income (in order to effectively exclude the taxes attributable to the FSI).[1315]

The formula was depicted as follows by the AG:[1316]

$$\text{Amount of tax reduction under exemption} = \text{Tax on total income} \times \frac{\text{Foreign gross income}}{\text{Total gross income}}$$

The issue arose from the difference between the steps. The first step was based on the *net* income, including *fully* taking into account all relevant personal allowances and circumstances (in this case, 'the maintenance payments made by the taxpayer and his tax-free allowance').[1317] The second step used the *gross* income in the denominator, with the (intended) effect of apportioning some of the expenses and personal allowances to the FSI.[1318] This 'apportionment' meant that a portion of the personal expenses, corresponding to the amount of FSI, was excluded in such a way that the final (not theoretical) tax liability no longer reflected the initial taking into account of the full personal circumstances.[1319]

1312. *Id.*, at 218–219 (2000) (Wattel was prescient, in that he predicted that precisely the issue discussed in *De Groot* would eventually arrive - after first being invoked, yet in his view overlooked, in *Gilly* - before the CJEU more explicitly).
1313. CJEU, Case C-385/00, *de Groot*, 12 Dec. 2002, ECLI:EU:C:2002:750.
1314. CJEU, Case C-168/11, *Beker*, 28 Feb. 2013, ECLI:EU:C:2013:117.
1315. CJEU, Case C-385/00, *de Groot*, 12 Dec. 2002, ECLI:EU:C:2002:750, at paras 20–26.
1316. Opinion of AG Léger in Case C-385/00, *de Groot*, 20 Jun. 2002, ECLI:EU:C:2002:389, at paras 9–10.
1317. *Id.*
1318. CJEU, Case C-385/00, *de Groot*, 12 Dec. 2002, ECLI:EU:C:2002:750, at paras 25–26; Opinion of AG Léger in Case C-385/00, *de Groot*, 20 Jun. 2002, ECLI:EU:C:2002:389, at paras 9–10.
1319. CJEU, Case C-385/00, *de Groot*, 12 Dec. 2002, ECLI:EU:C:2002:750, at para. 83 ('Secondly, it is clear that the parties to the main proceedings are agreed that, due to the application of the proportionality factor, a portion of the personal tax relief to which Mr de Groot was entitled did not give rise to an actual tax reduction in the Netherlands. He therefore suffered a real disadvantage as a result of the application of the proportionality factor since he derived from his maintenance payments and from the tax-free allowance a lesser tax advantage than he

To offer a simplified example, *De Groot* earns 200 in the Netherlands, 100 in Germany and 100 in France:

- On the total taxable income of 400, assume De Groot can deduct 40 of personal expenses, and this net income (360) would be effectively taxed at 20% on the progressive scale, thus leading to a theoretical tax liability of 72 (= (400–40) × 20%).
- This amount (72) is reduced by 36 (= tax liability × gross foreign-source income/gross worldwide taxable income = 72 × (200/400)).
- Hypothetically, if the net worldwide income that reflects personal circumstances (360) were in the denominator, instead of gross income (400), the amount would be reduced by more, i.e., 40 (= 72 × (200/360)).
- The Netherlands collects 36 (= 72–36) under its apportionment, while the taxpayer argued the Netherlands should collect only 32 (= 72–40).

To assess the effects of the Netherlands' fraction, notice that if the 40 of personal expenses are spread over the entire income, 20 would correspond to the 200 of DSI and 20 would correspond to the 200 of FSI. The difference in the amount of the tax reduction of 4 (40–36 = 4) happens to be equal to the tax savings of 4 that would result from the deduction of the 20 of personal expenses attributable to the FSI multiplied by the tax rate in the Netherlands of 20% (20 × 20% = 4). This means that, by granting 4 less in its tax reduction, the Netherlands effectively excludes, at the stage of the taxes due, an amount that corresponds to denying the personal deductions in proportion to the FSI, thereby granting personal deductions only to the extent of the income earned in the Netherlands.

The CJEU decided in favour of the taxpayer, mostly on the basis of the *Schumacker* rule that the state of residence is generally responsible for taking into account personal and family circumstances 'in full'.[1320] The *Schumacker* exception did *not* apply since the taxpayer did not earn the majority of his income (> 90%) outside the state of residence. Thus, the state of residence, not the other states, remained responsible.

Similar to the *Schumacker* case, the disadvantage could be directly attributed to the calculation in the Netherlands, *not* to disparities.[1321] However, it could be argued

would have received had he received his entire income for 1994 in the Netherlands') and para. 91 ('In this case, even if, as the Netherlands Government claims, the maintenance payments made by Mr de Groot and the tax-free allowance were taken into account in calculating the theoretical amount of tax payable on his total income, it is plain that, as a result of the application of the proportionality factor, Mr de Groot benefited from the allowances relating to his personal and family circumstances only in proportion to the income which he had received in the Netherlands. Thus, as a consequence of his exercise of his right to freedom of movement, he forfeited part of the tax allowances provided for by Netherlands law to which he was entitled as a resident of the Netherlands').

1320. CJEU, Case C-385/00, *de Groot*, 12 Dec. 2002, ECLI:EU:C:2002:750, at paras 88–90, 99.

1321. *Id.*, at para. 84 ('That disadvantage caused by the application by the Member State of residence of its rules on the avoidance of double taxation is liable to discourage a national of that State from leaving it in order to take up paid employment, within the meaning of the Treaty, in the territory of another Member State') and para. 85 ('Contrary to what the

that the Netherlands approach is a disadvantage only because of the *Schumacker* rule. More specifically, it could be argued that the Netherlands calculation creates a disadvantage only because all other MSs do not apply the same one, and the very reason why MSs cannot do so relates to the *Schumacker* decision. As the Netherlands proposed[1322] and some scholars agree,[1323] if *all* MSs applied the *same* proportional apportionment system of the Netherlands, it could be better from an internal market perspective.

The CJEU provided a compromise or a 'way out' for MSs such as the Netherlands to remedy its incompatible tax measure. One option is that the state of residence may *bilaterally agree* with other MSs to share the responsibility, to each proportionally allocate personal and family circumstances. Alternatively, if the state of residence simply discovers that the other MS *unilaterally* (without any joint, coordinated, agreement) offers a proportion of personal and family circumstances to the taxpayer, then the residence state 'may' reapportion accordingly.[1324] These options were reiterated in *Beker*.[1325] It is notable that the CJEU expands its analysis from a one-state perspective to a two-state perspective. This theme will reoccur, as the CJEU offers a similar option for remedying an incompatible tax law under the 'neutralization' line of case law (discussed below in Section 4.2.5.), with the difference that *bilateral* agreement is mandatory (thus allowing only the first option above but not the second).

In the *Beker* case, Germany calculated its credit in the following way:

- it calculated a resident's tax liability on the basis of its total worldwide taxable income, and
- it reduced the taxes owed by the amount of taxes paid abroad, up to the maximum amount calculated by means of the following formula: total tax liability multiplied by the ratio of FSI over total worldwide income.[1326]

Netherlands Government maintains when it relies on Gilly, the disadvantage suffered by Mr de Groot is attributable neither to the disparities between the tax systems of the Member States of residence and employment nor to the tax systems of the various States in which Mr de Groot was employed').

1322. CJEU, Case C-385/00, *de Groot*, 12 Dec. 2002, ECLI:EU:C:2002:750, at para. 59.

1323. *See*, e.g., Hein Vermeulen (update of 6th ed.), *Chapter 21: Individual Income Taxation*, *in* 1 *Terra/Wattel European Tax Law* 851, 861–864 (Peter J. Wattel, Otto Marres & Hein Vermeulen eds, Wolters Kluwer 7th ed. 2019).

1324. CJEU, Case C-385/00, *de Groot*, 12 Dec. 2002, ECLI:EU:C:2002:750, at paras 99–100. *See also* Peter J. Wattel, *Progressive Taxation of Non-residents and Intra-EC Allocation of Personal Tax Allowances: Why Schumacker, Asscher, Gilly and Gschwind Do Not Suffice*, 40(6) Eur. Tax'n 210, 223 (2000) (this would seem to create space for Wattel's preferred solution, quoted at *infra* note 1334, to function, especially if MSs would coordinate to take up the CJEU on this possibility).

1325. CJEU, Case C-168/11, *Beker*, 28 Feb. 2013, ECLI:EU:C:2013:117, at para. 56.

1326. *Id.*, at para. 7 ('Paragraph 34c(1) EStG states: "In the case of taxpayers with unlimited tax liability whose foreign income is liable to tax corresponding to German income tax in the State in which the income originates, the tax assessed and paid abroad, subject to a reduction to which a right has been acquired, shall be offset against German income tax due in respect of income from that State. The German tax on foreign income shall be calculated by apportioning the German tax on the taxable income (zu versteuerndes Einkommen) including foreign income [...] in the proportion that that foreign income bears to total income (Summe der Einkünfte).[...]"') and at para. 17 (the CJEU described the formula as follows: 'By its question

The difference between the two steps was depicted in the case as follows:[1327]

Maximum amount of credit	=	Income tax according to income tax scale (taxable worldwide income)	×	Foreign income / Total income
		↑		↑
		Calculated after deduction from total income of special expenditure and extraordinary costs		Calculated without taking into account special expenditure and extraordinary costs[1328]

As can be seen, it was similar to the contested *De Groot* calculation. To offer more practical numbers, the amounts cited in this case were: total dividends received from abroad of EUR 24,111.29 on which total foreign WHTs of EUR 2,853.02 were levied;[1329] the MCA was capped at EUR 1,282,[1330] leading to an excess of 1,571.02 in non-creditable foreign taxes. According to the AG, '[i]f taxable income rather than total income were used as the denominator of the fraction, the tax credit could, as far as can be understood, be around EUR 1 650'.[1331] The AG offered a clear and concise example to demonstrate the effects:[1332]

> '35. A straightforward example may, perhaps, help explain the situation better. Let us imagine total revenue of EUR 100, of which EUR 70 is produced at home and

the national court asks, in essence, whether Article 63 TFEU must be interpreted as precluding rules of a Member State under which, in the context of a system aimed at limiting double taxation, where persons subject to unlimited tax liability pay on foreign income, in the State where that income originates, a tax equivalent to the income tax levied by the said Member State, the *foreign tax is offset against income tax* levied in that Member State *by multiplying the amount of tax due in respect of taxable income in the same Member State, including foreign income*, by the *proportion* that *that foreign income bears to total income*, the *latter not taking into account special expenditure or extraordinary costs* such as costs relating to lifestyle or to personal and family circumstances' (emphasis added)).

1327. CJEU, Case C-168/11, *Beker*, 28 Feb. 2013, ECLI:EU:C:2013:117, at para. 12.

1328. Opinion of AG Mengozzi in Case C-168/11, *Beker*, 12 Jul. 2012, ECLI:EU:C:2012:452, at para. 33 (more specifically, it appears that both the numerator and the denominator were gross figures: 'Since the total theoretical German tax is calculated not on the basis of the total income but rather a lower tax base (taxable income), the practical result of the formula is that the personal allowances, the application of which turns the total income into taxable income to be taxed (which is taken into account in determining the total theoretical German tax), is "spread" over all the income, both the German and the foreign part. In the fraction contained in the formula both the numerator and the denominator are, as it were, "gross" figures. Since personal allowances are not applied to foreign income, the German legislature considered it right to divide that income by the total income (foreign and German), gross of the personal allowances (on which it then used the total income and not the taxable income to be taxed). If, on the other hand, the denominator were taxable income, which is less than the total income, a higher value would be obtained for the "foreign" part of the theoretical German tax and the set-off for the taxpayer would consequently be greater').

1329. CJEU, Case C-168/11, *Beker*, 28 Feb. 2013, ECLI:EU:C:2013:117, at para. 9.

1330. *Id.*, at para. 10.

1331. Opinion of AG Mengozzi in Case C-168/11, *Beker*, 12 Jul. 2012, ECLI:EU:C:2012:452, at para. 16.

1332. *Id.*, at paras 35–36.

> EUR 30 abroad, a rate of 10% at home and abroad (for reasons of simplification, I will avoid introducing here an element of the progressive application of the tax, although it is generally present in reality) and an amount of possible personal allowances amounting to EUR 20. The result produced is as follows: Abroad, the taxpayer pays EUR 3 in tax (10% of EUR 30). In Germany a theoretical tax of EUR 8 is calculated (10% of EUR 80, which is the taxable income obtained by subtracting the personal allowances from the total income), and a tax credit of EUR 2.4 (8 × 30/100) is granted by applying the formula set out above. Therefore, the taxpayer pays in all EUR 5.6 in tax to the State of residence (EUR 8 – EUR 2.4 in tax credit), and EUR 3 to the foreign State where the income was produced, making a total of EUR 8.6. It is as if, on the EUR 70 of national income, a deduction were granted not of EUR 20, but of EUR 14, which is proportional to the income (70%) received within the country. It need scarcely be pointed out that if all the income were received in the State of residence, the tax paid would amount to EUR 8. If the foreign income did not exist, and the national income were was the only income, amounting to EUR 70, with personal allowances amounting to EUR 20, the tax to be paid in the State of residence would be EUR 5.
>
> 36. If the referring court's doubts were to be confirmed, and the formula for calculating the set-off were to use taxable income rather than total income in the denominator of the fraction, the maximum tax credit would amount to EUR 3 (8 × 30/80). Therefore, if the rates were the same at home and abroad, the total tax burden borne by the taxpayer would be the same, regardless of the location of his income.'

Thus, unsurprisingly, the CJEU decided that the findings in *De Groot* were 'fully transposable' to this case.[1333]

Returning to Wattel's plea, he argued that, ideally and contrary to what the CJEU held, both states would have shared responsibility for the personal and family circumstances. He explained it as follows:

> 'The home State is allowed to allocate a pro rata part of its personal allowances and deductions to the foreign-source income of its residents when calculating their double taxation relief and therefore to virtually refuse deduction *pro rata parte*. The host State must extend its personal allowances and deductions to non-residents living in EC Member States in proportion to the fraction: source income divided by total income. The host Member State is not required, but is allowed to (and in my opinion should, from the point of view of a just taxation) calculate its rate progression for the taxation of source income on the basis of the total income of the non-resident.'[1334]

In the meantime, however, short of MSs fully coordinating together towards this (or other more harmonized approaches in direct taxation), MSs must at least adapt

1333. CJEU, Case C-168/11, *Beker*, 28 Feb. 2013, ECLI:EU:C:2013:117, at paras 45–46 (notably, the findings were 'fully transposable' despite the differences such as the fact that this was a credit calculation, whereas *De Groot* dealt with an exemption calculation, and the fact that this case addressed the free movement of capital, whereas *De Groot* addressed the free movement of workers).

1334. Peter J. Wattel, *Progressive Taxation of Non-residents and Intra-EC Allocation of Personal Tax Allowances: Why Schumacker, Asscher, Gilly and Gschwind Do Not Suffice*, 40(6) Eur. Tax'n 210, 223 (2000).

individually or unilaterally in order to respect the rulings of the CJEU. With that in mind, the analysis turns to the implications for the credit method.

Although the CJEU tends not to explicitly instruct national governments (it merely declares that the fundamental freedom in question 'precludes' the national legislation in question), instructions can be inferred. What these findings suggest is that, in these cases, the MSs should have used taxable income, net of personal deductions (not 'total income'), in the denominator of their MCA calculation. To assess the impact of these decisions, the following example will test different ways of calculating the MCA in light of the outcome.

Example No. 25: Testing *De Groot* & *Beker* Situations

Facts	
10%	Tax rate in MS R
10%	Tax rate in MS S
70,000	DSI
30,000	FSI
100,000	Total WWI
10,000	Personal reliefs
90,000	Net WWI Income
9,000	Tax (10%)
3,000	Foreign tax (10%)
30%	Percentage of WWI that is FSI
3,000	Amount of personal reliefs related to FSI, if proportionately allocated

	Taxes on WWI	×	**(FSI/WWI)**	=	**MCA of FTC**	
1	9,000	×	$\frac{30{,}000}{100{,}000}$	=	2,700	*Numerator and denominator = gross figures, thus apportions the taxes and personal deductions proportionately between the FSI and other income; Effect: by attributing the personal deductions proportionately to the FSI, the MCA has the effect of cancelling out that portion.*[1335]

1335. As described above, *see* CJEU, Case C-385/00, *de Groot*, 12 Dec. 2002, ECLI:EU:C:2002:750; CJEU, Case C-168/11, *Beker*, 28 Feb. 2013, ECLI:EU:C:2013:117 (this is based on the calculations used in the *De Groot* and *Beker* cases).

2	9,000	×	$\frac{27,000}{90,000}$	=	2,700	*Numerator = FSI figure net of a proportionate allocation of the personal deductions to the FSI, thereby assuming these deductions are spread evenly over the entire WWI; denominator = net figure; Effect: same as above.*
3	9,000	×	$\frac{27,000}{100,000}$	=	2,430	*Numerator = FSI figure net of the proportion of personal deductions attributable to FSI, thereby assuming these deductions are spread evenly over the entire WWI; denominator = gross figure; Effect: this fraction also cancels out personal deductions.*
4	9,000	×	$\frac{20,000}{90,000}$	=	2,000	*Numerator = over-allocating the personal deductions to the FSI because it allocates the entire 10,000 deduction to FSI even though the 10,000 is presumably either spread out over the full WWI or entirely attributable to DSI.*[1336]
5	9,000	×	$\frac{30,000}{90,000}$	=	3,000	*Numerator = gross figure; denominator = net figure; thus numerator is increased in proportion to the denominator; Effect: allocates personal deductions entirely to DSI; increases the amount of the FSI vis-à-vis the net WWI, which increases the amount of the FTC.*[1337]

In these cases relating to personal and family circumstances, these decisions seem to advocate for calculation 5. As can be seen, the calculation should result in the personal benefits being provided in full. In mathematical terms, this requires that the fraction treats such deductions as being fully attributable to the DSI. It seems intuitive to spread personal deductions over all the income earned by the taxpayer, as that is how the tax liability on the worldwide income is calculated. Yet, to the extent that the fraction assumes personal deductions are allocated to the FSI, even where the

1336. *See*, e.g., Marjaana Helminen, *Chapter 23: Finland – The Effect of Losses on the Foreign Tax Credit*, *in Tax Treaty Case Law Around the Globe 2012* 255 (Eric C.C.M. Kemmeren et al. eds, IBFD/Linde 2013) (this calculation is roughly based on a calculation used by Finland. However, one difference is that the mechanism described in this article by Helminen was used in the context of capital losses and other expenses, and not in the context of deductions related to personal and family circumstances).

1337. If converting the mechanism described by Paul Farmer into a fraction, this version would seem to reflect the result that could be achieved in the UK. *See*, e.g., Paul Farmer, *EC Law and National Rules on Direct Taxation: A Phoney War?*, 7(1) EC Tax Rev. 13, 15–16 (1998).

allocation is proportionate, it has the effect, ultimately, of neutralizing personal deductions. Thus, these decisions explicitly rejected or 'precluded' calculation 1. By extension, they would reject calculation 2, which leads to the same result as calculation 1. Although calculations 3 and 4 were not addressed, it would seem possible to argue *a fortiori* to reject them, calculation 4 seeming especially problematic, as it allocates personal deductions disproportionately to the FSI. This, therefore, as mentioned, leaves calculation 5 as the most acceptable. It seems that Kolfer's analysis in *Article 23B – Methods for Elimination of Double Taxation* in the *Global Tax Treaty Commentaries* also supports this conclusion.[1338]

The scope of this case law was expanded. In addition to personal and family circumstances, a state of non-residence may have the obligation to grant other deductions from the tax assessment basis. In *Renneberg*, the reasoning also applied to the right of a non-resident (who earned all of his employment income in the Netherlands, but resided in Belgium) to deduct the negative income related to a personal home in another MS, in the same way as a resident. It was debated the extent to which this could qualify as a 'personal and family circumstance'.[1339] According to this decision:

> 'In paragraph 34 of *Lakebrink and Peters-Lakebrink*, the Court stated that the scope of the case-law arising from *Schumacker* extends to *all* the *tax advantages connected with* the non-resident's *ability to pay* tax which are granted neither in the State of residence nor in the State of employment' (emphasis added).[1340]

As of 2014, the EU Commission seemed to be taking these findings yet further. It issued a formal notice against France due to its similar method of calculating the credit method. The EU Commission contested three aspects of France's credit method: (1) 'part of the benefits associated to the personal and family situation is lost'; (2) 'the FTC is forfeited when the taxpayer is in a global deficit position; and' (3) 'the FTC may be forfeited as a result of the combination of domestic tax allowance or credits and FTCs'.[1341] The first point seems to directly follow from the above case law; the third point may follow only indirectly. The third point relates to the fact that, under French

1338. Georg Kofler, *Article 23B: Methods for Elimination of Double Taxation, in Global Tax Treaty Commentaries* Section 3.2.2.3.3 (Richard Vann ed.-in-chief, Pasquale Pistone et al. eds, Global Topics IBFD updated as of February 2019).

1339. *See*, e.g., CJEU, Case C-527/06, *Renneberg*, 16 Oct. 2008, ECLI:EU:C:2008:566, at paras 29–30; Opinion of AG Mengozzi in Case C-527/06, *Renneberg*, 9 Jul. 2008, ECLI:EU:C:2008:362, at paras 52–57.

1340. CJEU, Case C-527/06, *Renneberg*, 16 Oct. 2008, ECLI:EU:C:2008:566, at para. 63. For further case law references and analysis of the scope of personal and family circumstances, *see*, e.g., Ivan Lazarov, *Chapter 3: The Relevance of the Fundamental Freedoms for Direct Taxation, in Introduction to European Tax Law on Direct Taxation* m.no. 48 (Michael Lang et al. eds, Linde 5th ed. 2018) (Lazarov explains, among other things, that '[t]he line of case law that followed Schumacker,[100] has been *delimiting the scope* of such personal deductions to include e.g. costs incurred in obtaining tax advice, mortgage payments, spousal income "splitting" schemes, contributions to a pension reserve, maintenance payments, allowances corresponding to special costs and extraordinary charges, as well as losses. […]').

1341. Philippe Derouin, *France Updates Foreign Tax Relief Rules for Residents*, 180 Tax Notes Int'l 261, 263 (19 Oct. 2015) (citing 'a formal notice to this effect on October 16, 2014 (TAXU 2013/4287)').

law, which could be relevant for other states, the FTC cannot be carried forward.[1342] In states where a credit carryforward is refused, then the FTC should be calculated and deducted *before* any personal allowances/credits which carry forward to future years.[1343] The second point, though, seems inspired from the *Haribo & Salinen* decision. However, what is surprising is that the EU Commission appears to want to stretch that decision beyond indirect tax credits to direct tax credits. The possibility for such an expansion regarding LCFs will be discussed further below (in Section 4.2.7.).

In addition to these CJEU decisions, the European Free Trade Association (EFTA) Court on 7 May 2008 decided a case that refers to and builds upon the above case law of the CJEU. It differs in one important respect, namely that, while the taxpayers in the CJEU cases were natural persons, the taxpayer in the EFTA case was a company. This case combines aspects of the above cases on the MCA calculation and the *Gerritse/Scorpio* or deductible expenses line of case law (discussed below in Section 4.2.6.).

The *Seabrokers v. Norway* case expressly addressed the 'maximum credit allowance' calculation in Norway. More precisely, it dealt with the 'attribution of expenses in accordance with the principle of net income taxation when calculating the maximum credit allowance for tax paid by a company in a foreign State'.[1344] A Norwegian company operated a branch in the UK and thus paid income taxes to the UK.[1345] Norway applied the credit method.[1346] The Norwegian company therefore included the income from the UK branch in the tax base in Norway, in accordance with Norway's 'principle of global income taxation',[1347] and claimed an FTC for the amount of income taxes paid to the UK.[1348]

The Norwegian tax authorities later reduced the amount of the FTC that could be claimed: 'The reduction was based on a calculation of the maximum credit allowance in accordance with *the principle of net income taxation*' (emphasis added).[1349] In order to determine the net income for the credit method, Norway applied specific rules for the

1342. *Id.*
1343. *Id.* ('As an exception to the general rule that tax allowances apply before tax credits, the new guidelines state that under double taxation treaties, the tax credit – equivalent to the French tax on foreign-source income – applies before the domestic tax allowances that can be carried forward into later years', *citing* 'See BOFIP, "IR – Réductions et crédits d'impôt," BOI-IRRICI-20150729 (Jul. 29, 2015), section 35 as amended').
1344. EFTA, Case E-7/07, *Seabrokers v. Norway*, 7 May 2008, at para. 29. *See also* Report for the Hearing EFTA, 1 Feb. 2008, in EFTA, Case E-7/07, *Seabrokers v. Norway*, 7 May 2008, at para. 2.
1345. EFTA, Case E-7/07, *Seabrokers v. Norway*, 7 May 2008, at para. 4, para. 7; Report for the Hearing EFTA, 1 Feb. 2008, in EFTA, Case E-7/07, *Seabrokers v. Norway*, 7 May 2008, at paras 3–7.
1346. EFTA, Case E-7/07, *Seabrokers v. Norway*, 7 May 2008, at paras 15–16; Report for the Hearing EFTA, 1 Feb. 2008, in EFTA, Case E-7/07, *Seabrokers v. Norway*, 7 May 2008, at paras 16–18.
1347. Report for the Hearing EFTA, 1 Feb. 2008, in EFTA, Case E-7/07, *Seabrokers v. Norway*, 7 May 2008, at para. 21.
1348. *Id.*, at para. 7.
1349. *Id.*, at para. 8. *See also* EFTA, Case E-7/07, *Seabrokers v. Norway*, 7 May 2008, at paras 8–10, 15.

allocation of expenses related to 'debt interest and group contributions'.[1350] In short, the rules spread out the allocation of interest expenses and group contributions evenly, in proportion to the net income.

The branch in the UK, however, kept proper records of its interest expenses and had only 'low debt interest costs'.[1351] Nearly all of the interest expenses were directly linked to the head office in Norway. The Norway rules ended up allocating more interest expenses to the UK branch than it actually had. Importantly, in addition to any minimal interest expenses that the UK branch actually incurred, this allocated some costs to the UK branch that were in fact incurred solely in Norway. As a consequence, Norway reduced the FSI attributable, from its perspective, to the UK branch, which in turn reduced the amount of the FTC that could be claimed. To offer an example, adapted from the Judge-Rapporteur Report,[1352] using simpler numbers and focusing only on the interest expenses:

Worldwide income *before* deduction of interest expenses	15,000,000
Foreign income *before* deduction of interest expenses	10,000,000
All interest expenses, including those from abroad	3,000,000
Actual interest expenses incurred by UK branch	250,000
Actual interest expenses incurred by Norway head office	2,750,000
Apportionment formula for interest expenses:	

$$3{,}000{,}000 \times \frac{10{,}000{,}000}{15{,}000{,}000} = 2{,}000{,}000$$

On the basis of actual foreign income	After recalculation of foreign income
10,000,000 (foreign income) – 250,000 (actual interest expense) = 9,750,000 (net foreign income)	10,000,000 (foreign income) – 2,000,000 (proportionate interest expense) = 8,000,000 (net foreign income)
Maximum creditable amount	**Maximum creditable amount**
Net foreign income × Norwegian tax rate = Maximum creditable amount 9,750,000 × 28% = 2,730,000	Net foreign income × Norwegian tax rate = Maximum creditable amount 8,000,000 × 28% = 2,240,000
Difference: 490,000	

The authorities from the government of Norway argued that this difference stems from: (1) the different tax rates in the UK (30%) and in Norway (28%) and (2) from the different ways of calculating the tax base in the UK and in Norway.[1353] In Norway, they

1350. Report for the Hearing EFTA, 1 Feb. 2008, in EFTA, Case E-7/07, *Seabrokers v. Norway*, 7 May 2008, at para. 9.
1351. *Id.*, at para. 4 and at para. 6.
1352. *Id.*, at para. 9.
1353. *Id.*, at para. 46; EFTA, Case E-7/07, *Seabrokers v. Norway*, 7 May 2008, at para. 33.

argued, the full amount of interest expenses and group contribution expenses are taken into account in the same way for all taxpayers.[1354] If the UK did not allow deductions from the branch's tax base for interest expenses and group contributions, this is merely because its rules for the tax base differed. Moreover, as for the EU/EEA (European Economic Area) law perspective to adopt in the case, the authorities from the government of Norway rejected the comparison with the *De Groot* case, which they argued applied to the obligation to take into account personal and family circumstances.[1355] In their view, the situation was, rather, similar to the *Gilly* case and the *Kerckhaert and Morres* case.[1356] They contended that this is juridical double taxation resulting from disparities - merely from 'a taxpayer exposing himself to two tax jurisdictions'.[1357] There is no obligation under the EEA Agreement to remedy this and it would amount to interfering with the right of the state of residence to determine its own tax base and tax rates.[1358]

Regarding the tax rate differential, this is not so convincing. It was a strategic argument for Norway to make because a mere tax rate differential would qualify the measure as a disparity, rather than a discrimination. However, whether this was the real underlying cause of the higher tax burden is questionable.[1359] To isolate the effect of the tax rates, one can assume the same tax base, such as that of the above example of 9,750,000. Norway would levy 28% on 9,750,000, i.e., 2,730,000 and the UK would levy 30% on 9,750,000, i.e., 2,925,000. Any excess credit that can be attributable solely to the tax rate differential would be maximum 195,000.

Regarding the tax base argument, the Norwegian company countered that the UK could *not* take into account the expenses since those expenses were domestic ones linked exclusively to the business activities in Norway and *not* the UK.[1360] The Norwegian company also put forward *De-Groot*-and-*Beker*-esque arguments. By virtue of allocating a portion of the expenses that were actually incurred domestically to the income abroad, via the MCA formula, this leads to a result where the final taxes due do not fully and accurately reflect the deductible expenses of the company. The Norwegian company expressed this in terms of 'forfeiting' part of its deductible expenses.[1361] To the extent that a portion of domestically incurred expenses are allocated to the foreign income, they are 'forfeited' in that the final taxes due under the credit method calculation do not reflect a full accounting of the expenses. Logically the more expenses a company has, the less net income it has, and thus the less taxes due. In this case,

1354. Report for the Hearing EFTA, 1 Feb. 2008, in EFTA, Case E-7/07, *Seabrokers v. Norway*, 7 May 2008, at para. 45.
1355. *Id.*, at para. 52.
1356. *Id.*, at paras 49–51; EFTA, Case E-7/07, *Seabrokers v. Norway*, 7 May 2008, at paras 33–34.
1357. Report for the Hearing EFTA, 1 Feb. 2008, in EFTA, Case E-7/07, *Seabrokers v. Norway*, 7 May 2008, at para. 49.
1358. *Id.*, at paras 49–51.
1359. Agreeing, *see* EFTA, Case E-7/07, *Seabrokers v. Norway*, 7 May 2008, at para. 52; Report for the Hearing EFTA, 1 Feb. 2008, in EFTA, Case E-7/07, *Seabrokers v. Norway*, 7 May 2008, at para. 38.
1360. Report for the Hearing EFTA, 1 Feb. 2008, in EFTA, Case E-7/07, *Seabrokers v. Norway*, 7 May 2008, at para. 38.
1361. *Id.*, at paras 42–43.

based on the way the expenses are allocated between the domestic source and FSI, Norway's calculation increases the total taxes due, through the back door of reducing the FTC.

Various explanations were put forward regarding the effects of this calculation of the credit limitation and how this mirrors the *De Groot* situation.[1362] For example, according to the EFTA surveillance authority:

> 'In the given situation, the effect of the Norwegian tax rules is that expenses considered partially attributable to the branch in the UK are deductible from the tax payable in Norway only in proportion to the income of the Norwegian head office. This means that the tax base for the Norwegian head office increases with an amount equal to the deduction attributed to the UK branch. In ESA's view, this situation is comparable to that examined in *de Groot* and the considerations of the ECJ in that case are applicable in this case.'[1363]

The EFTA Court agreed with the overall assessment of the effects of Norway's calculation of the MCA:

> 'In effect, this is the same as if Norway, for such taxpayers, would allow deduction only of a portion of expenses such as debt interest when calculating the global net income on which Norwegian income tax is assessed (cf. paragraphs 43–44 above). This means that the Norwegian rules on maximum credit allowance have the potential of leading to a more burdensome result for taxpayers with income earned through a branch in another EEA State than would have been the case had the taxpayers not exercised their freedom of establishment. After having been granted a credit allowance from the Norwegian global income tax, such taxpayers may not be able to enjoy, in effect, the same deduction of expenses as taxpayers with the same total income, but earned in Norway only. This places taxpayers with a branch in another EEA State in a less favourable position for the sole reason that they made use of their right of establishment under the EEA Agreement.'[1364]

The Norwegian company complained that this results in double taxation.[1365] The (at that time, EC) Commission also submitted that 'while a company doing business solely in Norway would enjoy a full deduction for the expenses in question, the Plaintiff has suffered double taxation by reason of the fact that part of its income is earned in another EEA State'.[1366] In this way, the Commission pointed out that this was double

1362. *Id.*, at para. 38 ('The Plaintiff refers to Case C-385/00 *de Groot*, according to which the Member States cannot deprive a citizen from the benefit of a tax deduction based on the assumption that he will receive a similar deduction in the other State where he performed work') and at para. 79 ('In the Commission's view, the logic of the *de Groot* judgment,[33] relied on by the Plaintiff, is transferable to this case to the extent that it shows that a State cannot withdraw normal tax advantages where a taxpayer earns income which is taxed in another State').

1363. Report for the Hearing EFTA, 1 Feb. 2008, in EFTA, Case E-7/07, *Seabrokers v. Norway*, 7 May 2008, at para. 68. *See also* the Commission's view, at para. 76 ('The Commission holds that by attributing part of the interest expenses to the Scottish branch, the Norwegian tax authorities reduced the amount of tax that should be paid by that branch and hence the amount of the tax credit to be granted to the Plaintiff in Norway').

1364. EFTA, Case E-7/07, *Seabrokers v. Norway*, 7 May 2008, at para. 47 and para. 64.

1365. Report for the Hearing EFTA, 1 Feb. 2008, in EFTA, Case E-7/07, *Seabrokers v. Norway*, 7 May 2008, at para. 10, para. 40.

1366. *Id.*, at para. 74.

taxation and, most importantly, *not* caused by a disparity (thus, not a *Gilly* or *Kerckhaert and Morres* situation), but caused by different treatment by Norway of income earned in another MS. The EFTA surveillance authority agreed.[1367]

Ultimately, the debate centred on the types of expenses. A first distinction was made between the interest expenses and the group contribution costs (for which the Court came to the same outcome). A second and more decisive distinction was made between: (i) costs incurred solely by the foreign branch in the host state, (ii) general costs incurred by the company as a whole, and (iii) costs incurred solely by the head office in the home state.[1368]

As regards general costs, or expenses that are *not* clearly linked to any specific activity, the EFTA surveillance authority opined that Norway's legislation is *not* contrary.[1369] It makes sense that expenses 'incurred for the company as a whole' would be proportionately allocated throughout the company.[1370] Presumably, the UK could also consider taking into account such general shared expenses. The Commission assumed as much.[1371] Thus, in that case, any higher tax burden stems from a difference in the calculation of the tax base of the two states.[1372]

As regards expenses that are solely linked to the business activity in Norway, Norway's legislation constitutes an infringement.[1373] It does not make sense to allocate them to the branch since the expenses solely linked to the activity in Norway do not actually 'increase or decrease in proportion to the income of the branch'.[1374] Also, the UK clearly cannot take into account such expenses.[1375] In part, what these arguments seem to boil down to is: identifying which are the expenses that only the state of residence can, or should, take into account (which has subtle echoes of the *Schumacker* reasoning).

The principles underlying the arguments and final decision were only vaguely articulated. The 'principle of net income taxation' was referred to multiple times throughout the judgment, especially by the Norwegian authorities.[1376] The Commission, after declaring that Norway's allocation of expenses is 'discriminatory', added that '[a]llocating debt interest expenses independently of the purpose for which the debt was incurred does not correspond to the situation of the taxpayer'.[1377] The EFTA Court also adopted this correspondence-to-the-situation-of-the-taxpayer as its benchmark for comparability.[1378] The question for establishing comparability in the view of

1367. *Id.*, at para. 69.
1368. EFTA, Case E-7/07, *Seabrokers v. Norway*, 7 May 2008, at paras 52–57.
1369. Report for the Hearing EFTA, 1 Feb. 2008, in EFTA, Case E-7/07, *Seabrokers v. Norway*, 7 May 2008, at para. 63.
1370. *Id.*, at para. 75.
1371. *Id.*, at para. 75.
1372. *Id.*, at paras 63–65.
1373. *Id.*, at para. 66.
1374. *Id.*, at para. 67.
1375. *Id.*, at paras 67–68.
1376. *See*, e.g., EFTA, Case E-7/07, *Seabrokers v. Norway*, 7 May 2008, at para. 8, para. 14, para. 15, para. 29, para. 43, para. 59, para. 70.
1377. Report for the Hearing EFTA, 1 Feb. 2008, in EFTA, Case E-7/07, *Seabrokers v. Norway*, 7 May 2008, at para. 76.
1378. EFTA, Case E-7/07, *Seabrokers v. Norway*, 7 May 2008, at para. 54 and para. 68.

the EFTA Court was 'whether a company with a branch in another EEA State is in a situation which is, with regard to those expenses, objectively comparable to the one of a company having all its business within the home State'.[1379] Attributing the expenses generated solely by the foreign PE or the general expenses which should be shared proportionately by the foreign PE *to the PE* (in calculating the MCA) is acceptable, as it corresponds to the situation of the taxpayer.[1380] As regards these particular expenses, the taxpayer (with a foreign PE) 'is *not* in a comparable situation to a taxpayer whose expenses are *all incurred in the home State*' (emphasis added).[1381] The EFTA Court concluded, on comparability, that:

> 'a company conducting all its business in its home State and having all its debt interest expenses linked to that State, and a company conducting its business in its home State and through a branch in another EEA State (the host State) but having all its debt interest expenses linked to the home State, are in a comparable situation with respect to these expenses. Thus, they should get the same tax treatment in the home State with respect to these expenses. As described in paragraphs 46 and 47 above, the rules at issue do not guarantee this'.[1382]

Although the link is not explicitly made, the 'principle of net income' seems to be implicit in the reasoning of both the Commission and the EFTA Court, by incorporating the idea that the deductibility of expenses should correspond to the taxpayer's situation (and thus their deductibility should not be thwarted or partially excluded at the stage of the credit calculation). Moreover, there seems to be what could be described as principle of causation, by incorporating the idea that the allocation of deductible expenses should be aligned with where and for what purpose they are actually incurred.

As for the decision, the EFTA Court rejected Norway's argument that Norway is free to design its legislation in this way because there is no obligation to grant (juridical) double taxation relief. While it is true that there is no such obligation, this does not allow Norway, or any EU/EEA states, to disregard other obligations. The EFTA Court reiterated the distinction between the allocation of taxation powers and the exercise of its taxation powers.[1383] While the states are free to decide on how best to allocate them, states must exercise them in accordance with the fundamental freedoms. Thus, once a state decides to grant relief, it must do so in a way that is not discriminatory.[1384] Having found that the situations were comparable, as regards 'expenses [that] can only be linked to the company's business' in the home state, Norway's legislation 'constitutes a restriction' on the freedom of establishment.[1385] No justifications were put forward, so the EFTA Court could not assess that aspect (which

1379. *Id.*, at para. 52.
1380. *Id.*, at paras 54–55.
1381. *Id.*, at para. 54.
1382. *Id.*, at para. 56.
1383. *See*, e.g., CJEU, Case C-307/97, *Saint Gobain*, 21 Sep. 1999, ECLI:EU:C:1999:438, at para. 58.
1384. EFTA, Case E-7/07, *Seabrokers v. Norway*, 7 May 2008, at para. 49.
1385. *Id.*, at para. 68.

leaves open the question of whether justifications exist).[1386] For these reasons, the EFTA Court held in favour of the taxpayer.

Interim Summary

This line of case law combines the perspectives of the state of residence and the state of non-residence. The foundations were laid by the *Schumacker* case, which established that in certain exceptional circumstances, the obligation to provide tax-related benefits for personal and family circumstances is transferred from the state of residence to the state of non-residence. The decision placed such personal tax-related benefits on a pedestal, elevating their importance from an EU law perspective by declaring that they must be taken into account *in full* somewhere. The decision placed the responsibility for this, as a general rule, on the state of residence and, as an exception, where all or nearly all the taxpayer's income is generated in the state of non-residence and insufficient income is generated in the state of residence, on the state of non-residence.

Although the decision addressed the state of *non*-residence, questions quickly arose as to the impact on the state of residence and, in particular, on the methods for relief of double taxation. As the state of residence in the *Schumacker* case exempted the income under the tax treaty in question, this underscored the state of residence's inability to provide allowances for personal and family circumstances. It would be less evident in cases where the credit method applies since this method entails including FSI into the tax base in the state of residence. The *Gilly* case could be read as implying that, where the credit method applies, the *Schumacker* exception does not. However, if this were applied as a general rule, it could undermine the CJEU's requirement that personal and family circumstances are taken into account in full somewhere. Examples above demonstrated that in cases where the state of residence is unable to fully credit the foreign taxes, namely in 'excess' credit situations, there is a risk that the personal and family circumstances are partially lost at the stage of the taxes due. In addition to demonstrating this by means of examples, ratios and general indicators were derived, as general guidance for MSs to detect when a *Schumacker* situation may be occurring under the credit method (*see* Example No. 21 and the explanation that follows).

In addition, given that explicit instructions were not directed at states of residence in such *Schumacker* situations (as the CJEU addressed the state of non-residence in that case), examples of possible ways in which a credit method state may respond to the decision were explored. In sum, there were four possible responses discussed, i.e., three possible responses of a credit-granting state, acting alone, and at least one possible coordinated response. First, if the obligation to grant tax-related benefits for personal and family circumstances has transferred to the state of *non*-residence, the state of residence could decide to fully disregard the personal and family circumstances of the taxpayer, assured that they are now taken care of by the other MS. The decision of the CJEU would seem to allow this, according to Farmer; however, the problem is that the credit method could have the effect of cancelling out the personal benefits extended under the *Schumacker* obligation in the other MS (as seen in Example

1386. *Id.*, at para. 58 and para. 69.

No. 22 and the explanation that follows). Thus, second, recognizing the risk that this first response could counteract the *Schumacker* obligation in the other MS, the state of residence could possibly continue to grant, to the extent possible, its own personal and family circumstances (by definition, in a *Schumacker* situation, it is unable to grant them in full) (but *see,* e.g., *supra* note 1306). Third, recognizing this risk, alternatively, the state of residence could adapt the amount of the credit it grants, by devising a notional credit, proposed by Farmer, for the taxes relinquished by the other MS under its *Schumacker* obligation. Examples were used to compare the relative advantages and disadvantages of these responses by a credit method state (*see* Example No. 22, Example No. 23, and Example No. 24). Fourth, as Wattel suggests, it may be possible for the MSs to coordinate in order to each grant a proportionate amount of allowances for personal and family circumstances (*see,* e.g., *supra* note 1311 and note 1324).

The ways in which the credit method can potentially have the effect of (partially) excluding tax-related personal and family considerations became even clearer in subsequent cases, namely the *De Groot* and *Beker* cases. Notably, as the *Schumacker* exception did not apply, the states of residence were responsible for all personal and family circumstances of the taxpayer. Also, as these cases were decided from the perspective of the state of residence, much more explicit instructions for the credit method (and a tax exemption method) can be inferred. The problem was caused by the way in which the MCA was calculated. From these decisions, examples were created in order to compare and contrast different approaches to calculating the MCA and the impact of these decisions on whether they are in line with EU law (*see* Example No. 25). In sum, the approach that the CJEU's decisions advocate for is one in which the tax liability on the basis of worldwide income (taking into account personal and family circumstances) is multiplied by a fraction with the gross FSI in the numerator (gross of allowances for personal and family circumstances) and the net taxable income in the denominator.

Comparing these decisions with those in the *Gilly* line of case law, what can be concluded is that, while the state of residence is under no obligation to eliminate juridical double taxation – meaning that it need not implement any direct credit method (or other methods) at all – as soon as the state of residence opts to do so, its direct credit method must be designed in a non-discriminatory way. What can also be concluded is that the distinction between disparities and discrimination seeps into these design considerations. For example, an 'ordinary' direct tax credit that is based on an MCA is, in principle, perfectly in line with EU law. However, as this line of case law revealed, an 'excess' credit requires closer scrutiny in order to determine the extent to which the excess is attributable to a mere difference in tax rates (compatible with the current state of EU law) and the extent to which it is attributable to other factors that may indicate, for example, a loss of personal reliefs (incompatible with the current state of EU law).

A case of the EFTA Court considered similar questions in circumstances involving companies and business-related expenses. Similar to the above cases, the issue did not revolve around an 'excess' credit per se, but rather revolved around what this 'excess' credit represented. In this case, *Seabrokers v. Norway,* the excess represented higher taxes as a result of a restrictive or discriminatory calculation of the credit that *indirectly* excluded some of the deductible expenses from the tax base in proportion to the FSI – merely at a later stage, when calculating the taxes ultimately due and the FTC. It has the same final effect but through different means. As mentioned, an 'excess' credit is not contrary to EU/EEA law if it stems from disparities between the tax rate and tax base in the state of source and the state of residence, as revealed in the *Gilly* and *Kerckhaert* cases. An 'excess' credit is problematic where it stems from a discriminatory approach to the calculation, as revealed in the *De Groot* and *Beker* cases. This is what the debate revolved around in this case. Since the *De Groot* and *Beker* cases regarded natural persons and their right to have their personal and family circumstances taken into account, in line with the *Schumacker* doctrine, it was unclear the extent to which the findings of these cases could be extended to companies and deductible business expenses. According to the EFTA Court, on the basis of a provision of the EEA Agreement that corresponds to the freedom of establishment of the TFEU and on the basis of applying the CJEU's case law, there are also EU law constraints that can arise in these cases, as summarized in Chapter 5.

4.2.5. The *Amurta* or 'Neutralization' Line of Case Law

By comparison with the previously discussed cases, many of which were analysed from the perspective of the state of residence, this line of case law is analysed from the perspective of the state of source or, more accurately, the state of the subsidiary that is distributing profits or dividends to a shareholder (subsidiary state).[1387] Generally speaking, these cases share similar fact patterns and legal issues: they concern a subsidiary state's legislation that requires a tax to be withheld when the subsidiary distributes profits to a non-resident shareholder, whereas less tax, or no such tax, is withheld when the subsidiary distributes profits to a resident shareholder (or, if the tax is withheld, some other form of relief, such as a refund or credit, is offered to the resident shareholder). The CJEU consistently held that this legislation leads to higher taxation of dividends distributed to non-resident shareholders as compared to resident shareholders, which is likely to deter cross-border investments, and is therefore a restriction on the free movement of (in most cases) capital.

To remedy this, if the subsidiary state offers relief from additional charges of tax on distributions to resident shareholders, it must also extend this relief to non-resident shareholders. This is especially because it is the subsidiary state *itself* that creates the immediate cause of the higher taxation on cross-border dividends, by levying a WHT

1387. CJEU, Case C-170/05, *Denkavit Internationaal and Denkavit France*, 14 Dec. 2006, ECLI:EU:C:2006:783; CJEU, Case C-379/05, *Amurta*, 8 Nov. 2007, ECLI:EU:C:2007:655; CJEU, Case C-521/07, *Commission v. Netherlands*, 11 Jun. 2009, ECLI:EU:C:2009:360; CJEU, Case C-540/07, *Commission v. Italy*, 19 Nov. 2009, ECLI:EU:C:2009:717; CJEU, Case C-487/08, *Commission v. Spain*, 3 Jun. 2010, ECLI:EU:C:2010:310; CJEU, Case C-199/10, *Secilpar*, 22 Nov. 2010, ECLI:EU:C:2010:706; CJEU, Case C-284/09, *Commission v. Germany*, 20 Oct. 2011, ECLI:EU:C:2011:670; CJEU, Case C-384/11, *Tate & Lyle Investments*, 12 Jul. 2012, ECLI:EU:C:2012:463; CJEU, Joined Cases C-10/14, C-14/14 and C-17/14, *J. B. G. T. Miljoen, X, and Société Générale SA*, 17 Sep. 2015, ECLI:EU:C:2015:608.

on the non-resident shareholder in the first place. Since it creates the problem, it should provide the remedy.

What is most remarkable about this line of case law is that, at the stage of considering possible justifications for this restriction, the CJEU accepted another way out for the subsidiary state. If the subsidiary state has bilaterally agreed with the residence state of the shareholder that the WHT levied at source will be credited in the residence state, then the subsidiary may have succeeded in 'neutralizing' the effects of the restriction.[1388] If so, its WHT, in combination with a credit in the other state, could be compatible with EU law. In this way, the discrimination analysis, or more precisely the justification or remedy, is extended from its usual one-state perspective to a two-state perspective (or perhaps, it is rather a bilateral treaty-based perspective).[1389]

Since the prospect of 'neutralization' relies on the application of the credit method in the residence state, most follow-up questions naturally pertained to the credit method. A WHT followed by a credit is rather standard, but EU law may exert an influence on how this works. Often, under DTCs based on the OECD Model, for example, in the case of dividends, the source state may levy a WHT up to a limited amount (Article 10 of the OECD Model), and the residence state agrees to give a credit for this WHT (Article 23A(2) or Article 23B of the OECD Model).[1390] Some residence states even unilaterally offer an FTC under their own domestic law. In practice, though, the credit is not always provided. For example, in the *Denkavit* case,[1391] although the residence state agreed to a credit under the DTC, under its domestic law, it simply *exempted* the dividend income; thus, there was no tax against which a credit could be offset.[1392]

Some clarifications were thus provided in the *Amurta* case:[1393] first, the credit must *actually* be given and, second, it must be based on the DTC, bilaterally agreed, and *not* a unilateral credit under the residence state's domestic law.[1394] Then it was left to the national court 'to determine whether that convention enables the effects of the

1388. CJEU, Case C-379/05, *Amurta*, 8 Nov. 2007, ECLI:EU:C:2007:655, at paras 78–80, 83–84; CJEU, Case C-540/07, *Commission v. Italy*, 19 Nov. 2009, ECLI:EU:C:2009:717, at paras 35–41; CJEU, Case C-487/08, *Commission v. Spain*, 3 Jun. 2010, ECLI:EU:C:2010:310, at paras 58–67; CJEU, Case C-199/10, *Secilpar*, 22 Nov. 2010, ECLI:EU:C:2010:706, at paras 39–43; CJEU, Case C-384/11, *Tate & Lyle Investments*, 12 Jul. 2012, ECLI:EU:C:2012:463, at paras 43–46; CJEU, Joined Cases C-10/14, C-14/14 and C-17/14, *J. B. G. T. Miljoen, X, and Société Générale SA*, 17 Sep. 2015, ECLI:EU:C:2015:608, at paras 75–90.

1389. *See* Georg Kofler, *Tax Treaty 'Neutralization' of Source State Discrimination under the EU Fundamental Freedoms?*, 65(12) Bull. Int'l Tax'n 684, 684–686 (2011).

1390. *See also* Werner Haslehner, *Article 10 Dividends*, *in* 1 *Klaus Vogel on Double Taxation Conventions* 775 (Ekkehart Reimer & Alexander Rust eds, Kluwer Law International 4th ed. 2015).

1391. CJEU, Case C-170/05, *Denkavit Internationaal and Denkavit France*, 14 Dec. 2006, ECLI:EU:C:2006:783.

1392. *Id.*, at para. 46.

1393. CJEU, Case C-379/05, *Amurta*, 8 Nov. 2007, ECLI:EU:C:2007:655.

1394. *Id.*, at paras 78–79 ('Accordingly, the Kingdom of the Netherlands cannot rely on the existence of a tax advantage granted unilaterally by another Member State in order to escape its obligations under the Treaty. However, it cannot be excluded that a Member State may succeed in ensuring compliance with its obligations under the Treaty through the conclusion of a convention for the avoidance of double taxation with another Member State').

restriction on the free movement of capital [...] to be neutralised'.[1395] Thus, more questions arose.

Further clarification came in the *Commission v. Italy* case.[1396] The CJEU stated that the credit must allow the WHT to be set off in the 'full amount', for the difference in treatment to 'totally disappear'.[1397] If the dividends are *not* taxed in the residence MS (as in *Denkavit*, due to an exemption) or are not sufficiently taxed, such that the WHT - 'or a part thereof' - cannot be offset, then the MS has *not* succeeded in ensuring neutralization.[1398]

This leads to a bit of a confrontation with the credit limitation (or MCA). In the *Gilly* case, the CJEU accepted that the MCA may lead to some part of the taxes levied at source *not* being fully offset. One distinction is that *Gilly* concerned the residence state's legislation, whereas this line of case law concerned the subsidiary state's legislation. Thus, it is not a problem for the residence state, but it could be a problem for the source state.

Moreover, to 'offset in full'[1399] the restriction seems hard to guarantee in practice. For that to happen 100% of the time, two eventualities would have to occur, namely that: (1) the residence state and subsidiary state have the same, or very similar, tax systems (e.g., tax rates and tax base) and (2) the facts and figures - potentially volatile things - have to be aligned. Since EU law allows MSs to decide on their tax rates and tax base, it is likely that the tax systems will differ.[1400] In any given case, the exact amount of the credit depends on multiple factors, e.g., whether the shareholder is in an overall loss or profit situation, whether the tax base is net or gross, whether the MCA is on a per-country or overall basis. Consequently, in some instances, the amount of the credit will 'neutralize', and in others it will not, leading to laws whose compatibility with EU law depends on the ever-changing circumstances.

In 2015, the CJEU reaffirmed this neutralization case law.[1401] It further clarified the meaning of the requirement for a 'bilaterally-agreed' provision. In these cases, the method articles - Article 23(1) of the Belgium-Netherlands DTC and Article 24B of the France-Netherlands DTC - offered a credit in the residence state (Belgium and France, respectively). As regards the Belgium-Netherlands DTC, the CJEU observed that Article 23(1) is subject to Belgian *domestic* law for the application of the credit method. In effect, this means that the tax credit is offered *unilaterally* by Belgium, rather than

1395. *Id.*, at para. 83.
1396. CJEU, Case C-540/07, *Commission v. Italy*, 19 Nov. 2009, ECLI:EU:C:2009:717.
1397. *Id.*, at para. 37.
1398. *Id.*, at para. 38.
1399. *Id.*, at para. 37.
1400. Taking tax rates as one example, according to data compiled from the OECD by the Tax Foundation, a comparison of EU MSs reveals that nominal corporate tax rates range from 9% (Hungary) to 34.4% (France), as of 2019. Personal income tax rates include a flat 15% in Hungary and 55% top marginal rate in Austria, as of 2019, and vary depending on the progressive tax rate brackets, types of income, among other factors. *See*, e.g., Elke Asen, *Corporate Income Tax Rates in Europe*, Tax Foundation (7 Feb. 2019), https://taxfoundation.org/corporate-tax-rates-europe-2019/; OECD, *Table I.7. Top statutory personal income tax rates*, OECD.Stat, https://stats.oecd.org/index.aspx?DataSetCode=TABLE_I7.
1401. CJEU, Joined Cases C-10/14, C-14/14 and C-17/14, *J. B. G. T. Miljoen, X, and Société Générale SA*, 17 Sep. 2015, ECLI:EU:C:2015:608.

being guaranteed at the level of the DTC; for this reason, the Netherlands is *not* able to claim that *it* neutralizes the different treatment.[1402] As regards the French-Netherlands DTC, the CJEU observed that the wording of Article 24B offers the possibility for a full credit of the WHTs levied in the Netherlands; however, Article 24B of the French-Netherlands DTC provides for an MCA, which in practice may prevent an 'offset in full' in some circumstances. The Netherlands court was instructed to ascertain whether this was in fact the case.[1403]

Finally, the CJEU was asked to address a key timing issue under the credit method. It was asked to decide whether 'the possibility of offsetting that [excess] tax in subsequent years may have the effect of neutralising the effects of a restriction', but the Court declined to answer the question, after rejecting it as hypothetical and thus inadmissible.[1404]

Interim Summary

According to the *Amurta* or 'neutralization' line of case law, it is possible for a subsidiary state to justify a restrictive WHT on dividends distributed to non-resident shareholders if the subsidiary state has bilaterally agreed (e.g., in a DTC) upon a credit in the residence state that will offset the different treatment in full. As a result, precisely how the credit method in the DTC is designed becomes relevant for this subsidiary state. To briefly summarize the main points, the credit must: (1) actually be given (i.e., not be unavailable due to the income being exempt or insufficiently taxed in the residence state); (2) be bilaterally agreed (yet, credit method articles in DTCs that rely on domestic law do not meet this criterion); and (3) fully offset the restrictive effect of the WHT. Yet, the question regarding a credit carryforward - more specifically, whether part of the subsidiary state's WHT that is not neutralized by a credit in the residence state in the year in question can instead be neutralized across time by means of a credit carryforward - was raised but not answered in the joined *J. B. G. T. Miljoen, X, and Société Générale SA* cases. Thus, even after all of these decisions, open issues remain, as discussed below (in Chapter 5).

1402. *Id.*, at para. 82.

1403. *Id.*, at para. 86 ('In that regard, it is apparent from the first subparagraph of Article 24B(b) of that convention that, in relation to the dividends on which the Netherlands tax was charged, the French Republic grants resident taxpayers who received such income a tax credit of an amount equal to the Netherlands tax. Since the second subparagraph of that provision provides that that tax credit may not exceed the amount of the tax levied in France on the income in question, it is possible that the full amount of the tax on dividends paid in the Netherlands may not be neutralised, which does not satisfy the requirements arising out of the case-law of the Court cited in paragraph 79 above. However, it is for the national court to ascertain whether that is so in the case in the main proceedings').

1404. CJEU, Joined Cases C-10/14, C-14/14 and C-17/14, *J. B. G. T. Miljoen, X, and Société Générale SA*, 17 Sep. 2015, ECLI:EU:C:2015:608, at para. 88. This paragraph is based on a summary written by this author for an update to the Vogel Commentary Online.

4.2.6. The *Gerritse/Scorpio* or Deductible Expenses Line of Case Law

As the 'neutralization' line of case law reinforced, there is an obvious link between the taxation in the state of source and the credit method in the state of residence. A common cause of 'excess' credits and therefore complaints against the credit method originates in the discrepancy between the tax base in the state of source and the tax base in the state of residence. WHTs often feature in such cases since they tend to be levied on a gross basis in the state of source, whereas the credit method is granted on a net basis in the state of residence.

From a credit method perspective, this may be problematic where the taxpayer has expenses related to a given stream of income, such that the amount of taxes levied in the state of source on a gross basis exceeds the amount of taxes levied in the state of residence on a net basis, thus leaving some of the foreign taxes uncredited. This state of affairs has become rather institutionalized, as this was the compromise reached after decades of deliberations under the organization that eventually became the OECD (as discussed in Chapter 2), in which nearly all EU MSs and now the EU Commission take part.[1405] The Commentary on the OECD Model, too, has flagged the issue of gross versus net-basis taxation, but quite explicitly allows it under its influential Model. In particular, under Articles 10 and 11, the state of source has the option to levy taxes on a gross basis on dividends and interest, and the state of residence applies the 'ordinary' tax credit (which 'shall not ... exceed that part of the income tax or capital tax, as computed before the deduction is given, which is attributable, as the case may be, to the income or the capital which may be taxed in that other State') and the details of computing taxable income are to be determined on the basis of domestic law.[1406]

Thus, there are discrepancies between two different states, with two different procedures for levying tax and two different tax bases. When this difference leads to higher taxation in a cross-border context as compared to a domestic one, as may be expected, complaints will be brought by taxpayers. Either one can seek to blame the state of residence for this or the state of source. Both attempts have been made. As this section shows, the CJEU seems to have largely pinpointed the state of source.

1405. *See* Chapter 2, at *supra* note 439; OECD, *Members and Partners*, http://www.oecd.org/about/membersandpartners/ (last visited 1 Dec. 2018); OECD, *Status of the European Commission Within the OECD*, Legal Affairs, https://www.oecd.org/legal/europeancommissionstatus.htm (last visited 1 Dec. 2018) ('The status of the European Commission within the OECD is unique. Supplementary Protocol No. 1 to the OECD Convention states that "The European Commission shall take part in the work of the Organisation". This has been summarised as follows: "The representative of the Commission has almost the same rights as Member countries. He or she has the right to speak at any point and not just at the end of a session as is often the case for observers. He or she may be elected as a member of the bureau of subsdiary [sic] bodies, participate fully in the preparation of texts, including legal acts and has an unrestricted right to make proposals and suggest changes". However, the representative of the Commission does not have the right to vote and does not officially take part in the adoption of legal acts submitted to the Council').

1406. OECD, *Model Tax Convention on Income and on Capital 2017: Condensed Version* Commentary on Articles 23 A and 23 B, para. 60 and para. 63 (OECD Publishing 2017). *See also* Werner Haslehner, *Article 10 Dividends*, *in* 1 *Klaus Vogel on Double Taxation Conventions* 775, m.nos 11, 72, 75 (Ekkehart Reimer & Alexander Rust eds, Kluwer Law International 4th ed. 2015).

Complaints against the state of residence have been unsuccessful (both before the CJEU, as, for example, the *Gilly* case highlights, and before domestic courts, as will be discussed below in this section).

In this case, if the state of source tends to be held responsible from an EU law perspective, the question that this section aims to explore is whether and to what extent the obligations that the CJEU places on the state of source in this context help to alleviate the aforementioned discrepancies, which, in turn, could reduce 'excess' credits, and would support more successful 'neutralization' claims. To do so, the discussion turns, first, to a study of this CJEU case law and, second, returns to the link with credit method in the summary of this section.

As for some preliminary remarks, the CJEU recognized, in the *Schumacker* case, that '[i]n relation to direct taxes, the situations of residents and of non-residents are not, as a rule, comparable' and, therefore, certain rules that govern the taxation of non-residents may differ from those of residents.[1407] Generally speaking, persons who are deemed resident taxpayers are subject to 'unlimited tax liability' on their worldwide income and persons who are deemed non-resident taxpayers are subject to 'limited tax liability' only on income that is earned in the territory or has some sort of economic or legal nexus with the territory.[1408] The procedures, or methods for levying income tax, tend to differ accordingly. Generally speaking, residents are assessed by means of an annual tax return where all of their income and expenses can be taken into account – and, thus, taxed on a net basis – and often, especially for individuals, on a progressive tax rate scale. Non-residents, for which the state does not have a global view of their circumstances and over which it has less enforcement power, are more likely to have taxes withheld automatically at source from income paid to them, often on the gross amount of the payment and at a flat rate. This is especially the case for investment income or for cases where a non-resident has only a temporary or insignificant presence in the state, while it is less often the case for business income.[1409] In some cases, a state enforces this by requiring a resident person who is paying the non-resident to retain the tax at source and potentially holds the resident payer legally liable if it fails to do so.[1410] On nearly all these aspects of the taxation of non-resident

1407. CJEU, Case C-279/93, *Schumacker*, 14 Feb. 1995, ECLI:EU:C:1995:31, at paras 31–35.

1408. *Id.*, at paras 3–5 (citing Germany's national legislation); CJEU, Case C-270/83, *Commission v. France (Avoir Fiscal)*, 28 Jan. 1986, ECLI:EU:C:1986:37, at para. 17 (the French government argued that 'The difference in question is based on the distinction between "residents" and "non-residents", which is to be found in all legal systems and is internationally accepted. It is an essential distinction in tax law'). On these general rules and some exceptions, in general, *see*, e.g., Brian J. Arnold, *International Tax Primer*, 22, 29, 83–87 (Wolters Kluwer 3d ed. 2016); Hugh J. Ault & Brian J. Arnold, *Comparative Income Taxation: A Structural Analysis*, 345, 395–411 (Kluwer Law International 2d ed. 2004).

1409. On these general rules and the exceptions, in general, *see*, e.g., Brian J. Arnold, *International Tax Primer* 85 (Wolters Kluwer 3d ed. 2016); Hugh J. Ault & Brian J. Arnold, *Comparative Income Taxation: A Structural Analysis* 395–411 (Kluwer Law International 2d ed. 2004).

1410. *See*, e.g., CJEU, Case C-290/04, *FKP Scorpio Konzertproduktionen*, 3 Oct. 2006, ECLI:EU:C:2006:630, at paras 9–14 (citing Germany's national legislation); Austria, Einkommensteuergesetz (EStG) 1988 (as amended), Section 95 (Income Tax Act 1988).

taxpayers, the CJEU has had an impact in this line of case law,[1411] in its efforts to sort out which differences in tax treatment amount to covert discrimination and which are appropriate, due to objective differences regarding residence, or are otherwise justified.

One of the landmark cases is the 2003 *Gerritse* case.[1412] Mr Gerritse, resident in the Netherlands, earned approximately DEM 6,000 playing music in Germany with expenses of approximately DEM 900.[1413] Under German law, non-residents that earned income in Germany, for example, for a sports or artistic performance, were taxed by means of a withholding at source at a fixed rate of 25%, and no deduction of business expenses was permitted, unless they amounted to more than 50% of the income earned.[1414] By comparison, residents were taxed on 'net profit after deducting business expenses' and at a progressive tax rate.[1415] In this case, the CJEU established that, as regards business expenses that are directly linked to generating (taxable) revenue in a MS, non-residents and residents are in a comparable situation. Therefore, like resident taxpayers, non-resident taxpayers should be able to deduct directly related business expenses.[1416]

Also, as regards the compatibility of applying a flat tax rate (of 25%) to non-residents, while applying progressive tax rates to residents, it is not prohibited outright to apply a different approach to the taxation of residents and non-residents.[1417] What is incompatible, however, is applying a higher tax rate to non-residents than to residents, as this would constitute 'indirect discrimination prohibited by Community law'.[1418] The MS in question, Germany, must calculate whether the flat tax rate leads

1411. Regarding individuals, *see*, e.g., CJEU, Case C-152/73, *Sotgiu*, 12 Feb. 1974, ECLI:EU:C:1974:13; CJEU, Case C-175/88, *Biehl*, 8 May 1990, ECLI:EU:C:1990:186; CJEU, Case C-279/93, *Schumacker*, 14 Feb. 1995, ECLI:EU:C:1995:31; CJEU, Case C-391/97, *Gschwind*, 14 Sep. 1999, ECLI:EU:C:1999:409; CJEU, Case C-169/03, *Wallentin*, 1 Jul. 2004, ECLI:EU:C:2004:403; CJEU, Case C-376/03, *D*, 5 Jul. 2005, ECLI:EU:C:2005:424; CJEU, Case C-234/01, *Gerritse*, 12 Jun. 2003, ECLI:EU:C:2003:340; CJEU, Case C-346/04, *Conijn*, 6 Jul. 2006, ECLI:EU:C:2006:445; CJEU, Case C-290/04, *FKP Scorpio Konzertproduktionen*, 3 Oct. 2006, ECLI:EU:C:2006:630. Regarding companies, *see*, e.g., CJEU, Case C-270/83, *Commission v. France (Avoir Fiscal)*, 28 Jan. 1986, ECLI:EU:C:1986:37; CJEU, Case C-307/97, *Saint Gobain*, 21 Sep. 1999, ECLI:EU:C:1999:438; CJEU, Case C-311/97, *Royal Bank of Scotland*, 29 Apr. 1999, ECLI:EU:C:1999:216; CJEU, Case C-253/03, *CLT-UFA*, 23 Feb. 2006, ECLI:EU:C:2006:129; CJEU, Case C-282/07, *Truck Center*, 22 Dec. 2008, ECLI:EU:C:2008:762; CJEU, Case C-385/12, *Hervis Sport- és Divatkereskedelmi*, 5 Feb. 2014, ECLI:EU:C:2014:47.
1412. CJEU, Case C-234/01, *Gerritse*, 12 Jun. 2003, ECLI:EU:C:2003:340 (regarding the freedom to provide services).
1413. *Id.*, at para. 9.
1414. *Id.*, at paras 3–8.
1415. *Id.*, at para. 8.
1416. *Id.*, at paras 25–29, 55.
1417. *Id.*, at para. 55.
1418. *Id.*, at paras 52–53 (as an aside, in this case, the methods of relief for double taxation form part of the legal background used in the reasoning for establishing comparability. According to the CJEU, the comparability follows from the 'tax exemption' method applied in the state of residence, the Netherlands. Notably, the CJEU takes into account the Netherland's relief mechanism on this point, despite the fact that the CJEU is assessing the EU law compatibility of *Germany's* tax laws in this case. As in the *Schumacker* case, the CJEU seems to take into account what is happening in the state of residence, including or in particular the method of relief, for these cases on individual non-residents. The CJEU reasoned that '52. Moreover, as

to taxation that is higher for non-residents.[1419] Of course, in practice, a flat tax rate can sometimes lead to more advantageous treatment and other times lead to disadvantageous treatment, depending on the amount of expenses.[1420] Therefore, it would seem inevitable that this decision entails adjustments to be made to MSs' rules for non-residents (e.g., allowing non-residents to opt for progressive tax rates or to request refunds when taxed at a higher rate), since MSs can never fully guarantee that no disadvantageous treatment will arise.

In the 2006 *Conijn* case,[1421] the CJEU confirmed the *Gerritse* finding that in so far as expenditure is directly linked to the business income that is taxable in the state of source, then residents and non-residents are comparable.[1422] In the same year, in the

regards the application to non-residents of a flat rate of tax of 25% while residents are subject to a progressive table, as the Commission has pointed out, the Netherlands as State of residence, pursuant to the bilateral convention, integrates the income in respect of which the right to tax belongs to Germany into the basis of assessment, in accordance with the progressivity rule. It does, however, take account of the tax levied in Germany, by deducting from the Netherlands tax a fraction which corresponds to the relation between the income taxed in Germany and worldwide income. 53. That means that, with regard to the progressivity rule, non-residents and residents are in a comparable situation, so that application to the former of a higher rate of income tax than that applicable to the latter and to taxpayers who are assimilated to them would constitute indirect discrimination prohibited by Community law, in particular by Article 60 of the Treaty (see, by analogy, *Asscher*, paragraph 49)'); CJEU, Case C-107/94, *Asscher*, 27 Jun. 1996, ECLI:EU:C:1996:251, at paras 14–15, 46–49 (the *Asscher* case sheds more light on this. In that case, the Netherlands applied a special regime to the taxation of non-residents, against which Mr Asscher brought a complaint once he became resident in Belgium and exercised self-employed activities in the Netherlands. Under the Belgium-Netherlands tax treaty, Belgium applied an exemption with progression system. The CJEU elaborates a bit further on the relevance of this fact for its reasoning, where it can be more clearly seen that the CJEU's statement is basically in direct response to one argument put forward by the Netherlands: '46 According to the Netherlands Government, the higher rate of tax is intended to offset the fact that certain non-residents escape the progressive nature of the tax because their tax obligations are confined to income received in the Netherlands. 47 It must be noted in that regard that, under Article 24(2)(1) of the Convention, modelled on Article 23A(1) and (3) of the OECD Model Convention (exemption with maintenance of progressivity), income received in a State in which the taxpayer pursues an economic activity but does not reside is taxable exclusively in that State and exempt in the State of residence. The State in which the taxpayer resides may nevertheless take that income into account in calculating the amount of tax on the remaining income in order, inter alia, to apply the rule of progressivity. 48 The fact that a taxpayer is a non-resident thus does not enable him, in the circumstances under consideration, to escape the application of the rule of progressivity. Both categories of taxpayer are therefore in comparable situations with regard to that rule. 49 In those circumstances, the application of a higher rate of tax to the income of certain non-residents than is applicable to those who are resident or treated as such constitutes indirect discrimination prohibited by Article 52 of the Treaty').

1419. CJEU, Case C-234/01, *Gerritse*, 12 Jun. 2003, ECLI:EU:C:2003:340, at para. 54.

1420. *Id.*, at para. 20.

1421. CJEU, Case C-346/04, *Conijn*, 6 Jul. 2006, ECLI:EU:C:2006:445 (regarding the freedom of establishment).

1422. *Id.*, at paras 7–8, 20, 21–24 (Mr Conijn, a national and resident of the Netherlands, was deemed to carry on business via his holding in a tax-transparent partnership (KG) in Germany. He requested to deduct from his taxable income the costs that he incurred for obtaining tax advice in order to prepare his German tax return, in the same way as resident persons with unlimited tax liability. The CJEU reaffirmed that residents and non-residents are comparable as regards expenses directly linked with the business income liable to tax in the state of source (or establishment). It also confirmed the comparability on another ground,

Scorpio case,[1423] the CJEU, in addition to again confirming previous case law regarding the right of non-residents to deduct business expenses that are 'economically connected' to the income in question,[1424] decided on further questions regarding the procedures for taxing non-residents.

In *Scorpio*, three aspects of Germany's procedures were assessed: (1) obliging the resident payer to withhold at source the taxes due on the income paid to a non-resident taxpayer;[1425] (2) allowing a non-resident to take into account expenses - not at source - but only by means of a subsequent refund procedure;[1426] (3) requiring a special application to be filed by the non-resident in order to benefit from the exemption under the DTC.[1427] In this case, the resident payer neglected to withhold the taxes on a payment to a non-resident and was held liable.[1428] The resident payer complained that this was against EU law and against the tax treaty.[1429]

The CJEU noted that a different procedure ('a procedure of retention of tax at source')[1430] applied depending on whether the provider of services resided in Germany or in another MS.[1431] This procedure, and its corresponding increased risk of liability for the payer, constitutes an obstacle to the freedom to provide services because it is 'liable to deter companies such as Scorpio from calling on providers of services residing in other Member States'.[1432] However, at the stage of justifications, the CJEU held it was justified by 'the need to ensure the effective collection of income tax'.[1433] As regards proportionality, indeed a retention at source is a proportionate means.[1434] It held the same as regards the liability for the payer (e.g., Scorpio) for a failure to withhold, '[s]ince that liability constitutes the corollary of that method of collecting

namely the purpose of the legislation in question. It noted that the purpose for allowing resident taxpayers to deduct expenses for professional help in preparing their tax returns is based on the complexity of the German tax law. Non-residents are also obliged to file a tax return when they earn income taxable in Germany and are in a comparable situation as regards the need to deal with the complexity of the German tax laws).

1423. CJEU, Case C-290/04, *FKP Scorpio Konzertproduktionen*, 3 Oct. 2006, ECLI:EU:C:2006:630 (regarding the freedom to provide services).
1424. *Id.*, at paras 42–44.
1425. *Id.*, at paras 8–10, 18–20 (in this case, a non-resident (a natural person doing business as 'Europop', that resided in the Netherlands) was taxed on income ('DEM 438 600') earned under a service contract relating to a music concert, by means of obliging the resident payer (a company, 'Scorpio', that resided in Germany) to withhold, or deduct, at source the amount of taxes due by the non-resident on the income ('15% of the gross amount') and to pass it along to the tax authorities).
1426. *Id.*, at para. 45 (while the non-resident could not deduct any expenses at the time of withholding, the non-resident could apply for this later and obtain a refund of any difference).
1427. *Id.*, at paras 11–15 (under the Germany-Netherlands tax treaty, the right to tax this income was allocated to the Netherlands and not Germany. Nevertheless, the procedure in this case required a withholding at source, unless the non-resident filed a special application in Germany verifying that it meets the conditions for the exemption; otherwise, the non-resident could be later reimbursed upon application).
1428. *Id.*, at paras 19–20.
1429. *Id.*, at paras 23–24.
1430. *Id.*, at para. 28.
1431. *Id.*, at para. 29.
1432. *Id.*, at paras 33–34.
1433. *Id.*, at para. 35.
1434. *Id.*, at para. 37.

income tax, it too contributes in a proportionate manner to ensuring the effectiveness of collecting the tax'.[1435]

As regards the subsequent refund procedure for expenses to be taken into account, this 'involves expense and additional administrative and economic burdens'[1436] that are likely to impede cross-border services and, thus, is an obstacle.[1437] Germany can also allow a deduction for expenses reported at the time of withholding.[1438]

As regards the tax treaty procedure, the obligation for the service provider (Europop) to obtain a certificate in order to benefit from his tax exemption under the treaty and the liability of the service recipient (the payer, Scorpio) is likely to deter cross-border services and, therefore, is an obstacle.[1439] However, it is justified 'in order to ensure the proper functioning of the procedure for taxation at source'.[1440]

Regarding the right to hold the payer liable for a failure to withhold, according to the 2018 *TTL* case,[1441] it is even compatible to charge default interest or other penalties on payers that fail to uphold their WHT obligations. However, in the *TTL* case, the rules were too severe (e.g., the interest was non-recoverable, even if no WHT proved due); thus, the CJEU recalled that such penalties must be tailored to achieve their objective of 'the need to ensure the collection of withholding tax on cross-border payments and to ensure the effectiveness of fiscal supervision in cross-border situations' and must not go beyond what is necessary to achieve that objective.[1442]

Next, the 2007 *Centro Equestre da Lezíria Grande* case[1443] is interesting: (1) for the role that the credit method played in the reasoning and (2) for the CJEU's further clarification of the meaning of economically connected operating expenses. In this case, a Portuguese company organized equestrian shows and lessons in Germany. It was taxed at source. It requested to reassess its income, by taking into account its expenses, and asked for a corresponding refund of some of the CITs, which the German authorities refused.[1444] Other details aside, the CJEU reaffirmed the *Gerritse* rule obliging a MS to allow the deduction of 'operating expenses [that] have a direct economic connection' to the income taxable in that MS.[1445] It considered that 'travel

1435. *Id.*, at para. 38.
1436. *Id.*, at para. 46.
1437. *Id.*, at paras 46–47.
1438. *Id.*, at para. 48.
1439. *Id.*, at para. 58.
1440. *Id.*, at para. 59.
1441. CJEU, Case C-553/16, *TTL*, 25 Jul. 2018, ECLI:EU:C:2018:604.
1442. *Id.*, at paras 57–63 (this case assessed a Bulgarian law according to which a Bulgarian payer that was responsible for levying withholding tax on cross-border payments was charged interest until evidence was provided that a particular DTC, which reduced the withholding tax on the income, was applicable. The interest was charged even if it was proven that no withholding taxes whatsoever were due and the interest was non-recoverable. The CJEU held that this was neither suitable to achieve the aim nor the most proportionate means to do so).
1443. CJEU, Case C-345/04, *Centro Equestre da Lezíria Grande*, 15 Feb. 2007, ECLI:EU:C:2007:96.
1444. *Id.*, at paras 8–13.
1445. *Id.*, at paras 22–23 (in addition to referring to its settled *Gerritse* rule, the CJEU brought in a justification new in this context referred to as the principle of territoriality: 'It is clear from the Court's case-law that a tax system under which, for the purposes of calculating the basis of assessment for non-resident taxpayers in a particular Member State, only profits and losses

and accommodation costs' are examples that could fall under this category.[1446] The CJEU rejected Germany's justification that it is trying to prevent the 'double counting of costs'.[1447] Among the reasons for rejecting this was that, under the Germany-Portugal tax treaty, Portugal applied the 'offsetting method'.[1448] The other reason was the existence of the mutual assistance directive, which provided for the exchange of information.[1449]

On the first point (regarding the role of the credit method), the explanation as to why the concern of the double deduction of costs is resolved under the credit method was ambiguous. The wording of the judgment first calls attention to the fact that, under the credit method, the taxpayer will be 'taxed in Portugal on all of its income, including income from activities pursued in Germany, where that income is also taxed', but then proceeded to focus on another aspect; namely, it highlighted that the state of residence will be in a position to 'check the operating expenses that have been taken into account in calculating the tax paid in the second State'.[1450] This is presumably based on the reporting obligation under the credit method, stemming from the fact that a taxpayer declares its worldwide income to the state of residence. Thus, its reasoning seemed motivated by the risk that taxpayers could double deduct without being detected. The credit method could reduce this risk by equipping the state of residence with the relevant information so that it could adjust its taxation accordingly, where needed.

In the 2016 *Brisal and KBC Finance Ireland* judgment,[1451] the question arose again. Both the Opinion of the AG and the CJEU decision agreed that this double-deduction issue was not insurmountable, and thus it was unlikely that this justification could be relied upon. Unfortunately, Portugal's submissions did not, according to the CJEU, sufficiently clarify how this potential risk would manifest itself. It therefore did 'not make it possible for the Court to assess the scope of that argument'.[1452] Nevertheless, the AG further elaborated on this aspect:

arising from their activities in that State are taken into account is consistent with the principle of territoriality enshrined in international tax law and recognised by Community law (*see*, to that effect, *Futura Participations and Singer*, paragraphs 21 and 22)').

1446. *Id.*, at para. 25.
1447. *Id.*, at para. 33.
1448. *Id.*, at paras 34–35.
1449. *Id.*, at para. 36.
1450. *Id.*, at paras 34–35 ('Firstly, it should be noted that the Agreement between the Federal Republic of Germany and the Portuguese Republic for the prevention of double taxation in the field of income and wealth taxes of 15 July 1980 applies what is known as the offsetting method' and 'It follows that a Portuguese company is taxed in Portugal on all of its income, including income from activities pursued in Germany, where that income is also taxed. Double taxation is avoided through deduction in the first State of an amount equal to the tax paid in the second State. Such a mechanism is appropriate for preventing the double counting of costs since, where it is applied by the first State, that State can check the operating expenses that have been taken into account in calculating the tax paid in the second State').
1451. CJEU, Case C-18/15, *Brisal and KBC Finance Ireland*, 13 Jul. 2016, ECLI:EU:C:2016:549.
1452. *Id.*, at para. 38 ('Secondly, as regards the desire to prevent double deduction of business expenses, which may be linked to the fight against tax evasion, suffice it to state that, by merely relying on, without further clarification, the potential risk that the expenses in question may be deducted a second time in the State of residence of the service provider, without establishing how that risk was not prevented by the implementation of Council Directive 77/799/EEC of 19 December 1977 concerning mutual assistance by the competent

'b) Double deduction of operating costs

64. Nor can any justification arise out of the fact that in imposing a withholding tax Member States must prevent operating costs from being deducted twice, as the Portuguese Government in particular submitted.

65. Regardless of whether such a justification would in principle have to be recognised, it is in any event obvious that operating costs could always be deducted twice if two Member States – that is, the source State and the State of residence – taxed the income in question.[47],[1453]

Moreover, in a footnote, the AG added:

'47 For that reason, the Court's statements in its judgment in *Centro Equestre da Lezíria Grande* (C345/04, EU:C:2007:96, paragraphs 33 to 36), are liable to misunderstanding.'[1454]

Furthermore, although the Portuguese government did not submit sufficient information about the tax treaty provisions,[1455] based on its submission that Article 11 on interest of the Ireland-Portugal DTC applied in the case,[1456] it is not a far step to the credit method (if it is assumed that this part of the tax treaty is based on the OECD Model). The Opinion of the AG explains that, under tax treaties based on the OECD Model, an excessive taxation of interest payments may result from the fact that the state of residence taxes on a net basis under either Article 23B or Article 23A(2) and the state of source taxes on a gross basis. For this reason, the OECD Commentary itself underlines that many states choose to forego the taxation of interest at source, so as not to hamper cross-border financing. Crucially, according to the explanation of the AG, nothing under the OECD Model obliges the state of source to tax on a gross amount, which disallows all deductions of operating costs, nor to tax at all. In fact, it is clear that the Model 'merely sets a maximum amount as regards the outcome of the tax, and does not give the source State any instructions as regards taxation'.[1457] On the basis of the AG's description, it is evident that both states may tax a net figure, allowing for the deduction of costs – indeed, the state of residence tends to do so and the state of source may opt to do so.

On the aforementioned second point of *Centro Equestre da Lezíria Grande* (i.e., the CJEU's further clarification of the meaning of economically connected operating expenses), on the one hand, its holding could be tantamount to the CJEU providing

authorities of the Member States in the field of direct taxation and taxation of insurance premiums (OJ 1977 L 336, p. 15), as amended by Council Directive 2004/106/EC of 16 November 2004 (OJ 2004 L 359, p. 30), in force at the time of the facts at issue in the main proceedings, the Portuguese Republic does not make it possible for the Court to assess the scope of that argument (see, to that effect, judgment of 24 February 2015 in *Grünewald*, C559/13, EU:C:2015:109, paragraph 52)').

1453. Opinion of AG Kokott in Case C-18/15, *Brisal and KBC Finance Ireland*, 17 Mar. 2016, ECLI:EU:C:2016:182, at paras 64–65.

1454. *Id.*, at para. 65 n.47.

1455. *Id.*, at para. 60.

1456. CJEU, Case C-18/15, *Brisal and KBC Finance Ireland*, 13 Jul. 2016, ECLI:EU:C:2016:549, at para. 6.

1457. Opinion of AG Kokott in Case C-18/15, *Brisal and KBC Finance Ireland*, 17 Mar. 2016, ECLI:EU:C:2016:182, at paras 59–63.

expense rules for MSs, since it seemed to specify precisely which expenses (e.g., travel expenses) should be 'operating expenses'. On the other hand, it could be seen as merely exemplifying what is intended by the requirement of a direct link between the expenses and the taxable income. One could argue that the CJEU should not directly declare certain expenses to be operating expenses, but rather orient this determination based solely on a non-discrimination reasoning. That is, the CJEU should specify that, where the expenses in question would be deemed operating expenses if a resident taxpayer incurred them, they should be allowed as a 'directly connected' operating expense if a non-resident incurred them. This point arises again below in the discussions of, especially, the *J.B.G.T. Miljoen & others*[1458] case.

While the above cases firmly established the rule that non-residents have the right to deduct directly economically connected expenses, some questions remained open, such as precisely what those expenses are. Also, at this point in the development of the CJEU's case law, MSs had been receiving what seemed to be mixed messages regarding the permissibility of a WHT.

First, regarding WHTs, as seen above in the 'neutralization' line of case law,[1459] as well as other cases,[1460] there was a series of decisions regarding dividends in which WHTs at source were successfully challenged. Yet, in *Gerritse*, the CJEU was careful *not* to exclude the option for MSs to apply different methods of taxation to non-residents, so long as it did not result in higher taxation of non-residents as compared to residents.[1461] In *Scorpio*, the CJEU ruled more explicitly on the procedures, holding that a WHT at source is (an obstacle but) a justified and proportionate means to tax non-residents.[1462] Then, in a subsequent 2008 case, referred to as *Truck Center*,[1463] the CJEU ruled that Belgium could require a WHT to be retained on outgoing interest payments, paid from a Belgium company to a Luxembourg company (but with quite different reasoning[1464] than in the *Scorpio* case and without any reference to *Gerritse*

1458. CJEU, Joined Cases C-10/14, C-14/14 and C-17/14, *J. B. G. T. Miljoen, X, and Société Générale SA*, 17 Sep. 2015, ECLI:EU:C:2015:608 (decided on the basis of the free movement of capital).
1459. *See supra* note 1387.
1460. *See*, e.g., CJEU, Case C-303/07, *Aberdeen Property Fininvest Alpha*, 18 Jun. 2009, ECLI:EU:C:2009:377; CJEU, Case C-521/07, *Commission v. Netherlands*, 11 Jun. 2009, ECLI:EU:C:2009:360.
1461. *See supra* note 1417.
1462. *See supra* note 1432, note 1433 and note 1434.
1463. CJEU, Case C-282/07, *Truck Center*, 22 Dec. 2008, ECLI:EU:C:2008:762 (decided on the basis of the freedom of establishment and the free movement of capital).
1464. *Id.*, at paras 41–48 (the CJEU offered various reasons why residents and non-residents were not comparable in this case. 'Firstly, when both the company paying the interest and the company receiving that interest are resident in Belgium, the position of the Belgian State is different to that in which it finds itself when a company resident in Belgium pays interest to a non-resident company, because, in the first case, the Belgian State acts in its capacity as the State of residence of the companies concerned, while, in the second case, it acts in its capacity as the State in which the interest originates.' 'Secondly, the payment of interest by one resident company to another resident company and the payment of interest by a resident company to a non-resident company give rise to two distinct charges which rest on separate legal bases.' 'Finally, those different taxation arrangements reflect the difference in the situations in which those companies find themselves with regard to recovery of the tax.' On this point, 'While resident recipient companies are directly subject to the supervision of the Belgian tax authorities, which can ensure compulsory recovery of taxes, that is not the case

and *Scorpio*). In a 2012 case, *X NV*,[1465] a WHT obligation for payments made from a football club in the Netherlands to a service provider in the UK was upheld and, for essentially the same reasons as in *Scorpio*, it was an obstacle but justified and proportionate.

One reoccurring justification for different methods of taxation, such as WHTs at source, for non-residents was 'the need to ensure the effective collection of income tax'. One ongoing question was whether the expansion of legal instruments in the EU on mutual assistance in the exchange of tax information and recovery of tax claims would weaken this justification. In the *Scorpio* case, the CJEU expressly noted that, at the time, since the facts date back to before 1993, there was no mutual assistance directive in the EU.[1466] And, its *absence* was part of the reason for justifying *procedural* differences in the taxation of non-residents (*Scorpio*). On the other hand, its *existence* was part of the reason for rejecting a *substantive* difference in the taxation of non-residents (*Centro Equestre da Lezíria Grande*).[1467] Given the continuing expansion of the EU law instruments on this topic, this issue became more relevant. The *X NV* case clarified that the existence, and broader scope, of the Directives on mutual assistance[1468] did not render this justification for WHTs obsolete.[1469] Basically, the

with regard to non-resident recipient companies inasmuch as, in their case, recovery of the tax requires the assistance of the tax authorities of the other Member State') and at para. 49 (in addition to the lack of comparability, no disadvantageous treatment could be found because, first, resident companies also paid some tax upfront since they were obliged to make 'advance payments of corporation tax' and, second, non-resident companies were not subject to higher taxation, since 'the amount of withholding tax deducted from the interest paid to a non-resident company is significantly lower than the corporation tax charged on the income of resident companies which receive interest').

1465. CJEU, Case C-498/10, *X NV*, 18 Oct. 2012, ECLI:EU:C:2012:635.

1466. CJEU, Case C-290/04, *FKP Scorpio Konzertproduktionen*, 3 Oct. 2006, ECLI:EU:C:2006:630, at para. 36.

1467. CJEU, Case C-345/04, *Centro Equestre da Lezíria Grande*, 15 Feb. 2007, ECLI:EU:C:2007:96, at para. 36 ('[...] That mechanism for cooperation between the competent national authorities also makes it possible to prevent any double counting of costs. Similarly, Council Directive 77/799/EEC of 19 December 1977 concerning mutual assistance by the competent authorities of the Member States in the field of direct taxation (OJ 1977 L 336, p. 15) also contributes to the realisation of that objective by providing for the exchange of information between the tax authorities concerned') and para. 37 ('A restriction on the freedom to provide services cannot therefore be justified where it arises from national legislation which makes repayment of tax deducted at source on the income received in the Member State concerned by a taxpayer with restricted tax liability subject to the condition that the operating expenses directly connected to that income are greater than half of that income. It must therefore be concluded that Article 59 of the EC Treaty precludes such legislation').

1468. CJEU, Case C-498/10, *X NV*, 18 Oct. 2012, ECLI:EU:C:2012:635 (citing the mutual assistance directives in force at the time, namely the 'mutual assistance in the recovery of taxes presented by Council Directive 76/308/EEC of 15 March 1976 on mutual assistance for the recovery of claims relating to certain levies, duties, taxes and other measures, as amended by Council Directive 2001/44/EC of 15 June 2001').

1469. *Id.*, at para. 53 ('In the light of the foregoing, the answer to the second and third questions is that, in so far as the restriction on the freedom to provide services arising from national legislation, such as that at issue in the main proceedings, results from the obligation to withhold tax at source, in that it entails an additional administrative burden and related liability risks, that restriction can be justified by the need to ensure the effective collection of tax and does not go beyond what is necessary to achieve that purpose, even in the light of the opportunities for mutual assistance in the recovery of taxes presented by Directive 76/308').

CJEU and AG weighed up the pros and cons of the alternative: if a MS must renounce its WHT, in its place the MS would need to collect the tax directly from the non-resident, e.g., by obliging the non-resident to file a form. This comes with its own administrative burdens and, thus, is not necessarily an easier or less restrictive way to tax a non-resident.[1470]

From the above, as regards the compatibility of a WHT levied on non-residents, some patterns can be detected. Where the CJEU struck down WHTs, the cases involved dividends paid to non-resident shareholders and were usually viewed in connection with the relief for (economic) double taxation on dividends paid to resident shareholders. Viewed from this perspective, there was a difference in treatment between the non-resident shareholders and resident shareholders. In these cases, relief mechanisms existed so that resident shareholders would not ultimately be subject to further taxation or would benefit from reduced taxation. The CJEU continuously reasoned that if a MS decides that *resident* shareholders should *not* be subject to further taxation on the grounds that dividends are already taxed at the level of the distributing entity, then this MS should extend the same to a *non-resident* shareholder since those dividends were also taxed at the level of the distributing entity; instead, the MS was doing the opposite, namely *itself* creating an extra layer of taxation on that non-resident with a WHT on the dividends.[1471] If it does so, then it must either extend its relief (e.g., in the case of indirect credits) or otherwise ensure that this is 'neutralized' by the other MS (e.g., in the case of direct credits).

By comparison, where the CJEU upheld WHTs, the payments were, for example, remuneration for services or interest on debt. Whether the recipient of these payments was a resident or a non-resident, both would be ultimately taxed on the income received.[1472] Generally, unlike dividends which are already taxed at the level of the payer, these payments are deducted from the tax base of the payer and then taxed in the hands of the recipient. Thus, a difference of treatment did not stem from the overall taxation of residents versus non-residents, but instead boiled down to a different procedure or method of collecting the income tax. In these cases, the CJEU decided, for

1470. *Id.*, at para. 50 (acknowledging that this could 'lead to a serious burden on the foreign service provider in that he would have to submit a tax return in a foreign language and to familiarise himself with a tax system in a Member State other than that in which he is established') and at para. 52 ('In the light of all of those considerations, it must be held, as the Advocate General has observed in point 59 of her Opinion, that the collection of the tax directly from the non-resident service provider would not necessarily constitute a less severe means than deduction at source').

1471. *See*, e.g., CJEU, Joined Cases C-10/14, C-14/14 and C-17/14, *J. B. G. T. Miljoen, X, and Société Générale SA*, 17 Sep. 2015, ECLI:EU:C:2015:608, at paras 67–69.

1472. CJEU, Case C-575/17, *Sofina*, 22 Nov. 2018, ECLI:EU:C:2018:943, at para. 51 (this point was clarified in the 2018 *Sofina* case: 'Although the Court held, in paragraph 41 of the judgment of 22 December 2008, *Truck Center* (C282/07, EU:C:2008:762), that a difference in treatment consisting in the application of different taxation arrangements on the basis of the place of residence of the taxable person relates to situations which are not objectively comparable, it nevertheless made clear, in paragraphs 43 and 44 of that judgment, that the income at issue in the case which gave rise to that judgment was, in any event, subject to tax irrespective of whether it was received by a resident or non-resident taxable person').

different reasons (that did not always appear consistent),[1473] that generally speaking a WHT at source - albeit a different method with certain inconveniences - is an appropriate method for levying income tax on non-residents. While the WHT *as a method* was accepted in certain cases, the 'gross' nature of the WHT was challenged, and this now returns to the question of deductible expenses.

Regarding the question as to precisely which expenses MSs must consider - in order to remedy the different treatment that can stem from the fact that non-residents are taxed on a gross basis, without the deduction of expenses, whereas residents are taxed on a net basis, with the deduction of expenses - two points can be distilled from the *Gerritse* decision. First, at a minimum, expenses directly connected with earning the taxable income in the MS must be deductible for non-residents. Second, though the methods may differ, this should not lead to higher taxation on non-residents than on residents. In order to double-check this, it is for the MS to calculate and compare the respective burdens. Both points gave rise to further questions.

As regards the first point (the meaning of directly connected expenses), shortly after, in the *Conijn* case, the question arose as to whether a non-resident in Germany can deduct expenses for hiring professional tax advice to file a tax return in Germany in the same way as residents. This expense is not, strictly speaking, related to the *generation* of income in Germany, but rather related to the subsequent payment of taxes on that income. Moreover, under German tax law, this does not fall under the provisions for business expenses, but under the provisions for 'special' expenses. Nevertheless, the CJEU considered the *Gerritse* rule applicable. One reason was that the non-resident's duty to pay taxes is directly connected to the carrying on of business in Germany that generated taxable income there. The underlying idea seemed to be that, as soon as a non-resident generates income that is taxable in Germany, it is in a comparable position to residents in that they are both legally obliged to pay taxes in Germany. In particular, since the German government explained that the purpose of allowing residents to deduct expenses incurred for tax advice was related to the complexity of the German tax laws, the CJEU reasoned that non-residents are equally faced with the complexity of those laws once they become taxable in Germany, and thus are comparable in that respect. In the *Centro Equestre da Lezíria Grande* case, in further clarifying the meaning of 'direct connection', the CJEU decided that this must include all costs 'inextricably linked to those services', offering the examples of 'travel and accommodation costs', irrespective of 'the place and time at which the costs were incurred'. So if the Portuguese company prepaid all of its hotels and flights in Portugal before arriving in Germany to perform its services, this does not prejudice the classification of these travel and accommodation costs as directly connected.[1474]

1473. *See*, e.g., *supra* note 1464 (in *Truck Center*, the CJEU reasoned at the level of comparability, holding that residents and non-residents were not comparable as regards the methods that a given MS had at its disposal to collect tax from them) and *compare supra* note 1462 and note 1465 (in other cases, e.g., *Scorpio* and *X NV*, the CJEU reasoned at the justification level that, although residents and non-residents were comparable, a withholding tax was justified by the need to ensure the effective collection of tax and was a proportionate means to do so).

1474. CJEU, Case C-345/04, *Centro Equestre da Lezíria Grande*, 15 Feb. 2007, ECLI:EU:C:2007:96, at para. 25.

As regards the relationship between the two points (directly connected expenses and calculating whether there is different treatment), some cases from 2015 and 2016 highlighted the difficulties. The 2015 *J.B.G.T. Miljoen & others* case[1475] was discussed under the 'neutralization' line of case law and is also very relevant for deductible expenses. In this case, dividends were distributed from the Netherlands to three different shareholders, namely two individuals, Mr Miljoen and X, resident in Belgium and a company, Société Générale SA, resident in France, all of which held non-controlling shareholdings. In the Netherlands, on the basis of domestic law in combination with the limits under the tax treaties, a 'final' WHT of 15% of the gross amount was levied.[1476] For residents, a WHT was also levied but was not 'final' and any excess over the ultimate income tax due could be reimbursed.[1477] A key difference, according to the CJEU, revolved around the finality of the tax.[1478] Moreover, as for the company, Société Générale SA, very precise questions were asked regarding deductible expenses. The company was normally in a position to credit the WHT in full in France,[1479] but in 2008 the company suffered losses and therefore could not.[1480] In a loss situation, without any corporation taxes in France against which the WHT could be credited, the company argued that the Netherlands should reimburse it, just like for residents.

In order to assess whether these tax law provisions in the Netherlands were compatible with the free movement of capital, the national court was instructed to calculate the effective tax burden to test whether the non-residents were faced with a heavier tax burden:

> '[F]or the purposes of comparing the tax burden of resident companies and that of non-resident companies, the referring court seeks guidance on whether account should be taken of all expenses which are economically linked to the shares from which the dividends arise'[1481] or whether specific expenses should be taken into account.

To this end, three specific expenses were mentioned, namely: (1) 'the dividend included in the purchase price of the shares', (2) 'the possible financing charges resulting from ownership of the shares concerned', or (3) as proposed by Société Générale SA, 'in the case of hedging, ... also the negative effects of rates and transactions on shareholdings and positions other than those from which the dividends arise, but with which there is nonetheless a connection'.[1482]

1475. CJEU, Joined Cases C-10/14, C-14/14 and C-17/14, *J. B. G. T. Miljoen, X, and Société Générale SA*, 17 Sep. 2015, ECLI:EU:C:2015:608 (decided on the basis of the free movement of capital).
1476. *Id.*, at paras 19–35.
1477. *Id.*, at paras 45–47.
1478. *Id.*, at paras 44–47.
1479. *Id.*, at para. 33.
1480. *Id.*, at para. 34.
1481. *Id.*, at para. 55.
1482. *Id.*, at para. 56.

The CJEU reiterated its *Gerritse* rule[1483] and then stated how this rule applies in the specific case of dividends,[1484] which is that 'only expenses which are *directly* linked to the *actual payment* of the dividends must be taken into account'[1485] (emphasis added). Of the three expenses identified as candidates, none had such a link: (1) the deduction of a dividend included in the purchase price concerns the pricing of shares (not the actual payment), (2) financing costs concern the ownership of shares (not the actual payment),[1486] and (3) hedging-related costs were completely overlooked by the CJEU, but based on its reasoning it is safe to assume that hedging-related costs concern the management of risk, for example (not the actual payment). Indeed, there seem to be few, if any, expenses linked solely to the *actual payment* of the dividends. Perhaps, though very speculatively, this could include payment fees, if any, or custody fees, if any.

As can be seen, the approach of the CJEU regarding deductible expenses in connection with dividends is narrow so as to effectively leave the gross amount of the dividends intact. Consequently, it hardly changes anything for non-residents in that respect.

As mentioned above (at *supra* note 1458), to some extent, this seems to amount to the CJEU dictating aspects of the tax base or expense rules on behalf of MSs. Rather than pronouncing itself on specific expenses, if the fundamental freedoms require non-discrimination, then one guiding principle for what expenses should be deductible for non-residents would be whatever expenses are considered 'directly linked' to dividends for residents.[1487] On the other hand, it can be said that the CJEU was merely responding to the questions posed to it. Moreover, the CJEU indicates that this is a minimum – that is, MSs are *obliged* to allow deductions for *at least* those expenses that are directly connected, but of course MSs can *choose* to allow additional expenses to be

1483. *Id.*, at para. 57.
1484. *Id.*, at para. 58.
1485. *Id.*, at para. 59.
1486. *Id.*, at para. 60.
1487. More specifically, *see* Opinion of AG Wathelet in Case C-575/17, *Sofina*, 7 Aug. 2018, ECLI:EU:C:2018:650, at para. 51 (it seems to be a dual condition: 'However, it is for the national court to verify whether the expenses covered by the claim for deduction are expenses which are deductible for resident companies in receipt of nationally sourced dividends (16) and are *directly related* to the actual receipt of the income at issue in the main proceedings. (17)') and at para. 55 (also note that the deductible expenses issue is technically distinct from the overall tax burden issue. The deductible expenses that are directly linked to the income in question should be allowed regardless. 'In that situation, such a restriction on the free movement of capital "cannot be justified by the fact that [non-residents] are subject to a tax rate which is lower than the rate for [residents]". (21) There is therefore no need to compare the actual tax burden on dividends paid to residents and that on dividends paid to non-residents since even though the taxation rate for non-residents is lower than for residents, the amount of deductible expenses to which residents are entitled is uncertain and there is nothing to suggest that it would be equal to the difference resulting from the taxation of residents compared with the taxation of non-residents.' On this point, *see also* '13 July 2016, *Brisal and KBC Finance Ireland* (C18/15, EU:C:2016:549, paragraph 33)' and the Opinion of Advocate General Kokott on that case); Opinion of AG Kokott in Case C-18/15, *Brisal and KBC Finance Ireland*, 17 Mar. 2016, ECLI:EU:C:2016:182.

deducted.[1488] Nevertheless, by virtue of essentially finding little to no expenses to be directly connected to dividends, the outcome of this case does little to advance the prospects of 'neutralization'.

In 2016, the *Brisal and KBC Finance Ireland* decision[1489] seemed to follow a more principled route - by that, meaning a route guided more explicitly by a principle of non-discrimination. First, the CJEU held, again, that a WHT on non-residents (when none is withheld on residents) is not an infringement as long as it 'is justified by an overriding reason in the general interest and does not go beyond what is necessary to attain the objective pursued'.[1490] Second, non-residents must be given the opportunity to deduct expenses from the interest income in question in the same way as residents.[1491] Third, when asked more precisely about whether the deductible expenses for non-residents could simply be estimated based on an average interest rate, such as the Euro Interbank Offered Rate or the London Interbank Offered Rate,[1492] the CJEU held that the deductible expenses should be based on those actually incurred[1493] and on what residents are allowed to deduct.[1494]

The CJEU, in *Pensioenfonds Metaal en Techniek*,[1495] also left it to the domestic court to determine which expenses should be deductible. The CJEU was asked whether Swedish laws that establish different ways of taxing resident pension funds as compared to non-resident pension funds are discriminatory in light of the free movement of capital. When non-resident pension funds (in this case, in the Netherlands) received dividends from Swedish companies, a WHT of 30% - reduced to 15% under the Netherlands-Sweden tax treaty - was levied on the gross amount. By contrast, resident pension funds were taxed on a notional yield at the rate of 15%, irrespective of any distribution of dividends.[1496] One key element of the alleged different treatment revolved around deductions from the tax base, namely that the laws allowed the deduction of financial liabilities from the tax base for resident pensions funds, but did not allow the same deductions from dividends paid to non-resident pension funds.[1497] The CJEU accepted Sweden's different approach to taxing resident

1488. To this effect, *see* CJEU, Case C-290/04, *FKP Scorpio Konzertproduktionen*, 3 Oct. 2006, ECLI:EU:C:2006:630, at para. 51 ('While the expenses which the provider of services has reported to his debtor must be deducted in the procedure for the retention of tax at source, Articles 59 and 60 of the EEC Treaty do not preclude the taking into account if appropriate of expenses that are not directly linked, within the meaning of the *Gerritse* line of case-law, to the economic activity that generated the taxable income, in a subsequent refund procedure') and CJEU, Case C-345/04, *Centro Equestre da Lezíria Grande*, 15 Feb. 2007, ECLI:EU:C:2007:96, at para. 24 ('In that connection, Community law does not preclude a Member State from going further, by allowing costs that do not have such a connection to be taken into account (see, to that effect, *FKP Scorpio Konzertproduktionen*, paragraphs 50 to 52)').

1489. CJEU, Case C-18/15, *Brisal and KBC Finance Ireland*, 13 Jul. 2016, ECLI:EU:C:2016:549.

1490. *Id.*, at para. 55.

1491. *Id.*

1492. CJEU, Case C-18/15, *Brisal and KBC Finance Ireland*, 13 Jul. 2016, ECLI:EU:C:2016:549, at para. 16.

1493. *Id.*, at para. 54.

1494. *Id.*, at para. 45 and para. 53.

1495. CJEU, Case C-252/14, *Pensioenfonds Metaal en Techniek*, 2 Jun. 2016, ECLI:EU:C:2016:402.

1496. *Id.*, at para. 31.

1497. *Id.*, at para. 32.

pension funds in general, but on the specific point of the deductibility of expenses, the CJEU held that the free movement of capital 'precludes non-resident pension funds being prevented from taking into account any professional expenses directly linked to the receipt of dividends, where the calculation method for the tax base of resident pension funds allows them to be taken into account, that being a matter for the referring court to determine'.[1498]

Another challenge that became particularly acute in *Pensioenfonds Metaal en Techniek*, after also arising in *J.B.G.T. Miljoen & others*, was how exactly to compare the effective tax burden of residents and non-residents.[1499] Indeed, while the CJEU has

1498. *Id.*, at para. 66.

1499. For another case that also demonstrates the difficulties, *see*, e.g., CJEU, Case C-105/08, *Commission v. Portugal*, 17 Jun. 2010, ECLI:EU:C:2010:345 (this case offers some precise ideas as to how gross taxation can be worse than net taxation, in particular for financial institutions. In this case, the Commission brought an infringement procedure against Portugal regarding its different tax treatment of non-residents as compared to residents on interest income. In the case of non-residents, Portugal levied a gross withholding tax at a flat rate of 20% (or more precisely, between 10% and 20% when taking into account DTCs). In the case of residents, Portugal assessed their net profits, taxed at a rate of 25%. The Commission needed to prove that non-residents were taxed in a more burdensome way, but ultimately failed in its burden of proof to bring forward sufficient evidence to support its arguments. Nevertheless, the arguments underline some key problems that can arise in the gross taxation of non-residents: '13 By providing for a withholding tax of between 10% and 20% on the gross amount of interest obtained in Portugal, the legislation at issue discourages any foreign credit institution from offering its services in Portugal unless its profit margin for the transactions concerned is significantly higher than the rate of withholding tax. However, in the light of the extremely competitive nature of the international financial markets, of the context created by the existence of a common currency in the euro zone, and of the similar levels of interest rates in most Member States, it is very unlikely that a foreign financial institution would be able to achieve a profit margin greater than 10%. Furthermore, in order to restore equality with resident financial institutions, which are taxed at 25% on their net income, non-resident financial institutions would have to achieve profit margins four times higher than those obtained by resident financial institutions in their respective activities pursued in Portugal. 14 [...] It follows from the Court's case-law, and in particular from Case C- 234/01 *Gerritse* [2003] ECR I5933, paragraph 27, and Case C-345/04 *Centro Equestre da Lezíria Grande* [2007] ECR I1425, paragraph 24, that, with regard to operating expenses which have a direct connection to the activity, pursued by a non-resident in a Member State, which generated taxable income in that country, residents and non-residents are placed in a comparable situation. Accordingly, those expenses must, as a rule, be taken into account in that country since residents are taxed there on their net income, that is, after the deduction of such expenses. According to the judgment in *Hollmann* (paragraphs 50 and 51), the principle of nondiscrimination requires, moreover, that, where the same tax is applied to residents and non-residents, the income of non-residents should not be taxed at a higher rate than that applied to residents' income and that the tax base should not be broader than that provided for residents. Non-resident financial institutions should therefore, at the very least, be allowed to deduct the amount of the interest which they have had to pay to third parties in order to obtain the capital used in the credit transactions completed in Portugal.' However, despite the problems, it is not so easy to find a solution, as this paragraph demonstrates: '18 The Commission acknowledges that it is not possible to ascertain which capital obtained from third parties has been used specifically by a legal entity in order to finance individual credit transactions completed in a given State. It submits, however, that it is not impossible to calculate the amounts of net income obtained by that entity for the purposes of taxation in the source State. In the present case, the Portuguese Republic would simply need to allow the taxpayer to deduct from the amount of gross income obtained within the territory of that Member State an amount corresponding to the average costs which are generally borne by that taxpayer in order to obtain similar income

accepted different approaches to the taxation of non-residents (such as a WHT at source), it holds the MS responsible for ensuring that this does not lead to a heavier burden of taxation on non-residents. This proves difficult in practice.

In the *J.B.G.T. Miljoen & others* case, the Netherlands was mostly concerned about this 'standard of comparison' for the effective tax burden. One factor that rendered the comparison (between natural persons who were residents and those who were non-residents) challenging in this case was that residents were taxed on an entirely different tax basis, namely on a notional amount of investment income (based on 4 % of the average value of the shares held)[1500] regardless of any actual distribution. In Sweden, in the *Pensioenfonds Metaal en Techniek* case, the situation was similar regarding the taxation of resident pension funds as compared to non-resident pension funds. While non-resident pension funds paid a WHT on the amount of an *actual* distribution, resident pension funds paid a 'capital yield tax' on 'a notional yield' (based on 'the average government bond yield') 'taxed at the rate of 15 %'.[1501] Yet faced with similar systems, the CJEU nevertheless came to different conclusions in the two cases.[1502] While the CJEU held that the Netherlands is responsible for making the comparison of the effective tax burdens between residents and non-residents in order to determine the EU-law-compatibility of its legislation, the CJEU held that the Swedish legislation was 'justified by the difference in situation of these two categories of taxpayers',[1503] residents and non-residents, 'in the light of the aim pursued by the national legislation, and of its purpose and content too'.[1504]

It is unclear precisely what made the difference, but one possibility is the emphasis on the purpose of the legislation. It seems that, more than the Netherlands, the Swedish government underlined the purpose and policy objectives of its legislation, a purpose which could only be achieved for residents.[1505] Since the CJEU often assesses

---

in the State of residence. In order to prevent nonresident financial institutions from deducting average costs which might be regarded as excessive by the source Member State, that latter State could limit the deduction of costs to a maximum amount fixed, for example, on the basis of the average costs borne by resident banks for similar transactions. In any event, the difficulty of attributing particular costs to certain specific income does not constitute valid justification for taxing the gross income of nonresidents in the source State or for applying to such income an actual tax burden which is higher than that levied on the similar income received by resident taxpayers'). *See also* Opinion of AG Kokott in Case C-18/15, *Brisal and KBC Finance Ireland*, 17 Mar. 2016, ECLI:EU:C:2016:182, at para. 2 (referring to Case C105/08 and the Commission's burden of proof).

1500. CJEU, Joined Cases C-10/14, C-14/14 and C-17/14, *J. B. G. T. Miljoen, X, and Société Générale SA*, 17 Sep. 2015, ECLI:EU:C:2015:608, at para. 46.

1501. More precisely, for a description of the two-step calculation, *see* CJEU, Case C-252/14, *Pensioenfonds Metaal en Techniek*, 2 Jun. 2016, ECLI:EU:C:2016:402, at para. 31.

1502. For a criticism of this point, *see*, e.g., Peter J. Wattel, *Commentary on Chapter 12: Anathema to the Internal Market, in European Tax Integration: Law, Policy and Politics* Section 5 (Pasquale Pistone ed., IBFD 2018) ('Anathema to the internal market (3) – Inconsistency and contradiction').

1503. CJEU, Case C-252/14, *Pensioenfonds Metaal en Techniek*, 2 Jun. 2016, ECLI:EU:C:2016:402, at para. 64.

1504. *Id.*, at para. 63.

1505. *Id.*, at paras 53–54, 37 (the purpose was rather vaguely expressed as 'neutral taxation independent of the economic climate surrounding various kinds of assets and all of the kinds of pension products concerned' (para. 53) and 'to achieve a uniform taxation of direct and

comparability in light of the purpose of the legislation in question,[1506] perhaps MSs' pleading strategy could be to more clearly articulate the tax policy objectives underlying their legislation, as Sweden did. That said, this is merely speculative. Given the similarities of the two national legislations, yet the difference in the decisions of the CJEU, future cases will have to shed further light on this. In any case, it goes beyond the scope of study here; rather, the main aim was to give concrete form to some of the difficulties in comparing the effective tax burden.

From this, some general remarks can be made. In theory, the CJEU leaves intact a MS's freedom to design its taxation system for its residents. This is a treasured area of sovereignty as numerous policy considerations (economic, political, social, etc.) play a role in designing how best to tax a certain type of income or wealth. Technically, this case law addresses the taxation of non-residents and not that of the MS's residents. Yet, under this case law, certain ways in which a MS would like to tax its own residents may become unviable or seriously constrained in practice. This is because it is possible that certain ways of taxing residents, such as the Netherlands' or Sweden's taxation of a notional yield of all assets, cannot feasibly, or legally (e.g., taking into account tax treaty obligations), be extended to non-residents. If so, this would necessarily entail a different approach for non-residents. Under this case law, different approaches to the taxation of non-residents may be compatible with EU law, as long as they do not result in higher taxation of non-residents. However, the tax base could be so different as to make it impracticable to precisely compare the ultimate burden. It becomes seemingly impossible to ensure that the burden will, in no cases, be higher.[1507] If so, consequently, taxation that may be ideal for residents, for various policy reasons, becomes

indirect savings and level out taxation over time' (para. 37). One possible effect of this legislation is that the choice of assets that pension funds invest in should be less distorted by taxation. If assets are taxed based on the amount of distributions or income streams, it is more likely that the selection of assets will be based on how often and how much a given asset pays out income to its investors. By taxing all assets, regardless of any distributions, on the basis of a notional income approximated to be at a risk-free rate so that the level of taxation is levelled out over time, it may support more long-term thinking in the selection of assets to invest in. Crucially, the design of the legislation corresponded to its objective: *see*, e.g., 'In order to achieve such an objective, all the assets of a resident pension fund are subject to yearly lump sum taxation, reflecting the yield of those assets, irrespective of the receipt of income generated by those assets, in particular the receipt of dividends' (para. 54). Arguably, this could be achieved only in the case of residents. The reason is that Sweden can only tax its own residents on all assets, and would have no right to tax non-residents on their assets held worldwide, but could only tax non-residents on their assets in Sweden, as confirmed in tax treaties).

1506. *See* especially, e.g., the 'equivalence' line of case law, discussed in Section 4.2.3. and the 'neutralization' line of case law, discussed in Section 4.2.5.

1507. CJEU, Case C-252/14, *Pensioenfonds Metaal en Techniek*, 2 Jun. 2016, ECLI:EU:C:2016:402, at para. 38 (this seems to be what the CJEU requires, namely an assessment whether it *ever* results in a higher burden, not an assessment whether it *on average* results in a higher burden: 'Moreover, the Court has already held that, regarding the freedom of establishment, even if a Member State's tax system is favourable to non-resident companies more often than not, that does not prevent it leading, where that system proves disadvantageous for those companies, to an inequality of treatment in relation to resident taxpayers and thus creating a hindrance to the freedom of establishment (*see*, to that effect, judgments of 14 December 2000 in *AMID*, C141/99, EU:C:2000:696, paragraph 27, and 22 March 2007 in *Talotta*, C383/05, EU:C:2007:181, paragraph 31). Similarly, the Court has previously held that the fact that the

contingent upon two factors: (1) whether this same approach is legally or practically feasible for non-residents and (2) whether the MS's system ever leads to a higher taxation of a non-resident. This is yet another demonstration of the limits of what the CJEU can do and the resulting indirect constraints that may be placed on MSs' tax design. There may be strong underlying policy considerations, but the CJEU cannot set MSs' tax policy and must restrain itself to the EU law - in these cases essentially non-discrimination - considerations. If a given approach cannot be extended to cross-border cases, then it increases the difficulty for a MS to retain that approach for its own residents, thus constraining its domestic tax policy options. MSs may have no choice but to make amendments in such cases, either to bring the taxation of their own residents more in line with that of non-residents or vice versa. A similar theme arises in the *Manninen* or ill-fated imputation method line of case law (discussed below in Section 4.2.8.). Interestingly, in the Swedish case, the comparability test *in light of the purpose of the legislation* acted, it seems, as a 'back door' way for policy considerations to play a role in the reasoning of the CJEU.

As for one other general remark, similar to, for example, the 'neutralization' line of case law, this approach (i.e., determining the compatibility of a given MS's law on the basis of the effective tax burden) could be seen as resulting in a given law being discriminatory in some cases (where it leads in practice to a heavier effective tax burden) and in other cases, not. However, '[t]he Court has previously held that the fact that the applicable national rules place non-residents at a disadvantage cannot be compensated for by the fact that, in other situations, that same legislation does not discriminate between non-residents and residents'.[1508]

Finally, the *Sofina* case, decided in November 2018, touched upon and reiterated some of the above case law while bringing in a new consideration. To present it briefly, three companies incorporated in Belgium, i.e., Sofina SA, Rebelco SA and Sidro SA, complained that the French tax rules discriminated against them as non-resident shareholders as compared to resident shareholders.[1509] The main issue was that a WHT was levied in France on dividends paid to non-resident companies, regardless of the companies' profitability or lack thereof, whereas no taxes were levied on dividends paid to resident companies when they were in a loss-making position.[1510] In the case of resident companies that generated losses, they would not pay taxes on the dividends received until they generated profits. In the case of non-resident companies, they were 'subject to immediate and definitive taxation irrespective of their results'.[1511] These three Belgian companies were in a loss-making position and therefore requested a refund of the French WHT levied on their dividends, which the French tax authorities

applicable national rules place non-residents at a disadvantage cannot be compensated for by the fact that, in other situations, that same legislation does not discriminate between non-residents and residents (judgment of 18 July 2007 in *Lakebrink and Peters-Lakebrink*, C182/06, EU:C:2007:452, paragraph 23)').

1508. CJEU, Case C-575/17, *Sofina*, 22 Nov. 2018, ECLI:EU:C:2018:943, at para. 39.
1509. *Id.*, at paras 12–17.
1510. *Id.*, at para. 22.
1511. *Id.*, at para. 34.

refused. The issue eventually came before the Conseil d'État, which referred questions to the CJEU.[1512]

The CJEU observed that the legislation in question allowed resident companies to benefit from deferral on the taxation of dividends received if they suffered losses and, moreover, taxation could be deferred indefinitely – meaning it could even convert into an exemption – if those resident companies never recovered profitability. The CJEU thus pinpointed the benefit of deferral as the core issue.[1513] It was not limited to the question of whether a WHT per se was acceptable,[1514] nor whether the 15 % gross-basis withholding taxation on non-residents, as compared to the 33.33 % net-basis corporate income taxation on residents, was acceptable.[1515] This benefit of deferral for dividends received from France granted to loss-making resident companies while refused to loss-making non-resident companies was deemed a restriction on the free movement of capital.[1516] The grounds for this were, *inter alia*, that: (1) it led to a 'cash-flow advantage' for the domestic situation, which was excluded for the equivalent cross-border situation; (2) it is irrelevant whether the difference in treatment in terms of the actual tax burden somehow equals out over time, since the relevant point in time for the comparison is 'each tax year, taken individually';[1517] and (3) this is all the clearer in this case since in some cases the deferral transforms into a 'definitive exemption' for resident companies, which is not possible for the non-resident companies.[1518]

The CJEU held that France could extend this deferral to non-resident companies, without undermining the balanced allocation of the powers of taxation between

1512. *Id.*, at paras 12–17.
1513. *Id.*, at para. 34 and para. 69.
1514. *Id.*, at para. 53.
1515. *Id.*, at paras 38–39.
1516. *Id.*, at para. 41.
1517. *Id.*, at para. 30.
1518. *Id.*, at paras 29–34 ('29 First, the exclusion of a cash-flow advantage in a cross-border situation when it is granted in an equivalent situation on national territory constitutes a restriction on the free movement of capital (*see*, by analogy, judgments of 13 December 2005, *Marks & Spencer*, C446/03, EU:C:2005:763, paragraph 33, and of 12 July 2012, *Commission* v *Spain*, C269/09, EU:C:2012:439, paragraph 59).

30 Secondly, the assessment of whether there exists a potentially less favourable treatment of the dividends paid to non-resident companies must be undertaken for each tax year, taken individually (judgment of 2 June 2016, *Pensioenfonds Metaal en Techniek*, C252/14, EU:C:2016:402, paragraph 41).

31 Since the dividends received by a non-resident company are taxed at the time when they are distributed, the financial year in which the distribution of those dividends occurs must be taken into account in order to compare the tax burden on such dividends and that on dividends paid to a resident company.

32 It should be noted that there is no such tax burden when the resident company is loss-making at the end of such a financial year.

33 Thirdly, such a deferral of taxation will be a definitive exemption of the dividends paid to a resident company if the latter does not become profitable before it ceases trading.

34 Accordingly, the national legislation at issue in the main proceedings is liable to procure an advantage for loss-making resident companies, since it gives rise, at the very least, to a cash-flow advantage, or even an exemption in the event of that company ceasing trading, whereas non-resident companies are subject to immediate and definitive taxation irrespective of their results').

MSs[1519] and without undermining the effective collection of tax.[1520] Thus, this legislation was precluded by the free movement of capital.[1521]

Interim Summary

Due to the above-mentioned link between the taxes in the state of 'source' and the credit in the state of residence, made all the more prominent from an EU law perspective under the 'neutralization' line of case law, this section presents some CJEU cases that further explore the impact of EU law on this link. Also, as mentioned, gross-basis WHTs in a state of source combined with an 'ordinary' credit in a state of residence may result in overall higher taxation of a cross-border context than of a purely domestic one. Naturally, taxpayers have brought complaints. Whether and how this can be tackled under EU law emerges from these cases. First, some conclusions and comparisons can be made regarding this link, in general, and, second, some conclusions can be made regarding the more specific question mentioned at the beginning of this section, namely whether the decisions in this line of case law help better align the tax base used in the state of source with the tax base used in the state of residence, so as to potentially reduce 'excess' credit cases and potentially facilitate the aim of 'neutralization'.

As for the state of residence, taxpayers have brought cases before domestic courts and largely failed. For example, in the UK, the *Yates v. GCA International Limited* case highlighted a particularly striking discrepancy between the taxes levied in Venezuela and the limited amount of FTC that could be claimed in the UK (discussed in Chapter 2, at *supra* note 361). As discussed, Philip Baker observed at that time that this was but one of an increasing number of cases where taxes levied abroad on a gross basis, especially on 'interest, royalties or technical service fees', were not fully creditable in the UK (in Chapter 2, at *supra* note 362). Arguments have been made that the credit limitation could reasonably be based on the tax base used in the state of source (in Chapter 2, at *supra* note 358). In fact, both in the UK and in the US, as the historical analysis showed, there were initial debates as to how the FSI should be calculated for the purposes of the credit limitation, though legislators in both states ended up settling on applying the rules of the state of residence, to the extent possible, for calculating the income. Additional examples of cases came before domestic courts, such as France and Hungary, where taxpayers challenged the state of residence because of the foreign taxes that could not be credited.[1522] Before the Conseil d'État in France, for example, a

1519. *Id.*, at paras 58–59.
1520. *Id.*, at paras 70–77.
1521. *Id.*, at paras 78–79.
1522. *See*, e.g., Hungary, Kúria (Supreme Court), No. Kfv.V.35.806/2013, 26 Feb. 2015; France, Conseil d'État (Supreme Administrative Court), N° 357189, *SA Crédit Industriel et Commercial*, 7 Dec. 2015. Although not an EU MS, *see also*, e.g., Canada, Tax Court of Canada, 2016 TCC 131, *Société Générale Valeurs Mobilières Inc. v. The Queen*, 26 May 2016, aff'd 2017 FCA 3 (the question posed to the Court was: '... is the amount of Canadian income tax that is referred to in Article XXII(2) of the treaty as being "appropriate to the income which may be taxed in Brazil": a. equal to the Canadian income tax on the amount of such interest income that is or is deemed to be taxed in Brazil, which is a gross amount; and b. if the answer to (a) is yes, what is the proper test for determining the Canadian income tax payable on the gross

French company sought an outcome under which France would take into account a tax base, *without* deducting certain expenses, more aligned with that of the state of source, Italy, so that the company could fully credit the Italian WHTs on dividends.[1523] In all of these cases, the courts decided (in one way or another) that the state of residence should tax the income on a net basis, taking into account expenses, in the same way as for domestic income, and fully accepted that this may have the effect of reducing the amount of taxes that can be credited.

As seen in the cases decided by the CJEU, this is also accepted under EU law. After all, the state of residence is applying the same rules to the FSI and the DSI. The CJEU has expressly accepted a credit limitation (as discussed in Section 4.2.2. and Section 4.2.3.). It seems generally accepted – by the OECD, by domestic courts, and by the CJEU – that states in general have the right to determine how to calculate taxable income and thus, by extension, the state of residence has the same right when it calculates taxable income for the purposes of levying tax and for crediting foreign taxes.[1524] However, it is clear that there are some instructions for the state of residence as regards the calculation of the credit limitation, flowing from the *De Groot*, *Beker*, and *Seabrokers v. Norway* cases (as discussed in Section 4.2.4.).

As for the state of 'source', this is where the CJEU has had more influence. Based on its decisions, the state of source is largely the cause of the difference of treatment. Differences could be more readily detected, as non-resident taxpayers brought cases in order to be able to claim the deduction of expenses in the same way as residents or, as seen, *inter alia*, in the 'neutralization' cases, even to challenge the WHTs themselves. Indeed, from an EU law perspective, it may be hard to 'blame' the state of residence, as

---

amount of income derived from Brazil; c. if the answer to (a) is no, what is the proper test for determining which amounts of the Canadian resident taxpayer should be included and/or deducted from the gross income arising from sources in Brazil?').

1523. France, Conseil d'État (Supreme Administrative Court), N° 357189, *SA Crédit Industriel et Commercial*, 7 Dec. 2015 (in this case, a French company earned dividends from an Italian company, on which withholding taxes were levied at source in Italy and for which the French company was eligible for a credit. The issue was to determine 'the amount of French tax attributable to' the dividend income, which in turn revolved around determining which expenses should be deducted from the dividends in order to calculate the net taxable income in France. The French company held these shares only temporarily, i.e., a few weeks, since it held the shares under a securities lending agreement with a UK bank, Goldman Sachs International London. The French company credited the amount of the Italian withholding tax from its corporate income tax due in France, but the tax authorities contested this, arguing that the full amount cannot be credited since France does not collect any taxes on this dividend income, once the expenses related to the securities lending agreement are taken into account. The transaction overall resulted in a net income of near zero. There were debates about which expenses should be considered linked to the dividends. Ultimately, the Conseil d'État held in favour of the tax authorities). *See also*, e.g., Hungary, Kúria (Supreme Court), No. Kfv.V.35.806/2013, 26 Feb. 2015; Dániel Dea´k, *Chapter 30: Hungary – Application of Article 23 on Foreign Tax Credit for Lack of Taxable Net Income*, *in Tax Treaty Case Law Around the Globe 2016* 359 (Eric C.C.M. Kemmeren et al. eds, IBFD/Linde 2017) (the case decided by the Supreme Court of Hungary was based on a similar set of facts, regarding the extent to which taxes withheld in Brazil on interest income could be credited in Hungary, since the net income in Hungary was low due to expenses related to SWAP agreements taken out in relation to the loan).

1524. The CJEU has since confirmed this in a 2021 decision. *See* CJEU, Case C-403/19, *Société Générale SA*, 25 Feb. 2021, ECLI:EU:C:2021:136, at paras 26, 37–38.

it would require arguing that, while the state of residence taxes all of its residents equally on the basis of their net income, uniquely in the case of residents who earn FSI, the gross amount should be taken into account - an argument which could be less tenable from a non-discrimination standpoint. As the CJEU has observed (e.g., *Schumacker*), income taxes are generally viewed as taxes based on the ability to pay of a taxpayer. What follows is that income taxes generally seek to reach only the net income that makes the taxpayer better off, thereby increasing the taxpayer's capacity to contribute. Thus far, the CJEU has been more inclined to require a state of source to bring its taxation of non-residents (which is often on a gross basis) more in line with its taxation of residents. This would seem to encourage, among other things, more net-basis WHTs in the EU. Such a development would be in line with some of the discussions on the future of WHTs, which was one of the main subjects of the 2018 IFA Congress.[1525]

As a result of the responsibility being placed predominantly on the state of source's taxation of non-residents, these cases had a less direct impact on the design of the methods themselves. The methods occasionally, however, played an ancillary role in the reasoning. For example, the methods for relief of double taxation played a minor role in the CJEU's reasoning for rejecting objective differences (on this, *see* further explanation in the footnote at *supra* note 1418) and for rejecting justifications (on this, *see supra* note 1448). In this way, the CJEU also subtly recognized other links between the two (taxation at source and the methods of relief).

As regards the second question posed above (i.e., whether this case law creates alignment in the tax bases in such a way that reduces risks of 'excess' credits and improves chances of 'neutralization'), what clearly results from these cases is the right of non-residents to deduct expenses 'economically connected' to earning the income subject to tax at source in a MS. Indeed, the CJEU itself now refers to 'the *Gerritse* line of case-law', implying that this rule is rather settled.[1526] On the one hand, by rejecting unabated gross-basis taxation, and requiring the deduction of some expenses, this case law moves one step closer towards net-based taxation in the source state, with the potential of more closely aligning the tax bases in the states of source and residence, and thereby mitigating the risk of excess credits and advancing the prospects of 'neutralization'. On the other hand, the actual size of this step seemed to vary in different contexts. In the case of cross-border services and business activities, this figurative step is bigger, in that more and different kinds of expenses were declared to have a direct connection with the income earned in the state of source, such as the deduction of expenses for hiring professional tax advisory services and the deduction of related travel and accommodation expenses. In the case of dividends, the CJEU specified that the expenses be directly connected *to the payment of the dividends*. Having tested different expenses invoked by the parties against this narrower criterion,

1525. For the views discussed on this possibility at the 2018 IFA Congress, *see*, e.g., Robert Goulder, *Rethinking Withholding: An Analog Tax for the Digital Age?*, 92 Tax Notes Int'l 129 (1 Oct. 2018).

1526. CJEU, Case C-290/04, *FKP Scorpio Konzertproduktionen*, 3 Oct. 2006, ECLI:EU:C:2006:630, at para. 51.

it was hard to detect any relevant expenses that qualified. This undermines the prospects of 'neutralization'. Of course, MSs can opt to be more generous. The CJEU made it abundantly clear that 'Community law does not preclude a Member State from going further, by allowing costs that do not have such a connection to be taken into account.'[1527]

At one point in the midst of the development of these cases, the question was raised whether this is the 'death of withholding taxes' in the EU.[1528] If this would have been the outcome, this could have indirectly altered the tax base used for non-residents. Admittedly, it is only a *means* for levying the tax, rather than the *substantive* aspects of the tax base and tax rates (and it is the *latter* which are more relevant for excess credits or 'neutralization'). However, they are often interrelated: that is, the mechanism of a WHT (i.e., this particular means) is well suited to gross taxation (i.e., this particular base), as it is often levied at the moment of a given payment made by a payer, who is likely unaware of the other income and expenses of the non-resident taxpayer. Thus, gross taxation may have become more difficult to sustain had WHTs been banned.

This was evidently not the outcome, however. The right to levy a WHT was largely left intact, with the exception of certain dividend cases. Simader explained the distinction as follows:

> 'In *Denkavit Internationaal* (C-170/05),[3] *Amurta* (C-379/ 05)[4] and *Aberdeen* (C-303/07),[5] the ECJ held that EC law prohibits the levying of withholding taxes. All three cases dealt with the taxation of dividends. According to the national provisions in question, economic double taxation was avoided for domestic dividends, but not for outbound dividends. Consequently, whilst outbound dividends were taxed by way of a withholding, no taxes were due on domestic dividends. This [led] to discrimination, not only in terms of taxation by way of a withholding, but also with regard to the taxation itself.[6] Accordingly, the ECJ did not accept any justification for the discrimination in these cases.'[1529]

In other cases, such as *Scorpio* and *Truck Center*, both residents and non-residents were indeed taxed in respect of the payments. Thus, the difference centred on the method of levying the tax. The WHT as a method was not found to be incompatible with EU law, as it was justified by 'the need to ensure the effective collection of taxes'.[1530] However, although it was substantially the same outcome, the CJEU reached it through different reasoning, as mentioned above.[1531]

1527. To this effect, CJEU, Case C-345/04, *Centro Equestre da Lezíria Grande*, 15 Feb. 2007, ECLI:EU:C:2007:96, at para. 24; CJEU, Case C-290/04, *FKP Scorpio Konzertproduktionen*, 3 Oct. 2006, ECLI:EU:C:2006:630, at para. 51.
1528. *See*, e.g., Karin Simader, *Withholding Taxes and the Effectiveness of Fiscal Supervision and Tax Collection*, 64(2) Bull. Int'l Tax'n 115 (2010) (summarizing the IFA/EU Seminar on 'The Death of Withholding Taxes?').
1529. Karin Simader, *Withholding Taxes and the Effectiveness of Fiscal Supervision and Tax Collection*, 64(2) Bull. Int'l Tax'n 115, 115 (2010).
1530. *See supra* note 1469. *See also* Karin Simader, *Withholding Taxes and the Effectiveness of Fiscal Supervision and Tax Collection*, 64(2) Bull. Int'l Tax'n 115, 115 (2010).
1531. *See also* Karin Simader, *Withholding Taxes and the Effectiveness of Fiscal Supervision and Tax Collection*, 64(2) Bull. Int'l Tax'n 115, 115 (2010).

Even in cases where WHTs were permitted, the CJEU required some modifications to the procedure, largely to allow for better taking into account directly connected expenses. For such expenses, according to the *Scorpio* decision, it should be possible to declare them to the payer before payment, rather than requiring the non-resident taxpayer to undertake a subsequent reporting-and-refund mechanism. In any case, it is not clear that a ban on WHTs as a procedure would, on balance, lead to a less restrictive means for taxing non-resident taxpayers. As the CJEU noted in *X NV*, if a MS were forced to abolish its WHT mechanism, it is likely that, in its place, the MS would ask non-residents to follow a tax procedure that is similar to the one for residents, which is often the filing of a tax return. This could merely replace existing burdens with other new burdens (e.g., it may 'lead to a serious burden on the foreign service provider in that he would have to submit a tax return in a foreign language and to familiarise himself with a tax system in a Member State other than that in which he is established').[1532] In sum, WHTs are not dead in the EU.

From a comparison of this line of case law with the *Schumacker* line of case law, some authors draw a distinction between the deductibility of personal expenses, relating to the 'subjective ability-to-pay' (usually a state of residence issue, concerning individuals) versus the deductibility of business-related expenses, relating to the 'objective ability-to-pay' (usually a state of non-residence issue, concerning both individuals and companies, under the case law).[1533] Although the state of source, or non-residence, is obliged to allow deductions for the latter if they are 'directly connected' to the income generated there, the cases do not go so far as to require net-basis taxation and thus, on balance, would not seem to be harbingers of a future free of 'excess' credits and thus successful 'neutralization'.

4.2.7. The *Marks & Spencer* or Losses Line of Case Law

An extension of the discussion of deductible expenses (in Section 4.2.6.) can morph into the issue of losses, as once deductible expenses exceed revenues, a loss is generated. Since questions regarding the amount of FSI to include are central to the calculation of the credit limitation, a negative amount in the form of losses inevitably also has an impact on the credit method. For this reason, the well-known *Marks & Spencer* line of case law may be one place to search for clues as to how losses may be treated under the credit method from an EU law perspective.

As regards the scope of analysis, this section focuses on losses more generally; thus, it is deliberately broader than the issue of 'final losses' alone. The precise degree

1532. CJEU, Case C-498/10, *X NV*, 18 Oct. 2012, ECLI:EU:C:2012:635, at para. 50.

1533. *See*, e.g., Alexander Rust, *Pending Cases Filed by German Courts II: The Scorpio, Centro Equestre, Conijn, Schwarz, and Meindl Cases Pending Cases Involving Germany: Commission v Germany*, *in ECJ Recent Developments in Direct Taxation* 175, 187 (Michael Lang, Josef Schuch & Claus Staringer eds, Linde/Kluwer Law International 2006); Alexander Rust, *Germany II: Case C-20/16 (Bechtel & Bechtel)*, *in CJEU Recent Developments in Direct Taxation 2016* 79, 82–84 (Michael Lang et al. eds, Linde 2016).

to which some of the cases selected reiterate the *Marks & Spencer* novelty of 'final losses' varies, but the common thread is the use of losses.

This line of case law grappled with the treatment of cross-border losses. To begin, in the watershed case of this series, the UK-based retail store, Marks & Spencer, brought a complaint regarding, in particular, the use of foreign losses. The company's business was successful in its state of residence, the UK, but did not manage to succeed in other EU MSs, such as Belgium, France and Germany.[1534] For this reason, it sold or shut down its subsidiaries in those states. Marks & Spencer sought to claim relief for the losses incurred by these subsidiaries, under the UK's 'group tax relief' regime.[1535] This was denied, as the 'group relief could only be granted for losses recorded in the United Kingdom'.[1536]

In this decision of the CJEU, this difference in treatment was held to be a restriction on the freedom of establishment,[1537] yet it was justified by reasons in the public interest.[1538] Nevertheless, even if justified, denying the losses would be disproportionate in certain circumstances. On this point, according to the CJEU, 'the restrictive measure goes beyond what is necessary to attain the objectives pursued'[1539] under two cumulative circumstances: (1) the non-resident has exhausted the possibilities available in its MS to have the losses taken into account and (2) there is no possibility for the subsidiary's losses to be taken into account in future periods.[1540] In other words, when the losses are 'final', the MS must take them into account. The decision seemed to be a compromise in this case, which showed the CJEU to be hesitant to force MSs to accept cross-border losses, unless 'final', with the precise meaning of 'final' thereafter being subject to much interpretation.[1541]

A next major decision occurred in the 2008 *Lidl Belgium* case.[1542] A complaint was brought by a limited partnership established in Germany with losses incurred by its PE in Luxembourg. The same basic rule as in *Marks & Spencer*, regarding subsidiaries in other MSs, was now extended to the cross-border case of PEs in another MS. Importantly, one of Germany's main contentions in this case was that, under the

1534. CJEU, Case C-446/03, *Marks & Spencer*, 13 Dec. 2005, ECLI:EU:C:2005:763, at paras 18–21.
1535. *Id.*, at para. 22.
1536. *Id.*, at para. 24.
1537. *Id.*, at para. 34.
1538. *Id.*, at para. 51.
1539. *Id.*, at para. 53.
1540. *Id.*, at para. 55 (the conditions read as follows: 'where:

- the non-resident subsidiary has exhausted the possibilities available in its State of residence of having the losses taken into account for the accounting period concerned by the claim for relief and also for previous accounting periods, if necessary by transferring those losses to a third party or by offsetting the losses against the profits made by the subsidiary in previous periods, and
- there is no possibility for the foreign subsidiary's losses to be taken into account in its State of residence for future periods either by the subsidiary itself or by a third party, in particular where the subsidiary has been sold to that third party').

1541. Most recently, *see*, e.g., CJEU, Case C-607/17, *Memira Holding*, 19 Jun. 2019, ECLI:EU:C:2019:510; CJEU, Case C-608/17, *Holmen*, 19 Jun. 2019, ECLI:EU:C:2019:511.
1542. CJEU, Case C-414/06, *Lidl Belgium*, 15 May 2008, ECLI:EU:C:2008:278.

tax treaty with Luxembourg, Germany fully *exempted* the profits earned by the PE in Luxembourg. In its view, Germany is not allowed to tax the profits and, thus, should also be permitted to disregard the losses.[1543] The CJEU agreed, on the basis of various justifications,[1544] as long as the losses were *not* 'final'[1545] (which in this case they were not; in fact, the losses had already been used in Luxembourg).[1546] Had the credit method applied, the losses attributable to a foreign PE would not give rise to the same problems since the fundamental starting point of the credit method is to take into account the worldwide profits and losses of the taxpayer.

Nevertheless, under the credit method, although the constellation of domestic profits and foreign losses could be less problematic (from the perspective of the taxpayer), one constellation that could give rise to problems is that of domestic losses and foreign profits (or more broadly, overall losses and foreign profits). If the losses are greater than the profits, the consequence is: no taxable income in the state of residence and thus no taxes in the state of residence against which any foreign taxes levied abroad on the foreign profits can be credited (a scenario further elaborated below in this section). One CJEU decision dealt with such a constellation, namely the *AMID* case.[1547] Due to its factual pattern, it is worth briefly summarizing. As for the legal pattern, it was the exemption method that applied, instead of the credit method, and the contested legal provisions were loss-ordering rules. These rules dictated the order in which a given foreign loss could offset other profits and, vice versa, the order in which a given domestic loss could offset other profits.

As for the facts, a Belgian company had a PE in Luxembourg. In 1981, the Belgian company generated losses in Belgium, while its PE in Luxembourg generated profits. In 1982, the Belgian company was successful again domestically and generated profits in Belgium. In 1982, the Belgian company requested to carry forward the losses from 1981 against its profits in 1982. The LCF rules in Belgium, in general, allowed business losses to be carried forward for up to five years. The Belgian tax authorities refused this.[1548] The reason for the refusal was the loss-ordering rule, 'on the ground that those losses should have been set off against the profits made by its Luxembourg establishment in the previous accounting year'.[1549] According to the loss-ordering rule: Belgian losses must be used, first, against other 'Belgian profits', then against foreign 'profits taxed at a lower rate', then against foreign 'profits exempted by treaty'.[1550] In this case, the Luxembourg profits were exempt under the Belgium-Luxembourg DTC.[1551]

The combination of the exemption method and these loss-ordering rules resulted in adverse effects from the fact that the loss-ordering rules would require offsetting

1543. *Id.*, at paras 11, 28–29.
1544. *Id.*, at para. 52.
1545. *Id.*, at paras 47–48.
1546. *Id.*, at paras 49–51.
1547. CJEU, Case C-141/99, *AMID*, 14 Dec. 2000, ECLI:EU:C:2000:696.
1548. *Id.*, at paras 2–3, 9–10.
1549. *Id.*, at para. 2.
1550. *Id.*, at para. 4.
1551. *Id.*, at paras 6–8 (citing the 'convention between the Kingdom of Belgium and the Grand Duchy of Luxembourg for the avoidance of double taxation ("the Convention") ... concluded on 17 September 1970').

between taxable sources and exempt sources – in this case, losses from taxable sources against income from exempt sources. Because the Luxembourg profits in 1981 neutralized the Belgian losses in 1981, thereby eliminating any possibility of a LCF, this meant that the Belgian profits in 1982 were left intact (i.e., not reduced by a LCF, which would have otherwise occurred in a purely domestic scenario) to the extent of the Luxembourg profits of the previous year. Thus, the losses could not be used in Belgium.[1552] Under this system, the Luxembourg profits were, in an economic sense, taxed.[1553] Also, Luxembourg would not take into account the losses, as they were not attributable to the PE there but only to the head office over which it has no jurisdiction. Thus, the losses were not taken into account in either Belgium or Luxembourg.[1554] If no Luxembourg PE had been established, the Belgian losses would have been tax deductible against future Belgian profits; in this way, the scenario was worse off by virtue of the existence of a PE in another EU MS. The CJEU held that this amounted to a difference of treatment contrary to the freedom of establishment.[1555]

Example No. 26: *AMID* Case

	Cross-border: ***Assume 25% tax rate and same tax base in BE & LU***	**Hypothetical 1:** ***No PE in LU – Domestic scenario alone***	**Hypothetical 2:** ***No PE in LU – PE in BE instead of in LU***
1981	BE: –100 Exempt PE in LU: 100	BE: –100	BE: –100 + 100
	Income recorded for tax purposes: –100 + 100 = 0	Income recorded for tax purposes: –100 (LCF generated)	Income recorded for tax purposes: 0
	Tax BE: 0 Tax LU: 25	Tax BE: 0	Tax BE: 0

1552. *Id.*, at paras 14–17.
1553. European Parliament, Jacques Malherbe, Philippe Malherbe, Isabelle Richelle, Edoardo Traversa, with the contribution of Daphné de Laveleye, *The Impact of the Rulings of the European Court of Justice in the Area of Direct Taxation 2010*, PE 457.367, IP/A/ECON/ST/2010-18, para. 72 and para. 90 (April 2011).
1554. CJEU, Case C-141/99, *AMID*, 14 Dec. 2000, ECLI:EU:C:2000:696, at para. 33; Opinion of AG Alber in Case C-141/99, *AMID*, 8 Jun. 2000, ECLI:EU:C:2000:309, at para. 1 and para. 24.
1555. CJEU, Case C-141/99, *AMID*, 14 Dec. 2000, ECLI:EU:C:2000:696, at paras 26–33.

1982	BE: 100 Exempt PE in LU: 100 Income recorded for tax purposes: 100 + LU exempt = 100 Tax BE: 25 Tax LU: 25	BE: 100 Income recorded for tax purposes: 100 – LCF of 100 = 0 Tax BE: 0	BE: 100 + 100 Income recorded for tax purposes: 200 Tax BE: 50
Over 2 years	Economic result in BE: 0 Economic result WW: 200 Taxable result in BE: 100 Taxable result WW: 300 (100 taxed in BE in Y2, 100 taxed in LU in Y1, 100 taxed in LU in Y2) Tax BE: 0 + 25 Tax LU: 25 + 25 Total: 75	Economic result: 0 Taxable result: 0 Tax BE: 0 + 0 Total: 0	Economic result: 200 Taxable result: 200 Tax BE: 0 + 50 Total: 50

Against this background, the two cases that expressly and rather prominently feature the credit method, thereby showing its interaction with this line of case law, are the *Nordea Bank*[1556] case and the *NN*[1557] case.

Regarding *Nordea Bank*, according to AG Kokott, this case 'gives the Court an opportunity to develop further its case-law on cross-border loss relief in general and the provision of such relief by way of the credit method in particular'.[1558] As for the facts, Nordea Bank, resident in Denmark, operated PEs in Finland, Norway and Sweden,[1559] all of which continuously operated at a loss.[1560] Since Denmark applied the credit method, under Article 25 of the Nordic Convention,[1561] those losses were taken into account in Denmark annually for the purposes of calculating Nordea Bank's taxes on the basis of the worldwide income and offering an FTC. Eventually, Nordea Bank decided to restructure by selling the loss-making PEs to some of its subsidiaries in those

1556. CJEU, Case C-48/13, *Nordea Bank*, 17 Jul. 2014, ECLI:EU:C:2014:2087.
1557. CJEU, Case C-28/17, *NN*, 4 Jul. 2018, ECLI:EU:C:2018:526.
1558. Opinion of AG Kokott in Case C-48/13, *Nordea Bank*, 13 Mar. 2014, ECLI:EU:C:2014:153, at para. 3.
1559. *Id.*, at paras 9–10.
1560. *Id.*, at para. 10.
1561. CJEU, Case C-48/13, *Nordea Bank*, 17 Jul. 2014, ECLI:EU:C:2014:2087, at para. 4.

states (Finland, Norway and Sweden).[1562] Under Danish law, due to this 'partial sale', two tax consequences followed: first, Denmark taxed the gains from the sale[1563] and, second, because Denmark would no longer have taxation rights over the PEs' future profits, the losses that were previously deducted were all recaptured – that is, added back into the taxable income of Nordea Bank in Denmark.[1564] This recapture mechanism amounted, in effect, to a (subsequent) denial of the use of foreign losses. The national court also made it explicit, directly in the wording of the question posed to the CJEU, that 'it must be assumed that the possibilities for applying the losses in question have been exhausted'.[1565] In other words, it was agreed that the losses were final.[1566]

As for the reasoning of the CJEU, the comparability of PEs at home and PEs abroad, in essence, stemmed indirectly from the application of the credit method, even if the CJEU did not explicitly express it in these terms. In the CJEU's words, 'by making the profits of permanent establishments situated in Finland, Sweden and Norway subject to Danish tax, the Kingdom of Denmark has equated those establishments with resident permanent establishments so far as concerns the deduction of losses'.[1567]

To be more precise, the comparability analysis was composed of two statements, both of which contain implicit messages about the credit method. To begin, the comparison selected by the CJEU was between a resident company with a PE at home and a resident company with a PE in another EU/EEA state. Thus, Denmark was in the position of the state of residence of the taxpayer. As regards this comparison, the two statements of the CJEU are analysed in turn and then assessed as to their relevance for the credit method.

First, the CJEU began by declaring that, in principle, the two situations are *not* comparable, in light of – essentially – the credit method:

> 'in principle, permanent establishments situated in another Member State or in another State that is party to the EEA Agreement are not in a situation comparable to that of resident permanent establishments in relation to measures laid down by a Member State in order to prevent or mitigate the double taxation of a resident company's profits'.[1568]

The CJEU offered no further reason or explanation for this statement. It is possible that this statement was inspired from the Opinion of the AG. The Opinion also stated that the two situations are not comparable, but the AG was clearer on this point. First, the AG specified that the starting point is often whether situations are comparable 'having regard to the aim pursued by the national provisions at issue'.[1569] Shortly thereafter, the AG stated that:

1562. *Id.*, at para. 11.
1563. *Id.*, at paras 6–7.
1564. *Id.*, at paras 12–13, 15.
1565. *Id.*, at para. 15.
1566. Opinion of AG Kokott in Case C-48/13, *Nordea Bank*, 13 Mar. 2014, ECLI:EU:C:2014:153, at para. 11.
1567. CJEU, Case C-48/13, *Nordea Bank*, 17 Jul. 2014, ECLI:EU:C:2014:2087, at para. 24.
1568. *Id.*
1569. Opinion of AG Kokott in Case C-48/13, *Nordea Bank*, 13 Mar. 2014, ECLI:EU:C:2014:153, at para. 21.

> 'In the present case, for example, it must be concluded that the situations of a foreign branch and of a domestic branch are objectively different, because only in the case of a foreign branch can foreign tax be offset against Danish tax. The question is, however, which criteria are to be used to decide whether that difference is relevant from the point of view of the recapture of loss relief.'[1570]

Notably, it was not the credit method that was under scrutiny; it was the loss rules. This brings the discussion to the next statement of the CJEU.

Second, the CJEU continued with a more standard comparability benchmark,[1571] which encompasses an amalgamation of reoccurring ideas, namely that, if the MS exercises its tax jurisdiction over the income in question (this idea has been used in the case of income flowing out to non-residents, as, e.g., in the 'neutralization' line of case law) or taxes the income in a similar way (this idea has been used in the case of PEs of non-resident companies, as, e.g., in the *Avoir Fiscal/Saint Gobain* line of case law), then the MS should offer tax treatment equal with that of its own residents (e.g., relief from an extra charge to tax such as a WHT or, e.g., the grant of an imputation credit). This precise formulation ('by making the profits ... subject to Danish tax') was often used in the context of *non*-residents and, indeed, the CJEU, in connection with this second statement, cites 'by analogy, the judgment in *Denkavit Internationaal and Denkavit France*, C170/05, EU:C:2006:783, paragraphs 34 and 35'. And, when one follows the trail, these paragraphs of *Denkavit*, in turn, cite 'Case C-374/04 *Test Claimants in Class IV of the ACT Group Litigation* [2006] ECR I-0000 [...]'. Based on these citations, the CJEU is applying 'by analogy' to the *Nordea Bank* case, reasoning that applied to cases concerning MSs from which dividends were distributed, wherein different treatment arose, basically, on the basis of whether the recipient of this distribution was resident or non-resident (*see* the respective discussions of these cases in Section 4.2.5. and in Section 4.2.8. for more details and precisions). However, the *Nordea Bank* case concerns a resident company, which generates FSI (or losses) via a foreign PE.

This shows just how far-reaching this *subject-to-tax/same-taxation-same-relief* reasoning is. Under the credit method, a MS is by definition, in a first step, exercising its jurisdiction over foreign income. Therefore, 'so far as concerns the deduction of losses', comparability between a resident with income from its domestic operations and a resident with income from its foreign operations is all but guaranteed.

What would this have meant then for the exemption method under the *Lidl Belgium* case? Technically, that decision could have ended sooner, then. The CJEU could have held that a restriction on the freedom of establishment (which was found to exist in both *Nordea Bank* and *Lidl Belgium*) 'is permissible *only if* it relates to situations which are *not objectively comparable* or if it is *justified* by an overriding reason in the public interest' (emphasis added).[1572] Then, it could have simply rejected the objective comparability of the situations. Instead, in *Lidl Belgium*, the CJEU overlooked the objective comparability analysis altogether and headed straight to the

1570. *Id.*, at para. 26.
1571. CJEU, Case C-48/13, *Nordea Bank*, 17 Jul. 2014, ECLI:EU:C:2014:2087, at para. 24.
1572. *Id.*, at para. 23.

public interest justifications (i.e., the decision states that a restriction 'is permissible only if it is justified by overriding reasons in the public interest';[1573] remarkably, the word 'compare' or 'comparability' does not make any appearance in the decision). It is perhaps somewhat surprising that despite the unambiguous and extensive criticism of the CJEU's comparability analysis by AG Kokott in her Opinion on *Nordea Bank* – describing it as a 'doctrinal vestige' that is no longer useful and lamenting that the CJEU's 'entire case-law does not make it clear in which circumstances a difference in the situations compared should preclude their objective comparability', citing various examples of divergent analyses[1574] – the CJEU yet again proceeded with what was arguably a divergent analysis.

To assist navigating through this to garner possible takeaways for the credit method, what could be said is that, from the two statements in the *Nordea Bank* case, the comparability analysis implies that: (1) in light of the purpose of a direct credit method, a resident with a PE at home and a resident with a PE abroad are not comparable, in principle; and (2) in light of rules regarding loss deductions, they are comparable because the relevant factor for the comparison is whether the profits are subject to tax and, evidently, this is the case under the credit method.

As for justifications, Denmark invoked 'the need to ensure a balanced allocation of the power to impose taxes between Member States in connection with the prevention of tax avoidance'.[1575] Its government officials argued that the recapture occurs because Denmark loses its taxation rights over the profits from that point forward and seeks to prevent base-eroding strategies wherein Danish taxpayers deduct foreign losses for many years and then, as soon as their business becomes profitable, sell it to a related party to avoid taxation.[1576]

After acknowledging these justifications, the CJEU reckoned that 'the legislation goes beyond what is necessary to attain that objective'.[1577] The CJEU explained that 'the balanced allocation of the power to impose taxes has the objective of safeguarding the symmetry between the right to tax profits and the right to deduct losses'.[1578] In this case, the symmetry between profits and losses[1579] was ensured since the profits of the PEs had always been under the tax jurisdiction of Denmark by virtue of applying the credit method (notwithstanding the fact that this entailed relief).[1580] Moreover, Denmark also subjected the gains of the sale of the PEs to tax.[1581]

The Opinion of AG Kokott is more explicit regarding the relevance of the credit method, especially in the following excerpts:[1582]

1573. CJEU, Case C-414/06, *Lidl Belgium*, 15 May 2008, ECLI:EU:C:2008:278, at para. 27.
1574. Opinion of AG Kokott in Case C-48/13, *Nordea Bank*, 13 Mar. 2014, ECLI:EU:C:2014:153, at paras 21–28.
1575. CJEU, Case C-48/13, *Nordea Bank*, 17 Jul. 2014, ECLI:EU:C:2014:2087, at para. 26.
1576. *Id.*, at paras 26–30.
1577. *Id.*, at para. 31.
1578. *Id.*, at para. 32.
1579. *Id.*, at para. 33.
1580. *Id.*, at para. 34.
1581. *Id.*, at para. 35.
1582. Opinion of AG Kokott in Case C-48/13, *Nordea Bank*, 13 Mar. 2014, ECLI:EU:C:2014:153, at paras 49–54.

'49. In the present case, however, as the Commission has rightly submitted, the symmetry of taking into account the profits and losses arising from a taxed activity is in principle safeguarded without there being any need for the loss relief to be recaptured. This is because, during the period relevant to the main proceedings, the Kingdom of Denmark had chosen to tax foreign permanent establishments and therefore had to take account of both profits and losses arising from such activities. [...]

51. The fact, as the Kingdom of the Netherlands, for example, argues by way of objection, that, in the absence of the Danish recapture rule, taxable persons would have to be granted relief on their losses while subsequent profits made by them would not be amenable to taxation is irrelevant in this regard. In the context of the taxation of an activity, the possibility that any future profits may no longer be amenable to taxation, because of the economic failure of the activity or because a Member State loses its power to impose taxes following the relocation of the company's seat, for example, is normal.

52. However, the Republic of Austria in particular has contested that there is symmetry by submitting that the taxation of profits in the present case is more in the nature of a formality. Since the Kingdom of Denmark applies the credit method to the taxation of foreign permanent establishments, tax already paid in the source State must be offset. If the tax rate in Denmark is equal to or lower than that in the source State, profits made by foreign permanent establishments will ultimately not be taxed at all in Denmark. Even if the tax rate in the source State is lower, however, Denmark will still not have a full right of taxation.

53. That objection is justified in so far as, in the context of the credit method, the taxation of a foreign permanent establishment gives rise to fiscal results different from those that would arise under the normal taxation of domestic activities. The revenue that Denmark receives from the taxation of foreign permanent establishments will, as a rule, be comparatively lower. There is also some imbalance between the full relief on the losses they incur and the taxation - ultimately, of only some at most - of their profits.

54. Nevertheless, the taxation of a foreign permanent establishment by way of the credit method cannot be regarded as being the same as its non-taxation under the exemption method. The Court looked at the latter situation in *Krankenheim Ruhesitz am Wannsee-Seniorenheimstatt*, and ultimately allowed the Member State in question to recapture *ex post* loss relief which had been granted notwithstanding the fact that there was no power of taxation because income from a foreign permanent establishment was exempt from tax. (38) Contrary to the view taken by the Federal Republic of Germany, however, that judgment cannot be transposed to the present case, since the Kingdom of Denmark *did* wish to exercise its power of taxation in respect of foreign permanent establishments and there was at least a possibility that some of their profits would also be taxed.'

According to the AG, the justification often referred to as the 'preservation of the allocation of the power to impose taxes between Member States' is actually a broader label that is composed, more precisely, of two more specialized grounds of justification, namely the 'preservation of the coherence of a tax system' and the 'prevention of tax avoidance'.[1583] In the view of the AG, the credit method safeguards the 'preservation of the *coherence* of a tax system' essentially because, as quoted in paragraph 49,

1583. *Id.*, at paras 38–46.

the credit method safeguards the *symmetry* between profits and losses.[1584] This 'preservation' power of the credit method is *not* undermined by the fact that the credit method – in the *second* step, by virtue of allowing the deduction of foreign taxes from the taxes due in Denmark – ultimately, in effect, results in Denmark not fully (if at all) collecting taxes on the profits. This is because, basically, what is at stake under this justification is merely to ensure that a MS's ability to tax profits is not jeopardized, i.e., that MSs may 'ensure that they are not divested of their power to tax income through the transfer of that income to another Member State'.[1585] This 'includes the ability to combat fictitious and fraudulent arrangements' that leads to profit shifting. This also includes 'conversely' that a MS is '*not* required to take into account losses arising from an activity which is taxed *not* by it but by another Member State' (emphasis added), which is related to the idea that taxpayers should not be allowed to 'choose the Member State in which their losses are taken into account' – both of which are manifestations of the need for 'symmetry between the right to tax profits and the right to deduct losses'.[1586] As can be seen, the reasoning seems to revolve mostly around tax base transfers (in this way, this echoes concerns of the BEPS Project). Since the credit method captures the tax base, everything is secured from the perspective of this coherence justification.

From the above, one conclusion that could be drawn is that, if EU MSs apply the credit method to foreign PEs, it is generally not permissible under EU law to deny the deduction of foreign losses (as Denmark tried to do at a later stage at the moment of sale). However, the CJEU seemed more circumspect in both its reasoning[1587] and its final conclusions. An exacerbating factor that was emphasized more in the CJEU's reasoning (than in the Opinion of the AG) was that, in this case of a transfer of a PE, Denmark also taxed the gains from the sale.[1588] For this purpose, all the PE's assets were valued at market value.[1589] These gains could be seen as comprising the future expected profits of the PE.[1590] This contributed to the disproportionate nature of

1584. For other cases on the relationship between the credit method and coherence, *see*, e.g., the *Manninen* case, at *infra* note 1652 and the *Bouanich* case, at *infra* note 1851.
1585. Opinion of AG Kokott in Case C-48/13, *Nordea Bank*, 13 Mar. 2014, ECLI:EU:C:2014:153, at para. 40.
1586. *Id.*, at para. 41.
1587. *Compare* Opinion of AG Kokott in Case C-48/13, *Nordea Bank*, 13 Mar. 2014, ECLI:EU:C:2014:153, at paras 57, 62–65 (of the two prongs of the 'preservation of the allocation of the power to impose taxes between Member States' justification analysed by the Advocate General, Kokott rejected the first one, the 'need to preserve the coherence of a tax system', and as regards the second, the 'prevention of tax avoidance', held that it failed the principle of proportionality) and CJEU, Case C-48/13, *Nordea Bank*, 17 Jul. 2014, ECLI:EU:C:2014:2087, at paras 30–31 (the CJEU seemed to accept the combined justification of 'the need to ensure a balanced allocation of the power to impose taxes between Member States in connection with the prevention of tax avoidance', but ruled that the law failed the proportionality test).
1588. CJEU, Case C-48/13, *Nordea Bank*, 17 Jul. 2014, ECLI:EU:C:2014:2087, at para. 6.
1589. *Id.*, at para. 7.
1590. Opinion of AG Kokott in Case C-48/13, *Nordea Bank*, 13 Mar. 2014, ECLI:EU:C:2014:153, at para. 63. *See also* Ana Paula Dourado (update of 6th ed.), *Chapter 18: Cross-Border Loss Relief in* 1 *Terra/Wattel European Tax Law* 757, 793 (Peter J. Wattel, Otto Marres & Hein Vermeulen eds, Wolters Kluwer 7th ed. 2019).

Denmark's regime.[1591] The CJEU identified both elements – the previous taxation of (potential) profits (made possible by the credit method) *and* the taxation of gains – as problematic in its final conclusion.[1592]

The decision gives rise to two questions. First, if Denmark did *not also* tax the gains from the sale, would the credit method alone suffice for the CJEU to find a full recapture of losses disproportionate? On the one hand, the wording of the decision proposed by AG Kokott would be more readily amenable to this conclusion.[1593] It would seem that the application of the credit method alone could suffice, in order for the CJEU to be coherent with its *subject-to-tax* reasoning and with its *symmetry-between-profits-and-losses* reasoning. During all the previous tax years in question, under the credit method, this symmetry was technically intact.

On the other hand, rules on loss offsets generally have the aim of compensating for or offsetting results over time. Connected to that, the taxation of the gains at the moment of the sale of the PE could capture a timing aspect, namely the potential future profits, to which the loss offset *would have* eventually corresponded, whereas in the meantime those losses merely reduced DSI. Bearing that in mind, if hypothetically a MS does *not* tax the gains upon sale,[1594] perhaps the MS could be justified in some partial recapture of previously deducted losses – because it had applied credit method to annual (negative) results, but then effectively applies an exemption to some of the 'future' results – to the extent that potential future profits are captured by the gains upon sale. In other words, the decision leaves open the possibility that this case law would permit a partial recapture, e.g., to the extent of the value of the gains exempted or untaxed.

1591. CJEU, Case C-48/13, *Nordea Bank*, 17 Jul. 2014, ECLI:EU:C:2014:2087, at paras 35–36.

1592. *Compare* CJEU, Case C-48/13, *Nordea Bank*, 17 Jul. 2014, ECLI:EU:C:2014:2087, at para. 40 ('It follows from the foregoing considerations that Articles 49 TFEU and 54 TFEU and Articles 31 and 34 of the EEA Agreement preclude legislation of a Member State under which, in the event of transfer by a resident company to a non-resident company in the same group of a permanent establishment situated in another Member State or in another State that is party to the EEA Agreement, the losses previously deducted in respect of the establishment transferred are reincorporated into the transferring company's taxable profit, *in so far as* the first Member State taxes *both* the profits made by that establishment before its transfer *and* those resulting from the gain made upon the transfer' (emphasis added)) and Opinion of AG Kokott in Case C-48/13, *Nordea Bank*, 13 Mar. 2014, ECLI:EU:C:2014:153, at para. 67 ('The reply to the question referred must therefore be as follows: Article 43 EC in conjunction with Article 48 EC and Article 31 of the EEA Agreement in conjunction with Article 34 thereof preclude a Member State which, using the credit method, allows a company resident in that State to deduct on an ongoing basis losses made by a permanent establishment situated in another Member State, from making full recapture in respect of the losses made by that permanent establishment (in so far as they are not matched by profits in subsequent years) if recapture is provided for whenever part of that company's business is transferred to an affiliated company which is resident in the same State as the permanent establishment').

1593. Opinion of AG Kokott in Case C-48/13, *Nordea Bank*, 13 Mar. 2014, ECLI:EU:C:2014:153, at para. 67.

1594. *See*, e.g., OECD, *Model Tax Convention on Income and on Capital 2017: Condensed Version* Article 13(1)/(2) (OECD Publishing 2017) (if one could assume that the OECD Model could be an indication of the general tendency, then perhaps, in practice, this does not arise often, since states of residence of a taxpayer would tend to tax gains from the sale of business assets).

Second, the AG also raised a similar open issue in her Opinion, namely whether some loss restrictions could apply if they were somehow calibrated:

> '55. In the present case, however, there is *no need to decide whether*, for the purposes of fiscal coherence, *a Member State's power of taxation* which is *limited by the credit method* also *entitles that Member State to take account of losses incurred only to a limited extent*. For it is *not* the stated and recognisable objective of *the Danish recapture rule* to establish *an appropriate ratio* between the taking into account of profits and losses arising from activities taxed by way of the credit method. Rather, the rule is intended only – as also the Kingdom of Denmark itself has submitted – to prevent the *full* loss relief available under the credit method from being abused in a particular case. [...]' (emphasis added).[1595]

If the 'stated and recognisable objective' of the Danish recapture rule were different, how could losses be taken into account 'to a limited extent' or how could it be possible 'to establish an appropriate ratio between the taking into account of profits and losses arising from activities taxed by way of the credit method'? The types of rules that, it seems, would need to be considered in light of these statements include, for example, dual consolidated loss rules (such as those in the US[1596] and in Germany[1597]) and overall loss recapture rules (such as those in the US, discussed at, e.g., *supra* note 225, and possibly rules similar to those in the Netherlands, under its 'tax exemption' method as described in the *Renneberg* case[1598]). From the above cases, it seems

1595. Opinion of AG Kokott in Case C-48/13, *Nordea Bank*, 13 Mar. 2014, ECLI:EU:C:2014:153, at para. 55.

1596. United States, Internal Revenue Code, Section 904(f).

1597. Germany, Körperschaftsteuergesetz (KStG) (as amended), Section 14(1) No. 5 (Corporate Income Tax Act).

1598. CJEU, Case C-527/06, *Renneberg*, 16 Oct. 2008, ECLI:EU:C:2008:566, at para. 6 ('Article 24(1)(1) and (2) of the Bilateral Tax Convention provides: "With regard to residents of the Netherlands, double taxation is avoided in the following manner:

1. [The Kingdom of the] Netherlands may, when taxing [its] residents, include in the basis of assessment the items of income or capital which, in accordance with the provisions of this Convention, are taxable in Belgium;
2. Subject to the application of the provisions relating to compensation for losses laid down in the domestic rules for the avoidance of double taxation, the Kingdom of the Netherlands will make a reduction in the amount of tax calculated in accordance with [subparagraph] (1). The reduction is to be equal to the amount of tax corresponding to the ratio between the amount of income or capital included in the basis of assessment referred to in [subparagraph] (1) and taxable in Belgium under [in particular, Article] 6 of the Bilateral Tax Convention, and the amount of the total income or total capital constituting the basis of assessment referred to in [subparagraph] (1)"') and para. 14 ('As the national court notes, if a resident taxpayer has a negative income from immovable property located in Belgium, that negative income component may be deducted from the income taxable in the Netherlands. However, in a subsequent year in which a positive income is derived from that immovable property, the reduction in order to avoid double taxation on that income will be calculated by deducting that prior loss from that positive income, by application of Paragraph 24(1)(2) of the Bilateral Tax Convention, in conjunction with Article 3(4) of the Decree on the Avoidance of Double Taxation 1989 (Besluit voorkoming dubbele belasting 1989, Staatsblad 1989, No 594; 'the Decree of 1989)') and para. 55 ('More precisely, with regard to positive income from immovable property in Belgium which is included in the basis of assessment of the tax payable in the Netherlands under Article 24(1)(1) of the Bilateral Tax Convention, a reduction in the

possible to derive two guiding rules or constraints on the design of such laws, namely that: (1) in the case of dual consolidated loss type rules, any such rules must be targeted only at 'double dips' (not, e.g., triggered merely on the basis of a more general event, such as a cross-border sale); (2) in the case of overall loss recapture rules (and likely any loss recapture rules, more broadly speaking), previously deducted foreign losses may be recaptured only to the extent of previous deductions from DSI (not, e.g., to the extent of previous deductions from other FSI, which could occur under a credit method system with different credit limitation 'baskets') and only against related taxable profits (e.g., to adhere to the aforementioned notion of 'symmetry').

In the *NN* case,[1599] the CJEU received another preliminary ruling from Denmark, again regarding laws that restrict the use of losses in the case of PEs. The difference was that this case involved *local* PEs of *non*-resident companies (by contrast with Nordea Bank, a Danish resident company with PEs *abroad*). The CJEU's decision gives an indication of the role that the credit method in a tax treaty may play in assessing this particular law's compatibility with EU law.

tax proportional to the amount of that income in the basis of assessment is to be granted, in accordance with the rules in Article 24(1)(2) of that Convention, in order to avoid double taxation') and para. 56 ('As regards negative income from immovable property in Belgium, it is apparent ... that it may be taken into account in the determination of the taxable income of resident taxpayers and that, provided that positive income is received from that property in a subsequent year, the reduction intended to avoid double taxation is calculated by deducting the earlier negative income from that positive income in accordance with Article 3(4) of the Decree of 1989, which follows the provisions on the setting-off of losses in the Netherlands legislation on avoidance of double taxation, to which Article 24(1)(2) of the Bilateral Tax Convention refers') and para. 76 ('Furthermore, the Court must reject another argument raised in that respect by the Netherlands Government, at the hearing, alleging, in essence, that there is a risk that losses related to a non-resident taxpayer's immovable property located in Belgium could be taken into account twice') and para. 77 ('Firstly, the national legislation on double taxation, read in conjunction with Article 24(1)(2) of the Bilateral Tax Convention, seeks to avoid that risk becoming reality with regard to resident taxpayers who suffer losses of income relating to a property located in Belgium, whose situation may be compared with that of a non-resident taxpayer such as Mr Renneberg').

1599. CJEU, Case C-28/17, *NN*, 4 Jul. 2018, ECLI:EU:C:2018:526.

Diagrams can help visualize the differences between the two cases:

Illustration: *Nordea Bank* case

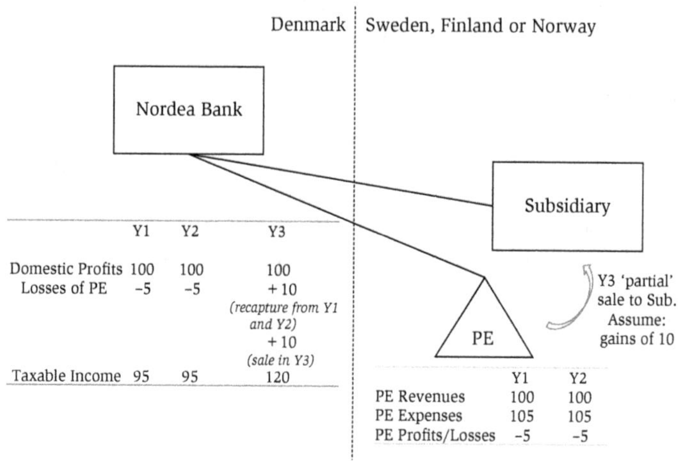

Illustration: *NN* case

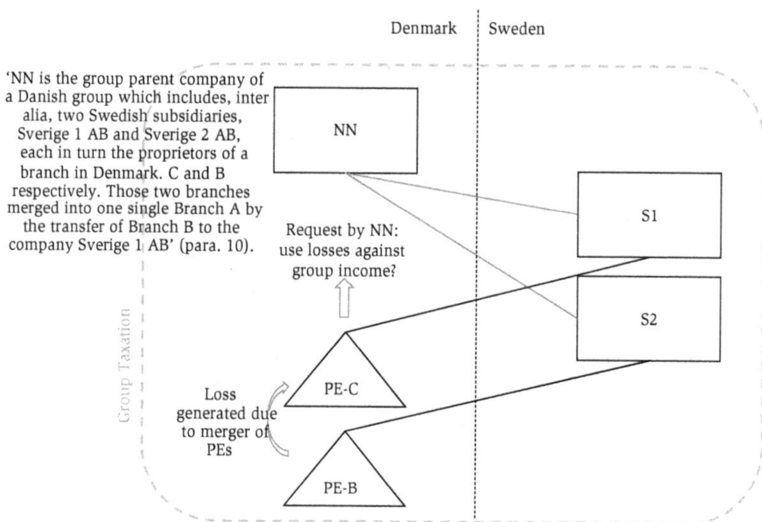

In this case, two companies residing in Sweden established branches (PEs) in Denmark. The Swedish companies were in turn subsidiaries of a Danish company, and they formed part of a group with their Danish parent company, NN.[1600] A decision was made to merge the two PEs which, setting aside the details, generated a loss. The Danish parent company, NN, applied to offset the losses 'against the overall group taxation income'.[1601] The Danish tax authorities refused this, citing 'Paragraph 31(2)(2) of the Law on corporation tax' under which '[a] loss in a permanent establishment may be set off against the income of other companies *only if* the rules in the *foreign* State ... *in which the company is resident* provide that a loss *cannot* be set off in the calculation of the company's income in the foreign State ... or if group taxation has been chosen pursuant to Paragraph 31 A ...' (emphasis added).[1602] In other words, the losses could be used by NN in Denmark only if the rules in Sweden, where the companies that established the PEs resided, did not already allow the loss to be taken into account in the calculation of those Swedish companies' income.

Notably, although the PEs belonged to *non*-resident Swedish companies, the PEs were located in Denmark. Thus, the CJEU had to scrutinize why Denmark would add an extra condition, or restriction, on the use of losses connected with branches on its own territory. But, also notably, this was a case of group taxation. Moreover, because the credit method applied in the Nordic Convention, the PEs were technically subject to the tax jurisdiction of *both* states, first in Denmark on the profits attributable to the PE and then in Sweden accompanied by an FTC for the Danish taxes. This is one of the main factors, it seems, that gave rise to the additional condition in Denmark. Since Sweden could normally take the worldwide income and losses of the PEs into account, there was a risk that the PE losses were already used in Sweden - hence, the extra condition, which required a verification that this was not the case.

As for the reasoning of the CJEU, since such a condition did not exist in a purely domestic context, there was different treatment[1603] of objectively comparable situations.[1604] In the next stage of reasoning, one of the justifications put forward by Denmark was that its law was justified by the need to prevent the double deduction of

1600. *Id.*, at para. 10.
1601. *Id.*, at para. 13.
1602. *Id.*, at para. 7 and para. 13.
1603. *Id.*, at paras 28–30 ('28 NN explains that the losses of a permanent establishment, situated in Denmark, of a resident company in the group are deductible without restriction from the group's taxable profits in Denmark. In the case in the main proceedings, NN points out that, if the Danish permanent establishment had been owned by one of its Danish subsidiaries, its losses could, in any event, have been set off against the group's profits.

29 In that regard, it should be noted that the tax legislation at issue in the main proceedings does indeed establish such a difference in treatment. The tax treatment of a Danish group which owns a permanent establishment in Denmark through a non-resident subsidiary is, under Paragraph 31(2)(2) of the Law on corporation tax, less favourable than that of a group in which all of the companies have their registered offices in Denmark.

30 That difference in treatment is liable to render less attractive the exercise of freedom of establishment through the creation of subsidiaries in other Member States. It is, however, incompatible with the provisions of the Treaty only if it concerns situations which are objectively comparable').
1604. *Id.*, at paras 31–38.

losses.[1605] On this point, the Court incorporated the credit method in Article 25 of the Nordic Convention into its reasoning. The reasoning seemed to be that if the income is *taxed twice* in both MSs, then it is not a problem if the losses are deducted twice – indeed, the latter would appear 'justified' according to the CJEU.[1606] By implication, if the income is *not* taxed twice, then it is a problem if the losses are deducted twice. In this case, where relief of double taxation is offered under a tax treaty by means of a credit, both states exercise their tax jurisdiction, but due to the credit mechanism, the income is *not* ultimately *taxed twice*. For that reason, the use of losses twice 'does not appear to be justified'. Thus, the justification stood.[1607] The CJEU also included the credit method in its conclusions, holding that 'Article 49 TFEU must be interpreted as *not* precluding, in principle, national legislation, such as that at issue in the main proceedings ... when the application of that legislation *is combined with* that of a *convention preventing double taxation allowing*, in the latter Member State, *the deduction from the income tax payable by the subsidiary of a sum corresponding to the income tax paid*, in the Member State on the territory of which that permanent establishment is situated, in respect of the latter's activity [...]' (emphasis added).[1608]

The relevant paragraphs establishing the connection between the compatibility of the legislation in question and the credit method are as follows:

> '43 It is true that, in a situation in which a permanent establishment's income is *taxed* by two Member States, it appears justified that the charges borne by that establishment should be capable of being deducted from that income in one and the other tax systems, in accordance with national rules.
>
> 44 However, the existence of such a situation *cannot* simply be inferred from the fact that two Member States *concurrently exercise their power of taxation over the profits* of the same permanent establishment, as is the case, in the dispute in the main proceedings, with regard to the Kingdom of Denmark and the Kingdom of Sweden.
>
> 45 The tax agreements between Member States specifically designed to prevent double taxation *cannot* be disregarded. [...]
>
> 46 Under Article 25 of [the Nordic] convention, if a person residing in Sweden receives income that is taxable in another contracting State, the Kingdom of Sweden *allows the deduction from income tax* of a sum corresponding to the income tax paid in the other State.
>
> 47 *In the light of that mechanism*, the parallel exercise of the powers of taxation of the Kingdom of Denmark and the Kingdom of Sweden does *not* entail an obligation for the Swedish company which has a permanent establishment in Denmark *to pay income tax twice*. In those circumstances, the ability, claimed by the *Danish group*

1605. *Id.*, at paras 39, 41.
1606. *Id.*, at para. 43.
1607. *Id.*, at paras 45–47.
1608. *Id.*, at para. 57 (however, it continued, the legislation becomes incompatible if it does not in fact allow the losses to be used even 'where it is not possible to set off those losses against that subsidiary's profits in the Member State [Sweden] on the territory of which that subsidiary is established, these being matters for the referring court to verify').

to which the Swedish company belongs, to deduct the losses of such an establishment *twice*, that is to say, in one and the other national tax systems, does *not* appear to be *justified*.

48 Paragraph 31(2)(2) of the Law on corporation tax is *specifically intended to prevent* the *group* concerned from *exploiting the same loss twice*. In the absence of such a provision, as noted by the Advocate General in point 75 of his Opinion, cross-border situations would confer an *unjustified advantage* over comparable national situations, in which a double deduction is not possible. The difference in treatment established by national legislation thus appears to be justified' (emphasis added).[1609]

The logical chain seems to be:

- If taxed 2x, then loss 2x = justified.
- If taxed 1x, then loss 2x ≠ justified.
- Credit method = taxed 1x, thus loss 2x ≠ justified.

Based on the general way it is formulated, it is not immediately clear whether this reasoning is intended to apply more broadly to the credit method and the treatment of losses in general, or whether it is confined to the unique circumstances and legislation at issue, as paragraph 47 quoted above implies, and confined to circumstances where the double deduction would lead to a calculable unjustified advantage, as paragraph 48 quoted above implies. It is likely, and should be, the latter, i.e., confined.[1610] As regards the unique aspect, the facts and laws operated within the specific context of group taxation. This is arguably what was most decisive. What the taxpayer requested was to use the losses in question against the overall group income in Denmark,[1611] and potentially (via the credit method in Sweden) the losses could be used against income of a group member in Sweden *at the same time*. Even the losses themselves were generated as a result of the unique combination of the laws in the two states and the valuation of the merged PEs.[1612] As regards the 'unjustified advantage' aspect ('an *unjustified advantage* over comparable national situations'), it is true that it is hard to imagine a situation in which a loss could be used in this same way twice within a purely *domestic* group context; thus, it is an opportunity rendered possible due to the cross-border element.

Otherwise, outside of this case (such as in non-group contexts), taking into account either losses twice or especially expenses twice, where the same income is

1609. CJEU, Case C-28/17, *NN*, 4 Jul. 2018, ECLI:EU:C:2018:526, at paras 43–48.

1610. Indeed, due to the many unique circumstances in this case, extrapolation would be risky. Without a careful reading, one could think, at very first glance, that the existence of the credit method opens the door to rules restricting losses. However, it is notable that the loss rule applied in Denmark and the credit method applied in Sweden. The two regimes were not in one and the same state; thus, this case does not give insight into what a credit-granting state may do vis-à-vis losses under EU law. Moreover, the losses technically belonged to a non-resident taxpayer; they were not losses of a Denmark resident. It was the applicability of the group regime that made the losses relevant for the Denmark resident. Moreover, any inclination that the credit method alone suffices as grounds for refusing losses is contrary to the very defining features of the credit method. It would also contradict the *Nordea Bank* case.

1611. CJEU, Case C-28/17, *NN*, 4 Jul. 2018, ECLI:EU:C:2018:526, at para. 13.

1612. *Id.*, at paras 11–12.

included in the tax base twice under the credit method, does not tend to lead to an unjustified advantage, as some simple numerical examples can demonstrate (*see* Example No. 27 below). Generally speaking, the use of an expense or a loss twice can be considered unjustified or excessive in at least two scenarios. First, one scenario is where a loss is used against different income; i.e., the same loss is used to reduce two different sets of income. If a loss is used twice against two different unrelated sets of income, then one loss is reducing two distinct taxable bases.[1613] Second, another scenario is where the same loss can be double counted against one and the same income, i.e., basically multiplied by two and deducted from the same income, which could potentially happen under a group taxation regime. Of course, anytime losses or expenses are artificially generated, this is problematic.

By comparison, if the same income is taken into account twice and a legitimate expense or loss related to that income is taken into account twice, then all the income, expenses and taxation are aligned.[1614] Indeed, to deny that both the state of source (or of a PE, etc.) and the state of residence, when taxing the same income, can allow the taxpayer to deduct the expenses related to that income would be to deny both states the right to tax on a net basis, thus interfering with sound tax base rules. This would be a counterproductive development. Net-basis taxation is fundamental to income taxation, as it ensures that taxpayers are taxed on an amount that better reflects their 'tax-paying capacity', which incidentally was a principle expressly mentioned in this judgment (at paragraph 35).

As can be seen, there is some ambiguity in this decision. As one law firm observed, it is not immediately clear how such reasoning will interact with certain ATAD rules on double deduction, which 'provides that it should be the State of the investor (i.e. the residence State) to deny the use of the losses'.[1615] Moreover, construed too broadly, the way in which parts of the reasoning were formulated could

1613. *See*, e.g., United States, Internal Revenue Code, Section 1503(d); United States, Internal Revenue Service, Internal Revenue Manuals, Part 4, Chapter 61, Section 13, https://www.irs.gov/irm/part4/irm_04-061-013 (last visited 24 Jul. 2019) (this can be referred to as 'double dipping'. The US devised 'dual consolidated loss' rules to counteract this. According to the IRS, 'The dual consolidated loss ("DCL") provisions of the Internal Revenue Code ("IRC") and regulations are intended to prevent an entity from using a loss to offset income of a domestic affiliate in the United States while using the same loss to offset income of a foreign affiliate which is not subject to U.S. tax. The DCL provisions are intended to prevent the "double dipping" of a single loss').

1614. *See* Opinion of AG Campos Sánchez-Bordona in Case C-28/17, *NN*, 21 Feb. 2018, ECLI:EU:C:2018:86, at para. 10 and CJEU, Case C-28/17, *NN*, 4 Jul. 2018, ECLI:EU:C:2018:526, at para. 9 (one of Denmark's laws quoted in the case implied this: 'Paragraph 5G(1) reads: "Taxable persons ... cannot claim a deduction for expenditure which under foreign tax rules can be deducted *from income that is not included in the calculation of Danish tax*. The same applies if the deduction for expenditure can be transferred under foreign tax rules to a deduction from the income calculated by companies etc. in the group *if the income is not included in the calculation of Danish tax*"' (emphasis added)). *See*, e.g., ATAD II, Article 1 amending Article 2(9)(g) and Article 9(1) (this also appears to be the reason behind an exclusion for 'dual inclusion income' in the ATAD).

1615. Maisto e Associati, *Case C-28/17, NN, CJEU Issued its Judgment on the Compatibility with the TFEU of Danish Legislation Limiting the Use, Within Domestic Fiscal Units, of Losses Incurred by Danish PEs of EU Companies*, EU Tax Alert 2018/14, https://www.maisto.it/en/newsletter/eu-tax-alert--47.html (last visited 18 Mar. 2019).

appear to give licence to states where PEs of non-residents are established to deny deductions for expenses or losses whenever the credit method applies in the state of residence. On this point, however, as argued above, the statements are best understood within, and confined to, their legal context of the group taxation regime.

Example No. 27: Credit Method and Double Use of Losses

Facts: Based on the facts depicted in the diagram below, this example illustrates the use of losses under a basic credit method scenario (first scenario) as compared to a use of losses under the credit method that could be considered problematic (second scenario).[1616]

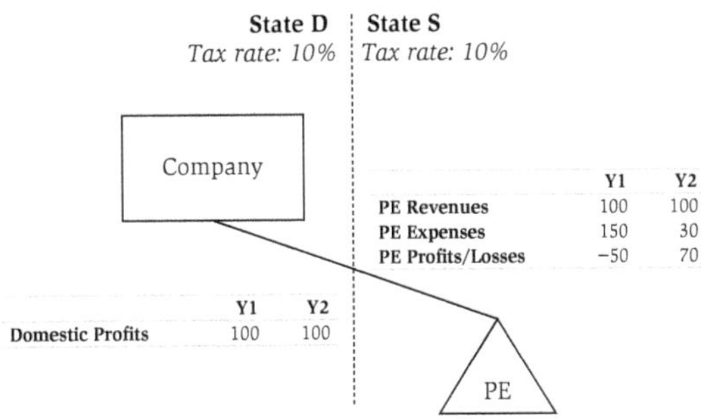

1616. As an explanatory note, these scenarios are intentionally simplifying the diagram, thereby not illustrating the whole group structure of the *NN* case. Rather, it aims to isolate numerically what happens if the losses are unduly counted twice in a credit method scenario. Despite not replicating the whole structure, it aims to show essentially what the taxpayer would have achieved numerically (*see* especially the second scenario, year 2).

Basic credit method scenario (non-group-taxation-regime context)

State D

	Year 1	Year 2
Domestic Profits of Company	100	100
Losses/Profits of PE	50	70
Taxable Income	**-50**	**170**
Tax Rate	10%	10%
Taxes	**5**	**17**
Credit for Taxes Paid by PE	0	2
Total Taxes Paid to State D	**5**	**15**

State S

	Year 1	Year 2
PE Revenues	100	100
PE Expenses	150	30
PE Profits/Losses	**-50**	**70**
LCF	N/A	-50
Taxable Income	0	20
Tax Rate	10%	10%
Total Taxes Paid to State S	**0**	**2**

Total tax burden over Y1 and Y2

Y1-Taxes Paid to State D	5
Y2-Taxes Paid to State D	15
Total Taxes Paid to State D (Y1 + Y2)	**20**
Y1-Taxes Paid to State S	0
Y2-Taxes Paid to State S	2
Total Taxes Paid to State S (Y1 + Y2)	**2**
Total Taxes Paid	**22**

Hypothetical: If purely domestic scenario, what would total taxes paid have been?

	D	S		
Year 1	100	-50	**50**	
Year 2	100	70	**170**	*No LCF would have occurred b/c the 100 in Y1 was already reduced by the losses.*
Total Income over 2 Years			220	
Taxes over 2 Years		*10%*	**22**	

Double deduction that leads to unjustified advantage over domestic situations

State D

	Year 1	Year 2
Domestic Profits of Company	100	100
Losses/Profits of PE	-50	20
Taxable Income	**50**	**120**
Tax Rate	10%	10%
Taxes	**5**	**12**
Credit for Taxes Paid by PE	0	2
Total Taxes Paid to State D	**5**	**10**

State S

	Year 1	Year 2
PE Revenues	100	100
PE Expenses	150	30
PE Profits/Losses	**-50**	**70**
LCF	N/A	-50
Taxable Income	0	20
Tax Rate	10%	10%
Total Taxes Paid to State S	**0**	**2**

Total tax burden over Y1 and Y2

Y1-Taxes Paid to State D	5
Y2-Taxes Paid to State D	10
Total Taxes Paid to State D (Y1 + Y2)	**15**
Y1-Taxes Paid to State S	0
Y2-Taxes Paid to State S	2
Total Taxes Paid to State S (Y1 + Y2)	**2**
Total Taxes Paid	**17**

Hypothetical: If purely domestic scenario, what total taxes would have been paid?

	D	S		
Year 1	100	-50	**50**	
Year 2	100	70	**170**	*No LCF would have occurred b/c the 100 in Y1 was already reduced by the losses.*
Total Income over 2 Years			220	
Taxes over 2 Years		*10%*	**22**	*Compare: 22 would have been paid, but only 17 is paid.*

In both *Nordea Bank* and *NN*, the credit method formed an integral part of the legal background that was used for determining whether *other* national laws, regarding the treatment of losses, were compatible with EU law. Consequently, these cases brought insight into the role of the credit method in the CJEU's analysis of comparability or of justifications. However, they remained rather vague in addressing the compatibility of the credit method itself or its design components.

Losses do, however, give rise to more credit-design-specific questions. This was one issue identified in the *Haribo & Salinen* case in Austria (discussed above in Section 4.2.3.) under the 'equivalence' line of case law. In sum, the credit method itself was criticized for giving rise to a double disadvantage in certain cases of overall losses. First, if a stream of positive income flows in from a foreign state, on which taxes were levied in that foreign state, but overall the taxpayer is in a loss-making situation, then, naturally, there are no domestic taxes against which those foreign taxes can be deducted. Second, given that this positive stream of foreign income is included in the tax base in the residence state under the credit method, the positive income reduces the amount of overall losses, which in turn reduces the amount of a LCF against future profits.

Upon closer inspection, this first aspect is not per se a problem. On the contrary, if a residence state *were* to collect taxes in the situation where a taxpayer suffered an overall loss, this would be more problematic. The fact that, under the credit method, the residence state takes into account the worldwide income of a taxpayer wherever generated and, as a corollary, fully recognizes its losses wherever generated - thereby reducing the tax base and taxing accordingly in that year - is generally speaking an advantage. Under EU law, according to the CJEU in *Nordea Bank*, the ability to take into account foreign losses constitutes a 'tax advantage'.[1617] It is true that the taxpayer is currently stuck with its *foreign* tax bill that cannot (yet) be credited, but it has no current *domestic* tax bill, leaving it with one tax bill in total and thus no *current* double taxation. Incidentally, this would be the same under the exemption method.

Thus, it is only in combination with the second aspect that a more distinctive disadvantage may arise. The extent to which the foreign profits soak up or shrink some of the losses and thus reduce the LCF (in year 1) directly corresponds to the amount by which the taxable profits in a future year are increased (in year 2). Since the foreign profits (of year 1) lead to a corresponding increase in the overall profits taxed later (in year 2), a taxpayer may argue that this is effectively double taxation. Hence, in *Haribo & Salinen*, it was observed that Austria ended up taxing those foreign profits merely at a later time (in year 2), without carrying forward any corresponding tax credit. In this way, it is a timing issue. Austria did not allow the creditable foreign taxes that could not

1617. CJEU, Case C-48/13, *Nordea Bank*, 17 Jul. 2014, ECLI:EU:C:2014:2087, at para. 20 ('20 A provision which allows losses incurred by a permanent establishment situated in another Member State or in another State that is party to the EEA Agreement to be taken into account in calculating the profits and taxable income of the principal company constitutes a tax advantage (see, to this effect, the judgment in *Lidl Belgium*, EU:C:2008:278, paragraph 23)').

be used in year 1 to be carried forward to year 2. This is the problem. And a solution, as the CJEU rightfully discerned, is a credit carryforward.[1618]

This problem is not unique to Austria. Other MSs have been challenged by taxpayers in cases involving losses and the credit method. For example, in 2011, in Finland, a taxpayer brought its complaint up to the Supreme Administrative Court, after the amount of foreign taxes it could claim as a credit was reduced by the fact that a LCF was taken into account in calculating the credit limitation.[1619] In 2014, in Belgium, the Constitutional Court decided on the case of a Belgian company that paid foreign taxes on interest income from Australia, but, due to being in an overall loss position, was not able to benefit from the Belgian FTC mechanism. The company, nevertheless, was forced to include the grossed-up interest income in its tax base, thereby reducing its LCF, without any possibility for a credit carryforward. The company put forward various grounds for violations of the (non-discrimination rule of the) Australia-Belgium tax treaty and the Belgian Constitution.[1620] In 2014, even post-*Haribo & Salinen* in Austria, the Supreme Administrative Court held that losses in the tax base can lead to the loss of the taxpayer's (direct) FTC, as there are no Austrian taxes against which the credit can be taken and there is no credit carryforward.[1621] In 2016, Portugal's Supreme Administrative Court decided on a case in which a taxpayer paid foreign taxes on the profits of its PEs located abroad, but was overall in a loss-making position, and, for this reason, did not owe any taxes in Portugal against which the foreign taxes could be credited.[1622] In all of the cases, the national courts reiterated that a credit was not possible in these loss scenarios.

1618. CJEU, Joined Cases C-436/08 and C-437/08, *Haribo Lakritzen Hans Riegel BetriebsgmbH and Österreichische Salinen AG*, 10 Feb. 2011, ECLI:EU:C:2011:61, at para. 173.

1619. Finland, Korkein Hallinto-oikeus (Supreme Administrative Court), KHO:2011:45, 18 May 2011. *See* Marjaana Helminen, *Chapter 23: Finland – The Effect of Losses on the Foreign Tax Credit, in Tax Treaty Case Law Around the Globe 2012* 255 (Eric C.C.M. Kemmeren et al. eds, IBFD/Linde 2013) (regarding the facts, in a previous year (2003), the taxpayer generated capital losses. In a subsequent year (2004), the taxpayer sold real estate property in the US at a gain, on which taxes were levied in the US. When calculating the taxable income in Finland, the loss carryforward from 2003 reduced the relevant taxable income in 2004, for the purposes of determining both the amount of Finnish income tax and the maximum amount of foreign tax credit that could be deducted therefrom. Normally, such loss carryforwards are beneficial, as they aim to take into account that, over a period of more than one year, a taxpayer has earned overall less taxable income and therefore should pay less income taxes than a strict one-calendar-year period might dictate. However, for the purposes of the credit, this meant that the tax base used in Finland, comprising the previous losses, was smaller than the tax base in the US on which the foreign taxes were levied, leading to the result that not all of the taxes levied in the US could be credited in Finland).

1620. Belgium, Grondwettelijk Hof, Cour constitutionnelle (Constitutional Court), No. 14/2014, 29 Jan. 2014. *See* Edoardo Traversa & Gaëtan Zeyen, *Belgium: Constitutionality of Interest Credit in Belgium-Australia DTC, in Tax Treaty Case Law Around the Globe 2015* 293 (Michael Lang et al. eds, Linde/IBFD 2016).

1621. Austria, Verwaltungsgerichtshof (Supreme Administrative Court), 2011/15/0112, 30 Oct. 2014 and Austria, Verwaltungsgerichtshof (Supreme Administrative Court), 2012/15/0002, 27 Nov. 2014. *See* Veronika Daurer & Nicole Tüchler, *Foreign Tax Credit: Is a Carry-Forward Obligatory?*, 66(10) Bull. Int'l Tax'n 563 (2012).

1622. Portugal, Supremo Tribunal Administrativo (Supreme Administrative Court), 0351/14, 5 Nov. 2016. *See* Ana Paula Dourado, *Portugal: Domestic Losses and Worldwide Gross Income, in Tax Treaty Case Law Around the Globe 2017* 63 (Michael Lang et al. eds, IBFD/Linde 2018).

These cases reveal that the intersection between the credit method and losses is a recurring issue in EU MSs. Numerous possible permutations of losses emerge: e.g., domestic losses with foreign income, foreign losses with domestic income, losses carried forward from a previous year versus losses generated in the current year (perhaps not surprisingly, as varied as the unique circumstances of taxpayers, which are potentially infinite). Depending on how these different axes intersect, credit method concerns can arise (especially in cases of overall losses with foreign profits).

Taking the last-mentioned case as an example, the problem can be illustrated (as in Example No. 28 below). According to the facts, a Portuguese company operated three PEs abroad (in the UK; in Zhuhai, China; and in Macau, China) each of which generated profits and paid taxes on those profits.[1623] Under the credit method, the tax base of the Portuguese company was its worldwide income calculated in accordance with national law. In the tax year in question, the Portuguese company had losses overall. Thus, it could not credit the taxes paid by its PEs abroad, but nevertheless had to include their income in its tax base. This reduced its LCF and Portugal did not offer a credit carryforward.[1624] What happens in cases like this one is that international juridical double taxation is not fully relieved.

Example No. 28: Losses and Credit Carryforward

	Cross-border scenario	Domestic scenario
Year 1	Assume the same 25% tax rate and the same tax base in all states.	
	Domestic loss: –100 PE-UK: 20 (tax-UK: 5) PE-CH: 20 (tax-CH: 5) PE-M: 20 (tax-M: 5) Overall profits/loss: –40	Domestic loss: –100 PE-Domestic 1: 20 PE-Domestic 2: 20 PE-Domestic 3: 20 Overall profits/loss: –40
	In year 1, both companies have the same amount of losses and, thus, a loss carryforward (LCF) of –40. In both cases, the state of residence does not levy any taxes. The tax burden on the cross-border scenario was 15 (taxes of 5 paid to 3 foreign jurisdictions) while the tax burden on the domestic scenario was 0.	

1623. Ana Paula Dourado, *Portugal: Domestic Losses and Worldwide Gross Income, in Tax Treaty Case Law Around the Globe 2017* 63 (Michael Lang et al. eds, IBFD/Linde 2018).
1624. *Id.*

Year 2	Domestic profit: +100 PE-UK: 0 PE-CH: 0 PE-M: 0 LCF: –40 Overall profits/loss: +60 Taxes: 60 × 25% = 15 taxes	Domestic profit: +100 PE-Dom 1: 0 PE-Dom 2: 0 PE-Dom 3: 0 LCF: –40 Overall profits/loss: +60 Taxes: 60 × 25% = 15 taxes
Over the 2-year period	30 taxes total = paid 15 taxes in PE states in Year 1 + 15 taxes in R State in Year 2	15 in taxes total
Solution	If a credit carryforward is provided, a credit for the 15 paid to PE states in year 1 is offered against the 15 owed to R State, now that the company is profitable = 15 in taxes total. This is the result that would have been obtained if the foreign PEs' profits had not been taken into account in year 1, since no taxes would be collected this year, as the tax base would be –100 + 100 = 0. Also, it is the result that would have been obtained had the R State been able to fully collect taxes on the PEs profits in year 1, since it would collect 15 and offer a credit for 15.	

One could view the concept of international juridical double taxation in a narrow formal way, looking only at the one-year tax period in question and overlooking effects on the tax burden across more than one tax period. It is true that, formally, there was no juridical double taxation in year 1, given that only the PE states levied taxes and not the state of residence (i.e., only one state taxed each of the profits of 20). The disadvantage for the taxpayer in year 1 is that it paid taxes on its PE profits, despite being in an overall loss-making situation from a worldwide perspective – a situation that would not arise had everything occurred in one state. The disadvantage persists, over a longer period (of 2 years, for example), since the situation leads to a larger aggregate tax burden for the cross-border situation as compared to the domestic situation.

As seen in the *Haribo & Salinen* case, one possible solution is a credit carryforward. Crucially, a distinction between these (above-cited domestic) cases and the *Haribo & Salinen* case is that, while the former concerned juridical double taxation, the *Haribo & Salinen* case concerned the economic double taxation of dividends. In the *Haribo & Salinen* case, the CJEU reiterated that the non-discrimination principles of the

EU fundamental freedoms cannot resolve juridical double taxation.[1625] Thus, this solution of the CJEU seems confined to the specific scenario where a MS applies the exemption method in the domestic scenario, applies an indirect credit in the cross-border scenario and needs to re-establish the 'equivalence' of the two methods. In this scenario, an indirect credit should be accompanied by a credit carryforward.

However, although CJEU case law tends to have less to offer in the cases of juridical double taxation, in the particular case of losses, the findings of the *AMID* case could arguably be relevant not only under the exemption method but also under the credit method.[1626] One could view the *AMID* decision as a finding that: if legal provisions allow for losses to be carried forward against future profits in the domestic context, then legal provisions on losses, in connection with the relief mechanism (in the case of *AMID*, exemption), cannot have the *effect* of preventing (domestic) losses from being used, merely because the company has activities abroad that are generating foreign profits. If one were to compare Example No. 26 (regarding the *AMID* case) with the above Example No. 28, or if one were to adapt Example No. 26 to replace it with the credit method, the ultimate tax effect is mathematically the same: the interaction of the LCF and the credit method *without* a credit carryforward is the same as under the *AMID* rules, whereas the interaction of the LCF and the credit method *with* a credit carryforward aligns the results with the domestic scenario where the LCF would be fully effective.

1625. CJEU, Joined Cases C-436/08 and C-437/08, *Haribo Lakritzen Hans Riegel BetriebsgmbH and Österreichische Salinen AG*, 10 Feb. 2011, ECLI:EU:C:2011:61, at paras 166–172. *See also*, e.g., Georg Kofler, *Article 23B: Methods for Elimination of Double Taxation, in Global Tax Treaty Commentaries* Section 3.2.2.3.5 (Richard Vann ed.-in-chief, Pasquale Pistone et al. eds, Global Topics IBFD updated as of February 2019) ('However, such measures [i.e. the carrying over unused tax credits] have been viewed as being required neither by article 23B of the OECD Model$_{[563]}$ nor by domestic constitutional law$_{[564]}$ or the EU/EEA fundamental freedoms,$_{[565]}$ although not granting a carry-forward or other form of relief may lead to intertemporal double taxation').

1626. European Parliament, Jacques Malherbe, Philippe Malherbe, Isabelle Richelle, Edoardo Traversa, with the contribution of Daphné de Laveleye, *The Impact of the Rulings of the European Court of Justice in the Area of Direct Taxation 2010*, PE 457.367, IP/A/ECON/ST/2010-18, para. 90 (April 2011).

Example No. 29: *AMID* Case Applied to the Credit Method

	NO Credit Carryforward (assume 25% tax rate and same tax base in BE & LU)	*Credit Carryforward*	*Purely Domestic Scenario*
1981	BE: –100 PE in LU: 100	BE: –100 PE in LU: 100	BE: –100 + 100
	Income recorded for tax purposes: –100 + 100 = 0	Income recorded for tax purposes: –100 + 100 = 0	Income recorded for tax purposes: 0
	Tax BE: 0 Tax LU: 25	Tax BE: 0 Tax LU: 25	Tax BE: 0
1982	BE: 100 PE in LU: 100	BE: 100 PE in LU: 100	BE: 100 + 100
	Income recorded for tax purposes: 100 + 100 = 200	Income recorded for tax purposes: 100 + 100 = 200	Income recorded for tax purposes: 200
	Tax BE: 50 – FTC 25 = 25 Tax LU: 25	Tax BE: 50 – FTC 25 – CCF 25 = 0 Tax LU: 25	Tax BE: 50
Over 2 years	Economic result in BE: 0 Economic result WW: 200	Economic result in BE: 0 Economic result WW: 200	Economic result: 200 Taxable result: 200
	Taxable result WW: 300 (**100** taxed in LU in Y1, 0 taxed in BE in Y1, **100** in Luxembourg in Y2, 200 taxed in BE in Y2, but FTC in BE for 25 LU taxes in Y2 = as though **100** were taxed in BE)	Taxable result WW: 200 (**100** taxed in LU in Y1, 0 taxed in BE in Y1, **100** in Luxembourg in Y2, 200 taxed in BE in Y2, but FTC in BE for 25 LU taxes in Y2 & CCF for 25 LU taxes in Y1 = as though **0** were taxed in BE)	
	Tax BE: 0 + 25 Tax LU: 25 + 25 Total: 75	Tax BE: 0 + 0 Tax LU: 25 + 25 Total: 50	Tax BE: 0 + 50 Total: 50

Interim Summary

The issue of the cross-border offsetting of losses has featured quite prominently in CJEU case law and, more recently (2014 and 2018), the credit method has featured in such cases. The *Nordea Bank* decision offers a first indication that, if a MS applies the credit method, the CJEU is less likely to accept that the MS may deny a resident company's right to use the losses of its PEs in other EEA/EU MSs. However, as mentioned, the final conclusions of the CJEU were more narrowly formulated, by comparison with the suggestion of the AG which focused more broadly on the credit method. A recapture of losses of a PE in another EEA/EU MS at the moment of sale is not proportionate, to the extent that the MS of residence of the head office *both* (1) 'taxes ... the profits made by that establishment' prior to the sale, in this case due to the credit method under Article 25 of the Nordic Convention; *and* (2) taxes the gains made from the sale.

The credit method was implicitly relevant in the comparability analysis where the CJEU reasoned that 'by making the profits of permanent establishments situated in Finland, Sweden and Norway subject to Danish tax, the Kingdom of Denmark has equated those establishments with resident permanent establishments so far as concerns the deduction of losses'[1627] and it was a key reason for finding the legislation disproportionate.[1628] This finding was not changed by the fact that, as argued by the government officials of Austria, the worldwide tax jurisdiction exercised under the credit method could be regarded as restricted, in reality, because, by its nature, the credit granted to relieve double taxation means that the MS will not always collect taxes on the FSI, despite including it.[1629]

However, as mentioned, two open questions include: (1) whether the credit method in isolation (without the taxation of the gains from the sale) would have sufficed as a grounds to argue that losses should be taken into account (thus, not recaptured), and (2) the question expressly left open by the AG (in paragraph 55 of her Opinion) as to whether 'a Member State's power of taxation which is limited by the credit method also entitles that Member State to take account of losses incurred only to a limited extent'. Some possible answers to these questions were discussed above (at *supra* note 1593) and are summarized in the 'Synthesis of Findings and Lessons for EU MSs' in Chapter 5.

In the *NN* decision, by contrast with the *Nordea Bank* decision, reasoning resembling that contended above by the Austrian government officials was accepted. The CJEU reasoned that, if the credit method applies, by virtue of the fact that it reduces the taxes due in the state of residence in order to relieve double taxation, the FSI cannot be considered taxed twice; as a result, it appears justified to deny the deduction of losses twice. In other words, if the income is taxed only once, then the losses should *not* be used twice. At first glance, it is not easy to reconcile these two positions, but there are at least three features which set the *NN* case apart from the *Nordea Bank* case: (1) while *Nordea Bank* was decided from the perspective of the state of residence, *NN* was decided from the perspective of the state of the PE of a non-resident company; (2) the existence of the loss seemed to have been recognized by only one MS; (3) the issues arose in the specific context of group taxation (*see also supra* note 1610). While this

1627. CJEU, Case C-48/13, *Nordea Bank*, 17 Jul. 2014, ECLI:EU:C:2014:2087, at para. 24.
1628. *Id.*, at paras 31–34.
1629. Opinion of AG Kokott in Case C-48/13, *Nordea Bank*, 13 Mar. 2014, ECLI:EU:C:2014:153, at paras 52–56; CJEU, Case C-48/13, *Nordea Bank*, 17 Jul. 2014, ECLI:EU:C:2014:2087, at para. 34.

reasoning maps itself more accurately onto the exemption method, especially in the context of a tax base exemption, it should not be overgeneralized in the context of the credit method. To support this, a brief demonstration in examples showed when deductions taken into account twice are potentially excessive and when they are potentially justifiable and intended (*see* Example No. 27). Moreover, it is questionable whether the PE state should be the one to deny losses in such cases, considering PE-non-discrimination rules, tax treaty rules and the ATAD rule under Article 9(1) (*see*, e.g., *supra* note 1615). Against this background, the third feature seems particularly decisive, namely that this was a question within the context of group taxation, where the risks of unintended double uses of losses are heightened.

While these two cases explored new developments in this losses line of case law, the analysis showed that they are more ancillary as regards the question of the design of the credit method. That is, the credit method played a bigger structural role in these cases than these cases played for the credit method in terms of its compatibility and design (this is especially so in the *NN* case; by comparison, the *Nordea Bank* gives some insight into the relation between the credit method and losses, as elaborated above).

Rather, the design-relevant and clearly reoccurring example of losses and the credit method was posed in the *Haribo & Salinen* case and, as cited above, on more than one occasion, before domestic courts of MSs. The CJEU made a positive contribution to the design, by prescribing a credit carryforward. However, the ruling was made in the specific context of the elimination of economic double taxation, or a series of charges to tax, on the distribution of profits, thus limited to the indirect credit method, and in the specific context of ensuring 'equivalence' between the exemption method and indirect credit method.

From this, what can be seen is that the refusal of a credit carryforward is not an inherent problem of the credit method, but rather a design issue (arguably, a design flaw) attributable to the MS implementing it. Even if non-discrimination arguments would not prevail, hopefully policy ones eventually will. If the objective of the direct credit method is to eliminate juridical double taxation, then it seems hard to justify the lack of a credit carryforward in the situation depicted in Example No. 28 above. It is not justified by the credit limitation, or MCA, because this limit serves to protect domestic taxes collected on DSI, an objective that is not undermined by a credit carryforward (i.e., the ability to collect taxes on DSI is not undermined to the extent that the taxes collected in future years correspond to an amount of DSI that was simply not sheltered by a LCF due to foreign profits in the previous year; in the absence of those foreign profits in year 1, no taxes would be collected on that portion of DSI in year 2). Moreover, it can be pointed out that, in most jurisdictions, businesses have the right to a LCF. Generally speaking, the purpose of these LCF rules is to serve as an exception to the normal rule of annual taxation of income earned within the calendar year (or any other one-year period), an exception which is intended to recognize that a strict application of this rule may not always correctly reflect the true ability to pay of the taxpayer.[1630] For example, taxation on an annual basis cannot fully capture the economic situation of a business if, in one year, the business loses 100 and, in the following year, it gains 100. In year 2, the business would be taxed in the same way as any other company that earned 100 in that year, despite the fact that over the two-year period, the business actually had zero income and therefore may not be in the same financial or economic situation. In year 2, it earned only enough to cover its losses and not necessarily enough to contribute as much as any other company earning 100 on an annual basis. One can argue that it is inconsistent that an income tax law treats the one-year period as too strict as regards the tax base and ignores its potentially strict effects as regards double taxation relief. Otherwise, the credit method operates on a strict one-year basis while the tax base on which it is calculated does not. Thus, a credit carryforward merely realigns the two.

Some EU law arguments can be made in favour of this realignment between LCF rules and credit carryforward rules, even in the context of a direct credit. First, the *AMID* case could be a solid basis to rely on in order to argue this point from a fundamental freedom perspective (*see* the above comparison of Example No. 26 and Example No. 29). Second, albeit from secondary EU law (not the fundamental freedoms), the definition of 'double taxation' in the Tax Dispute Resolution Directive portrays this as a problematic issue. According to Article 2(1)(c), '"double taxation" means the imposition by two or more Member States of taxes covered by an agreement or convention referred to in Article 1 in respect of the same taxable income or capital when it gives rise to either: (i) an additional tax charge; (ii) an increase in tax liabilities; or (iii) *the cancellation or reduction of losses that could be used to offset taxable profits*' (emphasis added). Point (iii) of the definition does *not* seem to endorse a narrow one-year view of double taxation. Although the definition is of course contained within the scope of the Directive (i.e., for 'disputes aris[ing] from the interpretation and application of agreements and conventions that provide for the elimination of double taxation of income and, where applicable, capital' according to Article 1), perhaps it is one indication of the general policy direction in which the EU and thus the MSs are, or *should* be, heading, or at least a direction in which they may be nudged in the tax treaty dispute resolution process.

4.2.8. The *Manninen* or the Ill-fated Imputation Method Line of Case Law

Non-discrimination and a state's desired tax policy evidently do not always coincide. Of those discussed thus far, none reveals this more discernibly than this line of case law.[1631] As explained above (in Chapter 2, at *supra* note 291 and note 293), the taxation

1630. CJEU, Case C-575/17, *Sofina*, 22 Nov. 2018, ECLI:EU:C:2018:943, at para. 71 (this was also viewed in a similar way by the CJEU in the *Sofina* case: 'In the first place, the rules on the deferral of taxation in the event of losses constitute, inherently, a derogation to the principle of taxation during the tax year in which the dividends are distributed, so that those rules are not intended to apply to the majority of companies which receive dividends').

1631. CJEU, Case C-319/02, *Manninen*, 7 Sep. 2004, ECLI:EU:C:2004:484; CJEU, Case C-292/04, *Meilicke*, 6 Mar. 2007, ECLI:EU:C:2007:132; EFTA, Case E-1/04, *Fokus Bank v. Norway*, 23

of corporations and their shareholders exists on a continuum, depending on how a given country conceptualizes the relationship between them. On one end, corporations and shareholders may be treated as entirely separate taxpayers with entirely separate tax bases (reflecting their separate legal existence and legal liabilities), with the consequence that taxation is levied on the corporation upon its own profits. Then, when those after-tax profits are distributed to shareholders, this is a distinct stream of income attributable to those shareholders as income from their investment, and taxation is levied on those shareholders in accordance with their distinct ability to pay. With this viewpoint, it could even be congruous to offer no relief whatsoever.[1632] After all, these are two stand-alone unrelated taxes on different taxpayers with different incomes. This approach is often referred to as the 'classical' CIT system. On the other end, corporations and shareholders may be treated as entirely integrated (reflecting the fact that corporations are mere legal fictions and ultimately constituted by shareholders). This adopts a more economic view, aligning the tax treatment with the fact that the profits that are generated by the corporation are the same ones that are passed up to the shareholders. From this viewpoint, taxes should be levied only once. Therefore, relief should be offered. To do so, the profits can be fully exempt from any further taxation when distributed to the shareholders or the imputation credit method or the indirect tax credit method can be designed to achieve this. This approach is sometimes referred to as an 'integrated' CIT system. There can be sound policy reasons for adopting either approach, or anything in between. Regardless of where a state stands on this continuum, and the potentially cogent policy reasons that led it there, the law of non-discrimination of the CJEU is blind to it – that is, the broader tax policy reasons (e.g., the aim of integration) do not factor in, which may have altered the comparisons selected by the CJEU for determining whether discrimination exists.[1633] In the end, this line of case law seems to have (inadvertently) acted like a wrecking ball for the imputation credit system (for better or for worse, depending on one's view of shareholder-corporate taxation, which is not the debate here).

In the words of AG Geelhoed, in his Opinion on the 'legality under Community law' of the 'partial imputation system' that previously existed in the UK, the different systems existing in the EU MSs were:[1634]

> 'In deciding whether and how to achieve such an aim [of providing a measure of relief for shareholders from economic double taxation], there are essentially four

Nov. 2004; CJEU, Joined Cases C-397/98 and C-410/98, *Metallgesellschaft Ltd and Others, Hoechst AG, Hoechst UK Ltd*, 8 Mar. 2001, ECLI:EU:C:2001:134; CJEU, Case C-374/04, *ACT Test Claimants*, 12 Dec. 2006, ECLI:EU:C:2006:773; CJEU, Case C-446/04, *Test Claimants in the FII Group Litigation*, 12 Dec. 2006, ECLI:EU:C:2006:774; CJEU, Case C-310/09, *Accor*, 15 Sep. 2011, ECLI:EU:C:2011:581; CJEU, Case C-35/11, *Test Claimants in the FII Group Litigation*, 13 Nov. 2012, ECLI:EU:C:2012:707; CJEU, Case C-416/17, *Commission v. France (Précompte mobilier)*, 4 Oct. 2018, ECLI:EU:C:2018:811.

1632. *See also* Opinion of AG Geelhoed in Case C-446/04, *Test Claimants in the FII Group Litigation*, 6 Apr. 2006, ECLI:EU:C:2006:240, at para. 43.

1633. *See*, e.g., Michael J. Graetz & Alvin C. Warren Jr., *Dividend Taxation in Europe: When the ECJ Makes Tax Policy*, 44(6) Common Mkt. L. Rev. 1577, 1578 and 1594 (2007).

1634. Opinion of AG Geelhoed in Case C-446/04, *Test Claimants in the FII Group Litigation*, 6 Apr. 2006, ECLI:EU:C:2006:240, at paras 4–5.

> systems open to Member States, which may be termed the "classical", "schedular", "exemption" and "imputation" systems. States with a classical system of dividend taxation tax have chosen not to relieve economic double taxation: company profits are subjected to corporation tax, and distributed profit is taxed once again at the shareholder level as income tax. In contrast, schedular, exemption and imputation systems aim at fully or partially relieving economic double taxation. (4) States with schedular systems (of which various forms exist) choose to subject company profits to corporation tax, but tax dividends as a separate category of income. Those with exemption systems choose to exempt dividend income from income taxation. Finally, under imputation systems, corporation tax at company level is fully or partially imputed onto the income tax due on the dividends at shareholder level, such that the corporation tax serves as a prepayment for (part of) this income tax. Thus, shareholders receive an imputation credit for all or part of the corporation tax attributable to the profits out of which the dividends were paid, which credit can be set against the income tax due on these dividends.'

In studying the interaction between the EU principle of non-discrimination and the imputation credit system, the aim is to highlight what it is about the design of these systems that seems to run headstrong into EU law problems. This line of case law shows what appeared to be the progressive dismantling of the imputation credit system, but also shows that not *all* is lost (actually, the case law just made such systems too expensive, it seems[1635]). On this point, this section will conclude with the example of Malta, which in 2006 reformed its imputation credit method after agreement with the European Commission, thus indicating that such systems can pass EU law scrutiny. This means that it is a question of design.

The *Manninen* and *Meilicke* cases: relief for economic double taxation from the state of residence perspective

In Finland, Mr Manninen held shares in a company in Sweden, from which he received dividends.[1636] For dividends received from companies in Finland, a tax credit was granted for the underlying CIT paid by a Finnish company. A Finnish company would pay a 29% CIT and then, upon distribution to its shareholders, the shareholders were granted 'a tax credit equal to 29/71sts of the amount of the dividends they received'.[1637] For the dividends that Mr Manninen received from a company in Sweden, he was taxed at a rate of 29% and a credit was offered for the WHT levied in Sweden (capped at 15% under the Nordic tax treaty).[1638] No credit was available to take into account the underlying CIT paid in Sweden.[1639]

In Germany, the 'late' Mr Meilicke held shares in companies in the Netherlands and Denmark.[1640] In Germany, a tax credit was granted for the underlying CIT paid by a Germany company. A German company would pay a 30% CIT and, thus, the credit,

1635. In agreement, *see* Ben J.M. Terra & Peter J. Wattel, *European Tax Law* 223 (Wolters Kluwer 6th ed. 2012).
1636. CJEU, Case C-319/02, *Manninen*, 7 Sep. 2004, ECLI:EU:C:2004:484, at para. 12.
1637. *Id.*, at paras 6–11.
1638. *Id.*, at para. 13.
1639. *Id.*, at para. 10.
1640. CJEU, Case C-292/04, *Meilicke*, 6 Mar. 2007, ECLI:EU:C:2007:132, at para. 2.

in the same way as the *Manninen* case, was equal to 3/7ths of the amount of the dividends.[1641] This credit was denied for the dividends coming from the Netherlands and Denmark.[1642]

According to the CJEU, this difference in treatment could 'deter' fully taxable persons in Finland (or in Germany) from investing in companies in other MSs and, conversely, it could hinder the ability of companies in other MSs to raise capital in Finland (or in Germany).[1643] It is therefore a 'restriction' on the free movement of capital.[1644] This can be justified only if: (1) there is an objective difference that calls for a different treatment or (2) there are 'overriding reasons in the general interest'.[1645] Even if justified, the restrictive measure must be proportionate: it must achieve its goal and not go beyond what is necessary to do so.[1646]

Regarding whether there is an objective difference 'according to whether [a shareholder] receives dividends from companies established in that Member State or from companies established in other Member States',[1647] the CJEU uses the objective of the legislation as the factor. Citing the *Manninen* case, which was decided first:

> '... the Finnish tax legislation is designed to prevent double taxation of company profits by granting to a shareholder who receives dividends a tax advantage linked to the taking into account of the corporation tax due from the company distributing the dividends'.[1648]

In light of that objective, *comparability* exists where: the dividends received by the shareholder were from a company that was subject to CIT in Finland and from a company in Sweden that was subject to CIT. The position of the shareholder that receives them is the same because both sets of dividends were subject to the same type of double taxation.[1649] In light of that objective, an *objective difference* would exist where: the shareholder receives dividends from Finland, which had been subject to CIT, and receives dividends from Sweden, which had *not* been subject to CIT (e.g., if Sweden, for example, 'already eliminated the risk of double taxation of company profits distributed in the form of dividends, by, for example, subjecting to corporation tax only such profits by the company concerned as were not distributed').[1650]

Regarding other justifications, such as 'the need to safeguard the coherence of the [Finnish] tax system',[1651] these were rejected by the CJEU (although the CJEU's reasoning implied that the credit system could be characterized as a 'coherent' one,[1652]

1641. *Id.*, at paras 9–10.
1642. *Id.*, at para. 11.
1643. CJEU, Case C-319/02, *Manninen*, 7 Sep. 2004, ECLI:EU:C:2004:484, at paras 22–23; CJEU, Case C-292/04, *Meilicke*, 6 Mar. 2007, ECLI:EU:C:2007:132, at paras 23–24.
1644. CJEU, Case C-319/02, *Manninen*, 7 Sep. 2004, ECLI:EU:C:2004:484, at para. 24; CJEU, Case C-292/04, *Meilicke*, 6 Mar. 2007, ECLI:EU:C:2007:132, at para. 20.
1645. CJEU, Case C-319/02, *Manninen*, 7 Sep. 2004, ECLI:EU:C:2004:484, at para. 29.
1646. *Id.*
1647. CJEU, Case C-319/02, *Manninen*, 7 Sep. 2004, ECLI:EU:C:2004:484, at para. 32.
1648. *Id.*, at para. 33.
1649. *Id.*, at para. 34 and para. 36.
1650. *Id.*, at paras 34–35.
1651. *Id.*, at para. 29.
1652. *Id.*, at paras 42–48.

see also infra note 1851). The reason for the shareholder tax credit is that the Finnish company paid CIT. However, whether the underlying taxes are paid by a Finnish company or a Swedish one should not matter. In both cases, granting the credit achieves the objective of eliminating the economic double taxation stemming from the fact that CITs were already levied.[1653] Concerns over extending the credit to dividends from another EU MS, the CJEU's reasoning implies, merely relate to a concern of losing some revenue, which is not an acceptable justification for infringements of the fundamental freedoms:[1654]

> 'Having regard to the objective pursued by the Finnish tax legislation, the cohesion of that tax system is assured as long as the correlation between the tax advantage granted in favour of the shareholder and the tax due by way of corporation tax is maintained. Therefore, in a case such as that at issue in the main proceedings, the granting to a shareholder who is fully taxable in Finland and who holds shares in a company established in Sweden of a tax credit calculated by reference to the corporation tax owed by that company in Sweden would not threaten the cohesion of the Finnish tax system and would constitute a measure less restrictive of the free movement of capital than that laid down by the Finnish tax legislation.'[1655]

Regarding the calculation of the credit, because the Finnish credit is based on the amount of tax actually paid,[1656] then 'the calculation of a tax credit' for 'dividends from a company established in Sweden, *must* take account of the *tax actually paid* by the company established in that other Member State' (emphasis added).[1657] The choice of 'must' is an interesting one, as it excludes any form of notional or matching credit or lump sum credit (as mentioned, albeit in a different context, under the 'equivalence' case law). By way of example, in *Meilicke*, the CJEU clarified that the shareholders should receive equal treatment regarding the tax credit: this does *not* mean it is equal to the *same* 3/7ths of the amount of dividends as provided for dividends from German companies based on the 30% corporate tax rate there, but rather it would be '34/66 of that income for the dividends of Danish origin' and '35/65 for those originating from the Netherlands' based on the corporate tax rates of '34% in Denmark and 35% in the Netherlands'.[1658]

Moreover, the *Meilicke* case came before the CJEU a second time in 2011 with compliants of various procedural blockages that Germany was alleged to have erected to prevent the claimants from obtaining the credit (discussed further in Section 4.2.9.).[1659] In addition to the largely procedural issues presented, it reinforced these calculation discussions, and reiterated that EU law permits a credit limitation, or MCA. As a result, the CJEU has accepted credit limitations in the direct credit, indirect credit and imputation credit context. The CJEU's reasoning on this point became clearer:

1653. *Id.*, at para. 48.
1654. *Id.*, at para. 49.
1655. *Id.*, at para. 46.
1656. *Id.*, at paras 52–53.
1657. *Id.*, at para. 54.
1658. CJEU, Case C-292/04, *Meilicke*, 6 Mar. 2007, ECLI:EU:C:2007:132, at para. 16.
1659. CJEU, Case C-262/09, *Meilicke*, 30 Jun. 2011, ECLI:EU:C:2011:438.

> 'the principle of free movement of capital ... cannot have the effect of requiring Member States to go beyond the cancelling of national income tax payable by a shareholder on dividends of foreign origin received and the reimbursing of a sum whose origin is in the tax system of another Member State (see, by analogy, Case C-446/04 *Test Claimants in the FII Group Litigation* [2006] ECR I-11753, paragraph 52), if the first Member State is not to see its fiscal autonomy limited by the exercise of fiscal power of the other Member State ... .'.[1660]

These were cases from the perspective of a state of residence and its tax treatment of resident shareholders investing in another MS, thus receiving dividends from abroad. These cases, along with other such dividend cases, e.g., *Lenz* and *Verkooijen*, all established the comparability of shareholders receiving dividends from home and from abroad. It is settled case law 'that the granting of imputation credits cannot be limited to domestically sourced dividends without falling foul of the free movement of capital'.[1661]

The *Metallgesellschaft* case: relief for economic double taxation from the state of source perspective

By comparison with the above cases, the perspective changes here. In the *Metallgesellschaft* case,[1662] the CJEU dealt with economic double taxation relief from the perspective of the state of the company distributing the dividends (the state of source), in this case the UK. The comparison was between 'the situation of resident subsidiaries of resident parent companies' and 'resident subsidiaries of non-resident parent companies'. In other words, there were complaints of a difference of treatment of UK subsidiaries on the basis of the seat of the parent company being established abroad.

The UK tax system that gave rise to this complaint, and numerous others analysed below (e.g., the *ACT* case, the *FII I* case, the *FII II* case), was its partial imputation system. This case, however, focused only on one subpart of it, explained here. Upon a distribution of dividends to a shareholder, UK subsidiaries paid 'advance corporation tax' (ACT). Details aside, ACT served as, exactly as the term suggests, a payment of their own CIT in advance, which would eventually be set off against their 'mainstream corporation tax' (MCT).[1663]

As an exception, it was possible to opt for a group taxation regime, under certain conditions: if both the subsidiary and the parent were residents in the UK and if there was a majority shareholding of at least 51%. Under this group taxation regime, *no* ACT needed to be paid by the subsidiary when distributing dividends to the parent.[1664] If a UK subsidiary was owned 51% or more by a non-resident parent, the pair could *not* opt for this regime. The UK subsidiaries that initiated the case had parent companies established in Germany. They argued that this difference of treatment led to a cash-flow disadvantage. If they could opt for the group taxation regime, only the final

1660. *Id.*, at para. 33.
1661. Ben J.M. Terra & Peter J. Wattel, *European Tax Law* 228 (Wolters Kluwer 6th ed. 2012).
1662. CJEU, Joined Cases C-397/98 and C-410/98, *Metallgesellschaft Ltd and Others, Hoechst AG, Hoechst UK Ltd*, 8 Mar. 2001, ECLI:EU:C:2001:134.
1663. *Id.*, at paras 5–10.
1664. *Id.*, at paras 21–24.

corporate tax liability was paid, so the cash needed in advance to pay the ACT was kept in the meantime.[1665] As they were denied the group taxation regime, UK subsidiaries with non-resident parents had to pay corporate tax in advance, while UK subsidiaries with UK-parent companies had the option to avoid this.

The CJEU reasoned that this was incompatible with EU law. As established in the 1986 *Avoir Fiscal* case (discussed in Section 4.2.1.),[1666] the seat of a company is tantamount to its nationality.[1667] Thus, a difference of treatment *solely* on this basis is tantamount to discrimination on the basis of nationality, prohibited by the TFEU. Here, two UK subsidiaries are treated differently on the basis of the seat of their parent companies.[1668] To avoid the accusation of discrimination, there must be some *other* basis (other than the corporate seat) to justify this - for example, there must be some *objective difference* between the two situations. Part of the reasoning (the main reason) that the CJEU established comparability and rejected any objective difference between the two situations is because: the two subsidiaries are both liable to tax under UK CIT.[1669] If the ACT is an advance payment of the subsidiaries' later corporate tax liability and if the two subsidiaries are both fully subject to this later corporate tax liability (irrespective of their parent company), then they are the same in light of this payment. Therefore, there is no reason to grant one subsidiary the option to forego the advanced tax payment, and thus to make only one final tax payment, while forcing the other one to make the advanced tax payment and to only later be able to offset it against another final tax payment.

This difference in treatment, resulting in a cash-flow disadvantage, was incompatible with EU law.[1670] The subsidiaries were therefore entitled to remedies for the financial loss they suffered.[1671]

1665. *Id.*, at para. 30.
1666. CJEU, Case C-270/83, *Commission v. France (Avoir Fiscal)*, 28 Jan. 1986, ECLI:EU:C:1986:37.
1667. CJEU, Joined Cases C-397/98 and C-410/98, *Metallgesellschaft Ltd and Others, Hoechst AG, Hoechst UK Ltd*, 8 Mar. 2001, ECLI:EU:C:2001:134, at para. 42 (when analysing the freedom of establishment, the seat 'serves as the connecting factor with the legal system of a particular State, like nationality in the case of natural persons').
1668. CJEU, Joined Cases C-397/98 and C-410/98, *Metallgesellschaft Ltd and Others, Hoechst AG, Hoechst UK Ltd*, 8 Mar. 2001, ECLI:EU:C:2001:134, at para. 43.
1669. *Id.*, at para. 60 ('Consequently, as the Advocate General has pointed out in paragraph 25 of his Opinion, the difference in the tax treatment of parent companies depending on whether or not they are resident cannot justify denial of a tax advantage to subsidiaries, resident in the United Kingdom, of parent companies having their seat in another Member State where that advantage is available to subsidiaries, resident in the United Kingdom, of parent companies also resident in the United Kingdom, *since all those subsidiaries are liable to MCT on their profits irrespective of the place of residence of their parent companies*' (emphasis added)).
1670. CJEU, Joined Cases C-397/98 and C-410/98, *Metallgesellschaft Ltd and Others, Hoechst AG, Hoechst UK Ltd*, 8 Mar. 2001, ECLI:EU:C:2001:134 (among other parts of the final holding, *see* in particular: 'It is contrary to Article 52 of the EC Treaty (now, after amendment, Article 43 EC) for the tax legislation of a Member State, such as that in issue in the main proceedings, to afford companies resident in that Member State the possibility of benefiting from a taxation regime allowing them to pay dividends to their parent company without having to pay advance corporation tax where their parent company is also resident in that Member State but to deny them that possibility where their parent company has its seat in another Member State').
1671. CJEU, Joined Cases C-397/98 and C-410/98, *Metallgesellschaft Ltd and Others, Hoechst AG, Hoechst UK Ltd*, 8 Mar. 2001, ECLI:EU:C:2001:134 (among other parts of the final holding, *see* in particular: 'Where a subsidiary resident in one Member State has been obliged to pay

The *ACT Test Claimants*: relief for economic double taxation from the state of source perspective – the UK saga continues

Following up on the *Metallgesellschaft* case, in the *ACT Test Claimants* case,[1672] the UK again referred a preliminary question to the CJEU regarding its approach to the taxation of corporations and shareholders. In the facts, its 'partial imputation' system was described concisely in the following way:

> 'From 1973 onwards, the United Kingdom of Great Britain and Northern Ireland operated a system of taxation known as "partial imputation", under which, in order to avoid economic double taxation when a resident company distributed profits, part of the corporation tax paid by that company was imputed to its shareholders. Until 6 April 1999, the basis of that system was, on the one hand, advance payment of corporation tax by the company making the distribution, and, on the other hand, a tax credit granted to shareholders who had received a dividend.'[1673]

As in the *Metallgesellschaft* case, the UK in the *ACT Test Claimants* case was again in the position of the state of the subsidiary distributing the dividends (the state of source) to shareholders, thus comparing UK subsidiaries with resident shareholders and those with non-resident shareholders. By contrast, this time, multiple taxpayers complained about another component of this imputation system, namely against the UK's refusal to extend a tax credit to the non-resident corporate shareholders. This underlines another difference between the two cases. The *Metallgesellschaft* case targeted a difference of treatment that affected a *UK subsidiary*, upon distribution of dividends, based on whether its shareholder was resident or not. The *ACT Test Claimants* case targeted a difference of treatment of the *shareholders themselves* by the subsidiary state, upon distribution of dividends from a UK subsidiary. In total, 28 groups of companies complained. Four were selected as 'test cases'.[1674]

The CJEU elaborated a lengthy (and in some aspects unnecessarily convoluted) reasoning as to why – with respect to 'a system for preventing or mitigating a series of charges to tax or economic double taxation for dividends', when comparing the shareholders and considering a MS's obligations vis-à-vis those shareholders – the *state of the subsidiary* distributing the profits is *not* in the same position as *the state of the shareholder* receiving dividends. The CJEU went further and made a distinction between: (1) the position of the MS in which *both* the subsidiary making the distribution *and* the ultimate shareholders are resident and (2) the position of the MS

---

advance corporation tax in respect of dividends paid to its parent company having its seat in another Member State even though, in similar circumstances, the subsidiaries of parent companies resident in the first Member State were entitled to opt for a taxation regime that allowed them to avoid that obligation, Article 52 of the Treaty requires that resident subsidiaries and their non-resident parent companies should have an effective legal remedy in order to obtain reimbursement or reparation of the financial loss which they have sustained and from which the authorities of the Member State concerned have benefited as a result of the advance payment of tax by the subsidiaries').

1672. CJEU, Case C-374/04, *ACT Test Claimants*, 12 Dec. 2006, ECLI:EU:C:2006:773.

1673. *Id.*, at para. 5.

1674. *Id.*, at paras 25–26.

in which the subsidiary alone is resident, i.e., where the MS is only the state in which the profits arise.[1675] To elucidate the reasons for this distinction, some reorganization of the reasoning helps.

First, one reason put forward was that, reaffirming its finding in *Schumacker*, the residence state is in a better position to take into account the ability to pay of its own residents, implying that it is therefore also in a better position to eliminate economic double taxation on its own residents.[1676] It supported this viewpoint by citing the Parent-Subsidiary Directive. Under the Parent-Subsidiary Directive, it is the residence state of the shareholder, or recipient of the distribution of profits, that is obliged to either exempt or offer an indirect FTC for the profits received.[1677]

A second reason was, essentially, that a source state should be able to tax profits generated on its territory. This was a reason for which there was no EU case law or other legal basis cited, but rather was motivated by, it seems, the CJEU forecasting the potential practical impact of its decision:

> 'It must be held in that regard, first, that to require *the Member State in which the company making the distribution is resident* to ensure that profits distributed to a *non-resident shareholder* are *not liable to a series of charges to tax or to economic double taxation*, either by exempting those profits from tax at the level of the company making the distribution or by granting the shareholder a tax advantage equal to the tax paid on those profits by the company making the distribution, *would mean in point of fact* that that *State would be obliged to abandon its right to tax a profit generated through an economic activity undertaken on its territory*' (emphasis added).[1678]

A third reason is that the UK refrained from taxing the outgoing dividends, meaning it was not responsible for causing double taxation and therefore did not have to extend the relief. More precisely, in the description of the UK legislation, it was clear that the UK would not levy a tax on outgoing dividends when it did not grant the tax credit to the non-resident shareholder, and, vice versa, the UK would levy a tax on outgoing dividends only if it granted the tax credit to the non-resident shareholder (by means of a DTC).[1679] This seems loosely based on the converse of the idea from the

1675. *Id.*, at paras 57–58 ('57 However, although the situation of those shareholders must be treated as being comparable as regards the application to them of the tax legislation of the Member State in which they are resident, the same is not necessarily true, as regards the application of the tax legislation of the Member State in which the company making the distribution is resident, of the situations in which shareholders receiving dividends resident in that Member State and shareholders receiving dividends resident in another Member State are placed.

58 Where the company making the distribution and the shareholder to whom it is paid are not resident in the same Member State, the Member State in which the company making the distribution is resident, that is to say the Member State in which the profits are derived, is not in the same position, as regards the prevention or mitigation of a series of charges to tax and of economic double taxation, as the Member State in which the shareholder receiving the distribution is resident').

1676. *Id.*, at para. 60.

1677. *Id.*, at para. 60.

1678. *Id.*, at para. 59.

1679. *Id.*, at paras 14–16.

Avoir Fiscal case (*see* Section 4.2.1.).[1680] In this 1986 case, the CJEU established an approach to 'legal' comparability between a local branch of a non-resident company and a company incorporated in France because France taxed them both in the same way under its CIT laws. In this UK case, the CJEU reformulated this idea: '[O]nce a Member State, unilaterally or by a convention, imposes a charge to income tax not only on resident shareholders but also on nonresident shareholders in respect of dividends which they receive from a resident company, the position of those non-resident shareholders becomes comparable to that of resident shareholders'[1681] (in light of legislation designed to relieve a series of charges to tax).

Ultimately, the finding of the CJEU turned mostly on this third point. The UK legislation, it held, did *not* violate the freedom of establishment and the free movement of capital. Since the UK did *not* tax the outgoing dividends, it was acceptable:

> 'The answer to Question 1(a) must therefore be that Articles 43 EC and 56 EC do *not* prevent a Member State, on a distribution of dividends by a company resident in that State, from granting companies receiving those dividends which are also resident in that State a tax credit equal to the fraction of the corporation tax paid on the distributed profits by the company making the distribution, when it does *not* grant such a *tax credit* to companies receiving such dividends which are resident in another Member State *and* are *not subject to tax on dividends* in the first State' (emphasis added).[1682]

There were other questions that arose in this case regarding, *inter alia*, tax treaties. In some cases, the UK would negotiate an extension of the tax credit in its tax treaties. In this case, the UK would tax the outgoing dividends to the extent agreed upon in the tax treaties and based upon the amount of the credit (e.g., partial or full) extended. There were arguments about whether different versions of these tax treaty provisions led to different treatment. Here, the comparison is between non-resident shareholders in different EU MSs, e.g., a UK subsidiary with a Germany shareholder versus a UK subsidiary with a Netherlands shareholder. For example, non-resident shareholders in Germany would not get any credit because the tax treaty between the UK and Germany did not provide one, whereas non-resident shareholders in the Netherlands could get a tax credit because the tax treaty between the UK and the Netherlands provided for one under certain conditions. By contrast with a comparison between a purely domestic pair and a cross-border pair, this is more of a 'most favoured nation' comparison. The CJEU reiterated its settled case law, according to which no sort of 'most favoured nation' obligation can be derived from EU law that requires the benefits granted to residents of one EU MS under one DTC to be extended to residents of another EU MS under another DTC (or no DTC). The way the CJEU avoided this was via its comparability analysis, by deeming the two situations incomparable:

> 'As the Court noted in paragraph 54 of *D.*, the scope of a bilateral tax convention is limited to the natural or legal persons referred to in it.' and 'The fact that those

1680. CJEU, Case C-270/83, *Commission v. France (Avoir Fiscal)*, 28 Jan. 1986, ECLI:EU:C:1986:37.
1681. CJEU, Case C-374/04, *ACT Test Claimants*, 12 Dec. 2006, ECLI:EU:C:2006:773, at para. 68.
1682. *Id.*, at para. 74.

reciprocal rights and obligations apply only to persons resident in one of the two contracting Member States is an inherent consequence of bilateral double taxation conventions. It follows, as regards the taxation of dividends paid by a company resident in the United Kingdom, that a company resident in a Member State which has concluded a DTC with the United Kingdom which does not provide for such a tax credit is not in the same situation as a company resident in a Member State which has concluded a DTC which does provide for one (see, to that effect, *D.*, paragraph 61).'[1683]

The decision of the CJEU in this case was in favour of the UK. In addition to confirming past case law, two particularly relevant points emerge especially from this case. First, it seems, the obligation falls more heavily on the state of residence of the shareholder in cases of economic double taxation. Second, regarding the state of the subsidiary, if this MS taxes the outgoing dividends, it should extend its domestic relief; if this MS refrains from taxing, it need not extend the relief.

The *Test Claimants in the FII Group Litigation* case: relief for economic double taxation from the state of residence perspective – the UK saga continues

EU law questions regarding this imputation system continued to flow in from the UK. The *FII Group Litigation* case[1684] looked at the same imputation system for relief of economic double taxation, this time from the perspective of the residence state. Based on the above *ACT Test Claimants* case, it can already be predicted that the CJEU will adopt a stricter view vis-à-vis the residence state, on which the CJEU places more responsibility for the relief of economic double taxation.

Before discussing the questions posed to the CJEU, a simple example can help explain the very basics of the relief mechanism (focused more on the shareholder perspective) in operation in the UK. Assume a UK company, UK-Co., that owns 100% of the shares of two different subsidiaries, namely 100% of UK-Sub. and 100% of EU-Sub. To understand the imputation system, two distributions have to be studied: first, the tax treatment of the distribution from the subsidiaries that are received by UK-Co. and, second, the tax treatment of the redistribution of these dividends by UK-Co. to its shareholders. In sum, UK-Co. in this case is, first, the recipient of dividends and, second, the distributor of dividends.

In the UK domestic context, UK-Sub. generates profits on which it will be liable for CIT in the UK.[1685] During the year, UK-Sub. distributes dividends to its parent, UK-Co., and, at this moment, it must pay ACT[1686] (to be precise, ACT would be due 14 days after the end of the quarter in which the dividends were paid).[1687] Later on, when the normal 'mainstream corporation tax' (MCT) falls due, the ACT is credited against the MCT.[1688] As for the parent, UK-Co., the dividends from UK-Sub. are exempt from

1683. *Id.*, at para. 84 and para. 91.
1684. CJEU, Case C-446/04, *Test Claimants in the FII Group Litigation*, 12 Dec. 2006, ECLI: EU:C:2006:774.
1685. *Id.*, at para. 6.
1686. *Id.*, at para. 8.
1687. *Id.*, at para. 24.
1688. *Id.*, at para. 9.

CIT. Nevertheless, UK-Co. gets a 'tax credit' in its name, which is equal to the ACT paid by its subsidiary (or to some fraction of the ACT, as it was a 'partial imputation' system, but details and numbered examples are not provided in the case, so this is deliberately simplified just to illustrate the basic mechanism). In total, the parent company, UK-Co., is considered to have earned 'franked investment income' (FII) equal to the amount of the distribution plus the tax credit.[1689] This becomes relevant upon redistribution of the dividends. When UK-Co. redistributes the dividends to its own shareholders, it also should pay ACT on the amount of the distribution; however, as a result of the tax credit, any ACT due by UK-Co. on this distribution can be reduced by the amount of ACT paid by UK-Sub. ('with the result that [UK-Co] was liable for ACT only on the excess').[1690] As for the ultimate individual shareholders, they would be subject to tax on the dividends, but entitled to a tax credit equal to the fraction of the ACT paid by UK-Co., and they would deduct this tax credit from their taxes due and could receive cash for any excess.[1691]

In the cross-border context, the subsidiary, EU-Sub., generates profits on which it will be liable for CIT in its respective MS of residence. During the year, EU-Sub. distributes dividends to UK-Co., its parent company. In this case, the dividends are *not* exempt from CIT at the level of UK-Co.[1692] Instead, UK-Co. includes them as taxable income, but receives relief for economic double taxation by means of an indirect FTC for its share of underlying CIT paid by EU-Sub. to the other EU MS (and also for juridical double taxation, due to any potential WHTs levied at source in that EU MS).[1693] Next, when UK-Co. redistributes these dividends to its own shareholders, it must pay ACT on the amount of the dividends. Finally, when UK-Co. must pay its MCT, it can offset the ACT against this MCT. However, the MCT is reduced by the indirect FTC, and then any remainder of MCT can be reduced by the ACT, making it more likely to have 'surplus ACT'.[1694]

As can already be seen, in the domestic scenario, relief was basically offered twice: first, the dividends were exempt at the level of UK-Co. and then, upon redistribution, ACT was due but offset by the tax credit at each layer in the corporate chain. In the cross-border scenario, the dividends were taxed first, and offered relief by means of an indirect FTC, but, since the '[r]elief on that foreign tax was available only on the amount due in the United Kingdom by way of corporation tax on the income concerned',[1695] then, upon redistribution, ACT was levied, without any further tax credit to offset it.

1689. *Id.*, at para. 12.
1690. *Id.*, at para. 13.
1691. *Id.*, at para. 14 ('Under Schedule F of ICTA, individual shareholders resident in the United Kingdom were liable to income tax on dividends received from a company resident in that Member State. Those shareholders were, nevertheless, entitled to a tax credit equal to the fraction of the ACT paid by that company. That tax credit could be deducted from the amount owed by that shareholder by way of income tax on the dividend or could be paid to that person in cash if the amount of the tax credit exceeded the amount of his tax liability').
1692. *Id.*, at para. 15.
1693. *Id.*, at para. 16.
1694. *Id.*, at paras 20–22.
1695. *Id.*, at para. 17.

The first question posed by the UK Court to the CJEU related to the first stage, namely the *receipt* of the dividends by UK-Co. from its subsidiaries. The UK Court asked whether it was compatible with EU law (the freedom of establishment and the free movement of capital) to apply the exemption method for dividends received from a UK subsidiary and to apply the credit method (both direct and indirect) for dividends received from a subsidiary in another EU MS.[1696] As discussed already at length above (*see* Section 4.2.2.), this is compatible and, indeed, one of the most important findings of this case was that of establishing the equivalence between the (indirect) credit method and the exemption method. It was a controversial matter, considering the Opinion of AG Geelhoed did not agree.[1697]

The second[1698] and third[1699] questions posed by the UK Court to the CJEU related to the second stage, namely the *redistribution* of dividends by UK-Co. to its own

1696. *Id.*, at para. 31 ('Is it contrary to Article 43 or [Article] 56 EC for a Member State to keep in force and apply measures which exempt from corporation tax dividends received by a company resident in that Member State ("the resident company") from other resident companies and which subject dividends received by the resident company from companies resident in other Member States ("nonresident companies") to corporation tax (after giving double taxation relief for any withholding tax payable on the dividend and, under certain conditions, for the underlying tax paid by the non-resident companies on their profits in their country of residence)?').

1697. Opinion of AG Geelhoed in Case C-446/04, *Test Claimants in the FII Group Litigation*, 6 Apr. 2006, ECLI:EU:C:2006:240, at paras 49, 50, 52, 56.

1698. CJEU, Case C-446/04, *Test Claimants in the FII Group Litigation*, 12 Dec. 2006, ECLI:EU:C:2006:774, at para. 75 (as reformulated by the CJEU, 'By Question 2, the national court essentially asks whether Articles 43 EC and 56 EC, and/or Articles 4(1) and 6 of Directive 90/435 must be interpreted as meaning that they preclude national legislation such as that at issue in the main proceedings which, in granting a tax credit to a resident company receiving dividends from another resident company by reference to the ACT paid by the latter in respect of the distribution, allows the former company to pay dividends to its own shareholders without being obliged to account for the ACT, whereas a resident company which has received dividends from a non-resident company must, in a similar case, pay the ACT in full') and at para. 31 ('2. Where a Member State has a system which in certain circumstances imposes advance corporation tax ... on the payment of dividends by a resident company to its shareholders and grants a tax credit to shareholders resident in that Member State in respect of those dividends, is it contrary to Article 43 or [Article] 56 EC or Article 4(1) or [Article] 6 of [Directive 90/435] for the Member State to keep in force and apply measures which provide for the resident company to pay dividends to its shareholders without being liable to pay ACT to the extent that it has received dividends from companies resident in that Member State (either directly or indirectly through other companies resident in that Member State) and do not provide for the resident company to pay dividends to its shareholders without being liable to pay ACT to the extent that it has received dividends from non-resident companies?').

1699. *Id.*, at para. 113 (as reformulated by the CJEU, 'By Question 3, the national court essentially asks whether Articles 43 EC and 56 EC and/or Articles 4(1) and 6 of Directive 90/435 must be interpreted as meaning that they preclude legislation such as that at issue in the main proceedings:

- which provides that any relief made available to a resident company which has received foreign-sourced dividends in respect of tax paid abroad is to reduce the amount of corporation tax against which it may offset the ACT which is due, and
- which does not allow a resident company to surrender the amount of ACT paid which cannot be set off against the corporation tax due for the current accounting period or for previous or subsequent accounting periods to non-resident subsidiaries in order that they may offset it against the corporation tax for which they are liable') and at para. 31 ('3. Is

shareholders, and the possibilities to offset the ACT, or lack thereof in the case of dividends from non-resident companies. The difference in treatment could not be justified based on any relevant objective difference. The situations were comparable in light of the objective of the legislation:

> '[A] national measure which is designed to avoid a series of charges to tax on distributed profits *only* as regards companies [UK-Co.] receiving dividends from other resident companies [UK-Sub.], while exposing companies [UK-Co.] receiving dividends from non-resident companies [EU-Sub.] to a cash-flow disadvantage, cannot be justified by a relevant difference in the situation of those companies' because both subsidiaries, namely subsidiaries that are '... resident companies distributing dividends to other resident companies' [UK-Sub.] and subsidiaries that are 'non-resident companies making such a distribution' [EU-Sub.] are 'subject, in the State in which they are resident, to corporation tax' (emphasis added).[1700]

The cash-flow disadvantage resulted from the fact that when UK-Co. redistributed profits *from a resident subsidiary*, ACT due could be *immediately* offset, whereas when UK-Co. redistributed profits *from a non-resident subsidiary*, the ACT had to be borne in full up front. In principle, later on, the ACT would be able to be compensated against any eventual MCT due. Yet, because the cross-border situation tended to amount in more 'surplus' ACT than the domestic one, there was a higher risk that the ACT would not all eventually be used. Moreover, there were less opportunities to offset the ACT in general. For example, surplus ACT could be transferred, or 'surrendered', to UK resident subsidiaries but not to non-resident subsidiaries. As seen in the above *Metallgesellschaft* case, there was also a 'group taxation' regime option available to resident companies, from which non-resident companies were excluded (which was deemed an infringement of EU law by the CJEU). It was also in the above *Metallgesellschaft* case that the CJEU decided that such unjustifiable cash-flow disadvantages were problematic under EU law.

On these questions, the CJEU held that:

> 'The answer to Question 2 must therefore be that Articles 43 EC and 56 EC preclude legislation of a Member State which allows a resident company receiving dividends from another resident company to deduct from the amount which the former company is liable to pay by way of advance corporation tax the amount of

---

it contrary to the provisions of EC law referred to in Question 2 above for the Member State to keep in force and apply measures which provide for the ACT liability to be set against the liability of the dividend-paying company, and that of other companies in the group resident in that Member State, to corporation tax in that Member State upon their profits:

(a) but which do not provide for any form of set-off of the ACT liability or some equivalent relief (such as the refund of ACT) in respect of profits earned, whether in that State or in other Member States, by companies in the group which are not residents in that Member State; and/or

(b) which provide that any double tax relief which a company resident in that Member State enjoys reduces the liability to corporation tax against which the ACT liability can be set?').

1700. *Id.*, at para. 91.

> that tax paid by the latter company, whereas no such deduction is permitted in the case of a resident company receiving dividends from a non-resident company as regards the corresponding tax on distributed profits paid by the latter company in the State in which it is resident.'[1701]
>
> 'The answer to Question 3 must therefore be that …': 'Article 43 EC precludes legislation of a Member State which allows a resident company to surrender to resident subsidiaries the amount of advance corporation tax paid which cannot be offset against the liability of that company to corporation tax for the current accounting period or previous or subsequent accounting periods, so that those subsidiaries may offset it against their liability to corporation tax, but does not allow a resident company to surrender such an amount to non-resident subsidiaries where the latter are taxable in that Member State on the profits which they made there.'[1702]
>
> '… Articles 43 EC and 56 EC do *not* preclude legislation of a Member State which provides that any relief for tax paid abroad made available to a resident company which has received foreignsourced dividends is to reduce the amount of corporation tax against which that company may offset advance corporation tax' (emphasis added).[1703]

A fourth question posed by the UK Court related to one other special regime called the 'foreign income dividend' (FID) regime.[1704] The goal of this regime was to remedy the disadvantage caused by the treatment of dividends that stem from non-resident subsidiaries. It was an optional regime. If a taxpayer opted for the FID regime, two consequences followed. First, the regime would permit UK-Co. to, later, get reimbursed for any surplus ACT.[1705] However, the time between paying the ACT (14 days after the end of the quarter in which the dividends were distributed) and the possibility to recoup the ACT later when it proved impossible to offset it against MCT (9 months after the end of the accounting period) could range from '8 ½ months and 17 ½ months'.[1706] Although it improved the situation, it still resulted in a cash-flow disadvantage,[1707] so it was not an acceptable way to remedy the situation.

Second, as regards the ultimate shareholders, 'a shareholder receiving a payment of dividends from a resident company which has its *origin in foreign-sourced dividends* treated as FIDs, is *not* entitled to a tax credit, but is treated as having received income which has been taxed at the *lower rate* for the tax year in question' (emphasis added).[1708] Precisely what this 'lower rate' treatment means (e.g., could it mean that the income is treated as falling in the lowest progressive income tax rate bracket?) is not clarified, neither in the judgment nor in the Opinion of the AG. In fact, on this point, the AG simply stated that 'it is for the national court to assess, in a particular case, whether

1701. *Id.*, at para. 112.
1702. *Id.*, at paras 138–139.
1703. *Id.*, at para. 138.
1704. *Id.*, at paras 23–26.
1705. *Id.*, at para. 144 ('That regime permits resident companies receiving foreignsourced dividends to obtain a repayment of the amount of surplus ACT, that is to say, the amount of ACT which could not be offset against the amount due by way of corporation tax').
1706. *Id.*, at para. 146.
1707. *Id.*, at para. 153.
1708. *Id.*, at para. 148.

such treatment actually had the effect that double economic taxation was relieved in an equivalent manner as for domesticsource dividends'.[1709] More importantly, the disadvantage was that, because there was no tax credit for the ultimate shareholders, 'such a shareholder has no right to any repayment if he is not liable to income tax or where the income tax due is less than the tax on the dividend at the lower rate'.[1710] For these reasons, the CJEU held that:

> 'The answer to Question 4 must therefore be that Articles 43 EC and 56 EC preclude legislation of a Member State which, while exempting from advance corporation tax resident companies paying dividends to their shareholders which have their origin in nationallysourced dividends received by them, allows resident companies distributing dividends to their shareholders which have their origin in foreign-sourced dividends received by them to elect to be taxed under a regime which permits them to recover the advance corporation tax paid but, first, obliges those companies to pay that advance corporation tax and subsequently to claim repayment and, secondly, does not provide a tax credit for their shareholders, whereas those shareholders would have received such a tax credit in the case of a distribution made by a resident company which had its origin in nationally-sourced dividends.'[1711]

Clearly, the answer to this fourth question excludes one possibility for designing the imputation system to remedy a different treatment. From this case, it also becomes clear that because there is a prohibition of a cash-flow disadvantage, remedying this relief mechanism requires equal treatment from the start (rather than by means of later reimbursements). To accomplish this, it would seem that the UK system would have to accept the payment of CIT to another MS as equivalent to the payment of CIT to the UK, thus treating it as though it were ACT paid by the subsidiary on the distribution of dividends to UK-Co., which in turn gives rise to a tax credit in favour of UK-Co. against the ACT due by the UK-Co. upon its own subsequent redistribution of those dividends.

The remaining questions (there were nine questions in total) dealt with the remedies available to the taxpayers if the CJEU were to find the UK measures incompatible with EU law. Thus, having found this incompatibility, remedies had to be offered to the companies that brought the complaint (e.g., in the UK government's estimate, the 'potential value of claims at issue could amount to £ 7 billion'; in the claimant's estimate, it was 'in the region of £ 100 million and £ 2 billion'[1712]). The last remnant of this UK system was abolished in 2016.[1713]

1709. Opinion of AG Geelhoed in Case C-446/04, *Test Claimants in the FII Group Litigation*, 6 Apr. 2006, ECLI:EU:C:2006:240, at para. 99.

1710. CJEU, Case C-446/04, *Test Claimants in the FII Group Litigation*, 12 Dec. 2006, ECLI:EU:C:2006:774, at para. 148.

1711. *Id.*, at para. 173.

1712. Opinion of AG Geelhoed in Case C-446/04, *Test Claimants in the FII Group Litigation*, 6 Apr. 2006, ECLI:EU:C:2006:240, at paras 140–141.

1713. For more information, *see*, e.g., United Kingdom, Parliament, Economic Affairs Committee, *The Draft Finance Bill 2016*, 2nd Report of Session 2015-16, HL Paper 108 (4 Mar. 2016), https://publications.parliament.uk/pa/ld201516/ldselect/ldeconaf/108/10806.htm (last visited 19 Mar. 2019).

The *Accor* case: imputation issues for recipient parent company upon redistribution

Two related cases regarding an 'imputation' credit system that existed in France were decided in 2011 and in 2018.[1714] To better clarify the findings, it is useful to first explain in a simple manner how the French relief mechanism worked (since abolished). The judgment itself cites the legislation and explains the mechanism only in so far as necessary for carrying out its reasoning and rendering its decision. The full picture therefore has to be pieced together, through reading both AG opinions and both cases from 2011 and 2018. This is now summarized here by means of an example.

ACo. (subbing for *Accor*) is a company resident in France. It is the 100% shareholder of a subsidiary in France, France-Sub., and of a subsidiary in another EU MS, EU-Sub. From its subsidiaries, ACo. receives dividends. In turn, ACo. eventually redistributes those dividends to its own shareholders.

Both of the subsidiaries generate their operating profits, pay CIT on those profits and eventually decide to distribute any profits remaining after tax to ACo. France-Sub. has paid CIT of 33.33%. The taxes paid by the EU-Sub. are (currently) unknown from the perspective of the French relief mechanism.

Upon receipt of the dividends by ACo., they are actually exempt, both the dividends from France and those from the other EU MS. France has implemented the Parent-Subsidiary Directive and has opted to exempt dividends in the hands of ACo.[1715] Still, at the same time, for dividends received from France-Sub., ACo. gets a 'tax credit' that is basically recorded at the Treasury. This tax credit is equal to 'half of the sums actually paid' to ACo., i.e., 50% of the dividend. Nothing happens with this credit for now. It sits at the Treasury on ACo.'s behalf.

Upon redistribution of dividends by A Co. to its own shareholders, an imputation credit system applies. A Co. must make an 'advance payment',[1716] in respect of the redistribution of dividends. This advance payment is equal to half of the dividends redistributed. This redistribution includes the underlying dividends *both* from France and from other EU MSs. To eliminate this layer of tax, the tax credit previously recorded at the Treasury directly reduces the advance payment. However, this tax credit was recorded only in respect of the dividends from France-Sub. and it results in fully eliminating the advance payment that relates to those dividends. No tax credit exists

1714. CJEU, Case C-310/09, *Accor*, 15 Sep. 2011, ECLI:EU:C:2011:581; CJEU, Case C-416/17, *Commission v. France (Précompte mobilier)*, 4 Oct. 2018, ECLI:EU:C:2018:811.

1715. Opinion of AG Mengozzi in Case C-310/09, *Accor*, 22 Dec. 2010, ECLI:EU:C:2010:813, at para. 7 n.4 ('Excluding the payment of a portion for fees and costs, determined in accordance with Article 216 of the CGI, which is not relevant in the main proceedings, and which, during the period at issue in the main proceedings, was fixed at 2.5% of the total income from shareholdings, including the tax credits, until 2000 and at 5% from 2001').

1716. Opinion of AG Mengozzi in Case C-310/09, *Accor*, 22 Dec. 2010, ECLI:EU:C:2010:813, at paras 1–5.

for the dividends from other EU MSs. In this way, the advance payment results in a layer of corporate tax imposed on the basis of those latter dividends.[1717]

The way in which this imputation system relieves economic double taxation for the distribution between French companies can be illustrated with simple numbers. To begin, in designing an imputation credit, one question is what the amount of the credit should be. In this case, it helps to explain why France granted a credit equal to 50% of the dividends. It is directly connected to the 33.33% CIT rate in France. Notice that if a French subsidiary generates profits of 100, it pays 33.33, or one-third (33.33%), of its profits as CIT. As a result, the subsidiary has 66.67 of after-tax profits, or two-thirds of its profits left, to distribute to its French parent (ACo.). It distributes the entire amount of 66.67 to its parent. Notice that 50% (one-half) of that after-tax amount of 66.67 (of two-thirds) is essentially equal to the initial taxes of 33.33 (one-third) paid on the original underlying profit. In this way, France designed a full imputation credit, to fully impute the CIT paid at the level of the subsidiary to the parent company.

To express it numerically, the credit in this case is equal to the CIT rate divided by one minus the tax rate: CIT rate/(1 – CIT rate) = imputation credit. In this case, 33.33%/(1 – 33.33%) = 33.33%/66.67% ≈ 0.5 = 50%. This appears to be the calculation used in the *Manninen* case and *Meilicke* case: the tax rate in Finland was 29% and the credit was equal to 29/71 of the dividends; the tax rate in Germany was 30% and the credit was equal to 3/7 of the dividends; the tax rate in Denmark was 34%, and thus the CJEU reckoned the credit should be equal to 34/66 of the dividends; the tax rate in the Netherlands was 35%, and thus the CJEU reckoned the credit should be equal to 35/65 of the dividends.[1718]

To illustrate, the recent AG opinion shares a diagram submitted by the French authorities,[1719] which is slightly reorganized and translated here in Example No. 30 (author's translation):

1717. This raises the question of whether it is in line with the Parent-Subsidiary Directive, a question raised both in this case and in the *FII Group Litigation* case; however, the analysis here focuses on fundamental freedom aspects.

1718. CJEU, Case C-319/02, *Manninen*, 7 Sep. 2004, ECLI:EU:C:2004:484, at paras 6–11 and CJEU, Case C-292/04, *Meilicke*, 6 Mar. 2007, ECLI:EU:C:2007:132, at para. 16.

1719. Opinion of AG Wathelet in Case C-416/17, *Commission v. France*, 25 Jul. 2018, ECLI:EU:C:2018:626, at para. 74. At the time of writing, the Opinion was not available in English; it has since been translated into English.

Example No. 30: The Imputation Credit System in France Depicted in the *Accor* Case

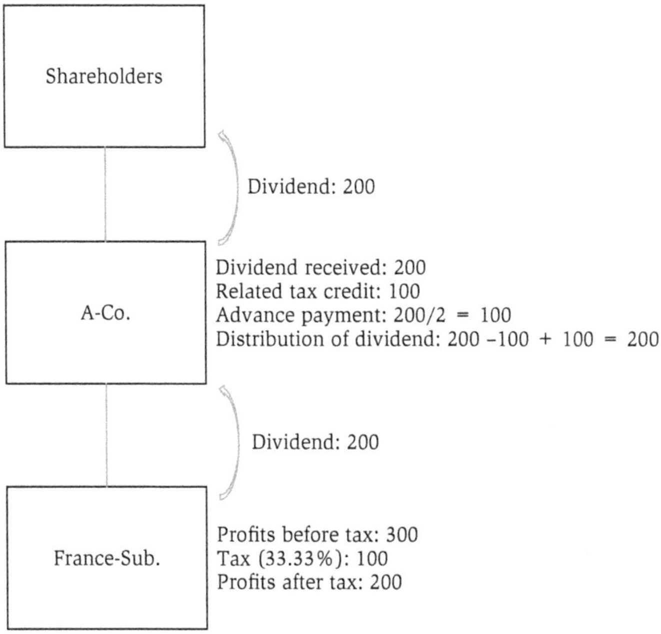

As an aside, to offer a brief comparison, it appears that the 'advance payment' under the French regime differs, in subtle ways at least, from the ACT under the UK regime. In the French regime, the tax credit precedes the advance payment, or seems to be perceived this way. The tax credit was more closely linked to the fact that the French subsidiary already paid CIT. The advance payment was conceived, it seems, more as a payment taken from the dividends owed to the shareholders, rather than an ACT levied on the French corporation paying them out.[1720] In the UK regime, the ACT was its own special institution in a way, a special tax asset. The ACT preceded the tax credit; according to the arguments of the UK government, the ACT was the reason for the tax credit. The ACT was paid upon distribution of a dividend regardless of what the ultimate corporate tax liability would be. This was evidenced in part by the fact that the ACT could be used in different ways: it could be set off against the future corporate tax

1720. CJEU, Case C-310/09, *Accor*, 15 Sep. 2011, ECLI:EU:C:2011:581, at paras 70–76 (when considering the question of 'unjust enrichment', it was suggested that, under France's imputation regime, 'the sum paid by the parent company does not constitute an accounting or tax charge for it but is set off against the total of the sums which may be redistributed to its shareholders').

liability of the subsidiary, carried forward or backward, or transferred to other UK subsidiaries.

Against this background, the French Court asked three questions. In essence, the first question asked whether this imputation system was in line with EU law (the freedom of establishment and the free movement of capital) and the second two questions related to the remedies. Considering the fate of the UK imputation system, it will come as no surprise that the French regime was found contrary to EU law. On the first question, the CJEU held that:

> 'Articles 49 TFEU and 63 TFEU preclude legislation of a Member State intended to eliminate economic double taxation of dividends, such as that at issue in the main proceedings, which allows a parent company to set off against the advance payment, for which it is liable when it redistributes to its shareholders dividends paid by its subsidiaries, the tax credit applied to the distribution of those dividends if they originate from a subsidiary established in that Member State, but does not offer that option if those dividends originate from a subsidiary established in another Member State, since, in that case, that legislation does not give entitlement to a tax credit applied to the distribution of those dividends by that subsidiary.'[1721]

As a consequence, remedies were needed, making the second and third questions more relevant in terms of providing further insights from this line of case law.[1722] The second question considered the remedy for the past breaches, while the third question considered the remedy moving forward.

In particular, the second question asked about reimbursement of the sums already levied under the regime and whether this reimbursement could be refused to the extent that such reimbursement would lead to 'unjust enrichment' of the French parent company (Accor, in this case). This question calls attention to one of the *raisons d'être* of such an imputation regime, which is to treat the corporation and its shareholders as integrated. In doing so, by linking their tax liabilities together so closely (via advance tax payments and directly associated tax credits), it becomes harder to unravel which parties are truly affected by the levy of the advance payment.

The French government argued that the advance payment was a charge upon redistribution that does *not* affect the profits of the French parent company (Accor) but affects *only* the redistributed profits owed to the shareholders. It is a cost 'born in full by the shareholders who received a reduced dividend', the government argued, and '[t]he parent company was not therefore affected by the regime'.[1723] The French government conceded that 'the contested regime does not result in the passing-on of a tax to a third party by the taxable person [as can be the case with indirect taxes] and does not therefore fall into the "classic" pattern of unjust enrichment',[1724] but under

1721. CJEU, Case C-310/09, *Accor*, 15 Sep. 2011, ECLI:EU:C:2011:581.

1722. For other questions regarding remedies, *see also* CJEU, Joined Cases C-397/98 and C-410/98, *Metallgesellschaft Ltd and Others, Hoechst AG, Hoechst UK Ltd*, 8 Mar. 2001, ECLI:EU:C:2001:134, at para. 84; CJEU, Case C-446/04, *Test Claimants in the FII Group Litigation*, 12 Dec. 2006, ECLI:EU:C:2006:774, at para. 202.

1723. Opinion of AG Mengozzi in Case C-310/09, *Accor*, 22 Dec. 2010, ECLI:EU:C:2010:813, at para. 38.

1724. *Id.*, at para. 63.

French administrative law there is a well-founded reason for its argument. That is, its own Supreme Administrative Court had held that the payment fell on the distributed income:

> 'The Conseil d'État has held that the advance payment does not constitute a charge which may be deducted from the company's net profit since that levy was introduced to prevent companies which, under conditions conferring entitlement to the tax credit, distribute profits which have not been liable to corporation tax at the normal rate from benefiting, for that reason, from an undue tax advantage. (35) Thus, by setting off solely against the total distributable income, the advance payment does not affect the parent company making the distribution but is levied on the shareholders' assets.'[1725]

However, the AG explained how this treatment is likely to actually economically affect the parent company, despite what the French government argues.[1726] For example, the French company may have dipped into its own cash in order to increase the dividends itself: it is possible that the 'company had borne the full burden of that levy by drawing on its reserves in order to avoid disrupting its distribution policy and altering the price of its shares on the stock market'.[1727] There could be some unjust enrichment, but it is for the national court to determine this – to measure the extent to which 'the person concerned had not himself borne the full economic burden of the sums which he had to pay'.[1728] However, then the AG observed that, nonetheless, a reimbursement seemed to be permitted in the purely domestic context; i.e., when a French company had overpaid the advance payment, it got a direct reimbursement from the French government. In this way, the French government's own practice could undermine its argument of concerns over unjust enrichment resulting from a reimbursement. If so, then the 'principle of equivalence' may require a similar treatment (reimbursement) for the case of foreign-source dividends.

While the AG was open to the possibility of a broader perspective on unjust enrichment,[1729] the CJEU ultimately rejected the French government's arguments. The CJEU cited the obligations of EU MSs, flowing from the 'principle of sincere cooperation laid down in Article 4 TEU', to 'ensure judicial protection' to safeguard 'an individual's rights under EU law' and to provide for a proper remedy for restrictions on the free movements; but in the absence of EU rules, national procedural rules carry this out,

1725. *Id.*, at para. 64.
1726. *Id.*, at paras 48–49, 64–67, 78–80.
1727. *Id.*, at para. 70.
1728. *Id.*, at para. 66.
1729. *Id.*, at para. 67 ('Thus, with regard to the main proceedings, I do not believe that it is possible to reject from the outset, as the European Commission and Accor attempt to do, the very existence of the possible unjust enrichment of the parent company which would result in the reimbursement of the sums paid in breach of Article 56 EC on the sole ground that, in legal terms, it is that company which is liable to make the advance payment. As I have stressed, the case-law of the Court favours an economic rather than a strictly legal approach to possible unjust enrichment resulting from the reimbursement of sums unduly paid by an economic operator').

subject to the principles of equivalence and effectiveness.[1730] For these reasons, in *Accor*, the CJEU held that:

> 'Where a national tax regime such as that at issue in the main proceedings does not of itself lead to the passing on to a third party of the tax unduly paid by the person liable for that tax, EU law precludes a Member State refusing to reimburse sums paid by the parent company on the grounds either that such reimbursement would lead to the unjust enrichment of the parent company, or that the sum paid by the parent company does not constitute an accounting or tax charge for it but is set off against the total of the sums which may be redistributed to its shareholders.'

The third question was the most relevant in terms of the design of the imputation regime moving forward, in order to correct it from an EU law perspective. In the Opinion of the AG, there were indications that perhaps the better way to re-establish equal treatment is – not by reimbursement of the advance payment to Accor (which as can be seen above raises numerous questions regarding who this advance payment actually affected, i.e., Accor or its shareholders, and thus questions of unjust enrichment), but – by granting a tax credit against that advance payment, as it would in the domestic context.[1731] So this is where the reasoning becomes relevant from the credit method design perspective. If the state is to now extend the benefit of the tax credit, how should it do so? What requirements are acceptable? That is what is discussed here.

First, as a starting point, the AG recalls two constraints on MSs' action, or rather principles governing MSs' action, namely the aforementioned 'principles of equivalence and effectiveness'.[1732] More specifically, when determining how to redesign or adjust the relief mechanism, the MS must respect the 'principle of equivalence' – meaning 'such rules are not less favourable than those governing similar domestic actions'[1733] – and the 'principle of effectiveness' – meaning 'that they do not render virtually impossible or excessively difficult the exercise of rights conferred by [EU] law'.[1734]

As regards the principle of effectiveness, some related debates included the type of proof required to obtain the credit, the overall burden of proof, what constitutes an undue administrative burden by comparison with the purely domestic situation, and

1730. CJEU, Case C-310/09, *Accor*, 15 Sep. 2011, ECLI:EU:C:2011:581, at paras 78–80.

1731. Opinion of AG Mengozzi in Case C-310/09, *Accor*, 22 Dec. 2010, ECLI:EU:C:2010:813, at para. 90 ('As the Commission rightly argued in its written observations, that question appears to arise only if the national court, to re-establish equal treatment, opts not for the reimbursement of the advance payment – which would, to some degree, amount to releasing the parent company from that advance payment without it first having benefited from the tax credit – but for the recognition of the benefit of the tax credit (after the parent company has paid the advance payment), such as it would have been granted in a purely domestic situation. For, as the Commission indicates in its written observations, referring to *Test Claimants in the FII Group Litigation*, paragraphs 50 to 52, in that second case, the parent company should receive a tax credit reflecting the rate of the corporation tax for which the subsidiary is liable in the Member State in which it is established').

1732. Opinion of AG Mengozzi in Case C-310/09, *Accor*, 22 Dec. 2010, ECLI:EU:C:2010:813, at para. 91.

1733. *See*, e.g., CJEU, Case C-446/04, *Test Claimants in the FII Group Litigation*, 12 Dec. 2006, ECLI:EU:C:2006:774, at para. 203 (and references cited therein).

1734. *Id.*

the role of the exchange of information and mutual assistance directive.[1735] As regards equivalence, the CJEU reiterated that technically the exemption method and imputation method can both achieve this equivalence.[1736]

Related debates resurfaced such as whether the credit should be based on the actual taxes paid versus based on a statutory rate,[1737] i.e., a debate over nominal versus effective taxation (as discussed in Section 4.2.3.). The Commission and Accor argued that 'since the tax credit is always equal to 50% of the dividends distributed', 'there is no strict correspondence between the amount of tax paid and the amount of the tax credit and that it is sufficient to refer to the statutory tax rate in the State in which the subsidiary is established'.[1738] The CJEU reiterated that the credit can be based on the taxes actually paid and can be limited to the amount of tax payable in the residence state (as discussed in Section 4.2.2. and Section 4.2.3.).[1739]

This led to an interesting part of the reasoning, where CJEU stressed that, while France is required to offer equal treatment, France is not required to create an *advantage* for the cross-border situation:[1740]

> '91 As regards the regime at issue in the main proceedings, *if* a Member State *were* to grant recipients of dividends from a company established in another Member State *a tax credit which was always equal to half of those dividends*, as sought by Accor, that would amount to granting those dividends *more favourable treatment* than that received by dividends from the first Member State, where the rate of tax to which the company distributing those dividends was liable in the State in which it was established was lower than the rate of tax applied in the first Member State.
>
> 92 Consequently, a Member State *must be in a position to determine the amount of the corporation tax paid* in the State in which the distributing company is established that *must be the subject of the tax credit* granted to the recipient parent company. Therefore, contrary to what Accor maintains, it is *not* sufficient to provide evidence that the distributing company has been taxed, in the Member State in which it is established, on the profits underlying the dividends distributed, *without* providing information relating to the nature and rate of the *tax actually charged* on those profits' (emphasis added).[1741]

These paragraphs address the relationship between the design of the credit method and EU law. Their exact import is unclear due to the shift in language moving from conditional to obligatory ('must').

Regarding the conditional part: as mentioned,[1742] the EU law obligation of equal treatment does *not* entail an obligation for MSs to offer an advantage to the cross-border situation. Of course, to say that MSs are not obliged means that it is merely

1735. CJEU, Case C-310/09, *Accor*, 15 Sep. 2011, ECLI:EU:C:2011:581, at paras 96–98.
1736. *Id.*, at para. 88.
1737. *Id.*, at paras 83–88.
1738. *Id.*, at paras 83–84.
1739. *Id.*, at paras 89–90.
1740. *Id.*, at para. 87.
1741. *Id.*, at paras 91–92.
1742. *Id.*, at para. 87 ('However, whilst it follows from the case-law that EU law requires a Member State which has a system for the avoidance of double economic taxation as regards dividends paid to residents by resident companies to treat dividends paid to residents by resident

optional. Thus, MSs *could* offer more advantageous treatment to cross-border situations, but they do *not have to*. This is not a surprise. It has been established that reverse discrimination, where domestic situations are treated worse than cross-border situations, is generally not covered by the fundamental freedoms.[1743] For this reason, the more refined understanding of this EU law equal treatment obligation is that it does not technically require equal treatment, but is generally an obligation not to treat the cross-border situation worse.

Regarding the obligatory part: according to paragraphs 91–92 cited above,[1744] the logic changes. The Court observed that, in the case of this specific French imputation regime, if France were to grant the same exact treatment, i.e., a credit in the amount of one-half, to the cross-border situation, the result would be more favourable treatment for the cross-border situation – if, the Court added, the tax rate is lower in the other MSs than in France. Since extending the same one-half credit would lead to a more advantageous treatment, '[c]onsequently', the Court reasoned, the MS 'must be in a position' (mandatory language is also used in French '*doit pouvoir être en mesure de*') to determine the amount actually paid. The language used does not make it clear whether the Court is saying: (1) France has an obligation to check the actual amount of taxes paid and base the tax credit on this amount, in order to avoid offering a more advantageous treatment; or (2) assuming France does not wish to extend the exact same one-half credit to the cross-border context in all cases because it would lead to a more advantageous treatment, this is acceptable under EU law and, in that case, France 'must be in a position' to determine the taxes actually paid (since that is the only way France can achieve this). The wording could seem to point towards the first, while the current understanding of EU law would seem to point to the second.

The key question is how to grant the credit in a way that is in line with both the principle of equivalence and the principle of effectiveness. In this 2011 case, the CJEU gave some answers and then, in a case of October 2018, gave further clarification.

To summarize, in this 2011 *Accor* case, as regards the fundamental freedoms (freedom of establishment and free movement of capital), the holding is: as usual, EU MSs have the sovereignty to design their tax laws and methods to relief double or multiple layers of taxation, as long as this design is not discriminatory. Thus, what is not compatible is to design legislation to relieve economic double taxation of dividends that applies only to dividends from France and not to dividends from other EU MSs. What makes it particularly problematic is that France would levy the advance payment upon redistribution of both sets of dividends, both from France and from other EU MSs. In this way, France was the cause of taxation of those dividends, but then only offered relief for the advance payment by means of a tax credit for the French dividends and

companies *in the same way* as dividends paid to residents by non-resident companies (see *Test Claimants in the FII Group Litigation*, paragraph 72), that law does *not require* Member States to give taxpayers that have invested in foreign companies an *advantage* compared with those having invested in domestic companies (see, to that effect, Case C-298/05 *Columbus Container Services* [2007] ECR I-10451, paragraphs 39 and 40, and *Haribo Lakritzen Hans Riegel and Österreichische Salinen*, paragraph 89)' (emphasis added)).

1743. *See*, e.g., *infra* note 1764.

1744. CJEU, Case C-310/09, *Accor*, 15 Sep. 2011, ECLI:EU:C:2011:581, at paras 91–92.

not for the EU dividends (had France exempted the dividends stemming from other EU MSs, upon redistribution, from any further tax, this issue would likely not have arisen). Thus, France must find a way to treat the dividends equal again.

To remedy the difference in treatment, first, looking backward, France was obliged to offer a remedy for the previously levied advance payments, as they were levied in breach of EU law. Next, France had a few choices moving forward. It could:

- stop levying the advanced payment on the proportion of redistributed dividends that stem from other EU MSs; or
- reimburse the advanced payment (but immediately, to avoid a cash-flow disadvantage) on the proportion of redistributed dividends that stem from other EU MSs; or
- extend the tax credit designed to offset the amount of the advanced payment; or
- abolish the whole imputation system.

EU MSs with imputation systems tended to opt for the last fix, including France.

As regards the principle of equivalence and effectiveness, the holding is: whatever method of relief is designed for restoring the 'equivalence' of treatment, France cannot impose conditions that, in practice, make it impossible for the taxpayers affected to actually obtain this relief. The taxpayer (basically) tried to argue that, since no special conditions were required in the domestic context, none can be required in the cross-border context. The Court rejected this. It is not unequal treatment to ask the taxpayer to provide evidence regarding the amount of tax paid by subsidiaries in other MSs, whereas 'with respect to subsidiaries established in France, that evidence, known to the administration, is not required'. In fact, the Court went so far as to state that not only may French tax authorities ask for such evidence but also that 'the evidence required should enable the tax authorities of the Member State of taxation to ascertain, clearly and precisely, whether the conditions for obtaining a tax advantage are met'.[1745] In order to respect the principle of effectiveness, the evidence required should not be disproportionately burdensome or too formalistic.[1746] The Court then gave some guidance by means of examples of circumstances that may give rise to difficulties in producing the evidence:

> 'Production of that evidence may however be required only if it does not prove virtually impossible or excessively difficult to furnish proof of payment of the tax by the subsidiaries established in the other Member States, in the light in particular of the provisions of the legislation of those Member States concerning the avoidance of double taxation, the recording of the corporation tax which must be paid and the retention of administrative documents. It is for the national court to determine whether those conditions are met in the case before the national court.'[1747]

1745. *Id.*, at para. 99.
1746. *Id.* ('... but it does not need to take any particular form and the assessment must not be conducted too formalistically (see, to that effect, *Meilicke and Others*, paragraph 46)').
1747. CJEU, Case C-310/09, *Accor*, 15 Sep. 2011, ECLI:EU:C:2011:581, at para. 102.

The *Accor* Case: a follow-up infringement procedure by the Commission

After the CJEU decision in the *Accor* case, the Conseil d'État (highest administrative court) in France rendered its decisions in 2012[1748] to give effect to the CJEU's pronouncements. France had opted to reimburse the advance payments unlawfully collected. After, the Commission received complaints from French companies about the conditions imposed by these 2012 decisions for the reimbursement and, upon further investigation, decided to launch infringement proceedings against France.[1749]

For the purpose of this analysis, the main points of this case are reordered and three issues will be discussed here. Of the three, two questions concerned the scope of the reimbursement for the advance payment offered by France, namely: (1) whether there is an obligation for the amount of the reimbursement to take into account underlying taxes paid by *sub*-subsidiaries, and (2) whether the reimbursement may be limited to maximum one-third of the dividends from the subsidiary in the other EU MS. The third question asked (3) whether the administrative requirements, such as *what* evidence to provide and *when*, in order to claim the reimbursement, were in line with the principles of equivalence and effectiveness. Although these questions were asked in the context of the reimbursement of the advance payment, based on the reasoning adopted by the CJEU, which applied by analogy case law on the credit method (e.g., *FII*, *Haribo & Salinen*, *Meilicke*), it can convincingly be argued that it could equally apply to a context where France instead opted to extend the tax credit.

Also, beyond its relevance for the credit method specifically, as regards EU law in general: this is the first time the Commission had ever brought an infringement case against a state for the failure of one of its national courts of last resort to fulfil its obligation to send a preliminary reference question to the CJEU when confronting a question that required the CJEU's interpretation of EU law.[1750]

Regarding the first issue: the Commission pointed out that, in a purely domestic chain of companies, relief was offered at every level, so that economic double (or multiple) taxation was fully neutralized throughout the entire chain, whereas in a cross-border context, France considered only the first-tier subsidiary for the reimbursement.[1751] This leads to a difference of treatment based on where the *sub*-subsidiary has its seat (thus, a discrimination based on the 'nationality' of the sub-subsidiary) and the origin of the dividends from outside of France.[1752] The French government admitted that it explicitly takes into account *only* the first-tier subsidiary and excludes lower-tier subsidiaries, but France asserted that this does not amount to a difference of treatment.

1748. CJEU, Case C-416/17, *Commission v. France (Précompte mobilier)*, 4 Oct. 2018, ECLI:EU:C:2018:811, at paras 11–13; Opinion of AG Wathelet in Case C-416/17, *Commission v. France*, 25 Jul. 2018, ECLI:EU:C:2018:626, at paras 15–17 (citing Conseil d'État, 10 Dec. 2012, *Rhodia*, FR:XX:2012:317074.20121210 and *Accor*, FR:CESSR:2012:317075.20121210).
1749. CJEU, Case C-416/17, *Commission v. France (Précompte mobilier)*, 4 Oct. 2018, ECLI:EU:C:2018:811, at paras 14–17; Opinion of AG Wathelet in Case C-416/17, *Commission v. France*, 25 Jul. 2018, ECLI:EU:C:2018:626, at paras 18–22.
1750. Opinion of AG Wathelet in Case C-416/17, *Commission v. France*, 25 Jul. 2018, ECLI:EU:C:2018:626, at para. 3.
1751. *Id.*, at para. 24.
1752. *Id.*, at para. 25.

The reason is that the French relief system applies *separately* to each layer in the corporate chain; the French government conceives of its relief system as looking at only one parent-subsidiary pair at a time, *not* the entire chain, even in the domestic scenario.[1753] Thus, when the French government extends its domestic treatment to the cross-border scenario (or rather corrects its previous unequal treatment), it likewise need *only* look at *one level* of parent-subsidiary relationship at a time. In other words, according to the French government, its relief system lacks any concept of 'sub-subsidiary'.[1754]

The AG described France's approach as formalistic, restrictive and erroneous (author's translation of 'une application formaliste, restrictive et, à mon sens, erronée').[1755] The AG employed the well-established same-taxation-same-relief reasoning to condemn this approach from an EU law perspective:[1756] i.e., France is exercising its jurisdiction to tax over those dividends, namely dividends which include dividends passed up from sub-subsidiaries abroad; if France exercises its taxation right over dividends, stemming both from the *domestic* context and from the *cross-border* context, and if it fully relieves the former, then 'equivalent' relief (or reimbursement) must be extended to the latter. Moreover, the wording used by the CJEU in past judgments could be read as implying relief for lower tiers in the chain: in these cases, in France as well as the past cases in the UK, namely *FII I* and *FII II*, the CJEU used the wording 'the mechanism adopted to prevent or mitigate a series of charges to tax or economic double taxation' (translated from 'le mécanisme adopté pour prévenir ou atténuer l'imposition en chaîne ou la double imposition économique').[1757]

The second issue addressed the reimbursement limitation of one-third in the cross-border context versus the credit fixed at a flat rate of one-half in the domestic context.[1758] First, the CJEU has already accepted that an MCA, up to the limit of what the MS would levy, is compatible with EU law. Second, France demonstrated convincingly that its approach re-equilibrates the different treatment (*see* the diagram slightly reorganized and translated in Example No. 31):[1759]

1753. *Id.*, at paras 26–28.
1754. CJEU, Case C-416/17, *Commission v. France (Précompte mobilier)*, 4 Oct. 2018, ECLI:EU:C:2018:811, at para. 21 and para. 38; Opinion of AG Wathelet in Case C-416/17, *Commission v. France*, 25 Jul. 2018, ECLI:EU:C:2018:626, at para. 28.
1755. Opinion of AG Wathelet in Case C-416/17, *Commission v. France*, 25 Jul. 2018, ECLI:EU:C:2018:626, at para. 30. At the time of writing, the Opinion was not available in English; it has since been translated into English.
1756. Opinion of AG Wathelet in Case C-416/17, *Commission v. France*, 25 Jul. 2018, ECLI:EU:C:2018:626, at para. 34.
1757. *Id.*, at para. 36 (citing 'Test Claimants in the FII Group Litigation (C446/04, EU:C:2006:774, point 46)').
1758. *Id.*, at para. 68.
1759. *Id.*, at para. 74.

Example No. 31: The Post-*Accor* Remedy to the Imputation Credit System in France

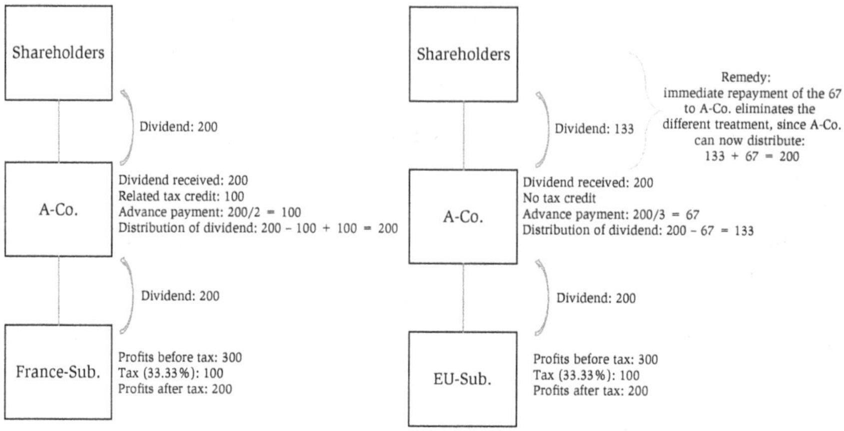

Regarding the third issue, the AG did not believe that the Commission had met its requisite burden to prove that France had violated the principles of equivalence and effectiveness, by creating disproportionately burdensome or impossible requirements in order to claim a reimbursement for taxpayers. The Commission seemed to have misinterpreted, or overstretched, the two decisions of the French Conseil d'Etat. From its interpretation of those decisions, the Commission derived strict obligations, for example, to produce extremely precise forms of evidence (e.g., accounting records of distributed dividends that matched sums discussed in the minutes of the General Assembly, an allegedly impossible task if the accounting records reflect dividends actually *distributed*, whereas the General Assembly discussed more aggregate accounting figures of *distributable* dividends, which may include sums from previous periods not yet distributed, etc.)[1760] or to hold onto certain documents even after the legal expiry period for the retention of such documents had passed.[1761] According to the AG, the mere fact that the Conseil d'Etat was citing those documents in the case is *not* proof of an obligation. The Conseil d'Etat discussed accounting records, for example, because they were put forward as evidence by the parties, and was not necessarily declaring them obligations for the taxpayer.[1762] The Commission was, among other things, equating mentions of those documents in the case with obligations flowing from the case. Thus, all the grounds of the Commission were dismissed. As a result,

1760. *Id.*, at para. 43.
1761. *Id.*, at para. 45.
1762. *Id.*, at paras 53–54.

there is no definitively conclusive insight regarding whether some of those requirements would have been too burdensome, in contravention of the principles of equivalence and effectiveness.

The CJEU followed the Opinion of the AG. The CJEU decided that the reimbursement limitation is acceptable under EU law. However, the CJEU held that France 'failed' its EU law obligations in two ways: first, by refusing to take into account the underlying CIT of sub-subsidiaries and, second, by failing to refer this question regarding the sub-subsidiaries to the CJEU in order to ask whether this was acceptable under EU law *before* pronouncing a decision by a court of last resort (the Conseil d'État) on the matter. Thus, in *Commission v. France*, the CJEU 'hereby':

> '1. Declares that, by refusing to take into account, in order to calculate the reimbursement of the advance payment made by a resident company in respect of the distribution of dividends paid by a non-resident company via a non-resident subsidiary, the tax incurred by that second company on the profits underlying those dividends, even though the national mechanism for the avoidance of economic double taxation allows, in the case of a purely domestic chain of interests, the tax levied on the dividends distributed by a company at every level of that chain of interests to be offset, the French Republic has failed to fulfil its obligations under Articles 49 and 63 TFEU;
>
> 2. Declares that, since the Conseil d'État (Council of State, France) failed to make a reference to the Court of Justice of the European Union, in accordance with the procedure provided for in the third paragraph of Article 267 TFEU, in order to determine whether it was necessary to refuse to take into account, for the purpose of calculating the reimbursement of the advance payment made by a resident company in respect of the distribution of dividends paid by a non-resident company via a non-resident subsidiary, the tax incurred by that second company on the profits underlying those dividends, even though its interpretation of the provisions of EU law in the judgments of 10 December 2012, Rhodia (FR:CESSR:2012:317074.20121210), and of 10 December 2012, Accor (FR:CESSR:2012:317075.20121210), was not so obvious as to leave no scope for doubt, the French Republic failed to fulfil its obligations under the third paragraph of Article 267 TFEU'.

Interim Summary

Imputation credit systems are now a rarity among EU MSs. CJEU case law was one driving factor behind their dismantling.[1763] After briefly summarizing the main issues and findings from the above case law, the aim is to explore: (1) what made these

1763. Andrew Ainsworth, *Dividend Imputation: The International Experience*, 1 JASSA 58, 58 (2016) (countries listed as having a 'full imputation tax system' are Australia, Canada, Chile, Mexico and New Zealand, among OECD countries, and Malta, among non-OECD. 'The OECD lists Korea and the United Kingdom as operating partial imputation systems. However, as the tax credits provided in these countries are not linked to the amount of corporate tax paid, these are not true imputation tax systems. Many countries have shifted away from imputation systems, including the United Kingdom (1999), Ireland (1999), Germany (2001), Singapore (2003), Italy (2004), Finland (2005), France (2005), Norway (2006) and Malaysia (2008). Table 1 provides an overview of the changes.' EU law is cited as one of the main causes for removal among EU countries).

systems incompatible with EU law and (2) what can be learned from this about the design of credits to eliminate economic double taxation.

The CJEU assessed these systems both from the perspective of the state of residence of the company distributing profits to its shareholders (for ease of reference, the term 'state of source', albeit an oversimplification, is used here) and from the perspective of the state of residence of the shareholder. The EU law obligations differed depending on the perspective.

From the perspective of the state of source, as deliberated in, for example, the *Metallgesellschaft* and *ACT Test Claimants* cases, the pair of comparison selected was that between two resident subsidiaries, one with its parent company, or shareholder, residing in the same state and one with its shareholder residing abroad, e.g., UK-Sub. owned by UK-Co. versus UK-Sub. owned by EU-Co. in another EU MS. The different treatment in *Metallgesellschaft* affected the UK subsidiary. Whereas a UK subsidiary with a UK parent could, under certain conditions, opt for a group taxation regime that eliminated the UK subsidiary's obligation to pay ACT upon distribution, a UK subsidiary with a parent in another state did not have this option. The latter had no choice but to pay ACT immediately upon distribution of dividends to a non-resident. The disadvantageous element was identified as a cash-flow disadvantage. The subsidiaries were deemed comparable based on a combination of the reasoning initiated in *Avoir Fiscal*, recalling that the seat of a company is a proxy for its 'nationality' and discrimination solely on the basis of nationality is clearly prohibited, and the formula of same-taxation-same-relief or subject-to-tax (discussed, *inter alia*, in Section 4.2.1., *see*, e.g., *supra* note 1069). Both UK subsidiaries were fully subject to CIT in the UK, regardless of the location of their parent or shareholder, and, as there was no objective difference in that respect, there should be no different treatment in respect of a benefit related to that CIT liability. The benefit in this case revolved around *when* to pay the CIT, either immediately upfront upon distribution of profits or deferred until later. It was an infringement that the cross-border case (UK-Sub. distributing to EU-Co.) suffered a cash-flow disadvantage as compared to the domestic case (UK-Sub. distributing to UK-Co.).

In *ACT Test Claimants*, although the comparison was essentially the same, the different treatment in this case affected the *shareholders* (as opposed to the UK subsidiaries, as in *Metallgesellschaft*). The complaint was against the refusal to extend the imputed tax credit to non-resident shareholders. This changed the outcome because, as regards the tax treatment of shareholders, the state of the distributing company is *not* in the same position as the state of residence of the shareholders. Reasoning, *inter alia*, on the basis of *Schumacker* and the Parent-Subsidiary Directive, the CJEU regarded the state of residence as having the greater ability and therefore responsibility to eliminate economic double taxation. Another related reason was that, if the CJEU were to place responsibility on the state of source in this context, it would in effect be obliging the state of source to renounce its ability to tax profits generated by subsidiaries on its territory. This point will be returned to below when further exploring why imputation credit systems have not thrived under EU law. Most decisively, the UK's regime was ultimately acceptable because – reasoning along consistency or subject-to-tax lines – the UK levied WHT only on outgoing dividends in cases where it had agreed to extend the shareholder's tax credit to non-resident recipients; in the cases where the UK did not extend the tax credit to non-resident shareholders, it also refrained from taxing the outgoing dividends.

From the perspective of the state of residence of the shareholders, the CJEU assessed different treatment of shareholders or recipients of dividends on the basis of the source of those dividends or on the basis of the location of the seat of the distributing subsidiary. There were two different points in time at which a different treatment could occur: (1) upon the receipt of dividends and (2) upon the redistribution of those dividends.

The first point in time (i.e., receipt of dividends) was considered in, for example, the *Manninen* and *Meilicke* cases. The comparison selected was made between a shareholder that received dividends from a resident subsidiary and a shareholder that received dividends from a non-resident subsidiary. The different treatment arose from the fact that the former would be granted a credit for the underlying CITs levied on the profits of the subsidiary, whereas the latter would not. The credit sought to eliminate a series of charges to tax, or economic double taxation, on distributed profits. Given that both distributions of profits were subject to this same risk, regardless of whether they stem from the same state or from another state, the two situations were comparable in light of the purpose of the legislation. Thus, the MS should grant equal treatment to the shareholders, by extending a credit for the underlying corporate taxes to shareholders upon receipt of foreign-source dividends.

As seen in, for example, the *Manninen* and *Accor* cases, equal treatment does not mean granting the exact same credit. Often imputation credits are calculated on the basis of a fixed fraction or percentage of the dividends received, e.g., 3/7ths of the dividends or 50% of the dividends. However, this fraction is often set based upon the nominal rate of CIT, but often with an adjustment mechanism if the distributing company paid a different amount. In this way, it is actually based on the taxes effectively paid by the distributing company. Thus, equal treatment means, likewise, basing a credit on the foreign CIT paid abroad.

On this point, the CJEU used mandatory language, i.e., 'must'. The CJEU added that, if the MS were to merely extend, for example, a fixed 50% tax credit *regardless* of the amount of foreign CIT actually paid, this could amount to granting more favourable treatment to cross-border cases. Although reverse discrimination is not generally a problem under EU law,[1764] it appears that the way in which the equal treatment

1764. On reverse discrimination generally, *see*, e.g., Marjaana Helminen, *Chapter 2: Non-discrimination and Basic Freedoms, in EU Tax Law – Direct Taxation* Section 2.1.2 (IBFD 2018 ed. 2018) ('Article 18 of the TFEU does not cover reverse discrimination, i.e. discrimination of internal situations compared to cross-border situations.[288] Because of the lack of a cross-border nexus, the Member States may treat such own nationals that have not made use of the basic freedoms worse than nationals of other Member States.' She notes that more favourable treatment for cross-border situations could run up against State aid issues). On the relationship between reverse discrimination and State aid, *see*, e.g., Rita Szudoczky, *The Sources of EU Law and Their Relationships: Lessons for the Field of Taxation* 731 (32 Doctoral Series, IBFD 2014) ('In the case of reverse discrimination where a national measure treats cross-border situations more favourably than domestic ones, the differential treatment falls

obligation was expressed in the wording of these decisions would 'outlaw' it or make it impossible (but *see* discussion at *supra* note 1744). This is interesting in light of the fact that the CJEU has accepted, in the *Kronos* case, a credit for domestic dividends and a complete exemption for cross-border dividends.

The second point in time (i.e., redistribution of dividends) was considered in, for example, the *Test Claimants in the FII Group Litigation* and *Accor* cases. The CJEU held that, at the moment of redistribution, different treatment of a company based on source of dividends, or 'nationality' of the subsidiary from which it received the dividends, is not acceptable. Again comparability was established in light of legislation designed to mitigate a series of charges to tax since those subsidiaries both risk suffering taxation of the profits before distributing them to the company in question. The different treatment revolved mostly around the company's obligation to pay advance CIT (triggered by a redistribution event), which in turn stemmed from a different conceptualization of the underlying CIT paid by the subsidiaries. In the French system, there was a different treatment of a French company (France-Co.) upon redistribution of dividends: if redistributed profits stemmed from a French subsidiary (France-Sub.), then a tax credit offset the advance payment due by the French company, whereas if profits stemmed from a subsidiary in another state (EU-Sub.), then no tax credit was passed up to be used against the advance payment.

In the UK system, one way to describe it, so as to simplify it and attempt to highlight the aspects flagged as problematic by the CJEU, may be as follows:

- For the UK-parent, the underlying CIT of UK-Sub. = ACT, which transformed into a tax asset that offset immediately the ACT of the UK-parent upon redistribution.
- The underlying CIT of EU-Sub. = indirect credit, but did not generate ACT; thus, there was no immediate offset and, thus, the UK-parent paid its own ACT in full upon redistribution of foreign-sourced dividends, with the eventual prospect (or hope) of compensating it later against MCT due.
- The consequence was: this led to a cash-flow disadvantage that was not acceptable.
- In practice, sometimes this prospect (of later compensating ACT against MCT) did not even work out because of 'surplus ACT' that accumulated systematically more often in the cross-border context; this was mainly for two reasons: due to the order of crediting the various tax assets/credits (i.e., against MCT: (1) first the indirect FTC, then (2) the ACT could be credited) and due to overall less possibilities to transfer or surrender ACT, which could be transferred to UK-Sub. but not EU-Sub.
- The consequence was: these factors further exacerbated the above-mentioned cash-flow disadvantage.

outside the scope of the *lex specialis*, i.e. the fundamental freedoms, thus it falls back on the *lex generalis*, i.e. State aid rules').

- If it opted in for the 'FID' regime, the UK-parent could get reimbursement of the surplus ACT; however, this came months later, leading to too long a time between paying ACT upfront and eventual reimbursement.
- The consequence was: the cash-flow disadvantage was not resolved by this FID regime.

In the 2018 Commission infringement proceedings against France, following what was regarded as an incorrect implementation of the *Accor* decision, two substantive aspects of the imputation system were discussed and some procedural aspects. First, when France corrects the unequal treatment under its imputation system by means of a 'reimbursement of the advance payment' with respect to dividends sourced from outside France, then the amount must also take into account the taxes paid by sub-subsidiaries. It does not seem too far a stretch to assume that the exact same reasoning could be applied to the choice (rather than to reimburse) to simply extend the tax credit to foreign-source dividends. In the domestic context, the imputation credit system had the effect of eliminating economic double taxation at each layer of the corporate chain, and thus this had to be replicated for the cross-border context.

Second, if France decides to limit the amount of the reimbursement to a maximum of one-third of the dividends, this succeeds in remedying the difference treatment because: (1) it corresponds to the advance payment actually made (according to paragraph 95 of the judgment) and (2) by analogy previous decisions that allow an MCA establish the 'principle' that 'a Member State cannot be required to grant a tax credit in respect of tax paid, in another Member State, on distributed profits which exceeds the amount of tax resulting from the application of its own tax legislation' (according to paragraph 96 of the judgment).

Regarding procedural elements, there are some main takeaways from this 2018 decision as well as the *Accor* case (and two *Meilicke* cases, as will be reinforced below in Section 4.2.9.). From an equal treatment logic, one could argue that, since there are minimal, to no, requirements in the domestic context, the same should apply cross-border. However, although the CJEU recognizes the comparability of the situation on substantive points, the CJEU permits certain adjustments for the cross-border context on procedural points. Certain adjustments, such as requiring the taxpayer to provide the information needed to obtain the benefits, are not deemed to undermine the principle of effectiveness. Rather, it is part and parcel of enabling the MS to properly provide the substantive rights. On the one hand, the procedural requirements must be proportionate. The MS should not require information that is impossible for the taxpayer to obtain, nor be overly formalistic in how precisely the information is presented. On the other hand, the MS must be equipped with the information needed to determine precisely the amount of taxes paid in the other state.

The next question that arises is: what can be learned from the above as to why these imputation credit systems were particularly problematic under EU law?

One aspect of the reasoning in the *ACT Test Claimants* case was revealing in this respect. As regards the respective roles and obligations of a MS with respect to an imputed shareholder tax credit, the CJEU relied on the examples of *Schumacker* and the

Parent-Subsidiary Directive as support for, in essence, placing more responsibility on the state of residence of the shareholder.

It also gave a reason as to why it should *not* be placed on the state of source where the distributing subsidiary resides.[1765] Perhaps, the Parent-Subsidiary Directive was also the underlying inspiration for this part of the reasoning too. The final result of that Directive is that only one layer (or nearly only one layer) of tax remains, namely the state of the subsidiary taxes the profits generated by the subsidiary and any further layers of taxation on the parent are eliminated (as will be discussed in Section 4.3.). In this way, it incorporates a notion that the taxes should be levied where they are generated (only in an approximate way, since depending on one's notion of where profits are generated, this overlooks that the profits of a corporation may themselves be sourced from many different places and activities, active or passive, etc.). It is true that, if the state of the subsidiary were obliged to eliminate *this layer* of *its* contribution to the phenomenon of economic double (or multiple) taxation, when the profits are distributed out of its territory, it would effectively entail eliminating CIT – at least, on the portion of the profits that are distributed. As the CJEU stated, it would either mean 'exempting those profits' from CIT or extending the imputed tax credit upwards to non-residents, 'by granting the shareholder a tax advantage *equal to* the *tax paid* on those *profits by the company making the distribution*' (emphasis added).[1766] One way to depict what some imputation systems seek to do is, by imputing the corporate tax to the shareholder, they could be seen as merging or 'dissolving' the CIT *into* the taxation at the level of the shareholder, leaving only one tax, namely that levied on the individuals ultimately owning the company.[1767] If so, then when the tax credit is granted to non-resident shareholders, a state relinquishes its corporate tax claim to the extent that the corporate tax is imputed or given to a shareholder from which the state does not collect any residual income tax; it gives up the corporate tax collected from its subsidiary to a shareholder over which it has limited, to no, tax jurisdiction. The CJEU does not, it appears, believe that it can create an obligation for this particular sacrifice. Thus, there is an implicit priority given to the subsidiary state's right to tax corporate profits on its territory, which is present in the Parent-Subsidiary Directive and now also here in the CJEU's reasoning. In so far as an imputation system can be seen as 'dissolving' the CIT into the shareholder level tax, this is one subtle way in which certain aspects of EU law and imputation credit systems are at variance, in systematic or structural ways.

In proffering a broader explanation, Terra and Wattel remark that a classical CIT system is 'internationally neutral', whereas integration systems are not.[1768] Neutral with respect to what is the decisive question. Terra and Wattel specify that a classical

1765. CJEU, Case C-374/04, *ACT Test Claimants*, 12 Dec. 2006, ECLI:EU:C:2006:773, at para. 59.
1766. *Id.*
1767. *See*, e.g., Ben J.M. Terra & Peter J. Wattel, *European Tax Law* 227, Section 4.2.3.4 (Wolters Kluwer 6th ed. 2012), cited at *supra* note 296 (this is similar to the previously discussed descriptions of the imputation credit system, depicting them as similar to converting the corporate income tax into essentially an advanced withholding tax on the shareholders).
1768. Ben J.M. Terra & Peter J. Wattel, *European Tax Law* 223 and 228 (Wolters Kluwer 6th ed. 2012).

CIT system is *not* neutral with respect to the *type* of investment in a corporation, in that it makes equity investments (with returns in the form of distributions of profits, which are taxed at both the corporate and investor level) more expensive than debt investments (with returns in the form of interest, which are deductible from the corporate tax base and taxed once at the investor level).[1769] Rather, it is 'neutral' in another way. If everything is simply taxed (equally), then a difference of treatment does not arise – to be precise, a difference of treatment does not arise *from the legislation* of that one state. If all distributions of profits, from home or from abroad, incoming or outgoing, are all taxed at the same rate (or same relative rate), then the classical CIT system itself does not distinguish between and treat differently the domestic situation and the cross-border situation. Perhaps rather than 'neutral', the words more precisely might be 'indifferent' or 'non-discriminatory'.[1770] By contrast, an integration system based on the imputation credit method discussed in these cases is neutral regarding the type of investment in a corporation, but generally speaking, it will apply only in the domestic situation and not in the cross-border situation.[1771] Regardless of whether such an imputation system would be better policy, based on carefully weighing various factors,[1772] any discriminatory effect that attaches to, for example, the origin of a dividend or the seat of the corporation in another EU MS renders it incompatible with EU law.[1773] This recalls the limits of EU law and the limits of what the CJEU can do. The

1769. *Id.*
1770. The term 'neutral' in this context is often associated with using a benchmark for testing the influence of a measure, e.g., a tax law, on the behaviour of actors, e.g., taxpayers or investors, such as how it affects their decisions to invest. Here, it seems to be about the treatment of taxpayers or investors by a state, not necessarily about how it affects their behaviour. If two states tax a given taxpayer in the same way as all other comparable taxpayers, and thus both are not acting in a discriminatory way, such double taxation will not necessarily be neutral in terms of the taxpayer's behaviour or decisions in response to it.
1771. Ben J.M. Terra & Peter J. Wattel, *European Tax Law* 223 and 228 (Wolters Kluwer 6th ed. 2012).
1772. Michael J. Graetz & Alvin C. Warren Jr., *Dividend Taxation in Europe: When the ECJ Makes Tax Policy*, 44(6) Common Mkt. L. Rev. 1577, 1578–1579 (2007) (the authors consider 'seven potentially complicating factors that must be addressed in constructing a system for taxing corporate income and dividends that cross national borders').
1773. Of course, one may delve into the debate regarding whether the reasoning of the CJEU was well founded or convincing because whether a law is 'discriminatory' depends on layers of interlinked reasoning, which can be challenged at each link: e.g., whether it is deemed different treatment of comparable situations (or the same treatment of incomparable situations); whether it is deemed different treatment follows from what is selected as the relevant comparison, a selection which is far from free of criticisms; and within that comparison, what factors or attributes are irrelevant to the comparison and what factors relevant to detecting an objective difference. In many of these cases, the CJEU has selected two interrelated factors, namely the *objective of the legislation to prevent economic double taxation* and whether the state in question *exercises its taxing rights over the income* in question (e.g., subject-to-tax, e.g., same taxation, same relief). The CJEU excludes factors such as the *objective of the legislation to integrate the taxation of corporations and taxpayers*, which may require broadening the CJEU's analysis from narrowly looking at the receipt of the dividend to looking at the 'entire stream of corporate-source income flowing ultimately to the shareholders'; another example from other cases (especially *Avoir Fiscal*) is the 'non-taxability of distributions by the branch to its foreign parent', which it considered an irrelevant attribute, while the fact that the MS taxes the branches of foreign companies the same as domestic companies is relevant (Graetz & Warren, at 1594). On some of these points, *see*, e.g., Michael J. Graetz &

CJEU assesses a given national law presented to it by a national court, in light of the TFEU prohibition on discrimination or restrictions, on the specific grounds (e.g., nationality) listed therein. It has no legal basis for a tax policy analysis.

Although the CJEU case law has challenged the imputation credit systems, based on their tendency to discriminate between a domestic and cross-border situation, this tendency does *not* seem to be an inherent feature of an imputation credit method. Theoretically, it *could* be extended to foreign shareholders (outbound distributions/inbound investment) and to foreign subsidiaries (inbound distributions/outbound investment). As Graetz and Warren point out, the problem is: the CJEU does not dictate, and cannot dictate, on which end it should be extended, and extending it on both sides would lead to systematically treating the cross-border investments better than the domestic ones.[1774]

Although the CJEU cannot explicitly dictate policy in place of MSs, some suggestions can be inferred from the reasoning and the aspects held incompatible by the CJEU through its process of negative integration. As regards an imputed shareholder tax credit, the reasoning seems to exert more pressure on the state of residence of the shareholder (especially a state that finds itself in the position of being the state where both the distributing company and the shareholder are located). What seemed more decisive for the final decision was that, once profits come within its jurisdiction and it exercises its tax jurisdiction over them: (1) upon arrival to a resident and/or (2) as they are redistributed by a resident, that resident should receive relief for economic double (or multiple) taxation on the FSI if such relief is granted for DSI. The state of the distributing company (when it is solely the state 'in which the profits are derived') is less well positioned to pass up an imputation credit to foreign shareholders, based on the reasoning. However, based on the final decision, to be on the safe side, this state should follow the example of the UK in ensuring that, if it does not pass up any such credit to foreign shareholders, it should also not levy any tax on those outgoing dividends. As mentioned above, if the state of the subsidiary taxes the outgoing

Alvin C. Warren Jr., *Dividend Taxation in Europe: When the ECJ Makes Tax Policy*, 44(6) Common Mkt. L. Rev. 1577, 1594–1595 (2007). However, this is beyond the scope of the analysis here; while understanding certain main trends in the CJEU's reasoning is relevant for predicting how certain design features of a credit method would stay in line with EU law, the more detailed critiques as to how the CJEU could have decided differently are merely interesting.

1774. Michael J. Graetz & Alvin C. Warren Jr., *Dividend Taxation in Europe: When the ECJ Makes Tax Policy*, 44(6) Common Mkt. L. Rev. 1577, 1584 (2007) ('Extending credits to outgoing dividends would tend to promote capital import neutrality and reduce tax revenues of source countries. Extending credits to incoming dividends would tend to promote capital export neutrality and reduce tax revenues of residence countries. The first approach would reduce differences in treatment based on the origin of capital, while the second would reduce differences in treatment based on its destination.

The choice between these two approaches is certainly not obvious, and studies commissioned by the European Commission have sometimes recommended the first and sometimes the second.[13] Both approaches, however, cannot be implemented simultaneously unless the goal is not just to eliminate discrimination against cross-border income, but to tax international income *more favourably* than domestic income.[14] As we shall see, the ECJ's tax decisions have required the Court to resolve the dilemma presented by this choice, but do not offer any coherent rationale for choosing between the two approaches').

dividends, it may be obliged to extend its domestic relief; if this MS refrains from taxing, it need not extend the relief. Parts of the reasoning suggest that the CJEU leans in one direction, though its final decisions are understandably more circumspect.

The above suggests that one way in which an imputation system could be designed would be a system in which a MS grants and allows the passing up of an imputation credit with respect to all distributions that are received by shareholders within its territory (upon arrival and upon redistribution) and, if and when those profits leave its territory to go to foreign shareholders, it should refrain from levying any tax on them to the extent that it does not grant or impute any credit to foreign shareholders. This would seem to be in line with the above case law. If so, this would favour the extension of the regime on the side of inbound distributions and thus outbound investment, which indirectly implies policymaking preferences. Whether or not it would be feasible for a given MS is another question.

As explained above when France was confronted with this dilemma, overall the following options are available:

- if an imputed tax credit is not passed up to the extent that dividends are foreign-source, France would have to refrain from levying any advance payment on that portion of the dividends (leaving them exempt);
- or if a MS levies an advance payment or income tax on the entire amount of the distributed dividends in a first step, it would in a second step need to reimburse this to the extent of the foreign-source dividends, but, importantly, it would have to do so immediately in order to avoid a prohibited cash-flow disadvantage;
- alternatively, a MS could extend the imputed shareholder tax credit. This would amount to some sort of mutual recognition, by regarding CIT paid to other states as equally eligible as CIT in France and thus allowing it to be passed up the chain. Under this option, applying by analogy the CJEU's reasoning in the 2018 *Commission v. France* case (C-416/17), the amount of the credit should take into account underlying CIT of not only first-tier subsidiaries but also the sub-subsidiaries. However, it is permissible, where the foreign CIT is higher, to limit the amount of the credit to the tax credit that can be granted in the domestic context. On a related point, it was contended above that the decision, although made in the context of an imputation credit, is equally relevant for both an imputation credit and an indirect credit;
- since the obligations of tax relief correspond to tax collection on dividends, the options revolve around either extending the relief or refraining from taxing; if a MS is unwilling or unable to apply the same relief to both domestic-source and foreign-source dividends, then that system has to be abolished and potentially a new one put in its place.

An extension across the border is not a purely theoretical option, as in practice the UK had accomplished this in a targeted way by means of DTCs (before its imputation credit was abolished) and as Malta's current system demonstrates. Malta operates a full imputation credit system. The CIT rate is 35%, corresponding to the highest tax rate on the progressive scale for personal income tax of 35 %.[1775] In general, when resident companies distribute dividends to shareholders, a refundable tax credit is granted to shareholders (corporate and individual) in the amount of the CIT paid by the company. The amount of the dividend plus the tax credit (thus, it is 'franked' dividend income or grossed-up dividend income) is included in the tax base of the shareholder and then the tax credit is deducted from the shareholder's income tax liability.[1776] It opted to extend this system 'upwards' to both resident and non-resident shareholders. Thus, it extended the regime on the side of outgoing dividends, thereby favouring inbound investment, perhaps unsurprisingly for Malta's general tax policy priorities.

Of course, Malta's system must also be non-discriminatory on the incoming-dividend side. Upon receipt of foreign-source dividends, they are either exempt or brought into full imputation system, if these dividends stem from a qualifying 'participating holding'. The requirements for a 'participation holding' are broad and thus seemingly readily achieved: there are more than five alternative (not cumulative) criteria, ranging from a 5 % holding of share capital to a minimum investment of EUR 1,164,000.[1777]

In the cases that do not qualify as a 'participating holding', it is possible that some EU law issues regarding potential differences in treatment could be detected. Upon receipt of foreign-source dividends in these cases, there are multiple options for double taxation relief. Based on the IBFD Analysis of Malta's legal system, generally speaking, relief is based first and foremost on the DTCs and, if not, on unilateral relief.[1778] Thus, without an analysis of the interaction with each tax treaty, it is not readily ascertainable the extent to which there is different treatment; it would require a case-by-case assessment. Upon redistribution in these cases, the amount of the imputation credit/refund passed on to shareholders differs, i.e., equal to 6/7ths, 5/7ths, or 2/3rds of the underlying corporate tax, depending on certain conditions.[1779] Thus, it seems that incompatible different treatment could potentially occur if it is the case that, when the dividends are sourced domestically, the full imputation regime always applies regardless of the size of the shareholding, whereas when the dividends are sourced from abroad, the full imputation regime does not always apply (namely, in the cases falling outside of participating holdings or where equivalent relief is not extended under a DTC). Nevertheless, it appears that no taxpayers have bothered to bring a

---

1775. *See*, e.g., André Zarb & Pierre Portelli, *Malta: Individual Taxation*, Country Analyses IBFD Section 7 (last visited 10 Jul. 2018); Conrad Cassar Torregiani, *Malta: Corporate Taxation*, Country Analyses IBFD Section 7 (last visited 10 Jul. 2018).

1776. *Id.*

1777. *See*, e.g., Conrad Cassar Torregiani, *Malta: Corporate Taxation*, Country Analyses IBFD Section 7.2.1.3 (last visited 10 Jul. 2018) (citing Article 2 of Malta's Income Tax Act).

1778. *See*, e.g., André Zarb & Pierre Portelli, *Malta: Individual Taxation*, Country Analyses IBFD Section 7.1.4 (last visited 10 Jul. 2018); Conrad Cassar Torregiani, *Malta: Corporate Taxation*, Country Analyses IBFD Section 7.2.6 (last visited 10 Jul. 2018).

1779. For more details, *see*, e.g., André Zarb & Pierre Portelli, *Malta: Individual Taxation*, Country Analyses IBFD Section 1.5.1 (last visited 10 Jul. 2018); Conrad Cassar Torregiani, *Malta: Corporate Taxation*, Country Analyses IBFD Section 6.1.2 (last visited 10 Jul. 2018).

complaint, which is perhaps not surprising considering that the end result remains, on balance, a very generous one. Notably, the Commission has not either.

This regime was implemented in 2006, after agreement with the EU Commission in the process of discussing the reforms needed for Malta to avoid falling afoul of the Code of Conduct against harmful tax competition.[1780] Thus for now, to date, Malta's imputation method system is the only one that has survived EU scrutiny.[1781]

4.2.9. Other Relevant Case Law

In making the selection of cases, the aim is to explore the interaction between the credit method and EU law and discover those from which insight can be garnered on how MSs may design and apply the credit method or certain components of it. However, not all cases or issues fit within the rather-established lines of case law of the CJEU. The credit method makes an appearance in other cases. Thus, for the sake of a more comprehensive overview, this section discusses a few other 'miscellaneous' cases that also touch upon the credit method.

One case[1782] specifically addressed the administrative requirements for claiming a credit. It is thus helpful for further discussing the procedural issues raised in the *Accor* decision and especially the follow-up *Commission v. France* decision. Following up on the first *Meilicke* case decided in 2007,[1783] the same claimants brought a second case decided in 2011.[1784] While the first case determined the substantive rights of the claimants to obtain a tax credit for dividends received from companies in other MSs in the same way as dividends received from German companies, the second case focused more on certain procedural aspects for ensuring these rights.

There were two issues of a procedural nature. First, in order to obtain the credit for the underlying corporate tax paid, German law required a 'corporate tax certificate'.[1785] The certificate had to contain, *inter alia*, information regarding the corporate taxes paid and some other details regarding the 'composition' of the dividends. The 'composition' information related to special rules under German law regarding 'the various parts of the capital and reserves available for distribution on the basis of a special division of capital and reserves within the meaning of Paragraph 30 of the KStG

1780. *See*, e.g., European Commission, State Aids E 6/2005, NN 26/2005, E 11/2005 and NN 35/2005 – Malta Tax Incentives in Favour of 'International Trading Companies' and 'Companies with Foreign Income', C(2006)810 Final (22 Mar. 2006).

1781. For debates on whether it should remain free from EU scrutiny, *see*, e.g., Tommaso Faccio, *Is Malta a Tax Haven?: Implications for Europe During the Maltese Presidency and Beyond*, A Study Commissioned by the Greens/EFA Group in the European Parliament (11 Jan. 2017), https://www.greens-efa.eu/files/assets/docs/is_malta_a_tax_haven_.pdf (last visited 20 Aug. 2018); for a rebuttal, *see*, e.g., Tonio Zarb & André Zarb, *Malta's Tax System: Setting the Record Straight* (KPMG 26 May 2017), https://home.kpmg/mt/en/home/insights/2017/05/maltas-tax-system-setting-the-record-straight.html (last visited 20 Jun. 2018) (one of the authors of the IBFD Analysis decided to co-author a public response to negate what they refer to as 'sensationalistic articles which have appeared in the press recently').

1782. CJEU, Case C-262/09, *Meilicke*, 30 Jun. 2011, ECLI:EU:C:2011:438.

1783. *See supra* note 1640; CJEU, Case C-292/04, *Meilicke*, 6 Mar. 2007, ECLI:EU:C:2007:132.

1784. CJEU, Case C-262/09, *Meilicke*, 30 Jun. 2011, ECLI:EU:C:2011:438.

1785. *Id.*, at paras 10–11.

(in the version in force in the relevant years)'. In connection with these special rules, the credit was granted for dividends, excluding those that 'originate from distributions for which capital and reserves are deemed to have been used'. While it was standard for German companies, it was much more difficult for foreign companies. The German Court (Finanzgericht Köln), in fact, used the word 'impossible'.[1786]

Second, there was a change in the tax laws regarding the conditions under which tax assessments that had been deemed 'final' could be amended (i.e., new conditions 'in relation to the finality of tax assessments and their amendment in the case of events having a retroactive effect').[1787] Certain 'event(s) having retroactive effect' could be grounds for amending a final tax assessment. However, with effect from 28 October 2004, the above-mentioned 'corporate tax certificates' would no longer constitute such a 'retroactive event' capable of reopening the tax assessment. This effectively made it 'procedurally impossible' for the claimants to request an amendment of the tax assessments on the dividends, since even if they could obtain the certificate, it would be too late.[1788]

As regards the first procedural issue, the CJEU formulated the question as an enquiry into whether the same form of evidence with the same level of detail that is required in the domestic context in order to obtain the credit may also be applied to the cross-border context.[1789] If not, the follow-up questions arose as to what 'degree of detail' may be required as evidence and whether, 'where necessary', an estimation of the tax would suffice.[1790] By the very question itself, this recognizes some inherent difference between a domestic situation and a cross-border situation.

As regards procedural issues in general, the CJEU began with the overarching general principle that, although MSs have 'fiscal autonomy', which also covers their right to set the evidentiary requirements for obtaining a tax credit, MSs must do so in compliance with, in this case, the free movement of capital.[1791] Mere administrative difficulties in ascertaining the tax paid abroad cannot justify a restriction on the free movement of capital.[1792]

1786. *Id.*, at para. 23.
1787. *Id.*, at para. 13.
1788. *Id.*, at paras 12–14, 23 (*see* question 4).
1789. *Id.*, at para. 35 ('By its second and third questions, the referring court asks whether Articles 56 EC and 58 EC must be interpreted as precluding the application of a provision such as Paragraph 36(2), second sentence, point 3, fourth sentence, (b) of the EStG under which the degree of detail and the form of evidence to be adduced by a shareholder fully taxable in one Member State in order to benefit in that Member State from a tax credit in respect of receipt of dividends paid by a capital company established in another Member State must be the same as those required where the dividend-paying company is established in the first Member State. If the answer is affirmative, the referring court is uncertain what degree of detail is required of the evidence adduced in order to establish the foreign corporation tax rate imposed on dividends, with a view to establishing the amount of the tax credit to which the beneficiaries of such dividends are entitled and, where necessary, whether Articles 56 EC and 58 EC allow the national court to estimate that rate of tax').
1790. *Id.*, at para. 35.
1791. *Id.*, at paras 37–38.
1792. *Id.*, at para. 39 (*see also* the reference to '*Manninen*, paragraph 54, and *Test Claimants in the FII Group Litigation*, paragraph 70', which in turn references 'Case C-334/02 Commission v France [2004] ECR I-2229, paragraph 29', where it is stated 'Where debtors are resident in

As regards the type of evidence, placing a strict obligation to produce the specific tax certificate in question, 'without any opportunity for the shareholder of showing, by means of other factors and relevant information, the tax actually paid, constitutes a disguised restriction on the free movement of capital'.[1793] Although it can be justified by 'an overriding reason relating to the general interest', in this case 'the need to ensure the effectiveness of fiscal supervision', it also has to adhere to the 'principle of proportionality'.[1794] Strictly enforcing only one way of formally presenting the evidence, even where shareholders may be able to provide other forms of 'relevant documentary evidence enabling the tax authorities of the Member State of taxation to ascertain, clearly and precisely' the relevant information, goes beyond what is necessary to ensure the effectiveness of fiscal supervision and therefore fails the proportionality test.[1795]

'As regards the burden of proof and the degree of detail' of the evidence, the CJEU essentially held the same as above. First, MSs 'are entitled to require the taxpayer to provide such proof', thereby indicating that the burden of proof can be on the taxpayer.[1796] The CJEU reiterates that the existence of the Mutual Assistance Directive[1797] does not affect this. In other words, the CJEU implies that the Directive does not place the burden of proof on the MSs; i.e., it does not oblige the MS to have to seek the information themselves.[1798] The MS may instead rely on the taxpayer. However, the procedure should 'not be conducted too formalistically'.[1799] Ultimately it is not the precise presentation or certificate that is important but rather whether the information provided 'enables the tax authorities of the Member State of taxation to ascertain, clearly and precisely, whether the conditions for obtaining a tax advantage are met'.[1800]

As regards the second procedural issue, the CJEU again began with the overarching general principle, namely the balance between the 'principle of the procedural autonomy' and those of equivalence and effectiveness.[1801] The change in German law

other Member States, it may prove more difficult to ascertain whether all the conditions necessary for the application of a particular rate of levy have been met. However, that involves disadvantages of a purely administrative nature which are not, as the Advocate General has noted at points 29 and 30 of his Opinion, sufficient to justify a restriction on the freedom to provide services and on the free movement of capital of the type which the legislation in question gives rise to').

1793. CJEU, Case C-262/09, *Meilicke*, 30 Jun. 2011, ECLI:EU:C:2011:438, at para. 40.
1794. *Id.*, at paras 41–42.
1795. *Id.*, at paras 43–44.
1796. *Id.*, at para. 45.
1797. *Id.*, at paras 48–52 (at that time, the Directive was 'Directive 77/799, the objective of which is to prevent tax evasion').
1798. *Id.*, at paras 48–52.
1799. *Id.*, at para. 46.
1800. *Id.*, at paras 45–46.
1801. *Id.*, at para. 23 (the German Court, Finanzgericht Köln, used the phrase 'the principle of effectiveness and the principle of "effet utile"') and at para. 55 ('It must be borne in mind that, according to settled case-law, in the absence of relevant EU rules, the detailed procedural rules designed to ensure the protection of the rights which individuals acquire under EU law are a matter for the domestic legal order of each Member State, in accordance with the principle of the procedural autonomy of the Member States, provided that they are not less favourable than those governing similar domestic situations (principle of equivalence) and that they do not render impossible in practice or excessively difficult the exercise of rights conferred by the

that no longer allowed the taxpayers to present the tax certificate (or equivalent relevant information), in order to obtain the credit granted to them by EU law, infringed the principle of effectiveness. In particular, it was implemented 'retroactively and without any transitional period',[1802] which it seems safe to assume would 'render impossible in practice or excessively difficult the exercise of rights conferred by the EU legal order'.[1803]

In sum, as regards the credit method, a distinction must be made between the two main procedural issues. A procedural component that is inherent to the credit method is some form of evidence or reporting of the taxes actually paid abroad. The exact type of evidence, be it the tax certificate in question or self-reporting by the taxpayer, etc., and upon whom the burden falls can vary. Thus, any holding of the CJEU on this matter is relevant for EU MSs to keep in mind in setting the administrative requirements and procedures for obtaining a credit for taxes paid abroad. The main holding on this question is that the MS should not be needlessly formalistic because the priority is *not* a specific presentation or form, but rather the information relevant to ascertain accurately the credit to be granted. As for the changes to the rules regarding the finality of tax assessments, it touches upon a broader aspect that is less inherent to the credit method as such; indeed, it would be equally problematic under *any* tax-related right or benefit, which EU law would require, to make it 'procedurally impossible' to obtain it. Nevertheless, it reiterates that MSs cannot find 'back door' ways by means of other procedural mechanisms to block the benefit of the credit.

The other aforementioned question (at *supra* note 1790), regarding the 'estimation' of the tax, seems to straddle both procedural and substantive aspects since it deals with the amount of the credit. The German Court (Finanzgericht Köln) asked the CJEU how best to determine the amount of the credit. It presented three options.[1804] First, the credit amounting to 3/7ths granted under German law for dividends received from German companies could simply be extended. This would extend 'equal treatment' in the most literal sense, but not in effective sense in light of the objective of the legislation. The 3/7ths amount reflects the German CIT rate and, thus, would be divorced from the actual CITs levied in the other MSs. In some cases, this could be more favourable for the shareholder, where the CIT actually levied in the other state was lower, and in other cases, this could be less favourable, where the CIT actually levied in the other state was higher. The latter could be the concern from an EU law perspective, as implied in the first question posed by the German Court.[1805] Second, the credit could be based on 'an estimate of the rate of foreign corporation tax imposed on dividends of foreign origin'. Third, the credit could be based 'as precisely as possible [on] the amounts levied under the foreign corporation tax'. The first two amount to approximations or a form of notional credit. Only the third is a 'true' credit method.

EU legal order (principle of effectiveness) (see Case C-201/02 *Wells* [2004] ECR I-723, paragraph 67 and Joined Cases C-392/04 et C-422/04 *i-21 Germany and Arcor* [2006] ECR I-8559, paragraph 57)').

1802. *Id.*, at paras 58–59.

1803. *Id.*, at para. 55.

1804. *Id.*, at para. 22.

1805. *Id.*, at para. 23.

However, the German Court reckoned that, in practice, it would be impossible to determine 'the amounts actually paid under that corporation tax in the Netherlands and Denmark'.[1806]

As regards the CJEU's response, it unambiguously rejected the possibility of an estimation of tax as 'not permissible'.[1807] The CJEU declared that determining the rate that applied to the dividends 'as precisely as possible' is 'decisive' for this credit method.[1808] Thus the CJEU merely recalled its prior holdings (e.g., *Manninen*) that the MS 'must take account of the tax actually paid by the company established in that other Member State':[1809]

> 'It follows from the foregoing that, in its answer to the question referred in *Meilicke and Others*, recalled in paragraph 20 of this judgment, the Court *ruled out the possibility that* the calculation of *the tax credit* to which a shareholder who is fully taxable in a Member State as regards dividends distributed by a capital company established in another Member State *could be done on a basis other than that of the corporation tax rate on the distributed profits* applicable to the dividend-paying company according to law of the Member State of establishment' (other than the case reference, emphasis added).[1810]

One aspect of the legal and factual pattern in this case that is decisive for this finding is that, in Germany, the treatment that applied in the domestic context was an imputation credit. As Germany had decided to provide relief by means of this form of credit *in the domestic context*, the CJEU, by requiring the extension of equal treatment to the cross-border context, effectively dictated certain aspects of how it was designed or applied. If it is designed to credit the actual underlying CIT in the domestic context, then it must be designed to do the same in the cross-border context.

This prompts some further observations. What this means is that, presumably, if no relief for economic double taxation were offered in the domestic context, the issue would not arise. There are two possible responses. This could prompt EU MSs to abolish certain relief systems, as often happened with the imputation credit method. Also, given the 'equivalence' line of case law, the question arises as to whether Germany could simply exempt the dividends from other EU MSs, rather than extending the imputation credit to the cross-border context. In this way, it would continue the imputation credit for the domestic context and grant exemption for the cross-border context. As the *Kronos* case indicates, under an imputation credit method, this is certainly compatible at the moment of the *receipt* of the dividends, since an exemption and a credit for the underlying CITs are equivalent. However, under an imputation credit method, there are tax effects both upon receipt of dividends and upon subsequent distribution.[1811] So a complete answer also depends upon the tax treatment upon redistribution since EU law issues can still arise at the stage of passing on the dividends

---

1806. *Id.*, at para. 22.
1807. *Id.*, at para. 36.
1808. *Id.*
1809. CJEU, Case C-262/09, *Meilicke*, 30 Jun. 2011, ECLI:EU:C:2011:438, at para. 26.
1810. *Id.*, at para. 28.
1811. CJEU, Case C-47/12, *Kronos International Inc.*, 11 Sep. 2014, ECLI:EU:C:2014:2200, at *supra* note 1202.

(as discussed at *supra* notes 1698–1699). Although already discussed above in the 'equivalence' line of case law, the *Haribo & Salinen* joined cases[1812] and the *Test Claimants in the FII Group Litigation* case[1813] are worth returning to here because they went beyond the substantive 'equivalence' to address some procedural issues. It is possible to create a link between the procedural issues and 'equivalence'. A commonly held perception is that the credit method is more complicated in terms of the procedures than the exemption method (as discussed in Section 4.1.). If so, even if the two are substantively equivalent, might it be the case that the credit method is too complicated in comparison with the exemption method, thereby compromising 'equivalence', or is the credit method, alone, contrary to EU law because the requisite procedures (e.g., reporting requirements) place an excessive burden on the cross-border situation?

As regards the relative complications of the two methods, the debates in Section 4.1. indicate that this claim may be too overgeneralized in some cases (*see*, e.g., *supra* notes 996–1005). Indeed, in the *Haribo & Salinen* joined cases, complaints were lodged against the difficulties of the reporting obligations for both the exemption and the indirect credit, though more emphasis was placed on the indirect credit.[1814] As regards the exemption method, the complaint was that it was 'virtually impossible' to satisfy procedural requirements for certain 'portfolio dividends' (from holdings less than 10%), in order to benefit from an exemption. The taxpayer had to prove that the Austrian 'switch-over' provision was *not* fulfilled, which required it to: (i) assess whether foreign taxes are 'comparable', (ii) 'ascertain the applicable tax rate', (iii) check 'the personal and subject-based exemptions of the non-resident corporation', (iv) 'obtain the corresponding documentation and keep it available for any check by the tax authorities'.[1815] As regards the credit method, the rules in question in Austria stipulated that 'the taxpayer must supply the following information in order for the foreign tax to be credited against the tax payable in Austria:

- the exact name of the company making the distribution in which the taxpayer has the holding;
- a precise indication of the size of the holding;
- a precise indication of the rate of corporation tax to which the company making the distribution is subject in the State in which it is established. If it is not subject to the normal tax regime of the State in which it is established (in that, for example, it has the benefit of a more favourable rate of tax, a personal tax exemption or significant tax exemptions or reductions), the rate of tax actually applicable must be given;

1812. CJEU, Joined Cases C-436/08 and C-437/08, *Haribo Lakritzen Hans Riegel BetriebsgmbH and Österreichische Salinen AG*, 10 Feb. 2011, ECLI:EU:C:2011:61.
1813. CJEU, Case C-446/04, *Test Claimants in the FII Group Litigation*, 12 Dec. 2006, ECLI: EU:C:2006:774.
1814. CJEU, Joined Cases C-436/08 and C-437/08, *Haribo Lakritzen Hans Riegel BetriebsgmbH and Österreichische Salinen AG*, 10 Feb. 2011, ECLI:EU:C:2011:61, at paras 76 et seq., in particular para. 79 and para. 90.
1815. *Id.*, at para. 22.

- an indication of the amount of corporation tax charged on the taxpayer's holding, in the light of the above parameters;
- a precise indication of the rate of the withholding tax actually levied, restricted to the rate of withholding tax under the relevant double taxation convention;
- a calculation of the tax creditable'.[1816]

According to the CJEU, the differing administrative burdens, i.e., the sometimes additional burdens for credit method as compared to the exemption method, are not an infringement. It cited 'to this effect, *Test Claimants in the FII Group Litigation*, paragraph 53',[1817] and 'tax authorities of a Member State are entitled to require the taxpayer to provide such proof as they may consider necessary in order to determine whether the conditions for a tax advantage provided for in the legislation at issue have been met'.[1818] If the burden were so 'excessive' as to render it 'impossible' to obtain the credit, this would effectively deny relief and, consequently, an indirect credit - which cannot actually be obtained in practice - and an exemption method cannot be equivalent in that case.[1819] However, in general, and in particular the above-mentioned demands in connection with the indirect credit in Austria were not deemed excessive.[1820] Asking information from the taxpayer is not overly burdensome:

> 'the fact that the national tax authority demands information relating to the tax that has actually been charged on the profits of the company distributing dividends in the State in which the latter is resident, [is] an intrinsic part of the very operation of the imputation method and cannot be regarded as excessive (see, to this effect, *Test Claimants in the FII Group Litigation*, paragraphs 48 and 53)'.[1821]

This information must be obtained; otherwise, without it, the authorities do not know how much to credit.[1822] And, asking for proof of tax paid abroad is not excessive.[1823] According to the CJEU, it is to be expected from the taxpayers - the recipient and its subsidiary - that they establish between themselves suitable information sharing and cooperation. If not, the problem is 'connected *not* to the inherent complexity of the information *but* to a possible *lack of cooperation* on the part of the

1816. *Id.*, at para. 7.
1817. *Id.*, at para. 91.
1818. *Id.*, at para. 95.
1819. *Id.*, at para. 96.
1820. *Id.*, at para. 99 (as an additional factor, it appears that the CJEU considered the Austrian regime as *a fortiori* compatible since, by comparison with what could normally be expected, Austria had even 'simplified the evidence necessary in order to receive a credit for the foreign tax', in that Austria, it seems, allowed the taxpayer to rely on a 'nominal' rate and did not necessarily demand the precise CIT paid. According to the decision, Austria permitted use of the following formula: 'The profit of the company distributing dividends must be multiplied by the nominal rate of corporation tax applicable in the State where that company is established and by the holding of the recipient company in the capital of the company distributing dividends').
1821. *Id.*, at para. 97.
1822. *Id.*
1823. CJEU, Joined Cases C-436/08 and C-437/08, *Haribo Lakritzen Hans Riegel BetriebsgmbH and Österreichische Salinen AG*, 10 Feb. 2011, ECLI:EU:C:2011:61, at para. 103.

company that has the information' (emphasis added), a problem for which the MS should not be held responsible.[1824]

On another topic, the *Haribo & Salinen* joined cases and *Test Claimants in the FII Group Litigation* case also brought clarification, namely on a personal scope issue and its interaction with Directives (i.e., the Parent-Subsidiary Directive). One distinctive design component for indirect credits in particular (as discussed in Chapter 2) is the need to consider ownership requirements. As indirect credits are operative in the context of distributions of profits to shareholders, there is inevitably some ownership relationship; thus, an additional aspect of the personal scope includes setting the requisite ownership requirements in order for taxpayers to be eligible for the indirect credit.

The *Haribo & Salinen* joined cases offered the perfect opportunity to explore this issue because the Austrian laws on relief for economic double taxation could be divided into a handful of different relief regimes with different benefits and different eligibility requirements depending on: (1) the state in which the subsidiary was located (in Austria, in other EU MSs, in EEA states, in non-EU/nor-EEA third states) and (2) the percentage of ownership held in the subsidiary (10% or more, or below 10%).[1825] In sum, in the case of dividends from Austrian companies, the exemption method applied, regardless of the level of ownership, whereas for dividends from non-Austrian companies, stricter requirements applied in order to benefit from an exemption, most notably if the ownership threshold was below 10%. Where the requirements were not met, in some cases, a 'switch-over' to the indirect credit could apply, where, e.g., certain proof was not furnished or the foreign subsidiary was not subject to any 'comparable' CIT.[1826] Most notably, for the ownership threshold issue, for dividends from companies in certain third states (neither EU nor EEA), no relief whatsoever – neither in the form of an exemption nor an indirect credit – applied.

1824. *Id.*, at para. 98.

1825. *Id.*, at paras 3–8, 21, 25, 145 (in sum, the basic differences could be described in the following way: for dividends from Austrian subsidiaries, regardless of the ownership (from 0% to 100% ownership), exemption applied. For dividends from 'international' holdings ('international' meaning the regime could apply to qualifying subsidiaries in any state), which were defined as ownership of 10% or more that was held for one year or more, exemption applied. For all other international holdings that did not meet these ownership requirements, i.e., 'holdings of less than 10% of the share capital of a company – that is to say, portfolio dividends' – the requirements were stricter. For dividends from qualifying EU MS subsidiaries, if the ownership was less than 10%, exemption applied on the conditions of furnishing certain proof and record-keeping. For dividends from qualifying (non-EU) EEA state subsidiaries, if the ownership was less than 10%, exemption applied on the conditions of the same proof and record-keeping and, in addition, *only if* there were agreements for mutual assistance *and* enforcement in place. For dividends from certain third (non-EU-nor-EEA) state subsidiaries, if the ownership was less than 10%, no relief was granted, i.e., neither an exemption nor an indirect credit. Moreover, a 'switch-over' to the indirect credit method applied, in some cases, if the conditions for the exemption regimes were not met. The 'switch-over' in other words applied the credit method in place of the exemption method where, for example, the required proof for the exemption was not furnished or the taxes were deemed too low in the other state).

1826. *Id.*, at para. 4 (citing the Austrian provisions, '(4) Notwithstanding subparagraph 1, point 7, shares of profits ... from international holdings within the meaning of subparagraph 2 shall, in accordance with the following provisions, not be exempt from corporation tax if there are

On the question of the ownership requirements, according to CJEU, the general rule is that:

> 'Also, when introducing mechanisms designed to prevent or mitigate distributed profits being liable to a series of charges to tax, it is in principle for Member States to determine the category of taxpayers entitled to benefit from those mechanisms and, for that purpose, to set thresholds based on the shareholdings which taxpayers have in the companies making the distributions (*Test Claimants in the FII Group Litigation*, paragraph 67).'[1827]

However, the fundamental freedoms prohibit discrimination, i.e., different treatment of comparable situations. Settled case law (discussed numerous times above, *see*, e.g., *supra* note 1135 and note 1208) had already established comparability in such dividend cases.[1828] The free movement of capital, applicable in this case, covers both EU MSs and non-MSs.[1829] Against this background, it was prohibited to completely deny relief for dividends from non-MSs, merely because the ownership fell below 10%, when in the equivalent case in the domestic context, exemption was granted.[1830] Nothing can justify no relief in such cases.[1831] It may be possible to justify some different conditions (such as an agreement for the exchange of information, justified on the public interest ground of 'the need to guarantee the effectiveness of fiscal

---

grounds for the Federal Minister for Finance so to order by regulation in order to prevent tax evasion and abuses (Paragraph 22 of the Federal Tax Code). Such grounds may be taken to exist, in particular, where:

1. the foreign corporation's main business focus lies directly or indirectly in obtaining revenue from interest, from the assignment of movable tangible or intangible assets or from the sale of holdings, and
2. the foreign corporation's income is not subject to any foreign tax comparable to Austrian corporation tax in terms of determination of the tax base or tax rates.

(5) Notwithstanding subparagraph 1, points 5 and 6, shares of profits shall not be exempt from corporation tax if one of the following conditions applies:

1. the foreign corporation is not in fact subject abroad, directly or indirectly, to any tax comparable to Austrian corporation tax;
2. the profits of the foreign corporation are subject abroad to a tax comparable to Austrian corporation tax, the applicable rate of which is more than 10 percentage points lower than Austrian corporation tax ...
3. the foreign corporation enjoys a comprehensive personal or subject-based exemption abroad. ...

(6) In the cases under subparagraphs 4 and 5, relief from a foreign tax corresponding to [Austrian] corporation tax is to be brought about for shares of profits in the following manner: upon an application being made, the foreign tax to be considered an advance charge on the distribution [of profits] shall be credited against the domestic corporation tax charged on shares of profits of any kind derived from the international holding. When determining the income, the foreign tax creditable shall be added to the shares of profits of any kind from the international holding').

1827. *Id.*, at para. 142.
1828. *Id.*, at para. 113.
1829. *Id.*, at para. 127.
1830. *Id.*, at paras 109–111.
1831. *Id.*, at paras 132–133.

supervision'),[1832] but not a complete denial of any relief. Thus, the MS must extend relief to the cross-border case and, given their substantive 'equivalence' in principle, it is acceptable to do so by means of exemption or by means of an indirect credit.[1833]

Related to this, there is the question of whether the existence of a directive governing the tax matter in question has an influence. For example, in *Test Claimants in the FII Group Litigation*, such a question was raised because the Parent-Subsidiary Directive governs tax relief for distributions of profits between EU MSs. At that time, the ownership threshold was 25% (now 10%) in order for a qualifying EU company to benefit from the exemption or indirect credit provided by the Directive. A MS could argue that its laws, which granted an exemption or indirect credit for dividends received from abroad *only if* the ownership met this 25% threshold, were based on the implementation of the Directive; the Directive permitted this demarcation. However, as CJEU decisions have held, the way in which Directives (which are secondary law) are transposed into EU MSs' national legal systems must respect the fundamental freedoms (which are primary law). Indeed, merely because a cross-border situation falls below the ownership requirements of the Parent-Subsidiary Directive does not mean MSs can discriminate.[1834] In other words, because the Parent-Subsidiary Directive sets a minimum threshold of 25% (now 10%) over which a MS must grant relief from double economic taxation, a MS is technically free to legislate as it wishes for holdings less than 25%, subject, however, to the fundamental freedoms. This means that the MS must be sure that it treats the nationally sourced dividends and foreign-sourced dividends that fall below these ownership thresholds in the same way. If nationally sourced dividends for holdings under 25% (or 10%) are exempt, then foreign-sourced dividends should be granted equivalent relief.[1835]

The lesson of these findings is that: although it is permissible to require certain further conditions in cross-border cases (such as requesting the taxpayer to provide information relevant to the exemption/credit, requiring the existence of agreements for mutual assistance with countries outside the EU, etc., and, as always, as long as the requirements are suitable to the aim and proportionate), as regards the ownership conditions, the thresholds that apply for relief of economic double taxation in the domestic context are, in effect, by virtue of these decisions on the free movement of capital, extended to cross-border contexts, both for EU MSs and for non-EU states.

On another topic, but also indirectly related to the personal scope of the credit method, the *Riskin and Timmermans* case[1836] concerned a 'most-favoured-nation'

1832. *Id.*, at paras 129–131.
1833. *Id.*, at para. 143 ('Article 63 TFEU therefore does not preclude the practice of a national tax authority which, for dividends from certain non-member States, applies the imputation method where the holding of the recipient company in the capital of the company making the distribution is below a certain threshold and the exemption method above that threshold, whilst it systematically applies the exemption method for nationally-sourced dividends, provided, however, that the mechanisms in question designed to prevent or mitigate distributed profits being liable to a series of charges to tax lead to equivalent results').
1834. *See*, e.g., CJEU, Case C-379/05, *Amurta*, 8 Nov. 2007, ECLI:EU:C:2007:655, at paras 20–28.
1835. *See*, e.g., CJEU, Case C-446/04, *Test Claimants in the FII Group Litigation*, 12 Dec. 2006, ECLI:EU:C:2006:774, at paras 66–69.
1836. CJEU, Case C-176/15, *Riskin and Timmermans*, 30 Jun. 2016, ECLI:EU:C:2016:488.

issue, implicating the wording of the credit method in the tax treaty in question. This case dealt with dividends, the crediting of a foreign WHT on those dividends (thus a direct credit), and the free movement of capital.

As regards the facts, two individuals, Mr Riskin and Ms Timmermans, received dividends from Poland, on which a WHT was levied at source.[1837] According to the Belgium-Poland DTC, Belgium offered a tax credit on certain dividends, but it was '[s]ubject to the provisions of Belgian legislation regarding the allowance as a credit against Belgian tax of tax paid abroad'.[1838] Under Belgium's tax law, there was a restriction: only dividends received 'in the conduct of a professional activity' would be granted a credit.[1839] Mr Riskin and Ms Timmermans were considered to have received these dividends in their personal capacity and not as part of a business or professional activity. The two taxpayers observed, however, that some DTCs between Belgium and non-EU ('third') states did not include a reference to Belgian law, with the consequence that the DTC required the credit to be granted. This amounted to less favourable treatment for dividends from Poland, an EU MS, than for dividends from certain non-EU states.[1840] Rather than the comparison between a domestic situation, within Belgium, and a cross-border situation, this involves a comparison between two cross-border situations, one between Belgium and Poland and one between Belgium and other non-EU states.

The question posed to the CJEU was whether the free movement of capital, in connection with the principle of 'sincere cooperation',[1841] renders this incompatible with EU law. According to the CJEU, 'as regards the sincere cooperation prescribed by Article 4 TEU, it is sufficient to note that that article cannot be interpreted as giving rise to any independent obligations on Member States beyond those arising from Articles 63 TFEU and 65 TFEU'.[1842] As regards the difference of treatment resulting from the DTCs, in particular from different wording among the credit method articles, if this were

1837. *Id.*, at paras 1–2.
1838. *Id.*, at para. 9.
1839. *Id.*, at paras 11–13.
1840. *Id.*, at para. 14. Another question was also raised in this case but was rejected as inadmissible. For more on this, *see* CJEU, Case C-176/15, *Riskin and Timmermans*, 30 Jun. 2016, ECLI:EU:C:2016:488, at para. 16 and para. 18; Opinion of AG Kokott in Case C-176/15, *Riskin and Timmermans*, 12 Apr. 2016, ECLI:EU:C:2016:246, at para. 19 (in addition, the taxpayers questioned whether it was compatible with EU law to restrict the credit to only cases in which 'the capital and property from which the income is derived is applied in Belgium in the conduct of professional activity' (CJEU, at para. 16). According to the Opinion of Advocate General Kokott (at para. 19), 'In the light of the grounds of the order for reference, the second question should be understood to concern the difference in the application of tax credits depending on whether the professional activity (in the conduct of which a shareholding is applied) is carried out in the national territory or in a different Member State.' Regarding this second question, however, the facts did not involve the conduct of professional activity; it was 'hypothetical and [was], therefore, inadmissible' (CJEU, at para. 18)).
1841. Opinion of AG Kokott in Case C-176/15, *Riskin and Timmermans*, 12 Apr. 2016, ECLI:EU:C:2016:246, at para. 3 (Article 4(3) TEU states 'Pursuant to the principle of sincere cooperation, the Union and the Member States shall, in full mutual respect, assist each other in carrying out tasks which flow from the Treaties').
1842. CJEU, Case C-176/15, *Riskin and Timmermans*, 30 Jun. 2016, ECLI:EU:C:2016:488, at para. 36.

incompatible, it could imply that EU MSs, once they have concluded beneficial treatment with another state, must extend the same treatment to all other EU MSs. The *Riskin* decision simply reiterated the CJEU's previous finding (in the 2005 *D* case)[1843] that MSs do not have any such most-favoured-nation treatment obligation under their DTCs, and the fact that the DTCs are concluded with non-EU states does not change this finding. In its reasoning, the CJEU explained this both in terms of existing disparities and in terms of a lack of comparability. Given the MSs' competence and the lack of harmonization regarding direct taxation, disparities remain; this entitles MSs to adapt their tax treatment for dividends from different MSs in different ways 'so as to take account of those disparities'.[1844] DTCs are negotiated within this context:

> 'It follows from this that the scope of such a convention is limited to Belgian residents receiving dividends from such a third State and having had tax deducted at source by that third State. The fact that the benefit in question is granted only to Belgian residents falling within the scope of that convention cannot be classified as a benefit that is separable from that convention, given that, as has been mentioned in paragraph 31 of the present judgment, that benefit is an integral part of the convention rules and contributes to the overall balance of mutual relations between the two contracting States to that convention.'[1845]

One lesson to be derived is that: the personal scope of a direct FTC can be limited to the persons covered by a given DTC.

The credit method in a DTC, between France and Sweden, also made an appearance in the *Bouanich* case decided in 2014.[1846] However, although the credit method was expressly included in the question referred to the CJEU, the CJEU clearly stated that the issue in the case related to a different rule, namely a 'tax shield' under French tax law that capped the amount of direct taxes paid by taxpayers to a maximum amount of 50% (or 60% depending on the year in question) of the income they received in a given year.

> 'In that respect, it should be noted from the outset that the case in the main proceedings does not relate to the prevention of double taxation but to the national

1843. *Id.*, at para. 31 (The CJEU cited the 'judgments of 5 July 2005 in *D.*, C376/03, EU:C:2005:424, paragraphs 54 and 61 to 62, and of 20 May 2008 in *Orange European Smallcap Fund*, C194/06, EU:C:2008:289, paragraphs 50 to 51').

1844. *Id.*, at paras 29–30 ('29 In that respect, it must be borne in mind that it is for the Member States to organise, in compliance with EU law, their systems for taxing distributed profits and to define, in that context, the tax base and the tax rate which apply to the shareholder receiving them, and that, in the absence of any unifying or harmonising EU measures, Member States retain the power to define, by treaty or unilaterally, the criteria for allocating their powers of taxation (see, to that effect, judgment of 20 May 2008 in *Orange European Smallcap Fund*, C194/06, EU:C:2008:289, paragraph 48).

30 Consequently, given the resulting disparities between the tax laws of the various Member States, a Member State may find it necessary, by treaty or unilaterally, to treat dividends from the various Member States differently so as to take account of those disparities (see, to that effect, judgment of 20 May 2008 in *Orange European Smallcap Fund*, C194/06, EU:C:2008:289, paragraph 49)').

1845. CJEU, Case C-176/15, *Riskin and Timmermans*, 30 Jun. 2016, ECLI:EU:C:2016:488, at para. 33.

1846. CJEU, Case C-375/12, *Bouanich*, 13 Mar. 2014, ECLI:EU:C:2014:138.

> tax treatment in France of dividends distributed by a company established in Sweden, for the purposes of applying a mechanism capping various direct taxes.'[1847]

Further reiterating this point:

> '40 In order to reply to the first question, a distinction must be drawn between, first, the granting of a tax credit resulting from the Franco-Swedish Agreement and, secondly, the application of the tax shield at issue in the case in the main proceedings, because they constitute two separate tax benefits.
>
> 41 The granting, in France, of a tax credit for the withholding tax levied in Sweden results from the Franco-Swedish Agreement and is part of the parallel taxation, by the Kingdom of Sweden and by the French Republic, of Swedish investment income. The French Republic reserves the right to tax Swedish income and grants a tax credit to limit, or avoid, double taxation.
>
> 42 By contrast, a provision such as the tax shield is unrelated to the parallel exercise of tax jurisdiction and concerns only the French Republic's tax jurisdiction. That tax provision has the purpose and effect of reducing the level of taxation of the income on which that Member State exercises its powers of taxation.'[1848]

The credit method played only a supporting role, mostly related to France's (and other intervening governments') attempt to justify the fact that the 'tax shield' excluded certain *foreign* taxes from its calculation of whether the taxpayer reached the 50% (or 60%) cap (an exclusion which was held incompatible).[1849] Nevertheless, one side note can be drawn from the case, regarding insight on how the CJEU views the credit method. In discussing France's asserted justification based on 'the need to maintain the coherence of the tax system', the CJEU explains that this justification is contingent upon a 'direct link [that] has to be established between the tax advantage concerned and the offsetting of that advantage by a particular tax levy'.[1850] To illustrate what this means, the CJEU characterizes the credit method as a measure that fulfils such a 'direct link' criterion and is thus implied to be a measure that upholds 'coherence':

> 'As regards the tax credit resulting from the Franco-Swedish Agreement, there is a direct link between the tax advantage granted and the offsetting of that advantage by a particular levy, the one levied at source by the Kingdom of Sweden on Swedish investment income.'[1851]

This reiterates previously discussed cases that also associate the credit method with the CJEU's judicially developed 'coherence' concept, such as *Nordea Bank* (at *supra* note 1584) and *Manninen* (at *supra* note 1652). Moreover, implicitly, this recognizes that, in the view of the CJEU, the credit method is, generally, based on the taxes *actually* paid abroad (since this is what reinforces the 'direct' link criterion).

1847. *Id.*, at para. 37.
1848. *Id.*, at paras 40–42.
1849. *Id.*, at paras 56, 60, 87–88.
1850. *Id.*, at para. 69.
1851. *Id.*, at para. 71.

On another topic, but on a similar theme, namely the ways in which the credit method occasionally influences decisions of the CJEU as part of the legal background of a case, Haslehner on the issue of 'The Principle of Territoriality as a Justification for "Exit Taxation"'[1852] surmised that the credit method could have an impact on the obligations of the state of origin in cases concerning exit taxation. In particular, he addresses 'asset transfers to foreign permanent establishments' and the question as to whether the state of origin can disregard any future losses, or decreases in value, that occur abroad after the exit. In his view, 'when the two Member States have agreed on the application of the credit method in their bilateral tax treaty', 'the Member State of origin clearly retains a right to tax any future profits resulting from assets transferred to a permanent establishment in the other Member State and, thus, cannot claim the exclusive allocation of future decreases in value to that State'.[1853]

Similar to its role under the losses line of case law, this is another instance of the possible influence of the credit method on other related obligations under EU law, in this case on MSs' exit tax obligations. Thus, clearly the influence works in both ways. Having witnessed both ways throughout this exploration of the credit method in CJEU case law, this has provided a more comprehensive understanding of the role of the credit method and thus facilitates the effort to extract the potential lessons for the design of the credit method itself (as in the interim summaries following each line of case law and as in Chapter 5).

4.3. THE CREDIT METHOD UNDER SECONDARY EU LAW

Secondary EU law in direct tax matters, as discussed in Section 3.2., has relied on the legal basis of Article 115 TFEU, thus requiring unanimous support for Directives. On a few occasions, where EU MSs have reached such agreement, the Directives have included some provisions providing for a credit method. In these cases, MSs have in effect proactively created agreed-upon guidelines and constraints as to how the credit method should be designed.[1854] These can be found in the Parent-Subsidiary Directive, the Merger Directive and in the now repealed Savings Directive. More recently, provisions can be found in the ATAD.

1852. Werner Haslehner, *'Avoir Fiscal' and Its Legacy after Thirty Years of Direct Tax Jurisprudence of the Court of Justice*, 44(5) Intertax 374, 388–389 (2016).

1853. *Id.*, at 388 (citing *inter alia* 'DMC, C-164/12, EU:C:2014:20, para. 56').

1854. Regarding the scope of this Section, the focus is on Directives that have been enacted and transposed by EU MSs, thereby affecting their EU law obligations. For other proposals, which were not enacted, that also contain provisions relevant to relief for double taxation in general or the credit method in particular, *see*, e.g., European Commission, Proposal for a Council Directive on a Common Corporate Tax Base, COM(2016) 685 Final, Article 53 (25 Oct. 2016); European Commission, Proposal for a Council Directive on a Common Consolidated Corporate Tax Base (CCCTB), COM(2016) 683 Final, Article 72 (25 Oct. 2016); European Commission, Proposal for a Council Directive Concerning the Harmonization of Systems of Company Taxation and of Withholding Taxes on Dividends, COM(75) 392 Final, OJ C 253, 2–8 (5 Nov. 1975); European Commission, Proposal for a 'Europäischen Doppelbesteuerungsabkommen (Multilaterales abkommen der Mitgliedstaaten der Europäischen Gemeinschaften zur Vermeidung der Doppelsteuerung des Einkommens und des Vermögens und über gegenseitige umtshilfe auf dem Gebiet der directen Steuern)', Doc.11.414/XIV/68-F (1 Jul. 1968).

Beginning with the Parent-Subsidiary Directive,[1855] the most important in terms of the relatively broader scope of application of its credit method provisions, it seeks to eliminate both juridical and economic double taxation on distributions of profits between eligible companies of different EU MSs.[1856] In doing so, this should facilitate the establishment of subsidiaries in other EU MSs and overall the 'grouping together of companies' within the EU, which creates 'conditions analogous to those of an internal market'.[1857] As demonstrated with a hypothetical example under Section 2.1.1.3. (*see* Example No. 11), potentially three layers of taxation can occur: first, CIT paid at the level of the subsidiary to the subsidiary state; second, a WHT levied at source on the distribution to the parent company, paid to the state of the subsidiary; and, third, CIT paid at the level of the parent company to the state of the parent. The Directive eliminates (or addresses) two of those three layers. It prohibits the state of the subsidiary from levying any WHT on distributions of profits (Article 5), and it requires the state of the parent to eliminate double taxation either by means of an exemption method or by means of an indirect tax credit (Article 4); thus, the second and third layers are removed or reduced, leaving only (or nearly only) the first layer of CIT paid by the subsidiary. The provisions regarding the credit method are in Article 4.

In the first version of the Directive in 1990,[1858] the main paragraph of Article 4 read as follows:

> '1. Where a parent company, by virtue of its association with its subsidiary, receives distributed profits, the State of the parent company shall, except when the latter is liquidated, either:
>
> - refrain from taxing such profits, or
> - tax such profits while authorizing the parent company to deduct from the amount of tax due that fraction of the corporation tax paid by the subsidiary which relates to those profits [...][1859] up to the limit of the amount of the corresponding domestic tax.'

1855. Council Directive 2011/96/EU of 30 November 2011 on the Common System of Taxation Applicable in the Case of Parent Companies and Subsidiaries of Different Member States, OJ L 345, 8–16 (29 Dec. 2011); Council Directive 2014/86/EU of 8 July 2014 amending Directive 2011/96/EU on the Common System of Taxation Applicable in the Case of Parent Companies and Subsidiaries of Different Member States, OJ L 219, 40–41 (25 Jul. 2014) (Parent-Subsidiary Directive).

1856. For more on the Parent-Subsidiary Directive, *see*, e.g., Otto Marres (update of 6th ed.), *Chapter 6: The Parent-Subsidiary Directive in* 1 *Terra/Wattel European Tax Law* 219, 219 et seq. (Peter J. Wattel, Otto Marres & Hein Vermeulen eds, Wolters Kluwer 7th ed. 2019); Mario Tenore, *The Parent-Subsidiary Directive, in Introduction to European Tax Law on Direct Taxation* 143 (Michael Lang et al. eds, Linde 5th ed. 2018); Fred C. de Hosson, *The Parent-Subsidiary Directive*, 18(10) Intertax 414 (1990).

1857. Parent-Subsidiary Directive, preamble recital 4.

1858. Council Directive 90/435/EEC of 23 July 1990 on the Common System of Taxation Applicable in the Case of Parent Companies and Subsidiaries of Different Member States, OJ L 225, 6–9 (20 Aug. 1990).

1859. *Id.* (the wording here also included the following: 'and, if appropriate, the amount of the withholding tax levied by the Member State in which the subsidiary is resident, pursuant to the derogations provided for in Article 5'. However, the derogations referred to in that wording were temporary).

As mentioned, and seen above in the wording, it is state of the parent company to which the obligation is addressed. Importantly, this state may choose between those two options, of exempting the profits or taxing the profits while granting a credit. In the latter case, there is a two-step operation in that the parent company determines its tax due and then deducts a certain amount of taxes from that amount. The creditable taxes are those that were levied on the subsidiary, so it is a tax credit for the underlying CITs on the distribution. As regards the amount, it is the 'fraction ... which relates to' the distributed profits, thereby leaving broad discretion as to any further details of the calculation. Finally, it provides for an MCA (on this point, notice that the language is not optional, such as the state 'may' limit it). The precise scope of the credit is dictated by the scope of the Directive itself. It answers some questions as regards the personal scope of eligible taxpayers. It applies only to eligible companies, with the requisite ownership or association (under Articles 2 and 3). For example, the 'parent company' must hold at least 10% (quantitative element) in the 'capital' (qualitative element) of the subsidiary. As regards the material scope, it is granted upon receipt of 'distributed profits', but as the wording of Article 4 states, the proceeds of liquidation are excluded. On this point, it is aligned with the conceptual issues discussed by Owens (*see supra* note 426).

After various updates to the Directive, a consolidated version was published in 2011. The main paragraph of Article 4 read as follows:

> '1. Where a parent company *or its permanent establishment*, by virtue of the association of the parent company with its subsidiary, receives distributed profits, the Member State of the parent company *and the Member State of its permanent establishment* shall, except when the subsidiary is liquidated, either:
>
> (a) refrain from taxing such profits; or
> (b) tax such profits while authorising the parent company *and the permanent establishment* to deduct from the amount of tax due that fraction of the corporation tax related to those profits and paid by the subsidiary *and any lower-tier subsidiary, subject to the condition that at each tier a company and its lower-tier subsidiary fall within the definitions laid down in Article 2 and meet the requirements provided for in Article 3*, up to the limit of the amount of the corresponding tax due' (emphasis added).

In the updated text, there are two main changes. First, both the state of the parent company and the state of its PE (when it is considered to receive the distributed profits) are the addressees and both thus have the obligation of granting the credit. As it mentions two separate states, this is evidently referring to a constellation where the parent company of one EU MS has a PE in another EU MS, which entails that it is a non-resident taxpayer in that other MS.[1860] Having studied the *Avoir Fiscal* and *Saint*

1860. More precisely, the Directive applies in the following constellations, which can be depicted simply as: MS S MS P, MS S MS PE, MS S = MS P MS PE, but not where MS S = MS PE. *See* Parent-Subsidiary Directive, preamble recital 9 ('The payment of profit distributions to, and their receipt by, a permanent establishment of a parent company should give rise to the same treatment as that applying between a subsidiary and its parent. This should include the

Gobain lines of case law (Section 4.2.7.), this case law sheds light on the reasons for this change. The basic idea is that, as PEs of non-resident companies are generally treated in the same way as resident companies for the purposes of levying taxes, those PEs should also be granted the same related benefits. As a result, EU MSs in the position of the state of non-residence may have to extend relief for double taxation to non-residents.

Second, another substantial change is the extension of the indirect credit to sub-subsidiaries. This gives insight into the understanding of double taxation in these cases. As discussed in *Commission v. France* (2018), which followed up on *Accor* (2011), this is the only way to ensure that the aim of relief for economic double (or multiple) taxation is achieved to the greatest extent possible.

There was a third relevant change in Article 4, not to the first paragraph, but by means of adding a new paragraph to Article 4 to address 'fiscally transparent' entities. It expands the scope of the credit method (or the exemption method, depending on which is chosen) to scenarios of 'fiscally transparent' subsidiaries. Directly related to this, it moves the timing of the benefits to an earlier stage, similar to CFC rules. As the change is made under Article 4, it is based on the perspective of the state of the parent company, as to its characterization of the subsidiary. It addresses only the state of the parent company, not that of its PE (it is a solution similar to that of paragraph 69.2 of the OECD Commentary on Articles 23 A and 23 B, but is clearer in this context of the elimination of double taxation).

To explain it further, the genesis of the issue is the widely known fact that states may characterize entities differently for the purposes of tax treatment.[1861] States offer a diversity of different legal forms through which taxpayers can conduct business or make investments. Depending on how a given state characterizes a given entity, it may determine that the entity itself is a taxable one or it may determine that the entity does not exist for tax purposes and deem the partners or owners of the entity the only relevant tax subjects. Thus, the state of the parent company may view the subsidiary as 'transparent', rather than as a distinct taxable entity. The consequence is that the state of the parent company considers the income generated in the state of the subsidiary to be directly attributable to the parent, on an ongoing basis. For the state of the parent company, there is no distinct distribution of profits. Rather, they accrue to the parent automatically and the state of the parent thus taxes them as regular corporate income. In instances where this occurs, this frustrates the objectives of the Directive. To avoid this, the Directive indicates that, while EU MSs would not go so far as to interfere with entity classification for tax purposes ('Nothing in this Directive shall prevent the Member State of the parent company from considering a subsidiary to be

situation where a parent company and its subsidiary are in the same Member State and the permanent establishment is in another Member State. On the other hand, it appears that situations where the permanent establishment and the subsidiary are situated in the same Member State can, without prejudice to the application of the Treaty principles, be dealt with on the basis of national legislation by the Member State concerned').

1861. *See*, e.g., OECD, *The Application of the OECD Model Tax Convention to Partnerships*, Issues in International Taxation, No. 6 (OECD Publishing 1999). Similarly, *see also*, e.g., *supra* note 752 and note 755.

fiscally transparent on the basis of that Member State's assessment of the legal characteristics of that subsidiary arising from the law under which it is constituted'), EU MSs could agree to expand the scope of relief to these situations. If the state of the parent company takes into account the profits of the subsidiary as they arise, it is also obliged to either exempt or offer an indirect tax credit:

> 'When assessing the parent company's share of the profits of its subsidiary as they arise the Member State of the parent company shall either exempt those profits or authorise the parent company to deduct from the amount of tax due that fraction of the corporation tax related to the parent company's share of profits and paid by its subsidiary and any lower-tier subsidiary, subject to the condition that at each tier a company and its lower-tier subsidiary fall within the definitions laid down in Article 2 and meet the requirements provided for in Article 3, up to the limit of the amount of the corresponding tax due.'[1862]

A second possible taxable event still remains, namely a later distribution of profits from the subsidiary. As the state of the parent company has already assessed those profits, it must not do so again: 'In this case the Member State of the parent company *shall refrain from taxing the distributed profits* of the subsidiary' (emphasis added). This is similar to the question under CFC rules as to how to treat previously taxed income when it is later distributed.[1863] The Directive opted for the exemption method in this case.

Against the background of growing concerns over double non-taxation, in 2014, an amendment was made to the Directive, in order to prevent certain hybrid mismatch arrangements from benefiting from the Directive. According to the preamble, recital 2: 'The benefits of Directive 2011/96/EU should not lead to situations of double non-taxation and, therefore, generate unintended tax benefits for groups of parent companies and subsidiaries of different Member States when compared to groups of companies of the same Member State.' In cases where the profits distributed were deductible from the tax base in the state of the subsidiary, they were not subject to CIT there. The intended result of the Directive is to leave essentially one layer of taxation, namely that of the subsidiary. When this no longer occurs, then the distribution should not benefit from an exemption in the state of the parent (or PE). Thus, the wording of 'Article 4(1), point (a)' was 'replaced by the following':

> '(a) refrain from taxing such profits to the extent that such profits are not deductible by the subsidiary, and tax such profits to the extent that such profits are deductible by the subsidiary ...'.

1862. Parent-Subsidiary Directive, Article 4(2).

1863. *See*, e.g., OECD, *Designing Effective Controlled Foreign Company Rules, Action 3 – 2015 Final Report*, OECD/G20 Base Erosion and Profit Shifting Project (OECD Publishing 2015); United States, Internal Revenue Code, Section 959; *supra* note 797 and note 798.

Notably, it is only the exemption method that is affected. Indeed, if the state opts for the indirect credit, this issue is already precluded. This underscores the credit method's role in this realm of double non-taxation concerns.[1864]

The Merger Directive[1865] also strives to create conditions more analogous to those of an internal market.[1866] As a general rule, when assets are sold, if the sale generates a profit (or capital gains), those are taxed. In cases of mergers, acquisitions and other forms of business reorganizations, assets may be sold or swapped or otherwise disposed of, potentially giving rise to capital gains (or deemed capital gains) and thus potentially substantial tax bills on the hidden reserves (generally, the value at the moment of the transaction minus the cost of acquisition). When assets are merely transferred in some way in the context of a reorganization, it may not be the case that any gains were actually realized. As states tend to want to facilitate the ability of companies to reorganize, to be nimble and efficient, to grow or shrink, according to their business needs, such reorganizations can benefit, often within the domestic context, from a deferral of taxation. The businesses involved respect certain rules regarding how to record the value of the assets in question and then, only later when the assets are actually disposed of, and capital gains are actually realized, will taxation be triggered. The Merger Directive seeks to extend similar deferral benefits to mergers, acquisitions and other reorganizations that take place among companies of EU MSs. The main, most basic rule of the Directive is that, when there is a cross-border EU reorganization (of a type covered by the Directive),[1867] all assets that remain in the original MS, effectively connected to a PE there, will benefit from a deferral of taxation.[1868]

The credit method plays a more ancillary role, but a unique one. It appears in Article 10(2) of the Directive.[1869] In certain instances where a state ends up taxing prior to the actual realization event, this state should basically grant a credit in advance on a notional amount, not yet levied. More precisely, Article 10(2) addresses the 'Special

1864. For more, in general, on this change, *see*, e.g., Christoph Marchgraber, *Cross-Border Tax Arbitrage, the Parent-Subsidiary Directive (2011/96) and Double Tax Treaty Law*, 70(3) Bull. Int'l Tax'n 123, 123–126 (2016); Werner Haslehner, *Anti-hybrid Measures in the Parent Subsidiary Directive and the EU's Competence to Harmonise*, Kluwer International Tax Blog (31 Aug. 2015), http://kluwertaxblog.com/2015/08/31/anti-hybrid-measures-in-the-parent-subsidiary-directive-and-the-eus-competence-to-harmonise/ (last visited 20 Aug. 2018).

1865. *See supra* note 831.

1866. Merger Directive, preamble recital 2.

1867. Merger Directive (as covered by Article 1, namely 'mergers, divisions, partial divisions, transfers of assets and exchanges', and defined by Article 2).

1868. For more details on the Merger Directive, *see*, e.g., Frederik Boulogne (update of 6th ed.), *Chapter 7: The Tax Merger Directive*, *in* 1 *Terra/Wattel European Tax Law* 279 (Peter J. Wattel, Otto Marres & Hein Vermeulen eds, Wolters Kluwer 7th ed. 2019); Matthias Hofstätter & Daniela Hohenwarter-Mayr, *The Merger Directive*, *in Introduction to European Tax Law on Direct Taxation* 169–197 (Michael Lang et al. eds, Linde 5th ed. 2018); Jime´nez-Valladolid de L'Hotellerie-Fallois, Domingo Jesús & Félix Alberto Vega Borrego, *Elimination of Double Taxation and Tax Deferral: The Example of the Merger Directive*, *in Tax Treaties: Building Bridges Between Law and Economics* (Michael Lang et al. eds, IBFD 2010) Online Books IBFD (last visited 2 Aug. 2016).

1869. Merger Directive, Article 10 (it is entitled 'Special Case of the Transfer of a Permanent Establishment' and the paragraphs read as follows:

Case of the Transfer of a Permanent Establishment'. It applies in situations where a company resident in one MS has a PE in another MS and 'where the Member State of the transferring company applies a system of taxing worldwide profits'; i.e., the residence state of the company applies the credit method. When the company undertakes a reorganization and the state where the PE is located grants a deferral, on the basis of the Merger Directive, the residence state of the company may tax the hidden reserves of the assets attributable to the PE, but it must grant a credit for the fictitious taxes of the PE state (which could have been levied by the PE state without the existence of the Merger Directive). It represents a compromise between a given state's right to tax and the ideal to uphold deferral – in line with the phrase of the preamble (recital 5) 'while at the same time safeguarding the financial interests of the Member State of the transferring or acquired company'. A similar rule is provided under Article 11 in the 'Special Case of Transparent Entities'. There is also a transparent entity rule in the Directive. Unlike in the Parent-Subsidiary Directive, there are no design elements whatsoever. The Merger Directive merely states the obligation. It is a form of notional credit, in that it is granted on the basis of what *would have been levied* in the state of the PE. Nothing is mentioned about whether there is a readjustment mechanism to adjust the amount of this initial credit on the basis of the amount actually collected, later on, by the state of the PE, if ever. What is notable is that the Merger Directive in this instance showcases the more unique forms of relief that can be accomplished in the EU given the closer ties (which ties back to the themes of regional integration brought up in the historical development of Chapter 2, *see*, e.g., Section 2.1.2.2. and *supra* note 449).

The Savings Directive is also mentioned here due to its special credit method, albeit briefly, as this Directive has since been repealed (as from 1 January 2016, with some transitional provisions extending into 2017). The general rule was the exchange of information on account holders, in order to prevent tax evasion. Some MSs, under

---

'1. Where the assets transferred in a merger, a division, a partial division or a transfer of assets include a permanent establishment of the transferring company which is situated in a Member State other than that of the transferring company, the Member State of the transferring company shall renounce any right to tax that permanent establishment.The Member State of the transferring company may reinstate in the taxable profits of that company such losses of the permanent establishment as may previously have been set off against the taxable profits of the company in that Member State and which have not been recovered.The Member State in which the permanent establishment is situated and the Member State of the receiving company shall apply the provisions of this Directive to such a transfer as if the Member State where the permanent establishment is situated were the Member State of the transferring company.This paragraph shall also apply in the case where the permanent establishment is situated in the same Member State as that in which the receiving company is resident.

2. By way of derogation from paragraph 1, where the Member State of the transferring company applies a system of taxing worldwide profits, that Member State shall have the right to tax any profits or capital gains of the permanent establishment resulting from the merger, division, partial division or transfer of assets, on condition that it gives relief for the tax that, but for the provisions of this Directive, would have been charged on those profits or capital gains in the Member State in which that permanent establishment is situated, in the same way and in the same amount as it would have done if that tax had actually been charged and paid').

their national banking secrecy laws, managed to negotiate rules for special, temporary exceptions under the Directive. These were Austria, Belgium, and Luxembourg. Rather than report information on account holders to their respective MSs of residence, in violation of their banking secrecy laws, these three MSs agreed to withhold tax on certain payments made to the account holders (Article 11) and pass along a portion of the revenue to the MS of residence (Article 12). The relevant provisions of the Directive are the following:

> Preamble recital 21: 'The Member State of residence for tax purposes of the beneficial owner should ensure the elimination of any double taxation of the interest payments which might result from the imposition of this withholding tax in accordance with the procedures laid down in this Directive. It should do so by crediting this withholding tax up to the amount of tax due in its territory and by reimbursing to the beneficial owner any excess amount of tax withheld. It may, however, instead of applying this tax credit mechanism, grant a refund of the withholding tax.'
>
> Article 14: 'Elimination of double taxation
> 1. The Member State of residence for tax purposes of the beneficial owner shall ensure the elimination of any double taxation which might result from the imposition of the withholding tax referred to in Article 11, in accordance with the provisions of paragraphs 2 and 3.
> 2. If interest received by a beneficial owner has been subject to withholding tax in the Member State of the paying agent, the Member State of residence for tax purposes of the beneficial owner shall grant him a tax credit equal to the amount of the tax withheld in accordance with its national law. Where this amount exceeds the amount of tax due in accordance with its national law, the Member State of residence for tax purposes shall repay the excess amount of tax withheld to the beneficial owner.
> 3. If, in addition to the withholding tax referred to in Article 11, interest received by a beneficial owner has been subject to any other type of withholding tax and the Member State of residence for tax purposes grants a tax credit for such withholding tax in accordance with its national law or double taxation conventions, such other withholding tax shall be credited before the procedure in paragraph 2 is applied.
> 4. The Member State of residence for tax purposes of the beneficial owner may replace the tax credit mechanism referred to in paragraphs 2 and 3 by a refund of the withholding tax referred to in Article 11.'

As can be seen, what is particularly interesting about the (temporary) credit method agreed upon under the Savings Directive is that the MSs of residence would grant a full credit and refund any excess. Thus, the Savings Directive contains more explicit design features, more than the Merger Directive, for example. This showcases the varieties of forms of relief and the more precise rules that cooperation under EU law renders possible, when the MSs are willing to act together.

The ATAD is the most recent act of secondary EU law to contain a credit method. As mentioned in the introduction (Chapter 1), there are two places in the ATAD that are relevant for the credit method, namely the preamble and the CFC rules under Article 7 and Article 8 (in particular Article 8(7) ATAD).

First, it is useful to quote again the preamble here because, in addition to its reference to a credit method, it also presents an overview of the Directive as a whole:

> '(5) It is necessary to lay down rules against the erosion of tax bases in the internal market and the shifting of profits out of the internal market. Rules in the following areas are necessary in order to contribute to achieving that objective: limitations to the deductibility of interest, exit taxation, a general anti-abuse rule, controlled foreign company rules and rules to tackle hybrid mismatches. Where the application of those rules gives rise to double taxation, taxpayers should receive relief through a deduction for the tax paid in another Member State or third country, as the case may be. Thus, the rules should not only aim to counter tax avoidance practices but also avoid creating other obstacles to the market, such as double taxation.'

Two observations can be made. First, the credit method broadly speaking, potentially either direct or indirect, is relevant for the document as a whole, in the context of all 'those rules' wherever double taxation may arise as a result. As this Directive represents new territory for the EU,[1870] upon first enacting these new rules, it is difficult to predict in what ways they may overlap in the future, especially given the numerous options in the Directive and that it is a 'minimum level of protection' (Article 3) allowing MSs to go further to protect their tax bases. As a result, it would be challenging to specify the myriad potential constellations and, perhaps, for this reason, only the general principle, or commitment, is stated in the Directive.[1871] Second, it indicates the role of the credit method in this evolving international context. It can, if properly designed, strike the balance between the concerns of (unintended) double non-taxation and double taxation. In a context where the overarching goal is anti-base-erosion-and-profit-shifting, with rules for recapturing parts of the tax base, an exemption method that excludes parts of the tax base is at odds with that objective and,

---

1870. *See*, e.g., *supra* note 61.

1871. Regarding the wording of recital (5), it could also be read as referring to a deduction of the foreign taxes from the tax base since it merely mentions 'taxpayers should receive relief through a deduction for the tax paid' without specifying whether that is a deduction from the taxes due in the state applying the ATAD rule. Applying a contextual interpretation, a reading of this wording in the context of the Directive as a whole indicates otherwise. Recital (5) refers to all the rules, including the CFC rules. Under the CFC rules, found in Article 7 and Article 8 of the ATAD, it unambiguously provides for 'a deduction of the tax paid ... from the tax liability of the taxpayer', i.e., a credit method, in Article 8(7). It would be inconsistent to refer to a mere deduction of foreign taxes from the tax base in the recital, including in the context of the CFC rules. A conceptual argument could also be put forward. A deduction of the foreign taxes from the tax base, generally speaking, while it does offer relief, arguably does not solve the problem of 'double taxation'. Rather, it treats foreign taxes as a cost of doing business abroad, like any other business-related expense. Thus, rather than, strictly speaking, being a method for relief of double taxation, it can be perceived as offering relief more incidentally and only partially, to the extent of *the foreign taxes multiplied by the tax rate in the state granting relief*. If 'double taxation' is seen as an obstacle, then to the extent it still remains, the objective is not obtained. One caveat is: although uncommon, there may be instances where a deduction would be more beneficial than a credit, e.g., in some cases where foreign taxes are particularly high. In the context of CFC rules applying to 'low-taxed' income, this will not be the case. Also, it depends on the meaning of double taxation. Based on its use in other parts of the Directive, *see*, e.g., Article 8(5) and Article 8(6), it seems to refer to a full elimination of double taxation rather than only partial relief.

instead, the credit method can be relied upon, where the aim is to include the tax base while eliminating as fully as possible any resulting double taxation.

The second place in the ATAD where the credit method plays a crucial role is under the CFC rules, under Article 7 and Article 8.[1872] Article 7 specifies the scope, options and possible exclusions from the CFC rules. Article 8 specifies the '[c]omputation of controlled foreign company income', including the instances where relief for double taxation is required. The CFC rules result in two main taxable events where relief for double taxation is required: (1) the inclusion of the CFC's income in the tax base of the 'taxpayer' and (2) any later distribution of profits from the CFC or, according to the Directive, a later sale of the participation in the entity.

Regarding the first, an indirect credit is required. Though, it could also operate as a direct credit, in certain cases where a PE is treated as a CFC. The wording, found in Article 8(7), is as follows:

> '7. The Member State of the taxpayer shall allow a deduction of the tax paid by the entity or permanent establishment from the tax liability of the taxpayer in its state of tax residence or location. The deduction shall be calculated in accordance with national law.'

It seems fair to characterize this as offering minimal to no guidance whatsoever. It dictates which MS is responsible, but this logically flows from the CFC rules themselves. It dictates a deduction of the CFC's taxes 'from the tax liability of the taxpayer', clearly indicating which method, namely a credit method, as opposed to a mere deduction of the CFC's taxes from the tax base. As mentioned before, an exemption method is logically excluded.[1873] Everything else is left to the domestic law of the MS, under the second sentence.

Regarding the second taxable event, an exclusion from the tax base is required. By means of a form of partial dividends-received-deduction, the effect is a complete exemption. The wording is as follows:

> '5. Where the entity distributes profits to the taxpayer, and those distributed profits are included in the taxable income of the taxpayer, the amounts of income previously included in the tax base pursuant to Article 7 shall be deducted from the tax base when calculating the amount of tax due on the distributed profits, in order to ensure there is no double taxation.
>
> 6. Where the taxpayer disposes of its participation in the entity or of the business carried out by the permanent establishment, and any part of the proceeds from the disposal previously has been included in the tax base pursuant to Article 7, that amount shall be deducted from the tax base when calculating the amount of tax due on those proceeds, in order to ensure there is no double taxation.'

1872. For more details on the ATAD, *see*, e.g., Daniël Smit, *Chapter 12: The Anti-tax-Avoidance Directive (ATAD)*, *in* 1 *Terra/Wattel European Tax Law* 485 (Peter J. Wattel, Otto Marres & Hein Vermeulen eds, Wolters Kluwer 7th ed. 2019); Sriram Govind & Stephanie Zolles, *Chapter 8: The Anti-tax Avoidance Directive, in Introduction to European Tax Law on Direct Taxation* 217, 217–254 (Michael Lang et al. eds, Linde 5th ed. 2018).

1873. In agreement, *see* OECD, *Designing Effective Controlled Foreign Company Rules, Action 3 – 2015 Final Report*, OECD/G20 Base Erosion and Profit Shifting Project (OECD Publishing 2015).

According to the wording in paragraph 5, it applies if 'those distributed profits are included in the taxable income of the taxpayer'. Thus, it would seem that, if a participation exemption applies to dividends, further relief would not be needed. Where an exemption does not apply to the dividends, then there is a requirement to ascertain the amount of previously taxed income and actively deduct it.

A few critical remarks can be made. First, according to the OECD Report on 'Designing Effective Controlled Foreign Company Rules',[1874] 'difficulties with the exemption method' can arise under two scenarios: (1) 'if only part of the CFC income has been attributed to a resident taxpayer' or (2) 'if a CFC is indirectly held through another non-resident company which does not have attributable CFC income'.[1875] The reason for difficulties is that: 'In these cases it may be hard to determine whether dividends have, in fact, been paid out of attributed CFC income and are therefore subject to double taxation.'[1876] Although it does not explicitly put it forward as a recommendation, it cites how other states have addressed these potential difficulties:

> 'To address these difficulties, countries tend to adopt relatively mechanical approaches that assume that dividends are likely to have been paid out of previously attributed CFC income. These approaches include, for example, limiting the dividend exemption to the amount of profits generated by the CFC during the tax years when CFC rules have applied.'

Both of these issues are sure to arise under the ATAD-based CFC rules, given that the scope of income covered is likely to be partial under both options (a) and (b) of Article 7(2). Also, the ownership, or association, threshold can be met 'directly or indirectly'.

Another reasonable way to avoid double taxation when profits are later distributed (portions of which were previously taxed under a CFC inclusion) is to include them in the tax base, calculate the tax owed and offer a credit for all taxes previously paid at the moment of the earlier CFC inclusion. This was the approach formerly used by the UK under its CFC legislation.[1877] This would eschew the need to determine precisely the amount of income that was previously included. It relies instead on information that is already known, namely the taxes already previously paid at the first stage.

1874. *Id.*
1875. *Id.*, at 68, para. 132.
1876. *Id.*
1877. CJEU, Case C-196/04, *Cadbury Schweppes and Cadbury Schweppes Overseas*, 12 Sep. 2006, ECLI:EU:C:2006:544, at para. 6 ('That legislation, which is contained in sections 747 to 756 and Schedules 24 to 26 of the Income and Corporation Taxes Act 1988, provides that the profits of a CFC – namely, under the version of that legislation applicable at the time of the facts in the main proceedings ("the legislation on CFCs"), a foreign company in which the resident company owns a holding of more than 50% – are attributed to the resident company and taxed in its hands, by means of a tax credit for the tax paid by the CFC in the State in which it is established. If those same profits are then distributed in the form of dividends to the resident company, the tax paid by the latter in the United Kingdom on the profits of the CFC is treated as additional tax paid by the latter abroad and gives rise to a tax credit payable in respect of the tax owed by the resident company on those dividends').

Moreover, although the ATAD is intended to implement or be consistent with the OECD BEPS recommendations,[1878] it neglected to include one of the recommendations regarding double taxation relief. In its Action 3 Report, the OECD discussed three main instances of double taxation that can occur under CFC rules:

> '(i) situations where the attributed CFC income is also subject to foreign corporate taxes; (ii) situations where CFC rules in more than one jurisdiction apply to the same CFC income; and (iii) situations where a CFC actually distributes dividends out of income that has already been attributed to its resident shareholders under the CFC rules or a resident shareholder disposes of the shares in the CFC'.[1879]

While the ATAD clearly addressed situations (i) and (iii), it did not address situation (ii), a situation which may occur with increasing frequency as more and more states implement CFC rules, and are obliged to do so under the ATAD. One of the issues that could arise from not explicitly addressing situation (ii) is that it could influence the distribution policies of CFCs. This is because CFCs could try to avoid double taxation of this sort by, e.g., distributing its profits immediately (with the consequence that the CFC rules will not apply because Article 7(2) applies to 'non-distributed income'). The solution recommended by the OECD was to insert a hierarchy rule. For example, 'this hierarchy could prioritise the CFC rules of the jurisdiction whose resident shareholder is closer to the CFC in the chain of ownership'.[1880]

In this connection, the scope of the CFC rules under Article 7 extends to 'indirect' ownership, meaning possibly also to sub-subsidiaries, which may lead to situation (ii). Yet, the double taxation relief under Article 8 does not follow through by likewise extending an indirect credit to sub-subsidiaries.[1881] This is surprising considering such was already agreed upon under the Parent-Subsidiary Directive; it would seem feasible to include it in the ATAD as well. The OECD recommends that states grant a credit for all eligible taxes levied on the CFC, including those on sub-tiers, excluding or subtracting any previous relief already granted at other levels:

> 'The recommendation for addressing the first two situations is to allow a credit for foreign taxes actually paid, including CFC tax assessed on intermediate companies. The actual tax paid (this can also include withholding taxes) should include all taxes borne by the CFC that are taxes on income that have not qualified for other relief, and that are not higher than the taxes due on the same income in the parent jurisdiction.'[1882]

1878. ATAD I, preamble recitals 1 and 2.
1879. OECD, *Designing Effective Controlled Foreign Company Rules, Action 3 – 2015 Final Report*, OECD/G20 Base Erosion and Profit Shifting Project, 65, para. 122 (OECD Publishing 2015).
1880. *Id.*, at 66, para. 126.
1881. To achieve this end, one could try to argue that a credit for lower tiers is perhaps implied in the definition of the term 'controlled foreign company' under Article 7(1), which by virtue of covering indirectly owned entities encompasses sub-tiers, and therefore the relief rule should also implicitly extend to sub-tiers; however, there is no clear reason for *not* being more explicit in this respect and, given the objective of the ATAD to coordinate its rules within the EU, a superior approach would be to simply be more explicit, in order to leave less room to the risk of different interpretations.
1882. OECD, *Designing Effective Controlled Foreign Company Rules, Action 3 – 2015 Final Report*, OECD/G20 Base Erosion and Profit Shifting Project, 65, para. 123 (OECD Publishing 2015).

In conclusion, as can be seen, in the cases where Directives provide for the credit method, the guidance on its design varies, but in all cases is rather meagre. On the one hand, it is intentional, in order to allow transposition in accordance with national legal systems. On the other hand, it is possible to go a little further without compromising this flexibility. This is especially the case under the ATAD, since unlike under the Parent-Subsidiary Directive, the credit method is *not* optional. Less experience in some MSs with an indirect credit[1883] and the diversity of approaches to a direct credit that currently exists in MSs,[1884] yet the commitment under the preamble of the ATAD to ensure that these new obligations to tax do not create new obstacles to the internal market, are symptomatic of a slight deficiency in this area, which could be remedied with (at least) even a few higher-level general considerations or framework.

1883. *See supra* note 57.
1884. *See supra* note 56.

CHAPTER 5
Synthesis of Findings and Lessons for EU MSs

5.1. OVERVIEW AND STRUCTURE

A wave of changes to international tax rules, predominantly driven by the OECD/G20 BEPS Project, entail increased reliance on the credit method (as the observations discussed in Chapter 1 indicate), especially to the extent that jurisdictions hope to close loopholes and expand the reach of international tax rules, *without* erecting barriers such as double taxation. The EU explicitly espouses the aim to achieve this balance in its Anti-Tax-Avoidance Directive. In the EU, achieving this balance is arguably necessary in light of its foundational aim of an 'internal market' inscribed in its Treaties, which stands on two main pillars of dismantling barriers to cross-border movements and preventing distortions to free and fair competition (as discussed in Chapter 3).

As the credit method is one of the essential tools in this balancing act, and as it has given rise to numerous legal questions under EU law over time (including whether the credit method itself was contrary to the internal market, as discussed in Section 4.1.), this research project set out to conduct a more comprehensive study of the compatibility of this method and the constraints on its design under EU law. Thus, it formulated the following research question: to what extent and in what ways does EU law influence the design of the credit method? It concentrated, in particular, on compliance with the fundamental freedoms as interpreted by the CJEU, as most EU law issues in the area of 'direct' taxation flowed from this process of legal interpretation and 'negative integration' (as discussed in Chapter 3).

In this period of change, much guidance has centred on the various technical mechanics of the anti-BEPS rules, while less has centred on those of the relief for double taxation. Even within the EU Directives that purport to protect against double taxation, the provisions offer only a general sketch of the credit method. Fortunately, on the relief-related mechanics, much insight can be garnered from studying what has been written on the details of the design of the credit method in the course of its historical legislative development, especially in jurisdictions with longer histories with it, such as the US (as discussed in Chapter 2); however, this guidance, unsurprisingly, does not contemplate the unique legal issues that arise under EU law. Yet, as EU MSs implement and apply the proposals of the BEPS Project, transposing Directives into national law and updating or redesigning other aspects of national law to accord with these changes, they are legally obliged to do so in a way that is in line with EU law and, to this end, must heed the judgments of the CJEU. The challenge is to navigate the vast array of an evergrowing body of case law on direct taxation, seeking the common threads and themes in what can otherwise sometimes appear disparate or divergent (as, e.g., at least one AG has acknowledged and criticized, at *supra* note 1574). Thus, by bringing together and distilling the lessons from these two – i.e., from accounts of the various technicalities of the credit method that arose throughout its legislative development (in Chapter 2) and from a thorough study of the credit method in the case law of the CJEU (in Chapter 4) – this book contributes further clarity and structure to the ongoing academic and policy considerations for EU MSs.

Against this background, this final Chapter (Chapter 5), which aims to synthesize the findings and lessons for EU MSs, proceeds in the following way:

(1) First, it identifies the various EU law questions that were raised in the core chapter, Chapter 4, throughout the analysis of the credit method under the case law of the CJEU (as part of the general overview in this section, Section 5.1.).

(2) Second, it combines the findings of Chapter 2 on the definition and key component parts of the credit method with the EU law questions of Chapter 4, by listing which of the design components of the credit method were, in some way, explicitly discussed in the case law of the CJEU and which were not (also here in Section 5.1.).

(3) Third, it elaborates on the influence of these EU law questions on the design components listed, focusing in particular on the open questions. Based on the case law analysis, there are four facets or axes of analysis to keep in mind, along which the findings are structured. The main two axes around which the findings revolve are, as developed in Chapter 2, those relevant for the direct credit and those relevant for the indirect credit (a credit for the underlying income taxes paid by another entity). In addition, there are two scenarios that entailed particular EU-specific design instructions, as revealed in Chapter 4, namely the design of the credit method in tax treaties to achieve 'neutralization' and the design features needed for an indirect credit to achieve 'equivalence'. Taking into account all four, the subsequent sections are therefore dedicated to:
    - the direct credit method (Section 5.2.);
    - the requirements of a direct credit under the 'neutralization' line of case law (Section 5.3.), and

- the indirect credit method and the requirements stemming from the 'equivalence' line of case law (Section 5.4.).

As this chapter highlights, there were numerous EU law questions that arose throughout this study of the credit method. The questions ranged from the most foundational - such as whether the credit method as a whole is compatible with EU law - to the design-specific questions - such as those implicating the MCA or the treatment of 'excess' credits. In answering these questions, the results, likewise, ranged drastically - from the explicit guidance that could be derived in certain cases (such as how to treat 'personal and family circumstances' in the MCA) to, in some cases, only the broadest sketches of boundaries. This range stems from the function of the principle of non-discrimination as a tool of 'negative' integration flowing from the CJEU case law. The CJEU, by assessing incompatibilities with EU law, in effect 'strikes down' certain aspects of tax laws. From this, the process of legal reasoning is therefore to try to assess - based on what is ruled *out*, under the *negative* integration process - which constraints exist and, if possible, whether explicit *positive* guidance or at least broader lessons can be derived from this.

To begin, the analysis of CJEU case law (in Chapter 4) uncovered numerous EU law questions concerning the credit method, some of which may now be considered settled and some of which remain open. These include:

- First and most fundamentally, one question that was actively debated for a period of time (as discussed in Section 4.1.) was: is the credit method compatible with EU law?
  - For example, does it constitute a prohibited obstacle to investment in another EU MS that the credit method - in the specific case where the taxes are lower in the other MS - cancels out the benefit of the lower taxes by raising the amount of taxes up to the level due in the credit-granting state?
- How does the concept of 'disparities' affect the relationship of the credit method with EU law?
- If the credit method is in principle compatible with EU law, could the procedural requirements 'intrinsic' to the credit method (as, at its core, it is based on taxes actually owed or levied abroad, thereby entailing some form of reporting obligation) themselves constitute burdens that hinder the fundamental freedoms?
- If the credit method is in principle compatible with EU law, is it compatible to design the credit method so as to restrict the amount of the credit (i.e., to set a 'maximum creditable amount' or 'credit limitation'), even though this sometimes has the effect that it is not possible to deduct all of the creditable foreign taxes paid to the other MS from the taxes due in the credit-granting MS?
- If a credit limitation is in principle compatible with EU law, are there indications, given the myriad ways to calculate it, as to which calculations are in line with EU law?

  - Regarding one such indication, the interaction between the '*Schumacker* doctrine' and the *De Groot* and *Beker* cases effectively ruled out one way of calculating the amount of the FTC – one which seemed rather intuitive, namely multiplying the tax liability on the worldwide income by a balanced fraction that used gross figures for both the FSI in the numerator and the worldwide income in the denominator. An open question therefore is: because the CJEU only indicates which approach is *in*compatible, what lessons can be derived regarding which calculation is compatible?
- As the legal and fact patterns of this case law (stemming from *Schumacker*) related only to personal and family circumstances, one open question is whether these findings can be extended to other circumstances, such as business-related expenses. How should business expenses be taken into account when calculating the FTC? What guiding principles or general rules may apply (e.g., the CJEU established what could be referred to as a *somewhere-in-full* rule for personal and family circumstances; what would govern business-related expenses)?
- As the legal and fact patterns resulting in the '*Schumacker* doctrine' included that the state of residence applied the exemption method (thus seemingly rendering it less feasible, if not impossible, that the state of residence could take into account the personal and family circumstances of the frontier worker in question), one open question is: does the *Schumacker* doctrine apply if the state of residence of the frontier worker applies the credit method? Put differently, since under the credit method, the state of residence first takes into account the worldwide income of the taxpayer, does this resolve the *Schumacker*-based risk by guaranteeing that the personal and family circumstances are taken into account?
- A follow-up question then is: if not, what is the effect of the credit method in the state of residence on the application of the *Schumacker* doctrine in the state of source or employment (i.e., in cases where the obligation is transferred to this latter state to fully take into account personal and family circumstances)? An open question is: must the credit method be adapted in some way to respect the *Schumacker* doctrine?
- If a credit limitation is in principle compatible with EU law, then open questions remain regarding how MSs must treat the excess amount of foreign taxes that could not be credited. One option is a credit carryforward, as seen, most notably, in *Haribo & Salinen*; however, as the legal and fact patterns of this case law addressed only relief for economic double taxation, are these findings transposable to relief for juridical double taxation, i.e., the direct credit?
- If not, are there any other EU law indications as to the treatment of 'excess' credits?
- A widely recognized cause of 'excess' credits relates to expenses, namely the divergence between the gross taxation of non-residents by the state of source/performance/etc. (disallowing the deduction of expenses) versus the

net taxation of that income by the state of residence of the taxpayer (allowing the deduction of expenses). Based on the interpretation of the fundamental freedoms, does one of the states end up responsible for the fact that not all foreign taxes will be creditable in such situations? If it is the state of residence, does this entail a 'full' credit? If it is the state of source, does this entail 'net' taxation at source?

- Going beyond mere expenses, are there EU law indications as to how a state that applies the credit method must treat losses?
- One open question, stemming from the *Nordea Bank* case and the Opinion of AG Kokott (at paragraph 55), is: if the CJEU considers that a MS that applies the credit method acts disproportionately if it *fully* recaptures foreign losses that were previously deducted, thereby indicating that said MS is clearly obliged to permit the deduction of foreign losses to some extent (if not fully), what is the extent of this obligation? In particular, does this leave open the possibility that the credit-granting state could 'take account of losses incurred only to a limited extent' under the credit method?
- Although it seems generally recognized (e.g., OECD Model, at Article 23; Parent-Subsidiary Directive, at Article 4; *Test Claimants in Class IV of the ACT Group Litigation*, Case C-374/04, at paragraph 60) that relief is the responsibility of the home state, or state of residence, is it acceptable under EU law to grant a credit only to residents?
- Regarding this point, as the legal and fact patterns in this case law (the *Avoir Fiscal/Saint Gobain* line of case law) related only to issues of relief for economic double taxation, e.g., an imputation credit and an indirect credit, one open question is: are the findings equally transposable to a direct credit?
- One open question, which the 'disparity' line of case law provokes but leaves unanswered, is: would it be compatible with EU law if a MS grants a full credit in a purely domestic situation, whereas it grants a credit capped with an MCA in the cross-border situation? For example, it is not uncommon for a state to impose upfront a WHT on interest and dividends at a rate of, e.g., 30% that, in the domestic context, is fully creditable against the final tax liability on interest and dividends, whereas, in the cross-border situation, any foreign WHTs levied abroad on interest and dividends are creditable only up to the MCA. Would this amount to incompatible different treatment?
- Stemming from the 'neutralization' case law, a number of open questions arise:
  - The overarching question is: what design features of the credit method would be needed for the *other* state, the state of source of the distribution, to declare that 'neutralization' is achieved?
  - If the credit method in the state of residence does not allow a WHT in the state of source to be offset 'in full' (due to a credit limitation) in the year in question, would it meet the 'neutralization' requirement if the state of residence offers a credit carryforward of the excess amount into future years? What about a credit carrybackward?

- In particular, must the credit method in the DTC be self-executing or may it refer to the domestic law of the credit-granting state, as is commonly the case?
- Regarding credit method articles in DTCs that make reference to domestic law on the credit method, yet include a caveat that any amendments to the credit method under domestic law must be made 'without changing the general principle thereof', would such wording respect the 'neutralization' requirement that the credit be 'bilaterally' provided?
- If the credit method in the state of residence does not allow a WHT in the state of source to be offset 'in full' (due to a credit limitation), may the state of source simply refund the excess credit or would this be considered merely a 'partial neutralization'?
- Does this case law seem to announce the 'death' of WHTs? Do the requirements of the *Gerritse/Scorpio* line of case law fix the issue (by moving WHTs more towards net-basis taxation)?

Additional questions that arose specifically in the context of an 'indirect' credit include the following:

- If a MS applies the exemption method to eliminate economic double taxation - or what the CJEU sometimes refers to as the mitigation of a series of charges to tax - for dividends received from a domestic company, but applies an indirect credit for dividends received from abroad, does this amount to discriminatory different treatment?
- Do the EU law requirements change if it is the other way around, namely an imputation credit or indirect credit for dividends received from a domestic company, but an exemption for dividends received from abroad?
- Similar to the questions raised in the direct credit context, is a credit limitation acceptable under indirect credits or imputation credits?
- If so, are there EU law indications as to how to treat the 'excess' credits?
- In what circumstances or under what conditions is there some form of 'equivalence' between an exemption for dividends and an indirect/imputation credit for dividends?
- As relief for economic double taxation of dividends implies an ownership relationship, are there EU law constraints on the ownership requirements?
- Considering that economic double taxation - or the mitigation of a series of charges to tax - can occur at multiple different levels of taxpayers, are there requirements to extend relief to lower-tier entities?
- One of the reoccurring complaints was that of a cash-flow disadvantage caused by timing differences between when the tax is levied and when it is refunded or credited. Under what circumstances does this disadvantage arise and which aspects of the credit method does this affect?

From the list of questions that arose under the CJEU case law in Chapter 4, it can be seen that, among the design features identified in Chapter 2 (*see* a condensed version of the findings in the table below), the following explicitly raised an EU law issue:

- eligible taxpayers, e.g., as the CJEU requires the extension of the personal scope to non-resident taxpayers under certain circumstances;
- amount of creditable taxes, on the questions of a credit limitation and of the treatment of the 'excess';
- FSI, on the questions of the allocation of expenses and of losses;
- procedural issues, on the questions of the proof required and, by implication, of redetermination or reimbursement mechanisms.

The design features that have not, to date, been *explicitly* addressed in CJEU case law are therefore:

- eligible taxes;
- amount of creditable taxes, on the questions of the permissibility of a partial credit (versus a EUR-for-EUR credit) and on the type of credit limitation, i.e., per-country versus overall;
- FSI, on the questions of a gross-up, of whether the sums should be based on foreign law or recalculated under domestic law, of divergences in notions of taxable income, of the progressive tax rate issue (e.g., whether the FSI constitutes the 'bottom-slice', 'top-slice', etc.);
- timing issues, on the questions of divergencies in taxable years or of exchange rate differences.

As regards the additional considerations that arise under an 'indirect' credit, the only points that were more explicitly addressed by the case law of the CJEU were:

- of course, any issues from the above list that are equally relevant for the indirect credit, such as the eligible taxpayers, the credit limitation, losses, and procedural requirements;
- furthermore, regarding the scope of eligible taxpayers, the ownership requirements have come under some scrutiny;
- the type of CIT system, as the integrated corporate-shareholder approach has evidently confronted more EU law challenges than the classical approach.

Other technical details of the 'indirect' credit are left undiscussed by the CJEU's fundamental freedom case law: e.g., the scope as regards the eligible distributions (qualifying distributions of profits, such as dividends) and the calculation issues as regards the rules to be used for calculating the FSI.

Although it was explained in detail in Chapter 2 (*see* especially Section 2.2., and Sections 2.1.1.4. and 2.1.2.4.), those findings are condensed again here for convenience to reiterate some of the most important design questions that arose. To highlight the interaction with Chapter 4, the aspects of the credit method listed above, which were explicitly addressed by the CJEU, are shown more prominently in bold text.

Core of the Credit Method

- basic two-step operation, such that the relief operates at level of taxes due

- relief for 'actual' double taxation

Direct Credit	**Indirect Credit** (Additional Considerations)

- **eligible taxpayers**
- eligible taxes
  - type, e.g., income, capital, estate
  - territory, e.g., dominions, all states, the other Contracting State
  - status, e.g., paid or payable
- **amount of creditable taxes**
  - e.g., 'dollar-for-dollar' vs. partial, **unlimited vs. limited**
  - if limited, type of limit, e.g., overall, per-country, per-item
  - **if limited, treatment of excess**
- **foreign-source income (FSI)**
  - calculation of tax base, e.g., gross-up, sums based on foreign law vs. sums recalculated under domestic law, **allocation of expenses, losses**, divergences in notions of taxable income
  - progressive tax rate issue, e.g., 'bottom-slice', 'top-slice'
	- as regards **eligible taxpayers**
	  - type, e.g., individuals, corporations
	  - **relationship, e.g., ownership threshold (quantitative)**, ownership type (qualitative)
	- as regards eligible distributions
	  - qualifying distributions of profits
	  - deemed distributions or inclusions
	- as regards figures in calculation
	  - 'gross-up'
	  - 'apportionment fraction' (especially FSI in denominator): (1) content, e.g., accounting figure, taxable income, E&P; (2) applicable laws, i.e., credit-granting state or foreign state
	- as regards timing and other operational issues
	  - annual determination[1885] vs. pooling approach

1885. As explained in Chapter 2, in making this selection between an annual determination versus a pooling approach, additional considerations include that the annual determination requires more detailed rules for tracing the distribution to the underlying profits and corresponding tax year ('attribution of dividends to annual profits of foreign corporation') and an 'annual calculation of the [indirect] tax credit' (*see*, e.g., Example No. 16, Option 2).

- timing issues - e.g., divergent taxable years, exchange rate differences - **procedural issues** - **e.g., proof, a redetermination mechanism**	- a 'recording' mechanism - by time, *see* above (annual vs. pooling) - by type, e.g., category of income (e.g., active vs. passive), high-taxed vs. low-taxed income, item-by-item[1886] - an 'ordering rule' - e.g., pro rata basis, FIFO, LIFO[1887] - date of distribution of the dividends - attribute dividend to: (i) entire taxable year in which dividends were paid, (ii) accumulated profits up to point of distribution, or (iii) 'profits for the last full taxable year' - if divergence of taxable years, verify if foreign tax has been paid 'on or with respect to' profits of a given year - losses at the level of the subsidiary - especially carryback or carryforward, based on credit-granting state or foreign state laws - **type of CIT system** - **e.g., integrated vs. classical**

This renders it easier to see at a glance the aspects of the credit method for which there are more explicit constraints from the CJEU's case law and the aspects for which there is relative freedom in design. As regards these undiscussed or less discussed aspects, however, this does not necessarily mean that MSs are entirely free. In some cases, Directives constrain MSs' design freedom, for those cases that fall within the scope of application of a given Directive (as seen in Section 4.3.). For example, for the

1886. As explained in Chapter 2, in making this selection, an additional consideration is that the need for look-through rules takes on increased importance.
1887. As explained in Chapter 2, in making this selection, an additional consideration is the possible incentive to strategically time the distribution of dividends to inflate the foreign tax credit.

'indirect' credit, the Parent-Subsidiary Directive explicitly specifies the ownership requirements (both quantitative, a holding of a minimum of 10%, and qualitative, 'in the capital' of the subsidiary) and extends an indirect credit to sub-tier subsidiaries. In all cases, including those covered by Directives, the principle of non-discrimination as embodied in the EU fundamental freedoms has to be kept in mind, even in the absence of a CJEU decision on a design question. Consequently, to try to trace the EU-law contours in which they are operating, MSs must rely on the answers that can be found *implicitly* in the CJEU case law – in that some guidance can be deduced from the general principles or rules emanating from its decisions – or on the answers that can be found explicitly in the Directives (e.g., questions regarding the scope of eligible distributions or income inclusions are dictated in the Parent-Subsidiary Directive or in the ATAD), or on a combination of both.

In the very broadest sense of the contours, one of the main functions of the fundamental freedoms could be viewed as setting a sort of 'floor' for the design, namely that, at a minimum, MSs should generally check that their tax measures align the treatment of FSI or of non-residents with the treatment granted to DSI or to residents in a domestic context. However, this floor only becomes operable or sturdy enough to stand on when the relief in question can or does operate in both contexts (both domestically and cross-border). This tends to be the case for an indirect credit or an imputation credit, as most (if not all) states tend to offer relief for economic double taxation or a series of charges to tax on distributions of profits in the domestic context. Consequently, the floor is rather clearly situated in the case of an indirect credit, whereas the floor is very low to non-existent in the case of a direct credit.

From a fundamental freedom perspective, there does not seem to be a 'ceiling' on the generosity. That is, a MS is seemingly free to devise a generous credit, e.g., with a broad scope. For example, Malta's imputation regime (discussed at *supra* notes 1775 et seq.) is generous and endures to this day. This is all the more the case to the extent that 'reverse discrimination' is not captured by the fundamental freedoms. However, ceilings come from other areas of EU law, such as the State Aid rules (provided that an element of 'selectivity' can be found), but so far, this has been more relevant for the exemption method than for the credit method (*see*, e.g., *supra* notes 45–46). Notably, in a way, the ATAD rules also now serve as a ceiling on generous tax treatment in that MSs have constraints on the extent to which certain income and activities can be exempted from taxation since MSs must adhere to the ATAD's minimum standard.

These general considerations will serve as a tacit framework, below, in the exploration of some examples and open questions regarding design components for which the CJEU has not yet itself provided explicit guidance (e.g., when enquiring into whether the credit limitation for a direct credit should be calculated per-country, per-item or overall). In particular, for the direct credit, the issue regarding FSI and progressive tax rates (e.g., 'bottom-slice', 'top-slice') is selected as an example to explore the above-mentioned contours and, for the indirect tax credit, one of the most frequently debated issues, namely the figure to be used for the FSI, is selected as an example.

5.2. LESSONS FOR THE DIRECT CREDIT

As regards the direct credit, MSs retain a great deal of freedom. Since a direct credit addresses international 'juridical double taxation', which in turn often arises from 'disparities' between the tax laws of MSs or the 'exercise in parallel' of MSs' taxation rights, with which the CJEU allegedly cannot interfere, indeed, nothing in the CJEU case law to date requires the state of residence to implement one at all. Yet, if the state of residence does so, then (perhaps somewhat ironically, though logically) it must ensure that it operates in a non-discriminatory way.

The question arises as to whether and how the credit method can result in discriminatory treatment. After all, it appears to treat all residents the same regardless of the source (domestic or foreign) of their income. In fact, this is often one of its aims, be it on the grounds of the ability-to-pay principle or, some may emphasize, on the grounds of CEN, to mention just two prime examples. And, this is often the comparison selected by the CJEU when assessing whether the law of a state of residence causes different treatment, namely that between a resident that, by virtue of exercising one of its fundamental freedoms, earned income from abroad and a resident that earned all income in the domestic context. This comparison effectively precludes a finding that the credit method in general is discriminatory.

From this vantage point, the mere fact that the credit method may have the effect in certain cases of 'topping up' the tax rate to the level of the rate in the MS of residence (i.e., the same that applies to all residents regardless of the source of their income) is not deemed an infringement. Where the tax rate is *lower* in the MS of source (e.g., the MS where the taxpayer exercises cross-border employment, the MS where the taxpayer carries on cross-border business via a partnership, the MS where a company is located from which the taxpayer receives dividends), the MS of residence includes the foreign income in the tax base similar to all domestic income and then offers relief by deducting from the tax liability an FTC equal to the lower taxes paid in the MS of source, thereby reducing the amount that the MS of residence collects on the FSI and leaving the overall tax burden at the rate that applies to all residents. Where the tax rate is *higher* in the MS of source, the MS of residence does the same, but in this case a question could arise. This is because not all of the taxes paid in the MS of source may be credited. The MS of residence will reduce the taxes it would otherwise collect on the FSI down to zero, but some of the (higher) taxes levied in the MS of source are not credited, with the consequence that the overall burden paid by the taxpayer is higher than other residents in the MS of residence. Instead the overall burden is equal to the higher tax rate in the MS of source. The MS of residence is confronted with two main options under the credit method: either to credit the entirety of source-MS taxes (a 'full' credit) or to limit the creditable amount to that which the MS of residence would levy domestically on the income in question (an 'ordinary' credit, with a credit limitation or MCA). The first option would equalize the overall *combined* cross-border burden to that of residents, while the latter allows the higher tax rate in the MS of source to stand. The CJEU allows the latter, i.e., for the credit method to be designed with an MCA.

There are two main reasons for this, according to the case law. First, the cause of the higher tax rate that applies to this resident does not stem from a different treatment attributable to the law of the MS of residence, but rather the cause is that the MS of source levies a higher tax rate on the income than the MS of residence, and – crucially – both MSs have the right under EU law to determine their income tax rates. Thus, it results from a 'disparity', not discrimination. Second, the CJEU declared itself unable to require the MS of residence, once it has already reduced its taxes to zero on the income in question, to go further, including eliminating some of its other taxes levied on DSI, for two reasons: (1) when both states exercise their legitimate right to tax the income in parallel, the CJEU refrains from dictating which of the two should have priority or should be blamed for the resulting double taxation, and apparently does not find any criteria within EU law upon which to make this determination; and (2) because in effect it would force the MS to adapt its tax system in response to other MSs' tax systems, a request that would impede on MSs' sovereignty in this area.

The CJEU holds that the authority remains with the MSs to take action to coordinate and resolve their overlapping taxation rights, as long as direct taxation remains within their field of competence under EU law. This was the balance struck by the CJEU in the current state of EU law. Regardless of whether one agrees with the reasoning, MSs are left with the outcome, as interpreted by the CJEU, and discerning its implications for their tax systems.

Yet, a measure that is compatible in terms of its substantive law aspects may nevertheless infringe EU law if, in terms of its procedural aspects, the administrative burden that it places on the taxpayer is prohibitive. At the core of the credit method is that it is based on the taxes actually due or levied abroad, which are credited against the taxes due on the worldwide income. Consequently, its basic functioning entails reporting obligations for the foreign taxes and the foreign income to which they correspond. The question has been raised whether undertaking such procedures 'intrinsic' to the credit method is an obstacle to cross-border movement. The CJEU has consistently held that: (1) it is acceptable to require a taxpayer to provide the information needed in order to obtain a tax benefit and, indeed, in some cases, the taxpayer should be expected to provide information that allows the benefit to be calculated precisely (this is especially the case where the MS grants relief, in the domestic context, by means of an indirect or imputation credit based on the actual underlying corporate taxes paid, since equal treatment of the cross-border context would require a credit for the actual underlying corporate taxes paid abroad); (2) yet the burden cannot be excessive. In other words, an administrative procedure which is simply necessary to the proper functioning of the tax relief (which itself is compatible) is compatible.

Any constraints therefore stem from determining wherever the threshold lies for deeming a procedure excessive. What could be considered excessive would be, *inter alia*, enforcing exacting standards as regards the formalistic aspects, such as paperwork requiring the information to be presented in one specific way, without room for deviation; demanding types of evidence unavailable in the other MS; or amending domestic laws so as to render it impossible to reopen a tax assessment to allow for the correct amount of credit to be granted or readjusted if needed in due course. In other words, the procedural demands should not, in effect, preclude the possibility to obtain the substantive benefit, to which the EU citizen is entitled, nor render it excessively difficult, which seems to occur when the procedural requirement is not truly necessary for ensuring the proper functioning of the relief (e.g., as long as the information provided by the taxpayer allows the MS to ascertain accurately the taxes paid abroad, the MS should not insist in an overly formalistic way on only one way of presenting the information).

Consequently, in principle, the credit method is compatible with EU law. In addition, the credit method calculated with an MCA is compatible with EU law. Nevertheless, this did not render the credit method unassailable.

As regards how the credit method can operate in a discriminatory way, one answer came from the general rule established in the *Schumacker* case, namely that the MS of residence is generally responsible for providing deductions to account for a taxpayer's personal and family circumstances in full. According to the CJEU, it cannot be the case that, by virtue of exercising EU free movement rights, a taxpayer loses such personal benefits, in part or in full. The way in which this general rule interacts with the credit method was uncovered in the 'calculation' line of case law (in Section 4.2.4.). It is not sufficient to grant allowances and deductions for personal circumstances at the level of the tax base if the MCA of the credit method has the effect that, at the level of taxes due, personal and family circumstances are disregarded or cancelled out in proportion to the FSI. In that case, the MS of residence is no longer upholding its obligation to treat residents the same regardless of the source of their income. According to this case law, the MCA must be calculated in a way that leaves intact the entirety of personal circumstances.

However, the CJEU generally pronounces itself only on what EU law prohibits, as opposed to how precisely a MS should adapt. As illustrated and explained fully above (in Section 4.2.4., *supra* note 1335), it is possible to study the calculation rejected by the CJEU and derive from its reasoning the calculation that is compatible for EU MSs. The lesson for EU MSs is that calculation 1 was explicitly rejected; calculations 2, 3, and 4 by implication are likely rejected; and calculation 5 is suggested as the most EU-law-aligned:

	Taxes on WWI	×	$\frac{\textbf{FSI}}{\textbf{WWI}}$	=	**MCA of FTC**	***This is the general formula for a maximum creditable amount. It does not answer the question as to whether the foreign-source income (FSI) in the numerator and the worldwide income (WWI) in the denominator are gross figures or net figures (meaning net of allowances/deductions for personal and family circumstances).***
1	Taxes on WWI	×	$\frac{\text{FSI (gross)}}{\text{WWI (gross)}}$	=	MCA of FTC	*Numerator and denominator = gross figures, thus apportioning the taxes and personal deductions proportionately between the FSI and other income; Effect: by attributing the personal deductions proportionately to the FSI, the MCA has the effect of cancelling out that portion.*
2	Taxes on WWI	×	$\frac{\text{FSI (net of proportion attributable to FSI)}}{\text{WWI (net)}}$	=	MCA of FTC	*Numerator = FSI figure net of the personal deductions allocated in proportion to the FSI, thereby assuming these deductions are spread evenly over the entire WWI; denominator = net figure; Effect: same as above.*

3	Taxes on WWI	×	FSI (net of proportion attributable to FSI) / WWI (gross)	=	MCA of FTC	*Numerator = FSI figure net of the proportion of personal deductions attributable to FSI, thereby assuming these deductions are spread evenly over the entire WWI; denominator = gross figure; Effect: this fraction also cancels out personal deductions.*
4	Taxes on WWI	×	FSI (net of entirety) / WWI (gross)	=	MCA of FTC	*Numerator = over-allocating the personal deductions to the FSI because it allocates the entire amount of personal deductions to FSI even though the personal deductions are presumably either spread out over the full WWI or entirely attributable to DSI.*
5	Taxes on WWI	×	FSI (gross) / WWI (net)	=	MCA of FTC	*Numerator = gross figure; denominator = net figure; thus numerator is increased in proportion to the denominator; Effect: allocates personal deductions entirely to DSI; thus, NONE are cancelled out in proportion to FSI; increases the amount of the FSI vis-à-vis the net WWI, which increases the amount of the FTC.*

This case law, though, was limited to individuals for whom personal and family circumstances exist. Whether this line of case law is also relevant for companies and for business expenses has been discussed, not by the CJEU, but by the EFTA Court in the *Seabrokers* case. This case specifically addressed the MCA. The taxpayer in this case was a company in Norway with a PE in the UK, and the expenses were business expenses, such as interest expenses and general overhead expenses. Under the calculation of the MCA, to the extent that expenses are attributed to the PE, it reduces the FSI in the numerator above and therefore reduces the credit. Mathematically, it is essentially the same as above, but the outcome as to what was acceptable in terms of the 'net' and 'gross' figures above was arrived at through different reasoning. Naturally, the *Schumacker*-type reasoning did not apply, but rather a reasoning based on the link between the expenses and the income. The rules in Norway, for example, pooled all interest expenses and allocated them proportionately to the FSI and DSI. If the expenses were actually economically spread out over all the income, as may be the case with general overhead expenses, it is reasonable to attribute some of them proportionately to the PE income earned abroad. If not, if, for example, the expenses were accompanied by proof showing that they were clearly attributed to the DSI, then to the extent these are nevertheless allocated to FSI, this results in partially disallowing those expenses, via the MCA calculation. In this way, by virtue of earning FSI, the company was denied the full deduction of expenses in the same way as other residents, at the stage of the taxes due. Among other arguments, Norway claimed that this was due to a disparity, arguing that it is merely that Norway and the UK diverge in their rules for calculating the tax base: if the UK also allowed the deduction of these interest expenses, then the FSI figure used for calculating the foreign taxes and the FSI figure used for calculating the credit would be better aligned. The EFTA Court rejected this, as the UK could not be expected to accept expenses that were solely attributable to the head office in Norway. From this decision, a distinction should be made between expenses that support the company as a whole in generating all income generally, such as general overhead expenses, and expenses with a clear link to specific parts of the company. The lesson is that, in the calculation of the MCA, expenses should be attributable to the FSI to the extent they were actually related to generating it and domestic expenses should not be over-allocated to the FSI. As Kofler succinctly summarized:

> 'The court distinguished three situations: (i) if expenses are "linked" to the foreign income, they can be applied to reduce the foreign income for the purposes of the limitation on credit, irrespective of whether the source state has granted a deduction;[549] (ii) if the "expenses cannot be linked to any particular business activities", then a proportionate rule is appropriate;[550] and (iii) it constitutes a restriction of the freedom of establishment if "debt interest expenses related solely to a taxpayer's business in the home State" are attributed "to the income of a branch situated in another EEA State when calculating the maximum credit allowance".[551],[1888]

1888. Georg Kofler, *Article 23B: Methods for Elimination of Double Taxation, in Global Tax Treaty Commentaries* Section 3.2.2.3.4 (Richard Vann ed.-in-chief, Pasquale Pistone et al. eds, Global Topics IBFD updated as of February 2019).

Taxes on WWI	×	FSI (net of directly linked expenses and/or proportionate share of general expenses) / WWI (net)	=	MCA of FTC	*Numerator = net figure, but net of expenses actually attributable to the FSI, excluding expenses solely attributable to DSI, but including a proportionate share of, e.g., general overhead expenses; denominator = net figure; Effect = avoids an over-attribution of expenses to FSI, thereby avoiding that otherwise-deductible expenses are cancelled out in proportion to FSI.*

While these questions were answered, nothing in the 'calculation' case law gives any clear indication as to whether the MCA should be calculated on a per-country, per-item or overall basis, so this gives MSs flexibility in design, to be stricter or more competitive, as they wish, under their credit formula. In contemplating responses to this question, a distinction can be made between what may be desirable, or EU-law-friendly, and what is technically legally required under EU law.

In Terra and Wattel's *European Tax Law*, it is argued that the credit method is complicated and one of the contributing factors that is pinpointed is a per-country limitation.[1889] The author observes that the per-country approach adds complications, disallows averaging or cross-crediting of excess credits between countries, and encourages the interposition of 'mixer' companies.[1890] Logically, the author would hold an even less favourable view of a per-item approach, which would by nature be even more complicated and more restrictive in terms of cross-crediting. An overall approach makes it possible that 'all credit space can be pooled and fully used'[1891] and makes the calculation easier. It has been acknowledged in the very-credit-method-experienced US that, although a per-transaction basis would be the 'theoretically purest' approach, it is eschewed due to the administrative challenges (*see*, e.g., *supra* note 205 and note 244). Thus, the smaller the divisions of the credit limitation baskets, the more administratively difficult it is to administer and the more protective it is of the home state tax base. Drawing inferences from the reasoning of Marres, Terra and Wattel, one EU-law-friendly design, or more accurately an internal-market-friendly design, is arguably to adopt an overall approach vis-à-vis other EU MSs. Such an approach, by allowing the averaging of rates among different MSs and not stopping the calculation at each border, would pretend or mathematically act as though it is one internal market and, to the extent that it is less complicated, this also renders cross-border activity smoother at the moment of calculating taxes. Of course, whether a given approach is truly more

1889. Otto Marres (update of 6th ed.), *Chapter 16: Division of Tax Jurisdiction; Double Tax Relief Mechanisms; Tax Treaty Issues*, *in* 1 *Terra/Wattel European Tax Law* 695, 699 and 705 (Peter J. Wattel, Otto Marres & Hein Vermeulen eds, Wolters Kluwer 7th ed. 2019).

1890. *Id.*

1891. *Id.*

favourable for a given taxpayer depends on the facts. As discussed in Chapter 2, where the taxpayer makes losses in one of the foreign states, a per-country limitation could be more favourable, as it would be more likely to ensure that those losses are siphoned off and limited to that one country, without reducing the profits from other foreign states against which taxes can be credited. Nevertheless, this does not technically impair the internal-market-friendliness since the same consequence (i.e., an overall pooling of profits and losses) would occur in a fully domestic internal context. In any case, it would be misguided to equate most-favourable-for-the-taxpayer in all circumstances with most-aligned-with-an-internal-market. Although this EU-overall approach may be desirable, it is not currently required. As Kofler explains:

> 'a discussion regarding whether the EU fundamental freedoms might require (at least) a "per-Union" approach to avoid fragmentation of the internal market,[593] [is] an idea that seems to have lost steam (and had already been rejected by domestic courts)[594] after the ECJ's decision in *D*,[595] where the court focused on the inter nation balance in each bilateral tax treaty'.[1892]

Another calculation question arose in a more limited, special EU-law-created circumstance, namely in a *Schumacker* situation where the obligation to grant tax-related concessions for personal and family circumstances is transferred to the MS of source. In this discussion, two issues were addressed, namely whether a *Schumacker* situation (which, notably, the exemption method in the state of residence contributed to creating) could also occur under the credit method and, if so, whether the credit-granting MS has any adjustments to make.

First, assuming the personal and family circumstances must be granted 'in full', it can be argued that a *Schumacker* scenario can arise even where the credit method applies. Despite the fact that the credit method, as a starting point, allows the MS of residence to take into account the worldwide income of the taxpayer, this does not guarantee that the MS of residence remains in a position to *fully* take into account the personal and family circumstances of the taxpayer. This was demonstrated numerically (*see* Example No. 21), and then ratios were proposed to assist in detecting when this particular EU law problem occurs. For example, all else equal:

$$\frac{\text{Net global income (= FSI + DSI – deductions for personal and family circumstances in MS R)}}{\text{Gross FSI (i.e., without any deductions for personal and family circumstances)}} < 1 \quad \text{MS R cannot absorb the personal and family circumstances in full} \rightarrow \text{MS S must do so.}$$

If so, second, it was argued that a MS of residence that applies the credit method is in a different position in these circumstances compared to one that applies the exemption method (as was the case in the CJEU decision) and thus may have to adapt

1892. Georg Kofler, *Article 23B: Methods for Elimination of Double Taxation, in Global Tax Treaty Commentaries* Section 3.2.2.3.6 (Richard Vann ed.-in-chief, Pasquale Pistone et al. eds, Global Topics IBFD updated as of February 2019).

accordingly in order to avoid inadvertently infringing the *Schumacker* rule to the detriment of its own resident. Following a *Schumacker*-transfer of obligations to the MS of source, the MS of residence should not, in response, refrain from granting any of its personal and family circumstances and, at the same time, apply its credit method as usual, as though it was operating in ordinary circumstances, disregarding their more exceptional nature. Three possibilities were discussed, one of which would require a more widespread active coordination effort among MSs (thus a potential first-best solution for a perhaps more distant future, if ever) and two of which address the more immediate implications of these cases (absent coordination) for a MS of residence that applies a credit method.

Regarding the first possibility (a potential first-best solution), Wattel argued that, rather than what was decided by the CJEU, MSs should share this responsibility and grant fractional or pro rata deductions for personal and family circumstances. Regarding a second possibility, a MS of residence that applies the credit method and thus continues to take all of the same income into its tax base under the credit method may, likewise, continue to grant its own benefits for personal and family circumstances to the extent possible, which will not be in full (*see* Example No. 23; such a possibility relies on a debatable assumption, though, as mentioned at *supra* note 1306, that the *Schumacker* decision results in an unconditional full transfer of obligations to the MS of source irrespective of what happens in the MS of residence). A third possibility, advocated by Farmer, and seemingly most in line with the case law, is that the MS could reconfigure its calculation to grant a form of notional credit for the amount of tax relinquished by the MS of source that corresponds to the revenue that it gave up for the personal and family circumstances (*see supra* note 1302). Calculated examples were offered to compare the effects of the latter two responses (in addition to Example No. 23 and *supra* note 1302, *see also* Example No. 24). Again, these are lessons or takeaways that are confined to the exception-to-the-general rule established in *Schumacker*. This is a prime example of the type of unique legal issues that can arise under EU law, which shape the credit method in ways that could be unexpected for non-EU MSs.

Having established that a credit limitation – provided that it is designed in accordance with the above constraints – is compatible with EU law, the next inevitable question occurs whenever the credit limitation is 'triggered': if the taxes in the other state are higher than the taxes that would be levied in the credit-granting state, such that some (or all) of the eligible foreign taxes cannot be credited, the question arises as to how to treat this 'excess'. The CJEU held in the *Haribo & Salinen* case that Austria must allow a credit carryforward. This was due to the impact of the (indirect) credit method on certain loss-making situations as compared to the exemption method. A relevant distinguishing factor of this case was that the legal and fact pattern was that of relief for economic double taxation; it was not a case of a direct credit for relief of juridical double taxation. As a result, thus far, the credit carryforward is expressly mandated only for the indirect credit, which applied to a cross-border case, and for the purpose of achieving 'equivalence' with the exemption method, which applied to a domestic case.

A question therefore is: are these findings transposable to the direct credit? Although these precise findings are not (since the 'equivalence' aspect is not present), other findings may be. In addition to sound policy arguments (as discussed in Section 4.2.7.), some legal ones may be found in the *AMID* case. Essentially, where the laws of a MS allow the offset and carry forward of losses against profits in the domestic context, it would be discriminatory to deny the use of those losses merely because the taxpayer has exercised its free movement rights. To the extent that foreign profits were included in the tax base under the credit method and thereby reduced the amount of a domestic LCF recorded by the taxpayer, the lack of a credit carryforward, in effect, amounts to disallowing the use of those losses (as shown in Example No. 26, Example No. 28, and Example No. 29). In addition, a relevant EU legislative development as of 2017 may strengthen the argument, in some cases. In the Tax Dispute Resolution Directive, the term 'double taxation' is defined broadly in Article 2(1)(c) to include scenarios that result in '(iii) the cancellation or reduction of losses that could be used to offset taxable profits'. Of course, this definition is confined to the scope of the Directive, i.e., essentially tax treaty disputes, and it would not amount to a fundamental freedom issue, but it can merely be hoped that, as taxpayers begin to utilize the Directive, bringing disputes on this basis, MSs will be compelled to more carefully consider this 'intertemporal double taxation' and how best to resolve the issue.

On the topic of 'excess' credits, one of the common culprits responsible for this issue relates to expenses. It is rather conventional, as embodied in the OECD Model, for example, that a state will levy a WHT on a payment going to a non-resident recipient and that this WHT will be imposed on the gross amount of the income, without the deduction of expenses, whereas the state of residence of this recipient will assess the income tax liability of its resident on the basis of its net income, taking into account expenses. The taxes levied on the gross amount in the state of source may be greater than the taxes levied on the net amount in the state of residence, leading to an 'excess' amount of foreign taxes that may not be credited. The result may be that the taxpayer faces a heavier tax burden in a cross-border context than in a domestic context. The question arises, from an EU law perspective, as to which state, if either, is responsible for the outcome. Should the credit-granting state be conferring a larger, or even full, credit for all eligible taxes levied in the state of source, as the Gilly couple would have liked and as some critics of the credit method have contended? Or should the credit-granting state adopt the same (gross) tax base figure as used in the foreign state, as has been argued in some domestic cases and literature (for further details and references, *see* the interim summary of Section 4.2.6.)? Complaints have been tested both against the credit method mechanism in the state of residence and against the withholding tax mechanism in the state of source.

Those against the credit method have been largely unsuccessful, including those brought before the CJEU (as discussed above, in the context of the 'disparity' line of case law and as reinforced in the 'equivalence' line of case law). From the perspective of the EU law fundamental freedoms, the main obligation on the state acting in its capacity as the home state or state of residence is to ensure that its own laws do not lead to a worse tax treatment of residents that, by virtue of exercising their EU law free movement rights, generate FSI as compared to residents with all activities and income in the domestic context. Thus, arguably, it should tax all residents the same, both in terms of net-based taxation, or deductible expenses (as implicit in, e.g., the EFTA *Seabrokers* case), and in terms of the tax rate charged and tax liability (*see*, e.g., *supra* note 1524). In principle, this is what the credit method achieves. The state of residence is not responsible for shielding its residents from all potential higher tax charges that other EU MSs have the right to levy in exercising their own tax sovereignty. For this reason, it is not obliged to grant a full credit; as already explained above, an MCA is acceptable. Similarly, for this reason, from a non-discrimination point of view, it would be difficult to argue that the tax base in the state of residence should adopt a gross figure for the FSI, while it would adopt a net figure for that same income if domestically sourced - for the purposes of determining the *overall tax liability*. It is true that the state of residence can (or rather, must) exclude certain expenses from the FSI - for the purposes of the *numerator of the credit limitation fraction*, i.e., expenses related to personal and family circumstances (e.g., *De Groot/Beker*) and expenses with a direct link to domestic profits (e.g., *Seabrokers*); however, to the extent the state of residence would disregard other additional expenses (e.g., expenses actually linked to the FSI under its rules) in order to inflate the FSI to be closer the gross amount used in the state of source (or origin or employment, etc., as the case may be), the corresponding increase in the size of the credit could lead to a corresponding decrease in the taxes attributable to DSI, beyond what is technically required by the fundamental freedoms. This might be an instance where the MS could opt to be more generous, but is not obliged to do so by EU law.

By contrast, complaints against the state of source, and the practice of levying gross-basis WHTs, have been more successful. As discussed in the 'neutralization' line of case law (Section 4.2.5.) - whose legal and fact patterns revolved around WHTs on distributions of *outbound* dividends, juxtaposed with (economic) double taxation relief for distributions of *domestically bound* dividends - WHTs on dividends paid to non-residents can be discriminatory if, in the domestic context, dividends paid to residents benefit from double taxation relief. The difference of treatment was visible to the CJEU in that, generally speaking, in both contexts, dividends are distributed from after-tax profits that have already borne CIT and thus both are liable to a series of charges to tax (both potentially suffer economic and juridical double taxation), yet in the domestic context, no further charges to tax are levied, whereas in the cross-border context the MS itself creates an additional tax charge for dividends destined to non-residents. To remedy this, either the MS would have to refrain from levying such WHTs (as incidentally was the solution reached in the Parent-Subsidiary Directive) or, if it insists on a WHT, the MS of source must ensure that the different treatment it causes can be 'neutralized' in the MS of residence by means of the credit method, which raises its own unique design issues (a topic returned to below).

By comparison, as discussed in the deductible expenses line of case law (Section 4.2.6.), the analysis of the CJEU changed for other payments, such as fees for services or interest (*see*, e.g., the discussion at *supra* note 1471 and note 1472). Although the CJEU does not explicitly distinguish the categories of cases, it is reasonable to assume that the different analysis corresponds to the different nature of the payments in question: as these payments are often deductible, the issue of relief for economic double, or multiple, taxation less often arises and, instead, income tax is charged only at the level of the recipient. In this case, if the state of source taxes its own resident recipients on, for example, interest received, then it is not discriminatory to tax non-resident recipients on interest received. The latter boils down to a fundamental question of allocation of jurisdiction to tax (e.g., whether it is the state of the debtor or that of the creditor that should have the right to tax interest), a competence that remains with the MSs according to the CJEU. In these cases, some regularly reoccurring questions therefore were: (1) the appropriateness of a different procedural mechanism for levying the tax on non-residents (e.g., withholding at source, often by the payer) and/or (2) the amount (e.g., whether non-residents ultimately suffer a higher tax burden than residents, due often to the question of deductible expenses or due to tax rates, such as flat rates for non-residents versus progressive rates for residents). Of these two sets of questions, the *second* is more relevant for the 'excess' credit issue.

To briefly address the first question regarding a WHT mechanism, the CJEU in effect held that, although it is a different procedure, it is one that is appropriate to the position that a state finds itself in when exercising its right to tax income paid out to non-residents (*see* the reasoning in, e.g., *Scorpio* and *X NV*, at *supra* notes 1430–1435, note 1461, note 1462, note 1465, as compared to that in *Truck Center*, at *supra* notes 1463–1464). The CJEU seems to recognize, especially in the context of procedures, that 'different' does not always equal more burdensome. Indeed, in some cases, a WHT mechanism, automatically deducted at source by a local payer familiar with the laws and language, is technically easier for a non-resident; it could arguably be more burdensome to require non-residents to adhere to the exact same procedures as residents in terms of filing annual forms, etc. (*see*, e.g., *supra* note 1470, citing *X NV*, at paragraph 50).

As for the second question, regarding the amount (i.e., resulting from the tax base and/or tax rate applied to non-residents), this has a greater impact on the possibility that taxes collected in the state of source can (or cannot) be credited in the state of residence. The CJEU holds the state of source responsible for allowing certain deductible expenses, but only those that are directly 'economically connected' to the income generated in that state. In some cases, for example, in the case of business income, this may bring the tax base closer to the net amount that would be taken into account in the state of residence. However, in other cases, such as one case regarding dividends, the CJEU held that the expenses must be directly connected to the *payment* of the dividends, finding thereafter very few such expenses and thus leaving essentially the gross amount of the dividends as the tax base (*see*, e.g., *J.B.G.T. Miljoen & others* case at *supra* note 1475). Consequently, not much (guaranteed) respite from potential 'excess' credit situations comes from the demands that fall on the state of source under this line of case law.

This may remain or become an increasingly important issue, as there have been discussions regarding the role that more widespread WHTs (e.g., on fees for technical services, on payments for digital advertising) could play in minimizing tax avoidance or in simply more effectively taxing the 'digital economy' (as observed in Chapter 1, at *supra* notes 38–41). Some aspire to more net-basis WHTs, precisely to avoid overtaxation or double taxation in this connection (*see*, e.g., *supra* note 1525). From an EU law perspective, as can be seen, although the CJEU case law moves part of the way in this direction, absent more precise coordination on WHTs and their creditability, 'excess' credit situations may persist.

Going beyond expenses to the topic of losses, the claim of taxpayers to use losses generated abroad has repeatedly occupied the CJEU's agenda. Often the legal patterns featured the exemption method, or other reasons for which the MS refrained from taxing the profits generated abroad (e.g., a foreign subsidiary over which the MS did not exercise tax jurisdiction). In those circumstances, the CJEU held, in essence, that MSs are not required to grant taxpayers the right to offset the foreign losses (thereby allowing a form of symmetry between the profits and losses), *unless* those losses are final, reasoning that it would be disproportionate to deny the losses once they could no longer be used in the other state.

Under the credit method, the analysis changes. As indicated in the *Nordea Bank* case, because the credit method involves, in a first step, exercising tax jurisdiction over the foreign profits, it becomes difficult - if not impossible - for a MS to deny the offset of foreign losses. By contrast with case law on the exemption method, a credit-granting MS should generally allow losses to be taken into account on an ongoing basis - assuming that the predominant reasoning in reaching the CJEU's decision was based on the *same-taxation-same-relief* or *subject-to-tax* precepts, various iterations of which have appeared throughout its case law, and perhaps also a corollary concept of the symmetry between profits and losses (for a more detailed discussion on the reasoning, *see*, e.g., *supra* note 1571, note 1579, note 1582, and note 1584).

Nevertheless, the decision seems to leave some room to manoeuvre to MSs as regards the treatment of foreign losses, even under the credit method. Two parts of the decision, taken together, raise questions (discussed at *supra* note 1593): (1) the fact that the CJEU's decision explicitly cited *two* factors contributing to the incompatible nature of Denmark's foreign-loss-recapture rule - namely because Denmark maintained its right to tax any foreign profits if and as they arose, under the operation of the credit method, *and* because Denmark taxed the gains upon the sale of the PE - combined with (2) the fact that the AG in her Opinion (paragraph 55) explicitly left open the question as to whether 'a Member State's power of taxation which is limited by the credit method also entitles that Member State to take account of losses incurred only to a limited extent'. What is the extent of the obligation to allow the use of foreign losses under the credit method and what could be meant by allowing their use 'only to a limited extent'?

One speculation would be that this is intended to leave room for rules designed to combat a double deduction of losses in a proportionate way, recapturing losses only to the extent necessary to neutralize an excessive amount. Although this double-deduction risk is more acute under the exemption method, there are some circumstances where, as illustrated by the *NN* case, even under the credit method, a double deduction of losses could arise. However, as demonstrated in Example No. 27, under the credit method, a distinction must be made between the situations where it is justifiable (e.g., where the income to which the losses are economically related is doubly included) and where it is unjustifiable (e.g., where a single loss reduces two different taxable bases). Examples of such rules exist, for example, in Germany (under Section 14(1) no. 5 of the Corporate Income Tax Code), which seem to be a modified version of the US dual consolidated loss rules (under Section 1503(d) of the Internal Revenue Code (IRC)). In order to respect the fundamental freedoms, according to these cases, the rules would have to be designed to achieve their legitimate aim, i.e., to apply only where a risk of an undesirable double deduction of losses actually materializes (not, e.g., merely when a foreign PE is sold, as in *Nordea Bank*, nor, e.g., when the use of the losses abroad is theoretical but does not actually occur in practice, as was potentially the case in *NN*), and in a proportionate way, i.e., the rules should not proceed with a full recapture (as in Denmark) but rather a recapture only to the extent of any 'double dip'. Another speculation could be that this refers to rules such as the US 'recapture of overall foreign losses' rules (under Section 904(f) of the IRC, discussed at *supra* note 225). Under these rules, to the extent foreign losses previously offset DSI, future foreign profits will be recharacterized as DSI for the purposes of calculating the credit limitation. These rules arguably do not necessarily amount to a loss restriction, but are rather loss-allocation and recharacterization rules, designed to ensure that the US is able to collect taxes on DSI, aligned with the objective of the credit limitation (a design feature expressly permitted by the CJEU under other lines of case law).

In addition to the above calculation and credit limitation issues, the CJEU addressed one fundamental aspect of the scope of the credit method, namely that of the personal scope, i.e., which taxpayers are eligible to claim an FTC. As seen in *Avoir Fiscal* and *Saint Gobain*, the personal scope is broadened: it is not acceptable to grant relief only to residents, as under certain circumstances, it must also be extended to non-residents. The fact patterns concerned the tax treatment of non-resident companies that established PEs in the host MS. According to the CJEU, given that the PEs were taxed in the exact same way as resident companies, it was discriminatory to treat those PEs differently only as regards relief. This amounted to a different treatment merely on the grounds that the PE belonged to a company with, for example, its seat in another MS.

Although the CJEU demanded this equal treatment in cases of an imputation credit and relief for economic double taxation in an international context, i.e., an exemption and an indirect credit for incoming dividends, one question is whether it is equally applicable to the direct credit method. As argued at the end of Section 4.2.1., because the CJEU's reasoning was predominantly based on a notion of *same-taxation-same-relief*, these findings should be equally applicable by analogy to a direct credit; if this form of relief is granted to resident companies, it should be extended to PEs of non-resident companies. More challenging is the question as to which tax rate should apply for the credit limitation. The challenge arises because there are three states involved, i.e., the EU MS of the PE, the EU MS of the company to which the PE belongs and the state of source of the income attributable to the PE. Assuming there are DTCs between these states, the question arises as to whether the credit for the WHT should be capped at the rate that applies under the DTC between the EU MS of the PE and the state of source or under the DTC between the EU MS of the company of the PE and the state of source. The 'national treatment' obligation as interpreted in the *Saint Gobain* decision suggests that the MS (where the PE is located) must extend the benefits provided under its own laws and tax treaties to which it is a party. While this guarantees legal equal treatment, in some cases (e.g., where the tax rates are higher under the DTC between the EU MS of the company of the PE and the state of source), it may not ensure effective equal treatment. This seems to be another area where the MS could opt for more generous treatment, but would not be obliged to do so.

The personal scope was also addressed indirectly in another instance, namely the *Riskin and Timmermans* case[1893] (discussed at *supra* note 1836). Confronted with a comparison of credit method articles in tax treaties, the CJEU reiterated its findings in the 2005 *D* case[1894] that there is no most-favoured-nation treatment obligation. This renders it possible for EU MSs to restrict the personal scope of an FTC to only those persons covered by a DTC.

One hypothetical scenario that was not explicitly addressed by the CJEU - which could merit a brief discussion, as it touches upon multiple lines of case law and the distinction between disparities and discrimination - is whether discrimination could arise under the credit method if a MS grants what appears to be a full credit in the domestic scenario but imposes a credit limitation in the cross-border scenario. The example given above (in Section 4.2.2. and in Section 5.1.) is that a MS may levy a WHT on, for example, dividends and interest, yet in the domestic context allow the WHT to be credited against the total tax liability of residents, whereas in the cross-border context interest and dividends are taxed upon receipt and benefit from a direct tax credit subject to a credit limitation. Assuming the credit-granting state is not levying a heavier tax burden on the cross-border situation - in other words, assuming that the WHT is merely an advance payment of tax and, thus, the refund or grant of a credit for this WHT in the domestic context merely serves to ensure that the final tax liability of residents represents the applicable domestic tax rates (and it does *not* serve as a mechanism for reducing the ETR on DSI) - and assuming that the credit method in the cross-border context accomplishes the same - in other words, it involves including the interest and dividends from abroad in the tax base, calculating the tax liability based on the same rates and rules applying to all income (domestic or foreign) and then allowing the foreign WHTs to be credited against this final tax liability - the state of residence is in essence treating both domestic and foreign WHTs as advance payments of tax (albeit to two different treasuries), which are creditable against the resident's final tax liability, and thereby treating both sets of income the same. Thus, all of the findings of the *Gilly* line of case law remain fully applicable here. Rather, any potential EU law problems that could arise in the hypothetical scenario would, as seen in the 'neutralization' line of case law (Section 4.2.5.) and in the deductible expenses

1893. CJEU, Case C-176/15, *Riskin and Timmermans*, 30 Jun. 2016, ECLI:EU:C:2016:488.
1894. *Id.*, at para. 31 (The CJEU cited the 'judgments of 5 July 2005 in *D.*, C376/03, EU:C:2005:424, paragraphs 54 and 61 to 62, and of 20 May 2008 in *Orange European Smallcap Fund*, C194/06, EU:C:2008:289, paragraphs 50 to 51').

line of case law (Section 4.2.6.), likely be attributable to the WHT (rather than the credit method) and the MS acting in its capacity as the state of source of the payment.[1895] As seen in cases regarding dividend distributions, if this credit-granting MS levied a WHT on dividends to non-residents and on dividends to residents, but subsequently granted a full refund or credit for this WHT to resident recipients, this WHT would likely violate the fundamental freedoms – either calling for its abolishment or its 'neutralization' by means of a credit in the *other* MS where the recipient resides. As seen in cases regarding, for example, interest distributions, notably the *Truck Center* case,[1896] if a MS taxes both residents and non-residents on the interest income, then the mere fact that a WHT is the mechanism used to tax non-residents, whereas no WHT (or the WHT is levied but refunded, which would have the same effect) is levied on residents, who are instead taxed by means of an assessment, is not discriminatory. As can be seen, upon closer inspection, this hypothetical scenario simply leads back full circle to the finding that the credit method, accompanied by an MCA, serves to tax residents in the same way regardless of the source of their income and, to the extent the taxes levied in the other MS are higher, any 'excess' credit would result from a disparity in, e.g., the tax rates between the two MSs. In some cases, it would also lead back to the 'neutralization' line of case law, to which the discussion turns in the next section (Section 5.3.).

While the above analysis shows that the CJEU has addressed numerous questions relating to the credit method, it also left some aspects open to debate (as enumerated in Section 5.1.). One such question concerns the treatment of FSI and, in particular, in a progressive tax rate system, to which tax rate bracket the FSI should be attributed. Should the FSI be attributed pro rata to all of the brackets or to the lowest bracket ('bottom-slicing') or to the highest bracket ('top-slicing')? In addition to the bottom-slicing, top-slicing and proportionate approaches, Harris describes a '[s]licing rule with taxpayer choice': another 'common approach is to permit taxpayers to order their limitation on credit calculations in such a way as will produce the least amount of residence country tax, that is to say, which maximizes the availability and use of foreign tax credits'.[1897] A bottom-slicing approach was initially the design inscribed in the wording of the League of Nations 1925 Report (*see supra* notes 588 et seq.). What was illustrated in the fictive 'Morania' example of the 1925 Report is that, first, at the stage of the tax base 'Morania' combined the FSI with all of the income and taxed the

1895. *Compare also*, e.g., Opinion of AG Kokott in Case C-540/07, *Commission v. Italy*, 16 Jul. 2009, ECLI:EU:C:2009:463, at paras 44–47 (in these paragraphs of the Opinion, the responsibility of the state of source in such cases is made clear) with Opinion of AG Kokott in Case C-48/13, *Nordea Bank*, 13 Mar. 2014, ECLI:EU:C:2014:153, at para. 26 (it was argued that, from a state of residence perspective, the situation of a domestic PE and a PE abroad are not comparable as regards the credit method, 'because only in the case of a foreign branch can foreign tax be offset against Danish tax').

1896. CJEU, Case C-282/07, *Truck Center*, 22 Dec. 2008, ECLI:EU:C:2008:762, at paras 34–35, 42, 44.

1897. Peter Harris, *Chapter III: Taxation of Residents on Foreign Source Income, in United Nations Handbook on Selected Issues in Administration of Double Tax Treaties for Developing Countries* 109, 130–133 (Alexander Trepelkov, Harry Tonino & Dominika Halka eds, United Nations 2013).

result at the rate applicable to this worldwide income figure, whereas, second, at the stage of calculating the credit against the taxes due, 'Morania' assumed that merely the lowest tax rate bracket applied to the FSI. This reduced the credit accordingly and it did so in a way that was divorced from the taxes actually imposed by 'Morania' on the FSI at the first stage. Generally speaking, such a system - wherein a MS first aggregates all the worldwide income together for the purposes of the tax base used for calculating the total taxes due, but then assumes that the FSI first fills the lowest bracket, thereby attracting the lowest amount of taxes, for FTC purposes - leads to the least generous treatment. If under the same circumstances the FSI first fills the highest bracket, this generally leads to the most generous treatment. In such circumstances, Rust argues that neither the top-bracket approach nor the lowest-bracket approach is convincing. Both mathematical reasoning and, in the context of DTCs, a reading of the Commentary would point towards using the average rate of tax. According to Rust:

> '[o]nce the material rate of tax applicable to a taxpayer's worldwide income has been determined by reference to the progressive scale of rates, the proportionate burden which application of that rate imposes on domestic and foreign income will be equal. The same would apply, mutatis mutandis, to a capital tax with a progressively increasing scale of rates. Therefore, the rate "attributable" to items of income derived from, or items of capital situated, abroad is the average tax rate applicable to the taxable totals (as also indicated in no. 62 OECD MC Comm. on Article 23). Some of the earlier German DTCs express this line of thinking by stipulating that the tax to be credited shall be "computed on the basis of an average rate of tax"' (original emphasis omitted).[1898]

In other words, there should be a correspondence between the treatment at the first stage and the assumption applied at the second stage for calculating the FTC. To be truly coherent, this correspondence should apply regardless of the approach adopted. The question is: do any of these approaches seem most aligned with EU law?

As for the 'bottom slicing' approach, a state could attempt to justify this on the grounds that it aligns with the non-resident taxation in the foreign state. For example, assume a taxpayer earns 80,000 of DSI and 20,000 of FSI. In the foreign state, the taxpayer earned only 20,000 and therefore was presumably taxed at the lowest rates on the progressive scale in the foreign state, thereby justifying the credit-granting state's approach to merely apply the same under its own tax rate scale.[1899] Moreover, the credit-granting state could espouse a comparison, as in the League of Nations 1925 Report, with a taxpayer that hypothetically earned only 20,000 in its own state, thereby disregarding the total income. As for the 'top slicing' approach, a state could justify opting for this on the grounds that it better ensures that more of the taxes levied in the foreign state can be credited and is thus more aligned with the aim of relief for double

1898. Alexander Rust, *Article 23 A Exemption Method and Article 23 B Credit Method, in 2 Klaus Vogel on Double Taxation Conventions* 1581, m.no. 56 (Ekkehart Reimer & Alexander Rust eds, Kluwer Law International 4th ed. 2015).

1899. But *see*, e.g., Section 4.2.6 and, in particular, *supra* note 1417 (such a presumption could be a stretch for this MS to sustain considering that the taxation of non-residents in the other state could, as is sometimes the case, be based on special flat tax rates and not on the progressive tax rates applicable to residents).

taxation. This approach was adopted in the UK and the explanation of John F. Avery Jones seemed to frame it in this way.[1900]

From an EU law perspective, there are two points to consider. First, the comparison is central to the assessment of whether a discrimination exists under the fundamental freedoms. It would be possible to compare taxpayer 1 that earns 100,000 in State R with taxpayer 2 that earns 80,000 in State R and, by virtue of exercising its free movement rights, 20,000 in State F; alternatively, if adopting the potential justification of a MS opting for a 'bottom slicing' approach, it would be possible to compare taxpayer 2 – *not* with respect to its true overall situation of 100,000 generated taking into account its cross-border activities – by looking *only* at its FSI of 20,000 in State F with a taxpayer 1 that earned only 20,000 in State R. The comparison in cases such as *Schumacker* suggests that the CJEU would opt for the first comparison, on the basis of the actual facts presented to it, and *not* for a purely hypothetical comparison that artificially isolates only the income earned in the other MS. Second, it is true that the CJEU case law on international juridical double taxation gives freedom to the MSs in that it would not require any FTC in the first place; however, as soon as a MS opts to provide one, it must do so in a way that is not discriminatory. If the MS aggregates the FSI in question with all other income to reach a worldwide income figure and taxes all the income, foreign and domestic, in the same way on the basis of its progressive income tax scale (as is the standard case under the credit method), then it upholds non-discriminatory treatment at this stage. If at the second stage of calculating the MCA to assess the taxes due, the MS opts to attribute a lower amount of taxes to the FSI than what was actually levied at the first stage, thereby reducing the FTC, it could be argued that, at this second stage, the MS's calculation results in a higher tax burden on the FSI. And, in this case, such a higher tax burden would not be attributable to a higher tax rate in the other MS, but rather would be attributable to the design of the MCA calculation (which taxes the FSI higher at the tax base stage than what it credits at the MCA stage).

Based on this reasoning, a 'bottom slicing' approach risks being found contrary to EU law. The approach that would seem most aligned with EU law would be the pro rata, or proportionate, approach. If the taxpayer had earned all the income within the same state, it would likely have formed part of the general pool of income, thus presumably taxed at the average rate; therefore, treating the FSI in this way in the tax base and within the MCA seems most aligned with the assumption of how DSI would be treated and, thus, aligned with the obligation to grant equal treatment. Of course, as the EU fundamental freedoms do not generally prevent a MS from granting more favourable treatment, it would also be in line with EU law to offer a 'top slicing' approach or even the '[s]licing rule with taxpayer choice' as illustrated by Harris in the *United Nations Handbook*. This is one demonstration of how the general principles derived from the CJEU case law can provide some answers to the open questions.

1900. John F. Avery Jones, *A Comment on 'Progressive Taxation of Non-residents and Intra-EC Allocation of Personal Tax Allowances'*, 40(8) Eur. Tax'n 375, 375 (2000) (Avery Jones explained how a 'top slice' approach was one of two factors that could help make the problem of 'excess' credits stemming from the 'host State tax' being 'higher than the home State' 'less likely to occur in practice').

5.3. SPECIAL ISSUE FOR THE DIRECT CREDIT: 'NEUTRALIZATION' – A CREDIT METHOD CHIMERA?

A MS that levies WHTs on profits distributed by entities or subsidiaries located in its territory to non-residents, while it grants relief for distributions to residents, risks infringing the fundamental freedoms. In spite of that, the CJEU proffered a way to remedy the situation. Under what has become known as the 'neutralization' line of case law, this MS is encouraged to bilaterally negotiate with the states of residence to offer a direct credit, i.e., via a tax treaty, and to design it in a way to enhance the chance that the credit will offset 'in full' the higher taxation on cross-border dividends that results from the WHTs in the state of the subsidiary.

While the CJEU has clarified some issues, other issues remain unclear. Recall that, for the subsidiary's state to rely on the 'neutralization' case law to justify a discriminatory WHT, there are three conditions. First, the credit must actually be given. According to AG Kokott, '[i]f the income is not taxed, or not taxed in an adequate amount, in the State of residence, there remains a part of the withholding tax from Italy that cannot be credited. In that eventuality the withholding tax on outgoing dividends results in a tax burden, attributable to Italy alone, which exceeds the tax that companies resident in Italy have to pay on such dividends'.[1901] Second, the credit must be bilaterally agreed. However, not all bilaterally agreed provisions are alike in this respect. Where, for example, the credit method article in the tax treaty is subject to the credit method provisions under the domestic laws of the state of residence, then it is rather a unilateral credit granted by the state of residence, rather than one that the state of source has secured through bilateral negotiations. Third, the credit must fully offset the disadvantageous effect of the WHT. The most secure way to achieve this is to design a 'full' credit, i.e., an unlimited credit method, in the tax treaty. On this point, this line of case law underlines a tension between the obligations the CJEU places on the state of the distributing entity and those on the state of residence. For example, according to the *Gilly* and *FII* cases, it is acceptable for a state of residence to employ an MCA calculation, but according to the CJEU in this 'neutralization' line of case law, such an MCA may jeopardize the 'neutralization' justification for the state of the distributing entity. In any case, as discussed (in Section 4.2.5.), how exactly this offset in full can be achieved in any truly consistent way is unclear.

Some open issues can be identified. First, regarding the requirement that the neutralization be bilaterally agreed, the 2015 *Miljoen* case could have far-reaching effects, as all DTCs whose credit method article makes reference to domestic law do *not* meet the standard of 'bilaterally agreed', presumably because the article merely confirms and solely relies on the credit method *unilaterally* provided under domestic law, without truly guaranteeing it *bilaterally*. As an example, the *Kerckhaert and Morres* and *Damseaux* cases revealed just how easily Belgium could completely

1901. Opinion of AG Kokott in Case C-540/07, *Commission v. Italy*, 16 Jul. 2009, ECLI:EU:C:2009:463, at para. 58.

disregard its FTC commitment under this type of credit method article in the Belgium-France DTC (as amended through 1971 and 1999, respectively), seemingly without infringing the DTC. Ensuring 'neutralization' via a DTC credit method article is evidently impossible to the extent that the wording of the article leaves open the possibility that the credit method could even be abolished under domestic law. However, this raises a question. Some DTCs' credit method articles include a caveat that, although the credit depends on domestic law, any amendments to the credit method should be made 'without changing the general principle thereof' (e.g., as in US DTCs with some EU MSs). Would this preserve the 'bilateral' nature of the credit since it at least implies that it will not be altogether abolished? The CJEU has not yet considered such wording since it was not quoted in the DTCs reviewed in the *Miljoen* case.

It seems highly unlikely that this reference to the 'general principle' would assuage the CJEU's concern. The vague nature of the term offers no concrete guarantee. Examples of how it has been interpreted reinforce this. For example, the 'principle of credit' is discussed in the OECD Commentary on Articles 23 A and 23 B of the OECD Model. It merely refers to what was identified as the core of the credit method in Chapter 2, namely that it has a basic two-step operation, such that the relief operates at level of taxes due, and it grants relief for 'actual' double taxation.[1902] As another example, in discussing US tax treaties, Shaheen inferred that the 'general principle' refers to 'a dollar-for-dollar reduction in the amount of U.S. tax on U.S.-taxable foreign-source income by the amount of foreign taxes paid'.[1903] Moreover, he observes that according to the Protocol of the Germany-US DTC:[1904]

> 'For purposes of paragraph 1 of Article 23, the "general principle hereof" means the avoidance of double taxation by allowing a credit for taxes imposed on items of income arising in the Federal Republic of Germany, as determined under the applicable United States source rules, as modified by the Convention. While the details and limitations of the credit pursuant to this paragraph may change as provisions of United States law change, any such changes must preserve a credit for German taxes imposed with respect to items of income that the Federal Republic of Germany may tax pursuant to the Convention.'

As a key example from a MS of the EU, in a case interpreted by the Belgian Supreme Court, the fact that the MCA was changed under national law to apply in a stricter way, namely by reducing the general fraction by an additional fraction known as the 'debt financing ratio' (to counteract certain abusive practices), did not infringe

1902. OECD, *Model Tax Convention on Income and on Capital 2017: Condensed Version* Commentary on Articles 23 A and 23 B, paras 15–16 (OECD Publishing 2017).

1903. Fadi Shaheen, *How Reform-Friendly Are U.S. Tax Treaties?*, 41(3) Brook. J. Int'l L. 1243, 1261 (2016).

1904. *Id.*, at 1255. *See* Convention between the United States and the Federal Republic of Germany for the Avoidance of Double Taxation and the Prevention of Fiscal Evasion with Respect to Taxes on Income and Capital and to Certain Other Taxes (1989), Protocol of 1989, para. 20 ('20. With reference to paragraph 1 of Article 23 (Relief from Double Taxation)'), https://www.irs.gov/pub/irs-trty/germany.pdf (last visited 19 Aug. 2018).

the 'principle' of the credit method under the Belgium-US DTC in question.[1905] Thus, despite this promise of adherence to a 'general principle', which would seem to offer some notion of stability, the MS of residence remains free to apply an MCA, of course, and, more importantly, to change the limitation as it deems best. In any case, due to the *Columbus Containers* case, which shows the ease of treaty override and that EU law does not counteract it, then under the standards of its own case law, the CJEU's insistence on the *bilaterally-agreed-in-a-DTC* neutralization is a rather flimsy guarantee.

A second open issue is the credit carryforward question. If the WHT is not offset in full, one possibility is for the residence state to allow any excess credits to be carried forward into future tax years. However, the CJEU has not explicitly addressed this question in the case of direct credits (only for *indirect* credits, as mentioned); thus little in the case law currently categorically compels cooperation from the state of residence in the form of a credit carryforward for *direct* credits (though, *see* the above discussion in connection with the *AMID* case). Under a credit carryforward, the residence state could offset the WHT over time. Thus, at first glance, it could be a potential solution. However, one question is whether there is perhaps a cash-flow disadvantage from not obtaining the credit (or from obtaining only a partial credit) in the same year as the WHT is levied.[1906] As for a third option, if the WHT is not offset in full, another possibility is for the state of source to refund that portion of the WHT in excess of the credit limitation in the residence state. Austria implemented this possibility.[1907] Would this be considered a mere 'partial neutralization' that does *not* fulfil the 'full neutralization' required by the CJEU[1908] or is the idea less formally stringent than that since such a solution would achieve the desirable outcome of eliminating the restriction?

To answer these questions, based on the CJEU case law, there are convincing reasons for arguing that a credit carryforward in the state of residence would not resolve the issue. First, it is highly unlikely to fulfil one of the main conditions for 'neutralization' mandated by the CJEU, namely the bilaterally agreed condition. A credit carryforward tends to be provided under the domestic laws of the state of

1905. Luc De Broe, *Chapter 27: Belgium – Limitation of Foreign Tax Credit Does Not Infringe Article 23 of the Former Belgium-US Treaty, in Tax Treaty Case Law Around the Globe 2014* 277 (Eric C.C.M. Kemmeren et al. eds, IBFD/Linde 2014) (regarding the 15 Mar. 2013 Belgian Supreme Court case decided under the 1970 US-Belgium DTC).

1906. On this point, *see*, e.g., CJEU, Case C-47/12, *Kronos International Inc.*, 11 Sep. 2014, ECLI:EU:C:2014:2200, para. 80 ('It is true that it follows from the Court's case-law that the exclusion of a cash-flow advantage in a cross-border situation where it is available in an equivalent domestic situation is a restriction on the free movement of capital (see, by analogy, judgment in *Commission v Spain*, C-269/09, EU:C:2012:439, paragraph 59 and the case-law cited)').

1907. Georg Kofler, *Tax Treaty 'Neutralization' of Source State Discrimination under the EU Fundamental Freedoms?*, 65(12) Bull. Int'l Tax'n 684, 689 (2011) ('Another substantive issue is whether or not "partial neutralization" is possible. For instance, in 2009, Austria amended its corporate tax act to comply with *Denkavit Internationaal* and *Amurta* and provide for a refund of (discriminatory) Austrian dividend withholding tax to certain non-resident corporate recipients "insofar as" no treaty credit for the withholding tax is available in the other state.71').

1908. *Id.*

residence.[1909] This is now rendered even less likely following the *Miljoen* case. Prior to this case, perhaps it could have been possible to argue that a credit method article in a DTC that makes reference to domestic law, which, in turn, is known by both Contracting States to provide for a credit carryforward and/or perhaps generous cross-crediting possibilities such that any excess WHT could have readily been used against excess-crediting capacity generated by other FSI. Following the *Miljoen* case, references to domestic law outright exclude the possibility to meet the bilaterally agreed condition since this means that the neutralization is rendered dependent upon the domestic law, or unilateral relief, of the state of residence, and any future changes to it. In this way, the state of source will have failed to secure this right in a way that has legal effect within its own legal system and agreements.

Second, it could also amount to a prohibited cash-flow disadvantage. On this issue, the CJEU has found a cash-flow disadvantage to exist in numerous contexts, tending to apply this reasoning 'by analogy'.[1910] For example, this was discussed in the context of an imputation credit from a residence state perspective (*Test Claimants in the FII Group Litigation*), in the context of an optional group-tax-treatment that allowed a later payment of CIT only to distributing entities with domestic parents (*Metallgesellschaft*), and in the context of a non-reimbursable WHT on non-residents in loss-making situations whereas tax was deferred for residents in loss-making situations from a source state perspective (*Sofina*), among various others.[1911] The CJEU 'has repeatedly held' that 'the exclusion of a cash-flow advantage in a cross-border situation when it is granted in an equivalent situation on national territory constitutes a restriction on the free movement of capital' and 'the freedom of establishment'.[1912] This statement would seem to map itself onto a case (such as the 'neutralization' cases) where a WHT is levied on non-residents, yet relief for any resulting heavier tax burden is provided only partially in that year and otherwise provided only possibly in future years, thereby

1909. *See*, e.g., OECD, *Model Tax Convention on Income and on Capital 2017: Condensed Version* Commentary on Articles 23 A and 23 B, paras 62–66 (OECD Publishing 2017); Alexander Rust, *Article 23 A Exemption Method and Article 23 B Credit Method*, *in* 2 *Klaus Vogel on Double Taxation Conventions* 1581, m.no. 58 (Ekkehart Reimer & Alexander Rust eds, Kluwer Law International 4th ed. 2015).

1910. *See*, e.g., CJEU, Case C-575/17, *Sofina*, 22 Nov. 2018, ECLI:EU:C:2018:943, at para. 29 (quoted above in Section 4.2.6).

1911. *Id.*, at paras 29–30 (quoted above in Section 4.2.6., in turn cites other cases, such as '12 July 2012, *Commission* v *Spain*, C269/09, EU:C:2012:439, paragraph 59', where the diversity of circumstances in which a cash-flow disadvantage is held to exist becomes clearer); CJEU, Case C-269/09, *Commission v. Spain*, 12 Jul. 2012, ECLI:EU:C:2012:439, at para. 59 ('However, it cannot be denied that the withdrawal of that advantage constitutes a clear disadvantage in terms of cash-flow. In this connection, the Court has repeatedly held that the exclusion of a cash-flow advantage in a cross-border situation where it is available in an equivalent domestic situation is a restriction on the freedom of establishment (see, to that effect, inter alia, Joined Cases C397/98 and C410/98 *Metallgesellschaft and Others* [2001] ECR I1727, paragraphs 44, 54 and 76; Case C436/00 *X and Y* [2002] ECR I10829, paragraphs 36 to 38; Case C446/03 *Marks & Spencer* [2005] ECR I10837, paragraph 32; and Case C347/04 *Rewe Zentralfinanz* [2007] ECR I2647, paragraph 29)').

1912. CJEU, Case C-575/17, *Sofina*, 22 Nov. 2018, ECLI:EU:C:2018:943, at paras 29–30; CJEU, Case C-269/09, *Commission v. Spain*, 12 Jul. 2012, ECLI:EU:C:2012:439, at para. 59.

requiring the *non*-resident to wait for the payment to remedy the different treatment, whereas residents would obtain relief immediately or within the same year.

Of course, in the process of reasoning by analogy or by distinction, caution should be exercised in extrapolating the CJEU's findings beyond their context. Upon closer inspection, the CJEU seems to take slightly different positions as regards cash-flow disadvantages depending on whether the case regards the taxation of a resident versus a non-resident. For example, the *Metallgesellschaft* case pinpointed different taxation of the *resident* distributing company itself – namely, whether it had to pay ACT upfront or not – based on where its parent was located. The *Test Claimants in the FII Group Litigation* case pinpointed different taxation of the *resident* distributing company itself – namely, whether it could offset the ACT it had to pay upfront or transfer the ACT to its subsidiaries, etc. – based on where its subsidiary was located or basically the source of dividends. The CJEU struck down this cash-flow disadvantage even where it was readjusted later within the same tax period.

By comparison, the combination of the 'neutralization' line of case law and the 'deductible expenses' line of case law indicates that the CJEU allows a timing difference in the moment of levying tax on *non*-residents in that it accepts a WHT as a legitimate and proportionate means for levying tax on non-residents.[1913] Some potential cash-flow (dis)advantage is inherent in the timing difference of the procedure itself, yet the procedure has been accepted. Often a WHT is levied in a first step and later the taxation is then adjusted or recuperated, usually within the same tax period (e.g., the WHT is refunded upon request or upon filing at the end of the year or the WHT is credited against tax liability at the end of the year).

However, it is possible that once the timing difference extends beyond more than one tax period, the CJEU may view it differently. The *Sofina* case was an indication for this. The *Sofina* case differed from other cases of WHT on non-residents because the issue scrutinized by the CJEU was the tax treatment *across* tax periods (i.e., for residents, no taxation was levied when losses occurred and would not be levied until future tax periods where profitability recovered, if ever). The CJEU also reiterated that 'the assessment of whether there exists a potentially less favourable treatment of the dividends paid to non-resident companies must be undertaken for each tax year, taken

1913. *See* cases discussed in Section 4.2.6. *See also*, e.g., Opinion of AG Wathelet in Case C-575/17, *Sofina*, 7 Aug. 2018, ECLI:EU:C:2018:650, at paras 28–32. Of course, if the laws of a given MS levied a WHT on both residents and non-residents alike, then the timing would be more clearly aligned, in that both residents and non-residents would be subject to an upfront payment of tax on the dividends at the moment of distribution, with a subsequent adjustment of their tax liability on the dividends, likely at the moment of paying taxes at the end of the fiscal year. However, the cases that came before the CJEU did not always have this as their fact pattern, such as *Commission v. Italy* C540/07. On this, *see*, e.g., Opinion of AG Kokott in Case C-540/07, *Commission v. Italy*, 16 Jul. 2009, ECLI:EU:C:2009:463, at para. 46. There were cases where a WHT was levied on non-residents and no WHT was levied on residents and, still, the CJEU accepted that, theoretically, this would be acceptable as longer as the higher taxation caused by the MS of source is offset in full in a subsequent step in the MS of residence under a bilaterally agreed measure in, for example, a DTC.

individually'.[1914] In this case, the CJEU ruled that there was a cash-flow disadvantage that amounted to an infringement. In light of this reasoning, it seems likely that a credit carryforward may not withstand this CJEU scrutiny.

Another question is: if dependence on a credit carryforward could mount a cash-flow disadvantage, could a credit carrybackward be a solution? To the extent that the WHT could not be neutralized by means of the credit method in the year in question, the state of residence could agree to reopen previous tax assessments and carry the credit backward to reduce the tax liability in those previous tax years, thereby allowing the full benefit in that same year (rather than waiting on future years). This could resolve the cash-flow disadvantage issue. The state of residence would have to be rather generous in this respect since a credit carrybackward will generally be limited in time – for example, capped at one year in the US (as of 2019) or subject to statute of limitation rules preventing the reopening of past final assessments after a given period of time. The success of this solution would ultimately be contingent upon such time-barred limitations, as well as upon the facts and circumstances (which as stated in other parts of this book are notoriously and infinitely variable things). The 'neutralization' line of case law requires relief *in effect*, not merely the legal possibility. Thus, any time the circumstances of the taxpayer in the state of residence are such that previous years did not have sufficient tax liability against which the taxpayer could actually carry back the excess, 'neutralization' will not be achieved.

Regardless of where one stands on the cash-flow issue and how the case law will develop in this respect, it seems that the credit carryforward (or credit carrybackward for that matter) nevertheless would not satisfy bilaterally agreed condition, as discussed above. Against this background, the 'partial neutralization' solution seems more attractive as an option. This solution would seem more compatible with the CJEU's primary suggestion, which is that the MS of source remedy the different treatment itself (the 'neutralization' solution seemed to be presented by the CJEU as more of a secondary alternative solution).

Recent developments may have an influence on how these open issues should be resolved. It will likely be hard to convince a residence state that applies the credit method to relinquish its MCA, considering that such a move would force the residence state to potentially give up taxes on its own domestic income (as Section 4.2.2. demonstrated by means of an example). Up until the launch of the OECD/G20 BEPS Project, it may have been easier to convince subsidiary states in the EU to cease levying WHTs. After all, MSs had found unanimous agreement to do so under the Interest-Royalties Directive and the Parent-Subsidiary Directive. However, recent developments would suggest that this is not always ideal. Under one draft recommendation of the EU Parliament, for example, MSs were encouraged to use WHTs coupled with the credit method, as a better protection against 'double non-taxation and BEPS'.[1915] Under Action 1 of the OECD/G20 BEPS Project, the OECD cites, among the options – but not

1914. *See* CJEU, Case C-575/17, *Sofina*, 22 Nov. 2018, ECLI:EU:C:2018:943, at para. 30 (citing '(judgment of 2 June 2016, *Pensioenfonds Metaal en Techniek*, C252/14, EU:C:2016:402, paragraph 41)').

1915. As cited in Chapter 1, at *supra* note 38.

its official recommendations – for states, the possibility of 'a withholding tax on certain types of digital transactions'.[1916] Considering that either extreme end of the spectrum – either the subsidiary state abolishing its WHTs on outbound dividends or the residence state setting aside the MCA – entails politically challenging policy choices, the more feasible responses would be either the credit carryforward (or backward) solution or the 'partial neutralization' solution,[1917] which seem to represent a middle ground.

The main obstacle to the credit carryforward or backward solution, as mentioned above, is that, if it exists at all, it is normally provided only unilaterally under the state of residence's domestic laws, thereby failing the bilaterally agreed condition; therefore, to increase its chance of success, the two MSs would have to draft Article 23 (or its equivalent) without any reference to domestic law and explicitly providing a credit carryover on the basis of the DTC. Even so, the aforementioned risks of falling afoul of the cash-flow-disadvantage case law linger for the credit carryforward option. Thus, it may be the 'partial neutralization' by the state of source which seems more likely in line with CJEU case law. Ultimately, although the CJEU extended this reasonable and potentially enticing olive branch to MSs in the form of the possibility for 'neutralization', it currently seems to be more of a credit method chimera than a plausible outcome of the credit method in tax treaties.

5.4. LESSONS FOR THE INDIRECT CREDIT: THE PREDOMINANCE OF THE 'EQUIVALENCE' LINE OF CASE LAW

Many CJEU decisions that influence the design of the credit method pertained to the indirect credit. For example, the CJEU recommended a credit carryforward in the *Haribo & Salinen* joined cases or a credit based on the nominal rate in the *FII II* case. To better understand the impact of these cases, however, it is necessary to consider the specific factual and legal patterns in which these design suggestions were made. This helps ascertain which instructions of the CJEU or findings derived from its case law can be transposed to the indirect credit in general and which are contingent upon a specific legal system in a MS.

The reason that the legal system – or more specifically, the relief system – in place takes on particular importance in this line of case law is because, in many cases, these instructions were made for the purposes of assessing 'equivalence' between different methods for relief. As a result, such instructions are especially relevant if MSs apply both methods: one in a cross-border context (e.g., an indirect credit) and another in the domestic one (e.g., exemption). Furthermore, the CJEU's proposal to compute the indirect credit based on the nominal rate is arguably relevant only in the even more specific constellation of: (1) an exemption for domestic cases and an indirect credit for cross-border cases and (2) where domestic subsidiaries systematically benefit from lower rates than their parent companies. Thus, the analysis of the findings must be

1916. OECD, *Addressing the Tax Challenges of the Digital Economy, Action 1 – 2015 Final Report*, OECD/G20 Base Erosion and Profit Shifting Project, 13 (OECD Publishing 2015).
1917. For more on this option, *see* Georg Kofler, *Tax Treaty 'Neutralization' of Source State Discrimination under the EU Fundamental Freedoms?*, 65(12) Bull. Int'l Tax'n 684, 689 (2011).

structured according to the possible legal constellations that may exist in MSs' tax systems.

There are three main constellations to discuss here. In short, these can be referred to as: (i) the exemption-credit constellation, i.e., where a MS applies the exemption method to dividends paid between domestic companies, whereas it applies the indirect credit method (a credit for the underlying CIT paid by the subsidiary on the profits) to dividends received from foreign companies; (ii) the credit-exemption constellation, i.e., where a MS grants an indirect, or imputation, credit for dividends paid between domestic companies, whereas it exempts dividends received from foreign companies; and (iii) the credit-credit constellation, i.e., where a MS grants an indirect, or imputation, credit for dividends received both from domestic companies and from foreign companies.

The first constellation, an exemption for inter-company distributions in the domestic context and an indirect credit in the cross-border context, gave rise to the most explicit findings from the CJEU case law. If a MS has organized its tax system in this way, then according to the CJEU case law, this is acceptable as the two methods are, in principle, equivalent. However, of course, because the cross-border situation should not be disadvantaged vis-à-vis its comparable domestic counterpart, certain lessons for the indirect credit should be heeded by MSs to maintain this 'equivalence'. First, and most evidently, the MS of residence cannot blatantly apply a higher tax rate to the incoming foreign-source dividends. Although this is evident, what follows from this rule can be more difficult to detect and ensure, namely that the indirect credit cannot inadvertently result in a higher tax burden on the foreign-source dividends as compared to the exempted domestic-source dividends. This will be discussed in the next paragraph. Second, the MS of residence must grant a credit 'equal to' the taxes levied in the other state (*see supra* note 1230). It is contended (at *supra* notes 1232–1233) that this implies that the credit must be granted on a full unit-per-unit (e.g., EUR-per-EUR) basis and cannot, therefore, be a partial credit (e.g., a credit granted for 80% of the foreign taxes, for every EUR paid only 0.80 EUR is credited, as, e.g., under US GILTI rules). Third, however, the MS of residence is permitted to limit the amount of the credit to, maximum, the amount it would levy on the income, such that if the taxes levied by the foreign state are higher, the MS of residence is not required to both reduce the taxes it would levy down to zero *and* repay the difference. In other words, a credit limitation, or MCA, is permitted.

Despite the 'equivalence' in theory, what the CJEU was called upon to notice through a second round of questions in *FII II* were certain differences in the effects of the two methods in practice, which impacts the overall tax burden on the dividends. The exemption method, since no further tax at all is levied on the recipient, leaves only the layer of tax paid at the level of the distributing entity; thus, to the extent the subsidiary paid a lower rate than what its parent company would pay, this benefit is 'passed up' to the parent company. In the end, only this lower rate applies to the profits. The credit method brings the level of taxation up to that which applies to the parent company. The assumption of equivalence was thus based on the idea that the subsidiaries in the domestic context were paying the statutory rate of tax (the same as that which applies to their domestic parents) before passing up their dividends; under this assumption, the credit method applied to foreign dividends tends to equalize the rate applying to the two streams (*see*, e.g., *supra* note 1223, note 1238, note 1249). However, it turns out that, even within one and the same domestic tax system, there can be discrepancies between the statutory tax rate presumed to apply and what the subsidiary actually pays (e.g., due to special tax base rules, etc.). In this case, the exemption has the effect of allowing for an overall lower tax burden on the inter-company dividends in the domestic context, as compared to the credit method in the cross-border context, which will top it up to the statutory rate. The CJEU indicated that, if this is a mere exceptional occurrence, 'equivalence' is not automatically compromised, but if it is a widespread phenomenon, then equivalence becomes compromised. It is in this context that the CJEU's nominal rate proposal arose. Isabella de Groot estimates that 'there will be more Member States than just the United Kingdom where this effective rate is lower than the nominal rate in more than just exceptional circumstances', supported by the empirical evidence she gathered from Eurostat.[1918] Accordingly, to determine how this case law impacts its indirect tax credit, first, a MS must review its domestic tax system to check whether this is the case (i.e., whether the taxes paid at the level of subsidiaries in the domestic tax context diverge from the statutory rate) and how prevalent it is. If it is not the case, the MS may carry on with exemption in the domestic context and the indirect credit in the cross-border context. If it is the case, then in order to maintain equivalence, the MS of residence should adapt. It may: (1) change its tax system, such that domestic subsidiaries are not systematically benefitting from lower rates, which is likely a more comprehensive, potentially much harder, overhaul; (2) consider the CJEU's suggestion of a more proportionate application of the credit method, namely to grant an indirect credit on the basis of the nominal tax rate abroad (instead of the actual taxes paid abroad); (3) extend the exemption to the cross-border context; or (4) apply an indirect/imputation credit to both domestic and cross-border situations.

If the MS follows the CJEU's proposition of an indirect credit based on the nominal rate, the outcome is a form of matching credit – in other words, it is no longer a true credit method, but moves in the direction of a partial exemption (thus, straining the CJEU's 'equivalence' reasoning, as critically discussed at *supra* note 1249). Where the taxes actually paid abroad are lower than the amount estimated on the basis of the nominal foreign tax rate, the result is a form of partial exemption. In these cases, it ensures a bigger credit than taxes actually paid.

Another difference between the exemption method and the indirect credit method that the CJEU eventually examined was that of the effect of foreign-taxed profits on domestic or overall losses. The exemption method is generally neutral in that

1918. Isabella de Groot, *The Switch-Over Provision in the Proposal for an Anti-tax Avoidance Directive and Its Compatibility with the EU Treaty Freedoms*, 25(3) EC Tax Rev. 162, 166 (2016) ('Research from Eurostat shows that the average statutory corporate income tax rate in the Member States during the period 1998–2012 was each year higher than the average "effective average tax rate" (hereinafter: EATR). For example, in 2012 the average EATR was 20.9%, while the average corporate income tax rate was 23%.[20]').

respect, whereas the (indirect) credit method, by including all profits and losses in the tax base wherever derived, leads to a reduction in the LCF and consequently an increased tax liability in future tax periods (*see*, e.g., *supra* note 1252). This again would result in overall higher taxation of the cross-border context over time. To remedy the difference in treatment in such cases, a credit carryforward should be used in order to compensate for any reduction in the LCF (in this way, foreign taxes can be credited in the future against the future increased tax liability), in order to maintain equivalence with the exemption method used in the domestic case.

The second constellation is the reverse one, namely an imputation/indirect credit for inter-company distributions in the domestic context and an exemption in the cross-border context. As held in the *Kronos* case, there are essentially no adaptations that need to be made. According to the CJEU, the situations are not even comparable because, in such a set-up, the MS of residence does not exercise its tax jurisdiction over the FSI at all, whereas it fully taxes the DSI.

However, if the MS in question applies a form of imputation credit in the domestic context, then this MS would additionally have to heed the line of case law on the imputation method (discussed in Section 4.2.8.). The *Kronos* case concentrated only on the moment of the *receipt* of dividends and the treatment of the *recipient* at that moment. 'Imputation' credit systems could give rise to different treatment at a next stage, namely the stage of *re*distribution of dividends. This is the moment when an imputation credit could be attached to the dividends (sometimes referred to as franked dividends), to the benefit of the next recipient, nearly always a domestic shareholder. Sometimes, this is also the moment when a MS may require the (re)distributing entity to pay ACT in proportion to the dividends. What can be learned from the imputation line of case law is that the MS has to ensure that: (1) it does not treat the resident company that is redistributing profits differently on the basis of whether it is redistributing foreign-sourced profits or domestic-sourced profits and (2) it does not suddenly exercise its tax jurisdiction over the foreign-sourced profits at this second stage without also extending some sort of relief to the next recipient. If the MS charges ACT, for example, upon redistribution calculated with reference to the full amount of the profits redistributed, regardless of the underlying foreign or domestic source of the profits, then the MS has effectively brought the foreign-sourced profits (after initially being exempt upon arrival) into its tax jurisdiction upon redistribution and should therefore also extend upward a shareholders credit. Alternatively, upon redistribution, presumably the case law would allow the MS to trace the foreign-sourced portion of the dividends and continue to exempt them each time they are passed upward.

Having discussed the constellations applying *both* methods, another constellation, which the 'equivalence' line to some extent pushes MSs towards, is that of applying the *same* method to both domestic and cross-border cases. The 'equivalence' line of case law seems to encourage this, since a state that applies exclusively the indirect tax credit in both the domestic and cross-border situations is applying literally equivalent (i.e., the same) methods and, thus, would not have to grapple with the above-mentioned lessons stemming from the need to re-equalize (or maintain 'equivalence' between) two different methods. At first glance, it would seem therefore that the

MS could design the indirect credit how it wishes. Yet, applying the October 2018 *Commission v. France* case (C-416/17) by analogy, in connection with the foundations laid by earlier cases such as *Manninen*, some rules should be respected.

First and most evidently, the CJEU's reasoning requires that, where an 'imputation' tax credit – or by extension an indirect credit – is granted in the domestic context, it should be extended to the comparable cross-border context. In other words, more precisely, the constellation cannot be relief in the domestic context and no relief in the cross-border context. This constellation has been struck down numerous times (as seen, e.g., in Section 4.2.8.).

Second, although France argued otherwise (arguing *inter alia* that the credit could be conceived as appertaining to only one distributor-shareholder layer at a time, at *supra* notes 1751 et seq.), the CJEU held that the credit should also be extended to underlying corporate taxes levied on the profits of lower-tier subsidiaries, in order to relieve the possible multiple layers of taxation that compile at each level in a chain of companies. This is necessary if the goal is to ensure that the 'imputation' tax credit for foreign-source dividends is equivalent in effect to the 'imputation' system in the domestic context, which does ensure relief at each level. Although this finding was reached under a case regarding an 'imputation' credit, the same reasoning could be transposed to a situation in which the aim is to achieve equivalence with an exemption method applying to domestic chains of companies (since it, too, offers relief at each level). In other words, both the credit-credit and the exemption-credit constellations of relief for economic double taxation (or a series of charges to tax) should observe this finding. Secondary EU law would agree. Under the Parent-Subsidiary Directive, for the cases that fall under its scope, the EU MSs that opt for the indirect credit method are obliged to grant it to 'the subsidiary and any lower-tier subsidiary'.[1919] So, this design feature applies to cases falling under the Directive and, depending on the scope of relief in the domestic context, may apply to cases that fall outside of the Directive's scope, due to the combination of case law on the fundamental freedoms and on the Directive. Extending one of the general rules applied in *Haribo & Salinen* (elaborated further below at *infra* note 1926), if a MS, under the Parent-Subsidiary Directive, implements an indirect tax credit for dividends from shareholdings of 10% or more in qualifying EU subsidiaries, whereas the MS grants an indirect tax credit (or an exemption) for dividends from shareholdings of *all* sizes (thus, even portfolio holdings, below 10%) in domestic subsidiaries, then it can be argued that, as in *Haribo & Salinen*, to ensure equal treatment, the MS must also extend the indirect credit to shareholdings of less than 10% in qualifying subsidiaries abroad and, as in the 2018 *Commission v. France* case, the credit should extend to taxes paid by sub-tier subsidiaries.

1919. Parent-Subsidiary Directive (Article 4(1)(b) allows the parent state to 'tax such profits while authorising the parent company and the permanent establishment to deduct from the amount of tax due that fraction of the corporation tax related to those profits and paid by the subsidiary and any lower-tier subsidiary, subject to the condition that at each tier a company and its lower-tier subsidiary fall within the definitions laid down in Article 2 and meet the requirements provided for in Article 3, up to the limit of the amount of the corresponding tax due').

Third, in this credit-credit constellation, another question arose as to, in order to remediate the different treatment between the domestic and cross-border situations, what is the amount of the credit that should be extended. One argument could be that, if a credit is fixed at an amount of, e.g., 3/7ths of the dividends in the domestic context, the EU MS should extend the *exact same* amount, i.e., the same 3/7ths, to the cross-border context (an argument that was presented on more than one occasion, e.g., *Meilicke, Accor*). This *literal* equivalence, however, was rejected by the CJEU. This amount, e.g., 3/7ths in the domestic context, was set deliberately so that it corresponded to the 30% CIT paid by the domestic distributing entity. Thus, to truly fulfil the equal treatment obligation, the credit extended to the cross-border context 'must' also correspond to the taxes actually paid. It is rather a functional equivalence, based on the aim of the legislation: since the amount of the credit in the domestic context reflects the actual underlying CIT paid, the amount of the credit in the cross-border context should be based on the same, the actual underlying CIT paid in the other state, as only in that case is it designed to achieve the same aim.

Against this background, EU MSs would be forgiven if there was some confusion as to precisely what is required of them in the case of credits for the underlying taxes, since, at first glance, there seems to be a contradiction between the findings of the case law on the constellation of equivalence-between-exemption-method-and-indirect-credit-method and the findings on extending imputation/indirect credits across the border. Under the case law on the former, one of the findings of the CJEU was that, in some cases, it would be more proportionate for EU MSs to grant a credit based on the nominal tax rate abroad, rather than the taxes actually paid. Under the case law on imputation credits, one of the findings of the CJEU was that the credit *must* be based to the extent possible on the *actual* taxes paid abroad. This divergence could be puzzling; however, as this discussion reveals, the main explanation for this is that the cases on indirect credits were reasoned with the aim of establishing equivalence with an exemption method, a method which itself is not contingent upon the taxes paid abroad. By contrast, the amount of an imputation credit, often granted only in the domestic context, is contingent upon the CIT paid by the domestic entity and, consequently, in extending it across the border, it should likewise carry out this same relief function. Thus, perhaps unsurprisingly, the general rule of thumb is that EU MSs' obligations in designing their relief vary based on the features and effects of the relief it provides in the domestic context. In other words, two EU MSs that would both prefer to grant a credit for the underlying foreign CIT are faced with different design constraints stemming from CJEU case law depending on whether they grant exemptions or credits in their domestic context.

Since the enactment of the ATAD, there is a legal obligation to implement an indirect tax credit under the CFC rules of ATAD I.[1920] The question is whether EU MSs

1920. ATAD I, Article 8(7) ('7.The Member State of the taxpayer shall allow a deduction of the tax paid by the entity or permanent establishment from the tax liability of the taxpayer in its state of tax residence or location. The deduction shall be calculated in accordance with national law').

must design it in line with the findings of the 'equivalence' line and 'imputation' lines of case law.

As seen above, to assess their obligations, MSs have to consider under which of the above constellations their tax system falls: (1) an exemption in the domestic context and an indirect credit in the cross-border context, (2) the reverse, i.e., an indirect credit or imputation credit in the domestic context and an exemption in the cross-border context, (3) the same method in both the domestic context and the cross-border context, either (3a) extending the same form of indirect credit to the cross-border case or (3b) extending the exemption method to the cross-border case. Of these constellations, one effect of the ATAD is that: two of them can no longer fully apply, namely option (2) of an indirect/imputation-credit-and-exemption and option (3b) of exemption-and-exemption. As long as MSs apply CFC rules, exemption for all cross-border cases is no longer possible, as there will always be an indirect credit in the cross-border context for at least some limited cases. Thus, for this question, the exemption-credit and credit-credit constellations will be discussed here.

Under CFC rules, one of the findings under the first constellation could lead to a potentially odd result. Recall that the first constellation (seeking to uphold 'equivalence' between exemption in a domestic context and credits in a cross-border context) entailed a credit carryforward and, in some cases, potentially an indirect credit based on the nominal tax rate in the subsidiary state. A credit carryforward is to be welcome and, as argued above (in Section 4.2.7.), and as implied in the *Kronos* case, is a more coherent solution, whenever LCFs are involved. Indeed, this would be advisable if MSs intend to fully uphold the Directive's aims expressed in the preamble, i.e., that its rules do not lead to new internal market obstacles such as double taxation. As for an indirect credit based on nominal tax rates, this is less welcome: in the new anti-tax-avoidance, anti-BEPS environment, this seems ill-advised (since where it behaves like a 'matching credit', it leads to a partial exemption). To the extent the nominal rate is higher than what was paid abroad, it leaves some non-taxation, thereby undermining one of the BEPS concerns of recapturing lost or shifted tax base and undermining the effectiveness of the rules. Recall, however, that the nominal rate was proposed for a tax system with the particularity that domestic subsidiaries were more-often-than-not subject to lower taxes than their parents. Thus, technically, EU MSs have to undertake an assessment of their national tax systems to verify whether this is the case. If it is, it could be argued that those EU MSs may have to ensure the 'equivalence' of their CFC credit rules with their existing exemption regimes, by allowing a calculation based on the nominal tax rate in the CFC state.

However, this nominal rate dilemma can potentially be avoided if the CJEU applies a different analysis to measures that counteract BEPS or 'wholly artificial arrangements'.[1921] This is a reasonable possibility.[1922] The CJEU often forms its judgments in light of the purpose of the rules in question. While these 'equivalence'

1921. For the term 'wholly artificial arrangements', *see* the seminal case CJEU, Case C-196/04, *Cadbury Schweppes and Cadbury Schweppes Overseas*, 12 Sep. 2006, ECLI:EU:C:2006:544, at paras 51, 55, 61–70. *See also* CJEU, Case C-135/17, *X GmbH*, 26 Feb. 2019, ECLI:EU:C:2019:136, at paras 73, 80–84 (while the CJEU analysed the requirements to qualify as a 'wholly

cases examined rules more broadly aimed at the elimination of economic double taxation (or a series of charges to tax) on dividends, CFC rules comprise a different objective, which may call for the outcome to be adapted accordingly. They are more in the nature of targeted anti-diversion rules, with the aim to recapture certain mobile or 'tainted' income to the extent it has been improperly diverted from the state of the shareholder to a low-taxed state, as exemplified by the design options under the ATAD[1923] and as exemplified by CFC rules in the UK and in Germany analysed by the

artificial arrangement' in the context of the freedom of establishment in the *Cadbury Schweppes* case, in the *X GmbH* the CJEU analysed the requirements in the context of the free movement of capital).

1922. *See*, e.g., Isabella de Groot, *The Switch-Over Provision in the Proposal for an Anti-tax Avoidance Directive and Its Compatibility with the EU Treaty Freedoms*, 25(3) EC Tax Rev. 162 (2016) (in her article, de Groot convincingly argues that the 'equivalence' line of case law would be generally transposable to a switch-over clause – from exemption to an indirect credit – for dividends received by a taxpayer, designed to apply if its subsidiary were taxed below a certain threshold – in particular, taking the initial ATAD proposal (cited at *supra* note 43) for a switch-over clause as her object of study; she implied that one possible exception to the 'equivalence' case law requirements would be if the measure, rather than being broadly formulated to be triggered merely in cases of low taxation, were more narrowly formulated to tackle 'wholly artificial arrangements'). De Groot's argumentation that applies to the switch-over clause would seem to apply *a fortiori* to CFC measures. CFC rules could be approximated to a switch-over clause, in that they, in effect, amount to switching from a situation where the income is 'exempted' (to be precise, exempted in effect, but technically not by virtue of an exemption method per se but rather by virtue of the separate tax jurisdictions and separate legal personality of the subsidiary in question, that deem it a distinct resident taxpayer of another tax jurisdiction) to the credit method. A question to that effect was put forward in the *Cadbury Schweppes* case. *See Cadbury Schweppes* case, *supra* note 1921, at para. 25 ('Should that legislation be viewed as involving a restriction on the freedoms enshrined by the Treaty, the national court asks, thirdly, whether the fact that CS may pay no more tax than what CSTS and CSTI would have paid if they had been established in the United Kingdom means that there is no such restriction'). As compared to a switch-over clause that applies in the case of dividend distributions, the key operational difference is the timing: this switch-over clause applies only upon receipt of dividends, whereas the CFC rules apply immediately, by attributing the income to the shareholder on an ongoing or annual basis irrespective of any distribution. Indeed, it is precisely this aspect that the CJEU highlighted as the key contributor to the restrictive or disadvantageous nature of CFC rules. *See Cadbury Schweppes* case, *supra* note 1921, at para. 45; *X-GmbH* case, *supra* note 1921, at paras 56–57. In this way, the CJEU gave deference to the separate entity status, which would otherwise be fully respected, if not for the CFC rules. Alternatively, CFC rules could be approximated to a switch-over clause in the case of a PE abroad in certain respects. On the one hand, they may be conceived as anti-deferral rules, which in effect would treat a CFC abroad similar to a PE abroad. However, on the other hand, they are often conceived as anti-diversion rules; this tends to be the stronger motivation underlying the rules, as was shown in the two examples of CFC rules in the UK and in Germany analysed by the CJEU. *See infra* note 1924. To compare and contrast the two further, it can be observed that, in the case of a standard PE abroad, i.e., assuming no avoidance issues, there is the assumption that the income is legitimately earned in the PE state and, as it is therefore foreign-source income, either the credit method or the exemption method – both 'equivalent' – may apply to provide relief for double taxation, whereas, in the case of CFC rules, the idea is that the income was not truly earned in the other state, but rather was artificially diverted from the taxpayer's state to the subsidiary's state and deliberately quarantined within the legal form of a subsidiary precisely in order to exploit the legal fiction according to which states treat subsidiaries as separate taxpayers, compelling them to refrain from exercising their tax jurisdiction over it.

1923. ATAD I, preamble recital 12 and Article 7(2)(a) 2nd sentence (in particular, for CFCs in other EU MSs, the rules are even more narrowly targeted, by virtue of an exclusion if the CFC

CJEU.[1924] To the extent the design of the rules is aligned with this objective, this would make a partial exemption unfitting or potentially counterproductive. Rather, both the preamble and the articles of the ATAD on the CFC rules call for a more precise targeted exercise - that is, MSs should be as precise as possible as regards the income that is intended to be recaptured and as regards the relief (as according to the wording, they '*shall* allow a deduction of the tax *paid*', i.e., thus, actually paid, not nominally payable, by the CFC).[1925]

Similar issues do not arise under the constellation of some form of indirect credit in both domestic and cross-border cases. According to the main findings, the MS 'must' base the credit on the actual underlying CIT paid (thereby rejecting the argument to extend the *same* amount as in the domestic context, which in the cross-border context would result in a form of notional credit unrelated to either the tax paid or the tax rate in the other state and, thus, disconnected from the aim and effect of eliminating economic double taxation that it achieves in the domestic context). Adhering to this finding would be in line with both the aims and wording of the ATAD. As mentioned above, in connection with the 2018 *Commission v. France* case, the tax credit should also cover taxes paid by lower-tier subsidiaries.

On this latter point, one rather conspicuous gap left open by the ATAD is the question of multiple layers of taxes resulting from taxes paid by lower-tier subsidiaries. While this is addressed in the Parent-Subsidiary Directive, the ATAD does not *explicitly* address this, not even in Article 8 on the indirect credit under the CFC rules (as mentioned at *supra* note 1881). However, it seems unlikely that it would be compatible for MSs to passively accept this oversight and therefore ignore this issue; rather, rules for regulating what happens in the case of taxes paid by lower-tier CFCs should also be

'carries on a substantive economic activity supported by staff, equipment, assets and premises, as evidenced by relevant facts and circumstances').

1924. CJEU, Case C-196/04, *Cadbury Schweppes and Cadbury Schweppes Overseas*, 12 Sep. 2006, ECLI:EU:C:2006:544, at para. 26 ('... given its objective to prevent the reduction or diversion of profits liable to United Kingdom tax'); CJEU, Case C-135/17, *X GmbH*, 26 Feb. 2019, ECLI:EU:C:2019:136, at para. 65 and at para. 67 ('In that regard, according to the referring court's explanations, the objective of the legislation at issue in the main proceedings is "to prevent or offset the transfer of (passive) income of persons with unlimited tax liability to States with a low tax rate". According to the German Government, that legislation is also designed to prevent tax avoidance by the artificial transfer of income to third countries which have a low tax rate.' Another aim of the rules, according to the Advocate General and cited by the CJEU, was similar to the equal treatment rationale that sometimes is invoked for the credit method: 'However, as observed by the Advocate General in point 71 of his Opinion, the purpose of the legislation at issue in the main proceedings is, so far as possible, to treat the situation of resident companies which have invested capital in a company established in a third country with a "low" tax rate in the same way as that of resident companies which have invested their capital in another company resident in Germany, with a view, inter alia, to offsetting any tax advantages which the former might obtain from investing their capital in a third country').

1925. ATAD I, preamble recital 12 ('In particular, in order to ensure that CFC rules are a proportionate response to BEPS concerns, it is critical that Member States that limit their CFC rules to income which has been artificially diverted to the subsidiary precisely target situations where most of the decision-making functions which generated diverted income at the level of the controlled subsidiary are carried out in the Member State of the taxpayer') and Article 8(7).

specified when implementing the ATAD's CFC rules. There are grounds to support this not only on the basis of the aforementioned case law, but also on the basis of the recommendations under Action 3 (cited at *supra* note 1882), since the ATAD purports to be 'consistent' with the BEPS Actions (as expressed in recitals 1 and 2 in the preamble), and on the basis of the aim to eliminate 'double taxation' under the Directive (as expressed both in recital 5 of the preamble and in the substantive provisions of Article 8(5), (6) and (7) of the CFC rules).

Another question that takes on particular importance in designing credits for underlying CIT is that of the ownership requirements. This affects the personal scope of taxpayers eligible for the credit, based on whether they hold a sufficient level of ownership in a given entity. On this question, there are two sources of EU law indications. First, the Directives that grant an indirect credit stipulate ownership requirements rather comprehensively. The Parent-Subsidiary Directive, for instance, currently stipulates: regarding the type of shareholder, a corporate shareholder that is a 'parent company', as defined by Article 3, and, regarding the threshold of ownership, a minimum of a 10% holding. Second, the CJEU has pronounced itself on questions of ownership requirements (as discussed in Section 4.2.9.). The CJEU has held that, in principle, the MSs are free to establish the 'category of taxpayers' and the levels of ownership required to benefit from an indirect credit. However, in doing so, it must respect the fundamental freedoms.[1926] Thus, the tax treatment that applies to the comparable cross-border context cannot be worse than the tax treatment that applies to the domestic context. As regards 'comparable', with respect to the need for relief for economic double taxation, recipients are in a comparable situation regardless of whether they earn dividends from domestic sources or from abroad, in so far as both streams of dividends stem from profits that have been taxed already at the level of the subsidiary. Consequently, the crux of any given MS's obligation, therefore, revolves around what system, if any, is in place in the domestic context. As seen in *Haribo & Salinen*, because Austria granted an exemption for dividends in the domestic context for *all percentages* of ownership, it could not then require a higher 10% threshold of ownership in order to benefit from relief in the cross-border context.[1927] Moreover, the Directives cannot shield a MS in this respect. A MS cannot rely on the existence of the 10% threshold in the Parent-Subsidiary Directive in order to justify requiring a 10% threshold for cross-border contexts if the MS does not have any threshold in the domestic context.[1928] Both national laws and the transposition of Directives into national laws pay heed to the higher ranking fundamental freedoms. In this way, any ownership thresholds established in the domestic context essentially dictate the design of the indirect credit that would apply in the cross-border context. Given this general rule, what this means is that, only in the circumstance that a MS offers *no* relief for

1926. CJEU, Joined Cases C-436/08 and C-437/08, *Haribo Lakritzen Hans Riegel BetriebsgmbH and Österreichische Salinen AG*, 10 Feb. 2011, ECLI:EU:C:2011:61, at para. 142.
1927. *Id.*, at paras 109–111.
1928. *See*, e.g., CJEU, Case C-446/04, *Test Claimants in the FII Group Litigation*, 12 Dec. 2006, ECLI:EU:C:2006:774, at paras 66–69; CJEU, Case C-379/05, *Amurta*, 8 Nov. 2007, ECLI:EU:C:2007:655, at paras 20–28.

economic double taxation of dividends in the domestic context, is it fully free in its design in the cross-border context. For this reason, given the unlikelihood of a complete lack of any relief in the domestic context, it is highly likely that a MS's system will be influenced to some degree by this case law.

Despite the numerous cases referred to the CJEU on credits for underlying CIT (both imputation and indirect) in the 'equivalence' and 'imputation' lines, certain aspects or details of the credit method have not been expressly examined by the CJEU. The above discussion (on the ownership issues) offers an example of the way in which MSs will have to proceed in filling in some of the gaps left open by the case law as regards the various design components of the credit method: in some cases, the Directives shape part of the answers and, in all cases, MSs have to derive the contours of what is permissible based on any reoccurring themes in the reasoning of the CJEU (e.g., credit method cases were often prone to reasoning based on notions of *subject-to-tax* or *same-taxation-same-relief*) and any general rules or principles that can be inferred from its more settled case law.

To offer one final important illustration of this, take, for example, the fact that the MSs must determine the precise procedures to put in place, as well as the rules for calculating the credit, in particular the figure that should be used for the FSI. In fact, in the case of CFC rules, the Directive explicitly states that the credit 'shall be calculated in accordance with national law' (under Article 8(7) ATAD). This statement may seem to definitively answer this question, thus leaving MSs fully free in how this is determined; yet, as seen repeatedly above, the national law itself is subject to the fundamental freedoms of the TFEU, and Directives do not constitute a carte blanche escape from their obligations. Thus, are there any further lessons that can be derived indirectly from the CJEU's case law on this crucial question?

As discussed above (in Section 5.2.), on a few occasions the CJEU has been confronted with cases regarding the procedural requirements for the credit method. Although it is relevant for both the direct and indirect credits, the issue has arisen predominantly under cases regarding indirect or imputation credit systems. The overarching principles governing this are the principle of procedural autonomy versus the principles of equivalence and effectiveness (*see*, e.g., *supra* note 1732). Sometimes there is a clash between equivalence, e.g., extending the exact same procedural requirements as in the domestic case to the cross-border one, and effectiveness, e.g., enabling access to the EU-law-granted rights to the credit. This is because to the extent that the requirements in the domestic context would be too difficult to fulfil in the cross-border context, too literal an application of *equivalence* as regards the *procedure* may impede *effectiveness* as regards the *substantive* right.

Also, as mentioned (in Section 5.2.), the CJEU has held that it is not a violation of free movement rights to require the taxpayer to provide the information needed to obtain a tax benefit such as an FTC. In fact, the information must be such that the MS is able to ascertain *precisely* the amount of taxes paid abroad for the credit. However, the MS cannot require a strict adherence to exact forms and narrowly construe the types of evidence to be provided, or ask for evidence and information that is not available under the legal system of another MS. A MS cannot insist on one specific format, in an overly formalistic way. In other words, the precise forms and types of evidence are less relevant than the quality and relevance of the information for the credit calculation. Having reiterated these general principles from the CJEU's case law on the procedural topic, the discussion can now explore the interaction with substantive calculation question.

As the historical developments revealed (in Chapter 2), one of the most fraught questions was the calculation of FSI for the purposes of the credit, in particular for the apportionment fraction. There were debates as to whether the figure should be based on the sums as calculated under the law of the subsidiary's state (e.g., since this alignment could better ensure that more of the eligible foreign taxes could be credited, arguably better in line with the aim of relief for double taxation) or whether the figure should be based on the sums as calculated under the law of the shareholder's state that grants the credit (e.g., since this is more in line with one of the often-cited aims of the credit method to ensure the equal treatment of residents). Even if it were decided that the figure should be based on the laws of the credit-granting state, this still leaves open different possibilities, such as whether the income earned by the subsidiary should be recalculated in line with local accounting rules or whether the income should be recalculated in line with the rules defining taxable income in the credit-granting state or whether the income should be recalculated in line with rules that determine the profits legally available for distribution (similar to the idea of the 'earnings and profits' figure used in the US). For this reason, even if the ATAD gives part of the answer – in that it repeatedly specifies that 'the rules of the Member State of the taxpayer' govern the computations[1929] – MSs still may have some constraints.

Some constraints stem from the aforementioned principles governing the procedure. To some extent, MSs remain stuck 'between a rock and a hard place', so to speak, because if the process for claiming the credit requires the application of the *exact* same rules for calculations as in the domestic context, in what circumstances does this go too far as to become 'excessive', such that equivalence is impeding effectiveness. The CJEU has dodged this crucial question on a few occasions. For example, in the *Meilicke* case[1930] (discussed at *supra* note 1784), the rules in Germany for granting the credit required a certificate that had to include the taxes paid abroad, among other things, and in particular had to include information regarding the 'composition' of the dividends. The reason for requesting this information was, essentially, in order to apply the same rules as in the German context, namely that, within Germany, a credit would be granted for distributions, provided that they had been distributed out of 'parts of the capital and reserves' deemed legally 'available for distribution'. Such 'composition'

1929. ATAD I, Article 7(1) 2nd sentence ('Furthermore the corporate tax that would have been charged in the Member State of the taxpayer means as computed according to the rules of the Member State of the taxpayer'); Article 7(3) ('Where, under the rules of a Member State, the tax base of a taxpayer is calculated according to point (a) [...]'); Article 8(1) ('[...] the income to be included in the tax base of the taxpayer shall be calculated in accordance with the rules of the corporate tax law of the Member State where the taxpayer is resident for tax purposes or situated [...]'); Article 8(7) ('The deduction shall be calculated in accordance with national law').

1930. CJEU, Case C-262/09, *Meilicke*, 30 Jun. 2011, ECLI:EU:C:2011:438.

rules do not appear to be so different from the computation rules in the US that require recalculating the foreign subsidiary's income in line with its domestic rules for 'earnings and profits', which are also related to determining the amounts available for distribution as dividends, and, similar to in the German context, some scholars complained of the complexities in undertaking such recalculations (*see*, e.g., *supra* notes 337–347, notes 349–350, notes 363–365). The taxpayer complained that it was 'impossible' to maintain such 'composition' information for foreign subsidiaries. However, the CJEU did not directly respond to this 'composition' question, as to whether it would be acceptable to require such information. It merely reiterated the broader principles and mentioned that the 'tax authorities of a Member State are entitled to require the taxpayer to provide such proof as they may consider necessary in order to determine whether the conditions for a tax advantage provided for in the legislation at issue have been met' and can request the information needed to ascertain precisely 'the reality and nature of tax deductions made in other Member States'.[1931]

Related questions arose in a case regarding CFC rules, namely the *Cadbury Schweppes* case, where the 'national court states that it is faced with a series of uncertainties as to the application of Community law to the case before it',[1932] including:

> '[The UK Court] also asks whether it is relevant that on the one hand there are differences in some respects between the rules for calculating the tax liability in respect of the income of CSTS and CSTI [the foreign subsidiaries in question] and the ordinary rules applicable to United Kingdom subsidiaries of CS and on the other the fact that losses of a CFC cannot be deducted from the profits of another CFC or from the profits of CS and its United Kingdom subsidiaries, whereas such a deduction would have been available if CSTS and CSTI had been established in the United Kingdom.'[1933]

The phrasing of the UK Court's question suggests its view that, from the perspective of the state of residence of the taxpayer, the non-discrimination principle would require that the rules for calculations in the cross-border context should be the same as those that apply for residents in the domestic context, yet it wonders to what extent certain deviations are appropriate. In its decision, the CJEU entirely neglected to respond to this uncertainty.

The closest the CJEU came to providing a response was in a case regarding the calculation of losses generated abroad, for the purposes of taking them into account in the state of residence. Both profits and losses give rise to similar concerns in this respect.[1934] In the *A Oy* case, the AG was clear in her view that the losses 'must *in*

1931. *Id.*, at paras 44–45.
1932. CJEU, Case C-196/04, *Cadbury Schweppes and Cadbury Schweppes Overseas*, 12 Sep. 2006, ECLI:EU:C:2006:544, at para. 22.
1933. *Id.*, at para. 25.
1934. Michael Lang, *Has the Case Law of the ECJ on Final Losses Reached the End of the Line?*, 54(12) Eur. Tax'n 530, 535 (2014) ('The ECJ regularly refers to the "losses" suffered by the foreign company or foreign PE as such, which must be taken into account under certain circumstances. Thus, the ECJ is acting as if these losses had a clear predefined value. The amount of a loss, however – just as that of a profit – is merely the result of an arithmetic operation. This

principle be calculated according to the tax law of the receiving company's State of residence'.[1935] According to the decision of the CJEU:

> 'The rules for calculating the non-resident subsidiary's losses for the purpose of their being taken over by the resident parent company, in an operation such as that at issue in the main proceedings, must not constitute unequal treatment compared with the rules of calculation which would be applicable if the merger were with a resident subsidiary.'[1936]

As Lang observes, the CJEU expresses a preference for this 'discrimination approach' but yet in other parts of its reasoning, the CJEU equivocates, thereby leaving some room for doubts as to when there may be compromises in applying the rules of the state of residence.[1937]

The persistent reoccurrence of this question, both throughout the historical developments in Chapter 2 and in the cases before the CJEU, illustrates its importance and, with the implementation of the ATAD, among other recent developments to recapture 'lost' or shifted tax bases, the question seems bound to confront the CJEU yet again in future cases. In the meantime, MSs must already grapple with it and, from the sparse guidance that can be garnered, based on the clear wording of the ATAD in connection with the, albeit more vaguely endorsed, principled approach embedded in the credit-granting state's non-discrimination obligation, it is safe to assume that MSs should require computations in accordance with their national laws, in the same way as for residents, and that they may oblige taxpayers to provide precise information so as to ascertain the amount of the credit; the only clear limits on this appear to be that the credit cannot be refused on grounds of mere formalities (e.g., where a taxpayer cannot present the information in the exact way obliged on a given form) and cannot be refused where the information requested proves impossible to obtain in the other state. Given that it is information at stake, other recent developments may also play a role. On the one hand, the scope for arguments based on impossibilities to obtain information or match records for reporting obligations may be increasingly constricted in the future (as, e.g., *X-GmbH* indicates) given the rapid legal developments in extending the scope of the exchange of information and mutual assistance, legal developments on reporting and disclosure rules, and possibly also technological

---

result will depend on the respective relevant provisions defining what is taxable at all and how the assessment is to be addressed, as well as which deductions will be taken into account in which period. The profits and losses established for tax law purposes may, therefore, considerably differ from those determined, for instance, under corporate, social or other provisions of different jurisdictions. A loss is never a factual value but depends on the relevant provisions of positive law. Since the tax assessment basis is not harmonized within the European Union, the amount of a loss from the same economic activity can be completely different depending on the applicable legislation. What may appear as a loss under one piece of legislation may even prove to be a profit according to another. The reasoning given by the ECJ for its case law on final losses does not make it easier to answer the question as to whether the tax law of the residence state or that of the source state applies').

1935. Opinion of AG Kokott in Case C-123/11, *A Oy*, 19 Jul. 2012, ECLI:EU:C:2012:488, at para. 73.

1936. CJEU, Case C-123/11, *A Oy*, 21 Feb. 2013, ECLI:EU:C:2013:84.

1937. Michael Lang, *Has the Case Law of the ECJ on Final Losses Reached the End of the Line?*, 54(12) Eur. Tax'n 530, 535–536 (2014).

solutions. On the other hand, on a cautiously optimistic note, it is hoped that such developments, once properly functioning, could render these credit method procedures more precise and efficient, hopefully for taxpayers and tax administrations alike.

As can be seen from the findings presented in this chapter, there was a wide range of results. In some cases, the guidance that can be derived from the CJEU's case law is very precise; in others, it is much broader. Some aspects of the credit method have been scrutinized by the CJEU, while others have not been explicitly addressed by its case law at all. This variation serves as a reminder of the limitations of the process of 'negative integration' on the basis of the fundamental freedoms. This process merely closes some doors or legal avenues (namely, those found incompatible with EU law) while leaving others either partially or wide open. For this reason, this research project sought to address the challenges that EU MSs themselves face when trying to ascertain how to adapt their tax systems to the CJEU's pronouncements. Thus, the aim was to detect where these EU law boundaries lie, no matter how precise or how wide, when designing and applying the credit method.

In sum, as presented in Chapter 1, relevant recent developments such as the ATAD have implications for the credit method in the EU. In some cases, it becomes a legal obligation. In other cases, it simply becomes one of the inevitable recourses to which MSs will have to turn in situations where they seek to 'recapture' parts of the tax base without creating double taxation. Historically, as outlined in Chapter 2, it was double taxation that was brought to centre stage by phenomena ranging from the desire for deeper regional integration or for increased international trade to calamitous and costly wars. The credit method and the exemption method eventually surfaced as the prevailing responses to offer relief for double taxation. Generally speaking, as detailed in Section 4.1., the exemption method has been the preferred approach in the EU. More recently, as Chapter 3 demonstrated in a longitudinal study of EU Directives, the legislative focus in the EU has expanded from one on eliminating barriers to the internal market, such as double taxation, to one on combating double non-taxation, BEPS and tax evasion, which, it is feared, threaten to fragment and undermine the internal market. Thus, despite the relative lack of popularity of the credit method in the EU, the credit method may now be reinforced as a relevant tool in this context where concerns over both double taxation and double non-taxation abound,[1938] as it has the potential to address both sides of this coin, newly minted (or at least now more widely circulated) by the OECD and EU, potentially increasing its appeal or perhaps its begrudging use. For this reason, Chapter 2 studied historical reports on the credit method and its key legislative developments, in order to define this relief mechanism and distinguish its main components, as these constitute the design features that legislators of EU MSs may have to adapt or implement. After Chapter 3 established that the leading influence shaping MSs' EU law obligations in the field of direct taxation stems from the case law of the CJEU on the fundamental freedoms, Chapter 4 thoroughly examined this prodigious and growing source of EU law. In doing so, it

1938. For a comprehensive analysis of double non-taxation in the EU context, *see* Christoph Marchgraber, *Double (Non-)Taxation and EU Law* (Kluwer Law International 2017).

analysed the compatibility of and the constraints on the credit method, and, in particular, its design components, under EU law. Finally, as summarized here in Chapter 5, this book derived the relevant legal findings and lessons for MSs that can guide the design of both the direct and indirect credit method in line with the fundamental freedoms of EU law. Overall, the aim was to offer this first comprehensive study of constraints on the design of the credit method, in order to provide a basic analytical framework, to lay foundations for future research, and to support MSs in their current balancing act of implementing the anti-BEPS and double non-taxation measures, while aiming to avoid double taxation.

Table of Cases

Case Law

(organized in chronological order)

SERIES ON INTERNATIONAL TAXATION

1. Alberto Xavier, *The Taxation of Foreign Investment in Brazil*, 1980 (ISBN 90-200-0582-0).
2. Hugh J. Ault & Albert J. Rädler, *The German Corporation Tax Law with 1980 Amendments*, 1981 (ISBN 90-200-0642-8).
3. Paul R. McDaniel & Hugh J. Ault, *Introduction to United States International Taxation*, 1981 (ISBN 90-6544-004-6).
4. Albert J. Rädler, *German Transfer Pricing/Prix de Transfer en Allemagne*, 1984 (ISBN 90-6544-143-3).
5. Paul R. McDaniel & Stanley S. Surrey, *International Aspects of Tax Expenditures: A Comparative Study*, 1985 (ISBN 90-654-4163-8).
6. Kees van Raad, *Nondiscrimination in International Tax Law*, 1986 (ISBN 90-6544-266-9).
7. Sijbren Cnossen (ed.), *Tax Coordination in the European Community*, 1987 (ISBN 90-6544-272-3).
8. Ben Terra, *Sales Taxation. The Case of Value Added Tax in the European Community*, 1989 (ISBN 90-6544-381-9).
9. Rutsel S.J. Martha, *The Jurisdiction to Tax in International Law: Theory and Practice of Legislative Fiscal Jurisdiction*, 1989 (ISBN 90-654-4416-5).
10. Paul R. McDaniel & Hugh J. Ault, *Introduction to United States International Taxation* (3rd revised edition), 1989 (ISBN 90-6544-423-8).
11. Manuel Pires, *International Juridicial Double Taxation of Income*, 1989 (ISBN 90-6544-426-2).
12. A.H.M. Daniels, *Issues in International Partnership Taxation*, 1991 (ISBN 90-654-4577-3).
13. Arvid A. Skaar, *Permanent Establishment: Erosion of a Tax Treaty Principle*, 1992 (ISBN 90-6544-594-3).
14. Cyrille David & Geerten M.M. Michielse (eds), *Tax Treatment of Financial Instruments*, 1996 (ISBN 90-654-4666-4).
15. Herbert H. Alpert & Kees van Raad (eds), *Essays on International Taxation*, 1993 (ISBN 90-654-4781-4).
16. Wolfgang Gassner, Michael Lang & Eduard Lechner (eds), *Tax Treaties and EC Law*, 1997 (ISBN 90-411-0680-4).
17. Glória Teixeira, *Taxing Corporate Profits in the EU*, 1997 (ISBN 90-411-0703-7).
18. Michael Lang et al. (eds), *Multilateral Tax Treaties*, 1998 (ISBN 90-411-0704-5).
19. Stef van Weeghel, *The Improper Use of Tax Treaties*, 1998 (ISBN 90-411-0737-1).

20. Klaus Vogel (ed.), *Interpretation of Tax Law and Treaties and Transfer Pricing in Japan and Germany,* 1998 (ISBN 90-411-9655-2).
21. Bertil Wiman (ed.), *International Studies in Taxation: Law and Economics; Liber Amicorum Leif Mutén,* 1999 (ISBN 90-411-9692-7).
22. Alfonso J. Martín Jiménez, *Towards Corporate Tax Harmonization in the European Community,* 1999 (ISBN 90-411-9690-0).
23. Ramon J. Jeffery, *The Impact of State Sovereignty on Global Trade and International Taxation,* 1999 (ISBN 90-411-9703-6).
24. A.J. Easson, *Taxation of Foreign Direct Investment,* 1999 (ISBN 90-411-9741-9).
25. Marjaana Helminen, *The Dividend Concept in International Tax Law: Dividend Payments Between Corporate Entities,* 1999 (ISBN 90-411-9765-6).
26. Paul Kirchhof, Moris Lehner, Kees van Raad, Arndt Raupach & Michael-Rodi (eds), *International and Comparative Taxation: Essays in Honour of Klaus Vogel,* 2002 (ISBN 90-411-9841-5).
27. Krister Andersson, Peter Melz & Christer Silfverberg (eds), *Liber Amicorum Sven-Olof Lodin,* 2001 (ISBN 90-411-9850-4).
28. Juan Martín Jovanovich, *Customs Valuation and Transfer Pricing: Is It Possible to Harmonize Customs and Tax Rules?,* Second Edition, 2018 (ISBN 978-90-411-6134-5).
29. Stefano Simontacchi, *Taxation of Capital Gains under the OECD Model Convention: With Special Regard to Immovable Property,* 2007 (ISBN 978-90-411-2549-1).
30. Michael Lang, Josef Schuch, & Claus Staringer (eds), *Tax Treaty Law and EC Law,* 2007 (ISBN 978-90-411-2629-0).
31. Duncan Bentley, *Taxpayers' Rights: Theory Origin and Implementation,* 2007 (ISBN 978-90-411-2650-4).
32. Sergio André Rocha, *Interpretation of Double Taxation Conventions: General Theory and Brazilian Perspective,* 2008 (ISBN 978-90-411-2822-5).
33. Robert F. van Brederode, *Systems of General Sales Taxation: Theory, Policy and Practice,* 2009 (ISBN 978-90-411-2832-4).
34. John G. Head & Richard Krever (eds), *Tax Reform in the 21st Century: A Volume in Memory of Richard Musgrave,* 2009 (ISBN 978-90-411-2829-4).
35. Jens Wittendorff, *Transfer Pricing and the Arm's Length Principle in International Tax Law,* 2010 (ISBN 978-90-411-3270-3).
36. Marjaana Helminen, *The International Tax Law Concept of Dividend,* Second Edition, 2017 (ISBN 978-90-411-8394-1).
37. Robert F. van Brederode (ed.), *Immovable Property under VAT: A Comparative Global Analysis,* 2011 (ISBN 978-90-411-3126-3).
38. Dennis Weber & Stef van Weeghel, *The 2010 OECD Updates: Model Tax Convention & Transfer Pricing Guidelines - A Critical Review,* 2011 (ISBN 978-90-411-3812-5).
39. Yariv Brauner & Martin James McMahon, Jr. (eds), *The Proper Tax Base: Structural Fairness from an International and Comparative Perspective— Essays in Honour of Paul McDaniel,* 2012 (ISBN 978-90-411-3286-4).
40. Robert F. van Brederode (ed.), *Science, Technology and Taxation,* 2012 (ISBN 978-90-411-3125-6).

41. Oskar Henkow, *The VAT/GST Treatment of Public Bodies*, 2013 (ISBN 978-90-411-4663-2).
42. Jean Schaffner, *How Fixed Is a Permanent Establishment?*, 2013 (ISBN 978-90-411-4662-5).
43. Miguel Correia, *Taxation of Corporate Groups*, 2013 (ISBN 978-90-411-4841-4).
44. Veronika Daurer, *Tax Treaties and Developing Countries*, 2014 (ISBN 978-90-411-4982-4).
45. Claire Micheau, *State Aid, Subsidy and Tax Incentives under EU and WTO Law*, 2014 (ISBN 978-90-411-4555-0).
46. Robert F. van Brederode & Richard Krever (eds), *Legal Interpretation of Tax Law*, 2014 (ISBN 978-90-411-4945-9).
47. Radhakishan Rawal, *Taxation of Cross-border Services*, 2014 (ISBN 978-90-411-4947-3).
48. João Dácio Rolim, *Proportionality and Fair Taxation*, 2014 (ISBN 978-90-411-5838-3).
49. Paulo Rosenblatt, *General Anti-avoidance Rules for Major Developing Countries*, 2015 (ISBN 978-90-411-5839-0).
50. Gaspar Lopes Dias V.S., *Tax Arbitrage through Cross-Border Financial Engineering*, 2015 (ISBN 978-90-411-5875-8).
51. Geerten M.M. Michielse & Victor Thuronyi (eds), *Tax Design Issues Worldwide*, 2015 (ISBN 978-90-411-5610-5).
52. Oktavia Weidmann, *Taxation of Derivatives*, 2015 (ISBN 978-90-411-5977-9).
53. Chris Evans, Richard Krever & Peter Mellor (eds), *Tax Simplification*, 2015 (ISBN 978-90-411-5976-2).
54. Reuven Avi-Yonah & Joel Slemrod (eds), *Taxation and Migration*, 2015 (ISBN 978-90-411-6136-9).
55. Alexander Bosman, *Other Income under Tax Treaties: An Analysis of Article 21 of the OECD Model Convention*, 2015 (ISBN 978-90-411-6610-4).
56. John Abrahamson, *International Taxation of Manufacturing and Distribution*, 2016 (ISBN 978-90-411-6664-7).
57. Frederik Boulogne, *Shortcomings in the EU Merger Directive*, 2016 (ISBN 978-90-411-6713-2).
58. Angelika Meindl-Ringler, *Beneficial Ownership in International Tax Law*, 2016 (ISBN 978-90-411-6833-7).
59. Andreas Waltrich, *Cross-Border Taxation of Permanent Establishments: An International Comparison*, 2016 (ISBN 978-90-411-6832-0).
60. Sergio André Rocha & Allison Christians (eds), *Tax Sovereignty in the BEPS Era*, 2017 (ISBN 978-90-411-6707-1).
61. Peter Antony Wilson, *BRICS and International Tax Law*, 2018 (ISBN 978-90-411-9435-0).
62. Louise Otis, Brigitte Alepin & Blanca Moreno-Dodson (eds), *Winning the Tax Wars: Tax Competition and Cooperation*, 2018 (ISBN 978-90-411-9460-2).
63. Marta Castelon, *International Taxation of Income from Services under Double Taxation Conventions: Development, Practice and Policy*, 2018 (ISBN 978-90-411-9594-4).

64. D.M. Broekhuijsen, *A Multilateral Tax Treaty: Designing an Instrument to Modernise International Tax Law*, 2018 (ISBN 978-90-411-9872-3).
65. John Abrahamson, *International Taxation of Energy Production and Distribution*, 2018 (ISBN 978-90-411-9101-4).
66. Leopoldo Parada, *Double Non-taxation and the Use of Hybrid Entities: An Alternative Approach in the New Era of BEPS*, 2018 (ISBN 978-90-411-9991-1).
67. Richard Snoeij, *International Tax Aspects of Sovereign Wealth Investors: A Source State Perspective*, 2018 (ISBN 978-90-411-9431-2).
68. Aleksandra Bal, *Taxation, Virtual Currency and Blockchain*, 2019 (ISBN 978-94-035-0103-1).
69. Werner Haslehner, Georg Kofler, Katerina Pantazatou & Alexander Rust (eds), *Tax and the Digital Economy: Challenges and Proposals for Reform*, 2019 (ISBN 978-94-035-0361-5).
70. Eva Escribano, *Jurisdiction to Tax Corporate Income Pursuant to the Presumptive Benefit Principle: A Critical Analysis of Structural Paradigms Underlying Corporate Income Taxation and Proposals for Reform*, 2019 (ISBN 978-94-035-0640-1).
71. Jérôme Monsenego & Jan Bjuvberg (eds), *International Taxation in a Changing Landscape: Liber Amicorum in Honour of Bertil Wiman*, 2019 (ISBN 978-90-411-9234-9).
72. Kasper Dziurdź, *Non-discrimination in Tax Treaty Law and World Trade Law: The Impact of Formal, Substantive and Subjective Approaches*, 2019 (ISBN 978-94-035-0904-4).
73. Félix Daniel Martínez Laguna, *Hybrid Financial Instruments, Double Nontaxation and Linking Rules*, 2019 (ISBN 978-94-035-1074-3).
74. Jan Gooijer, *Tax Treaty Residence of Entities*, 2019 (ISBN 978-94-035-1301-0).
75. John Abrahamson, *International Taxation of Banking*, 2020 (ISBN 978-94-035-1094-1).
76. Richard Krever & François Vaillancourt (eds), *The Allocation of Multinational Business Income: Reassessing the Formulary Apportionment Option*, 2020 (ISBN 978-94-035-0614-2).
77. Ajit Kumar Singh, *Exploring the Nexus Doctrine in International Tax Law*, 2021 (ISBN 978-94-035-3363-6).
78. Galya Savir, *Regulation and Tax in Space*, 2021 (ISBN 978-94-035-3393-3).
79. Rita Julien, *Credit Method Compatibility and Constraints under EU Law: An Analysis of the Case Law of the CJEU*, 2022 (ISBN 978-94-035-2363-7).

www.ingramcontent.com/pod-product-compliance
Lightning Source LLC
LaVergne TN
LVHW020003031026
849161LV00023B/856
* 9 7 8 9 4 0 3 5 2 3 6 3 7 *